Agricultural Trade Conflicts
and GATT

Agricultural Trade Conflicts and GATT

New Dimensions in U.S.-European Agricultural Trade Relations

EDITED BY

Giovanni Anania, Colin A. Carter, and Alex F. McCalla

Routledge
Taylor & Francis Group

LONDON AND NEW YORK

First published 1994 by Westview Press

Published 2018 by Routledge
52 Vanderbilt Avenue, New York, NY 10017
2 Park Square, Milton Park, Abingdon, Oxon OX14 4RN

Routledge is an imprint of the Taylor & Francis Group, an informa business

A CIP catalog record for this book is available from the Library of Congress.
ISBN 0-8133-2354-1

ISBN 13: 978-0-367-01000-3 (hbk)
ISBN 13: 978-0-367-15987-0 (pbk)

Contents

Preface

The chapters in this book result from a conference on *New Dimensions in North American-European Agricultural Trade Relations* held in Isola Capo Rizzuto (Calabria, Italy) on June 20-23, 1993. All chapters but the first one were selected from the over 50 papers presented at the conference. All final chapters but the first one were completed before the conclusion of the Uruguay Round of GATT in December 1993. In this book, a group of leading experts present a comprehensive set of analyses of U.S.-E.C. agricultural trade issues. These provide a unique perspective on the U.S.-E.C. agricultural trade conflict in recent years which may help explain the final GATT agreement reached and offer insights into forthcoming agricultural trade issues.

There is no doubt that agricultural trade will continue to be an abrasive issue in the years to come. Trade liberalization achieved with the GATT agreement is only partial and the agreement itself calls for a continuation of the negotiation process to achieve the long-run goal of a *"substantial reduction in agricultural support and protection."* U.S.-E.C. agricultural trade relations will remain central to any future negotiation.

This book explores this subject from a number of perspectives. First, the issue is addressed in a broad historical context (Chapters 1 and 2). The next section of the book is focused on changes in U.S. trade and agricultural policies and their implications for global agricultural markets (Chapters 3 and 4). A similar evaluation of changes in European agricultural policy in the 1980s (Chapter 5) and in the early 1990s (Chapter 6) is undertaken to determine the ramifications for U.S.-E.C. trade relations. Chapter 7 discusses the E.C. integration and enlargement processes and the consequences likely for agriculture and trade relations. Future GATT negotiations will build on past experiences; thus, there is much to be learned from the experience of the Uruguay Round. This experience is looked at from the U.S. perspective (Chapter 8), the E.C. perspective (Chapter 9), and from third party perspectives (Chapter 10). Chapter 11 explores future possible directions in U.S.-E.C. agricultural trade relations.

The remainder of the book is devoted to more specific analyses of some additional dimensions of the U.S.-E.C. agricultural trade conflict. These include: analyses of the effects of the CAP reform and of the expected GATT agreement (Chapters 12 and 13); of the implications of likely developments in the relationship between the E.C. and Central European countries (Chapter 14); and of the likely effectiveness of the E.C. set-aside programs (Chapters 15 and 16). Chapters 17, 18, and 19 provide a better understanding of the mechanisms and forces which determine agricultural policy formation in the United States and the E.C. The environmental dimensions of E.C. agricultural policies are addressed in Chapter 20 and impacts are compared with those of some specific environmental policy interventions. Finally, Chapters 21 and 22 analyze the U.S.-E.C. conflict with reference to two specific commodity markets: seafood and durum wheat markets.

The June 1993 conference and this book were made possible by the support received from several sponsors. Among them we want to acknowledge the Banca Popolare di Crotone; the Department of Economics, University of Calabria (Italy); the Department of Agricultural Economics, University of California, Davis (USA); the Economic Research Service of the United States Department of Agriculture; the International Agricultural Trade Research Consortium; the Italian National Institute of Agricultural Economics (INEA); the Italian National Research Council and its Special Project "Advanced Research for Innovation in the Agricultural System" (RAISA); and Rubbettino.

The support of Bob Robinson and John Lee of the USDA is gratefully acknowledged. Bob Robinson also served on the conference organizing committee.

In addition to the authors of the papers, two other people were critical to the success of the conference and to the production of this book. Rosanna Peluso's invaluable support was crucial in making the conference in Calabria a success, while Nancy Ottum provided us with editorial assistance and the careful and skillful preparation of the camera-ready text.

Giovanni Anania
Colin A. Carter
Alex F. McCalla

This book is publication No. 1393 of the Special Project RAISA of the Italian National Research Council, Sub-project 1.

1

Agricultural Policy Changes, GATT Negotiations, and the U.S.-E.C. Agricultural Trade Conflict

Giovanni Anania, Colin A. Carter, and Alex F. McCalla

Introduction

The conclusion of the Eighth Round of the General Agreement on Tariffs and Trade (GATT) negotiations included an agreement designed to "bring agriculture into the GATT." Agriculture was not set aside at the eleventh hour as it was in the preceding two rounds (Kennedy and Tokyo). However, the actual agreement is a far cry from the desired outcome sought by the United States and the countries of the Cairns Group[1] in the optimistic environment of the opening declaration in Punta del Este, Uruguay, in September 1986. After seven years and three months of intermittent negotiating and substantial acrimony, the agreement on agriculture was being hailed by some as a significant success but by others as a disappointing compromise likely to have limited impact.

As in previous rounds, the latter part of the Uruguay Round negotiations were essentially bilateral, between the United States and the European Community (E.C.), or the European Union, as it is now known, as a consequence of the implementation of the Maastricht Treaty. This is why understanding this bilateral trade conflict is central to answering many other questions. Why did we end up with the particular Uruguay Round agreement in agriculture that we did? Why is agricultural trade such a big issue for the United States and the European Union, the world's two largest traders? Why is agricultural trade so difficult to liberalize when it is a small and declining share of world trade?

During the course of the Uruguay Round many things changed—the Soviet Union collapsed and the Eastern Bloc disintegrated, the Berlin Wall fell and Germany was unified, European integration became more complete with the signing of the Maastricht Treaty and the completion of Europe 1992, a Canada-United States Free Trade Agreement (CUSTA) was signed in 1988, a North American Free Trade Agreement (NAFTA) was completed in 1993, a major reform of the Common Agricultural Policy (CAP) of the European Communities (the so-called MacSharry Reform) was agreed upon in 1992, and reforms in U.S. agricultural policy initiated in 1985 evolved further under the Food, Agriculture, Conservation, and Trade Act (FACTA) of 1990.

How should the GATT conclusion be judged? Should it be compared to 1986 or to 1993? Compared to 1986, today's world agricultural trade and market structures are significantly different. But how much can be attributed to the GATT negotiations and how much to other events such as the ones listed above? For example, opinions differ sharply (including in this volume) on whether GATT pressure "caused CAP reform" or whether it was a purely European event independent of GATT.

In the post-Uruguay Round world, agricultural trade relations will change only slowly. Agricultural intervention will remain substantial despite the GATT agreement. For example the Canadians are proposing to replace an essentially zero quota on butter with a prohibitive *ad valorem* duty of 351 percent. "Liberalization" under GATT will lower that duty to 298 percent by the year 2000. Without doubt, today's agriculture will continue to be a contentious issue, particularly across the North Atlantic.

Thus, the issues addressed in this volume are relevant in terms of understanding the character of past U.S.-E.C. agricultural trade conflicts and will remain relevant and dominant in future world agricultural trade relations. The GATT agreement itself calls for a continuation of the negotiations (to restart in the year 2000) to move towards the long term objective, as agreed at the Mid Term Review of the Uruguay Round in April 1989, "...to provide for substantial progressive reduction in agricultural support and protection...."

This chapter's goal is twofold. It attempts to summarize some of the findings presented in the book and to put the recent U.S.-E.C. agricultural trade conflict and the GATT agreement in agriculture in a historical perspective. In the next section some of the developments in the U.S.-E.C. political and economic relations since the end of World War II are recalled. The following three sections outline first the evolution of U.S. agricultural policy, then that of the European Common Agricultural Policy, and, finally, the nature and evolution of the conflict. The last section of the chapter reviews the tortuous path of the Uruguay Round of GATT negotiations as it tried to resolve U.S.-E.C. global agricultural trade conflicts.

U.S.-E.C. Agricultural Trade Conflicts in the
Broader North Atlantic Context

Agricultural trade conflicts between the United States and the European Community occur as part of a broader and more complex set of economic, political, and monetary relations. This web of relations is the result of a long history of interaction and growing interdependence between Western Europe and North America that has evolved since World War II. Further, this North Atlantic relationship has evolved in the context of radical changes in the global setting. This section presents a brief overview of the evolution of the complex set of economic and political relations in the North Atlantic scene in the post-World War II period.

The past 50 years have seen enormous global economic changes. A new economic order was plotted at Bretton-Woods in 1944, which set the stage for managed financial and monetary affairs. A massive aid effort under the Marshall Plan accelerated the rebuilding of Europe and Japan. By the 1960s the number of independent countries in the world had more than doubled as colonial empires—British, Dutch, French, Belgian, and Portuguese—collapsed.

The 1970s saw the end of the Bretton-Woods regime of fixed exchange rates and massive increases in international capital movements, in part because of the recycling of petrodollars garnered by the OPEC cartel. The 1970s also saw unprecedented rates of growth in global GNP and trade.

The 1980s brought a hangover of debt, slowed growth (global recession), and contracting trade. The late 1980s and early 1990s saw a protracted recession in the United States and the highest postwar unemployment rates in Western Europe and Japan as these countries experienced continuing slowdowns in growth, rising debt, and growing concerns about their fiscal capacity to support social program commitments.

Throughout the period until 1989-90, however, an overriding constant in this sea of change was "bipolar/cold war international politics" (Featherstone and Ginsberg, 1993, p. 10). The "Cold War" also was the driving force in the evolving relations between the United States and Western Europe that stood on the front line against possible Soviet expansion. A strong military, economic, and political alliance between North America and Europe was seen on both sides of the Atlantic as the natural (and necessary) thing to do to contain communism and foster the rapid development of an integrated system of market economies.

Following Featherstone and Ginsberg, the evolution of the U.S.-E.C. relations in the past 50 years can be divided in three periods. The first one, which covers the 20 years from the end of the war to the mid-1960s, is characterized by the hegemonic leadership of the United States. A hegemon can be defined as having a preponderance of material resources and being stronger than anybody else. The second period, which covers the 20 years from 1965 to 1985, is characterized according to Featherstone and Ginsberg by the progressive decline in the U.S. hegemony, but U.S.-E.C. relations were still dominated by the United States. The third period, which started in the mid-1980s, is the post-hegemony period, where the hegemony of the United States is no longer recognized.

The United States emerged from World War II as the clearly dominant military and economic power of the Western World. It became a hegemonic leader (Keohane, 1984). Thus in this period (1945-65) the U.S.-E.C. relationship could be defined as a "patron-client," one where the United States bore the costs of international leadership in return for European acquiescence. Clearly the United States was dominant militarily, politically, and economically.

However, European recovery occurred quickly. European integration started with the establishment of the European Coal and Steel Community (ECSC) under the Schuman Plan in 1951 and the signing of the Treaty of Rome in 1957. By the mid-1960s Europe was economically and politically much stronger and this led to the period of "hegemonic decline" where the dominance of the United States diminished but the United States continued to treat Europe as a junior partner/client. The period after 1986 can be defined as post-hegemony, resulting in the evolution of a relationship of "complex interdependence." Therefore over the postwar period U.S.-European relations shifted from extreme asymmetry to symmetry economically and politically, if not militarily.

Throughout this period, multilateral institutions, in which the United States was dominant, framed U.S.-E.C. relations, for example:

- NATO—North Atlantic Treaty Organization—an organization for military cooperation to present a united front against the Soviet Union.
- Organization for European Economic Cooperation (OEEC), which became the Organization for Economic Cooperation and Development (OECD)—the OEEC was originally designed to provide a European input into postwar aid. With European recovery the OEEC became the OECD, an association of developed countries who attempt to liberalize trade and harmonize policies.
- GATT—General Agreement on Tariffs and Trade—a long standing organization devoted to nondiscriminatory and liberalized trade.
- IMF—International Monetary Fund—the mechanism originally designed to administer exchange rates. Latterly a short-term financing mechanism for structural adjustment.
- More recently the so-called G-7 countries—United States, Japan, Germany, U.K., France, Italy, and Canada—where E.C. participates as a regular observer, has sought economic policy harmonization.

Economically the European Community (EC-12) emerged as roughly comparable to the United States in terms of GNP, though per capita income still lagged behind. The European Community has accounted for around 40 percent of world trade since 1965, with the United States accounting for about 15 percent (Featherstone and Ginsberg, 1993). Thus these two economic giants continue to account for more than half of world trade.

But of far greater magnitude are the bilateral flows of investment. Mastrostefano in this book provides a discussion of the recent dynamics of U.S. and E.C. direct investments in each others' agrifood sectors, and of the motivation behind such investments. Sales of affiliates of U.S. companies in the E.C. exceed U.S. exports to the E.C. by a factor of 10. Overall ". . . total two-way trade and investment coupled with sales generated from investment surpassed $1 trillion in 1980 . . ." (Featherstone and Ginsberg, 1993, p. 115).

The E.C. is the largest trading partner of the United States. In 1990 the sum of the two-way trade was equal to $183.9 billion. U.S. trade with the next two largest trade partners, Canada and Japan, was $170.2 and $134.9 billion, respectively. The Community is the largest importer from the United States ($93.1 billion; Canada is second with $78.2, and Japan is a distant third with $46.1 billion), while Canada is the largest exporter to the United States (exports from Canada to the United States were $92.0 billion, and exports from the E.C. and Japan to the United States were $90.8 and $88.8 billion respectively) (Featherstone and Ginsberg, 1993).

In 1990, U.S.-E.C. agricultural trade accounted for only 6-7 percent of the total bilateral trade—the U.S. ships about $7 billion worth of agricultural exports to the E.C., while the E.C. sells about $4.5 billion worth of exports to the United States. But despite its relatively small role in U.S.-E.C. bilateral trading, agriculture has been by far the most acrimonious area of dispute between the two. As is noted later on in this chapter, 12 out of 17 of all GATT disputes between the United States and the E.C. have involved agricultural trade issues. While most have been resolved, many resulted in countervailing or antidumping duties and much heated rhetoric.

The question that must be raised is why such a small portion of bilateral trade should be such a difficult and divisive issue across the North Atlantic. Part of the answer lies in a long history of domestic producer income support (Anderson, Ch. 10).

Agricultural protectionism has a long history that predates GATT (McCalla, 1969), but modern policies of income transfer to producers via the price system have their origins in the Depression of the 1930s. Agricultural policy changed dramatically on both sides of the Atlantic with the onset of the Depression, which followed the price skid of 1925-29. In

Europe, country after country resorted to raising tariffs and controlling imports (Tracy, 1993, McCalla, 1993). In the United States direct price guarantees were granted in return for reducing acreage. In addition, high tariffs were implemented under the Hawley-Smoot Tariff. At that time neither side worried much about export markets as policies were protectionist and inward-looking.

North Atlantic agricultural trade conflicts became much more acute in the 1960s as the United States joined Canada as a major exporter of grains (and oilseeds). At the same time, the establishment of the European Community portended a high-priced protectionist Common Agricultural Policy that would clearly expand output. In time the two policies would be in conflict, as Europe was transformed from the world's largest importer of agricultural products into the world's largest exporter in less than 25 years. Therefore, in the next two sections we explore, in some detail, the evolution of U.S. and E.C. policies.

U.S. Agricultural and Trade Policies and
U.S.-E.C. Agricultural Trade Relations

The U.S. original proposal to GATT in 1987 to eliminate all trade distorting subsidies, internal supports, and border protection (the zero option) might have been perceived as a logical extension of a long-standing U.S. commitment to free trade in agriculture. Clearly that was not true. The championing of free trade by the United States is a fairly recent and only partial phenomenon. In an effort to understand the U.S. position, this section reviews briefly U.S. agricultural policy evolution since the 1930s.

Until 1933 U.S. government support for agriculture was indirect (e.g. public support of research, extension, marketing regulations, credit assistance, etc.) and did not involve direct market intervention. That changed with the passage of the Agricultural Adjustment Act (AAA) of 1933. The essential characteristics of that act—acreage control to reduce supply, minimum price guarantees (loan rate), demand expansion, and stock holdings by the Commodity Credit Corporation (CCC)—remain to this day. The explicit purpose of the policy was to reduce supply and expand demand to raise farm prices and therefore, it must have been assumed, farm incomes.

Necessary adjuncts to such a policy were border measures to protect domestic programs from low-priced imports and mechanisms to distribute excess production. The now infamous Section 22 of the AAA provided the border protection by authorizing the Secretary of Agriculture to use import quotas and/or other quantitative restrictions to isolate domestic markets. Section 32 of the AAA committed a portion of U.S. tariff revenue for the purpose of purchasing surplus commodities for distribution domestically and potentially abroad. The United States, as a condition for signing GATT in 1947, insisted on the introduction of an exception (Section XI of GATT) that allowed continued use of Section 22.

During World War II the loan rate was used as the basic price-support vehicle and was raised to 90 percent of parity (Steagall Amendments) for the duration of the War and two years afterwards. High loan rates continued into the Korean War and through the 1950s. U.S. agricultural output grew and stocks began to build in the early 1950s. The first internationally oriented response was PL480 (Agricultural Trade Development and Assistance Act) in 1954, which was an implicit export subsidy program targeted at selected developing countries. But despite PL480, and the Soil Bank of 1956, stocks by 1960 exceeded all previous record levels.

The 1960s were an important decade for the international dimensions of U.S. agriculture. Prior to the early 1960s the United States was a net *importer* of agricultural products. Exports were relatively unimportant except in a few selected commodities, e.g. wheat. During the 1960s exports and imports were about equal with the U.S. showing a positive agricultural trade balance of about $1 billion by the end of the decade. In 1965 the United States began to adjust its policy, prevalent since the 1930s, of income support via high loan rates, stock holding, export subsidies, and land diversion. Loan rates were sharply lowered and a system of direct "deficiency payments" were introduced to transfer income to agriculture directly from the Treasury rather than from consumers through the marketplace. The result was that U.S. exports became competitive at market prices. This change in policy was codified into a two price system of target prices and loan rates with direct payments in the Agriculture and Consumer Protection Act of 1973 and has continued in every piece of legislation since.

In the 1970s trade expanded rapidly. U.S. exports including agriculture grew after two back-to-back dollar devaluations, rising international demand, and steady commodity price increases. The United States became a major agricultural exporter only in the 1970s. The positive agricultural trade balance shifted from about $1 billion in the 1960s to a high of over $25 billion in 1980/81.

Dependence of U.S. agriculture on exports doubled during the 1970s. This subjected the U.S. government to political pressure from domestic producers and agribusiness to introduce (or preserve) policies to maintain export market share. Agricultural interest groups in the U.S. now had a stake in influencing trade policy because about one-third of U.S. cropland was planted for export and approximately 30 percent of farm cash receipts came from exports. U.S. agricultural exports have fluctuated around $40 billion per year in the 1990s. Although U.S. agriculture accounts for only about 2 percent of domestic GNP, food exports account now for about 10 percent of U.S. total current account exports. The agricultural industry ranks fifth among the earners of foreign exchange (a net trade balance of $18 billion per year).

Grains and oilseeds account for a large percentage of the value of U.S. farm exports (about 50 percent) and a large proportion of the trade friction between the United States and the E.C. Figure 1.1 displays grain production, area, stocks, and exports for the United States. Figure 1.2 charts market shares for the United States versus the E.C. The trade conflict between the U.S. and the E.C. was exacerbated by events in the early 1980s when U.S. domestic grain stockpiles increased, exports fell, and at the same time E.C. export market share rose. As shown in Figures 1.1 and 1.2, the volume of U.S. grain exports (and international market share) in 1979 was historically very high. It is therefore shortsighted to focus only on the period of decline from 1981 to 1985. The volume of U.S. exports in 1985 were no lower than exports in the early 1970s and export volume rebounded in the latter half of the 1980s and early 1990s.

In the early 1980s, U.S. grain surplus situation was determined as much by domestic policy (the 1981 Farm Bill) and the appreciating dollar as by declines in international demand and increased competition from the E.C. As part of the 1981 Farm Bill, loan rates and target prices were raised under the expectation of continuing inflation and buoyant export markets. These optimistic expectations were based on the experience of the 1970s. United States grain exports fell from 114 million tons (mmt) in fiscal 1980 to 63 mmt in 1985. Part of this decline was attributed by the U.S. government to "unfair" export subsidies by the E.C. Despite a massive land removal scheme under the P.I.K. program in 1983, stocks grew large again.

In order to regain "lost" market share, the Food Security Act of 1985 simultaneously lowered loan rates and introduced the Export Enhancement Program (EEP). The EEP program was established in order to reduce CCC stocks and meet subsidized competition from the E.C. in certain targeted markets. This program has played an important role in U.S. grain exports. For example, in 1992, approximately 70 percent of all U.S. wheat exports were EEP sales. However, the 1985 Farm Bill kept target prices high and thus production remained high.

As part of the Uruguay Round of GATT negotiations, the United States administration pressed for global agricultural trade reform. While GATT negotiations dragged on, two new trade agreements were negotiated in North America—the Canada-U.S. Free Trade Agreement (CUSTA) was signed in 1988 and the North American Free Trade Agreement (NAFTA) in 1993. These regional agreements were generally consistent with the

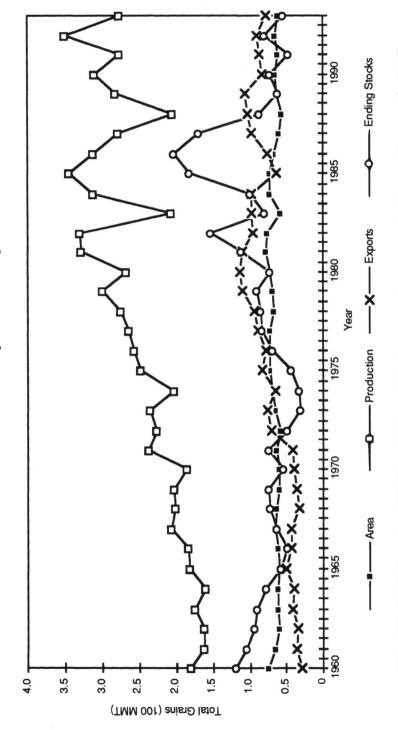

FIGURE 1.1 United States Total Grains: Area, Production, Export, and Ending Stocks.

Source: USDA ERS, PS&D View, Oct. 1993. *Note:* Grains include wheat, rye, rice, corn, oats, barley, sorghum, and feedstuffs.

FIGURE 1.2 U.S. and E.C. Market Shares of World Grain Trade.

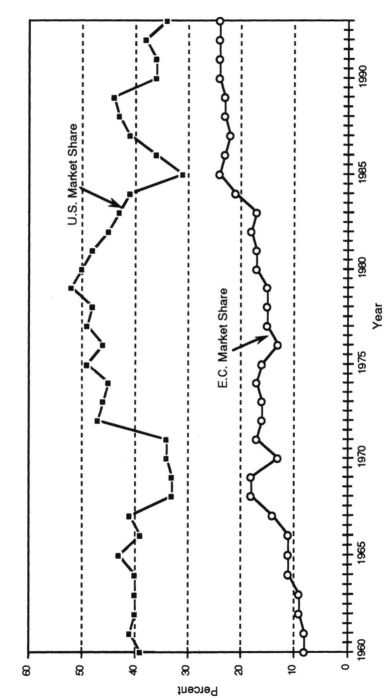

Source: Derived from USDA ERS, PS&D View, Oct. 1993.

Reagan/Bush administrations' free trade philosophy, but, compared to manufactured goods, most of the thorny agricultural issues were either left out or reforms were to be implemented over an extra long transition period. Issues of tariffication of supply control commodities (Canada) and quotas (beef, sugar, peanuts, etc., in the U.S.) were left to GATT negotiations. The reason was that Canada and the United States tend to be competitors in agricultural trade, thus removing trade barriers between these two countries was not seen to result in large gains. With the completion of a GATT agreement interesting questions arise about the interface between NAFTA and GATT. For example, GATT requires tariffication of quotas such as those used by Canadian supply control marketing boards. NAFTA requires reducing tariffs to zero. Does this mean that, when Canada converts quotas to tariffs under GATT, the tariffs on dairy and poultry between the United States and Canada must be eliminated? The implications of NAFTA and CUSTA for North Atlantic agricultural trade relations are less clear. The U.S., Canadian, and Mexican markets will become more closely linked, necessitating continued efforts for North America policy harmonization.

In summary, it is clear that U.S. agricultural policy has been evolving since 1965 towards a policy that is less market distorting (i.e. decoupled). The shift to a two-price system (target prices and loan rates) coupled with direct payments freed U.S. market prices to reflect global conditions. Gradual additional changes such as (1) using historical rather than current yields to calculate deficiency payments, (2) implementing the "triple base" where the production for a portion of the base acreage beyond the set-aside requirement is made ineligible for deficiency payments, and (3) increased planting flexibility, have moved U.S. policy to something approaching being decoupled (Gardner, Ch. 3). These changes, plus fiscal constraints that have frozen or lowered support levels in nominal terms, have clearly reduced levels of real price support. A consequence of this is that the United States, like the E.C., should have relatively little difficulty in meeting the requirements of the final GATT agreement.

Recent Changes in the CAP

The early developments of CAP are well known. Although the European Economic Community was established on January 1, 1958, it was not until 1962 that the form of the Common Agricultural Policy began to emerge. The common market for cereals, the first one to be put in place, was not completed until 1968. The process was not easy. It involved lengthy negotiations on the instruments to be used, on the level of support to be granted, on the role to be given to structural policies relative to market intervention, and on the decision mechanisms.

The outcome was a system based on market-specific domestic support instruments that involved insulation from the world market by the use of variable import levies and export restitutions. Border measures associated with the CAP were meant to be (and have been used) as instruments needed to implement agreed-upon domestic farm support prices, not primarily as border instruments to achieve trade-related goals. It is useful to recall that the distortionary domestic effects of the policy interventions that were going to be introduced were not ignored. It was recognized that the CAP could lead to rapid productivity growth, to large surpluses that could not be absorbed domestically at prevailing prices, and to a large budget expenditure. But these were not addressed at the outset.

The 1970s saw a rapid expansion of agricultural production in the Community resulting from price-induced increases in yields and significant capital investments (Figure 1.3 shows U.S., E.C., and average world wheat yields since 1960). Prices independent of world market dynamics, and increasing in real terms, led to large surpluses that were either absorbed through massive intervention buying or through different forms of subsidized exports. The most blatant result of this process was the E.C. moving from being a large importer of wheat to being a net exporter at the end of the 1970s (and the second largest wheat exporter today). This change implied the need to subsidize the export of excess production. A policy that was originally income generating (as a result of the variable levy) soon became a budget cost for the E.C. The increasing cost of the CAP was a major factor in providing momentum for a change in its mechanisms. Despite rapidly increasing agricultural production in the E.C., U.S. exports to the Community continued to grow.

The focus of the remainder of this section is on policy changes in the 1980s and early 1990s. Many observers believe that policy changes in the 1980s were more radical than those occurring under the CAP reform of 1992. However they were not fully understood outside of the Community.

These changes are well described in Chapter 5, by De Benedictis, De Filippis, and Salvatici. Their view is that the CAP in the 1980s appears to have been driven by a sort of "conjunctural gradualism" (as opposed to a clear-cut plan for a radical reform). All of the changes in E.C. market policies were implemented through partial adjustments and corrections of the policies in place. These changes appear to have been dictated by strong contingent necessities and constraints that could not be accommodated otherwise. These changes were put in place without explicit reference to a long-run view of a new policy scenario.

The impossibility of coping with an expenditure that was growing out of control, led to the introduction of a production quota system for milk in March 1984[2] and to the limiting of all prices for the 1984/1985 campaign in nominal terms at, or below, the level in the previous year. In July 1985 the

FIGURE 1.3 World, United States, and E.C. Wheat Yields.

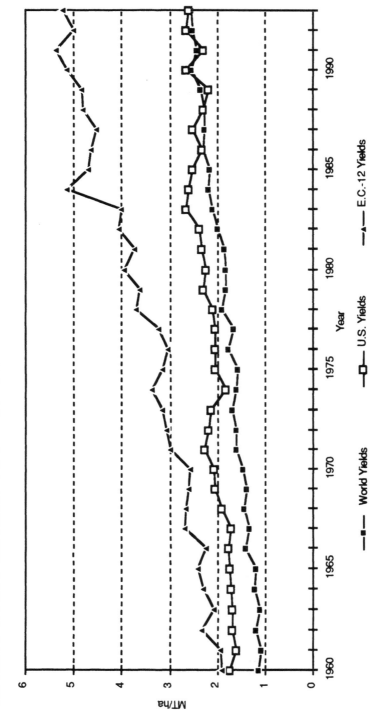

Source: USDA, ERS, PS&D View, Oct. 1993.

"Green Book" indicated what in the Commission's opinion were the two main options faced by the CAP: a severe price reduction with the intent of slowly driving E.C. prices to world market levels, while leaving domestic production free to grow, or the introduction of constraints on the quantity produced, while maintaining domestic prices well above world price levels. No decision was made until February 1988, when the Council of Ministers introduced the so-called automatic financial stabilizers.[3]

With the stabilizers, the choice between the two options indicated in the Green Book—a choice that policymakers proved to be unable to make—was transferred to producers. In fact, the stabilizers linked CAP prices to quantities produced. When production in the E.C. exceeded a pre-fixed limit—which was set at or below production in the previous years—the so-called Maximum Guaranteed Quantity (MGQ), prices were automatically reduced. Actual mechanisms were different among commodities. For example, the wheat price reduction was applied in the marketing year following the one in which production exceeded the MGQ; the price cut could not exceed 3 percent, but it was permanent, i.e., it was not to be removed in the following years even if production was to remain within the MGQ. On the contrary, oilseed price cuts, due to the stabilizer mechanism, applied in the same marketing year in which the overproduction took place; the percentage price cut was given by the percentage of the overproduction, but it was not permanent, i.e. if production in the following years remained within the MGQ, guaranteed support prices went back to the original levels. Price reductions due to the stabilizers were substantial. Figure 1.4 shows wheat and corn minimum guaranteed prices in the E.C. (in nominal terms), while Figure 1.5 shows theoretical and actual (i.e. after the correction due to the stabilizer) soybean "guide" and minimum prices during the 1980s.

Early in the past decade, E.C. agricultural prices were still increasing in real terms, but they have been rapidly declining since the 1983/1984 marketing year as a consequence of the changes that occurred in the CAP. In marketing year 1991/1992 E.C. agricultural prices in real terms were 24.1 percent below those in 1980/1981. The stabilizers caused the gap between U.S. and E.C. prices for wheat and oilseeds to decrease after 1987. The trend toward a realignment is particularly strong for oilseeds. The ratio between the U.S. average production price and the E.C. target price for soybean and sunflower seeds, because of the stabilizers, declined by 18 percent and 34 percent, respectively, between 1987/88 and the 1991/1992 marketing years (Anania and Gatto, 1993).

The changes introduced in the CAP between 1984 and 1988—production quotas, the price freeze, and self-adjusting stabilizer mechanisms—were mainly driven by strongly binding financial constraints and by a growing domestic dissatisfaction with CAP. In addition to its financial

FIGURE 1.4 E.C. Intervention Price for Wheat and Corn.

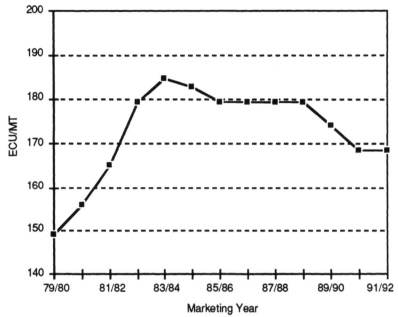

Source: Anania and Gatto, 1993.

unsustainability, the most important areas of concern were the very high levels of the stocks held by the Community in the mid-1980s, a widespread recognition of the inefficiency and inequity of the policy instruments used, and a growing awareness of negative environmental effects.

Although the changes did not bring a reduction in CAP expenditure, they were able to put its rate of growth under control, a control that seemed lost in the early 1980s. On the other hand, quotas created valuable rents and introduced additional rigidities in factor mobility and inefficiencies in the use of the resources. After a strong decline in the second half of the 1980s, stocks again reached very high levels in the early 1990s. The changes introduced in the 1980s certainly did not solve the inefficiency and inequity problems faced by the CAP. However, these changes allowed a transition from a period of unlimited support to a new phase in which the Community regained control over policy interventions that at the beginning of the past decade were mostly driven by its own internal dynamics.

The drastic policy changes introduced in 1991 for oilseeds and in 1992 for cereals and meats are well known. These included a large reduction in minimum guaranteed prices, compensated for with direct payments[4] and set-aside provisions for large producers. As with the pre-reform CAP,

FIGURE 1.5. E.C. Soybeans Theoretical and Actual (Stabilized) "Guide" Prices and Minimum Prices.

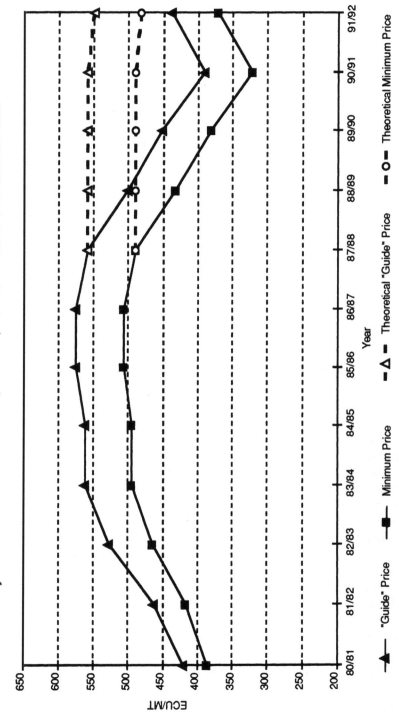

Source: Anania and Gatto, 1993.

border measures continued to be used for the successful implementation of the domestic policies.

Expectations are that the 1992 CAP reform will bring lower production, larger domestic consumption, lower exports, and less harmful environmental impacts of agricultural practices in the Community. The CAP reform should significantly change the role played by the E.C. on the world market by reducing the confrontation with other exporters.

Many believe that the 1992 CAP reform was introduced as a result of the strong external political pressure for liberalization of agricultural markets that grew within and around the ongoing GATT negotiations (Guyomard et al., Ch. 6; Sumner, Ch. 4). While such pressure was certainly a factor, the central role played by internal forces, the same forces that guided the conjunctural gradualism of CAP adjustments in the 1980s, should not be underestimated (De Benedictis, De Filippis and Salvatici, Ch. 5).

Was the choice of reforming the CAP in 1992 the only option for the E.C.? This question does not yet have an answer. As discussed by De Benedictis, De Filippis and Salvatici, if the goal of the reform was to make a tactical move toward a reduction across the board of the level of support granted to farmers, then the changes introduced with the reform were needed. The role of these changes was to make the amount and the distribution of transfers to the farmers explicit. By so doing, it facilitated the emergence of a strong opposition to the CAP demanding its dismantling. However, if the goal was simply to limit the financial cost of the CAP and to reduce overproduction, then a recalibration of the instruments already in use was certainly a viable alternative. If instead the reform was a genuine effort to decouple agricultural subsidies, by reducing their less desirable effects while maintaining farm support, then, again, the choice made was the only one feasible.

This is not a secondary issue from the point of view of future U.S.-E.C. agricultural trade relations. If, as many believe, the 1992 CAP reform was an intermediate step toward its dismantling—allowing in its place decoupled farm support to be channeled through national budgets—the tensions between the Community and other agricultural exporters will certainly be lower in the future, regardless of the likely implications of the GATT agreement. However, if this is not the case, the conflict within the E.C. about the direction the CAP should take, and the Community enlargement processes, will be central forces in determining the future scenarios for U.S.-E.C. agricultural trade relations.

The U.S.-E.C. Agricultural Trade Conflict

This section addresses the evolution of the U.S.-E.C. trade conflict in the context of the changes in domestic policies discussed above. The U.S.-E.C. confrontation has two components: what happened in bilateral trading and what happened in third-country markets. We address the conflict in third markets first, then move on to a discussion of what happened in bilateral trading.

The structure of U.S. and E.C. agricultural trade by country of destination of exports and of origin of imports (Figures 1.6 and 1.7) is substantially different. Further, it shows that the two countries play different roles in each other's market. While U.S. agricultural imports and exports are relatively concentrated, E.C. agricultural trade partners, both export

FIGURE 1.6 E.C. Agricultural Exports and Imports by Country of Destination or Origin. (1991 percentage values).

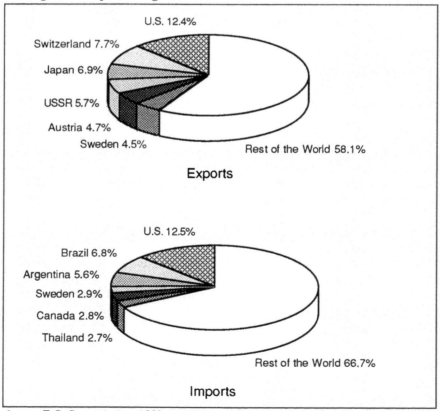

Exports

Imports

Source: E.C. Commission, 1993. Agricultural Situation in the Community, Brussels.

FIGURE 1.7 U.S. Agricultural Exports and Imports by Country of Destination or Origin. (1991 percentage values).

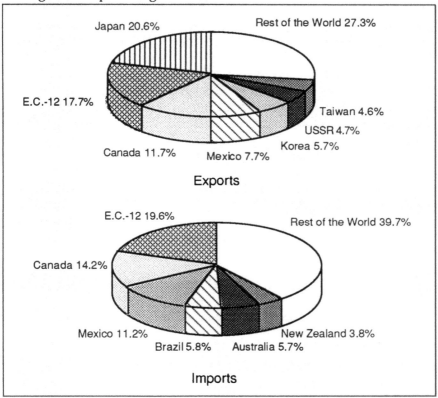

Exports

Imports

Source: USDA, *Agricultural Statistics,* 1992.

buyers and import sources, are much more diversified. In 1991 the three largest U.S. partners accounted for 50 percent of agricultural exports and for 45 percent of agricultural imports. For the E.C. the same percentages were equal to 27 percent and 24.9 percent, respectively.

In relative terms the role played by the E.C. as a destination for U.S. agricultural exports is larger than the role played by the United States as a destination for E.C. exports. The E.C. share of U.S. agricultural exports in 1991 was 17.7 percent (Figure 1.7). The E.C. is the major supplier of U.S. imports with 19.6 percent of the total market. The United States is also the largest supplier to the E.C. market, and the largest buyer of E.C. agricultural products, but the shares are lower than those of the E.C. in the U.S. trade (Figure 1.6).

In the 1970s U.S. agricultural exports increased from $18.2 to $48.1

billion and the U.S. share of the world market fluctuated between a low of 16.4 percent in 1977 and a high of 19.8 percent in 1974. During the early 1980s the United States rapidly lost market share in global agricultural trade, falling from over 19 percent of the market in 1981 to 12 percent in 1986 and 1987. Since 1987, U.S. share of the world market bounced back but has remained well below the values reached in the 1970s and early 1980s (Figure 1.8).

Many in the United States blamed the E.C.'s Common Agricultural Policy for most of the decrease in the U.S. agricultural exports in the past decade. The CAP was certainly a factor, but several other causes probably played even more important roles in explaining what happened. Among the leading reasons for a weaker international demand for U.S. agricultural commodities in the mid-1980s are: the slower rate of growth in the developing world; the debt crisis; the strong U.S. dollar; and the reduction of the wheat imports by China and U.S.S.R. as a result of initally being excluded from EEP export subsidies.

High CAP prices during the 1970s and most of the 1980s produced a rapid increase in E.C. domestic production and exports. However, in the

FIGURE 1.8 U.S. and E.C. Export Shares of the World Agricultural Market (1980-91).

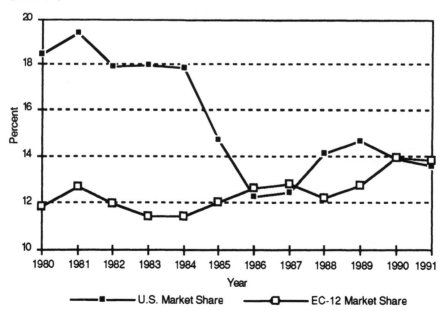

Source: FAO, *Trade Yearbook,* various issues and E.C. Commission, Brussels, *Agricultural Situation in the Community,* various issues. *Note:* E.C. data do not include intra-E.C. trading.

1970s both U.S. and E.C. agricultural exports to third countries grew because of the expansion of the market in developing and centrally planned countries (Cuffaro and De Filippis, 1992). Despite the implementation of the CAP, during the 1970s U.S. exports to the E.C. increased at a rate that was only slightly below the rate of growth of total U.S. agricultural exports (Baldwin, Ch. 2).

E.C.-12 agricultural exports grew from $28.8 billion in 1980 to $44.6 in 1991. E.C. imports increased as well, from $62.8 billion in 1980 and $53.6 in 1981 to $70.5 in 1991. As a result, the increase in the E.C. negative net trade position was not as large as the increase in its exports. As a matter of fact, the E.C. net agricultural trade position in 1989, 1990, and 1991 was little differ-ent than in 1981, 1982, or 1983. The E.C. increased its share of the world agricultural market in the 1980s (Figure 1.8). Its exports exceeded those of the United States both in 1986 and 1987 and in the early 1990s. However, the increases in the E.C. share of the world market remain well below the decreases in the U.S. share.

As argued by Baldwin, world structural conditions are to be held largely responsible for what happened to U.S. agricultural exports in the 1980s. In the early 1970s U.S. agricultural exports to developing countries accounted for about 10 percent of total U.S. agricultural exports; by 1981 they accounted for about 45 percent. Much of this growth in import demand was fueled by borrowing and by the declining value of the U.S. dollar. Higher interest rates and the appreciating dollar (which rose until 1985) raised debt service payments in the early 1980s and forced many LDCs to significantly reduce food imports, even in the presence of expanded food deficits. It seems plausible that changes in the macroeconomic environment in the last two decades—such as changes in the exchange rates, in the rate of income growth in the developing world, and the debt crisis—dominated any changes in trade policy.

When the EEP program was started in 1985, exports to the U.S.S.R. and China were excluded. As a result, both countries decided not to buy any wheat from the United States. In marketing years 1985/1986 and 1986/1987 the U.S. share of these two large markets dropped drastically, from 35 percent to less than 5 percent in China, and from over 20 percent to less than 5 percent in U.S.S.R. In the U.S.S.R. market, the E.C., Canada, and Australia all expanded their shares; Australia and Canada benefitted from the decision by China to discriminate against U.S. exports. When China and U.S.S.R. were included among the countries whose imports were eligible for EEP subsidies, both restarted importing wheat from the United States in large quantities, and the U.S. share in these two markets bounced back immediately (Anania, Bohman, and Carter, 1992).

In addition to conflicts in third-country markets, U.S.-E.C. bilateral trading has also been characterized by continuing conflicts. U.S. surplus in the bilateral agricultural trading with the E.C. is today much smaller than in the early 1980s. In 1992 it was equal only to \$2.451 billion (it was \$7.541 billion in 1982) (Figure 1.9). What explains the decline? The data presented in Figure 1.10 show the strong negative correlation between the \$/ECU exchange rate and U.S. agricultural exports to the E.C. But the exchange rate does not tell the entire story. There seems to be a structural asymmetry in bilateral agricultural trading between the United States and the E.C. While U.S. share of the E.C. agricultural imports declined steadily in the 1980s, the E.C. share of U.S. market increased until 1987 and has remained steady since then (Figure 1.11). E.C. exports to the United States include a much larger share of high value-added processed agricultural products than U.S. exports to the E.C. (Cuffaro and De Filippis, 1992; Guyomard et al., Ch. 6). It is important to note that they penetrate the U.S. market without substantial benefits from the CAP.

These data seem to imply that the problem is not, as many believe, the contraction of the E.C. import market because of the CAP (E.C. imports actually expanded) but may be due to the decline of U.S. competitiveness in the E.C. market. This is mainly due to two causes: the increasing difference between the composition of E.C. imports and U.S. exports,[5] and the trade preferences the E.C. grants to many third countries through the Lomé Convention and many other bilateral and multilateral agreements.[6]

FIGURE 1.9 U.S.-E.C. Bilateral Agricultural Trade (1982-92).

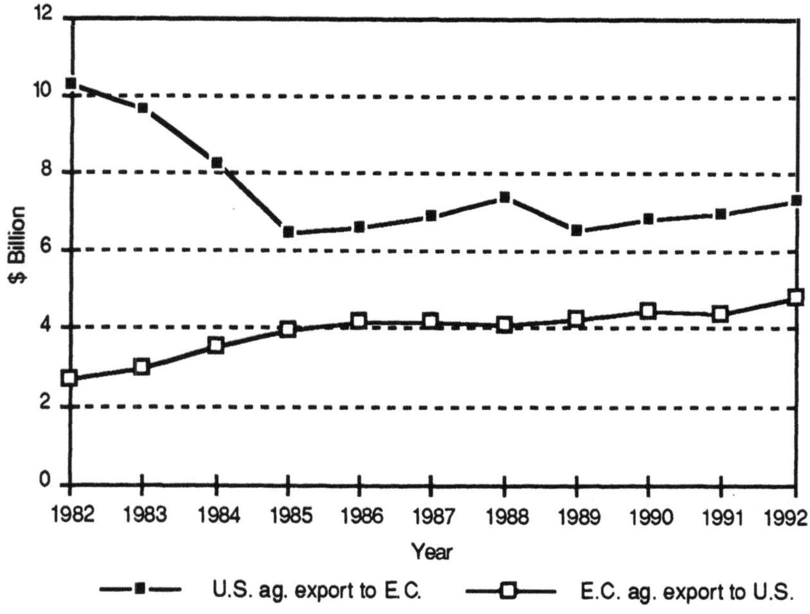

Source: USDA, ERS, *Foreign Agricultural Trade of the United States,* various issues.

FIGURE 1.10 U.S. Agricultural Exports to the E.C. and the $/ECU Exchange Rate (1982=100).

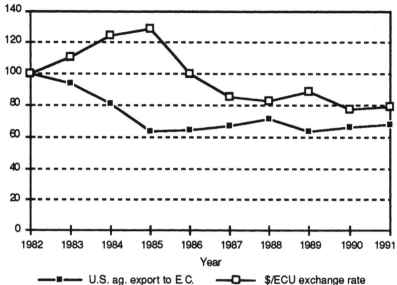

Source: USDA, ERS, *Foreign Agricultural Trade of the United States,* various issues.

FIGURE 1.11 U.S. and E.C. Market Shares in Bilateral Agricultural Trade (1982-91).

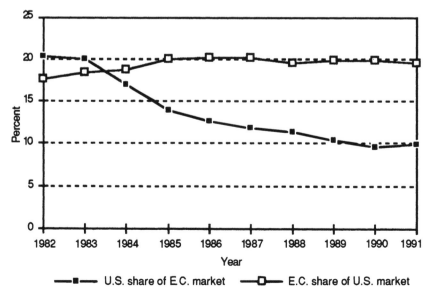

Source: USDA, ERS, *Foreign Agricultural Trade of the United States,* various issues.

As long as third countries enjoy a significant preferential tariff wedge in the E.C. market, increased market access in the E.C. is likely to induce only a small expansion of U.S. exports. Further, the CAP does not explain the fact that between 1980 and 1990 U.S. oilseed exports to the Community dropped by a little over 50 percent[7] while at the same time E.C. imports from Argentina, Brazil, and Paraguay increased by 80 percent. Today these three countries together deliver to the E.C. market almost as much as the United States, while in 1980 the U.S. market share was four times that of these three countries combined.

The recent confrontation between the United States and the E.C. over agricultural trade occurred in a period of generally strong political cooperation over many international crises, making the option of an escalation of the confrontation in a real trade war politically very costly. The changes that had occurred in the CAP since 1984 and the reform of May 1992 had the effect of decreasing the distortionary impact of E.C. interventions both on domestic and world markets. As a result, from the point of view of the bilateral agricultural trade relations, the main issue at stake in achieving a GATT agreement seemed to have been reaching an agreement on new rules to reduce the likelihood of the future resurgence of market-distorting interventions. Domestic policy adjustments, plus the drought of 1988, had significantly reduced tensions. As Guyomard et al. put it in Chapter 6 in this book, the importance for the United States of the GATT agreement in agriculture, from the point of view of its long-standing conflict with the E.C., was probably not much more than that of "putting a cap on the CAP."

The U.S.-E.C. Agricultural Trade Conflict Within GATT

Despite its relatively small importance—it now accounts for less than 6 percent of total bilateral merchandise trading—agriculture has always been the major area of trade conflict between the United States and the E.C. within the GATT (Hudec, 1988; Featherstone and Ginsberg, 1993). As noted above, since 1962 agriculture was involved in 12 out of the 17 major U.S.-E.C. GATT disputes.[8]

Agriculture has always been part of the ongoing general discussions within GATT, but it was not on the agenda of the first four Rounds of negotiations. However, it has been on the table in all four Rounds since then. Under GATT rules, the creation of the European Economic Community and the implementation of a Common Agricultural Policy required negotiations within GATT to reach an agreement over binding new common tariff levels. Among the agreements reached in the Dillon Round (1960-1962) was the acceptance by the Community of a zero tariff binding for cotton and oilseeds and a bound 6 percent tariff on nongrain feeding stuffs. However, no decision was made regarding target prices, export restitutions, and the variable import levies that were to be the instruments used to implement the CAP. The United States considered these instruments to be illegal under GATT rules. In the Kennedy Round (1963-1967) the United States proposed a "tariffication" of CAP variable levies and their reduction by half, but eventually it had to capitulate obtaining only modest concessions. In the Tokyo Round (1973-1979), after a long stalemate—with the E.C. being unwilling to negotiate its variable levy system and the United States being unwilling to accept the implementation of agreements on a commodity-by-commodity basis as proposed by the E.C.—agriculture was, once again, on the margins of the final agreement (Baldwin, Ch. 2; Guyomard et al., Ch. 6; McCalla, 1993; Petit, 1985).

It was with the Uruguay Round that for the first time agriculture took center stage in GATT negotiations. The long history of difficulties in previous attempts to bring agriculture within GATT portended that the negotiations would be very difficult, and they were difficult indeed.

The Round started with the Punta del Este declaration on September 20, 1986. The declaration itself must be considered an important step in the history of trying to resolve trade conflicts in agriculture. The major points of the declaration concerning agricultural trade were: (a) an agreement to make a specific effort to bring agriculture within GATT by achieving "greater liberalization of trade in agriculture;" and (b) an agreement to bring both border and domestic policies under scrutiny by "bringing all measures affecting agricultural trade under strengthened and more operationally effective GATT rules and disciplines."

The first U.S. proposal was put forward in July 1987. This is often referred to as the zero option because it proposed that over a ten-year period there should be a complete phase out of all forms of support to agricultural production that directly or indirectly affected trade and the removal of all import barriers. The E.C. proposal came in October of the same year. It was based on a two-stage approach: attacking first the most heavily intervened markets (cereals, sugar, and dairy products); and then, in a second stage, taking actions to reduce market distortions across a broader base. The E.C. proposal called for the monitoring of policy changes by means of an aggregate measure of support (AMS). By doing so the Community was making clear that it was not willing to negotiate specific policy instruments but rather a reduction in the overall level of support, leaving freedom to each country (and to itself) to decide how to achieve the agreed-upon reduction in support.

The favorable dynamics of world markets in 1988, with higher prices and low stocks for cereals and oilseeds—mainly due to the drought in North America—lowered the pressure for an agreement. The mid-term review meeting in December 1988 in Montreal did not produce any tangible results. The U.S. and the E.C. positions remained very far apart, and no real attempt was made to define acceptable boundaries within which future negotiations could occur. Thus halfway through the originally planned duration of the Round it was clear that the negotiations had not yet started.

The midterm review was kept formally going well after the December deadline, leading to an agreement in April 1989 on subsequent steps. The agreement stated that the Round's aim was to establish a fair and market-oriented agricultural trading system to be achieved through ". . .substantial progressive reduction in agricultural support and protection. . . ." In practice the only improvement with respect to the Punta del Este declaration was agreeing that the reduction in support and protection to be introduced was to be substantial. This may not seem to be a significant result, but actually it was a clear step forward, when compared to the limited amount of progress that had been achieved in the first two years of the Round. The request by the E.C., that countries should receive credit for policy changes that had occurred since the start of the Round, was accepted—solving one of the contentious issues in the first half of the negotiations—and all parties agreed to produce comprehensive proposals by the end of 1989.

The second U.S. proposal came in October 1989. It continued to take a strong position on export subsidies by demanding the elimination, in five years, of all such subsidies. It offered a minor concession on the reduction of border protection by proposing tariffication of all non-tariff barriers and their elimination, or at least their reduction to a low level, over ten years. The U.S. proposal called for the elimination of grossly distorting domestic agricultural policy instruments over the same time frame (the "red box" interventions) while nondistorting policies were allowed to stay ("green box"), and an intermediate group were to be put under GATT discipline and reduced ("amber box").

The E.C. comprehensive proposal was presented late, on December 20, 1989. It did not provide any significant changes over the initial one tabled in 1987. It did not mention any commitment to reduce export subsidies and confirmed the proposal for a reduction of policy interventions in agriculture to be measured by means of an AMS. The rationale for such a proposal was that a reduction in global support would implicitly result in lower market distortions and reduced export subsidies, while leaving each country a wide margin of choice for accomplishing the agreed upon support reduction by trading off domestic and border policy changes.[9]

In July 1990 all parties agreed to present specific final offers by October 15, to leave some time for final negotiations before the December 31st deadline. The final U.S. proposal (presented in October 1990) offered some concessions with respect to the one tabled in 1989. It was to reduce export subsidies by 90 percent and import tariffs and internal support by 75 percent over 10 years using the 1986-88 period as a base.

The final proposal by the E.C. came in November 1990. It proposed a reduction of internal support, measured by an AMS, by 30 percent by 1995, using 1986 as the base. The position of the E.C. with respect to export subsidies was, once again, that a reduction in support would lead to a reduction in the volume of subsidized exports, per unit subsidies, and subsidy expenditure. Such a "final" proposal came after almost four years of "negotiation" and almost at the deadline for the Round. At least, for the first time, the E.C. put a figure on the table, indicating how far it was willing to go in reducing domestic support.

Neither of the two "final" proposals seemed to provide possible grounds for reaching a final compromise. How can we explain the fact that both the United States and the E.C., four years into the Round, were still very close to their initial negotiation positions? There are two possible explanations for the U.S. behavior. First, U.S. experience in previous GATT Rounds was that starting with "reasonable" requests always ended up with no results. This may explain why the original U.S. position was so extreme. In addition, the low (or zero) probability that other countries would take the U.S. positions seriously muted potential domestic opposition from import-sensitive commodity groups. Second, because the E.C. was showing no willingness to move from its equally extreme position, the United States had no incentive to adjust its own. In the absence of any sign of willingness from the E.C. to move towards trade liberalization, a unilateral move by the United States to a modified position could be interpreted as a sign of weakness.

The E.C. "final" proposal came after a long and strenuous internal confrontation. It took seven meetings of the Council of Ministers of Agriculture (some of which involved the Ministers of Trade as well) to produce an agreement on the stand to be taken. A proposal by the Commission to offer tariffication of nontariff barriers and reduce them by 30 percent over a five-year period was rejected by several country members (Schlöder, 1992).

It should not then be surprising that the attempt by Matt Hellstrom, the Swedish Minister of Agriculture, to find a last-minute compromise in Brussels on December 6, 1990, failed to be accepted. His proposal called for a reduction of internal support by 30 percent over 5 years, using 1990 as a base; for a 30 percent reduction in all tariffs over five years after tariffication of nontariff barriers; for a minimum access equal to 5 percent of domestic consumption where import barriers remained in place; and for a 30 percent cut over 5 years in export subsidy expenditure, of per unit subsidies, or of the volume of subsidized exports.

On the same day that saw the failure of the GATT "final" meeting, the

MacSharry "nonpaper," which outlined the main ideas and proposals behind what in May 1992 became the CAP reform, surfaced in Brussels (Schlöder, 1992).

In December 1991, one year after the failure to meet the original deadline of the Round, Arthur Dunkel, at that time Director General of the GATT, presented a Draft Final Act for the GATT Agreement in Agriculture. This is often referred to as the Dunkel Text. *A posteriori* this proved to be the very much needed common base, until then missing, from which to start real negotiations for a final agreement. The main provisions of the Dunkel Text for agriculture were as follows:

- A reduction of domestic interventions in agriculture, as measured by an AMS on a commodity-by-commodity basis, by 20 percent in equal installments over a six-year implementation period (the implementation period was to start in 1993), taking the 1986-1988 period as a base;
- a tariffication of all nontariff barriers and a reduction over six years of the country's simple average tariff by 36 percent and of each tariff by at least 15 percent, taking the 1986-1988 period as a base;
- a minimum market access equal to 3 percent of domestic consumption in the base period in the first year of the implementation period, to increase up to 5 percent in equal installments over the length of the implementation period;
- a reduction by 36 percent of export subsidy expenditure and by 24 percent of the volume of subsidized exports over the implementation period, using the years 1986-1990 as a base.

There were three main concerns expressed by the E.C. with respect to the Dunkel Text. First, the direct compensatory payments the Community was going to introduce with CAP reform were to be included in the domestic support measures subject to reduction. This meant that the E.C. was to receive no credit for its 1992 reform. Second, the Dunkel proposal made no provision for the need expressed by the Community to rebalance protection levels of cereals and cereal substitutes to keep their use ratio relatively stable. Finally, the Dunkel Text did not provide any assurance that CAP instruments were not going to be challenged under GATT rules once an agreement was signed (Guth and Pankopf, Ch. 9).

An important development for the Uruguay Round came in May 1992, when the CAP reform took place. Some considered the reform to be a result of the ongoing GATT negotiations, but others saw it as the result of a political process mainly driven by internal forces (see De Benedictis, De Filippis, and Salvatici, Ch. 5, for this alternative explanation of the reform). Regardless of the driving forces behind it, its adoption implied a significant change in the E.C. negotiating position. The reform opened up the possibility for the E.C. to offer concessions not only in terms of a reduction in domestic support (as long as direct compensatory payments were to be put into the "green box" of policy tools), but also in terms of a reduction in the volume of subsidized exports and of export subsidy expenditures as well.

However, the most important turning point in the E.C.-U.S. confrontation in the Uruguay Round (and in the Round itself) was the agreement reached by the United States and the E.C. Commission on November 20, 1992, in Washington, known as the Blair House agreement (named after the Washington guesthouse where most of the negotiations took place).[10] The Blair House agreement had two parts: One focused on the solution of the long standing bilateral oilseed dispute; the other defined a mutually agreeable modification of the Dunkel Text, and, by doing so, designed a draft final text of the Round agreement in agriculture.

The Blair House agreement is discussed at length in the contributions by Sumner (Ch. 4), by Guth and Pankopf (Ch. 9), and by Anderson (Ch. 10). There were three important amendments of the Dunkel Text contained in the agreement. These were:

- Direct compensatory payments under production-limiting programs, such as those introduced with the CAP reform, were not to be considered among the policies whose level of support was to be reduced under the GATT agreement;
- domestic support reduction was to be based on a total (i.e. sector-wide) AMS (instead of on a commodity-by-commodity basis); and
- the volume of subsidized exports was to be reduced by 21 percent (instead of by 24 percent).

In addition, the Blair House agreement stated that the two groups were willing to enter in consultation if rebalancing at any point was to become an issue for the E.C. It was further agreed that as long as the provisions of the GATT agreement were respected, policy instruments that were in place, including export subsidies, could not be challenged in GATT during the six-year implementation period of the agreement (this is what is often referred to as the peace clause, although calling it a truce clause would perhaps be more accurate).

The first observation regarding the provisions of the Blair House agreement is that it did not change the Dunkel Text dramatically. Thus for the agreement to be reached something had to have changed in the U.S. or in the E.C. negotiation strategy, or in both. An implicit answer to the question of what changed may come from the distance that the Blair House compromise was from both parties' positions before the agreement. All major E.C. objections to the Dunkel Text appear to have been accommodated in the Blair House agreement, but it is considerably less radical than the requests tabled by the United States during the first six years of the Round.

The provisions in the Blair House agreement, which modified the Dunkel text to make the domestic support reduction commitment on an aggregate instead of a commodity-by-commodity basis, clearly made the emerging GATT agreement more saleable domestically both in the United States and in the E.C. In fact, this change provided implicit protection to the highly subsidized dairy and sugar sectors in both the United States and the E.C., which would have been hit hard by an across-the-board reduction of the level of support measured on a commodity specific basis. No doubt the desire of the Bush administration negotiating team to reach some agreement before the arrival of the Clinton administration had something to do with the outcome. An additional explanation could be the lower internal pressure in the United States compared to the early 1980s for a GATT agreement. U.S. exports were up again in the early 1990s, and stocks were down, which reduced internal resistance to a less demanding agreement for the most protected sectors such as dairy and sugar.[11]

Finally, a major force explaining why the United States accepted the Blair House agreement was the growing political pressure and concern about the negative consequences of not having a GATT agreement. The United States had too much at stake in the overall outcome to let agricultural disputes scuttle the entire Round but could not again let agriculture be taken off the table. Thus a modified agreement which included agriculture was a domestic political imperative.

Those who thought that the Blair House compromise would result in a quick overall GATT agreement in agriculture were soon disappointed. Even within the E.C. there were countries that were unwilling to sign a final GATT agreement containing the Blair House compromise. Such behavior led Hardy-Bass to describe the Community as a political body acting as a "13-headed dragon with 26 arms and 26 legs" (Ch. 8).

The E.C. Commission claimed that a conclusion of the GATT based on the Blair House agreement would not imply any significant change in the CAP. This claim is largely confirmed by the simulations conducted on the effects of CAP reform by Guyomard and Mahé (1992); Guyomard, Le Mouel, and Surry (1993); Guyomard et al. (Ch. 6); Gray, Storey, and Zacharias (Ch. 22); Helmar, Meyers, and Hayes (Ch. 12); Folmer et al. (1992); Josling and Tangermann (1992). These studies suggest that the sugar, cheese, and meat sectors were the only markets in which the provisions of the emerging GATT agreement would not be met by CAP reform.

However, France was not willing to buy the Commission's argument, arguing that such a compromise would imply significant costs to E.C. farmers in addition to those resulting from CAP reform. France—and the other member countries who have been free-riding with France, such as Ireland and Portugal—was able to win a difficult political battle in two steps, within the Community first, and then in the final E.C.-U.S. negotiations. The French victory within the E.C. came during the so-called Jumbo Council of September 20, 1993, where it was able to garner a resolution that mandated the Commission to ask the United States for a reinterpretation of the Blair House agreement. This was clearly nothing but asking for a partial renegotiation of the agreement. The final French victory came with the final GATT agreement, which incorporates some of the changes in the Blair House text for which the French had asked.

While the start of the Round and its first steps had been characterized by the active and effective role played by several other countries and country groups (such as the Cairns Group), such multilateral activism slowed down as the negotiations moved ahead. Bilateralism prevailed in the final crucial stages of the negotiations, which designed the final agreement. The role played in the last months of 1993 by the United States was central for the achievement of a GATT agreement on agriculture. The U.S. strategy in the final stages of the Round involved action on several bilateral fronts. The major of these fronts was certainly that with the E.C. Other bilateral negotiations, mostly behind the scenes, involved other individual countries—such as Japan and South Korea—and were essentially centered on determining what was needed for them to accept the compromise that was emerging in the E.C.-U.S. bilateral negotiation.

This strategy proved to be successful and an agreement was reached on December 15, 1993, in Geneva, on the final deadline dictated by the U.S. fast-track requirement. Not surprisingly, the final agreement on agriculture is not dramatically different from the Dunkel Text as modified by the Blair House agreement. The main features of the final Uruguay Round agreement on agriculture can be summarized as follows:

- Domestic interventions in agriculture, as measured by an aggregate ("total") AMS, are to be reduced by 20 percent over a six-year implementation period (this will start in 1995 and each country can choose to use fiscal, marketing, or calendar years) taking the 1986-88 period as a base;
- as long as they are based on fixed area and yields and are made on 85 percent or less of the base level of production, or they are based on livestock numbers, direct payments under production-limiting programs are not to be subject to the commitment to reduce domestic support (direct compensatory payments introduced with the 1992 CAP reform are included among such payments);

- all nontariff barriers are to be subject to tariffication (except for the cases specified below); in general equivalent tariffs will be calculated as the difference between the average c.i.f. unit value in the importing country and a representative wholesale price ruling in the domestic market;
- each country will reduce by 36 percent its simple (i.e. unweighted) average tariff over the implementation period and will reduce each tariff line by at least 15 percent, taking the 1986-88 period as a base;
- a country may choose not to replace a non-tariff barrier with a tariff as long as (i) its imports of the commodity considered are smaller than 3 percent of domestic consumption in the base period, (ii) no exports of the commodity have been subsidized, (iii) effective production-reducing policies are used, and (iv) a minimum market access equal to 4 percent of the domestic consumption in the base period will be allowed in the first year of the implementation period, which is to be increased in equal installments to reach 8 percent at the end of the implementation period;
- minimum market access equal to 3 percent of average domestic consumption in the base period (1986-1988) must be allowed in the first year of the implementation period and increased in equal installments up to 5 percent by the end of the implementation period (minimum access imports will be subject to an in-quota tariff equal to 32 percent of the basic tariff, i.e. of the tariff subject to reduction under the agreement);
- export subsidy expenditures are to be reduced by 36 percent and the volume of subsidized exports by 21 percent over the implementation period, using the years 1986-1990 as a base; some flexibility is allowed in the phasing of such reductions over the implementation period;
- food aid exports are exempt from this reduction commitment;
- a "safeguard clause" exists specifying the circumstances under which, if undesired import increases or import price decreases occur, countries are allowed to impose additional duties;
- developing countries will have to reduce export subsidy expenditures by 24 percent and the volume of subsidized exports by 14 percent;
- as far as reduction commitments are concerned, the length of the implementation period for developing countries is extended to ten years; least developed countries are exempt from undertaking any reduction commitment;
- as long as a country is fulfilling its commitments under the agreement, its current policy interventions in agriculture cannot be the object of countervailing duties or be challenged under existing GATT rules for nine years, commencing in 1995 (the so-called peace clause);

- all countries agree that negotiations to achieve the long-term objective of "substantial progressive reductions in support and protection" will start one year before the end of the implementation period; the possible extension of the special treatment under which a country can choose not to replace an import non-tariff barrier with a tariff (as specified above) will be part of this negotiation.

The final agreement is largely the result of the bilateral agreement between the United States and the E.C. reached in Brussels on December 6, 1993. In addition to the specifics of the final text, this agreement involved many important details of the two country "schedules."[12] The final U.S.-E.C. bilateral agreement essentially involved provisions to soften the impact of the implementation of the GATT agreement in the Community (with some spillover benefit for the United States as well) in exchange for concessions accommodating specific U.S. commodity interests. A quick look at the detailed list of the provisions of the agreement may offer some hints about the role interest groups may have played in the final hours of the negotiation.

For those commodities that experienced an increase in exports between 1986-90 and 1990-91, the accord allows for a phasing of the reduction of the volume of subsidized exports, and of subsidy expenditure, which permits larger subsidized exports over the implementation period. It does so by allowing reductions to be calculated taking the 1991/92 levels as the base instead of those in 1986/90.[13] However, the final levels to be reached have been left unchanged. Although this provision has been seen by many as a victory for France and the Community, U.S. producers are net gainers as well. Both countries will be able to subsidize significant additional volumes of agricultural exports between 1995 and 2001. The new schedule will allow the E.C. to subsidize an additional 8.1 million tons of wheat exports, over 100,000 tons of cheese exports, and 360,000 tons of beef exports over the implementation period. For the United States, additional subsidized exports will be equal to over 7.4 million tons of wheat, 1.2 million tons of vegetable oil, 0.7 million tons of rice, and 65 million dozen eggs.

The bilateral agreement includes the acceptance by the United States of the E.C. tariff schedule (tariffs are higher than those derived from a strict application of the guidelines for the tariffication of nontariff barriers specified in the text of the agreement); the preserving of existing market access conditions for U.S. exports to the E.C. for corn, rice, and wheat; larger than expected E.C. minimum access quotas for commodities like pork and "mozzarella-type" cheese; larger than expected E.C. tariff cuts in many commodities of specific interest to the United States (from processed turkey and fresh asparagus to shelled almonds and in-shell walnuts, from potato chips and cheddar cheese to grapes and apples, from orange juice to swine livers); the aggregation of meat products as part of the E.C.'s implementation of the minimum access provision (to offset increased market access in pork and poultry meat with already relatively high imports of sheep meat); and the modification of the "consultation agreement" reached in the Blair House agreement relating to the "rebalancing" issue by referencing increased E.C. nongrain feed ingredient imports to a 1990-92 base instead of 1986-90.

The main question regarding the agreement that has been reached is clearly how much it will impact on U.S. and E.C. agricultural production, consumption, and trade. The remainder of this section discusses the implications of the agreement for the two largest agricultural traders.

Tariffication and Tariff Reduction

The implications of tariffication and tariff reduction are no different for the E.C. and the United States than for anybody else. An important result of the agreement clearly is the reinstrumentation of nontariff barriers to equivalent tariffs. The E.C. will have to dismantle its variable levy/export restitution system, while the United States will not be able to impose import restrictions based on "Section 22" of the AAA. However, tariffication, by itself, cannot be expected to produce immediate significant results other than, perhaps, greater world price stability. The agreed-upon reduction in the tariff levels is not likely to result in significant changes in trade flows. Realistically, for the most sensitive commodities, the only binding constraint will be a reduction of each tariff line by at least 15 percent. This follows because all countries will achieve the 36 percent reduction in their simple average tariff by larger percentage reductions of tariffs imposed on relatively less sensitive commodities. A 15 percent minimum tariff line reduction over six years may be a significant change depending on the initial level of tariff chosen, but it is not likely to be large enough to drastically change country import behavior. Initial tariff levels being proposed by some countries seem well above the wedge between domestic and international prices; therefore a 15 percent tariff reduction may not result in any change in trade flows.

Minimum Access

The minimum market access provision of the agreement implies additional E.C. imports of meats, skimmed milk powder, butter, eggs, and wheat. However, the volume of additional imports needed to comply with the agreement's requirements are relatively small and far from being a problem.[14] In the United States the minimum access provision would likely apply to peanuts, nonfat dry and concentrated milk, cheese, and butter.

Export Subsidies and Subsidized Export Reduction

A 36 percent reduction in export subsidy expenditure should not be a binding constraint for the E.C. 1992 CAP reform will bring cereals and beef internal minimum guaranteed prices in ECU down by 30 percent and 15 percent, respectively, by 1995. This will drive market prices down as well and imply a significant reduction in the E.C. export restitution expenditure. The reform—as a consequence of lower market prices, the partially decoupled nature of the compensatory payments, and the set-aside constraint—is expected to reduce domestic production, and, by so doing, to reduce E.C. exports. However, the reduction of production because of CAP reform may not satisfy the 21 percent reduction in subsidized exports. This is so because compensatory payments are not fully decoupled as they are still linked to the area of cultivated land and to the number of livestock units; the impact of the set-aside provisions on production may be less than originally expected because of the large number of smaller farms that are not required to idle land; and because of slippage effects (Herlihy and Madell, Ch. 16; and Barbero and Zezza, Ch. 15). In addition, changes in relative domestic currency values within the E.C. mean that domestic prices have not been reduced to the same degree, and some have not been reduced at all.

In the United States, the Export Enhancement Program will likely have to be scaled down. An interesting question is whether or not it will be completely eliminated. The EEP was put in place partially as an instrument to force the E.C. to negotiate in the GATT Round and to force a reduction in its export subsidies. Now that an agreement has been reached there may be fewer compelling reasons for the EEP to be continued.

Domestic Support Reduction

The 1992 CAP reform lowered market support for cereals as measured by the agreed-upon AMS by much more than 20 percent. Additional reductions in support occurred as a result of the changes in the E.C. oilseed market intervention. The support reduction on these two markets will likely constitute a decrease larger than the needed 20 percent in the E.C. "total" AMS. In the United States, reductions in production eligible for deficiency payments and constant or decreasing nominal support prices have led most to conclude that the United States will have no difficulty in meeting this requirement (Sumner, Ch. 4).

The conclusion must be that in the near future no significant changes are likely in U.S. and E.C. agricultural production and trade patterns as a consequence of the Uruguay Round agreement. However, the final agreement should be a turning point in the long standing U.S.-E.C. bilateral confrontation over agricultural trade issues. The conclusion of the Uruguay Round provides both parties with greater certainty about the economic and institutional environment in which bilateral agricultural trading will take place.

A relevant question that remains unanswered at this point is whether the GATT agreement will force further changes in the CAP. However, any future CAP developments will be bound by current GATT commitments.

Any evaluation of the significance of the Uruguay Round agreement on agriculture is sensitive to the time horizon. In the longer term, bringing agriculture at least partially under GATT discipline will result in some modifications of current policy and will place constraints on future policy excesses. The agreement to convert non-tariff barriers to tariffs and the introduction of binding ceilings will limit both the forms and the levels of protection of domestic agricultural markets. The agreement involves all countries committing themselves to a continuing reform process and to the creation of a more powerful institutional framework to resolve trade conflicts—the World Trade Organization.

Despite these positive outcomes the provisions fall short of imposing immediate radical changes in agricultural policy interventions. Many country-specific exceptions, bilateral deals, and compromises had to be made in order to reach an agreement. Some of the provisions, such as those on minimum access, probably require increased trade management and the creation of significant rents to be distributed. Once again agriculture has proven difficult to integrate fully in the GATT. However, some progress is certainly better than no agreement at all. The lack of an agreement could have led to retrogression back towards increased protectionism.

Conclusions

Despite the importance of the GATT agreement, other factors are likely to remain critical in shaping U.S.-E.C. agricultural trade relations in the next decades. These include: (a) world economic growth; (b) exchange rates; (c) continuing fiscal pressure for a change in domestic policies, both in the E.C. and in the United States; (d) changes dictated in the CAP by the possible enlargement of the EU to EFTA countries and central European countries; and (e) economic integration in the Western Hemisphere. While the GATT agreement may channel future disputes into more open and manageable institutional arrangements, bilateral tensions across the Atlantic will no doubt continue. Thus, the analyses that are presented in the following chapters will have future as well as historical relevance.

Notes

1. Argentina, Australia, Brazil, Canada, Chile, Colombia, Hungary, Indonesia, Malaysia, New Zealand, Philippines, Thailand, and Uruguay.

2. An analysis of the political process that ended in the introduction of the milk quotas is in Petit et al., 1987.

3. An interesting analysis of the political debate that ended with the introduction of the stabilizers is in Moyer and Josling, 1990.

4. It should be pointed out that if stabilizers had remained in place and no reform took place, cereal prices in 1996 would have been close to those that will occur due to the reform, but no compensatory payments would have been made.

5. Of course, the decline of E.C. imports in basic food commodities, that are an important component of U.S. exports, was in large part due to the CAP.

6. Evidence of the negative impact of the first two Lomé Conventions on the competitiveness of U.S. agricultural exports on the E.C. market is provided in Aiello and Anania, 1990.

7. In part this decline is due to the changes which occurred in U.S. domestic oilseed policy.

8. The agricultural GATT disputes between the E.C. and the United States include those over E.C. production and/or export subsidies for canned fruit (twice, one in 1981, the other in 1989), poultry (the early 1960s so-called chicken war), wheat flour, pasta, and oilseeds; the preferential tariffs the E.C. granted to imports of citrus from Mediterranean countries; the U.S. wine equity act (this is the only dispute involving agriculture that has been initiated by a complaint by the E.C.); the E.C. restricting apple imports and imports of hormone growth-treated meats; and the Spain and Portugal accession to the E.C. A discussion of the developments in each of these disputes can be found in Featherstone and Ginsberg (1993).

9. A comparative analysis of all the comprehensive proposals tabled at the end of 1989 is in IATRC, 1990.

10. Apparently, the final agreement was actually reached over the telephone (AgraEurope, November 27, 1992).

11. Interesting insights about the possible role of domestic agriculture interest groups within the E.C. and the United States in shaping the GATT outcome can be found in the contributions by Brooks (Ch. 19), and by Marchant, Neff, and Xiao (Ch. 17), and in Johnson, Mahé, and Roe (1990).

12. Country schedules will be part of the agreement to be signed in April 1994. They will specify all the details regarding the commitments for the implementation of the agreement in each country, such as how tariffication will occur, minimum access quantities, in-quota tariffs, and the reduction in each tariff line, in the subsidized export volume and in the subsidy expenditure that will take place in each year over the implementation period.

13. For E.C. beef exports the base will be the 1986-92 period.

14. Because actual imports are between 3 and 5 percent of average domestic disappearance in 1986-88, additional imports of meats, butter, and wheat will not have to occur at the beginning of the implementation period.

References

Aiello, F., and G. Anania. 1990. "Protezionismo agricolo comunitario e politiche di preferenza commerciale per i paesi in via di sviluppo. Un'analisi della I e della II Convenzione di Lomé." *La Questione Agraria*. 37: 5-49.

Anania, G., M. Bohman, and C. Carter. 1992. "United States Export Subsidies in Wheat: Strategic Trade Policy or Expensive Beggar-Thy-Neighbor Tactic?" *American Journal of Agricultural Economics*. 74: 534-45.

Anania, G., and E. Gatto. 1993. "C'era davvero bisogno di una riforma della PAC? L'efficacia delle politiche comunitarie sui mercati agricoli negli anni '80." *La Questione Agraria*. 49: 71-118.

Cuffaro, N., and F. De Filippis. 1992. "A Comparative Market Share Analysis of E.C. and U.S. Agricultural Trade." Paper presented at the EAAE Seminar "Agricultural Trade and Economic Integration in Europe and North America," Frankfurt am Main, December 7-9.

Featherstone, K., and R. H. Ginsberg. 1993. *The United States and the European Community in the 1990s. Partners in Transition*. New York: St. Martin's Press.

Folmer, C. *et al*. 1992. "CAP Reform and Its Differential Impact on Member States." Centre for World Food Studies. Amsterdam, Staff Working Paper WP-92-02R, September (cited in Sarris).

Guyomard, H., and L. P. Mahé. 1992. "CAP Reform and E.C.-U.S. Agricultural Trade Relations." Mimeo, paper prepared for the E.C. Commission, September (cited in Sarris).

Guyomard, H., C. Le Mouel, and Y. Surry. 1993. "Les effets de la réforme de la PAC sur les marchés céréaliers communautaires." *Cahiers d'économie et sociologie rurale* 27: 7-41.

Hudec, R. E. 1988. "Legal Issues in U.S.-E.C. Trade Policy: GATT Litigation 1960-1985." In R. E. Baldwin, C. B. Hamilton, and A. Sapir (eds.), *Issues in U.S.-E.C. Trade Relations*. Chicago, IL: The University of Chicago Press. pp. 17-64.

IATRC. 1990. "Bringing Agriculture into the GATT. The Comprehensive Proposals for Negotiations in Agriculture." Commissioned Paper No. 7.

Johnson, M., L. P. Mahé, and T. Roe. 1990. "Politically Acceptable Trade Compromises Between the E.C. and the U.S.: A Game Theory Approach." International Agricultural Trade Research Consortium, Working Paper No. 90-5, October.

Josling, T., and S. Tangermann. 1992. "MacSharry or Dunkel: Which Plan Reforms the CAP?" International Agricultural Trade Research Consortium, Working Paper No. 92-10, July.

Keohane, R. O. 1984. *After Hegemony: Cooperation and Discord in the World Political Economy*. Princeton, N.J.: Princeton Univ. Press.

McCalla, A. F. 1969. "Protectionism in International Agricultural Trade, 1850-1968." Agricultural History 43: 329-343.

McCalla, A. 1993. "Agricultural Trade Liberalization: The Ever Elusive Grail." *American Journal of Agricultural Economics* 75: 1102-1112.

Moyer, H. W., and T. E. Josling. 1990. *Agricultural Policy Reform*. Ames: IA, Iowa State University Press.

Petit, M. 1985. "Determinants of Agricultural Policies in the United States and the European Community." Research Report No. 51, Washington, D.C.: International Food Policy Research Institute, November.

Petit, M., M. De Benedictis, D. Britton, M. de Groot, W. Henrichsmeyer, and F. Lechi. 1987. *Agricultural Policy Formation in the European Community: the Birth of Milk Quotas.* Amsterdam: Elsevier.

Sarris, A. 1988. "E.C.-U.S. Agricultural Trade Confrontation." In R. E. Baldwin, C. B. Hamilton, and A. Sapir (eds.) *Issues in U.S.-E.C. Trade Relations.* Chicago: The University of Chicago Press, pp. 101-31.

Schlöder, H. 1992. "The European Community's Position in the GATT Round." In T. Becker, R. Gray, and A. Schmitz (eds). *Improving Agricultural Trade Performance Under the GATT.* Kiel: Wissenschaftsverlag Vauk. pp. 279-85.

Tracy, M. 1993. *Food and Agriculture in a Market Economy.* Belgium: Agricultural Policy Studies, Chapters 8-9, pp. 148-184.

PART ONE

U.S.-E.C. Trade Relations in a Changing Global Context

2

U.S.-E.C. Trade Relations in a Changing Global Context

Robert E. Baldwin

Introduction

The United States and the countries of the European Community have been the key players in the liberal trading system that has developed through much of the world over the last 50 years. The willingness of these two large trading blocs to open their extensive internal markets to foreign-produced goods has been the major factor in inducing other countries to reciprocate by reducing their trade barriers. This joint commitment to promote a liberal trading order has also played an important role in resolving U.S.-E.C. differences on trade policies. The United States and the European Community have long recognized that, unless they compromise with each other on the issues over which they disagree, further global trade liberalization is not feasible.

Unfortunately, this implicit contract has been broken in the latest round of multilateral trade negotiations, the Uruguay Round, which began in 1986 and was scheduled to end in December 1990. The major issue of disagreement is, of course, agricultural trade liberalization. The United States is pressing for significant liberalization, while the Community wishes to liberalize only modestly. The parties appeared to reach a compromise in November, 1992, but efforts by the Bush Administration to wrap up the Uruguay Round negotiations failed before it left office in January. Furthermore, there is a danger that the agricultural agreement reached at that time may unravel. The French government strongly opposed the agricultural compromise at the outset, threatening to veto it in E.C. deliberations on the issue. However, this government later accepted that part of the agreement covering oilseeds after the European Community included the increase of payments to those farmers who would be required to take part of their land out of production. But the French continue to reject that portion of the agreement dealing with the reduction of E.C. export subsidies on agricultural products. In addition, the new American Administration has expressed dissatisfaction with some aspects of the agreement, complaining that its market access provisions do not go far enough in opening E.C. markets.

Other parts of the Uruguay Round agreement also are in jeopardy. The Clinton Administration has expressed dissatisfaction with agreements tentatively reached on such key issues as intellectual property rights, trade in services, dumping and countervailing duties, the environmental impact of trade, and the creation of a new institution (the Multilateral Trade Organization) to replace the General Agreement on Tariffs and Trade (GATT). While Congress agreed to extend the so-called "fast track" authority, which provides for an up-or-down, no-amendments vote on trade agreements negotiated by the Executive Branch, until December 1993, this timetable may be too short for completing the Round.

The first failure to complete a multilateral trade negotiation on schedule is, in itself, cause for concern, but other developments reinforce this apprehension over the prospects for the multilateral trading system. One is the greater use of regional agreements as the institutional means through which governments pursue their policy goals. In recent years, the European Community, for example, has expanded its membership and moved closer to becoming a single market by eliminating many internal barriers to trade and by initiating steps in the Maastricht Treaty to establish a common monetary policy and currency. It has also forged closer economic relations with members of the European Free Trade Association by creating the European Economic Area. The U.S. government has negotiated separate free trade agreements with Canada and Israel, and is now engaged in concluding the North American Free Trade Agreement with Canada and Mexico. The Bush Administration planned to expand this latter agreement to include other Latin American countries, and the Clinton Administration has also expressed some interest in such an expansion. The other major industrial power, Japan, has not concluded any formal agreements with other countries in East Asia but has established strong informal ties through direct investment activities in this region.

Another development has been the increased use of unilateral policies by a number of advanced industrial countries to achieve their trade objectives. Since the early 1980s, there has, for example, been an explosion in the use by the United States and the European Community of the dumping and countervailing duty provisions of the GATT to protect domestic producers against foreign competition. Even more significant has been the greater use of such measures as Section 301 and Super 301 of U.S. trade law to force other countries to open their internal markets or refrain from various allegedly unfair trading practices. Many U.S. government officials now seem to believe that this unilateral approach and a greater reliance on regional agreements are much more effective in achieving U.S. trade-policy goals than the multilateral methods embodied in the GATT.

While the frustrations of the United States and the European Community in settling their trade-policy differences, especially with regard to agricultural trade liberalization, have contributed to the movement by each away from multilateralism and toward unilateralism and regionalism, other inadequacies of the GATT system have also played an important role in bringing about these shifts. Among these factors have been the difficulty of opening the domestic markets of developing countries as these countries themselves became successful exporters of industrial products; the unwillingness of the advanced industrial countries to permit market conditions to determine the domestic size of such industries as textiles and apparel, steel, automobiles, and consumer electronic products and the resulting frustrations of the developing countries in trying to gain access to the international markets for these goods; the absence of GATT rules covering restrictive business practices and the existence of ineffective rules on government purchasing policies; the inability to reach agreement on rules covering so-called unfair trade; and the inability of GATT members to reach decisions in a timely fashion on matters ranging from trade disputes to rules in new areas of trade negotiations.

Unless these various weaknesses of the current multilateral trading regime are corrected, there is a serious possibility that the global trading system may become divided into three major blocs whose relations with each other become increasingly protectionist over time. In my view, the only feasible way of undertaking the needed reforms in the trading system is by seeking agreement among a subset of key GATT members to accept a higher level of GATT discipline and responsibilities along the line of the GATT-Plus organization proposed several years ago. This organization would be open to all GATT members at any time and would involve both greater responsibilities, e.g., an increased willingness to open domestic markets and accept GATT panel decision, and additional privileges, e.g., greater access to the markets of signatories and better safeguards against unilateral retaliation.[1]

As one would expect, the key members of this subset of current GATT members must be the three major trading powers, the United States, the European Community, and Japan, and a number of the newly industrializing countries. The expectation is that most other current GATT members would quickly join with these key countries in changing the conditions that are currently leading to the breakdown of GATT discipline and in establishing a new international regime that will maintain the multilateral nature of trading relations.

Before a GATT-Plus is possible, however, the three key players in global trade must achieve an acceptable degree of harmony in their relations with each other. Thus, resolving the current agricultural dispute between the United States and the European Community is important not only in itself but so that these two great trading powers can begin to tackle the larger problem of strengthening the multilateral trading system. The purpose of this chapter is to assist in the search for ways of settling the U.S.-E.C. agricultural dispute by analyzing various disputes that have arisen over the last 35 years between the United States and the European Community. An effort is made to determine the basic reasons for these disagreements and the means that have proved most successful in resolving them. Based on this analysis, various suggestions are then made for hastening the resolution of the current agricultural dispute.

Factors Underlying U.S.-E.C. Trade Tensions

There are two fundamental reasons why trade disputes between the United States and the European Community are sometimes contentious and difficult to resolve. First, although neither is now a hegemon, both are major economic powers accustomed to exerting great influence over most other countries with whom they negotiate on trade matters. In such negotiations, the United States and the European Community essentially establish the policy that best meets their own self-interests, and other countries accommodate to this policy in the best manner for them. However, in dealing with each other, the two trading blocs recognize their strategic interdependence, in the sense that the best policy for each to pursue is highly dependent on the policy followed by the other. Consequently, working out an equilibrium set of policies in which each believes its own policy is best for its own self-interest, given the policy being followed by the other, is likely to prove difficult in some circumstances.

A second reason is the different economic philosophies held by the policy-makers and electorates of the two trading powers concerning the proper role of the state in promoting various economic goals. In the United States, there is a widely held view that the nation's welfare is best promoted if the allocation of goods and services among individuals is largely decided through the free-market system. In most E.C. countries, in contrast, the electorate believes in the need for considerably more intervention in the form of state ownership and various price-fixing and tax-subsidy arrangements in order to change the allocation of goods and services from its free-market outcome. These differences of views sometimes lead to disputes over what kinds of trade measures are "fair" or best promote collective welfare, thus exacerbating the problem of finding mutually acceptable policy compromises.

The next section illustrates how the gradual shift in the power relationship between the two blocs, specifically, the decline of the United States as a hegemonic state and the concomitant rise in the power of the European Community, has led to an increasing number of disputes that have been difficult to resolve. The section after then explains how differences in economic philosophies also account for some of the disputes between the two trading partners.

U.S.-E.C. Trade Disputes in the Post-U.S. Hegemony Period

In the period from the end of World War II until the formation of the Community in 1957, the hegemonic status of the United States enabled this country to have its way, by and large, in shaping world trade policies. Two general factors account for the emergence of the United States as a hegemon in the postwar period. First, the destruction and obsolescence of capital facilities in both victorious countries such as the United Kingdom and France and defeated nations such as Germany and Japan turned out to be much greater than anticipated. The international organizations established to assist these countries in restoring their peacetime industrial capacities and in helping the developing countries to break their cycles of poverty, such as the World Bank and the International Monetary Fund, turned out to be completely inadequate for this task. Only the United States, whose industrial capacity at the end of the war was much larger than at the beginning, was capable of meeting even the most essential needs of these countries. Fearing a return to the international economic chaos of the 1930s, U.S. political leaders began soon after the war to support direct U.S. economic aid to these countries. An early example of such assistance was the U.S. loan of $3.75 billion to the United Kingdom in 1946.

A second, even more compelling, reason why the United States assumed a hegemonic role was the political threat posed by the Soviet Union. The expansion of Soviet political influence into Eastern Europe, Manchuria, and Northern Korea and the threat of communist take-overs in such nations as Turkey and Greece endangered the political benefits of the military victory. As in the economic area, only the United States had the military capability to contain Soviet geographic expansion. The strategy adopted involved both military and economic elements. On the military side, the United States promoted a series of defensive military alliances, such as the Atlantic Treaty, with countries around the world aimed at limiting Soviet expansion. On the economic front, the United States undertook a massive foreign aid program designed to strengthen the so-called "free world" so that it could better resist internal and external pressures from the communists. U.S. political leaders also took the lead in initiating a series of multilateral, tariff-reducing trade negotiations under the auspices of the GATT. It was the firm belief of these leaders that moving toward free trade not only increased the economic welfare of all nations but, by reducing discrimination against foreigners, increased the prospects for international political stability and peace.

Since the international economic policies promoted by the United States were generally in the collective interests of the free world and the United States provided financial aid to assist countries with any structural adjustments necessitated by these policies, there was little resistance to U.S. economic leadership in the early postwar years. Duties in the major industrial countries were reduced about 20 percent in the first multilateral trade negotiation in 1947 and another 10 percent in a series of smaller negotiations that followed in the 1950s and early 1960s (Baldwin, 1984). When objection to a U.S. policy position by a particular country was encountered, the United States was usually able to line up other countries to put pressure on the recalcitrant nation and thus force it into line. Furthermore, the United States was generally able to secure special privileges for itself, as the 1955 GATT agricultural waiver illustrates. In the early 1950s, the U.S. Congress passed legislation mandating quantitative import restrictions on dairy products that went beyond the special rules on agricultural products contained in Article XI of the GATT, which themselves had been incorporated in the GATT to accommodate the United States (Hudec, 1975). While President Truman opposed these provisions and attempted to repeal them in subsequent years, he was not completely successful and in 1955 the United States asked for a GATT waiver permitting these agricultural import restrictions (Jackson, 1989). Even though two-thirds of voting GATT members must approve such a request before it is granted, the United States had little difficulty in obtaining such approval.

The Tariff-Cutting Rule. The United States first began to encounter serious resistance to its leadership role in trade matters in the Kennedy Round of multilateral trade negotiations (1962-1967), which was the first major trade negotiation undertaken after the European Community had been formed. The dispute that arose over the tariff-cutting rule illustrates this resistance. While the average duty level for manufactured goods was about the same in both trading blocs, the United States had many more high- and low-duty items than the Community.[2] The United States proposed cutting all tariffs by 50 percent, with a minimum of exceptions being permitted. The Community responded by proposing a rule that cut high-duty items a greater percentage than low-duty products. Specifically, their suggested rule reduced tariffs on manufactured goods by 50 percent *of the difference* between their existing levels and 10 percent. Thus, a 40 percent duty would be cut by .5(40–10) = 15 percentage points to 25 percent, while a 20 percent duty would be cut by .5(20–10) = 5 percentage points to 15 percent. Duties on semi-manufactures and raw materials would be cut 50 percent *of the difference* between their existing levels and 5 percent and zero, respectively (Baldwin, 1965).[3]

The United States opposed the E.C. formula on the grounds that it would not yield a significant average duty reduction and involved a greater average percentage cut in U.S. than E.C. duties. A prime U.S. objective in the negotiation was to achieve a significant average duty cut and thereby reduce the margin of tariff preference for Community members against the rest of the world within Community markets. In contrast, the Community had only reluctantly agreed to a new negotiating round and did not wish to add the adjustment problems associated with large cuts in external tariffs to those that were taking place with the removal of duties among its members. E.C. negotiators also believed that the greater number of high-duty items in the U.S. than the E.C. tariff schedule caused trade to be diverted from the Community.[4] Consequently, they wanted these U.S. duties to be cut by a greater percentage in order to reduce the gap between the two sets of rates.

With the direct approval of President Kennedy, U.S. negotiators insisted on a rule involving a uniform percentage cut and were prepared to end the negotiations unless the American position was accepted. After a series of tense meetings, a compromise was accepted in which the 50 percent rule was accepted. However, the following provision was included in the agreement: "In those cases where there are significant disparities in tariff levels, the tariff reductions will be based upon special rules of general and automatic application" (see Baldwin, 1965). As it turned out, the U.S. negotiators were able to prevent the extensive application of this special provision by showing it would generally have an adverse effect on third countries. But the incident showed that the common negotiating positions adopted by the six European countries reduced the power of the United States to impose its own trade-policy objectives on GATT members.

Agricultural Liberalization. The Kennedy Round negotiations with the Community on agricultural products also illustrate the decreased negotiating power of the United States. Prior to the start of the Kennedy Round, U.S. negotiators repeatedly stated that improved market access for American agricultural products was an essential condition for the United States to sign any agreement, and they were successful in including the following in the ministerial statement initiating the Round: "The trade negotiations shall provide for acceptable conditions of access to world markets for agricultural products." (Preeg, 1970). However, the Community initially offered only to bind overall levels of support for farm products for three years and to establish an international set of reference prices for grains that would be used to determine import levies and export subsidies. No commitment on access to the E.C. market was included in the offer.

The response of the United States and other agricultural exporters was highly negative. U.S. negotiators insisted that any freezing of support levels must be accompanied by assurances of continued access to E.C. markets. Since E.C. negotiators were anxious to gain increased access to U.S. industrial markets through lower tariffs, U.S. negotiators linked progress in reducing trade barriers in manufacturing sectors to liberalization in agriculture. This strategy paid off partially, with the Community finally agreeing to modest tariff concessions on imports of nongrain agricultural products. However, Community negotiators refused to accept a grain agreement involving assurances about market access. The final agreement only set price ranges for international wheat trade and a joint food aid commitment. (See Preeg, ch. 9, for a detailed discussion of the agricultural negotiations.)

By the next GATT-sponsored multilateral trade negotiation, the Tokyo Round (1974-79), the decline in the international economic power of the United States had become even more evident. The U.S. share of world exports of manufactured goods had, for example, fallen to 13.4 percent by 1971, compared to 18.7 percent in 1959. U.S. dominance of international monetary matters had also come to an end, as the fixed exchange-rate system anchored to the dollar had collapsed and been replaced by a flexible-rate system. One consequence of this relative decline was that the United States had even greater difficulty in "getting its way" in dealing with trading powers such as the European Community and Japan.

Both the negotiations on the tariff-cutting formula and on agricultural liberalization during the Tokyo Round illustrate this point. The United States made a slight concession to the Community's objective of cutting high-duty rates more than low rates by proposing a rule that would reduce duties equal to, or greater than, 6.67 percent by 60 percent and those less than 6.67 percent by 50-60 percent. The formula proposed by the Community involved a much greater degree of tariff harmonization. The percentage cut in each duty would be the level of the duty itself. Moreover, this would be repeated four times. Thus, a 40 percent duty would be cut by 40 percent or by 16 percentage points to 24 percent. It would then be cut by 24 percent to 18.2 percent; the 18.2 percent figure would be reduced by 18.2 percent to 14.9 percent. The 14.9 rate would then be cut by 14.9 to reach the final level of 12.7 percent.

E.C. negotiators objected to the U.S. proposal for failing to provide sufficient tariff harmonization, while U.S. negotiators argued that the Community proposal would yield an average cut of only about 30 percent, even before any exceptions were applied. It was evident that this time the

United States did not possess enough international political clout to force the Community to accept its proposal. It was due to pressure from the other industrial countries, who wanted to move ahead with the negotiations, that the two major trading powers finally reached a compromise. Under the so-called Swiss formula that was accepted, the rate by which a duty was cut was the duty rate itself divided by the duty rate plus .14. Thus, a duty rate of .14 was cut by $.14/(.14+.14) = .5$ or 50 percent. The United States accepted the formula because its application produced a larger average cut (about 40 percent) than the E.C. proposal, while the Community accepted this tariff-cutting rule because it produced much more harmonization than the U.S. proposal.[5]

In the area of agriculture, the Tokyo Round started with the same wide divergence in U.S. and E.C. positions that characterized the Kennedy Round. The United States wanted to negotiate agricultural liberalization in a manner identical to that followed in industrial sectors. Furthermore, the United States wanted to eliminate agricultural export subsidies and increase access to world markets for agricultural products. In contrast, the European Community insisted that the principles and mechanisms of its Common Agricultural Policy were not subject to negotiation and that any discussions on agriculture must take place in a separate negotiating group. In addition, the Community stressed the importance of stabilizing international agricultural markets through a series of international commodity agreements.

The United States agreed to the creation of a separate negotiating group but balked at the Community's insistence on negotiating all types of trade measures, e.g., tariffs and price supports, in this group. The outcome was a lack of any progress in the agricultural negotiations from early 1975 until a compromise was finally reached in July 1977. Interestingly, the main reason for the compromise was the change in leadership of the U.S. Executive Branch from President Ford to President Carter. As Winham (1986) points out, the offensive against E.C. agricultural policies was nearly a theological position of the Ford administration. However, the U.S. Trade Representative appointed by President Carter, namely Robert Strauss, was much more pragmatic and less committed to agricultural interests. In exchange for a timetable for the rapid completion of the Tokyo Round, the United States dropped its insistence that agriculture be negotiated along with industry on the condition that there would be "substantial results for agriculture."

Bilateral negotiations between the United States and the European Community led to improved access to E.C. markets for high-quality U.S. beef as well as lower trade barriers against rice and tobacco in return for better access to U.S. markets for European dairy products and the elimination of a discriminatory U.S. tax on alcoholic beverages. An Arrangement

Regarding Bovine Meat and an International Dairy Arrangement were negotiated multilaterally, but these mainly involved an exchange of information among trading nations. The main multilateral effort in this area, namely the negotiation of a grain agreement to replace the International Wheat Agreement, failed. Thus, the final accomplishments of the Tokyo Round in agriculture were, like those of the Kennedy Round, modest.

By the time the Uruguay Round started in 1986, the United States no longer was interested in achieving a deep average reduction in manufacturing duties. The cut of about 30 percent achieved in the Tokyo Round brought average industrial tariffs in the advanced countries below 5 percent. There were still numerous high rates, but they were in politically sensitive product lines that U.S. negotiators would have difficulty cutting under any automatic tariff-cutting formula. Consequently, the United States proposed returning to the old item-by-item approach to tariff cutting that had been followed prior to the Kennedy Round. E.C. negotiators readily accepted this proposal, apparently satisfied that further tariff harmonization was not needed.

The main efforts of U.S. negotiators were directed at increasing trade in services, strengthening intellectual property rights internationally, and liberalizing agriculture. Opposition by the Community had largely been responsible for the failure of the Ministerial Meeting in 1982, when the United States first proposed negotiating on the first two topics. However, in the period between 1982 and 1986, the Community changed its views on these issues and joined the United States in pressing for negotiations in these areas. Consequently, the only major issue on which there has been serious disagreement between the United States and the European Community in the Uruguay Round has been agricultural liberalization.

Like the earlier Ford Administration, the Reagan Administration approached agricultural liberalization with a sense of religious zeal. Indeed, Clayton Yeutter, the U.S. Trade Representative, often said that "the angels are on our side on this issue."[6] The initial U.S. proposal called for the complete phase-out of agricultural subsidies and import barriers over a ten-year period. Community negotiators called the U.S. proposal unrealistic when it was made in July 1987 but did not respond with a proposal that included a commitment to reduce domestic supports by a certain percentage until July 1990, six months before the negotiations were scheduled to end. Thus, it was difficult for U.S. negotiators to modify their position significantly just before the December meeting, without being perceived by domestic agricultural interests as "caving in" to domestic manufacturing interests as well as the Community. Reducing the extent of liberalization sought over a ten-year period from 100 percent to 75 percent was about the extent of the "back-off" from their original proposal that was politically feasible.

But, if U.S. negotiators thought that E.C. negotiators would be willing and able to modify their negotiating position at the Ministerial meeting in December by agreeing to something like a 50 percent reduction in agricultural supports (a figure mentioned at the time of the initial proposal as being acceptable if it came down to complete liberalization or no liberalization), they were woefully misinformed about the political strength of agricultural interests in the Community and the difficulty of modifying Community policy positions, once they have been taken. Thus, the Ministerial Meeting in December 1990 failed. A compromise was finally reached two years later, in November 1992, but this is now in jeopardy, since, as already noted, the French are threatening to veto the compromise and even the new Clinton Administration apparently is dissatisfied with the agreement.

The Hegemonic Theory of Regime Stability. According to one well-known theory of international political economy, the hegemonic theory of regime stability, one should expect the disagreements that have arisen between the United States and the Community over agricultural liberalization. This theory maintains that the existence of a hegemonic power is a necessary condition for a liberal international trade and financial system (Gilpin, 1987; Kindleberger, 1981). The hegemon's trading and financial interests are so large that it gains under a system of free trade and stable exchange rates compared to a system of worldwide protection and unstable exchange rates, even if smaller states free ride by pursuing mercantilist trade and exchange rate policies. When, however, the country loses its dominant political position, as the United States has done, the costs to it of maintaining a liberal regime, which is like an international public good, are no longer less than its gains from such a system. Therefore, trade policy disputes arise, and protectionism and beggar-thy-neighbor trade and exchange rate policies emerge on a global basis.

Obviously, the dire predictions of this theory have not materialized. Despite the end of U.S. hegemony and the conflicts among large trading powers such as the United States, the European Community, and Japan, the world trading system has continued to be relatively open. Game theory and the theory of collective action indicate that stable, liberal trading equilibrium positions are possible among large trading nations both with and without explicit cooperation. The international institutions created during the hegemonic period, such as the GATT and International Monetary Fund, also have served as facilitators of cooperation in the post-hegemonic period.

The Role of Different Economic Philosophies in U.S.-E.C. Trade Disputes

As noted in the introduction to this section, disputes are highly likely between two large trading partners as they each pursue their economic self-interests. However, when these partners also disagree on such matters as what economic conditions further a country's self-interests and the economic policies that best promote a particular collective economic goal, these disputes are likely to be more difficult to resolve. This subsection illustrates how such differences in economic philosophies have played a role in various U.S.-E.C. disagreements.

The Disparities Issue. One of the most frustrating aspects of the U.S.-E.C. disagreement over the tariff-cutting formula in the Kennedy and Tokyo Rounds was the inability of U.S. negotiators to understand the rationale behind the E.C. position. As noted earlier, the average duty level in the United States and the Community was approximately the same at the outset of the Kennedy Round, but the United States had a larger number of both high- and low-tariff items. E.C. negotiators raised three objections to the proposal to cut all duties by 50 percent. First, they argued that an equal percentage cut in high U.S. and middle-level E.C. rates would increase U.S. exports to the Community much more than E.C. exports to the United States. They simultaneously maintained that 50 percent cuts in the larger number of low-duty U.S. items would not be worth much in terms of increasing E.C. exports, because these low duties are only a minor obstacle to trade. Secondly, they claimed that equal percentage cuts would divert exports from third countries away from the United States and towards the Community. Finally, they argued that the United States would end up with more high rates and thus have greater bargaining power for future negotiations.

The implication of the first two arguments is that the average elasticity of import demand is less in the United States than in the European Community due to the relative inelasticity of import demand for both high-duty and low-duty items in the U.S. tariff schedule. The only substantive argument Community officials made about high U.S. duties was that they were, in effect, prohibitive and would still remain so after a 50 percent cut. In other words, they claimed that there was considerable "water" in high U.S. duty items. However, no empirical evidence in the form of elasticity estimates was presented by Community negotiators to support this point. The logic behind the prohibitive nature of U.S. tariffs was also weak. Any "water" that existed in the very high duties established under the Smoot-Hawley Tariff Act of 1930 had likely long been eliminated in the trade negotiations of the 1930s, 1940s, and 1950s. During this period, the president had the power to reduce any tariff at least to its so-called "peril point," the level determined by the Tariff Commission at which further cuts would supposedly cause serious injury to domestic producers of the product. If the president reduced a duty below its "peril point," he or she was required to explain why. Since U.S. presidents were anxious to reduce duties significantly in the 1930s and 1940s, they cut most dutiable items to their "peril point" and many below this level.

E.C. officials also did not set forth any empirical evidence substantiating their claim that cuts in low duty items were not worth as much in terms of increased exports as cuts in middle-duty items. Actually, most low-duty items are primary products or semi-manufactures. Since these products tend to be homogeneous, a low duty can be fully as protective as a higher duty on a differentiated manufactured item.

The argument presented by E.C. spokespersons seemed to confuse the effect of a given percentage cut on the price of a product and the concept of price elasticity. A 50 percent cut on a 10 percent duty item, for example, will decrease the product's price relatively less, all other things being equal, than a 50 percent cut in a 50 percent tariff item.[7] Therefore, under the assumption that other things are equal, the relative increase in imports of the first product will be less than for the second. This has nothing to due with differences in elasticities. However, if import elasticities are the same in the United States and the Community, the smaller increase in imports for low-duty U.S. items would be offset by the larger import increase for high-duty U.S. items, since average duties and trading volumes were about the same in the two areas.

In the Kennedy Round, it was never possible to get Community negotiators to present their case in a manner that could be argued in terms of some common economic language or method of analysis nor that could be disputed in terms of different empirical methods used in reaching different conclusions. The issue seemed to be a matter of ideology for these officials and remained so through the Tokyo Round. In the Tokyo Round, however, U.S. officials decided it was not worth the effort to argue about the Community's harmonization ideas after empirical estimates of trade effects indicated no significant difference between a linear and harmonization rule, provided the average cut was about the same.

Assistance to Industry and Agriculture. More important in trade-volume terms than the disputes over tariff-cutting rules has been the disagreements between the United States and the Community over government assistance to various manufacturing sectors and agriculture. A basic reason for these disputes is the difference in viewpoint concerning the proper role of government in helping particular income groups or in pursuing some national economic goal.

In the post-World War II period, government intervention has been extensive in the European Community countries. For example, in the late 1950s, the French government drew up specific investment programs for several key industries and not only used controls over credit, raw materials, and imports to channel investment into targeted sectors but directly financed a large part of the desired investment. Similarly, in Great Britain under the Labor government, a number of industries were nationalized and controls over investment established for the private sector. By the early 1950s, about one-half of all investment in the country was directly or indirectly under government auspices. Germany adopted a policy of codetermination under which labor participated in the management of private corporations, and the government continued to control such industries as railroads, telegraph, telephone, radio, saving banks, and a number of industrial enterprises.

Although the extent of state intervention has eased in most E.C. countries since the early post-World War II years, government still plays a very active role in economic affairs. Subsidies are extensive in such relatively depressed industries as textiles, steel, shipbuilding, coal, and paper and pulp, and special regional grants are common to aid depressed regions. Most European governments also provide grants and other forms of assistance to foster high technology sectors such as computers, electronics, and aircraft.

The American political tradition is, in contrast, one in which there is considerable reluctance to intervene in industrial activities on a long-run basis. Temporary import protection has traditionally been granted to assist sectors injured by import competition, but even here the industry must show it has been seriously injured because of increased imports. Only one manufacturing sector, the politically powerful textiles and apparel industry, has been able to secure import protection on a long-run basis. The generally accepted view is that it is neither fair nor economically efficient to maintain production in a declining industry at artificially high levels for a long period. Promoting new manufacturing activities by means of low interest rate loans or direct grants for capital facilities and research efforts also has not been generally politically acceptable, although the Clinton Administration may change this tradition.

Agriculture is, however, one sector where long-run government assistance has been provided by both the United States and European Community countries, as well as by most other nations. Price support programs backed by quantitative import controls were introduced in Great Britain, Germany, and France in the 1920s. The United States provided special credit facilities to farmers and promoted orderly marketing agreements during this period, and, in the 1930s, followed the European countries in establishing agricultural price support programs. These programs continued in both Europe and the United States after World War II.

There seem to be several reasons why the electorate of most countries is willing to subsidize farmers over long periods of time. Because of the lower long-run rate of growth in the farm sector compared to the industrial sector in most countries, urban voters are receptive to providing adjustment assistance on income-distribution grounds. The long hours worked by farmers and their perceived simple lifestyle make their adjustment difficulties especially appealing to urban voters. These voters are prepared to provide assistance over longer periods than for most other sectors because they recognize the relative immobility of productive factors in agriculture. In addition, such factors as the essentiality of agricultural products at times of natural or political crises, a belief in the importance of family farming in contributing to the country's social stability, and the role of farmers in preserving the natural environment contribute to the appeal of the agricultural sector for special treatment. On a more practical level, the fact that farmers, their urban relatives, and the service sector employees who depend heavily on the spending of this group usually constitute an important political interest group in the constituencies of many legislators makes them a very effective lobbying group.

At least two factors account for the divergence in E.C. and U.S. agricultural policies since the 1960s. First, the United States became increasingly competitive as an agricultural exporter. In the 1950s, for example, U.S. agricultural imports exceeded U.S. agricultural exports by 17 percent. However, in the 1960s, the United States became a net exporter of agricultural goods, with exports exceeding imports by 37 percent. During the 1970s the percentage by which agricultural exports exceeded imports rose to 93 percent (*Economic Report of the President*, 1992). This favorable development took much of the political pressure off government officials for extensive agricultural support programs. Instead, many farmers began to urge the U.S. government to pressure foreign governments to open their internal markets to U.S. agricultural products.

The second factor is related to the creation of the European Economic Community. At the time the Community was formed, there was considerable variation among member nations in the degree to which they were subsidizing their agricultural sectors. To ensure that internal trade in agricultural goods would be free and a common level of protection against imports from nonmember nations would prevail, it was necessary to coordinate and centralize the agricultural support programs of the different members. Consequently, beginning in 1962, the Common Agricultural Policy (CAP) was gradually put into place. Under this policy, target prices (desired prices), intervention prices (floor prices guaranteed by the Community), and threshold prices (minimum prices at which imports can be sold) were established annually for commodities. Understandably, the politics of forming such a system tended to result in prices that maintained production levels in countries with the most inefficient farmers, while encouraging the expansion of output in members whose farmers were more efficient.

One might have expected growing opposition to the CAP among Community officials because of the rising budgetary costs of the program, but such was not so. In the early years, the CAP was regarded as the main feature that made the state of economic affairs among E.C. members different from the situation preceding the formation of the customs union. In other words, the CAP was regarded by some Community bureaucrats as the cement that bound members together economically. Consequently, rather than trying to curtail the program, Community officials seemed to push for its expansion as a means of strengthening the organization and increasing their own influence. They realized that, since the Community was a large importer of agricultural commodities, the producers who would lose under a program that kept expanding E.C. production would be foreign exporters, who did not participate in the internal decision-making process of the organization.

Despite the introduction and extension of the CAP in the 1960s and 1970s, U.S. exports of food products to Europe grew significantly, especially in the 1970s. U.S. food exports to the Community increased by 137 percent between 1973 and 1980, for example, and food exports to the rest of the world rose by 141 percent over this period. World exports of food products increased 102 percent between these years. However, as E.C. agricultural output under the CAP grew larger and larger in the 1980s, U.S. exports of agricultural products to the Community began to decline. For example, between 1980 and 1990, U.S. agricultural exports to the Community fell by 25 percent, whereas U.S. agricultural exports to the rest of the world increased by 19 percent. The fact that world exports of agricultural goods only rose 45 percent over the decade means that basic world structural conditions were largely responsible for the slowdown in the growth of U.S. agricultural exports, but the discriminatory impact of the CAP is evident from the figures.[8]   In view of the decline in U.S. agricultural exports to the Community in the 1980s, it is not surprising that U.S. negotiators pressed for significant E.C. agricultural liberalization in the Uruguay Round.

The negotiating strategies of both U.S. and E.C. negotiators in the agricultural sector can be faulted, however. The initial U.S. proposal turned out to be highly unrealistical in terms of the degree of liberalization that the Community was willing to grant. At the same time, E.C. negotiators significantly underestimated the seriousness of the U.S. resolve to achieve a significant degree of liberalization in the agricultural sector and failed to negotiate seriously on the matter in a timely fashion. Higher U.S. officials with greater foreign policy knowledge and responsibilities also failed to force the U.S. trade negotiators to adopt more realistic objectives before the negotiations proceeded to the stage where it became difficult to make major changes in their proposals.

Interestingly, the initial U.S. proposal calling for the complete phase-out of agricultural subsidies and import barriers over a ten-year period was not put forth as a consequence of intense domestic political pressures from agricultural interests. Instead, the main impetus for the proposal came from the Executive Branch. Trade officials in the Reagan Administration, like many in the agricultural sector, felt that agriculture had been "sold down the river" near the end of both the Kennedy and Tokyo Rounds of multilateral trade negotiations. The U.S. proposal also was not in response to commitments made in the Ministerial Declaration on the Uruguay Round. This declaration only calls for greater liberalization of agricultural trade and increased "discipline on the use of all direct and indirect subsidies and other measures affecting directly or indirectly agricultural trade, including the phased reduction of their negative effects and dealing with their causes" (GATT Press Release, September 25, 1986).

Resolving the U.S.-E.C. Agricultural Dispute and Strengthening the Multilateral Trading System

As the preceding section has shown, both relative size and differences in economic philosophies affect the ability of trading nations to resolve their disputes. Successful dispute resolution between two large trading blocs, such as the United States and the European Community, depends on the mutual recognition that both have much to gain from trade with each other and that the world trading system in general depends on reasonably harmonious relations between the large trading nations. When there are profound differences in economic ideologies between such trading blocs, as existed for many years between the United States and the European Community, on the one side, and the Soviet Union and the Peoples' Republic of China, on the other, substantial trade between such countries is usually not feasible.

Except for agriculture, U.S.-E.C. trading relations have, by and large, been reasonably harmonious. The agricultural conflicts have been the result of the weakening of GATT rules over this sector in the 1950s and the significant changes in economic and institutional conditions since that period. One of the major trading powers, the United States, and a number of smaller developed and developing countries would like GATT discipline restored to this sector, while the two other major trading powers, the European Community and Japan, would like to maintain the *status quo*. Furthermore, the United States no longer seems prepared to settle for largely symbolic liberalization in this field. Achieving a compromise that is acceptable to these three parties is a major test for the international trading system, not only because of the importance of this issue but because of the need for the United States and the European Community, as well as other key trading nations, to tackle jointly the problem of the threatened breakdown of the multilateral trading system.

The Agricultural Dispute

While the long-run adjustment problems faced by farmers and their special economic and social contributions make agricultural producers deserving of special consideration, there seems to be no convincing reason why agriculture should be treated completely differently from other sectors. In other words, as in the case of developing countries, agriculture should be given extra time to conform to GATT rules, but this does not mean that this sector should be excused indefinitely from the usual GATT obligations. If this view is accepted, the best way of making progress in the agricultural area may be to try to agree on the various GATT obligations this sector should eventually meet rather than concentrating on quantitative targets for liberalization.

Clearly, the most contentious aspect of the U.S.-E.C. agricultural dispute concerns the use of export subsidies by the Community. GATT rules currently ban the use of export subsidies for manufactured products and stipulate that granting export subsidies on agricultural products should not result in the subsidizing country obtaining more than an equitable share of world trade in these products. However, the agricultural agreement proposed by the Director-General of the GATT, Arthur Dunkel, as part of his proposed Final Act of the Uruguay Round (GATT Secretariat, 1991) stipulates that export subsidies on agricultural products shall be gradually reduced.

Since export subsidization is an obvious example of the kind of beggar-thy-neighbor policies that seriously undermine a multilateral trading system, the Dunkel proposal seems reasonable and is consistent with the notion that agriculture is basically no different from other sectors. It appears that the Community's opposition to the Dunkel proposal is based not so much on the principle that agricultural export subsidization should be phased out but rather on the speed with which they would be reduced under this proposal. Consequently, a compromise acceptable to all may be possible by focusing on gaining a commitment to this principle and being more flexible on the timetable for meeting it. However, should some governments refuse to reduce their agricultural subsidies, other GATT members should have the right to withdraw equivalent concessions on other products. But, rather than taking such action unilaterally, decisions on retaliation should be reached through the dispute settlement process of the GATT. Retaliatory actions taken as a result of the GATT dispute settlement process are much less likely to prevent cooperation on other matters than unilateral retaliation.

The other key principle contained in the Dunkel proposal is that any government support provided to farmers should have no, or at most, minimal, trade distortion effects or effects on production. This is another principle that the Community seems prepared to accept, and it is already considering replacing the current price support system with one involving direct income payments to farmers. Again, it is the speed with which this commitment would be carried out under the proposal, more than the principle itself, that seems to be the basis of the opposition of E.C. negotiators to the proposal. While direct income payments still distort the market in the long-term, they penalize foreign producers and consumers much less than export subsidies and domestic price support programs and make the extent of the assistance to agriculture more transparent. Thus, being more flexible on the schedule for liberalization, while gaining a commitment on the principle of nondistortionary assistance, may be the means of resolving this aspect of the dispute. It would seem that what matters most is to bring the agricultural sector under GATT discipline rather the speed with which this will be accomplished. However, international negotiations will still be needed to resolve the issue of the extent to which the agricultural sector deserves such income support on a long-term basis.

A GATT-Plus Agreement

Once the U.S.-E.C. agricultural dispute is settled, GATT members should be able to complete the Uruguay Round within a reasonable time and then begin to address the basic issues that are leading to the significant weakening of the multilateral system. The ideal solution would be to amend GATT rules to correct the deficiencies in the present system. However, the needed reforms are so significant that the chances of success through this route are remote. As argued in the introduction, the most promising means of achieving the desired result is for the key trading countries to negotiate a new agreement with a higher level of responsibilities and privileges than under the current system of rules.[9] This would involve, for example, changing the articles dealing with developing countries so that their preferential treatment does not continue after they successfully begin the industrialization process, integrating textiles and apparel into the GATT system, reforming the safeguard provisions, significantly reducing the degree of preferences given to domestic suppliers in the area of government procurement, introducing an effective set of rules covering trade-distorting business practices, and changing the fair trade laws to prevent their misuse to thwart legitimate competition but also to prevent firms from avoiding the legitimate purpose for which they were intended. Anticipating future GATT problems with environmental issues, new rules covering these matters should also be put in place.

In getting members to accept the greater responsibilities and privileges of the GATT-Plus agreement, we would rely on the same motivations that have driven countries toward greater regionalism. Some large industrial countries like the United States want new rules covering such areas as intellectual property rights, trade in services, special and differential treatment for developing countries, foreign investment opportunities, and dumping and subsidization, and, in return, are prepared to open further certain important domestic markets and to act in a less aggressive unilateral manner. Many developing countries and small industrial nations are attracted by the export possibilities associated with this market-opening and to the prospects of less arbitrary unilateral actions by the large industrial countries and, in turn, are willing to make some of the changes sought by the large industrial countries. Mutually beneficial gains can also be achieved among developed countries as well as among developing countries. Thus, such a new agreement would be attractive to most developed and developing countries and could slow down the trend toward exclusive trading blocs, while still furthering the trade liberalization being achieved in the current regional movement.

It is possible, of course, that the number of negotiating areas in which agreements on greater responsibilities and privileges could be reached would be too small to warrant a GATT-Plus agreement. Furthermore, even if an agreement along the lines described is negotiated, it may not be sufficient to halt the decline in the effectiveness of the GATT. But the disastrous outcome that is possible, if the erosion of a rule-based, multilateral system of international trade continues, makes a serious effort to negotiate a GATT-Plus type agreement very much worthwhile.

Notes

1. For an elaboration of the proposal, see Baldwin (1992).

2. In forming the European Economic Community in 1958, the six European countries averaged their individual duties on each item, thus creating a common external tariff schedule with less dispersion than the individual country tariff schedules.

3. Agricultural products were not covered by the E.C. formula.

4. Average duty levels for manufactures for both countries were between 13 and 14 percent (Preeg, 1970).

5. Since the U.S. Congress had limited the president's maximum cutting authority on any duty to 60 percent, the United States could only cut duties of 21 percent or more by 60 percent.

6. Interestingly, Yeutter was Deputy U.S. Trade Representative under the Ford Administration.

7. Suppose the free-trade price at which a product can be purchased in the international market is fixed at $1.00. A 10 percent duty will raise the domestic price of the product to $1.10, whereas a 50 percent duty will increase the domestic price to $1.50. Consequently, reducing the duty by 50 percent will cut the price in the first case to $1.05 or by 4.5 percent and cut the price in the second case to $1.25 or by 16.7 percent.

8. U.S. exports to the rest of the world were, of course, also adversely affected by the growing export subsidization that took place under the CAP.

9. An advisory panel of trade policy experts assembled by the Atlantic Council recommended this approach in a report first issued in 1974 (Atlantic Council of the United States, 1976).

References

Atlantic Council of the United States. 1976. *GATT Plus—A Proposal for Trade Reform*. Report of Special Advisory Panel to the Trade Committee of the Atlantic Council, New York: Praeger Publishers.

Baldwin, R. E. 1965. "Tariff-Cutting Techniques in the Kennedy Round." In *Trade, Growth, and the Balance of Payments*, edited by R.E. Cave, H.G. Johnson, and P.B. Kenen. Chicago: Rand McNally & Company.

———. 1984. "The Changing Nature of U.S. Trade Policy Since World War II." In *The Structure and Evolution of Recent U.S. Trade Policy*, edited by R. E. Baldwin and A. O. Krueger. Chicago: University of Chicago Press.

———. 1992. "Adapting the GATT to a More Regionalized World." In *Regional Integration and the Global Trading System*, edited by K. Anderson and R. Blackhurst. Geneva: General Agreement on Tariff and Trade, forthcoming.

Economic Report of the President. 1992. Washington, D.C.: U.S. Government Printing Office.

GATT Secretariat. 1991. *Draft Final Act Embodying the Results of the Uruguay Round of Multilateral Trade Negotiations*. Geneva: General Agreement on Tariffs and Trade (December 20).

General Agreement on Tariffs and Trade. 1986. *Press Release on Uruguay Round*. (September 25).

Gilpin, R. 1987. *The Political Economy of International Relations*. Princeton, N.J.: Princeton Univ. Press.

Hudec, R. E. 1975. *The GATT Legal System and World Trade Diplomacy*. New York: Prager Publishers.

Jackson, J. H. 1989. *The World Trading System: Law and Policy of International Economic Relations*, Cambridge: MIT Press.

Kindleberger, C. P. 1981. "Dominance and Leadership in the International Economy: Exploitation, Public Goods, and Free Rides." *International Studies Quarterly* 25: 242-53.

Preeg, E. H. 1970. *Traders and Diplomats: An Analysis of the Kennedy Round of Negotiations Under the General Agreement on Tariffs and Trade*. Washington, D.C.: Brookings Institution.

Winham, G. R. 1986. *International Trade and the Tokyo Round of Negotiations*. Princeton, N.J.: Princeton Univ. Press.

Discussion

Pier Carlo Padoan

Professor Baldwin's chapter offers a wide perspective on the current stage of trade disputes where agricultural trade negotiations play such a crucial role. Professor Baldwin stresses that, while the United States and Europe share a mutual interest in the strengthening of a multilateral trading system, they are also facing the risk that the current trend towards regional trade agreements may push in the opposite direction by breaking the global system into conflicting blocs. He also reminds us that the establishment of a multilateral regime is made more difficult by the fact that we are no longer in a situation of hegemony, i.e., a situation in which the cost of providing international public goods (of which an international trade regime is a major example) is more than proportionally borne by the larger and most powerful state.

I intend to develop this point by looking at two aspects. The first one deals with the conditions that are required for the provision of international public goods without hegemony. The second deals with the difficulty of treating Europe as a single and unified actor. Indeed I shall argue that some of the difficulties currently facing international trade negotiations are generated by the pressures and costs Europe is facing in this very peculiar period of her history.

International political economy scholars—drawing on both game theory and the theory of international regimes—have suggested some conditions that must be fulfilled in order to establish international regimes without hegemony (see Axelrod and Keohane, 1985; Guerrieri and Padoan, 1988). The most relevant for the topics of this conference are: (1) that actors involved in negotiations take a long-term horizon, i.e., they must be willing to interact repeatedly so that the incentives to defect are minimized; (2) that actors involved are willing to change their preferences (so that payoff matrices can be appropriately altered in order to make a cooperative solution feasible); and (3) the presence of institutions as instruments necessary for the exchange of information about each other's behavior and the formation of expectations about the chances of success in negotiations.

Conditions (1) and (3) seem to be fulfilled in the trade negotiation scene. As far as condition (1) is concerned, despite repeated frustration about advances in liberalization negotiations, there is no obvious sign of the intention of major trading partners to retreat, even temporarily, from negotiations. The level of global interdependence is such that the costs of "opting out" of negotiations are far larger than benefits. In this perspective one should consider the widely available evidence that shows that there is no real tendency towards regionalism in the world economy as far as trade flows are concerned. Rather, regionalism should be understood as a policy option pursued by the major trading partners as a possible alternative to multilateral agreements.

As far as condition (2) is concerned the wide number of international organizations, both at global and regional levels, is sufficient to provide plenty of information and reciprocal communication about the expected behavior of the negotiating parts.

What is really an obstacle to the formation of a new multilateral system is the unwillingness of trading partners to alter their preferences and hence give concessions, in order to achieve a cooperative solution. While the focus of this volume is on American-European trade disputes I argue that North Atlantic, and indeed global, trading disputes cannot be properly understood if one does not recognize that Europe and the Community in the first place cannot be regarded as a unitary actor, but rather as a group of distinct actors that often find it difficult to define a common preference. This is obviously a very broad topic and several contributions to this conference deal with it. In what follows I will consider one single, although rather general, aspect. Different E.C. members have different interests in trade and especially agricultural liberalization because of their different comparative advantages. In addition the current phase of deep institutional transformation Europe is facing—which involves three "institutional shocks," the Single Market, Monetary Unification, and enlargement—is bound to exacerbate rather than mitigate national differences.

To give a little substance to this point consider Table 2.1, which offers an impressionistic view of the specialization patterns in an enlarged Europe drawing on existing revealed comparative advantages (+) and disadvantages (−) based on Pavitt's (1984) taxonomy. If we assume that a process of integration in Europe will tend to deepen national specialization patterns in the direction of existing comparative advantages, the information summarized below provides a first indication of the mutual consistencies and/or inconsistencies implicit in such a process.

The comparative advantages of the three largest western European economies, Germany, United Kingdom, and France, are located in the sectors where the comparative disadvantages of Eastern Europe lie, and vice versa. The comparative advantages that the former countries enjoy in the science-based and specialized suppliers sectors suggests that they are in the position to produce and export the technology and equipment Eastern Europe needs to upgrade her competitive position, while they would become importers of the goods for which Eastern Europe enjoys a comparative advantage.

TABLE 2.1 Revealed Comparative Advantages: European Countries

	Science-based	Scale-intensive	Specialized Suppliers	Traditional	Agriculture	Resource Intensive	Energy
Germany	–	+	+	–	–	–	–
United Kingdom	+	–	+	–	–	–	+
France	+	+	+	–	+	–	–
Italy	–	–	+	+	+	–	–
Spain	–	+	–	+	+	–	–
Portugal, Greece	–	–	–	+	+	–	–
Czechoslovakia	–	+	–	+	–	+	–
Hungary	–	–	–	+	+	+	–
Poland	–	–	–	+	+	+	+
USSR	–	–	–	–	–	+	+
EFTA Countries	–	+	+	–	+	–	–

Note: "+" = comparative advantage; "–" = comparative disadvantage.
Source: Author's calculations and adapted from Guerrieri and Mastropasqua, 1993.

Let us now turn to the conflicting part of the scenario, i.e., let us look at those cases in which eastern and western countries reveal comparative advantages in the same sectors. France has a comparative advantage in agriculture while the United Kingdom enjoys a comparative advantage in the energy sector. On the eastern side Czechoslovakia reveals a comparative advantage in the scale intensive sector.

Problems are possibly more severe if we turn to the position of Italy and of the southern members of the European Community, Greece, Portugal, and Spain. Their comparative advantage lies in the traditional and agricultural sectors (with Spain acquiring one in the scale-intensive sector), and also in the specialized suppliers in the case of Italy. EFTA countries also enjoy comparative advantages in agriculture

As it is widely recognized, in order to accomplish full integration into the E.C., markets will have to be liberalized to allow access of the Eastern European economies in three crucial areas: agriculture, textiles and clothing, and steel, i.e., those sectors where protectionist resistance is the fiercest and where the action of the Community has been able, so far, to produce only a moderate amount of internal E.C. liberalization. Our evidence supports the view that liberalization in these sectors would favor the comparative advantage of eastern European countries.

While protectionist policies are implemented at the Community level, they actually reflect sectoral, rather than national, pressures. However, the current situation of "suspended liberalization" in Europe seems to suggest that special interest group pressures are strong enough to influence national and Community-wide policies, a fact that is quite common in regional trade agreements (De Benedictis and Padoan, 1993; Leidy and Hoekman, 1992). Looking at the evidence sketched in Table 2.1, only very few E.C. countries seem to have sectors whose comparative advantages would not represent a source of conflict in moving towards a liberal policy vis-à-vis Eastern Europe. In fact only one country seems to be in such a position, notably Germany (and not even Germany if we assume that the comparative advantage in scale-intensive sectors conflicts with the comparative advantage of Czechoslovakia).

A more liberal stance in global agricultural trade on the part of the Community requires the definition of a new place for agricultural trade in an enlarged Europe. We can single out a double level of trade negotiations and friction. The European Community will be ready to make progress in global trade liberalization as long as this does not generate unbearable pressures on some of its (most powerful) members. In this respect successful adjustment to a new division of labor within Europe is a prerequisite for a more liberal global system. On the other hand seeking a more liberal trade regime globally might be necessary for Europe in order to complete, as rapidly as possible, the full integration of the former planned economies into an enlarged market. European preferences must be changed both with respect to the global system and with respect to her own internal problems. Non European trading partners should exploit this point for the benefit of the international system at large.

References

Axelrod R., and R. Keohane. 1985. "Achieving Cooperation Under Anarchy." *Strategies and Institutions, World Politics*, vol. XXXVIII, pp. 226-54.

De Benedictis L., and P. C. Padoan. 1993. *The Integration of Eastern Europe into the E.C. National and Community Interests and Sectoral Resistances*, edited by S. Lombardini and P. C. Padoan, *Europe Between East and South*, Kluwer. Forthcoming.

Guerrieri P., and C. Mastropasqua. 1993. "Competitivita', specializzazione, e prospettive di integrazione commerciale dei paesi dell'Est europeo." in Bollino A. and P. C.Padoan. *Il circolo virtuoso trilaterale*. Il Mulino, Bologna.

Guerrieri P., and P. C. Padoan. 1988. *The Political Economy of European Integration*. New York: Barnes and Noble.

Leidy M., and B. Hoekman. 1992. "What to Expect From Multilateral Trade Negotiations, a Public Choice Perspective." CEPR Discussion Paper n.747, December.

Pavitt. K. 1984. Sectoral Patterns of Technical Change: Towards a Taxonomy and a Theory. *Research Policy* 13: 343-73.

PART TWO

U.S. Agricultural and Trade Policies and Their Implications for U.S.-E.C. Agricultural Trade Relations

3

U.S. Domestic Policy and U.S.-E.C. Trade

Bruce L. Gardner

Introduction

U.S. domestic policies have an impact on U.S.-E.C. trade in two ways: the policies change the supply and demand situation in the United States, which affects the U.S. exportable supply; and the policies influence the negotiating environment in which U.S.-E.C. trade policy issues are (sometimes) resolved. Economic analysis has most to contribute to the exportable supply issue, and this is the focus of the chapter.

Three main U.S. political objectives lie behind the policies to be analyzed: farm income support, environmental protection, and control of federal expenditures (budgetary restraint). Other objectives are sometimes important, but currently these are the ones that make the most difference for U.S. agricultural policies. Farm income support is traditionally the most influential objective. This objective is pursued through many avenues—credit programs, research and extension, crop insurance—but the most visible and probably most important is commodity programs. Environmental protection has long been on the agenda in the form of conservation programs. What brings the subject to fore at present is the fact that some environmentally directed policies have been enacted that farmers oppose, and more are in prospect. Control of expenditures has been on the agenda but has had a decisive impact on policy reform only in the last several years.

Commodity Support Programs and Exportable Supply

Not often does a practical policy debate turn on the sign of a result in economic comparative statistics, but this is close to being the case in agricultural policy disagreements between the E.C. and the United States. The E.C. view—a shorthand simplification since of course not all in the E.C. accept it—is that U.S. commodity programs in general, and for the grains in particular, cause U.S. agricultural output and exports to increase. This view is taken to justify the negotiating position that U.S. commodity programs are thus equivalent—in the sense of having the same effect—to the E.C.'s Common Agricultural Policy (CAP). The alternative view is that the U.S. programs reduce output and exports through their use of acreage reduction measures. The U.S. Export Enhancement Program (EEP) is agreed by both sides as equivalent to export subsidies in the CAP, but not the deficiency payment program (because receipt of these payments is tied to farmers' participation in acreage reduction).

In this section I devote a considerably detailed discussion to an attempt to determine which view is correct; that is, to provide an estimate of the output and trade effects of U.S. commodity programs in 1990-92 and the prospective effects in 1993 and beyond. The discussion takes as a paradigm commodity wheat, the main traded commodity that both the United States and E.C. subsidize heavily. But the structure of the analysis is similar for the corn, rice, sorghum, barley, oats, and cotton programs.

Farmers' receipts for the major grains and cotton are supported principally by means of "deficiency" payments, which make up the difference between the legislated target price and the market price. For wheat the target price has been fixed at $4.00 per bushel since 1990, where current law freezes its minimum level until 1995. This is a 9 percent reduction from the peak of $4.38 in 1985-88, and a 30 percent reduction in real terms from the 1979 peak (Figure 3.1). Other commodities have had similar reductions (see Table 3.1).

Since the wheat price received by U.S. farmers averaged about $2.95 per bushel during 1990-92, the program, recent cuts notwithstanding, might appear to have had the potential to provide a significant incentive for farmers to increase wheat production. There is about a 35 percent potential subsidy according to these figures ($1.05/2.95).

In order to forestall output expansion, however, and to hold down budgetary outlays, the wheat program has involved production control measures along with its payments since the payment approach began to be used in the 1960s. The specific mechanisms have varied over time. The mechanisms in use in the 1991-93 crop years will be described in detail here.

The payments received by a producer are equal to:

$$G = (P_T - P_m) \cdot A_P \cdot Y_P , \qquad (1)$$

where G is the payment received, P_T is the target price, P_m is the maximum

FIGURE 3.1 Wheat Target Price: Real and Nominal (Real: GDP Deflator, 1987=100).

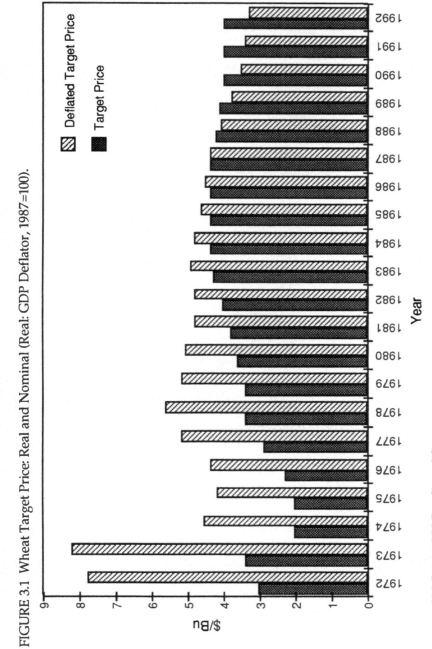

Source: U.S.D.A., ASCS Fact Sheet: Wheat.

TABLE 3.1 Features of U.S. Commodity Price Support Programs.

	1987	1988	1989	1990	1991	1992	1993
Target or Support Price							
Wheat ($/bu.)	4.38	4.23	4.10	4.00	4.00	4.00	4.00
Corn ($/bu.)	3.03	2.93	2.84	2.75	2.75	2.75	2.75
Rice ($/cwt.)	11.66	11.15	10.0	10.71	10.71	10.71	10.71
Cotton (¢/lb.)	79.4	75.9	73.4	72.9	72.9	72.9	72.9
Soybeans ($/bu.)	4.79	4.77	4.53	4.50	5.02	5.02	5.02
Milk ($/cwt.)	11.10	10.60	10.10	10.10	10.10	10.10	10.10
Idled Acres as a Fraction of ***Harvested Acres***							
Wheat	.43	.42	.23	.25	.46	.29	.25[a]
Corn	.39	.30	.20	.22	.18	.14	.20[a]
Rice	.67	.38	.44	.36	.32	.13	.16[a]
Cotton	.40	.18	.36	.17	.07	.11	.09[a]
Government Outlays ($ billion) ***Fiscal years (Oct.-Sept.)***							
Wheat	2.8	0.7	0.1	0.8	3.0	1.7	2.3[c]
Corn	12.3	8.2	2.9	2.4	2.4	2.1	5.2[c]
Rice	0.9	0.1	0.6	0.7	0.9	0.7	0.9[c]
Cotton	1.8	0.7	1.5	-0.1	0.4	1.4	2.4[c]
Milk	1.2	1.3	0.7	0.5	0.8	0.2	0.1[c]
Other[b]	0.9	-1.2	0.2	0.2	0.4	0.6	0.8[c]

[a] Author's estimate.
[b] Wool, peanuts, tobacco, honey, soybeans, barley, sorghum, oats.
[c] U.S.D.A.'s estimate for FY 1993, Oct. 1, 1992 to Sept. 30, 1993.
Source: U.S.D.A., July 1993.

of the market price and the "loan rate"—the price at which grain is valued to pay off loans from the government's Commodity Credit Corporation (CCC), which grants "nonrecourse" loans using commodities as security.[1] A_P is the farm's payment acreage, and Y_P is the farm's payment yield per acre. Any of the four right-hand-side variables can be manipulated to control payments. Their status is:

P_T : the target price is $4.00 per bushel in 1991-93.

P_m : the market price is defined as the average U.S. price received by farmers for the first five months of the marketing year (June-October) as estimated by the National Agricultural Statistics Service. This is the seasonally lowest price period. But this price has been above the loan rate since 1988.[2] The market price for payment purposes is the same for all farmers and for all types of wheat, even though farmers' wheat varies in quality and location, and different types of wheat have market premiums and discounts that vary substantially.

A new feature for 1993 is that a "marketing loan" program is being introduced. This would cause additional payments if the local market price—defined as a county-specific price for wheat at any time a farmer's CCC loan is repaid—falls below the loan rate. However, 1993 market prices appear high enough that payments under this program will not be triggered.

A_p: The farm's acreage base in any year is the average acreage planted[3] for the five preceding years, except that, for farms that have an established crop rotation plan, the acreage base is the average of the 3 preceding years corresponding to the current year in the rotation. The acreage on which payments are made is further reduced in two ways.

First, the Acreage Reduction Program (ARP) requires that a percentage of the acreage base be held in an "acreage conservation reserve" (ACR), and not planted to wheat, or any other harvested crop, or grazed during the growing season. The percentage is chosen by the Secretary of Agriculture within a range established by Congress in the 1990 Farm Act as follows:

> In the case of each of the 1992 through 1995 crops of wheat, if the Secretary estimates for a marketing year for the crop that the ratio of ending stocks of wheat to total disappearance of wheat for the preceding marketing year will be—
>
> (i) more than 40 percent, the Secretary shall provide for an acreage limitation program (as described in paragraph (2)) under which the acreage planted to wheat for harvest on a farm would be limited to the wheat crop acreage base for the farm for the crop reduced by not less than 10 percent nor more than 20 percent; or
>
> (ii) equal to or less than 40 percent, the Secretary may provide for such an acreage limitation program under which the acreage planted to wheat for harvest on a farm would be limited to the wheat crop acreage base for the farm for the crop reduced by not more than 0 to 15 percent.
>
> For the purpose of this subparagraph, the term "total disappearance" means all wheat utilization, including total domestic, total export, and total residual disappearance (U.S. Code, 104 Stat. 3390).

Since ending stocks have been about 20 percent of disappearance since 1990, the 0-15 percent range applies. For 1991, 15 percent was chosen (Congress overrode the Secretary's discretion via legislation in this case). In 1992, the acreage reduction percentage was 5 percent, and in 1993 it is zero.

The second reduction in payment acreage occurs because of a budgetary provision introduced in 1990, according to which no deficiency payments are made on 15 percent of the farmer's permitted acres (acreage base less ACR land as just described). This 15 percent is called "normal flex" acreage, to indicate that a wheat farmer can maintain wheat base on this land while planting either wheat or another crop (except fruits, nuts, vegetables, trees, peanuts, tobacco, or wild rice). An additional 10 percent "optional flex" acreage may be shifted from wheat to another crop, with loss of wheat payments, if the farmer chooses.

Combining both reductions, A_P is a maximum of 80 percent of the wheat acreage base in 1992 and 85 percent in 1993. If a producer plants less than the maximum payment acreage (permitted minus normal flex acres, or 85 percent of permitted), wheat payment acreage falls with acreage actually planted. However, producers have the option under the "0/92" program of devoting all or a portion of their permitted acreage to oilseed crops other than soybeans or to conservation uses—no other crops harvested or grazing—and still receive payments on 92 percent of the maximum payment acreage.[4]

Y_P: The yield per acre used to calculate payments has been frozen since 1985. The U.S. average payment yield for wheat is 33 bushels per acre, compared to 39 bushels per acre for actual production. This both limits budgetary outlays and forestalls producers' incentives to increase yield in pursuit of payments.

Production Incentive

What effect does this set of program provisions have on net returns for additional output? Consider a producer's marginal net revenue. Total net revenue is

$$\pi_i = P_m Q_i + G_i - TC_i , \tag{2}$$

where π_i is the return from growing quantity Q_i of wheat for the ith farmer. P_m is the market price, taken as given. G_i is government payments and TC_i is the cost of growing Q_i.

For a farmer who is not participating in the program, maximum net return is obtained where

$$\frac{d\pi_i}{dQ_i} = P_m - \frac{dTC_i}{dQ_i} = 0, \tag{3}$$

i.e., market price equals the marginal cost of growing wheat. The incentive price for output is marginal revenue, which equals P_m since a producer's output has no influence on market price.

For a program participant, revenue also includes deficiency payments, so marginal revenue (dropping the i subscript) is

$$\frac{dR}{dQ} = \frac{d(PQ + sQ' - C)}{dQ}, \tag{4}$$

where $s = P_T - P_m$, payment per unit of Q', program production, and C is costs of participation—mainly costs of idling land as required of partici-pants. Assuming the payment is P_T - P where P_T is the target price, we have the sum of market receipts and program payments as:

$$PQ + (P_T - P)Q' = P_T \cdot Q' + P(Q - Q'), \tag{5}$$

where $Q' = A_P Y_P$, program payment acreage times program yield. Then marginal revenue is

$$\frac{dR}{dQ} = \frac{d[P_T \cdot A_P \cdot Y_P + P(Q - A_P Y_P) - C]}{dQ}. \tag{6}$$

This expression has to be considered separately for a change in acreage and a change in yield.

The incentive price for an increase in acreage for a given yield is

$$\frac{dR}{dA} = \frac{d[P_T \cdot A_P \cdot Y_P + PAY - PA_P Y_P - C]}{dA}$$

$$= P_T \cdot Y_P \frac{dA_P}{dA} + PY - PY_P \frac{dA_P}{dA} - \frac{dC}{dA} \tag{7}$$

$$= (P_T - P)Y_P \frac{dA_P}{dA} + PY - \frac{dC}{dA},$$

where dC/dA is the change in costs of participation as A increases. Compliance costs depend on acreage held idle and are principally the opportunity returns (land rental value) that the acreage could have earned if cropped. The requirements are fixed by the producer's wheat acreage base and the ACR percentage, so $dC/dA = 0$ as long as the farmer stays within the farm's permitted acreage. However, if A exceeds the farm's permitted wheat acreage, the farmer must drop out of the program and all payments are lost in the current year. Maximum payment acreage (MPA) is fixed as described above, so $dA_P/dA = 0$ for acreage increases of above this level; but for A less than maximum payment acreage $dA_P/dA = 1$.

Consequently, there are several discrete ranges of revenue effects of increased acreage:

- if A < maximum payment acreage (80 percent of wheat base in 1992), added revenue is market revenue on actual yield plus deficiency payments on program yield
- if A is between maximum payment acreage and maximum permitted acreage (80 to 95 percent of wheat base in 1992), added revenue is market revenue on actual yield

- if A is at the maximum permitted acreage, added revenue is market revenue minus the loss of all payments
- if A is above the maximum permitted acreage, the producer is a non-participant and equation (3) applies.[5]

The preceding discussion has been couched in terms of an increase in acreage, but marginal revenue changes for acreage decreases are the same in magnitude except at the discrete switch points (where marginal revenue is not defined in any case). However, thinking about decreases seems more natural for acreage levels below maximum payment acreages. In the "optional flex" acreage range, between 70 and 80 percent of wheat base in 1992, the marginal revenue loss is market revenue plus deficiency payments times program yield, as stated above. Reducing acreage below the optional flex range causes the additional loss of one-fifth of the acreage reduction in the subsequent year's wheat base if the acreage is planted to another crop; however, if the acreage is not harvested or planted to oilseeds other than soybeans, then the reduced acreage is considered planted for program purposes and the producer maintains the wheat base, by signing up for the "0/92" program.

Figure 3.2 provides a summary sketch of the incentives a producer faces in deciding whether to change the acreage of a program crop. This structure of incentives is the same for wheat, rice, corn, sorghum, barley, oats, and upland cotton, but particulars vary—notably the relative distance between target price and market price, and between base and permitted acres. The most important points are: the program provides a greater than market incentive to keep producing at the MPA level, and a less than market incentive to increase acreage above the maximum permitted level. Therefore, the program will cause acreage to be concentrated between the MPA and maximum permitted levels.

An important qualification to Figure 3.2 is the effect of voluntary acreage diversion programs, in which the government offers to rent a farmer's land, which is then held idle. The only significant current program of this type is the Conservation Reserve Program (CRP). Farmers who have highly erodible land, or other land on which normal cropping practices can cause water quality problems, can rent this acreage under 10-year contracts that may pay the farmer a higher rental value than crop returns for this acreage. So the incentive price to grow crops on this acreage is less than the market price. About 36 million acres (11 million acres of wheat base) is enrolled in 1993.

The marginal revenue for an increase in yield is

$$\frac{dR}{dY} = (P_T - P)A_P \frac{dY_P}{dY} + P_m A - \frac{dC}{dY}. \tag{8}$$

FIGURE 3.2   Price Incentives for Production Decisions Under 1991-95
Target-Price Program.

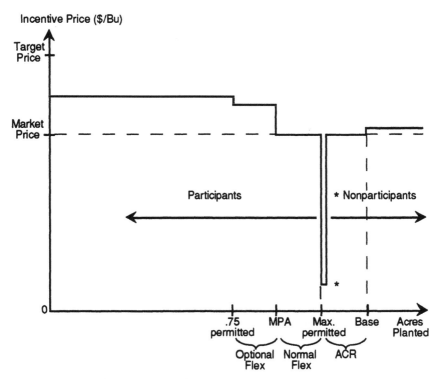

* Cost of losing all Payments, which is larger than shown here for the marginal acre.
If a producer moves from any acreage at or less than the maximum permitted to any
acreage level above, this loss is a fixed cost to be spread over the added acres.

   Since Y_P is fixed in current programs, $dY_P/dY = 0$. And, if the producer
increases fertilizer use or takes other steps to increase Y, this does not
change ARP requirements, so $dC/dY = 0$. Therefore the change in revenue
is just market revenue. Expressed in revenue per bushel, the price relevant
for producer optimization is the market price, as in equation (3).

Acreage Diversion and Supply Shifts

   A given percentage acreage reduction will have different effects on
output depending on participation and, given participation, on "slippage." Slippage is defined as

$$\lambda = 1 - \frac{\%\Delta Q}{\%\Delta A} , \tag{9}$$

where Q is actual output and A is the reduction in acreage planted. If, for example, acreage is reduced 10 percent and output is also reduced 10 percent, then slippage is zero. If output is not reduced at all, then $\lambda = 1$.

The main potential causes of slippage are: (a) use of additional nonland inputs, (b) farmers' choice of lower-quality land for diversion, (c) idling land that would not be used to produce the program crop in the absence of the program, and (d) noncompliance, e.g., planting a larger acreage than is allowed and hoping not to be detected. Item (a) is largely controlled by freezing program yield, (b) and (c), to some extent, by regulations on entering marginal lands in the programs,[6] and (d) by enforcement activity.

Taking λ as a constant, the supply effects of diversion programs depend on participation rates. In the case of voluntary diversion programs participation depends on the level of rental payments offered (the size of accepted bids in the CRP). For ARPs, participation depends on the size of the ARP percentage, the nonpayment base, and the expected size of the deficiency payment. The smaller the former reduction in payment acres, or the lower the expected market price, the more participation we expect. In wheat, the participation rate has been quite stable—78 to 88 percent of national base acres have been enrolled each year in 1987-1993.

To depict the commodity's supply function under an ARP program, consider participants and nonparticipants separately. Nonparticipants get no program benefits. They sell all they produce at the market price. So for them the supply function is the ordinary one given by their marginal costs. For participants, the supply curve has shifted because compliance requires holding α percentage of the crop's base acreage out of production. One complication is that the supply curve will shift by a smaller percentage than α because of slippage, as discussed earlier. The actual horizontal supply shift will be $\alpha(1-\lambda)\gamma$, where λ is slippage as defined earlier and γ is the participation rate.

In Gardner (1990) I presented estimates that U.S. output of grains generally was reduced by the programs as operated in 1987, and the same was true in the whole period of the Food Security Act of 1985. The situation is more complicated under the 1990 Farm Act, mainly because of the 15 percent nonpayment ("flex") provisions, which allow farmers to shift some production among the major crops in response to market signals if farmers wish to do so. Policies still affect acreage allocation to the extent that they distort *market* prices, but acreage flexibility makes inter-commodity price distortions less important also. The issue then becomes the effect of commodity programs on the *aggregate* output and prices of the crops sector.

The aggregate acreage idled in commodity programs is shown in Figure 3.3 for recent years, with commodity detail in Table 3.1. On an overall cropland basis, a time series regression of harvested acres on idled acres, 1948-1990, yields:

$$H_t = .331 - .799 \, I_t \tag{10}$$

$$(.118) \ (.053) \, .$$

where H_t is harvested acres in year t and I_t is total idled acres. The numbers in parentheses are standard errors of the coefficient estimates. The coefficient on I_t implies an aggregate "acreage slippage" coefficient of 0.2. It implies that if the 60 million acres held idle in 1991-1993 were no longer idled under the programs, harvested cropland would rise by 48 million acres, or about 15 percent.

Table 3.2 shows aggregate farm program outlays. The sum of deficiency, disaster, and other payments to producers averaged about $9 billion annually in 1991-93. This amounted to 11 percent of the $83 billion annual farm receipts for crops in those years, including market receipts for crops that had no payments (mainly fruits and vegetables). Because aggregate crop supply elasticities are estimated to be quite low, probably .1 to .3 (LaFrance and Burt, 1993), even if the payments were not tied to fixed bases they would induce only 1 to 3 percent additional output and thus are very unlikely to offset the 15 percent effective acreage reductions of 1991-93.

In short, the evidence is strong that U.S. programs for crops in the 1990s are output-reducing, perhaps by about 10 percent, although any quantitative estimate of the effect is very conjectural. To estimate the effect on the E.C., however, the effects of trade policies, particularly the EEP, must be added. This could well convert U.S. wheat policy as a whole to one that drives down world prices.

Livestock commodities present a different picture. The only significant price support programs are for milk and wool. These commodities together account for about 22 percent of the value of farmers' livestock receipts.

The wool program pays a subsidy that averaged over 100 percent of the market price of wool, over the 1980-91 period. In 1990-91 the market price averaged 67.5 cents per pound and the subsidy $1.85 per pound. This subsidy is paid on each farmer's actual sales. Therefore, it would be expected to have—and is intended to have—an output-increasing effect. But despite the steady support this program has provided since 1955, U.S. wool production is now one-third of its 1955 level and makes a trivial contribution (less than one-half of one percent) to U.S. farmers' livestock

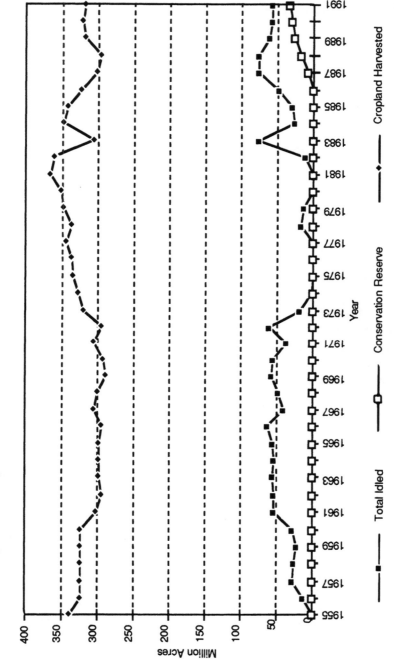

FIGURE 3.3 Cropland Acreage: Harvested and Idled.

Source: U.S.D.A., *Agricultural Statistics. Note:* Annual Programs and Conservation Reserve.

TABLE 3.2 U.S. Government Outlays for Agricultural Programs, Fiscal Years ($Billions)

	1987	1988	1989	1990	1991	1992	1993[a]
Deficiency and marketing loan payments	4.9	4.0	5.8	4.2	6.2	5.7	9.2
Export promotion	0.3	0.2	-0.1	-0.0	0.7	1.5	2.7
Acreage diversion and dairy buyout	1.0	0.3	0.2	0.2	0.1	0.0	0.0
Disaster payments and emergency assistance	0.0	0.0	3.9	0.2	0.1	1.1	1.2
Producer storage payments	0.8	0.7	0.2	0.2	0.0	0.0	0.0
Price support loans and purchases (net)	11.7	3.4	-0.8	-0.4	1.2	0.9	2.7
Section 32 purchases and other	0.7	2.0	0.4	0.9	0.5	0.2	1.3
Subtotal (commodities)	19.0	10.2	9.1	4.9	8.3	9.0	16.7
Program administrative and interest cost (ASCS and CCC)	4.2	2.8	2.0	2.3	2.5	1.5	1.1
Conservation Reserve Program and Agricultural Conservation Program	0.2	1.3	1.6	1.7	2.0	2.0	2.0
Federal crop insurance (subsidy and administrative)	0.6	0.6	0.9	0.7	1.0	0.9	0.8
Soil Conservation Service (programs and administrative)	0.4	0.5	0.5	0.5	0.5	0.6	0.7
Animal and Plant Health Inspection and Federal Grain Inspection Service	0.3	0.3	0.4	0.4	0.4	0.4	0.5
Information: Agricultural Marketing Service, Economic Research Service, and National Agricultural Statistics Service	0.1	0.1	0.2	0.2	0.3	0.3	0.3
Research: Agricultural Research Service, Cooperative State Research Service, and Extension Service	1.1	1.2	1.4	1.4	1.4	1.5	1.5
Total	26.3	17.4	16.6	12.5	16.8	16.6	23.9

[a]U.S. Official Estimates, April 1993.
Source: Budget of the United States, various years.

receipts. In the international picture, at least vis à vis the E.C., the program is negligible.

The dairy program, after a period in the 1980s when high support prices caused overproduction that required a dairy herd buyout to correct, has brought support prices down sufficiently that government acquisitions have largely ceased to present a chronic problem in 1991-93. Over the past decade U.S. milk production has grown at about a 0.7 percent annual rate, less than the rate of population growth, and does not appear to have been strongly stimulated by price supports. A key factor internationally continues to be fixed dairy import quotas at very low levels. Dairy product imports between 1985 and 1992 have varied only between 2.4 and 2.7 billion pounds of milk equivalent (fat basis), less than 2 percent of U.S. milk consumption.

The overall U.S. effort to produce agricultural output is best portrayed by the total commitment of inputs to farm production. Figure 3.4 shows the USDA total input index, including land, hired and family labor, capital, and purchased inputs of all kinds. After a rebound in the late 1970s, input use declined in the 1980s at a faster rate than the longer-term historical trend. U.S. agricultural policies may have played a role in keeping resources in agriculture that otherwise would have left in 1950-70. But the new production commitments of the 1970s were market driven. And clearly policies did not engender increased input use in the 1980s.

Environmental Protection and the Regulation of Agriculture

When the U.S. Supreme Court in 1936 ruled the first New Deal production controls unconstitutional, it left the door open for acreage controls

FIGURE 3.4 Farm Inputs.

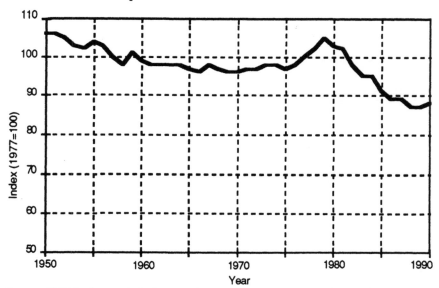

Source: USDA, *Economic Indicators of the Farm Sector,* various issues. *Note:* USDA. Index of all inputs used.

based on soil conservation. Subsequent legislation followed this path by generally linking conservation and supply management as joint goals of acreage-idling programs. However, the rationale shifted over time to a political one—wider political support exists for programs that arguably cause farmers to undertake environmentally beneficial activities in exchange for commodity program benefits.

During the 1980s, traditional political interest in soil conservation broadened to other environmental concerns. Wetlands protection ("swampbuster") was added to the 1985 Farm Act to discourage the draining and cultivation of wetlands that are unsuitable for agricultural production in their natural state. The sanction for draining and planting crops for harvest on wetlands is ineligibility for various farm program benefits.

The "sodbuster" provisions of the 1985 and 1990 Acts deny federal agricultural program benefits to any person who introduces crops on highly erodible land without following an approved soil conservation plan. This provision was aimed at limiting the conversion to cropland of an estimated 70 million acres of grassland or forests considered to have a significant crop-producing potential. To deal with erosion problems from land that had been cultivated prior to enactment of the 1985 Act, a "conservation compliance" provision was established. Under the 1985 Act, any farmer who produces an agricultural commodity on highly erodible land must use conservation practices determined by USDA's Soil Conservation Service to be appropriate for that land, as a condition of eligibility for commodity price support and other federal benefits. The determination of both "highly erodible" and "appropriate" conservation practices is difficult and requires ultimately arbitrary regulatory decisions. Contention over details and burdens on farmers caused delays, but, generally, the conservation planning must have been completed and the plan in effect as of December 31, 1989.

The "swampbuster" and "sodbuster" provisions are part of agricultural legislation. A development that has farmers even more worried is expansion of the regulatory agenda affecting agriculture beyond the protective sphere of the Congressional Agriculture Committees. Following is a summary of the main areas of contention.

The Clean Water Act

This is the principal legislation aimed at improving water quality. First enacted in 1972 and scheduled for re-authorization in 1993, the provisions that are most important for agriculture involve the regulation of wetlands and of agricultural pollutants that enter ground water and surface water (lakes, ponds, and streams) from eroded soils, chemical fertilizer, pesticides, or livestock operations. The main issue to date has been regulation of the use of wetlands.

It is possible that new amendments to this set will go further to address specific regulation of agricultural "nonpoint" sources of pollutants such as phosphorus, nitrogen, or leached pesticides. "Point" sources, such a city's sewage outlet or a factory's waste discharge pipe, have long been subject to Environmental Protection Agency (EPA) regulations on allowable emissions. Nonpoint sources, such as runoff from fields or forests, have not been regulated by EPA. But some states have taken substantive regulatory steps in agriculture in pursuit of water quality. Iowa has imposed a fertilizer tax, whose proceeds are used to finance the development and implementation of best management practices (BMPs) designed to reduce fertilizer and pesticide leaching into ground water. Nebraska restricts pumping in areas with falling water tables or high nitrate concentrations and has imposed restrictions on chemigration methods. Phosphate runoff controls are in the process of being implemented for South Florida, including taxing landowners to finance the purchase of catchment areas where vegetation could remove phosphates so that downstream areas (near the Everglades) would not be so affected by phosphate-rich water.

The Endangered Species Act

This is the chief statute to conserve and protect species determined to be endangered or threatened and to conserve the ecosystems upon which they depend. The Act establishes a uniform process for designating a plant or animal as being in danger of extinction, protecting that species from further decline in its number, and formulating a plan for the recovery of the species, i.e., for increasing the number of individuals to a viable population.

The Act as of December 1, 1992, protects 749 species of plants and animals found in the United States. In addition, some 950 species are candidates for inclusion because of substantial declines of population. The U.S. Fish and Wildlife Service of the Interior Department monitors species that are at significant risk of extinction, as well as "recovered" species, i.e., those that have been removed from the threatened/endangered list.

EPA's efforts to implement the Endangered Species Act as it applies to pesticide regulation illustrate how environmental and farm interests can come into serious conflict. The Act prohibits any action that places members or populations of an endangered species in jeopardy. These actions range from killing members of the species directly to destroying their habitat or food sources. Pesticides can kill endangered plants or invertebrates living in fields, and they can destroy habitat. Pesticide drift into weedy border areas or streams can also result in the death of members of endangered species or their food sources. For example, the snail kite (a hawk) that lives in Florida is on the Fish and Wildlife Service list of endangered species. One of its main sources of food is the apple snail, which during dry periods migrates into drainage/irrigation canals, where both snails and kites can be exposed to pesticides. Thus, EPA could prohibit the use of any pesticide with known toxicity toward either snails or kites, or which has adverse effects on either snail or kite habitat, in these areas.

A change in the political climate may be indicated by the Omnibus Reclamation Act, which became law on October 30, 1992. This Act funds projects that deliver water to farms and municipalities in Western states; but it also includes provisions for irrigation water allocations in the Central Valley Project of California to be adjusted to protect wildlife. The Act directs the Interior Department to increase the amount of water flowing into the Sacramento River by 800,000 acre-feet annually, for the sake of a salmon fishery. Water is also to be allocated to resting and breeding areas for migrating ducks and geese. California agricultural interests were strongly opposed to the bill's thrust toward tightening the availability of water to agriculture. Similar legislation dealing with western water projects and policies of the Bureau of Reclamation failed to pass because of opposition by the farming community during the 101st Congress (1989-90). So it is noteworthy that such legislation could become law in 1992.

The Federal Insecticide, Fungicide, and Rodenticide Act (FIFRA)

Originally enacted in 1947 as a means of assurance to farmers that pesticides sold would be effective as advertised, the focus of FIFRA shifted in the early 1970s to protection against human and wildlife health risks of pesticides. EPA must approve, or register, a pesticide for it to be used.

The regulatory process has been plagued by the volume of pesticide formulations on the market—some 35,000 according to the National Research Council. In the 1988 reauthorization of FIFRA, Congress mandated EPA to re-register all pesticides registered under earlier, more lax standards, gave it a tight deadline for doing so, and authorized EPA to impose registration fees to finance the extra personnel needed to accomplish re-registration in the allotted time. The results have been dramatic. Large numbers of registrations (a registration covers use of a chemical on a specific crop) were dropped for failure to pay the initial fees.

A particular issue at present is the effect on "minor use" pesticides that are targeted for specific applications for a small market. The issue is most important for fruits and vegetables. Overall expenditures on pesticides in this market are substantial, an estimated $660 million annually. But unlike chemicals used on major field crops, fruit and vegetable usage is spread over several thousand individual pesticide registrations covering several hundred different crops. Consequently revenues are measured in the thousands, not millions, of dollars. It is often not worthwhile economically for manufacturers to undergo the expenses of registration for the sake of access to such small markets. These expenses include the costs of carrying out a battery of toxicological tests and tests on residues and environmental fate as well as registration fees. A fact causing some rethinking is that relatively benign chemicals used in certain integrated pest management programs have been dropped for this reason (See Gianessi et al., 1992).

Food Safety

A June 1992 decision by a Circuit Court of Appeals reaffirmed that the Courts would take seriously the "Delaney Clause" of the Food, Drug, and Cosmetics Act, supporting a possible renewed thrust to keep pesticides and other chemicals out of foods if these substances have even the remotest chance of causing cancer in humans. EPA lost its appeal in a Supreme Court ruling in February 1993. Congress may yet legislatively permit the use of chemicals having "de minimus" (negligible, but possibly greater than zero) human health risks, an approach generally favored by the Clinton Administration. Whatever the outcome of this debate, certain to be contentious, the underlying concerns about food safety will continue to generate pressure for increased regulation.

These concerns affected the 1990 Farm Act through a pesticide record-keeping requirement for farmers, as well as research and studies on several pesticide issues. Also, "Circle of Poison" legislation almost became part of the Act. This title would have prohibited the export of pesticides not approved by EPA (under FIFRA) for use in the United States. Proponents of this prohibition argue that fewer products having residues of these pesticides would be imported into the United States. Opponents argue the risks are negligible, would not be changed by the prohibition anyway since manufacturers would move offshore, and the only sure effect is reduction of U.S. exports and costs to U.S. firms.

Regulation of Biotechnology

The term biotechnology is used narrowly to describe recombinant DNA research and more broadly to refer to a range of modern biological research and development efforts—synthetic growth hormones for animals, notably bovine somatotropin (bST) and porcine somatotropin (pST); transgenic plant pesticides, such as cotton that produces the bacteria *Bacillus thurigiensis* (Bt) to kill insects; the development of herbicide-tolerant crops such as glyphosate-tolerant soybeans, so that weeds can be eradicated more effectively; and laboratory-produced products that are synthetic but biochemically the same as plant or animal products.

No single law regulates biotechnology. The National Institutes of Health and the Animal and Plant Health and Inspection Service (APHIS) of USDA regulate the narrowly defined area of field testing of genetically engineered organisms. The Plant Pest Act gives APHIS oversight of the field testing of transgenic plants. More broadly, products of biotechnology are regulated under FIFRA and the Federal Food, Drugs and Cosmetics Act, mainly by EPA. Currently, plants, even transgenic plants, are excluded from FIFRA oversight and registration requirements, but this situation is likely to change through legislation or executive branch regulatory powers.

The Food Security Act of 1985 authorized USDA to establish controls over the development and use of biotechnology in agriculture. USDA's Office of Agricultural Biotechnology published guidelines for field testing of genetically altered organisms for institutions receiving USDA support, but these recommendations are not legally binding (see Larsen and Knudson, 1991). USDA has not yet exercised its authority to assume broader regulatory control over developments in agricultural biotechnology, but the Clinton Administration is planning substantially tighter regulations.

USDA, EPA, FDA, and other agencies will be seriously considering new and more comprehensive regulatory steps. One bill in Congress has proposed prohibiting USDA research support for the development of herbicide-resistant crops. The idea of this restriction is that such crops would encourage the heavier use of herbicides and this would have adverse environmental consequences. The counterargument is that much of the herbicide resistance research leads to a substitution of herbicides that are used at lower rates per acre for older, high rate-materials. Over the past ten years most of the new herbicides and insecticides registered are used at much lower rates and these are the ones being incorporated into crop plants.

Wisconsin has legislatively delayed the commercial use of bST in dairy, and bills to this effect have been introduced in Congress in 1993. Analogous anti-biotechnology efforts can be expected as other technically exotic products and production methods approach commercialization. The combination of farmers' worries about surplus production and consumers' fears of chemicals in foods is legislatively potent. The concerns on the consumer side appear sufficiently strong, if unpredictable, that regulation building consumers' confidence may be necessary for biotechnical innovations to succeed commercially. Even though the Food and Drug Administration found no reason to question the human consumption of milk from cows treated with bST, some dairies have thought it prudent to publicly announce they would sell no milk from bST trials.

The Clean Air Act Amendments of 1990

New clean air regulations being phased in during 1993-95 affect agriculture in several ways. The 1990 amendments require EPA to update its list of ozone-depleting chemicals and implement regulations to eliminate their use. In January 1993, EPA ordered the production and importation of the fumigant methyl bromide (used in soils and stored commodities) to be phased out by 1996. Other regulations will add to the cost of off-road diesel engines in some areas. The air pollution regulations, however, will have a larger, indirect effect on agriculture.

Most important is the requirement for cleaner-burning gasoline under the Act's reformulated fuel provisions. These provisions will increase the demand for ethanol because of its properties as an oxygenate (in gasohol or the ethanol blend ETBE) in fuels that can help attain the requirements that states must meet in the plans they submit to EPA to attain at least 2.7 percent oxygen in motor fuels during the winter months. Implementing the Act has proven contentious, however, because the dominant ethanol blend, 10 percent gasohol, was ruled out for the first round of reformulated fuel requirements for 1993. In October 1992 President Bush overruled this determination by EPA, thus opening up a potentially expanded ethanol market immediately in 1993. President Clinton has so far also been supportive of ethanol.

The substantive environmental questions involve how serious are the volatile emissions (from gas tanks of cold, stationary cars, and from hot engines of cars just turned off) from ethanol blends as compared to methanol-based fuel additives (which the oil industry favors) made from natural gas, and how ethanol blends perform on pollutants other than CO and CO_2. The stakes are high for agriculture because about 1.5 billion bushels of corn per year (about 15 percent of production) would be needed by the year 2000 to meet ethanol demand if these blends capture 20 percent of the reformulated fuel market (see House et al., 1993).

Exportable Surplus

As was the case with commodity policies, U.S. environmental policies have if anything reduced the exportable supply of U.S. farm goods since 1985. The conservation and preservation programs for erodible soil, wetlands, and endangered species have reduced cropland availability; pesticide and fertilizer regulation has increased farmers' costs, albeit only modestly to date; and ethanol policies have expanded the market for U.S. domestic use.

Prospects for Domestic Policy Changes

They key determinant of future farm policies is the economic health of the agricultural sector. Widespread economic losses will be mitigated one way or another. How then is the farm economy doing? Overall, quite well.

Figures 3.5 through 3.8 summarize the situation in its historical context. First, productivity growth continues unabated (Figure 3.5). Second, and related, real farm commodity prices continue to decline at about their long-term trend rate of about 1.5 percent annually (Figure 3.6). The growth in productivity has enabled U.S. agriculture to maintain its international competitiveness while U.S. manufacturing by and large has not. The U.S. trade balance in agriculture has featured growing net exports in the past 20 years, while the overall U.S. trade balance has moved decidedly to net imports (Figure 3.7). Finally, and most important for policy, the income of farm people (including both farm and nonfarm sources) has improved dramatically in the past 30 years relative to that of nonfarm households (Figure 3.8). The rebound from the farm crisis of the early 1980s made pressures to assist farmers as low as they have been in the post-World War II period. Neither party in the 1992 presidential election campaign felt the need to make any substantive promises to do more for farmers. Candidate Clinton even announced intentions to end a commodity program, granted a minor one, for honey.[7]

In the absence of pressure to do more for farmers, the general pressure to reduce governmental spending will mean further reductions in support for farm commodities. It is, however, difficult to make such cuts even when the political climate is most favorable. Figure 3.9 illustrates the

FIGURE 3.5 Agricultural Productivity (Output Per Unit of Total Inputs).

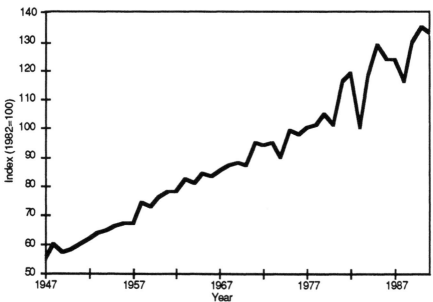

Source: USDA, *Economic Indicators of the Farm Sector.*

FIGURE 3.6 Real Farm Prices: All Commodities.

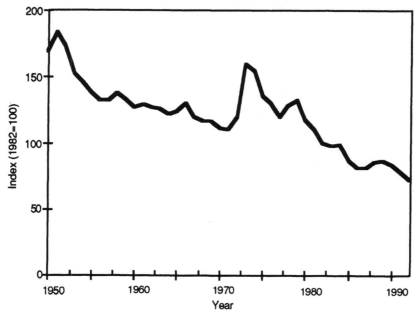

Source: USDA, *Agricultural Statistics. Note:* USDA prices received Index/CPI.

history of the 1990 budget cuts, achieved principally through the 15 percent reduction in payment acres.

The 1991-94 starred data points in Figure 3.9 show the official projections of commodity program spending that Congress had to work with after the Agriculture Committees had completed work on the 1990 Farm Act. Congress found itself unable to legislate in the Farm Act the $13.5 billion 5-year savings that had been agreed upon in the landmark 1990 budget agreement (for accepting which President Bush paid a heavy political price in 1992). The $13.5 billion savings were finally achieved in the Omnibus Budget Reconciliation Act of 1990. The savings followed the accepted procedure of being calculated with reference to a baseline. The particular savings pattern was achieved as shown in the bottom line of the 1991-94 projections (of Figure 3.9). The top line shows the actual outcomes for 1991 and 1992 and mid-1993 projections for 1993 and 1994. In the first two years of the budget agreement actual expenditures not only failed to achieve the cuts but exceeded the pre-agreement expenditure levels by about $2 billion; 1993 looks worse.

Nonetheless, it remains the case that, if payment acres had not been reduced, budgetary expenditures would be even higher than any of the projections shown in Figure 3.9.

FIGURE 3.7 Trade Balance: Net Exports.

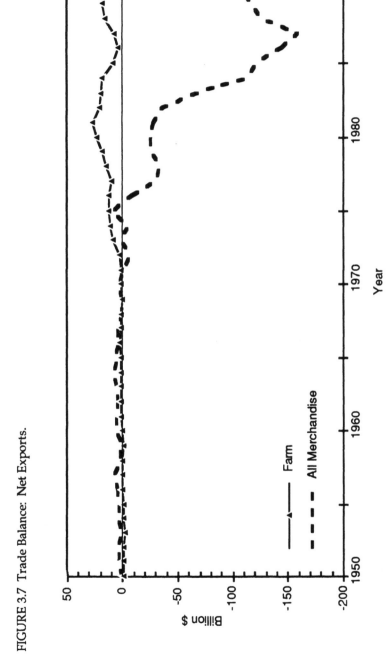

Source: U.S. Council of Economic Advisors, Economic Report of the President, Jan. 1993.

FIGURE 3.8 Farmers'/Nonfarmers' Income: Income From All Sources.

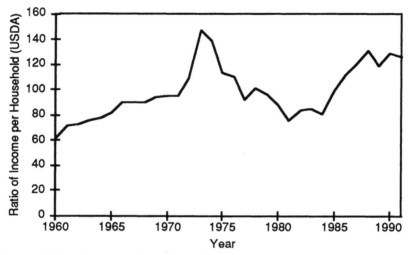

Source: USDA, Economic Indicators of the Farm Sector.

FIGURE 3.9 CCC Net Outlays.

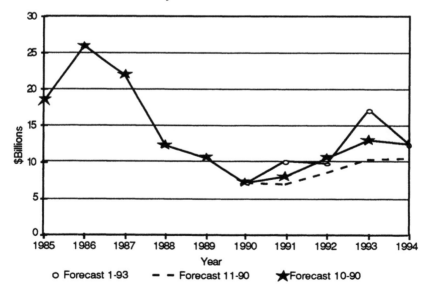

Source: Budget of the United States, Various years.

Conclusion

The main features of the U.S. policy situation as it bears on U.S.-E.C. agricultural trade are:

- U.S. farmers have become relatively prosperous
- Pressure to reduce governmental outlays keep building
- Environmental pressures may constrain output growth
- Productivity growth nonetheless continues unabated
- U.S. price support policies no longer increase U.S. output

The implications are somewhat reduced pressures for protection of U.S. farmers from foreign producers, less policy-generated exportable supply, and a maintained and perhaps enhanced capability to export U.S. commodities under liberalized trade.

Notes

1. "Nonrecourse" means the government has no choice but to accept grain valued at the loan rate, no matter what market conditions may be.

2. Beginning in 1994, the market price will be defined as the minimum of the five-month price plus 10 cents, or the 12 month (June-to-June) average price received by farmers. This change is budgeted to reduce deficiency payments by 10 cents per bushel.

3. This includes acreage "considered planted" for program purposes because it was idled or planted to another crop under program provisions discussed below.

4. Producers can "back in" to the "0/92" program after the growing season has begun if they have a crop failure. This converts the deficiency payment into a self-triggered crop disaster indemnity payment.

5. However, acreage above the wheat base will increase the base by one-fifth of A for the following year. So once a producer has exceeded the maximum permitted, there is an extra incentive above the market return to add acreage to "build base." This incentive is omitted from the algebraic representation.

6. It might be questioned whether slippage is particularly large on Conservation Reverse acreage because highly erodible land is less productive. However, a recent analysis of yields and rental values indicates that the average highly erodible acre has almost the same yield as U.S. average land (see Heimlich, 1989).

7. The Clinton Administration's FY 1994 budget carried through this intention, and also cut the wool program, the Rural Electric Administration, and payments to farmers who receive more than $100,000 annually from nonfarm sources. These steps and some adminstrative steps were budgeted to same $5.8 billion over five years. However, these proposals have met resistance in Congress and the savings will be greatly reduced.

References

Gardner, B. L. 1990. "The Why, How, and Consequences of Agricultural Policies: The United States." In *Agricultural Protectionism*, edited by Fred H. Sanderson, Washington D.C.: Resources for the Future, pp. 19-63.

Gianessi, L., C. Puffer, S. Deberhow, and D. Beach. 1992. "Pesticides: Balancing Risks, Benefits." *Agricultural Outlook* (May): 23-27.

Heimlich, R. E. 1989. "Productivity and Erodibility of U.S. Cropland," U.S.D.A., Economic Research Service, Agricultural Economic Report No. 604 (January).

House, R., M. Peters, H. Baumes, and W. T. Disney. 1993. "Ethanol and Agriculture." U.S.D.A. Economic Research Service, Agricultural Economic Report No. 667 (May).

LaFrance, J., and O. Burt. 1993. "A Modified Partial Adjustment Model of Aggregate U.S. Agricultural Supply." *West. Jour. Agr. Econ.* 8: 1-12.

Larson, B. A., and M. K. Knudson. 1991. "Public Regulation of Agricultural Biotechnology Field Tests." U.S.D.A., Economic Research Service, Technical Bulletin No. 1793 (August).

U.S.D.A. 1993. *Agricultural Outlook*, July.

Discussion

Giancarlo Moschini

I would like to congratulate Bruce Gardner for providing a thorough and lucid presentation of the main features of U.S. agricultural policies that affect agricultural trade. His main conclusion is that U.S. commodity programs no longer increase U.S. output; if anything, they result in less U.S. output for some major commodities. Thus, the implications of these policies for trading partners such as the Economic Community (E.C.) should be reassuring. Furthermore, Gardner notes that: (1) the income of U.S. farmers no longer provides a rationale for agricultural price support because farmers have become relatively prosperous; (2) there is continuous political pressure to reduce government spending; and, (3) emerging environmental concerns may further constrain agricultural output growth. All of this reinforces his main conclusion: The tendency of (current) U.S. agricultural support policies to decrease output is very likely to persist in the future. I find myself in substantial agreement with the theses presented in this chapter. I only have minor qualifications, which I would like to discuss briefly.

The basic elements leading to Gardner's conclusions are: first, a large proportion of U.S. cropland is currently being idled; second, there are no program-specific incentives to overproduce on the land being harvested because program yields are frozen[1] (so that deficiency payments are, essentially, decoupled); and third, a related point, "slippage" is an important feature but not enough to offset the effect of acreage reduction.

That a large fraction of land is being idled is clear. Whether or not this translates into a considerable reduction in production depends on the "slippage" coefficient. Quantifying slippage, of course, remains a difficult problem. Gardner's regression of harvested acres on idled acres provides evidence of "acreage slippage," as he correctly notes. What matters at the end of the day, however, is "production slippage," which may be considerably higher for a number of reasons. Love and Foster (1990) estimate slippage rates for wheat ranging from 29 percent to 37 percent and for corn ranging from 48 percent to 58 percent. The fact that idled land now is mostly land retired under the Conservation Reserve Program (CRP), a program that is most attractive for marginal land,[2] suggests that such relatively high slippage rates may in fact be the relevant ones. On the whole, however, Gardner appears on sound grounds in arguing that the acreage reduction effect dominates so that, *ceteris paribus*, output of program crops at present is being negatively affected by commodity programs.

The "loan rate" policy may deserve some additional comments. As pointed out by Gardner, the loan rate essentially makes U.S. domestic demand infinitely elastic and thus provides a floor for the market price. The fact that the 1990 Farm Bill set the loan rate for program crops at a low level makes this parameter less important than in the recent past. However, with government stocks of program commodities at fairly low historical levels, it remains to be seen whether the policy of low loan rates will continue in the future. At any rate, it should be clear that a floor price policy need not be binding to affect production decisions and the equilibrium market price. Given price uncertainty, a loan rate policy truncates the probability distribution and thus raises the expected price, which affects the output of both participants and nonparticipants alike.[3] Risk aversion on the part of producers is not necessary for such an effect, although it would increase its importance.

The discussion above clearly applies only to "program" commodities. For a number of other commodities not covered by these provisions, import quotas represent the main instrument of protection. Among these commodities, dairy and sugar are probably the most important from the point of view of U.S.-E.C. trade. The stiff import restrictions in these sectors allow for a considerable indirect price support for domestic producers. In addition, the arbitrary allocation of import quotas to exporting countries introduces an additional source of friction amongst trading partners.

Gardner's analysis of the potential impact of emerging environmental regulations attacks a potentially important new dimension of U.S. policies affecting agriculture, and his detailed exposition of the main issues in this matter are useful. Clearly, the eventual changes in agricultural output and trade due to environmental policies are difficult to gauge at the present time.

To conclude, I concur with Gardner that at present time U.S. policies are perhaps reducing, rather than increasing, for most commodities. Of course, this was not always the case. In the past, U.S. policies have often resulted in increased U.S. output for program crops. Perhaps the best evidence in support of this is the fact that the Commodity Credit Corporation has periodically accumulated large amount of stocks. Among the creative ways that the U.S. government has devised to dispose of these stocks, includes financing the ongoing Export Enhancement Program (EEP) and this has surely attracted the attention of trading partners. This suggests that, in analyzing the trade effects of U.S. policies, it may be wise to take a longer view. What U.S. domestic policies are capable of doing is perhaps just as important as what they are doing at the present time.

It remains true that supporting farm incomes in the United States is no longer a compelling rationale for intervention, as Gardner has persuasively argued here and elsewhere (Gardner, 1992). Whether this consideration will lead to a decrease in the proven political clout of the farm lobby remains to be seen. Given the current concerns on the size of the U.S. budget, however, it is very likely that the United States will not increase overall farm spending in the near future, and possibly look for ways to reduce financial outlays. A relevant implication for the issues addressed in this chapter of this somewhat new political attitude concerns the financing of the expensive CRP. Currently, CRP is responsible for most of the land that has been taken out of production, and the large amount of farmland being idled is crucial to the conclusions reached in this chapter. Whether it will continue to be feasible to keep a large share of U.S. farmland out of production as the ten-year contracts start expiring in a few years is an important and unsettled issue.

Notes

1. One could quibble with this simplification. Program yields have been frozen since 1985, but before that they were based on farmers' proven yields. Insofar as farmers expect program yields to be updated in future Farm Bills, the incentive to overproduce may still be present. However, I agree with Gardner's implicit assumption that such an effect is of secondary importance.

2. The program yield for the wheat acreage base retired under CRP is 28 bu/ acre, well below the national wheat program yield average of 33 bu/acre. In fact, the time profile of the wheat base acreage retired under CRP provides some support for the notion that the least productive land is the first to go in acreage reduction programs. The program yield of the wheat base acres retired in the first three sign-up periods (1986) was 26 bu/acre, whereas for the last three sign-up periods (1991-1992) it was 34 bu/acre (Osborn, Llacuna, and Linsenbigler, 1992).

3. Stock acquisition by the CCC through the loan rate program would work in this fashion if the stock is permanently removed from the market. If CCC stocks are released in the domestic market in periods of higher prices, then the program will be more like a stabilization program. If producers are risk averse, such stabilization effect may still have supply effects.

References

Gardner, B. 1992. "Changing Economic Perspectives on the Farm Problem." *Journal of Economic Literature*, (March): 62-101.

Love, H. A., and W. E. Foster. 1990. "Commodity Program Slippage Rates for Corn and Wheat." *West. J. of Agr. Econ.*, 15(December): 272-81.

Osborn, C. T., F. Llacuna, and M. Linsenbigler. 1992. *The Conservation Reserve Program.* U.S.D.A., E.R.S., Statistical Bulletin No. 843, November.

4

Agricultural Trade Relations Between the United States and the European Community: Recent Events and Current Policy

Daniel A. Sumner

Agricultural trade relations between the United States and the European Community were, unnaturally, headline news throughout much of 1992. Still, let us not be confused about why so much attention was paid to agricultural trade. It was not because the topic has intrinsic interest for the public (the lack of sex or violence [except in France] reduces its appeal in most countries). Nor is trade in farm goods the major share of aggregate economic activity—it is about 10 percent of world merchandise trade. But even farm trade can get media attention when the dispute is heated enough and when major parts of the economy seem to depend on the outcome. As 1992 drew to a close many believed that resolving some specific farm trade disputes and overcoming the bilateral impasse between the United States and the E.C. would lead to an expeditious conclusion of the whole multilateral General Agreement on Tariffs and Trade (GATT) Round.

In the so-called Blair House accord of November 20, 1992 (together with the clarifications in the following few weeks), the United States and the European Community dealt with the longstanding GATT oilseed case and settled on modifications to the "Dunkel text" to resolve the major U.S.-E.C. disagreements in agriculture that had been blocking the Uruguay Round talks. However, after an initial wave of optimism, trade observers realized that disagreements outside of agriculture were more troublesome than had been envisioned, and these were sufficient to block an Uruguay agreement during the remaining weeks of the Bush Administration.

The most important event in recent U.S.-E.C. agricultural relations has been the Blair House accord mentioned above. Accordingly, the largest part of this chapter reviews the economic content of the resolution of the oilseed dispute and the compromise on modifications of the draft Uruguay Round text on agriculture. Next, I review recent U.S. farm trade policy in the context of trade patterns and trade relations with Europe. U.S. policy issues related to the North American Free Trade Agreement (NAFTA), the Export Enhancement Program (EEP), and changes in farm program budgets are considered. The chapter does not forecast policies in any country or predict the likely outcome of the Uruguay Round—those topics are too difficult.

The Blair House Accord

Recent agricultural trade issues between the United States and the European Community have included both the multilateral trade negotiations and specific bilateral GATT cases. There has been an attempt to keep the issues officially separate even though it has been generally understood that the dispute on one issue affects, at least implicitly, the discussions in other areas. Throughout the 1990s, as the Uruguay Round continued, particular disputes, such as beef hormones, corn gluten feed, and oilseeds, have been prominent. In early November 1992, a deadline for dealing with the GATT oilseed case corresponded with the effort to conclude the Uruguay Round before the change in leadership in both Europe and the United States caused additional delays. The Blair House accord resolved the oilseed case and represented the status of the Uruguay Round negotiations on agriculture, as of June 1993.

Oilseeds

The oilseed dispute may be summarized briefly as follows. The E.C. had been found to have policies inconsistent with their longstanding zero tariff binding for imported oilseeds and products. For several years the E.C. provided subsidies to oilseed crushers to compensate them for the purchase of high-priced oilseeds produced in the Community. The most recent version of the program provided instead generous per hectare payments directly to producers of oilseeds in order to encourage planting oilseeds in the E.C. Over the past 15 years various forms of the subsidy scheme had encouraged E.C. oilseed production to increase from less than two million metric tons (mmt) to more than 13 mmt in 1992. This subsidized production allowed E.C. oilseeds to displace imports of oilseeds and products from the United States and other countries, especially Brazil and Argentina. It was therefore found to constitute a nullification and impairment of the original zero import duty commitment.

The oilseed dispute lasted several years as the E.C. resisted sufficient modifications of their policy to satisfy either the GATT or the affected parties. The 1992 settlement provides a GATT-bound agreement to phase down over three years the E.C. oilseed planting to 5.128 million hectares minus an amount based on the E.C. set-aside rate on arable cropland. For oilseed area that set-aside rate must be at least 10 percent. Therefore, by the 1995 marketing year the E.C. will be allowed no more than 4.615 million planted hectares of oilseeds compared to 5.75 million hectares this year. To assure that these area limits are met, the E.C. will impose reduced payment rates by one percent if the aggregate plantings exceed the limit by one percent. The reduced payment rate continues for the following year and is cumulative if the area again exceeds the limit.

The Blair House accord on oilseeds also allowed no payments for confectionary sunflower seed growers and limits on oilseeds planted for industrial uses on set-aside land. The E.C. is committed to take corrective action if this production exceeds one mmt in soybean meal equivalent and affects food or feed markets. Finally, the E.C. has agreed to undertake binding GATT arbitration if the United States believes there has been a violation of the agreement.

Though negotiated in November of 1992 and adjusted in further discussions in December the oilseed agreement was only ratified by the E.C. in June 1993 when the French finally accepted the agreement. The oilseed GATT case was again caught up in the middle of European debate over Common Agriculture Policy (CAP) reform and the Uruguay Round.

At the same time as the implementation of the new oilseed regime the new CAP reform policy was being introduced. CAP reform changed the incentive for planting grains and oilseeds by reducing payment rates, requiring set-asides, and lowering market prices for grains. The combination of set-aside rules, relative prices, and payment rates reduced the incentives for planting oilseeds relative to grains. The returns ratio for oilseeds to grains has recently been in the range of about 2.5 to 1, but under CAP reform that ratio has been calculated as about 2.1 to 1. Further, since the relative costs of oilseed production is likely to be rising, the implication is lowered plantings of oilseeds.

The Blair House accord for oilseeds stipulates that, once the planting limit has been reached, the payment rate per hectare must be reduced proportionately as the aggregate area planted increases. The industry faces an aggregate policy response curve that has a unitary elasticity of payment rate to planted area. If the payment rate declines by the same percentage that the area exceeds the trigger, current year payments are approximately constant as payment area expands (Figure 4.1). In the next year the payment rate begins at the new lower level, and if there is again excess area payment rates are again lowered proportionately. If excess

FIGURE 4.1 Oilseed Payment Rates and Planted Area: An Example for 1995.

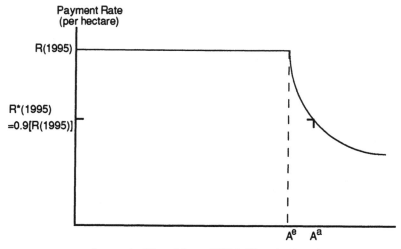

Aggregate Oilseed Area, 1995 (millions hectares)

Note: Assume a 15% set-aside so the area trigger A^e is 4.36 million hectares. If actual area (A^a) were 4.8, the 1995 payment rate would be 10 percent below the 1995 rate. The 1996 payment rate would also be 0.9(R1995), but, if 1996 area were below the trigger, the 1997 payment would snap back to the original.

area is not planted the payment rate reverts to the original level in the following year.

For growers, total revenue is derived from market sales in addition to payments, therefore total revenue in the initial year could rise or fall with added aggregate area, depending on the elasticity of market demand. However, since industry demand might be expected to be inelastic it is likely that aggregate market revenue also declines with more area. The incentive of individual growers with respect to payments is similar to those faced in a competitive market because individual payments rates do not depend on individual planting behavior just as growers are price takers in the commodity market.

The Blair House accord for oilseeds was a true compromise in the sense that no one was satisfied. The agricultural interests in the United States are aware that E.C. subsidies for oilseeds remain at very high levels relative to the prices in the United States and relative to subsidies for grain production in the E.C. Further, in order to get those income transfers E.C. growers are required to plant oilseeds. Producers of oilseeds in the E.C. will, of course, receive less in direct government transfers than previously, but even the lowered incentive to produce will remain high enough to keep most area in production and to reduce only yield growth rather than actual yields. Projected output in the range of 9 to 10 mmt by 1996 may appear appropriate. That production level is consistent with an average yield of about 2.1 tons and area at about 4.5 million hectares. In 1993, expected oilseed production in the E.C. is already down by about 2 mmt due to CAP reform.

Uruguay Round

The Uruguay Round bogged down at the end of 1990 over an impasse between the E.C. and those who wanted trade reform in agriculture. In December 1991, GATT Chairman Arthur Dunkel released the "Draft Final Act," a proposed Uruguay Round agreement that was based mostly on negotiated compromises between the major trading partners. Several parts of the agricultural text (as well as other areas) remained in dispute and so multilateral negotiations continued throughout 1992, particularly between the United States and the E.C.

Finally, in the Blair House accord, the United States and the E.C. put together a compromise package for agriculture. The tentative agreement in agriculture has met with the broad acceptance of the Cairns group and is now the basis for a GATT deal if difficulties outside of agriculture can be cleared up. Also, internal disputes must be resolved within the E.C. Council so that the agreement can be formally accepted by all GATT parties including members of the Community.

The Blair House accord was designed as amendments to the Dunkel text and it is the amended text that will be referred to here. I will summarize the tentative agreement in four categories. The first category is a requirement that trade restrictions that claim to be based on threats to human, animal, or plant health and safety be scientifically grounded. This part of the agreement has been generally in place since early 1992. As normal and straightforward trade barriers become less available there will be a natural tendency for governments to attempt to take recourse in nonstandard barriers. Under the new GATT rules, it will become more difficult to use sanitary and phytosanitary restrictions as substitute trade barriers when direct barriers are unavailable. This sanitary and phytosanitary part of the agreement will not end disputes on these issues; it will, however, allow those disputes to be conducted within a framework of rules.

The second category is import access. There are four parts to the access provisions:

1. Nontariff trade barriers will be converted to GATT bound tariffs. The actual difference between internal and external prices during

1986-88 will be used to determine tariff equivalents. This "tariffication" was used to open the Japanese beef market a few years ago and is being used in the NAFTA also. Tariffication means that barriers such as the Section 22 import quotas and the meat import law in the United States and variable levies in the E.C. will be converted to bound tariffs. The level of the new tariffs are supposed to be based on the current level of protection afforded by the nontariff barrier. This provision, while clear in principle, is vague enough that it provides ample room for dispute in its implementation.

2. Agricultural tariffs will be reduced by an average of 36 percent over six years. Each tariff line, including the newly created ones, will be reduced by at least 15 percent. The tariff agreement calls for a reduction of the average tariff, i.e., not weighted by trade flows. Because the tariff schedules in most nations include many high tariff lines that are little used, it is likely that the reduction of the tariffs on sensitive commodities will be limited to the 15 percent minimum.

3. In order to assure improved trade flows immediately in the most egregious cases, minimum import access of at least 3 percent of consumption for each commodity is required. The 3 percent figure grows to 5 percent over the six-year implementation period. The Dunkel text says that minimum access should be assured at the 4-digit level if possible and allocated back to tariff lines. For many commodities, consumption data is not available at this level of disaggregation. For example, if all grains were treated as a single commodity, imports into Japan would far exceed the 5 percent minimum and Japan would continue to keep out all imported rice with prohibitive tariffs. Such a broad aggregation has been clearly rejected by the major parties, but specifics of aggregation remains important because the more aggregated the commodity the less the implied access improvement.

4. Current access opportunities should be maintained as a part of the tariffication process (current is defined as the average access during 1986-88). Of course, since the amount of access that is now available is not obvious for many commodities, this provision also has room for interpretation in its application.

Because of sensitivity over rice, Japan and Korea have been the most· prominent countries uncomfortable with these access provisions. However, both the United States and the E.C. have sensitive commodities, such as dairy products, for which the minimum access commitments will be politically inconvenient and for which the tariffication principle is unpopular.

The third category of the prospective Uruguay Round agreement is export subsidies. The Dunkel text required that governments cut the value of export subsidies by 36 percent and the quantity of subsidized exports by 24 percent. Both cuts apply to a specific list of commodities, are based on the average subsidy levels during the 1986-1990 period, and are phased in over six years. The Blair House accord modified the Dunkel text by lowering the quantity cuts to 21 percent. This quantity discipline is likely to be the most binding for the United States and the E.C. It also has important affects on projected world commodity prices and trade flows of major agricultural commodities, especially now that CAP reform has lowered the differential between internal E.C. prices and world prices. It has been well understood that the quantity discipline had the potential to limit exports, and that was why the Commission negotiators demanded lower percentage cuts.

The final category of the Dunkel text and the Blair House accord is internal agricultural subsidy policies. This area was the subject of considerable disagreement between the United States and the European Community for most of 1991 and 1992. It was also the area for which the positions of the negotiating parties changed most over the course of the negotiations. The Blair House accord changed the Dunkel text substantially, and it is reasonable to consider the evolution of these provisions in some detail.

The Dunkel text has several related provisions related to internal agricultural subsidy programs. First, programs would be subject to discipline and reduction mainly through lowering the aggregate measure of support (AMS) for each commodity by 20 percent over 6 years. The base period of 1986-88 would be used for the reduction calculations and credit for reforms back to 1986 would be provided since that was when the Uruguay Round was begun. The AMS calculates support levels based on fixed reference prices to measure changes in the influence of policy separately from the influence of movements in commodity markets due to such nonpolicy factors as weather. A *de minimis* level of 5 percent for developed countries and 10 for developing countries would be used for exemptions from reduction commitments. Finally, programs judged to be in a "green box" category of sufficiently nonsubsidizing policies would be exempt from reduction commitments.

After initially urging strong limits on internal supports, in order to discipline U.S. programs, in 1992, the E.C. needed assurance that their new compensatory payments included in the reforms of the Common Agricultural Policy would not be subject to challenge in the GATT. Under the Blair House accord the internal subsidy provisions were weakened in two major ways. First, the 20 percent reduction commitment now applies only to a commodity total subsidy level defined as the sum of the AMS across commodities plus the farm-sector–wide AMS. Second, domestic support in the form of direct payments under production-limiting programs is not included in the aggregate AMS so long as payments are based on fixed areas and yields (or in the case of livestock a fixed number of head), or payments are made on no more than 85 percent of the base production.

The Blair House accord also modified the so-called "peace clause" in the Dunkel text as it relates to internal supports. These changes place some restraints on increasing commodity-specific subsidy rates. In particular, if the exempted direct payments conform with the agreement and if the level of support is not raised above its 1992 marketing year level for a specific commodity, then these measures are exempt from GATT actions against subsidies (Article XVI) or nullification and impairment.

The Dunkel text AMS summed the effects of each internal support policies for each commodity. It is defined in monetary units and uses budget costs, administered internal prices, and fixed nominal 1986-88 border prices to represent the level of support that is then to be reduced relative to support in the 1986-88 base period. The AMS for year t for commodity j may be represented as follows:

$$AMS_{j,t} = \left[P^s_{j,t} - P^b_{j,86-88}\right]Q^s_{jt} + \left[P^d_{j,t} - P^c_{j,86-88}\right]Q^d_{jt} + \left[W^m_{jt} - W^g_{jt}\right]L^g_{jt} + B_{jt} - A_{jt}, \quad (1)$$

where the superscript s refers to the support price and quantities, the superscript b refers to the associated border price, the superscript d indicates the target price and the quantity used for direct payments, the superscript c stands for the market price used in calculations of direct payments, and finally the superscripts m and g indicate the market price and government-subsidized price for subsidized inputs L, B refers to the budget outlays for farm benefits for program not otherwise specified, while A refers to farmer assessments to offset costs of providing the benefits.

Several features of this AMS specification deserve comment. First note that the reference prices for calculations of the subsidy component of price support and direct income payments $P^b_{j,86-88}$ and $P^c_{j,86-88}$ are fixed at the base-period levels, but that is not the case for input subsidies $W^m_{j,t}$ which use current-year estimated market prices to calculate the implicit subsidy. In addition, for both direct payments and for input subsidies governments can choose to use current-year budget cost to reflect the amount of the subsidy rather than calculated subsidy at either current- or base-year prices. The AMS is a flexible sum of current-year budget costs and calculated support to arrive at a money measure of subsidy that is then compared to the base year.

Calculation of AMS for time period t is compared to the 1986-1988 AMS to determine compliance with the 20 percent reduction commitment.

$$\frac{AMS_{j,86-88} - AMS_{j,t}}{AMS_{j,86-88}} \le 0.80 \ . \tag{2}$$

The Blair House Accord changes the internal support part of the Dunkel text in two major ways. First, it changes which policies go into the AMS, and second it limits discipline only to the cross-commodity total AMS. The new AMS is written as:

$$AMS_t = \sum_j \left[P^s_{j,t} - P^b_{j,86-88} \right] Q^s_{jt} + \left[P^d_{j,t} - P^c_{j,86-88} \right] Q^d_{jt} + \left[W^m_{jt} - W^g_{jt} \right] L^g_{jt} + B_{jt} - A_{jt} \ . \tag{3}$$

The Blair House accord effectively drops the term $\left[P^d_{jt} - P^c_{j,86-88} \right] Q^d_{jt}$ from the calculation of the AMS in the most important practical situations. This is similar to changing the criteria in the green box.

The green box is defined in Annex 2 of the Dunkel text. It was not changed in the Blair House accord. The attempt was to ensure that those policies that would be exempted from reduction commitments would conform generally to the notion of "minimally trade-distorting government programs," with an emphasis on a relatively short-term horizon. The first overriding condition is that such exempt policies may not include consumer-funded support and must not provide price support to producers. The list of criteria for exemption is specified in the Dunkel text at a much finer level of detail than other topics in that agreement, so only a sketch can be provided here.

Policies that qualify for exemption include such service programs as: (1) productivity improving services (such as research, extension, training, pest control, inspection, marketing information and promotion [but not price subsidies for buyers] infrastructure for transport, electricity, and water); (2) public stocks for food security; (3) domestic food aid (direct income aid to producers must meet several criteria and generally is expected to fall into one of the next eight categories); (4) decoupled income support (so long as it is based on criteria defined for a fixed-base period, is not related to volume of production or input use after the base period, and is not related to prices after the base period); (5) income insurance or safety nets (so long as the agricultural income loss exceeds 30 percent of gross income [or equivalent in net income] over a 3-year average [or the middle three of the last five years], payments cannot compensate for more than 70 percent of the lost income, and payments cannot be specific to type or amount of production, prices, or input use); (6) disaster payments (so long as an official disaster is declared, losses exceed 30 percent, payments do not exceed the amount of loss, and payments are not tied to future production); (7) producer retirement programs that require total and permanent exits from agriculture; (8) long-term resource retirement schemes (land must be retired for at least 3 years, livestock must be permanently removed, payments must not be conditional on using other land or on prices); (9) investment assistance for which assistance levels are not related to prices or future production; (10) environmental payments to compensate for meeting environmental or conservation regulations; (11) assistance for disadvantaged regions (so long as benefits are not related to prices or production but shall be linked to the extra costs of production in the disadvantaged area).

For the United States and the E.C., the level of overall support for agriculture has declined substantially for most major commodities since 1986 so that even a commodity-specific commitment would not affect many policies. The aggregation across commodities is enough to assure that no policy in the United States or the E.C. would be affected by the required 20 percent reduction. Further, now subsidies for any particular commodity can be raised substantially without violating the amended agreement. (However, if they increase past their 1992 levels they may be vulnerable to challenges of nullification or impairment.)

The major rationale for including internal subsidies in a trade agreement is that production subsidies can reduce imports or increase exports. However, in practice it is very expensive to use internal policies for this purpose and countries resort to border barriers and direct export subsidies to achieve these ends. In the E.C. oilseed case, the internal subsidy policy was found to be a GATT violation under nullification and impairment provisions and was disciplined, even under the current GATT rules. With the Blair House amendments the Uruguay Round no longer attempts to create meaningful binding internal support disciplines. This is itself not a major concern, but a more important problem with the Blair House disciplines on internal support is that a complicated set of provisions, even if they are designed to be nonbinding, may have unanticipated consequences either directly or by affecting the starting point for further negotiations. It seems likely that, compared even to the current GATT, it would be more difficult to pursue, under the amended Dunkel text, a subsidy or nullification and impairment case against internal subsidies that nonetheless have unwarranted trade effects.

Dropping any effective disciplines on internal supports from the package is the final step in the progression of internal supports from the center of the negotiations to the periphery. As negotiations continued it became clear that trying to create disciplines on internal support policies would be inordinately complicated and fraught with problems. These problems include the following: policies having similar trade effects would be treated differently, programs with different trade effects would be treated as though they were similar, and loopholes might well cause continuing policies to become more trade distorting rather than less. Further, when alternative schemes for progressive reduction of distortions were analyzed it became clear that most of the measurable effects of distortions on international trade were due to border measures and especially export subsidy programs (Office of Economics, 1991 and 1992).

Economists who considered disciplines on internal support policies a major goal of the Uruguay Round will be dismayed at the elimination of any real limits in the Blair House accord (see for example Sanderson, 1992). However, as I have argued elsewhere, international negotiations that focus too much on domestic reform are less likely to succeed in their main purpose (Sumner, 1992). Using an international forum to force domestic reform has substantial potential to backfire and increase the chance the trade agreement itself will be rejected. It is not just protectionists who may be troubled by the duplicity of negotiating internationally a policy that was not feasible through domestic policy channels.

Of course, international negotiations affect domestic policy change in several ways even without including internal subsidies in the agreement. The prospect of an impending international agreement can provide additional arguments and incentives for domestic policy reforms (as for example with CAP reform or with Mexican agricultural support policy changes prior to NAFTA). Also, when one of the rationales for a domestic support policy is to offset the impacts of policies of other countries, then reforming trade-distorting policies multilaterally may reduce the incentive for such a policy. And, in the opposite direction, during negotiations a country may increase the level of its subsidies in order to increase the pressure on its negotiating partners. This was the stated purpose of the so-called "GATT triggers" in the 1990 U.S. farm legislation. Under this provision, because the Uruguay Round was not completed by July 1, 1992, grains in the United States are now covered by marketing loans that provide added subsidies to program participants and reduce the market effects of price supports.

Agricultural economists were among those who urged the use of a summary AMS to cover internal and border policies so that the GATT could monitor and discipline all agricultural policies of its members. This early descriptive work probably encouraged the focus on the level of relative level of support across commodities and countries rather than the level of trade distortion caused by policies. When agricultural or trade ministers from the Cairns group or the United States pointed to the level of farm program outlays in Europe or the Producer Subsidy Equivalent (PSE) in Japan they made good rhetoric at home but probably set back progress in the negotiations. But beyond rhetoric, there was the notion that even a measure like the PSE could be used somehow in the negotiations or in GATT disciplines or bindings. Papers prepared for the International Agricultural Trade Research Consortium (1990) as well as the Economic Research Service (1989) seemed to envision the use of an overall

AMS, perhaps along the lines of a PSE. It became apparent that such an approach was not operational and was even counter to reducing effectively the trade-distorting aspects of agricultural policies. (For a more general and favorable treatment of the role of economists in the Uruguay Round and agricultural trade policy, as requested in the discussion on this chapter, see Sumner, 1993b.)

Uruguay Round Implementation Issues: Moving Towards Closure?

The Blair House accord settled the most important issues of dispute between the United States and the E.C. in the Uruguay Round. For export subsidies and internal supports how the remaining issues are resolved is unlikely to affect significantly the measurable projected impacts of the agreement for major markets or commodities. However, the Blair House amendments to the Dunkel text were silent about border protection and the Dunkel text leaves significant issues open to interpretation. The most important of these issues are: the amount of aggregation in the commitments for minimum access; the level at which tariff equivalents are set; and the mechanism used to assure there is no reduction of current access opportunities.

The United States and the Cairns group countries have argued for a relatively disaggregated approach to minimum access because any aggregation allows averaging commodities for which imports are more than 3 percent of consumption with those for which imports are less than 3 percent of consumption to bring the average over the limit and avoid improving access up to the minimum. Obviously, countries such as Japan and Korea would favor aggregation for at least rice and other grains. The Dunkel text seemed to imply that minimum access be applied by tariff line at a very detailed level, but this is simply not feasible because even if import data were available internal consumption data would not be available. Further, many tariff lines apply to narrow product categories; some may even have been created for import purposes. In these cases the import product has almost perfect substitutes in the domestic market (this applies, for example, to certain cheeses or other manufactured dairy products in the United States). For a specific tariff line the import share may be 100 percent, but the import may have a tiny share of the domestic market in the competing market with the protected domestic product. To complete the Uruguay Round will require some comprehensive, if limited, opportunities in markets that are now closed. That means these practical and politically charged questions must be dealt with carefully.

Tariffication naturally allows some flexibility in selecting the internal and external prices for the computations. Some amount of added protection created in the process of converting from nontariff barriers to tariffs is inevitable and likely a requirement of getting an agreement adopted in most protectionist countries. If such inflated tariff equivalents are too extreme the Uruguay Round could add to protection under the name of liberalization. Some GATT members have proposed methodologies for tariffication not based on internal and external market prices but rather with excess protection designed into the calculation. For example, using policy prices rather than actual prices would increase the tariff equivalent whenever the chosen policy price is above the internal market price. For example, the target price of cotton in the United States in 1988 was $1670 per ton, whereas the internal market price was $1245 per ton. If the chosen border price were $1000 per ton, using a target price for tariffication would raise the implied tariff from about 25 percent to 67 percent. This same argument applies to using the intervention price in calculating tariff equivalents when the intervention is above the market price or to using the variable levy when the levy is above the level needed to preclude imports. The E.C. also proposed explicitly adding 10 percent to the tariff and adding another 10 percent variable element. None of these proposals is consistent with the Dunkel text.

For products subject to tariff equivalents, one way to ensure current access opportunities are maintained is to introduce a two-tier tariff where the first tier, with a very low or zero duty, would apply to the import level, and the second tier at the tariff equivalent rate would apply to additional imports. With other approaches imports into a market will likely be lower in the years immediately following the Uruguay Round agreement than before. This would be the case for example if more than nominal tariffs were applied to the current access commodities and internal prices were lowered. A further complication of current access is deciding the quantity to which current access applies. Some markets are very sensitive to the base year and some to the specific policy interpretation. For example, for imports of beef into the United States current access could be determined as the legislated quota formula, the actual imports in base years (which are often above the quota), or the trigger level (which is 10 percent above the quota). It is not obvious which of these is most consistent with the Dunkel text.

Likely Uruguay Round Impacts

The anticipated impacts of various trade packages for agriculture have been estimated by several government agencies and university authors. (For an early example of projected impacts of full liberalization see Tyers and Anderson, 1986.) The United States Department of Agriculture released estimates for U.S. agricultural impacts of adopting the U.S.

proposal in May of 1991 and the impacts of adopting the Dunkel text in March of 1992. The Blair House accord has effects that are somewhat smaller than those of the Dunkel text. For a few significant U.S. export commodities the lack of an internal subsidy discipline implies larger E.C. production and more E.C. exports. But the major factor affecting farm prices, quantities, and revenues remains the reduction of the quantity of subsidized exports.

Overall, with the Blair House accord, the United States can expect about an additional $4 billion of annual agricultural exports, higher world prices for most farm commodities, and lower government outlays for farm subsidies by about $2 billion with no change in internal farm programs. Even with lower payments and higher costs from expanding output, net farm income will be about $1 billion higher than without an agreement because market revenue will be up about $4 billion. This is a significant gain, especially with the reduction of government payments. Cuts in payments to farmers are likely even with no GATT agreement, and the Uruguay Round can accomplish this while improving net farm income.

No full accounting of specific commodity effects is presented here; however, it may be useful to highlight two major commodities to indicate the kinds of impacts anticipated. For wheat the key factor in the agreement is lower subsidized exports from the European Community. In the 1980s the E.C. went from being a large importer of wheat to the second largest exporter of wheat, behind the United States. This was accomplished using trade barriers and export subsidies. Last year the E.C. subsidized about 22 mmt of wheat exports, compared to an average of about 15 million in the period 1985-1988. Under the Blair House compromise they will be allowed about 17 mmt in the first year and 14 mmt by the sixth year. These changes will imply an increase in world wheat prices of 10 percent to 15 percent (Office of Economics, 1992).

Of course the U.S. Export Enhancement Program for wheat will also be scaled back by 21 percent under the Blair House accord, but the EEP is focused on matching E.C. subsidies. All estimates are that simultaneously lowering E.C. subsidized exports and the EEP by 21 percent will produce expanded exports for the United States even though other exporters may gain more. EEP reductions for some other U.S. commodities that made little use of subsidies in the base period will likely have more impact. Commodities such as vegetable oil, meats, rice, and barley had only small tonnages exported with subsidy during the years 1986-1990; therefore the discipline in the Blair House accord may well reduce the export gains in these commodities, especially in the short run.

The U.S. beef industry would expect to benefit from both improved import access and lower E.C.-subsidized exports. As with wheat, the E.C. has become a major beef exporter on the basis of export subsidies. Lowering those subsidized exports and providing more access to imports will allow more low-priced beef from Australia and New Zealand to be exported outside of U.S. markets and allow better prices for the grain-fed beef that is the comparative advantage of the American industry. The exports of beef may be expected to be 5 to 10 percent higher and market prices 3 to 5 percent higher under the Blair House accord to be consistent with USDA figures under the original Dunkel text.

NAFTA

For agriculture, NAFTA is two bilateral agreements with Mexico—one United States and Mexico, and one between Canada and Mexico. NAFTA does almost nothing to change trade rules between the United States and Canada as these were modified under the Canadian-U.S. Free Trade Agreement (CUSTA) of 1989. I will focus on the U.S. impacts (see also Sumner, 1993a). Some observers have looked upon NAFTA as a competitor to improving trade relations with Europe or Asia. But, such an idea does not bare scrutiny mainly because the market is too small and because the policy changes are relatively minor in aggregate.

Mexico is an important trading partner for the United States accounting for about 10 percent of U.S. agricultural exports and a higher proportion of imports. However, the Mexican economy is only one-tenth the size of Japan and one-thirtieth the size of the E.C. The implications of NAFTA are not trivial but for most commodities they are an order of magnitude smaller than the potential impacts of the Uruguay Round. The Uruguay Round is more important because it deals with the whole world market and because trade between the United States and Mexico is already relatively open. In addition Mexico does not use export subsidies and NAFTA does not apply to U.S. export subsidies.

For wheat, NAFTA will eliminate the Mexican import licensing system and substitute a 15 percent *ad valorem* tariff, which will be reduced to zero over 10 years. Given that export programs and the deficiency payment programs are not disciplined, the significant consequence for the U.S. wheat industry is better access to the Mexican market. In the past, annual exports to Mexico have been quite variable, ranging from 50,000 mmt to over one mmt compared to total wheat exports of 35 mmt. Mexico is a significant market for wheat, but even if U.S. exports to Mexico remain consistently in the range of 1.3 mmt it will amount to only about 2 percent of U.S. production or 4 percent of exports. The net effect of NAFTA is likely to be a higher domestic wheat price by at most a few cents per bushel (Office of Economics, 1993).

The beef industries in the United States and Mexico have worked together for many years. Mexico supplies cattle to feedlots in the Southwest and some slaughter cattle and beef is shipped to Mexico. Relatively minor trade barriers for the beef and cattle trade existed recently until Mexico imposed new tariffs in November 1992. Now the tariff on live cattle is 15 percent, on fresh beef 20 percent, and on frozen beef 25 percent. These tariffs will be eliminated by NAFTA for the United States and Canada but are unaffected by NAFTA for imports from other suppliers.

NAFTA will increase cattle and beef prices by about one percent and raise revenues for the cattle industry by some $400 million or slightly more than 1 percent (Office of Economics, 1993). Among the most important consequences for the beef industry is the assurance that Mexico not raise barriers previously lowered. These results are significant but clearly not of a magnitude to cause one to abandon trade relations with other major trading partners.

Export Subsidy Programs

The export subsidy programs of the United States include the Export Enhancement Program and several other commodity specific programs. They all have similar objectives and origins and must be considered in the context of the other programs operating for those commodities. Wheat is the major commodity in the EEP program accounting for most of the export bonuses and most of the tonnage. The EEP was conceived when government grain stocks were high, grain prices were low, and government outlays excessive. The EEP was used to shift up the export demand curve while land-idling programs were used to shift back the supply curve. The impacts may be evaluated on several criteria, but they all depend on the export additionality of the program. Clearly a substantial portion of exports under the program would be made anyway and estimates of additionality hinge on the elasticity of the import demands. Plausible estimates of additionality have been made to range from about 15 percent to 40 percent for wheat depending on the market conditions. With this level of added exports, the wheat domestic price increase from EEP is enough so that deficiency payment savings offset the direct cost of export bonuses.

The export subsidy policy of the United States claims to be focused explicitly on combating the subsidized exports of the European Community. There are several ways to consider the effectiveness of the efforts to date. First is to ask if exports from Europe have been displaced by U.S. exports. The second is to examine the impact of the EEP on export subsidy costs in the E.C. If the EEP has reduced the export price for E.C. wheat, it will raise the per unit subsidy and the costs of any given level of subsidized exports. The elasticity of the export subsidy response function determines how much budget costs increase or exports decrease. A further effect may be to encourage policy change in the E.C. to reduce support prices and production of grain. The policy response to added export costs may be a less generous and more restrictive program. Finally, the EEP and related programs may have encouraged the E.C. and others to be more responsive in trade negotiations. Clearly there is evidence of E.C. changes in all these areas, but evidence of the direct impact of the EEP is difficult to obtain or interpret.

Acreage Reduction and Budgets

It is instructive to examine briefly recent proposals for reform of U.S. farm programs. The recent budget package included several revisions to farm programs as well as changes in the appropriations for operating ongoing programs. The impact on trade relations are affected by changes to those programs in the last two farm bills. The reforms in 1985 and 1990 changed substantially the trade and production impacts of U.S. commodity programs. For example, frozen payment yields, nonpayment acres, planting flexibility provisions, and the voluntary acreage idling under the 50-92 and 0-92 programs reduce significantly the production incentives and the negative environmental impacts of U.S. farm programs (Gardner, Ch. 3). With these provisions farmers make acreage and input decisions based on market prices not on the higher, government-set target prices (which may become simple accounting devices).

Marketing loans, which have been in place for cotton and rice since 1985, are now also available for wheat and feed grains. Marketing loans were added late in the legislative process as a part of the "GATT trigger" provision of 1990 farm legislation. (This provision is included in the Omnibus Budget Reconciliation package of 1990 that also included the flexibility provisions and other major farm program changes.) This legislation made implementing marketing loans in 1993 conditional on failure to conclude Uruguay Round negotiations in 1992 in order to pressure negotiating parties and minimize the export-limiting impacts of price supports.

Marketing loans allow commodities placed in the government loan program to be removed from the price support loan program with the loan repayment rate determined by the market price, not the initial loan rate. This means that, because the loan rate no longer acts as a support price, it does not limit downward movements in the market price, the government does not acquire stocks, and farmers receive, as a marketing loan payment, the difference between the loan rate and the market price. Further, this payment is paid on all of production, not just the amount eligible for regular deficiency payments. So, now, in making planting and input decisions, farmers take into consideration the incentive from these potential new payments. Unlike deficiency payments under the current program, marketing loans provide payments on all production, so provide incentives for more yield-increasing inputs and planting on all base area.

For wheat and feed grains (unlike cotton and rice), loan rates have been well below expected market prices. Therefore both the added production incentive and the added budget costs of marketing loans are small. Politically, there is significant interest in increasing the commodity loan rates on the part of both the Administration and Congress. This was not done in the budget act in 1993, in part, because of budget costs and environmental concerns.

The major proposed agricultural budget savings under active consideration in the United States are associated with a reduction in the amount of land available for deficiency payments. The 1993 proposal by the administration (which was not adopted) was for an increase from 15 percent to 25 percent of base acreage not eligible for payments. Under this proposal, those participating in the grains and cotton programs would have had more flexibility in what they plant and all growers would have lower payment incentives to participate in the farm programs. The flexibility to remain in the program but plant alternative crops clearly has positive efficiency and environmental effects. It would also allow the United States to produce and export more in response to market signals. Compared to other options to reduce outlays on farm programs this proposal has probably the strongest economic arguments.

The Administration also proposed eliminating payments for voluntary acreage reduction under 50-92 and 0-92 programs. (These programs allow participants to plant zero or 50 percent of eligible acreage and receive 92 percent of the anticipated government payment that would have been received had they planted the crop.) Eliminating these programs alone would add to program crop acreage and output, lower commodity prices, and increase total commodity program budget costs. The larger program acreage and lower market price raises deficiency payments. The increase in deficiency payments is larger than the direct saving from eliminating a category of government payments. However, the Administration proposed to offset the implied increase in budget outlays by requiring the released land to be idled under the mandatory Acreage Reduction Program (ARP). The proposal therefore was to shift from voluntary, paid land idling to more mandatory land idling for all participating farms. That combination of changes would obviously lower budget outlays. But increased mandatory land idling also reduces production efficiency and agricultural exports. Raising ARPs is a shortsighted and counterproductive proposal from the view of trade strategy or economic efficiency.

Conclusions

Both the United States and the E.C. have been engaged in changes to domestic subsidy programs. CAP reform was only mentioned in this chapter, but it promises to make an Uruguay Round agreement feasible. Most of the economic requirements in the amended Dunkel text are already met by CAP reform. Credible estimates suggest that, with CAP reform, E.C. subsidized grain exports will naturally decline to the levels required by the Blair House accord.

The United States reformed its internal farm programs in 1985 and 1990. In each case distortions and potential outlays for major crops were reduced. However, over the same period the United States began to use export subsidies in a major way. The next year will provide information about how the new Administration and Congress will conduct trade policy and also how farm programs will be changed. One signal suggests that acreage reductions may be increased and loan rates raised. If that path is pursued, the United States will be less of a force in world markets. At the same time, however, export subsidies may be used even more. These policies are almost contradictory and it seems clear that if the high acreage reduction and high loan rate policy is pursued exports will fall even with large export subsidy bonuses.

As has been true for 7 years, the Uruguay Round continues to dominate trade relations between the United States and Europe. The Blair House compromise, together with the Dunkel text that it amends, now provides a basis for concluding the Round. The results of such a resolution would be economically significant for agriculture in the United States and Europe mainly because concluding the Uruguay Round will allow some relaxation of the export subsidy competition in which the E.C. and the United States have been engaged. The other significant changes from such a conclusion of the Round would be a conversion of nontariff barriers to tariffs and at least a guaranteed minimum access for all agricultural goods into all markets. These changes have smaller market impacts but if implemented carefully could lead to substantial liberalization over a longer horizon. For both export subsidies and border barriers the Dunkel text provides the basis to begin a process of liberalization that could fully liberalize agricultural trade in less than two decades. Such a program would make bilateral efforts such as NAFTA irrelevant in the long run even as they provide significant benefits over a shorter horizon.

References

Economic Research Service. 1989. "GATT and Agriculture: the Concepts of PSEs and CSEs." Miscellaneous Publication No. 1468, Washington D.C.: USDA.

International Agricultural Trade Research Consortium. 1990. "Bringing Agriculture into the GATT: Potential Use of an Aggregate Measure of Support." Commissioned Paper No. 5, University of Missouri, Columbia.

Office of Economics. 1991. *Economic Implications of the Uruguay Round for U.S. Agriculture.* Washington, D.C.: USDA. May.

————. 1992. *Preliminary Analysis of the Economic Implications of the Dunkel Text for American Agriculture.* Washington, D.C.: USDA. March.

————. 1993. *Effects of the North American Free Trade Agreement on U.S. Agricultural Commodities.* Washington, D.C.: USDA. March.

Sanderson, Fred H. 1992. "Comment on Sumner." in T. Becker, R. Gray, and A. Schmitz, eds., *Improving Agricultural Trade Performance Under the GATT.* pp.251-253. Kiel: Wissenschaftsverlag Vauk.

Sumner, D. A. 1992. "The Economic Underpinnings of Uruguay Round Proposals." in T. Becker, R. Gray, and A. Schmitz, eds., *Improving Agricultural Trade Performance Under the GATT.* pp.239-250. Kiel: Wissenschaftsverlag Vauk.

————. 1993a. "How NAFTA Will Affect Agriculture in the United States:Regional Impacts," In *Increasing Understanding of Public Problems and Policies 1992.* pp.173-183. Oak Brook, Il: Farm Foundation.

————. 1993b. "Economic Analysis for Better Agricultural Trade Policy." The James N. Snyder Memorial Lecture, Department of Agricultural Economics, Purdue University, West Lafayette, Indiana.

Tyers, R., and K. Anderson. 1986. "Distortions in World Food Markets: A Quantitative Assessment," Background Paper No. 22, prepared for World Bank, *World Development Report 1986,* Washington, D.C.

Discussion

Nadia Cuffaro

Professor Sumner's chapter provides a very useful and timely discussion of two main themes: First, the Blair House agreement between the United States and the E.C., which dealt with both the oilseed case and the U.S.-E.C. confrontation over agriculture at the Uruguay Round; second, recent developments of U.S. agricultural policies, especially selected issues concerning such policies. The latter include: the likely impact of the North American Free Trade Agreement on U.S. trade relations with Europe and Asia, the export subsidy programs (specifically the Export Enhancement Program), and the recent proposals of the new administration.

The compromise agricultural package put together at Blair House in November 1992 is described as consisting of four main points: First, an attempt to curtail the use of sanitary and phytosanitary restrictions as trade barriers; second, import access (with a combination of tariffication, tariff reductions, and minimum import access provisions); third, the reduction of the value of export subsidies and of the quantity of subsidized exports. Finally, at the bottom of this list, we find the issue that agricultural economists have discussed most thoroughly in recent years: internal agricultural subsidy policies.

Professor Sumner makes some rather strong statements on this point arguing that as the accord now stands the limits to internal subsidy policies are merely cosmetic and suggesting that the Blair House agreement would be stronger if such a chapter were not included at all. However, I would argue that the fact that a measure of internal support is included, even if it is a cross-commodity average aggregate measure, remains, at least in principle, an important feature of the agreement.

As for U.S. agricultural trade policy, Professor Sumner absolves NAFTA from charges that it might hinder trade relations between the United States and other important partners. The EEP is evaluated as an effective, budget-neutral policy for increasing exports, while as for its effectiveness in combatting the subsidized exports of the Community, which was the program's intended purpose, the chapter finds no conclusive evidence. It could however be added that the program has harmed some nonprotectionist exporters. Finally we learn that the orientation of the new administration is toward stepping up acreage reductions, loan rates, and probably export subsidies.

On the whole, the chapter is informative and pertinent, but one is left with the impression that the analysis is not entirely convincing or could have been usefully carried further on two issues.

The first one relates to the "solution" of the GATT confrontation, if such a solution will actually be based on the Blair House agreement. Lengthy discussions about the need for a general move towards liberalization and the inclusion of internal support policies in the GATT have led to a quite different outcome. We have a trade agreement that benefits the United States and probably other exporters, while the initial extreme emphasis on internal policies has basically served to put pressure on the E.C. for CAP reform, in conjunction with subsidy policies such as the EEP and the marketing loans for wheat and feed grains, measures that have not rendered U.S. agricultural policy more liberal.

All of this may be fine, but one might wonder if anyone has ever believed in the zero option. In other words I believe that at this point it would be worthwhile to try to interpret the actual negotiating strategies at the Uruguay Round and their effectiveness. Professor Sumner's interpretation, as it emerges from the chapter, seems to be the following. The work of agricultural economists contributed to focusing the first negotiating stage of the Round on the level of support rather than the level of trade distortion caused by policies. Such focus set back progress in the negotiation. Later, as the United States realized that such an approach was not effective, internal support moved from the center to the periphery of the negotiations. What this account fails to acknowledge, however, is the fact that what set back progress in the negotiation was not the focus on internal policies as such but the initial U.S. insistence on the "elimination" or extremely drastic reduction of support policies, the much heralded zero option. Furthermore, Professor Sumner argues that international negotiations that focus too much on domestic reform are less likely to succeed in their main purpose. Here however there are some observations to be made. In the case of agriculture, one is faced with the fact that "protectionism" and the resulting trade distortions are in general, and in particular in the case of the CAP, mostly a byproduct of the internal policy of support and stabilization. Internal policy change can then be a precondition for accepting a drastic reduction of trade-distorting measures. In other words, it seems unlikely that the E.C. could have adhered to such measures as those contemplated by the Blair House agreement if it had not undertaken a process of reform that contemplates a partial decoupling of price support and product quantities. On the other hand, international pressure has been a very important force for the internal political process of reform.

My second criticism of the chapter concerns the section devoted to the discussion of the proposals of the new administration. Professor Sumner defines such proposals "almost contradictory" and as such they are perhaps difficult to clarify. However, it would have been interesting to have a more extended discussion of recent policies and to be able to establish some connections between such policies, the ongoing U.S. debate on trade policies, and the general orientation of the Clinton administration.

PART THREE

Changes in the Common Agricultural Policy and Their Implications for U.S.-E.C. Agricultural Trade Relations

5

Nature and Causes of CAP: Changes in the 1980s and a Tentative Exploration of Potential Scenarios

Michele De Benedictis, Fabrizio De Filippis,
and Luca Salvatici

Introduction

The aim of this chapter is to review the Common Agriculture Policy (CAP) reform process during the 1980s, up to the MacSharry package approved in May 1992. The interpretation of the sequence of events and of the technical solutions approved along the process is all but unique. On the one hand, one can see the reform as the embodiment of a reductive approach, and evolution of the CAP as a "conservative" process, aimed at preserving the hard core of the traditional (coupled) model of agricultural policy. According to this interpretation, the several changes introduced in the last decade could be considered as attempts to secure the survival of the traditional price policy, concentrating all efforts on limiting its negative effects in financial terms. On the other hand, a more "optimistic" interpretation stresses the emergence, within the CAP reform process, of a genuine attitude towards real change, the main focus being on the definition of new (decoupled) policies, capable of introducing greater market orientation in food production and of helping agriculture play the new roles assigned to it by society at large.

The next section highlights the driving forces, both at national and international levels, that explain the main changes introduced in the CAP during the 1980s. In this framework the major steps of the reform process are analyzed in the following section, with special attention devoted to the approval of the MacSharry reform (MSR). Some implications of the MSR are outlined in the section titled "Some Reflections on the MacSharry

Reform," together with a critical discussion of the most innovative features introduced in the CAP. The analysis is developed in the next section with reference to the general issue of the decoupling of agricultural policies and to the specific problems raised by the MSR in terms of implementation costs. In the final section, some tentative conclusions are drawn, looking at the MSR as a transition towards three possible future scenarios.

The Driving Forces in the CAP Reform Process: Two Dimensions

The CAP, as is well known, was created at the beginning of the 1960s and, during its first decade of application, proceeded securely in a general economic situation of rapid growth and in an European Community comprising only six countries joined in a common policy whose administration was relatively simple. The agricultural lobby was satisfied with the enactment, at the Community level, of a high price support policy, whose principal beneficiaries were the strongest and most efficient producers. Furthermore, costs of the CAP still appeared modest, also because the six-member Common Market was a net importer of practically all the regulated products.

Above all the CAP's effects and its very existence as the first (and for a long time the only) result of the European integration appeared politically very important to all member countries. At the international level, the United States, whose hegemony was uncontested at the time, looked favorably on the creation of a pole of economic and political integration in Western Europe, even at the price of the protectionist orientation of the CAP that would have reduced the outlets for U.S. agricultural exports.

Some problems emerged in the 1970s in a general economic context of rising prices of oil and raw materials, monetary disorder, progressive divergence between the economies, and the economic policies of the member countries, all within the framework of an international crisis characterized by the decline of U.S. hegemony. This period saw the partial failure of agricultural structural policy, as conceived by Mansholt in his Memorandum of 1968 (Commission of the E.C., 1968) and only partially enacted by the Directives of 1972. Market policy, on the other hand, continued to expand protected from the upheavals of the flexible exchange system through a complicated agrimonetary mechanism. This, however, caused distortions in intra-Community trade and, in effect, differentiated between the level of prices received by farmers of the different Member States. Moreover, some of the unequal effects of the CAP grew apparent: differences between strong support for continental products and weak protection for Mediterranean agriculture; disharmonies between regions or areas, between categories of producers, and, principally, between financial costs and benefits to Member States. It was as a result of these tensions regarding CAP costs and benefits, rendered more acute by England's intransigent position on budget issues, that in 1980 the long and difficult process of CAP revision began.

The CAP's difficulties at the beginning of the 1980s reflect a more general crisis of the model of agricultural policy that has been dominant in industrial countries. The crisis of this model, structured primarily on price support measures "coupled" to quantities of products, has two principal dimensions: an internal dimension that finds indefensible the attribution of costly and distortive supports to ever stronger and more productive agricultures; and an international dimension reflecting the growing interdependence between national agrifood systems that is incompatible with the protectionist component of the coupled model. These two dimensions explain the driving forces for reform of the CAP.

The Internal Dimension

The internal dimension that has, undoubtedly, been the most important for development of the CAP reform has the following aspects:

1. *Financial.* With growth of the production potential of agricultures of developed countries, the "coupled" model of agricultural policy produces costs that are intolerable. In fact, with progressive saturation of internal market outlets and stagnant consumption, there are structural problems of overproduction that require aggressive and, in any case, costly trade policies for disposal of the surplus abroad. The main driving force, as already mentioned, toward CAP reform is its financial incompatibility as regards both control of agricultural expenditures and the distribution of costs and benefits between Member States and between categories of beneficiaries. The question of the CAP's financial compatibility was posed energetically as far back as the late 1970s and, in fact, most of the remedies applied to the CAP during the 1980s aim at controlling agricultural expenditures (Moyer and Josling, 1990). At the beginning of the 1990s it continued to be perceived as the only really important problem. Moreover, the immediate effects of German reunification on the CAP budget and the perspective of integration with other Eastern European countries represented another blow for financial compatibility.

2. *Decline of the political importance of agriculture.* One of the catalysts of this decline in the E.C. was progress toward completion of the Single Market. There is a diminished role for agriculture and agricultural policy in the European integration process. According to the philosophy of integrated development of the rural world, the CAP, a

strictly sectorial policy, loses a part of its central and autonomous position even in the eyes of its traditional supporters. Politically, there is also full awareness of the CAP's economic and administrative inefficiency in attaining its objectives and of the disharmonies this has caused. Even among policy makers, there is growing intolerance for a costly, complicated policy that is difficult to administer, is continually accused of generating waste, and that, in any case, seems to satisfy no one. Given the fact that the fate of future European integration will largely be determined outside the agricultural sector, the CAP seems to have exhausted its historical role as the cement and cornerstone of European unity in the name of which, in the past, it was defended at any price. This type of reasoning was reinforced by the neoliberal currents of the 1980s; the CAP was an easy target for supporters of the virtues of the market and of the advantages of deregulation: it was transformed, in this perspective, from cornerstone to tombstone of the European Community (Salvatici, 1993; De Filippis, 1993).

3. *Environmental sustainability of the CAP.* The capacity of the CAP to defend and promote an agriculture producing good quality food with environmentally compatible techniques is a new objective/constraint. It is hard to define precisely such an objective, but the demand for "luxury goods" such as quality products and environmental services from agriculture is spreading rapidly among satiated and rich consumers, as Europeans are. In other words, in a context of overproduction, the traditional aim of "food security," which the CAP pursued with success, is replaced by "environmental security." Obviously, all this leads to profound revision of the philosophy of coupled intervention that puts quantity before quality of food products.

The International Dimension

The international dimension regards all the aspects of growing interdependence between CAP and agricultural policies in the rest of the world and the need to reduce the CAP's distorting effects on international markets and avoid trade conflicts. This problem, given the CAP's protectionist character, has always existed in theory, but perception of it has grown as the E.C. gradually became a net exporter of a large number of agricultural goods (Cuffaro and De Filippis, 1992). However, during the first half of the 1980s, the problem was limited and manageable in a bilateral framework with some specific episodes of contention with the United States and a series of agreements with Third World countries. With regard to relations with developing countries and, more recently, with the countries of Eastern Europe, the E.C. tends to utilize its agricultural surpluses strategically in economic and political relations and to adapt concessions on a case-by-case basis. Thus, on the one hand, it has conceded food aid and sales at favorable conditions to less developed country (LDC) importers; on the other hand, it has endeavored to maintain good relations with exporting countries, guaranteeing them bigger quotas of E.C. imports through a series of bilateral agreements (agreements with Mediterranean countries, the Lomé Convention with ACP countries, and more recent agreements with Eastern European countries). Such concessions have further exasperated relations with the United States and other developed countries that are exporters of agricultural goods. They accuse the E.C. of having contributed to destabilizing and depressing international prices by lowering import volumes and increasing subsidized exports on world markets. It is common knowledge how the E.C.-U.S. dispute, that was sporadic and concerned single questions in the past, has become generalized in the Uruguay Round of the General Agreement on Tariffs and Trade (GATT). Hence, from 1986 on, strong emphasis was put on agricultural trade liberalization and the CAP found itself involved—as the principal defendant—in a much more pervasive re-examination of policies at the world level and it faced strong pressure to reduce its protectionist components.

The Fundamental Steps of CAP Reform in the 1980s: Driving Forces at Work

Conjunctural Gradualism of the 1980s

The explicit need for reform of the CAP matured, as we have seen, between the 1970s and 1980s, largely due to the appearance of increasing production surpluses, the rising budget cost of price supports and the unequal distribution of benefits amongst countries, products, and regions. The Gundelach Report of December 1980 (Commission of the E.C., 1980) and the following Thorn Report (Commission of the E.C., 1981a, b) can be considered the documents that officially initiated the process of CAP reform.

The Community's reform action during the 1980s was a strategy that could be labeled as "conjunctural gradualism." With this term, we intend a pragmatic and often low-profile approach whose strengths have been flexibility and the capacity to use the emergency and the interests involved so as to accomplish the CAP's difficult survival. However, this approach has, in various way, been excessively reductive with respect to the complexity of the problems so that, to an external observer, the revision process appears hesitant and full of contradictions: a series of apparently disconnected measures that represent partial and provisional compromises reached by the protagonists to resolve the emergency of the moment.

The principal stages of this process over successive years can be described as follows:[1]

1983. The first operational attempt at CAP reform was a document issued in July 1983 (Commission of the E.C., 1983). With this, in a climate of great tension caused by the E.C.'s financial crisis resulting from agricultural expenditures, the Commission tried to pass a strong version of the "guarantee threshold" principle, meaning systematic imposition of constraints and limitations on supports conceded by price policy. The proposal was destined to be tabled but represented the germ of the budget stabilizers that were put into effect five years later.

1984. During the usual spring negotiations on agricultural prices, a turning point was reached in 1984. This consisted of a package of decisions for 1984-85 that was the most stringent ever to be passed. In particular, for the first time in CAP history, the nominal level of institutional support prices, expressed in ECU, diminished, and, more importantly, a quota regime was instituted for milk production. The same package included agrimonetary reform by creation of the Green ECU tied to strong currencies and also introduced the switch-over mechanism that cushioned price restrictions, assuring their rise (or preventing their fall) in national currencies. In the short run, this helped overcome the resistance of farmers of strong-currency countries to the freezing of ECU prices, which otherwise would have corresponded to their reduction in national currency terms. In the long-run, this also satisfied the weak-currency countries because it further widened the margins for agrimonetary devaluation as a cushion against price restrictions imposed by CAP reform.

1985. Regulation 797 initiated a new structural policy that started to take into consideration problems of consistency with market policies and their effects. In particular, in contrast to the productivist philosophy inherited from Mansholt, the need to keep production under control was recognized in structural policy. In the same year, the so-called *Green Book* was issued (Commission of the E.C., 1985a), in which the Commission brought price policy under serious discussion for the first time and explicitly recognized the need for market orientation of European agriculture. The long-term scenario toward which the *Green Book* was directed was progressive and represented a substantial realignment of internal prices with those of the world market, combined with a selective support system based on direct income aid to farmers and decoupled, as much as possible, from the quantity of production. The opposition of the agricultural lobby and of several national governments led to rapid rejection, at least for the time being, of the changes announced by the *Green Book*. A subsequent, more limited and operationally oriented, document was passed by the Commission (Commission of the E.C., 1985b).

1986-1989. Within the limits of reduced financial commitment and therefore somewhat marginal to CAP reform, structural "accompanying measures" appeared on the scene during this period. These were innovative structural interventions that experimented with some of the decoupled supports proposed by the *Green Book*. Included in this type of intervention were measures for control of production potential through regulation or limitation of the use of factors of production (extensification, retirement schemes, set-aside) as well as a program of direct income aid to alleviate situations of major social hardship (Commission of the E.C., 1989). In this new climate, as presented in the document *The Future of the Rural Society* (Commission of the E.C., 1988), measures in support of agriculture were viewed within the framework of an integrated approach to long-term development of the rural economy and society. In the meantime, the main road to CAP reform which involves price and market policies, reached the point, by 1988, of rationalization of the guarantee threshold principle through the budget stabilizers and extended them to almost all commodities. These were more or less automatic control mechanisms that set penalties of various types (proportional price cuts and/or increase in coresponsibility levies) when total production exceeded a given production ceiling ("maximum guaranteed quantity").

It can be said that the introduction of the stabilizers represented the most important change in the long process of CAP revision throughout the 1980s, even if their importance has been considerably underestimated. They were the most coherent culmination of the guarantee threshold principle and can be viewed as the final stages of the conjunctural gradualism that characterized the reform movement in the 1980s. The adoption of the stabilizers was an attempt to reform the CAP "with the train in motion," without shock and upheaval, as befits a slowly evolving, inertia-laden policy on which twelve national governments must find agreement. Furthermore, by combining control of production and price reduction, stabilizers can be considered a compromise—perhaps the only possible one at the time—between two different approaches to CAP reform and between the two alternatives already indicated by the *Green Book*. On the one hand, the strongly "regulated" approach of quotas theorizes that high and coupled support levels are in the nature of the CAP and are unrenounceable. Stressing the need to keep administered prices high, this approach supports the principle of guarantee thresholds and, particularly, generalized controls on production assuring, in this way, the CAP's survival, at least in terms of financial compatibility. The other alternative, at the opposite extreme, is for more radical reform along the lines indicated in the *Green Book*. This viewpoint gained momentum with the general crisis of the coupled model of agricultural policy as well as the neo-liberal trends of the 1980s. It theorized an effective market orientation of European agriculture with the need to reduce price supports drastically or, at least, to improve the role of prices as signals to farmers. In this perspective, most income support—in those cases and to the extent that was still deemed legitimate and necessary—would be in the form of selective and decoupled direct payments.[2]

It should be noted that the previously described accompanying measures are also part of the attempt to reform CAP silently and without trauma and, together with the stabilizers, were apparently successful (minor) ingredients of conjunctural gradualism. Though at the cost of further complicating CAP procedures, they offered the possibility of diversifying the instruments and occasions of support and thereby played an important role in the politics of negotiations: in fact these measures, providing small concessions to one country or another, acted as "sweeteners," easing the difficult road to agreement and compromise within the E.C. Council (Runge and von Witzke, 1987; Petit *et al.*,1987).

By the end of the 1980s, conjunctural gradualism seemed to have won the day within the CAP and the problem of financial compatibility seems, if not quite resolved, was at least on the way to solution. The only remaining but very real problem was with to regards international compatibility in terms of its effects on world agricultural markets, which were particularly damaging for the traditional exporting countries. This led to difficulties for agricultural negotiations in the Uruguay Round of the GATT that the United States is trying in every way to transform into a court of justice for European agriculture. However, this pressure is not perceived as having a determining effect on CAP reform, as shown by the strongly defensive stand of non-negotiability of the CAP with which the E.C. initially responded to the United States' "zero option" proposal in GATT negotiations. In fact, the CAP's history is an unequivocal demonstration that international pressure alone cannot push the twelve national governments to radically alter their agricultural policy if this is not in conformity with internal interests (Moyer and Josling, 1990).

The MacSharry Reform

The reform process that culminated in May 1992 had its start in January 1991 with the distribution of the so-called nonpaper, an anonymous document of reflections about the CAP, not yet officially adopted by the Commission but, in fact, attributed to the Commissioner for Agriculture, Ray MacSharry, whose name from that moment on is inseparably linked to the CAP reform package. The document's essential points are as follows:

- emphasis on defense of the European model of small family farm agriculture;

- partial refusal of the logic of stabilizers and (principally) of production quotas and return to the *Green Book* approach: market orientation through price reductions compensated by payments that are partially decoupled and decrease according to farm size;
- redefinition of the justification for supports and strong emphasis on their more equitable redistribution among farmers;
- strengthening of accompanying measures in areas regarding quality, the environment, forestation, and extensification, which are seen as new recipients of decoupled and selective supports.

At first appearance, the MacSharry proposal appeared *inevitable* and *impossible* at the same time: inevitable, in normative terms, as pointed out by a body of literature that stresses the need for reorienting agricultural policies of developed countries in the direction of greater decoupling; impossible, in positive terms, as past history demonstrated that inertia regarding decisions is a constituent and irremovable element of the CAP and makes it difficult to imagine a drastic break with conjunctural gradualism. As a result there are two possible readings of the MacSharry proposal: people who were aware of the necessity for radical reform, and believe it possible that this can be promoted within the Commission, considered it a real and true "Copernican revolution" and a demonstration of genuine willingness to liquidate the old CAP; people who held the opposite view, apparently more realistic and tied to the logic of conjunctural gradualism, tended to belittle the proposal as simply a tactical move. In this interpretation it is thought to be a show of goodwill in the framework of the GATT negotiations and, at the internal level, a threat to prepare the ground for a more restrictive use of stabilizers (De Filippis and Salvatici, 1991).

In February 1991, MacSharry's nonpaper was converted into an official document of the Commission (Commission of the E.C., 1991a) but still in the form of reflections and proposals. These were more generic and slightly "softened" with respect to the nonpaper, but the sense of the need for a strong turning point remains unaltered. In July 1991, the Commission's reflections were transformed into an official proposal (Commission of the E.C., 1991b) that became operative in October with proposals for changes in the official texts (Commission of the E.C., 1991c). The core of these changes applies mainly to arable crops and, to a lesser extent, to livestock:

- For cereals and oilseeds, a reduction of 35 percent of institutional prices and abolition of stabilizers and of coresponsibility are predicted; payments per hectare are fixed on the basis of past yields at the regional level. So-called large producers (whose production, on the basis of average regional yields, exceeds 92 tons) receive compensation on the condition of compulsory set-aside of 15 percent of farm area with compensation for a maximum of 7.5 hectares.

- A *base area* is established (to be administered at the farm or the national level) determined by the average number of hectares in grains and oilseeds for the three-year period 1989-1991. This represents the ceiling of the number of hectares eligible for compensation.
- For the dairy sector, reductions are foreseen in prices of butter (–15 percent), skimmed milk powder (–5 percent) and in quotas (–4 percent), whereas premiums are introduced for suckler cows in the case of extensive livestock activities.
- For beef, the proposed price reduction is 15 percent, compensated by reduced grain prices and by premiums per head in the case of extensive livestock activities. A *reference herd for livestock* is introduced, working in the same way as the base areas for cereals.

Internally, the Commission's proposals aroused the protest of farmers while negotiations were opened on the price package for 1992-93. In this package, changes in the regulations affecting oilseeds were already introduced for the current marketing year. At the same time MacSharry threatens, if his proposal is not approved, an 11 percent reduction in grain prices through exclusive application of stabilizers (that would be without any kind of compensation).

At the international level, GATT discussions began regarding compatibility between the new support mechanisms and the proposed agreement presented in December 1991 by the GATT Director General, Arthur Dunkel, at a time when completion of the Uruguay Round negotiations seemed imminent. The main problem, in this phase, was whether compensations per hectare foreseen by CAP reform could be considered decoupled and, therefore, excluded from the calculation of internal support indicators. On the other hand, as regards the reduction of internal prices and of differences between internal and world prices, the MacSharry proposal seemed to go even beyond Dunkel's compromise.

Debate on the reform reached a decisive phase in the Spring of 1992. By then, it is clear that the Commission was serious. Some farmer organizations—beyond the protests that are imposed by their role—began to see the MSR as the "lesser evil," compared to a scenario of more rigorously administered stabilizers and hardline defense of the CAP in GATT talks.

In May 1992, after relatively brief negotiations and contrary to expectations, the E.C. council reached agreement on the MSR. The May 1992 agreement contained, substantially, the initial proposal, though watered down by some important changes that were required to obtain almost full unanimity[3] from the agricultural ministers, as follows:

- as a result of opposition by Britain, Denmark, and the Netherlands, the support scheme was made less regressive through elimination of the limit (7.5 ha) on compensation to large farms for compulsory set-aside;
- E.C. preference rose from 10 percent to 40 percent at the request of France, probably to defend European agriculture from the effects of possible tariffication in the GATT;
- the package of measures was considerably softened in terms of price reductions while decisions about restrictions on milk quotas were postponed.

Some Reflections on the MacSharry Reform

Goals and Instruments

A verdict on the MSR cannot be global, but one must examine its parts. In our opinion, the objectives that one wishes to, or can, pursue with this reform should be kept distinct from the chosen instruments.

1. The verdict is positive with regard to the aims: partial decoupling of price supports and product quantities; the idea of giving more consideration to demand-supply mechanisms in the formation of prices; the declared aim to correct inequitable distribution of supports; the attempt to reinforce selective intervention through accompanying measures. Another positive element is the break with past inertia and its conjunctural gradualism. The small shock that derives from this reminds everyone that global debate is needed on the CAP's future and that yet another defensive regeneration is impracticable.
2. With regard to the chosen means for carrying out the reform, there is much perplexity about their effectiveness, selectivity, and manageability. This applies principally to the choice of using hectares or head of livestock as the criteria for distributing and limiting supports; the effects of the "freezing" of the present situation with regard to the extent and territorial distribution of support; the risk of bureaucratizing agricultural activities; the high administrative cost.

With these issues in mind, we propose the following points for discussion:

Decoupling. During the second half of the 1980s, at the margin of GATT negotiations and with the need to redesign agricultural support policies in less distorting ways, there was much discussion of the desirability and meaning of decoupling (Miner and Hathaway, 1988). A *strong* definition of decoupling considers only those support measures that are completely independent of production and/or are even explicitly intended for reducing production potential.[4] A *weak* definition, on the other hand, considers as decoupled even measures that grant support in ways that are not proportional to current production quantity. In other words, decoupling in the weak sense, although tied to the existence of production activity, should provide no incentive to increasing such activity.

The fact that compensation per hectare, as foreseen by CAP reform, is calculated according to past yields and not according to current yields, certainly gives it a decoupled character, at least in the weak sense, since the new mechanism reduces the incentive to increase production by improving yields. On the contrary, with this form of payment, farmers, in response to lower prices, are expected to reduce production.

But if the strong definition of decoupling is adopted, the compensation per hectare that the reform provides would not qualify as decoupled, because in order to receive it production must, in fact, continue. As a consequence, the effect is to keep those marginal farms on the market that could have been forced to give up their activity with lower prices. Production is probably not reduced as much in this case as it would have been by simply cutting prices. This measure, therefore, is not completely neutral in terms of production quantity and cannot be considered completely decoupled.

There has been much discussion, and perhaps there will be more, about the extent to which the compensation mechanism activated by the MSR can be considered decoupled. But the fact is that it has been judged to be so by the GATT, which has implicitly adopted a weak definition of decoupling: the E.C. succeeded in having payments per hectare included in the so-called green box and there is no doubt that this "international compatibility" of the MSR is one of the explanations for its rapid adoption by the E.C.

Effects of Redistribution. In the matter of redistribution, the MSR presents at least two aspects that deserve reflection:

1. With the new system, a large percentage of support that was previously paid by consumers through higher prices now explicitly weighs on the Community budget. This represents an important change in the distribution of intervention costs, implying an increase in efficiency and welfare in terms of traditional economic theory, but somewhat questionable when viewed in terms of public choice. Obviously, transfer of the burden of support from consumers to taxpayers is typical of decoupling but is also one of the reasons why this option is considered difficult politically. It must, however, be said that the final consumers of grains and oilseeds are very "distant" from the first buyers of these products—the industrial processors. Hence, the latter are the principal beneficiaries of the reform in terms of reduced costs of their raw materials, and it is doubtful if lower prices at production

will, in any significant degree, be transmitted to lower prices at final consumption. Given the pressure that can be exerted by the processors, this result could be in line with the public choice approach.

2. For the redistribution of support between beneficiaries, that is between farms, the question of definitions of regions becomes crucial because average yields, hence compensation, are calculated with respect to them. Clearly, the larger the regions in question, or rather the higher the variability of yields within the single regions, the stronger will be the redistributive impact. Producers with yields below the regional reference average will be overcompensated and those with yields above will be undercompensated. It is clear that the desirability of such redistribution depends on the variability of yields between types of farms. Which farms have the lowest yields? The smallest? The poorest? The most disengaged? Which, among these, are more deserving of public support? Much remains to be discussed on this point, which involves how the aims and the whole domain of agricultural policy are understood and the answer probably varies according to the different local contexts.

Base Area. With the fixing of base areas that serve as ceilings for the number of hectares that have the right to full compensation, the quota system or rather the guarantee threshold is moved back from output to input. The base area—above which the amount of subsidy per hectare or per head of cattle is proportionally reduced in the current year and the percentage of compulsory set-aside is increased for the next year—can be administered in two ways: at the farm level or at the regional and/or national level.

The individual level would probably be more efficient and fairer since each farmer would be responsible only for his or her own conduct with no problem of collective action. But, besides the administrative complications, it would probably lead to greater rigidity, as far as factor mobility is concerned, thereby creating a new "fixed factor" for each farm ("the right to compensation") and the associated rent.

Another impact of base areas concerns the redistributive effects of reform and has to do with the freezing of support distribution, between regions and between farms, to levels existing during the reference period. This freeze could make sense from the point of view of operations and cost control, but no justification can be advanced in terms of distribution. In fact, it cannot be assumed that the distribution, between regions and between farms, of the support assured by price and market policies for the three year period 1989-1991 is the best possible or most in line with the CAP's objectives. Indeed, it might be safe to assume that the opposite is true since one of the policy's declared aims is to correct the "shower" of support for farms and regions generated by a policy such as intervention on prices, which is, by definition, indiscriminate.[5]

On this same point, another less than convincing aspect has to do with how payments per hectare are calculated. Since they are considered as simple compensation to farmers for the loss of income due to price reductions, their possible use as more selective instruments of support to the beneficiaries is renounced. The chosen mechanisms not only fail to exploit this opportunity, but we are also facing a substantial risk that the drawbacks of decoupling, such as greater management difficulties—as compared to price intervention, will be heavily felt. Moreover, if payment is calculated as pure compensation—by multiplying price reduction by average *past yields*—and if the use of base areas allocates the right to compensation on the basis of past production, then it is obvious that who benefited more before the reform will continue to benefit more after it. The imbalances that one should be correcting thus risk becoming frozen and even rendered legitimate by the base area system.

The Problem of Bureaucratization. One of the most doubtful characteristics of the MSR is that, with the compensation per hectare mechanism, it loads the CAP with a mass of additional bureaucratic complications. Substantial bureaucratic burdens are put both on farmers—in terms of filling out forms and producing certificates—and on the public administration—in terms of millions of dossiers and controls. In some cases all this is for the purpose of disbursing trifling funds that may not even cover their administrative costs. On this issue it is interesting to quote at length Agra-Europe (April 30, 1993):

> As farmers struggle to complete their Integrated Administration and Control Scheme (IACS) forms before the May 15 deadline, it is only natural that they should seek to blame somebody for the horrendously complex and bureaucratic task that lies ahead. The majority of farmers have only a rudimentary knowledge of cartography and mathematics, yet they know that they have to draw up an accurate map of their land and withdraw precisely 15 percent of their total area from production if the vital E.C. compensatory subsidies are not to be put in jeopardy. This time-consuming task is not a one-off job: it looks set to become an annual springtime chore for the new post-MacSharry CAP.[6]

The Reform Budget. The partial shift of the financial burden from consumers to taxpayers implies a notable increase in CAP expenditures. The increase in budget costs will likely be higher than the (optimistic) forecasts of the Commission and perhaps impossible to sustain over the long run. From this point of view, it is curious to see how insensitive the MSR is to the main traditional reason for a CAP reform, that is budgetary problems. Moreover, it is hard to believe that E.C. financing of the costly mechanisms of compensation per hectare—assured, for now, until 1997—could be maintained indefinitely. With reference to conjunctural gradualism, this seems one of the main contradictions of the E.C. reform package and perhaps the most important problem whose implications cannot be ignored.

The Driving Forces Behind the MacSharry Reform

One could ask how the MSR could have been completed and passed so rapidly and with such relative ease in contrast with other, less important, changes in the past. As indicated, the changes brought in the CAP during the 1980s remained limited and aimed to revise the instruments of policy but did not call into question its aims and basic structure. The timing and processes of revision were indeed typical of a defensive action, reflecting the general political will to preserve the hard core of the CAP, modifying it piece by piece, without radical alterations, every time that change appeared inevitable and/or conditions permitted it. We have called this approach conjunctural gradualism, but its ingredients very much resemble those indicated by Moyer and Josling (1990) as constituent parts of CAP reform, such as *incrementalism, satisficing approach, acceptability, policy inertia*. According to these authors, E.C. policy makers "choose the first *acceptable* option," rather than the most *efficient* one, "act only when they must and only to the extent necessary to 'cope' with the crisis" (Moyer and Josling, 1990, p. 205). Moreover, "to the extent that change is necessary, a strong tendency exists to adapt familiar options (standard operating procedures) easier to deal with than new ideas which have more uncertain consequences and are likely to prove more difficult to implement" (Moyer and Josling, 1990, p. 205). In this connection they, generalizing the experience of milk quotas in 1984 and of stabilizers in 1988, go so far as to indicate the principal conditions that must be present before a supranational reform such as the CAP (even if only of a "defensive" or "incremental" nature) can pass (Moyer and Josling, pp. 100-101):

1. climate of crisis and especially of budget crisis (a subject on which policymakers as well as beneficiaries of policy are most sensitive), in order to "use the crisis as a justification for making sacrifices";
2. failure of a top-level summit meeting regarding the problem that highlights "the seriousness of the problem and generates political pressure to achieve a solution";
3. strong capacity for political initiative on the part of the country that holds the presidency of the E.C. Council;
4. piece-by-piece construction of the final package with an *elimination-satisfaction* mechanism and with the changes entrusted to tested instruments so as not to upset too much the familiar options of policy

(both quotas and stabilizers—the main changes adopted in the past—
can be traced back to the guarantee threshold principle, already
present in the CAP);

5. absolute priority of internal interests and almost total indifference to
   the international effects of the decisions that are taken;
6. continuation of the tendency toward increased regulation rather
   than deregulation of the CAP.

The first big difference is that the MSR was not decided in the wake of
an emergency. During the first months of 1992, immediately preceding
the May accord, the trend of agricultural outlays was well below the
budget forecasts (*Agra Europe* No.1490, 1992; *European Agribusiness* No.
312, 1992); while the Commission itself predicted that the reform would
lead to greater expenditures. Furthermore, with regard to points 2 and 3,
even the political climate was not one of an emergency. There were no
summit failures over reform, and the final debate took place under the
(first) presidency of Portugal, which certainly could not be considered a
strong presidency and was nearing its end as the final agreement was
signed.

The reform package seems to have no relation to the past "incrementalism" and to the elimination-satisficing approach. It provides for drastic
change in the support mechanism and presents the strong new idea of the
decoupling principle. The only remaining "familiar option" is the base
area, which resembles a variant of the guarantee threshold principle
shifted from output to inputs.

In addition, the MSR does not neglect the international dimension of
problems as was too often done in the past. On the contrary, we believe
that pressure generated by the GATT negotiations was a determining
factor, at least as a catalyst, for CAP reform thereby hastening events that
led to the 1992 agreement. The Uruguay Round probably had a double
effect: a direct political effect that gave European agricultural policy
makers the incentive to hasten reform by internal negotiations without too
many explicit constraints, so that they could present themselves at the
Round's final phase with their house in order and their consciences clear.
This also precluded the risk of having to submit to international obligations exerted from the outside and *a posteriori*. More indirectly, the severe
agricultural dispute that emerged in the Uruguay Round (and characterized the talks) increased pressure from interests outside agriculture "to do
something" so that agriculture should cease to be the main obstacle to
completing a comprehensive accord in the GATT.

The only important analogy between the MSR and the preceding changes
in the 1980s is that, although it moves toward market orientation of prices,
it involves additional bureaucratic regulation with the resulting complications. We will return to this point.

If all the above is true, we must conclude that we are, in fact, at a historical turning point stemming from the overall crisis of the (coupled) model on which CAP was based. This means that the hard core of its policy began to be questioned at the start of the 1990s. In other words, if this had been the usual "defensive" reform in response to one of the many budget emergencies (the only really important constraint throughout the 1980s), probably a slightly more rigorous management of stabilizers would have been more than enough (Anania and Gatto, 1993). So we should ask ourselves what happened, what new interests and perceptions entered the scene and led to the turning point that contradicts the past history of a policy whose basic characteristic had been conjunctural gradualism.

In the first place, the traditional productivity goals of the CAP, as embodied in the Treaty of Rome, became indefensible and anachronistic in their view that food production must assure "security of supply" and that this is the main justification for support to farmers. Now it is assumed that today's modernized and strengthened agricultural sector can accomplish this satisfactorily at market prices. But new reasons for support are seen in agriculture's contribution to public goods, such as food quality, environmental protection, and sustainable evolution of the rural world.

Despite the fact that much has been said about this for some time, the options remain vague and confused, even though public opinion is certainly aware, at all levels, that these problems are important and unavoidable. Perhaps this became evident to the E.C. Commission before it did to the national agricultural delegations in Brussels—the latter, in fact, are more in line with the defensive action of the pressure group of the CAP beneficiaries. This could explain why the strategy of conjunctural gradualism of the 1980s was abandoned. Though that strategy was fairly successful, it was not reproposed because there was no longer the widespread conviction that the "old" CAP, with its version of coupled support, should be defended at all costs.

On another level, agriculture's and CAP's declining political influence probably played an important part. The disaffection also increased during the debate on the Single Market, where it became clear that the role of agriculture in the E.C. of the 2000s would cease to be salient. This, of course, has brought in new interests groups, undermining any attempt at defense or "regeneration" of the CAP in ways that would leave it substantially unaltered.

One could also explain the MSR in terms of the interests of big industrial and marketing organizations that might, perhaps, benefit from reduced agricultural prices. This is undoubtedly a legitimate hypothesis, supported by the intense lobbying that goes on and that has been conducted in recent years by groups such as Unilever, who support the need to dismantle agricultural protectionism (Friedberg, 1989, 1992). However, it should be pointed out that the groups in question—especially the multinationals—had, after initial difficulties, fully adapted themselves to the old CAP and took ample advantage of its support mechanisms. This is particularly true for export subsidies that, with the lowering of prices foreseen by the MSR, will be drastically reduced (Mastrostefano, Ch. 18; Scoppola, 1993a and 1993b).

As for the relatively docile attitude of the agricultural lobby in the debate that ended with the decision of May 1992, it seems to us that a short-term viewpoint prevailed among pressure groups more directly tied to agriculture. It is, in fact, very probable that in the short run and for the purpose of defending the level of income support, the MSR package could be more acceptable than a rigid application of stabilizers or any reduction of support imposed by the GATT. This seems largely confirmed by the results of several models that compared the two scenarios (Card Staff, 1991; Helmar *et al.*, 1992; Loyat, 1991; Josling and Tangermann, 1992; Roningen, 1992). Apparently, the idea that there was not much choice took hold because, even in the absence of reform, there would have been anyway a considerable reduction in the support farmers receive. A significant difference would be that the reduction would come without the compensations provided by the MSR package. In other words, it could be that decoupling and its long-term dangers of greater transparency and less defensible support were exchanged for the more certain advantages the reform offers for the immediate future.

Different Interpretations and Possible Implications of the CAP Reform Process

Some General Caveats

The analysis of the reform process developed in the previous sections has shown that the MSR is a turning point with reference to the conjunctural gradualism of the 1980s, as far as it could represent a transition toward the decoupling of the CAP. As is well-known, decoupling can be considered a two-step process: on the one hand, it reduces domestic prices towards the free market level; on the other hand, it implies the creation of income transfer programs not based on production levels.

As far as the first step is concerned, it is quite clear that decoupling implies a market orientation, provided that, as a consequence of the reduction of the gap between internal and international prices, domestic prices would better reflect world supply and demand conditions. The second step deserves greater attention, since a policy measure decoupled from output does not imply that such a measure could be considered costless in terms of economic efficiency. Indeed, as far as decoupling is concerned, different measures can be ranked in a continuous spectrum and "the precise degree of economic distortion generated by a particular measure in given circumstances is an empirical question that needs to be examined on a case-by-case basis" (Burrell, 1992, 10). More generally, it cannot be taken for granted that the closer we get to decoupling, the greater the potential gain in economic efficiency. In other terms it should be stressed that it is misleading to consider "decoupling" and "market orientation" as synonymous, as long as the two processes are not always and ever mutually consistent.

Several contributions (Alston and Hurd, 1990; de Gorter and Meilke, 1989; Gardner, 1983) have made the point that an accurate account of the deadweight loss resulting from redistributive policy intervention in agricultural markets requires discarding the assumption that a dollar of government spending involves a net social cost of one dollar. Such an assumption, based on a partial equilibrium approach or on the hypothesis that there are no tax distortion costs, leads to a bias in favor of policies that involve government spending compared to alternatives that do not. In this perspective, even if decoupling permits income transfers to be achieved with minimal consequences in commodity markets, complete decoupling of existing policies could be undesirable because it causes distortion elsewhere in the economy due to raising of government revenue (Lewis, Feenstra, and Ware, 1989).

Misgivings about "transfer efficiency"—that is, the proportion of an extra dollar raised from consumers or taxpayers that is actually received by agricultural producers—of decoupled policies are reinforced if we take administrative costs into account. The trend toward bureaucratization of the CAP and the fragmented farm structure of the Community suggest in fact that these kinds of "transaction costs" could play a crucial role in the implementation of the MSR.

Decoupling, Transaction Costs, and CAP Reform

It is worthwhile to devote some attention to the nature of the costs associated with the specific form that decoupling has taken within the reform of the CAP, and to the likely impact of the decoupled measures on efficiency and redistribution. While it is quite obvious that alternative policies are likely to differ in the resources required for their implementation, the analytical implications of this issue have so far been largely ignored in the literature. As was demonstrated by Monke (1983), in one of the very few attempts to incorporate policy-implementation costs into the policy-choice problem, not only do different implementation costs imply different optimal tax/subsidy rates, but also "Government policies, like privately produced outputs, are likely to be subject to considerations of comparative advantage in the sense that some countries will be able to implement a given policy more efficiently than other countries" (Monke, 1989, p. 291).

Concentrating our attention on implications of the main technical and institutional solutions through which decoupling has been introduced into the CAP, it seems plausible to put forward the following hypotheses:

1. Implementation costs of the "new" CAP will be affected sharply, registering—with respect to the previous regime—substantial change both in the nature and size of the overall transaction costs.
2. This modification could considerably affect the operational implementation of the new CAP, so that its *ex-post* results, in terms of efficiency and redistribution, may deviate a great deal from the *ex-ante* expectations of European bureaucrats and policy makers. Without indulging in excessive pessimism, we could argue that the dimension and direction of this deviation, and its cumulative effects, may be such as to compromise, *ceteris paribus*, stability and persistence of the new CAP.

To provide analytical support to these hypotheses, but without any pretense to construct a comprehensive model, it may be useful to compare, from the point of view of their implementation costs, a set of policy programs composed of three representative options:

- P_1, corresponding to the "original" CAP: a high level of protection for domestic production associated with a high level of price support and without any form of supply control for those sectors in which the European Community was less than self-sufficient;
- P_2, corresponding roughly to the CAP during the era of conjunctural gradualism: high protection, high price support combined with some measures of supply control both on output and inputs;
- P_3, corresponding to the "reformed" CAP, in which decoupling has been conceived and designed along the lines described previously.

According to the intentions of the policy makers, these programs have been and are implemented with the purpose of generating respectively a flow of benefits: B_1, B_2, B_3. An implicit but strong equity criterion dictates that the enjoyment of these benefits by the producers eligible to participate in the programs should occur in a context of nonrivalry and nonexcludability in other words, B_1, B_2, and B_3 should share the characteristics of pure public goods, obviously restricted to the producers potentially eligible. The central point of our reasoning rests on the assertion that the differences in the implementation costs of the three programs—IC_1, IC_2, IC_3, respectively—are such that the above equity criterion may end up being violated for P_3 and, consequently, B_3 may lose the connotation of a pure public good.

In very schematic terms, we can envisage the implementation costs of any program IC_j as made up of two components:

$$IC_j = AC_Z + TC_j , \qquad (1)$$

where AC_Z are the administrative costs (personnel and other general expenses) of the bureaucratic structure, Z, responsible for implementing the policy package (in our case either P_1, or P_2, or P_3). TC_j are transaction costs that must be endured in order to implement P_j in such a way that B_j retains the connotation of a pure public good.

As always, transaction costs make up a category of costs that are far from homogeneous. A substantial portion is taken up by information costs, since any agricultural policy program is usually administered in a context of incomplete and asymmetric information. An ample fraction of the transaction costs must be supported by public intervention. Basically they amount to the value of the resources needed in order to: (a) spread information about the program; (b) design the program implementation in such a way as to minimize the potential insurgence of adverse selection and moral hazard; (c) ascertain the correspondence of the characteristics of the potential participants with those specified by the program; (d) control the compliance of individual and collective behavior with the constraints imposed by the program; (e) allocate in an equitable way the benefits of the program among the participants.

Another, not negligible, fraction of transaction costs must be supported by the private operators who are potential participants in the policy program. An indicative measure of these costs is given by the opportunity cost of the time spent by each individual producer: (a) to collect information about the nature of the program; (b) to calculate the convenience of joining the program; (c) to comply with the *ex-ante* and *ex-post* bureaucratic requirements needed in order to participate and to obtain the benefits; (d) in case the program offers alternative options, to devise strategic behavior aimed at maximizing potential benefits. In the likely eventuality that specific features of the program open the possibility of moral hazard, transaction costs generated by the detected opportunistic behavior of producers may take the form of pecuniary fines, exclusion from future benefits, or some other sanction.

We can therefore say that the overall transaction costs of a program TC_j result from the aggregation of the public (TC_{Zj}) and the private (TC_{Fj}) components:

$$TC_j = TC_{Zj} + TC_{Fj} . \qquad (2)$$

Without going into too many details, it should be intuitively evident that transaction costs of the programs under analysis not only differ widely but it is also reasonable to expect a ranking of the following order: $TC_1 < TC_2 < TC_3$.

A couple of considerations should be sufficient to support the plausibility of the above ranking. First, in the case of the coupled programs P_1 and P_2 the public component of transaction costs is essentially dependent on only one variable: the size of the output. In the case of P_1, TC_1 is positively correlated with the volume of output, but it is likely to become economically and politically significant only from the moment in which surpluses begin to pile up: for the CAP, management and disposal of surpluses have indeed become the main causes of the growth of both administrative and transaction costs (frauds, speculative arbitrages, etc.). In the case of P_2, we must add the costs required to carry out the controls on the size of the output, costs obviously greater if the checks have to be executed at the farm level. We can therefore conclude that $TC_2 > TC_1$.

It is also reasonable to assume that, for P_1, the AC component of the implementation cost (which, through the years, both at Community and National levels, has been designed to handle this kind of program) has an adequate operational capacity to cope with the public component of transaction costs even though they are certainly not trifling in a context of growing surpluses. Sharply different is the case of P_2, where the management capacity of the bureaucratic machine has encountered much greater difficulties, mainly in certain Member States.[7]

Secondly, in the case of the "decoupled" CAP, because of the technical and institutional solutions adopted, the transaction costs are instead affected by a multiplicity of variables, of which three seem to be particularly important: the size of the factors put under control (amount of land and of cattle), specific characteristics of participants in the program, and the number of participants. We can therefore expect a substantial increase in transaction costs, both in the public and private domain, so that: (a) TC_{Z3} is certainly not negligible; and (b) TC_{F3} is going to affect behavior, performance and income of the participants.

Since in the short run AC_Z is equivalent to a fixed cost, it follows that the same ranking also applies to implementation costs of the three programs:

$$IC_1 < IC_2 < IC_3 . \tag{3}$$

Bearing in mind the two hypotheses formulated at the beginning of this section, the next step is to explore the likely implications of this drastic change in the nature and size of implementation costs. It is important to stress again that the one fundamental difference amonst IC_1, IC_2, and IC_3 lies in the fact that, while the implementation costs of the first two programs, being tied to support to production, could be subject to economies of scale, this is certainly not the case for IC_3, which is directly related to the number of participants.

We must then add two crucial and related variables to the picture that, in our opinion, will affect considerably the level of efficiency and of equity of the "decoupled" CAP and, eventually, its economic and political sustainability: regional distribution of potential participants to the programs and regional capacity of the public structure charged with the implementation of P_3. It seems appropriate to frame our discussion in terms of a comparison between North and South.

With regard to the first variable, the issue of the presence of an administrative bias associated with disparity in regional distribution of producers and of production has recently been discussed by Sarris (1992). Also adopting a North-South dichotomy, he has measured the degree of "administrative bias" by means of "an index that computes the ratio between the relative number of holdings producing a given product under reform in the South versus the North, and the ratio between the total production of the relevant product in the South and the North" (p. 37). Values of the index are reported in Table 5.1. Since a value greater than one suggests an implementation-cost bias against the South, values for the main regulated products speak for themselves.

The implications stemming from this bias gain strength and evidence when we combine it with the constraints associated with the second variable: the differential in the operational capacity of public administration in the North versus the South.

In the case of the North, we can, in all likelihood, continue to assume, as we did for P_1 and P_2, that the burden of implementation costs falling on public administration can be adequately handled by its present structure (whose cost is AC_N), so that: (a) TC_{N3} will be negligible; (b) P_3 will be

TABLE 5.1 Index of Administrative Cost Bias of the CAP Reform

	South	North	Ratio South/North
Number of Holdings Producing or Having:	(Thousands, 1987)		
Cereals	2884.4	1437.7	2.01
Bovine Animals	1193.3	1456.7	0.82
Production of:	(Thousand tons, 1989)		
Cereals	45528	148272	0.31
Beef	1806	5655	0.32
Administrative Bias Index			
Cereals	6.53		
Beef	2.57		

Source: Sarris, 1992.

implemented with the same level of efficiency and equity than P_1 and P_2; and (c) the benefits distributed by P_3 to the entitled producers will retain the characteristics of a pure public good.

In all likelihood, the situation in the South will be substantially different: here the administration of P_3 will be somewhat—even perhaps greatly—affected by a structural disequilibrium between the dimension of the implementation costs and the capacity of local bureaucracies.

The gap between the demand for participation in P_3 and supply of public services needed to ensure, on an equitable basis, participation to all eligible producers might have manifold repercussions. The first consequence might be the emergence of a degree of *congestion* in the management of P_3, so that the associated B_3 will lose the properties of a pure public good. Rivalry and excludability enter the scene, become fertile ground for rationing, inevitably open, at this point, to a variety of forms of discriminatory selection . Secondly, we must also take into account a substantial increase in the private component of transaction costs. Three main potential causes of this increase merit attention:

1. In a scenario of congestion *with* discrimination, the individual producer will have to make greater and substantial efforts—also monetary—to be included in the privileged group. This kind of scenario may even be attractive from the point of view of the farm organizations, if they feel that they could play a significant part in controlling the management of the selection process;
2. In a more equitable scenario of congestion *without* discrimination, an inevitable consequence of the inability of the bureaucratic structure to handle the public component of transaction costs efficiently will be a dilution through time of the distribution of B_3: in this eventuality the increase in private transaction costs will take the form of a reduction in the present value of the flow of benefits;
3. In both scenarios, the unfavorable comparison between the dimension of expected benefits and expected transaction costs may induce a certain number of producers—having been enrolled in P_1 and P_2—to abstain from participating in P_3. In these cases the choice of "exit" (Hirschman, 1970) may be imputable to a form of "government failure," since it is a cost imposed upon the private sector by a sluggish bureaucratic apparatus that ultimately defeats the objectives of the public action.

As a third consequence of the limited capacity of public administration, producers could perceive that the enforcement of the technical constraints associated with participation in P_3 will be sporadic and superficial. This might turn out to be a strong incentive for opportunistic behavior: implementation of P_3 in the South could then become plagued with moral hazard problems, thereby increasing substantially the transaction costs in the public sphere.

It is certainly not easy at this point to predict how strongly the problems associated with implementation of the decoupled CAP will affect its economic and political sustainability. On the basis of the previous analysis we can draw some tentative conclusions.

First, it is plausible to expect that the degree of efficiency and equity with which the reformed CAP will be implemented will not be homogeneous throughout the Community. If decoupling has the well recognized merit of greater transparency with respect to the previous regime, the regional differences in implementation costs will, however, take the form of an invisible tax imposed on the South.

Secondly, global deadweight losses associated with the new CAP will differ between North and South: in terms of the surplus transformation curve between taxpayers and producers, the South will operate on a curve lying below the Northern one. If the gap between the two curves turns out to be sizable, a further grievance will be added to the traditional complaint of differential treatment between continental and Mediterranean products: Political cohesion within the Community might suffer and, depending on the evolution of the budgetary variable, the forces pushing for a less centralized CAP might gain strength and become more vocal. We can speculate, also on the basis of previous experience, that it may turn out that the richer North, eventually tired of a sluggish and morally hazardous South, looking at the problem from its stronger financial position, will push in favor of a renationalized CAP.

A third element of regional differentiation will be the degree of implementation of the accompanying measures, aimed at pursuing the less traditional objectives of the CAP (environmental quality and structural adjustment). As has already happened in the 1970s with the structural directives, we can expect that in the South the probable high priority assigned by the public administration to implementing income compensatory measures will inevitably crowd out those actions whose benefits are of a more collective nature and can only be reaped in the future.

Are We Going Towards a Market Orientation of the CAP?

In trying to provide a general evaluation of the decoupling introduced in the CAP by the MSR, criticisms can be raised both in terms of equity and efficiency. As far as equity is concerned, it can be pointed out that the shift of the burden of the cost from consumers to taxpayers, embedded in the idea of decoupling, makes the system less regressive. Nevertheless the distribution of benefits linked to the specific form of decoupling introduced with the MSR shows two main shortcomings:

- While decoupling should allow a better targeting of the beneficiaries of public intervention in comparison with coupled policies, decoupled aid when used only to compensate for price reduction does not change the previous distribution (see above);
- Implementation costs of the new instruments will differ between North and South of the Community, increasing regional imbalances fostered by the CAP.

From an efficiency point of view, it is necessary to evaluate the different components of the deadweight loss implied by the new mechanisms, considering that, in addition to changes in consumer surplus (ΔCS), we also have:

- Changes in producer surplus (ΔPS) that have to be corrected for the marginal deadweight loss in terms of transaction costs sustained by the private sector (tc_f);
- changes in administrative costs (ΔAC) that have to be added to changes in public transfers (ΔTX);
- both changes in government expenditure (AC and TX) that have to be corrected for the marginal deadweight loss of raising government revenue (μ) and the marginal deadweight loss in terms of transaction costs sustained by the public sector (tc_z).

Therefore, changes in deadweight loss (ΔDW) resulting from the introduction of decoupled policies can be expressed as follows:

$$\Delta DW = (1-tc_f)\,\Delta PS + \Delta CS - (1+\mu+tc_z)\,(\Delta TX+\Delta AC)\,. \tag{4}$$

As already mentioned, the definition of decoupling implies an increase not only in consumer surplus and public transfers but also in administrative costs provided that

> more vigorous eligibility and compliance conditions may increase administrative and information costs, and give rise to a need for stricter enforcement. Moreover, because these measures are closely related to specific objectives, monitoring their success in terms of their objectives is both possible and desirable (Burrell, 1992 p. 8).

In this regard, the literature has shown that the normative ranking of coupled and decoupled policies in terms of transfer efficiency becomes an empirical matter depending on μ, elasticities of supply and demand, the size of the PS, and, for traded goods, the fraction of consumption and production traded (Alston and Hurd, 1990).

Our claim, with reference to MacSharry's version of decoupling, is that administrative and especially transaction costs will turn out to be substantial, unevenly distributed within the Community, and not justified in terms of a more equitable distribution between farmers. If this is plausible, the fact that several economists (and the United States within the Uruguay Round of the GATT) had accepted the MSR as "less distortive" seems to reflect quite a narrow definition of distortion, more concerned with the limitation of subsidized exports than with an overall increase of economic efficiency covering both the international and the national dimension.

Finally, it should be emphasized that a more cautious judgment of the type of decoupling introduced by the MSR does not imply a negative evaluation of decoupled policies as a whole. In this perspective two points deserve our attention:

- Transaction costs are not peculiar to decoupled policies. Any kind of resource transfer within the economic system implies some kind of "intermediation" cost and, even if bureaucracy shows a great deal of "x-inefficiency," transfers managed by private agents are certainly not costless;
- The past evolution of the CAP reform process shows that the alternative to a radical reform of the CAP in terms of decoupling would be, according to conjunctural gradualism, the creation of additional measures with the aim of reducing the negative effects of current programs and trying to rescue traditional policies from obsolescence. In this case, as has been argued before, implementation costs might turn out to be comparable to those of a decoupled scheme.

If this is true, we can conclude that decoupling in general is neither a sufficient nor a necessary condition for market orientation and MacSharry's recipe for decoupling, in particular, could even push European agriculture in the opposite direction. Nevertheless, the design of efficient decoupled schemes still provides an interesting prospect in terms of future scenarios for the CAP.

Beyond MacSharry: Some Tentative Conclusions on Potential Scenarios

At the moment of its formulation, the reactions to MacSharry's proposal have been basically positive on the part of all those convinced that CAP could no longer proceed along its traditional course of high protection and high price support, even though somewhat mitigated by a variety of supply control measures. The initial optimism was also shared by the present authors, who saw in the logic and in the crucial features of the reform not only the culminating outcome of a process driven by a host of domestic and international forces but, more significantly, the onset of a radical change in the very essence and conception of CAP. The initial proposal seemed indeed firmly grounded both on a substantial market orientation and on the adoption of decoupled measures potentially able to ensure greater selectivity in income support as well as the pursuit of socio-economic objectives largely ignored by the traditional CAP.

As the reader will have noticed, the original optimism still permeates the first two sections of the chapter, since it seems appropriate, when one places the reform in a long-term retrospective of CAP's vicissitudes, to emphasize its elements of novelty and its apparent drastic departure from the old approach. A more sober appraisal is however appropriate when one looks at the sequence of events following the initial proposal, from the edulcorated version of reform approved by the Council of Ministers in May 1992 to the technical and administrative solutions adopted for its implementation. The considerations advanced in previous sections of this chapter have stressed, among other perplexing features, the weak nature conferred to decoupling, the nonselectivity of the compensatory measures whose philosophy remains strongly production-oriented, and the potential difficulties and inequities stemming from the bureaucratic burden.

Whatever the overall evaluation of the reform's innovative thrust, one thing is certain: the present configuration of the CAP, far from being the final destination of the reforming process, retains all the characteristics of a transitory solution. The degree of uncertainty that surrounds the future is undoubtedly not trivial: there is indeed no guarantee that the point of no return in the direction of a market-oriented and decoupled CAP has been crossed and that we are therefore slowly but surely moving toward one exclusive scenario. The picture is much more complicated: as things stand now, there are at least three alternative and drastically different scenarios that could materialize with some likelihood.

At one extreme we can envisage a somewhat somber scenario leading toward an essential *dismantling* of CAP. Though not easy to imagine at this stage, it cannot be excluded that the completion of MacSharry's experiment could be followed by a drastic cut in size and scope of the Community's intervention in agriculture. The synergetic impact of old and new driving forces could indeed create favorable conditions for such an outcome.

A crucial factor will be the prevailing European political climate at the end of the century: we have previously stressed the relevance of the decline of the political weight of agriculture during the 1980s as a domestic force pushing for reform. The persistence and perhaps the growth of this kind of attitude could represent the premise for a dismantling process, possibly reinforced by a double failure of the present reform. The first failure, not difficult to predict, might concern the old controversial issue of financial compatibility when it will become evident that the amount of resources required by the prolongation of price reduction with full compensation will be unsustainable. The second failure could take the form of an unbalanced North-South implementation of the reform , especially if it is large and controversial enough to contribute to a split in political cohesion within the Community.

A blend of these factors could then push disaffection toward the CAP to such a point as to view it as an unreformable policy, whose centralized design and management is inevitably destined to produce more costs than benefits. In such a scenario, the possibility of an extension, in the medium term, of full compensation measures, as conceived and implemented today, are undoubtedly quite dim. At most, in a dismantling perspective, a limited—in time and payments—extension of the program might be envisaged to ensure a softer socioeconomic landing.

Much more difficult to forecast are the general implications of a dismantling scenario for the future of European agriculture. Again the overall political climate will be a determining factor, after maintaining some levels of border protection compatible with international agreements, in choosing between two alternatives: a strong push in favor of a competitive renationalization of agricultural policies or a strategy of pure deregulation. There is no need to stress how radical these two alternatives would be: the former implying a basic incoherence with a single market, the latter fully coherent with a neoliberal concept of the single market. The lessons of the past would suggest that, even in a dismantling framework, one should not be surprised if European policy makers would eventually try to find some (politically) "efficient" compromise between the two roads.

A scriptwriter would probably be tempted to label the second scenario as *Conjunctural Gradualism II: The Revenge.* There are indeed several clues that point to the fact that the forces that supported conjunctural gradualism as the best long term feasible strategy for CAP reform not only are far from defeated but have been rather vigilant and active during all phases of the definition of MSR. First of all, we cannot ignore the fact that the markets of several important products (milk, tobacco, wine, and sugar) continue to be regulated through strongly coupled policies. As for the products involved in the reform, it seems appropriate to interpret the dilution of selectivity (from the initial proposal to the definitive regulations) and the adoption of the base area as elements more coherent with the conjunctural gradualism criterion of choosing familiar options than with a genuine reformist attitude.

On such premises if, at the end of the implementation period, European policy makers face a situation not only financially awkward but also holding stocks that exceed GATT's constraints, we cannot exclude an official revival of coupled policies, probably enacted through a return of the traditional guarantee threshold approach, reswitching input constraints into controls on output. Viewed under this light, even MSR could then be interpreted as a tactical move of conjunctural gradualism, achieving—within the logic of a satisficing approach—the important twofold objectives of a substantial reduction in prices within a relatively short time span and attainment of a bargainable position for the Uruguay Round.

It should be evident at this point that both scenarios discussed so far share a basically pessimistic outlook on the performance of MSR in terms of its intended objectives and unintended consequences. The very sharp difference in their respective outcomes lies essentially in the divergent political assessment of the worthiness of continuing a Communitarian effort of supporting agricultural producers toward traditional objectives and by means of coupled instruments.[8]

Moving now to the opposite extreme, an optimistic outlook permeates the third scenario, which could be labeled as *fully decoupled CAP*.

Its essential premises are both a satisfactory achievement in the short run of the objectives of the MSR and a containment within acceptable limits of its unintended consequences (financial and administrative mainly). Within this framework the new driving forces laboring for a redefinition of CAP's objectives, attaching higher priorities to goals such as environmental quality and integrated rural development, might gain strength and political support.

Indulging this time in some needed optimism, we could then envisage a CAP:

1. Extending gradually but firmly a decoupled approach to other products;
2. Searching for decoupled transfers hopefully endowed with higher efficiency and greater selectivity;
3. Enlarging, financially and technically, the scope of the accompanying measures, conceived and managed outside a purely compensatory logic.

The high desirability of this kind of scenario, merely suggested here, is evenly matched by the difficulty of its implementation on political and technical grounds. Without going into any detail, it cannot be ignored that the first and, perhaps, main stumbling block is institutional: the prosecution of a strongly Eurocentric CAP appears highly incompatible with a fully decoupled policy conceived along the lines indicated above. The real challenge posed by a fully decoupled CAP is designing a policy that, though pursuing general objectives chosen at Community level, could be implemented, with a satisfactory level of efficiency and equity, in the conditions of decentralization and flexibility demanded by the extreme variability of local contexts.

Our profession, so active and vocal in denouncing the distortions and inefficiencies of traditional coupled policies, has so far been relatively hesitant in exploring, from a positive and a normative angle, the complicated territory of decoupled policies. The time is ripe to commit ourselves to this front: avoidance of the first two scenarios and materialization of the third one may also depend, perhaps marginally, on our contribution in laying the analytical foundations of a fully decoupled CAP; in identifying, and possibly limiting, its implementation difficulties; and in evaluating its global efficiency and equity.

Notes

This research was supported by the National Research Council of Italy, Special Project RAISA, Sub-project No. 1, Paper No. 881. We gratefully acknowledge the editorial assistance of Anne Rossi-Doria.

1. There is a vast literature on the subject, but the work of Petit and others (1987) and Moyer and Josling (1990) deserve special attention. The latter, in particular, defines the general approach underlying our interpretation of the CAP reform process in the 1980s. Such an interpretation is discussed at length in De Filippis and Zezza, 1993.

2. In a certain sense, it could be affirmed that stabilizers were, in themselves, a first step in the direction of market orientation, even if partial and imperfect, because a kind of "administrative simulation" of the laws of demand and supply was set up whereby if production increased, price or aid was reduced.

3. In the final vote in the Council, only Italy abstained, emphasizing its dissatisfaction that the problem of Italy's quota for milk production remained unsolved.

4. Examples of the first type include production of public goods such as research and extension, environmental payments to farmers, and poverty aid; examples of the second type are such measures as set-aside and early retirement provisions.

5. In the preparatory documents of the Commission, there is repeated emphasis on the need to remedy the situation of unacceptable imbalance whereby 20 percent of European farms provide 80 percent of total production and capture the same proportion of (coupled) support from price policy.

6. In the case of Italy the bureaucratic chore imposed on farmers is more than ludicrous: just to give an example, each farmer is expected to present every year a notarized certificate of not belonging to the Mafia, which must be issued not earlier than 20 days from the May 15 deadline! While this chapter was being written, a campaign against CAP reform "bureaucracy" was orchestrated by British and German agriculture ministers with the likely support of the other members of the Council. As Agra-Europe rightly points out, these ministers "are now engaged in a rather duplicitous attempt to divert the criticism of their farmers away from themselves and towards the convenient scapegoat of Brussels."

7. An appropriate example is offered by the vicissitudes of the milk quotas in Italy, still far from being implemented after almost ten years from their enact-

ment. Italy is now being called to pay a fine of 4,000 billions of lire (equivalent to more than two-thirds of yearly Italian milk production in value).

8. It would be no surprise, at this point, to find the Communitarian bureaucracy as a potent and aggressive actor operating for its own survival and, therefore, for the continuation of a "strong" CAP.

References

Alston, J. M., and B. H. Hurd. 1990. "Some Neglected Social Costs of Government Spending in Farm Programs." *American Journal of Agricultural Economics* 72: 149-56.

Anania, G., and E. Gatto. 1993. "C'era davvero bisogno di una riforma della Pac?" *La Questione Agraria* 49: 71-118.

Burrell, A. 1992. "The Role of Direct Income Support in Agricultural Policy Reform." Paper presented at 30th EAAE Seminar *Direct Payments*, Château D'Oex, Switzerland, November 11-13.

Card Staff. 1991. "An Analysis of the E.C. Commission Plan for CAP Reform." Paper presented at meeting *Mechanism to Improve Agricultural Trade Performance under the GATT*, Kiel RFG, October 28-29.

Commission of the European Communities. 1968. *Memorandum on the Reform of Agriculture in the European Economic Community*. COM(68)1000, Part A, Brussels.

———. 1980. *Reflections on the Common Agricultural Policy*. COM(80)800, Brussels.

———. 1981a. *Commission Report on the Mandate*. COM(81), Brussels, June 24.

———. 1981b. *Guidelines for European Agriculture*. COM(81)608, Brussels.

———. 1983. *Common Agricultural Policy—Proposals of the Commission*. COM(83)500, Brussels.

———. 1985a. *Perspectives for the Common Agricultural Policy*. COM(83)500, Brussels.

———. 1985b. *A Future for Community Agriculture*. COM(85)750, Brussels.

———. 1988. *The Future of Rural Society*. COM(88)501 def., July.

———. 1989. *Guide to the Reform of the Community Structural Funds*. Luxembourg.

———. 1991a. *The Development and Future of the Common Agricultural Policy. Reflections Paper of the Commission*. COM(91)100, February.

———. 1991b. *The Development and Future of the Common Agricultural Policy*. COM(91)258, Brussels.

———. 1991c. *The CAP Reform. Legal Texts*. COM(91)379, Brussels.

Cuffaro, N., and F. De Filippis. 1992. "A Comparative Market Share Analysis of E.C. and U.S. Agricultural Trade." Paper presented at 31st EAAE seminar *Agricultural Trade and Economic Integration in Europe and North America*, Frankfurt am Main, December 7-9.

De Benedictis, M., F. De Filippis, and L. Salvatici. 1991. "Between Scylla and Charybdis: Agricultural Economists' Navigation around Protectionism and Free Trade." *European Review of Agricultural Economics* 18: 311-37.

De Filippis, F., and L. Salvatici. 1991. "La proposta Mac Sharry di revisione della Pac: un'occasione per discutere." *La Questione Agraria* 42: 175-208.

De Filippis, F., and A. Zezza. 1993. *La Pac prima e dopo la riforma Mac Sharry*. Mimeo, INEA, Rome.

Friedberg, A. S. 1989. "Protectionist Rebalancing or Market-Oriented Reform?" *Food Policy* 14: 301-07.

————. 1992. *Once Bitten, Twice Shy*. Rotterdam: Unilever.

Gardner, B. 1983. "Efficiency Redistribution Through Commodity Markets." *American Journal of Agricultural Economics* 65: 225-34.

de Gorter, H., and K. D. Meilke. 1989. "Efficiency of Alternative Policies for the EC's Common Agricultural Policy." *American Journal of Agricultural Economics* 71: 592-603.

Helmar, M. D., D. L. Stephens, K. Eswaramoorthy, D. J. Hayes, and W. H. Meyers. 1992. "An Analysis of the reform of the CAP." Paper presented at 31st EAAE seminar *Agricultural Trade and Economic Integration in Europe and North America*, Frankfurt am Main, December 7-9, 1992.

Hirschman, A. 1970. *Exit, Voice and Loyalty: Responses to Decline in Firms, Organizations and States*. Cambridge Mass: Harvard Univ. Press.

Josling, T., and S. Tangermann. 1992. "MacSharry or Dunkel: Which Plan Reforms the CAP?" IATRC Working Paper No. 92-10, July.

Lewis, T. R., R. Feenstra, and R. Ware. 1989. "Eliminating Price Supports. A Political Economy Perspective." *Journal of Public Economics* 40: 159-85.

Loyat, J. 1991. "La reforme de la politique agricole communitaire: une evaluation par le modele Ecam." Paper presented at Société Française de 'Economie Rurale meeting, Montpellier, November 28-29.

Miner, W. M., and D. E. Hathaway, eds. 1988. *World Agricultural Trade: Building a Consensus*. Institute for Research on Public Policy/Institute for International Economics, Ottawa and Washington D.C.

Monke, E. 1983. "Tariffs, Implementation Costs, and Optimal Policy Choice." *Weltwirtschaftliches Archiv* 19: 281-96.

Moyer, H. W., and T. E. Josling. 1990. *Agricultural Policy Reform—Politics and Process in the E.C. and USA*. Ames: Iowa State Univ. Press.

Petit, M., et al. 1987. *Agricultural Policy Formation in the European Community: The Birth of Milk Quotas and CAP Reform*. Amsterdam: Elsevier.

Roningen, V. O. 1992. "Whiter European Community Agricultural Policy, Mac Sharried or Dunkeled in the GATT?" IATRC Working Paper No. 92-3, April.

Runge, C. F., and H. von Witzke. 1987. "Institutional Change in the Common Agricultural Policy of the European Community." *American Journal of Agricultural Economics* 69: 213-22.

Salvatici, L., and F. De Filippis. 1993. "E.C. Single Market and Public Intervention in Agriculture: Re-regulation or Deregulation?" Paper presented at the VII EAAE Congress *Transition to an Integrated Agriculture Economy*, Stresa, Italy, September 6-10.

Sarris, A. H. 1992. "Implications of Economic Integration for Agriculture, Agricultural Trade, and Trade Policy." Paper presented at the 31st EAAE Seminar *Agricultural Trade and Economic Integration in Europe and North America*, Frankfurt am Main, December 7-9.

Scoppola, M. 1993a. "Gli interessi delle multinazionali e la politica agricola comunitaria." *La Questione Agraria* 51. Forthcoming.

———. 1993b. "Multinationals and Agricultural Policy in the E.C. and U.S.A." Paper presented at the International Conference *New Dimensions in North American-European Agricultural Trade Relations*, Isola Capo Rizzuto, Italy, June 23.

Discussion

Richard R. Barichello

This chapter takes on an ambitious task, to identify the causes of CAP reforms in the 1980s, with particular attention to the MacSharry reform (MSR). This focus is undertaken to understand the forces that led to and shaped the MSR, allowing an improved ability to forecast future developments. But the opportunity is also taken to appraise the MSR in terms of its specifics. This is partly to assess the extent to which it really represents a decoupled policy, and partly to anticipate its likely success after implementation. On both counts the authors are rather pessimistic. They then identify three possibilities for future developments in CAP reform. Running through them are two common themes: the institutional constraints to decoupling the CAP, and the insufficient attention paid by our profession to designing policies with low administrative or implementation costs, particularly in the case of decoupled policies.

The CAP reform process in the 1970s was dominated by domestic issues, notably the inequity of unequal effects on farmers in different regions and countries. The financial costs of the system were also rising, raising questions of the distortion of intra-E.C. agricultural trade and the differing levels of financial costs and benefits by country. These tensions led by 1980 to the process of revisions to the CAP. During the 1980s, the two problems, increasing costs and the unequal distribution of benefits, continued to dominate CAP reform, but were complicated by the increased productivity and surpluses of the E.C. farm sector. As these surpluses were often exported, farm producers in other countries were affected by the consequent fall in world market prices. This provoked new international pressures on the CAP, in the direction of reducing its level of protection. In addition, the last decade has seen a decline in the political importance of agriculture in maintaining European unity, and environmental sustainability has emerged as a more important political objective than food security.

With these forces at work, CAP reforms have gradually occurred, but in a piecemeal fashion that can be described as a series of inconsistent and partial compromises to deal with the emergencies at hand. The authors describe this process as "conjunctural gradualism."

In 1991, the introduction of the MacSharry Reform (MSR) appears to represent a major change in the CAP, toward increased market orientation via lower price supports and decoupled payments. The primary issue that is addressed in this chapter is to what extent is this reform a radical departure from the existing CAP, or a modest adaptation of the CAP, in line with the gradual reforms of the 1980s. This issue is raised in order to anticipate more accurately the future course of CAP reforms and agricultural policy changes.

To answer this question, the authors review the MSR in some detail, looking at its design and the incentives it offers, its likely effects, and also realistically at its implementation. In general, the authors are quite critical of the MSR, at least in the context of needed CAP reforms. It only decouples weakly and incompletely, offering little encouragement to farm producers to reduce production or exit from the industry. The redistributive effects are significant, transferring costs to taxpayers rather than consumers, and over-compensating farmers with below-average yields (and conversely) due to the use of regional averages for compensation. Although the use of historical data for compensation targets helps decouple the support, it also reduces flexibility in making income transfers. Fourth, the MSR has associated with it a level of bureaucratic complexity that is unusually high. This issue of the administrative costs of a policy, in general and specific to MSR, is dealt with at considerable length in the chapter to offer the reminder that these costs should not be assumed away and are not equal across policy alternatives. Finally, the reform shifts at least part of the financial burden away from consumers to taxpayers. This is seen as an ironic twist, given that one of the main reasons for CAP reform is to reduce the budgetary or taxpayer cost of the program. In fact, the authors do not believe that the budgetary load of the MSR is sustainable.

However, even if the MSR is problematic in its economic efficiency and operational dimensions, it seems in many ways to differ from previous CAP reforms in the circumstances surrounding its introduction. It did not take place in the wake of an emergency, its elements are quite different from previous reforms, it does not ignore international implications, and the interest groups that might benefit from reduced prices do not seem to have played a more significant role. Although the authors argue that policy goals appear to have changed from food security to the environment, broadly defined, and possible agreements in the Uruguay Round appeared more threatening, still the adoption of the MSR comes as quite a break with the past.

The chapter concludes by emphasizing the uncertainty surrounding future paths for the CAP. The authors can foresee either movement to a decoupled and market oriented CAP or largely maintaining the existing CAP, with fairly minor changes. Much depends upon implementation issues that have been too long ignored.

Commentary

Even without a clear conclusion on the main issue of whether the MSR is radical reform or minor incrementalism, this chapter gives an interesting and thoughtful review of CAP reform in the 1980s. It draws out nicely the main issues influencing the past process of CAP reform, highlighting the political economy issues as well as some of the program detail. On this basis alone the chapter is to be recommended. In addition, this historical context provides a useful perspective from which to re-appraise the MacSharry reforms. Although some of the judgments on the MSR may be a little negative, the emphasis given to implementation and administrative details in reviewing decoupled policies in general and the MSR in particular is overdue and appropriate. One of the first lessons one learns upon moving from academic offices to the policy-making arena is the critical importance of such issues in designing and deciding upon policies. Local institutions such as those dealing with markets (and the environment) cannot be left out of the analysis of government policies, and the little details of these institutions or policy implementation do indeed matter. Even if economists are not the only ones to give insufficient attention to such detail, implementation costs have clearly been missing from our agenda.

Having said that administrative and implementation costs are important, I would argue that some of the arguments against MSR on these grounds may be exaggerated. For one example, the authors argue that many of the potential gains to consumers from the MSR will be absorbed by processors in increased rents, resulting in no significant fall in prices at final consumption. However, processors with little competition would already be exploiting their market power under current policies, and it is not clear that they would be able to increase their market power under MSR. It is even in the interests of a monopoly processor to share any raw material price fall with consumers. For another example, under the issue of using base areas as the basis for compensation, the authors argue that this will create a new fixed factor, and the base area (the "right to compensation") will attract the associated economic rent. This is true, but currently the rents will be captured more generally in land values or in the price of other inelastically supplied factors. It is not only under the MSR that rents will be capitalized into higher asset prices, creating a certain amount of rigidity in addition to the more obvious distributional implications.

It is also likely that some of the implementation costs noted in the chapter are one-time costs of designing the program, and they will diminish with time and learning. An example might be the individual accounts needed to undertake farm-by-farm compensation in a decoupled program. Undoubtedly there will be substantial initial costs in setting these up, but once in operation with the early problems solved, the set-up costs should fall significantly, even if there remain the costs of enforcing their provisions.

Finally, the authors point out a number of shortcomings in the compensation mechanism suggested in the MSR. These criticisms are valid for the particular details laid out, but they are not necessarily so problematic for decoupled policies generally. With the care and attention to program design and implementation that is counseled in the chapter, a number of compensation possibilities are possible in a decoupled policy, including some flexibility. However, the criticism that our profession for too long has waved its hand at some of these administrative problems (design and enforcement) in decoupled policies is well taken.

6

The CAP Reform and E.C.-U.S. Relations: The GATT as a Cap on the CAP

*Hervè Guyomard, Louis P. Mahé, Terry L. Roe,
and Secondo Tarditi*

Introduction

The last ten years have witnessed a substantial reevaluation of agricultural policies in developed countries. The launching of the Uruguay Round and the insistence that agricultural issues be dealt with, under the pressure of the United States (U.S.) and other net exporters of temperate zone products, has created an environment for debate and action. The European Community's (E.C.) Common Agricultural Policy (CAP) has been the main target of attack that has resulted in E.C.-U.S. conflict with hot and cool moments according to the stages of the GATT (General Agreement on Tariffs and Trade) negotiations and to the various negotiation tactics employed in the Urugay Round.

The present chapter focuses on the interpretation of the CAP reform in the context of the Uruguay Round and the E.C.-U.S. agricultural trade conflict. The questions addressed are first to explain why agriculture has, for the first time, been given such a central role and why the CAP reform has developed in the way we have witnessed, tackling firmly the cash crop programs and leaving nearly untouched the most protected dairy and sugar sectors. Our main point is that changes in comparative advantages and the existence of big trade interests in cash crops, organized by the main player, i.e., the United States, were the main forces to circumvent the otherwise dominant special interest forces in favor of the status quo. This explains convincingly the actual design of the CAP reform and even the changes brought to the Commission projects by the E.C. Council.

The second point is that the GATT framework provides to the competitive exporters a means to constrain the CAP in the future. But, because the GATT is based on general principles and should not be commodity specific, the accord has to be stated more generally and should accordingly force all countries to reform their own highly protected and less competitive subsectors. The GATT would therefore put a cap on the CAP and on other protectionist farm policies as well.

However, all countries try to minimize the political cost of adjustment, and reforms of the CAP and of other policies still leave a lot of room for payments to be too tied to production incentives, at the expense of environmental amenities. Will the GATT be able to tame and reorient farm policies in socially desirable directions?

The next section briefly reviews the historical E.C.-U.S. trade debate. The following section deals with the E.C.-U.S. special interests and trade conflicts. Our next section analyzes the CAP reform implications on E.C.-U.S. relations and relates it to the expected GATT treaty. The final section addresses more long-run issues, stressing the shortcomings of the CAP reform and future prospects for the GATT as a framework to discipline domestic and trade farm policies, including their environmental dimensions.

The E.C.-U.S. Agricultural Conflict

The history and the role of agriculture in the GATT shows that the successive rounds of negotiations were dominated by E.C.-U.S. disputes. Several issues in the E.C.-U.S. agricultural trade conflict emerged soon after the creation of the Common Market and the implementation of the CAP. This conflict reached a new stage with the economic growth of E.C. agriculture, and it became the focus of negotiations in the Uruguay Round.

The trade balance in agricultural products between the E.C. and the United States has traditionally been in favor of the United States. U.S. exports to the E.C. reached about 10 billion U.S. dollars at the end of the seventies but fell to nearly 6 billion in 1985. It has slowly recovered over the rest of the decade (Figure 6.1).

The composition of bilateral trade flows in agricultural products is however quite different (Figure 6.2). The U.S. exports to the E.C. essentially basic commodities (grains, oilseeds products, and corn by-products) that are heavily regulated in both the E.C. and the United States with a generally higher level of protection granted in the E.C., except for corn by-products. E.C. exports to the United States include more processed food products with a high value added per ton. For the most part, they are non-CAP commodities, such as wine and beer. Meat and dairy products are also exported. The latter are supported in the E.C., but they are also subject to strict trade barriers in the United States.

FIGURE 6.1 Bilateral E.C.-U.S. Trade: Agricultural Products.

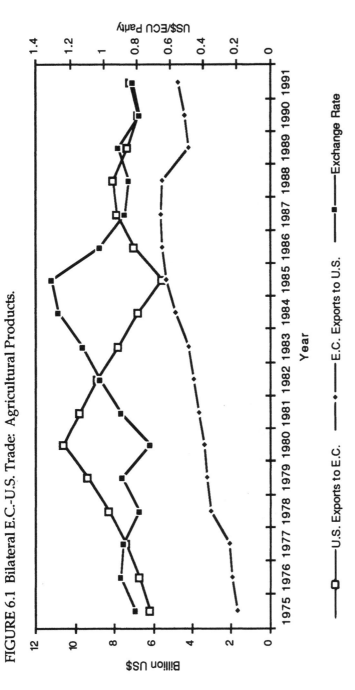

Sources: USDA ERS, various years and Commission of the European Communities, various years.

FIGURE 6.2 Structure of Bilateral Agricultural Trade (1990-91).

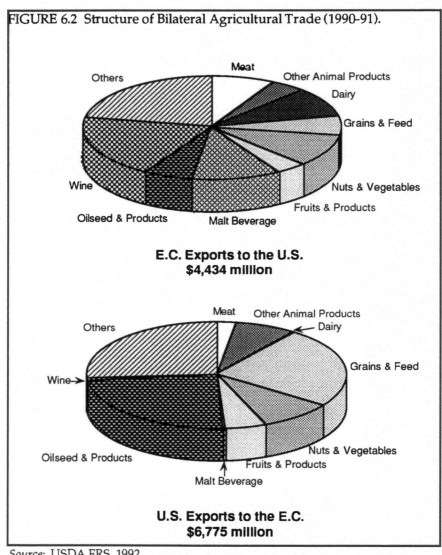

Source: USDA ERS, 1992.

The sources of the trade tensions between the E.C. and the United States originated in both the bilateral trade interests and in the competition for outlets in third countries. The latter source has gained momentum with the increasingly net exporting position of the E.C.

The major concern of the United States has always been to alleviate or reverse the consequences of the CAP on trade in cereals and related feed stuffs. The United States was in favor of European integration but has never really accepted the creation of the customs union and the subsequent principles of the CAP. The issue at stake is the high protection in the E.C. for grains that first reduced potential U.S. outlets for these products in the E.C. and made it necessary for the E.C. to protect other sectors too. Moreover, the use of the variable levy-restitution system, compared to a "gate on a dam" by U.S. Secretary Freeman, was constantly criticized by the United States and other exporters as being in contradiction with GATT principles. In the Kennedy Round, the United States wanted to modify the variable levy system, and in the Tokyo Round it wanted levies considered as nontariff measures and treated accordingly. The United States did not get preferential access to the E.C. for grains in negotiations following the first enlargement of the E.C. but did so in 1986 after the accession of Spain and Portugal.

Tensions increased when the E.C. turned to a net exporting position in grains in the early eighties. Variable restitutions, the major E.C.-protecting device, have been under constant pressure from the United States (the share of restitutions in E.C. agricultural expenditures has increased from 20 percent in 1975 to 35 percent in 1990). This new situation has launched a creeping trade war on the world grain market, with the United States developing a permanent program of export subsidies. In the Tokyo Round, the code for subsidies attempted to reinforce Article XVI with the "concept of an equitable share of world export," but the implementation of this vague limit did not prevent a rapid growth of E.C. grain exports. The United States has become increasingly frustrated by these developments, which explains its insistence on a separate negotiation on export subsidies in the Uruguay Round.

Two other major trade concerns of the United States, namely oilseeds and corn by-products, are indirectly determined by the E.C. grain policy. The E.C. conceded a bound zero tariff on oilseed products in the XXIV-6 Negotiation, on corn germ meal in 1962, and on corn gluten feed in the Kennedy Round in 1967. These concessions have proved over time to make it increasingly difficult for the E.C. to pursue its high grain price policy. First, the E.C. wanted to increase its capacity to produce oilseeds in order to reduce dependence on imports, a policy triggered by the U.S. soybean embargo and the peak world prices of 1972-74. Oilseed production in the E.C. has been stimulated by a price support and by a crushing subsidy mechanism (which works broadly as deficiency payments). This mechanism has proved to be very costly as production increased sharply. Increased production was further enhanced by the slowly diminishing support given to grains as a reaction to excess supply. As a result, the cost of the oilseed program has risen to 3.4 billion ECU in 1990.

Meanwhile, imports of by-products used in compound feeds have soared due to the price differential with domestic grains. This increased demand has created an attractive outlet for U.S. corn by-products that accounted for more than 1 billion U.S. dollars of imports in 1990. Because of the trade interests in soybean and corn gluten feed, the United States has resisted vigorously attempts by the E.C. to "rebalance" its external protection either by placing a tax on vegetable fats or by voluntary export restraint on grain substitutes. In the early eighties, the strong dollar and the emerging competition from Brazil and Argentina caused a general reduction in U.S. exports to the E.C. (Figure 6.1), particularly in U.S. trade shares of E.C. soybean imports (Figures 6.3 and 6.4). Pushed by the American Soybean Association, the United States filed a GATT complaint in 1988 alleging that the E.C. discriminated against the import of U.S. soybeans. The appointed panel concluded in 1989 that this was indeed the case. The Commission of the European Communities (CEC) accepted the conclusions, with some reservations, and implemented a subsidy per hectare of oilseeds produced.

These trade interests and the U.S. competitive advantage in crops explain its emphasis on reducing border protection first. The trap in which the E.C. has put itself is due to its long-standing grain policy and its direct (restitutions) and indirect (feed imports) consequences. This situation has recently given the United States a formidable leverage to press the E.C.

FIGURE 6.3 E.C.-12 Soybean Imports by Source.

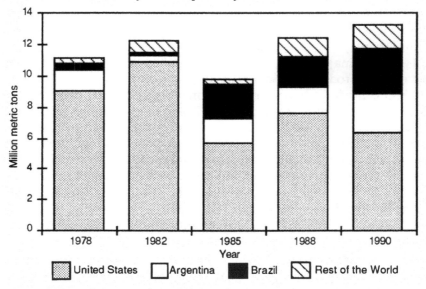

Source: USDA ERS, 1993; ISTA, various years.

FIGURE 6.4 E.C.-12 Soybean Meal Imports by Source.

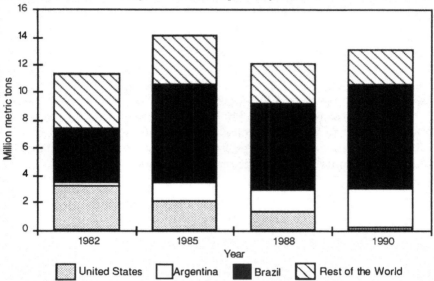

Source: USDA ERS, 1993; ISTA, various years.

towards reforming the CAP. The various recent skirmishes on other trade disputes (definition of corn gluten feed, delisting of U.S. beef and pork packing plants, the procymidone case, the E.C. sugar complaint...) can be considered as minor avatars to the central conflict. In contrast, the E.C.'s attitude in relation to the United States is not so much dictated by trade interests as it is by a continuous attempt to cope with the adverse consequences of earlier decisions in the framework of the CAP. The E.C. exports to the United States are mainly non-CAP products (Figure 6.2) that sell competitively and are designated targets for occasional retaliation. As a consequence, the behavior of the E.C. has been mainly passive or reactive to U.S. pressures. From the beginning, the E.C. considered the CAP as nonnegotiable, variable levies and restitutions being viewed as logical consequences of domestic policies emanating from domestic pressures. In the early stages of the Round, the E.C. constantly refused to negotiate separately on border measures.

Another distinctive feature in the E.C. approach to trade policy has been its desire to "organize world markets" through International Commodity Agreements (ICAs). These ICAs have not really worked and the United States has always been reluctant to manage world trade or to indulge in implicit cartellization of agricultural trade.

The so-called harmonization of border protection in the E.C. is another example where trade policy changes are dictated by the E.C. feeling the need to tackle the consequences of domestic policies. The cost of the grain and oilseed regimes has led to a recurrent debate in the E.C. about fat taxation, which evolved into the concept of harmonization of border protection (CEC, 1989) whereby domestic support would be reduced as a concession for import taxation of animal feeds. Hence, the inclusion of rebalancing in all of the E.C. GATT proposals, a demand that the United States was never willing to consider as a possible concession in the Round.

In sum, the recent reform of the CAP reflects the typical lagged response of the E.C. to the adverse effects of pressures created by past policies, except the extent of this reform seems to be in excess of that which would come about from domestic pressures alone.

The E.C.-U.S. Agricultural Trade Game and the Design of the CAP Reform

Sources of Domestic Pressures for a Reform of the CAP

In its introduction to the July 1991 "Communication to the Council" (CEC, COM(91) 258 final), the E.C. Commission repeats the conclusions of its previous reflections (CEC, COM(91) 100 final) on the current state of the CAP and on the need for fundamental changes. Quoted arguments include: (1) price guarantees lead to growing output; (2) extra output can be accommodated only by adding to stocks or by exports to already oversupplied world markets; (3) built-in incentives for high-input intensity places the environment at risk; and (4) rising budgetary expenditures, devoted in large part to a small minority of farms, provides no solution to the problems of farm incomes in general.

These reasons for CAP reform are well known. They reflect the outcome of policies that cannot be adjusted for various political reasons in the familiar agricultural context of rapid technical change—partly induced by the support—and of sluggish demand due to the staple nature of the products of the industry. The inefficiencies and market imbalances that result are also known, as well as the regressive distributional effects of the considerable and steadily rising budget expenditures. It is more difficult and conjectural to point out the actual causes for the recent reform, which, although not comprehensive, is the most drastic since the inception of the CAP.

Given the magnitude of the protests triggered by Commission pronouncements on reform and of the subsequent watering down of the reform by the Council, one can only be surprised that a significant reform still took place in a manner so central to the E.C. agriculture, and in such a market-oriented manner. One can also be surprised at the large price cut decided for grains and oilseeds while, in a similar domestic context, the course of action adopted in the dairy sector in 1984 was the other extreme, i.e., production quotas. Actually, the latter solution was highly supported by large producer groups and even by countries. So, in the current reform program, what prevented this idea from being applied to the crop sector?

It is our belief that domestic forces were unable to generate the current extent of reform even though it was eventually circumscribed to the main cash crops, to a lesser extent to beef, and accompanied by sizable compensation payments, which have become increasingly tied to the endowments of the farmers. The final package of CAP reform appears to be more the result of external pressures.[1] This view is supported by the observation that the dairy and sugar sectors, where trade conflicts do not concern trade interests of the big players, only experienced a cap on current policies. This view is also supported by the land set-aside program in the reformed CAP, which is mainly for purposes of reducing excess supply, and thus exports with little attention to environmental concerns.

E.C., United States, and the International Game

Our focus here is on how international pressure influenced the nature of CAP reform. Our general theme is that the legitimacy of the GATT rests on its principles, and that the broad based rejection of these principles for agriculture would continue to perpetuate shocks to international markets of magnitudes greater than the collective interests of either the United States or the E.C. were willing to accept. The role of special interests within each country, and the extent of interdependencies among exporting and importing countries, influenced the actual direction and magnitude of the CAP reform and the GATT compromise.

The Nature of Special Interests in Agriculture. The plethora of papers on the formation of special interests and their motivation to seek, through economic policy, income transfers that are not easily undone has clearly sharpened our understanding of their influence in forestalling and directing policy reform in agriculture. To suggest how international pressures influenced the nature and extent of CAP reform, it is useful to mention briefly several factors that strengthen the capacity of narrow-based interest groups to influence agricultural policy to a degree greater than would otherwise be suggested by their representation in the polity.[2] We group these factors into two broad categories: institutional and economic.

Institutional structures that are part of the policy making-policy implementation process cause an inertia to reform. Agriculture in many of the industrialized market economies tends to typify the extensiveness of these structures relative to the other traded goods sectors of their economies, and particularly so for the CAP. They tend to make reform more difficult because of the various channels of political connections, legislative committees, legal statutes, and other organizations at the regional and local levels that support, implement, and provide communication mechanisms to agriculture. Policy reform that entails a dismantling of this structure, particularly after it has been in place for an extended period of time, is often questioned on the grounds that it will expose the sector to the vagaries of the market without mechanisms in place to help farmers insure against future contingencies. This structure too has a vested interest in sustaining the status quo, while at the same time it has strong control over the public decisionmaking process. Consequently, it and its vested interests tend to dampen internal motivation for reform while, at the same time, increasing the difficulty for those outside the structure to induce reform.[3]

Several economic factors also provide agricultural interests with political influence beyond their relative number in the population. First, the cost of policy that supports incomes in agriculture tends to be dispersed over the entire economy while the benefits are concentrated on a few. As Olson (1965) has suggested, because farmers are small in number relative to a country's population, they have two major advantages. Their small number decreases their individual costs of arranging a group consensus to seek legislation in their favor and their specialization in one or two major activities allows them to earn per capita benefits from support that far exceed the per capita costs incurred by consumers and taxpayers. Hence, since food accounts for a small proportion of total household expenditures, producer groups tend to be more motivated to expend resources to achieve their narrower political interests than are consumers and taxpayers in general willing to countervail these forces.

Second, due to the uncertain and cyclical nature of agricultural markets caused by climatic, macroeconomic, and world trade shocks, agricultural support is often introduced in the presence of upturns in the macroeconomic business cycle. But, agricultural support tends to be only marginally withdrawn during downturns in the cycle and is generally increased during periods of macroeconomic uncertainty (Paarlberg, 1989). Part of the reason is that agricultural production is characterized by sector-specific resources such as land, buildings, and equipment that cannot be easily reallocated to other sectors during cyclical downturns in the agricultural economy. Consequently, the value of these resources can fall precipitously during decreasing cycles or lag behind the upturns in the macroeconomic economy, all of which places the welfare of rural households, financial institutions supplying credit to the sector, and variable input suppliers at some risk relative to the overall economy. This risk invariably induces support for agriculture (Orden, 1990). Part of the reason that support is only partially withdrawn appears to lie in the fact that, just as cyclical downturns affect the value of these resources, so too do the very economic policies designed to avert these effects on their value. That is, the value of agriculture's sector-specific assets embody the implicit value bestowed upon them by the instruments themselves.[4] Hence, when economic conditions improve, policies tend to remain in place. Producers are aware of the linkage between the value of sector-specific resources and economic support. They are aware of the potential decline in value if support is withdrawn, and therefore they have an incentive to engage in political actions to avert this eventuality. Hence, policies designed to offset the effects of uncertainty and cycles in the economy tend to turn into permanent support.

A third closely related incentive to maintain support after a cyclical downturn is that the increased value of the sector specific resources that support causes also provides incentives for capital deepening in land improvements, buildings, equipment, and so on. Since this capital deepening is induced by support, the returns to this new capital is dependent on maintaining support. Together, these two effects provide incentives for the racheting up of economic support for agriculture.

Fourth, agriculture is often associated with environmental amenities, rural development, and natural resources. It appears that the economic support to the producers of agricultural commodities is easily confused with the support for rural development, the country life in general, and the environment in particular, the more so as these amenities are public goods without a collectively organized constituency to promote their supply at the socially desirable level.

And, fifth, food is closely associated with security (an alleged reason for Japan's support of its rice producers) and health, particularly in the form of food safety. Food safety can easily serve as a justification for nontariff barriers and extensive regulation.

The culmination of these various factors tends to provide some sectors in agriculture with more political power to influence policy in their favor than others. Johnson *et al.* (1993) obtained empirical estimates of these relative influences for the United States and the E.C. based on data from 1986, while another study reaffirmed these approximate magnitudes using data from 1990. Sugar and dairy interests in both the United States and the E.C. exhibited the most influence, followed by producers of animal feeds and grains. Taxpayers (as reflected by the budget costs of agricultural programs) and consumers had the least influence. The influence of beef and pork and poultry producers tended to rank higher in the E.C. than in the United States. Hence, from an interest-group perspective alone, it is not surprising that (1) reform is likely to be more difficult to obtain in the sugar and dairy sectors of either the E.C. or the United States relative to the grain sector, and (2) if reform is to be obtained, some form of compensatory payments will surely be required. It is also apparent that acceptance of the GATT principles for agriculture, even if reform is modest, will be an important disciplinary cap to the influence of these interest groups.

The Nature of Interdependencies Between the Agricultural Economies of the Major Players. The interdependent effects of E.C.-U.S. agricultural policies are fairly well known. Effectively, the various studies are in general agreement that the effects of policy reform are greater than the indirect effects of reform in the E.C. (United States) on the agricultural economy of the United States (E.C.). For example, the results of Johnson *et al.* (1993) suggest that, if the U.S. reforms while the E.C. follows the status quo, the world prices of wheat and coarse grains, milk and milk by-products, and sugar will rise while the prices of animal feed concentrates (oil cakes and vegetable proteins), pork, and poultry will tend to fall. If the E.C. reforms while the United States follows the status quo, the world prices of wheat and coarse grains, milk and milk by-products, and sugar will also tend to rise, as will the prices of beef. The prices of animal feed concentrates, and pork and poultry will tend to fall. However, changes in domestic prices and quantities produced always tend to be greater from one's own reform than from indirect effects of reform in the other country. As a consequence, federal budget savings, the decline in producer quasi-rents, the increase in consumer surplus, and the net social gains in either the United States or the E.C. are always greater for own-policy reform than from the indirect effects of E.C. (United States) reform on the United States (E.C.). Since grains are the major traded commodities for the United States and for many members of the Cairns Group of countries, the greatest interdependence lies in the grain sector, which in turn impacts on animal feeds, beef, and pork and poultry. To exporters, this interdependence in grains has of course been the major cause for frustration with the CAP's variable levies, export subsidies, and other policies that distorted the E.C. grain sector. In turn, the E.C.'s commitment in the Dillon Round to bound tariffs on soy beans and meals at zero caused a large divergence in the relative feed grain-protein concentrate price ratios faced in the Community relative to the United States, and hence a disadvantageous cost structure for its livestock sector.

In another study, Mahé and Roe (1993) evaluated the importance of reforms in other industrialized agricultural importers on the willingness for the United States and the E.C. to compromise. The results suggested that concessions by these other countries had the effect of increasing their import demand and raising world market prices. In the context of a Nash game where budget savings are used to compensate the losers from reform, these effects in turn increased the domain of policy choice over which the United States and the E.C. could find agreement that made neither country worse off than the status quo. The domain was enlarged because the increase in demand for U.S. and E.C. exports caused smaller losses to U.S. and E.C. producers in the export-competing sectors for an increased range of U.S. and E.C. concessions. Moreover, the smaller losses allowed the budget savings from reform to compensate the losers more adequately. While free trade was not obtained, freer trade appeared to be a real possibility. Thus, the extent of reform in the Round, and reform of the CAP, may be strongly influenced by the willingness of the other countries mentioned to make concessions; and it is in the mutual interests of the United States and the E.C. to encourage this outcome.

Collective action at the international level also helps to explain why and how the various and often contradictory forces, channeled into the agricultural trade game of the Uruguay Round, contribute to delineating the contour of the final agreement and the nature of the reform of the CAP. Whether the incentives for reform are sufficient to trigger action at the national level depends in part on the prospects that a country can internalize the gains from reform. The Most Favored Nation principle that the benefit of a concession made by any country must be extended to all other contracting parties is akin to a concession being a public good. When a large number of countries are involved, and/or when they have approximately equal world market shares of the traded good, the incentive is reduced for an individual country to make a concession in return for a concession from another since the benefits of such concessions must be shared by all, i.e., the free-rider problem. This may be a partial explanation for the failure of the group of small and numerous countries that are low-cost producers of sugar to obtain reform of U.S. and E.C. sugar policies.

The proliferation of Free Trade Areas, bilateral trade agreements (e.g., NAFTA) and trade blocs may be seen as attempts to circumvent this external problem, as well as to circumvent the pressures of domestic interest groups (Paarlberg, 1987, p. 44). The existence of big players in the international game helps to safeguard the principle of multilateral trade agreements on which the GATT is based. Large players have incentives to negotiate concessions (i.e., to incur costs) because, even though they will need to share the "reformed market" with others, their relative size allows them to capture sizable benefits and to express credible threats that can force other reluctant players to move as well. It appears that the United States and other large agricultural exporters have such an incentive, particularly in the form of terms of trade gains in the grain sector. Hence their active role as a catalyst for collective action in the game of negotiations. A positive externality in this case is the extension of the pressure on others to reform this sector too, such as Japan, Korea, and the Nordic countries.

Summary. The major conclusion is that domestic and international forces appear sufficiently strong to explain why reform under the GATT and the CAP is to occur primarily in the grain sector and to some extent in the livestock sector through the feed grain-concentrate linkage. While there is more to the story, note that the domestic forces for reform of the CAP discussed above, the mentioned political influence in the grains being small relative to sugar and dairy, the major interdependencies between U.S. and E.C. policies occurring in grains, and lower incentives for countries to free-ride in making mutual concessions, together point to trade reform in the grain sector.

The GATT process has therefore been supported by countries with vested interests in the widely traded commodities (namely grains). While the E.C. was motivated to undertake reform, the approach is notable because the instruments chosen permit market forces to operate more effectively, which is in sharp contrast to the choice of production quotas for dairy in the 1984 reform of the CAP. The large cut in E.C. market prices in grains and oilseeds would have been unlikely if the domestic forces alone were the major motivating force for change. Discrepancies between the initial Commission proposals and the decisions of the Council support this view. The Council has constantly watered down the reform effort—and is still doing it—so as to attenuate price adjustments and to increase the level of compensation. Furthermore, the progressive drop of the measures to reform dairy and sugar envisaged by the Commission, and the relatively smaller shift toward direct payments in the beef sector, reflect, in our view, the lack of foreign pressure from big countries having trade interests in these areas. New Zealand's interests in dairy products and developing countries interests in sugar cane have not been able to develop a coalition in support of their interests as have the grain and oilseeds exporting countries. In sum, the changes in economic conditions and the resulting imbalances and inefficiencies in European agricultural policy developed sufficient pressure to induce reform of the CAP. But these pressures were not sufficient to counter those seeking to maintain or increase protection so as to produce a reform of the magnitude and of the market-oriented type we have witnessed.

E.C.-U.S. Agricultural Relations and the GATT Round: A Cap on the CAP

Within Commission circles, the CAP reform was officially presented as a separate process from the GATT negotiations. We have argued that the features eventually included in the reform package reveal a major effort to soothe anticipated international pressures on specific trade issues. This is illustrated by the sizable positive effects of the CAP reform on U.S. agricultural policy objectives. Our analysis (Table 6.1) suggests that the

TABLE 6.1 Main Effects of E.C. Reform Scenarios on the United States in 1999 (billion 1993 ECU)

	1993	1996				1999			
		Base-Run	Decoup.			Base-Run		Decoup.	
			Reform	Reform	Dunkel		Reform	Reform	Dunkel
Farm Income	77.5	76.0	76.0	75.7	76.0	74.8	74.1	73.7	74.9
Budget Costs									
Grains	7.1	6.1	4.9	4.4	5.4	5.0	3.5	3.1	4.0
Dairy	0.7	0.8	0.8	0.7	0.8	0.8	0.8	0.8	0.8
Trade Balance									
Grains	7.1	6.4	7.1	7.4	6.8	5.6	6.5	6.7	6.1
Oilseeds	4.2	4.3	4.1	4.5	4.1	4.4	4.7	4.8	4.4
CGF	0.7	0.7	0.6	0.6	0.6	0.8	0.6	0.6	0.6

strict implementation of the Dunkel compromise in the E.C. would not have provided larger benefits to the United States than those from the CAP reform. In this light, the continuing conflict to conclude the Round can be seen as an effort by the grain exporters to bring the CAP under the discipline of the GATT as a guarantee that future CAP developments be constrained more than in the past and as an assurance that the CAP reform would be more effective, i.e., a cap on the CAP. Moreover, as mentioned in the previous section, applying the discipline of the GATT to agriculture on a multilateral basis would also serve to countervail those interests in sectors of agriculture, such as sugar and dairy in the United States and to reform these sectors as well.

CAP Reforms, World Prices and Implications for Future E.C.-U.S. Trade Conflicts

The implications of the CAP reforms on the United States arise from at least three sources : (1) changes in U.S. exports to the E.C., (2) expected U.S. gains in export volume to the rest of the world as a result of reduced E.C. competition, and (3) some terms of trade gains on grain exports. The analyses of these linkages are based on MISS (Modèle International Simplifié de Simulation) (Guyomard and Mahé, 1993). MISS is a price equilibrium model that focuses in detail on the structure of U.S. and E.C. agriculture and agricultural policy and is extended to include a simplified "rest of the economy" supplying inputs to the farm sector at near infinitely elastic supply so that prices of inputs supplied by the nonfarm sector are led by the inflation rate. Technological change, growth trends in population and in per capita incomes, and other variables exogenous to the agricultural sector are factored into the analysis.

World Prices. The base-run scenario corresponds to a "continuation of the prereform" CAP. The results suggest that nearly all prices decline moderately in real terms. Prices of grains, of oilseeds, and particularly of grain substitutes decrease the most. The only significant exception is beef, which exhibits price increases in nominal and real terms due to a lower rate of technical change and a higher income elasticity than other food products. These results depend on the assumptions made regarding the evolution of the mentioned exogenous variables. They also depend on the changes in E.C. price support policies in the base-run. There is room for debate here, and alternative assumptions could be made on exogenous variables depending on world economic growth in the next decade with different results for the trends in world prices.

The main effect of the CAP reform is to reduce grain exports by stimulating domestic demand for feed and by controlling production growth. World grain prices are 5.3 percent higher in 1996 and 6.4 percent higher in 1999 with respect to the base-run scenario. Corn gluten feed price falls sharply and is 14 percent smaller than in the base-run. Prices of manioc and other grain substitutes fall less because their implicit protection is adjusted down and their supply elasticity is larger. From 1993 to 1999, the world price ratio of corn gluten feed to grains falls by about 5 percent in the base-run and by 22.5 percent in the CAP reform scenario. World prices of animal products are less affected by the CAP reform save for beef and, to a much smaller extent, milk prices, which would be respectively 5.2 and 2.7 percent higher than in the base-run.

In a decoupled CAP reform scenario,[5] world prices are not much different from their levels under the actual CAP. The slight difference, mainly visible until 1996, originates from a further contraction of E.C. output of crops and beef due to the complete decoupling of payments. The magnitude, however, is limited as the set-aside requirement, according to our interpretation and our parameters, partly offsets the incentives to produce created by acreage payments. World prices of grain-fed animal products and of grain substitutes would be slightly lower in a fully decoupled CAP reform because of the increased price competitiveness of grains. Sugar prices are basically unaffected since no policy change is expected. Sugar is otherwise little affected by the price of other crops because of its quota restriction. The same reason explains why world dairy prices are the same in the two CAP reform scenarios. It is also noticeable that the discrepancies in world prices between the actual and the decoupled CAP reforms fade over time and almost disappear at the end of the decade.

In the "Blair House" or GATT scenario, where the pre-accord is implemented in the E.C. only, the picture of world price effects is generally not much different, except for grains and feeds. World prices are lower in this GATT scenario because no set-aside is imposed on the arable land in the E.C. and only a limited cut in producer price is mandatory to meet the 20 percent reduction in aggregate measure of support (AMS) and the 36 percent tariff equivalent cut. The user price of grains in the E.C. has to be fully aligned on the world price since exports overshoot the allowed quantity of subsidized exports. Consequently, the E.C. is running large deficiency payments in grains, exporting at world prices, but much more than under the actual CAP reform scenario and, of course, much more than under the nearly free trade decoupled CAP reform scenario. Lower cereal and feed grain prices also drive world prices of proteins and grain by-products further down, but only to a small extent.

In conclusion, the overall picture of world price changes due to the three E.C. scenarios: the major impact of the decoupled reform is to moderately improve world grain prices (Table 6.2). In the CAP reform scenario, prices of oilseeds are a little below the level of the base-run scenario, but it is not the case in the decoupled reform. Corn gluten feed prices are driven down sharply in the two reform scenarios, and more so in the actual reform simulation. The prices of animal products are also raised by the reform projects, but only in 1996 for pork and poultry prices, which are thereafter heavily influenced by E.C. and world grain prices.

Implications for the United States. It is difficult to model correctly the complex U.S. farm programs. Our quantitative assessment meets clear limitations in that respect and will have to be supplemented by verbal comments based on the economic rationale of the policy instruments introduced in the Farm Act of 1990. In our representation, target prices of grains are exogenous, but loan rates follow the trends of world prices. The loan rate on soybeans is treated in the same way.[6] Market prices of pork and poultry, and of corn gluten feed also follow world prices. For dairy,[7] beef, and sugar, domestic prices are pegged in nominal terms, and therefore they decrease by the rate of inflation in real terms.

The effects of the three E.C. reform scenarios on the United States are

TABLE 6.2 Effects of E.C. Reform Scenarios on World Prices (ratio of 1996 world prices in the E.C. reform scenarios relative to the base-run)

	Reform	Decoupled Reform	Blair House
Grains	1.05	1.07	1.03
Protein Cakes	0.98	1.01	0.97
Oil	1.02	1.05	1.02
Corn Gluten Feed	0.86	0.84	0.84
Manioc	1.00	1.00	1.00
Other Grain Substitutes	1.01	0.99	1.00
Beef	1.05	1.06	1.01
Pork, Poultry, and Eggs	1.01	1.01	1.01
Milk	1.03	1.03	1.03
Sugar	1.00	1.00	1.01

summarized in Table 6.1. The main observation is that, except for budget costs and trade balance on grains, the difference between the various E.C. reform scenarios is significant but not huge in spite of the noticeable discrepancies in world prices highlighted previously.

Under the base-run scenario in the E.C., terms of trade for U.S. exports would deteriorate. The export value of grains would be 1.5 billion ECU (in 1993 ECU) lower in 1999 than in 1990. Net exports of oilseeds (and products) and of corn gluten feed would continue to grow slightly in value.

As expected, the actual CAP reform appears attractive to the United States. With respect to the base-run, better world prices for grains reduce the U.S. budget costs for grains by 1.2 billion ECU (in 1996) and net exports of grains are 0.6 billion higher in value. The only minor adverse effects are due to the loss of oilseeds (and products) and corn gluten feed export value because of the declining feed demand from the E.C. animal sector.

The consequences of the E.C. reform scenarios on U.S. agricultural incomes are small in relative terms, although they may be less reliable because of the way policy programs are expressed in the model.[8] World prices of grains affect the feed cost of U.S. livestock producers, and higher grain prices, as a result of the two CAP reform scenarios for example, translate into an income loss for the U.S. farm sector as a whole. This is the reason why the CAP reform looks better than the decoupled alternative from the U.S. farm income point of view. Because of the absence of an adequate representation of nonparticipants in the U.S. crop programs who would benefit directly from higher world prices, the result in Table 6.1 is probably too pessimistic for the United States.

Trade in Commodities, Trade in Livestock Products on a More Competitive Basis. The CAP reform has clearly been designed to solve the problems of E.C. cash crops. The global benefits to the United States in terms of budget or trade are clear-cut. The reform will also have drastic effects on price ratios in the livestock sector, which could potentially shift the contested E.C.-U.S. issues from the grains and feeds to livestock products.

Figure 6.5 shows the dramatic changes in the price ratio between grain-fed animals and grains in both the E.C. and United States. Similar patterns of evolution would be observed for other animal products and other feeds. Over the next decade, this price ratio will increase by about 30 percent in the E.C. and decrease by about 10 percent in the United States. By the end of the decade, both countries should export these products on a nearly competitive basis.

Trade in animal products and particularly in poultry and even in pork and dairy has increased more than in the basic commodities. The prospects for trade expansion in this area are good because these products are

FIGURE 6.5 Price Ratio Between Grain-fed Animals (Pork and Poultry) and Grains in the E.C. and the U.S. Under the CAP Reform Scenario.

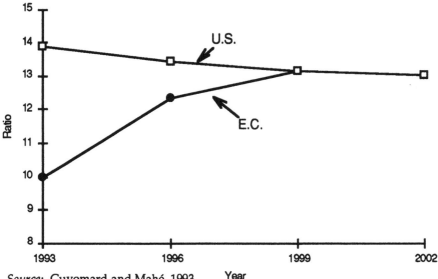

Source: Guyomard and Mahé, 1993.

income elastic and consumption should grow, as the upturn in the world economy gains momentum. It should particularly be the case in the fast growing newly industrial countries (NICs) of East Asia, where land is scarce and where environmental concerns will develop and increasingly constrain domestic production.

As the basic price cost ratios turn in favor of the E.C., one should expect that trade conflicts in livestock products, either on bilateral trade flows between the E.C. and United States or on third market outlets, might arise. The use of limited but targeted subsidies to capture market shares in this area are not an unrealistic scenario. E.C. dairy products also can potentially become competitive, as the general movement to lower opportunity cost of land in the E.C., dampened however by the acreage payments, and lower feed costs will drive the shadow price of milk in the E.C. in the vicinity of world prices. The E.C. will therefore be in a position to develop a more competitive position on cheese and other dairy products if the market organization is adjusted in an appropriate manner.

It is to be expected that nontariff barriers, new technologies (hormones) and sanitary regulations will become even more important issues in this area than they are now. The GATT should play an increased role in this area, and adequate surveillance procedures by the Secretariat will become a major stake as it is clear that few countries can resist the temptation to use nontariff barriers on such sensitive products.

The Operation of the CAP With Market Prices in the Vicinity of World Prices. The assessment of the implications on E.C.-U.S. relations based on the model has focused on long-term issues and basic trends. The major changes in E.C. market prices for grains and feeds do however raise short-run issues related to the operation of the CAP with domestic price support close to instable world prices.

First, the considerable reduction in exports is likely to change the self-sufficiency position in wheat and feed grains. It is probable that corn supplies, at some stage in the transition period at least, fall short of domestic demand while net wheat exports would remain positive. In such a case, the operation of the CAP would certainly create a wedge between wheat and corn prices because of Community preference. As Surry (1992) has shown, market prices are driven up to the threshold price in a net importing situation and driven down to the intervention price in a net exporting case. Higher prices for corn than for wheat in the E.C. would trigger outlets for U.S. corn but also make Community preference (45 ECU/tonne, which is much larger than the target-intervention price wedge of 10 ECU/tonne) more dissuasive. Skirmishes on the implementation of the minimum access as specified in the GATT Draft Final Act are therefore likely.

Such circumstances would also affect the issues on grain substitutes, and particularly trade in corn gluten feed (CGF). First, the continuation of unabated U.S. flows of CGF exports to the E.C., as projected by the model, calls for some qualifications (Figure 6.6). This outcome is probable as long as E.C. market prices for grains are significantly above U.S. and world prices. However, with world prices rising in nominal terms, our scenario of alignment of E.C. on world prices is likely. It would of course be even more likely if the dollar approached its PPP (purchasing power parity) value, if world economic growth accelerates, and if the E.C. set-aside is not adjusted quickly enough to changes in market or weather conditions. Such optimistic or booming prospects on world markets, which cannot be discarded, would drastically change the prospects for feed substitutes in the E.C. Even in the absence of rebalancing, transportation costs should provide some wedge between U.S. and E.C. values of CGF, both led by similar world prices. The use of CGF in the U.S. compound feed sector should take place under these circumstances because the E.C. price premium would disappear, potentially leading to a dramatic fall in exports of CGF to the E.C. A dollar appreciation would clearly enhance the probability of this course of events, but the rise of corn and feed grain prices in the E.C., due to low self-sufficiency after the CAP reform, would for some time retard this process.

The trend in world grain prices would also change the fundamentals of E.C. grain exports. The management of restitutions will be more subject to

FIGURE 6.6 Price Ratio Between Grains and Corn Gluten Feed in the E.C. and the U.S. Under the CAP Reform Scenario.

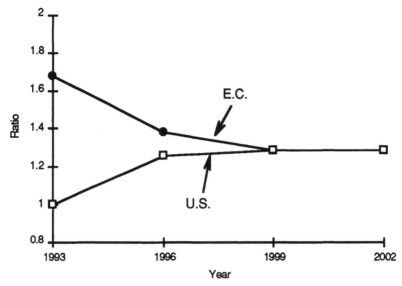

Source: Guyomard and Mahé, 1993.

world price shocks as the necessary level of subsidization becomes low or zero. The E.C. could then more precisely target its restitutions, as the United States does now, on specific markets to be contested or preserved.

Altogether, the likely picture of E.C. imports and exports in the grain and feed area is clearly moving toward more instability in prices, subsidies, and trade flows. The macroeconomic factors world wide, and in both the E.C. (through the working of the EMS [European Monetary System] and the switchover) and in the United States (exchange rate), will be essential elements of agricultural trade. Because of the likely shocks and ratchet effects on flows due to changing price relations, conditions are right for the development of conflicts between the two big players. Even the signing of a Peace Clause is not likely to overcome the potential trade conflicts created by the fundamentals.

The GATT as a Cap on the CAP

The United States and the so-called fair traders have obtained, with the CAP reform, a considerable reduction in E.C. competition in third markets by the cut in price incentives and by a freeze of resources in the cash crop sectors. Still, they are not satisfied with this unilateral reform because past experiences seem to have taught them that the E.C. is unable, in a timely way, to adjust price support levels to technical change and world market conditions in a manner that precludes a loss in their market shares. Hence, their response to this reform suggests that it does not provide the guarantees that the disciplines of the GATT will apply. This is likely why the United States and the Cairns Group firmly rejected the E.C. negotiating position that specific commitments on trade policies were unnecessary because they would result automatically from the cut in internal support.

This is one of the reasons for the U.S. proposals to have included specific and often different commitments on various trade barriers.[9] Therefore, two areas of negotiation were added to the PSE-AMS approach which had a more central role in the early rather than in the later stages of the Round. This is at variance with the expectation that the AMS would play an important role when, for the first time, domestic policies were supposed to be scrutinized in the negotiation process and then disciplined by the GATT.

The post midterm U.S. proposals (1989, 1990) focused on tariffication and export competition, insisting that export subsidies should be reduced at a faster pace than import barriers. Moreover, the concept of tariffication was also aimed at the elimination of the long-denounced variable levy-restitution system.

These elements are in fact consistent with the GATT philosophy, which promotes transparency of trade barriers and bound tariffs and which does not allow dumping practices. The GATT Secretariat and the President of the Trade Negotiation Group on Agriculture supported this line, as reflected in the De Zeeuw paper (1990) and more systematically in the Dunkel compromise (1991). The discrimination against export subsidization was justified by the GATT general principles but amounted to a disproportionate burden of adjustment on the E.C. as compared to United States for example (Guyomard and Mahé, 1991).

The lack of confidence among the more competitive exporters in the unilateral CAP reform is further illustrated by the introduction of a new concept in commitments, i.e., the obligation of results in trade liberalization. Hence, the introduction of the concept of minimum access to imports and the specified reduction in subsidized export quantities included in the Dunkel compromise.[10] These elements are clearly aimed at countervailing the temptation of the E.C. to maintain a sizable exporting activity based on subsidization and to further enhance self-sufficiency in the remaining importing sectors. In other words, the GATT Round was seen as an opportunity to discipline the E.C. decision-making and to "put a cap on the CAP."

Even if the Uruguay Round has often appeared as a "combat des chefs" between the two economic giants, it is also true that multilateralization of the reform process was a way to promote positive externalities in the reform process. Most studies (e.g., OECD, 1987; Johnson, *et al.* 1993) suggest that joint liberalization increases world prices. For most developed countries, this would reduce the cost of adjustment or increase the benefits of net exporters due to further improvements in terms of trade. Hence the efforts of the United States and the Carins countries to continue the multilateral process.

The GATT is Also a Means to Help So-called Fair Traders Do Some Housekeeping at Home

The process of negotiating a treaty for agriculture under GATT principles requires that negotiators reach agreement on rules. These rules, however, cannot be commodity-specific even if strategies were clearly designed so negotiators could maximize other countries' concessions while minimizing their own concessions.[11] The rules, tailored according to this strategy, must be in line with the GATT philosophy of reducing import barriers and especially reducing subsidies to exports that up to now were tolerated under Article XVI.

Rules, as they are specified in the Draft Final Act, are complex, and their differences according to policy instruments reflect the strategies of the various countries to capture trade gains at minimal political cost. Still, the protected sectors (sugar, dairy) should not escape the obligation of adjustment in the future. This is how the compromise will impose a revision of the CAP reform in a direction more consistent with the first Commission proposals and will help to reduce price supports in the dairy and sugar sectors, eventually enlarging the cap on the CAP. This change in the political balance of domestic forces between reform supporters and opponents will also extend to the countries who have a tendency to present themselves as free traders but who nonetheless have highly protected sectors that they have been unable to reform. Again, the United States is probably the best example of this case as illustrated by the commodities that are sheltered by the 1955 waiver in the GATT.

Whether these factors were an intended positive spillover effect of the U.S. administration in the early stages of the Round or a reflection of the economic philosophy of the republican administration is difficult to determine. The latter is doubtful, however, since otherwise the sugar policy in the United States would have been liberalized to the benefit of sugar cane producers from developing countries independently of the GATT process.

Summary

Our interpretation of the course of events observed in the agricultural component of the Round is therefore that expected trade gains in key sectors of key countries were the necessary circumstances to promote collective action at the international level. This action also served to countervail collective action at the domestic level that would otherwise have likely resulted in the status quo. Highly protectionist countries and groups like Japan and the E.C. (for even further reasons due to its supra-national nature) almost surely would not have promoted the discipline of agricultural policies under GATT rules, in spite of their general trade interest in sectors other than agriculture. The role the United States played in the early stages of the GATT treaty, such as insisting that agriculture be given a special treatment, and its efforts to obtain the waiver are ample pieces of evidence to suggest that it would not have pursued free trade on philosophical grounds alone. The changed economic conditions, particu-larly in comparative advantage, and the threats from the E.C. on trade interests in specific commodities were sufficient to induce her to seek an effective result in this Round.

Long-term Perspectives of E.C.-U.S. Trade

The CAP remains on the whole inefficient and inequitable to consum-ers, and taxpayers, and selected farmers whose incomes are supported unevenly. The main motivation for farm support in the E.C. is the existing low remuneration to resources, labor in particular, invested in farming. Consequently, in the long term, intersectoral mobility of resources is the natural remedy for low agricultural incomes, and policymakers should find ways of facilitating this transfer at the least social cost. A proper long-term policy favoring resource mobility and structural adjustment in agri-culture is then essential to reduce in the future justified claims for public support. Consequently, long-term perspectives on the E.C.-U.S. agricul-tural trade will be largely dependent on the impact of the CAP reform on the farm structure.

Conflicting Objectives: Structural Impact
of E.C. Common and National Policies

The traditional CAP has been focusing on price support, without a strategy for structural adjustment. The Guidance section of EAGGF has always accounted for less than 5 percent of the fund, even though, accord-ing to the initial views of E.C. policymakers, its size should have been at least one-third of common expenditure in agriculture. Structural policy has been left to the initiative of member states, whose main concerns were focused on safeguarding farm incomes and adequate levels of agricultural employment.

As a result, farm structure in the E.C., which was quite uneven before the institution of the E.C., has failed to become more homogeneous. In northern countries, farm structures have moderately improved along with labor productivity. In southern countries, farm structures have improved at a much lower rate and labor productivity is still very low. Notwithstanding considerable rates of labor outmigration (e.g., in Italy and Spain), farm structure has not changed substantially, and a large number of inefficient farms are still present together with a smaller number of larger and more competitive farms. In fact, the declared objective of some national policies has been to keep a large number of working people in agriculture. For example, the objectives of the Italian "Piano Agricolo Nazionale" are (1) to support and increase farm incomes and, (2) to safeguard agricultural employment, especially for young people and in less developed regions.

These objectives of the Italian agricultural policy are clearly hindering the intersectoral mobility of resources, and of labor in particular. This may help to explain why Italy, although importing almost one-fifth of her food needs, accounts for a labor share in total employment in terms of annual work units (AWUs) that is still double or triple that of other E.C. countries enjoying approximately the same level of economic development, such as the Netherlands and Belgium.

Unfortunately, in the E.C. as a whole, the distribution of farms per class of farmer's income is more similar to Italy than to the Netherlands. Family farm income per AWU in half of E.C. farms is still less than 5000 ECU per year, not withstanding the substantial price and income support granted by the CAP. This may explain, to a certain extent, the more liberal approach of Dutch policymakers and farmers' unions regarding the GATT negotiations as compared to the more conservative positions held by some other member states.

This excess labor retained in agriculture, especially in the less-developed regions, is likely to be the combined effect of both the E.C. price support policy and the pseudo-structural policies implemented at the national level. The invisible nature of most income transfers to farmers was disguising the real contribution of agricultural employment to social welfare.[12]

The 1992 CAP reform, by substituting explicit direct subsidies for invisible market transfers, substantially increased the transparency of the social productivity of farm labor, not only as perceived by consumers and taxpayers, but also as understood by farmers. On the contrary, in the dairy subsector where production quotas were introduced in 1984, the existing level of transparency has been further reduced, hindering the intersectoral mobility of resources and structural adjustment.

Long-term Effects of the CAP Reform

The long-term effects of the CAP reform are obviously very important in order to understand whether it will effectively contribute to solving the farm problems and favor a more efficient international allocation of resources, or whether it will be a palliative aiming at maintaining present economic rents in some farms and regions together with inefficient farm structures in other regions. "Gattopardismo" has been very frequent in past CAP reforms.

The E.C. Council of Ministers on May 1992 decided that the compensation of farmers for income losses due to reduced price support should be paid on a year-to-year basis. This decision is likely to have the following consequences:

1. The administrative costs of computing compensations and validating farmer's annual declarations will be a major burden on E.C. and national budgets, with wider possibilities for fraud.
2. It would not be advisable to modulate compensation according to farm size in the case where they are paid yearly without running the risk of hindering structural adjustment while they install incentives to meet the conditions to maximize payments. Maintaining smaller and less efficient farms would mean receiving higher compensations every year.
3. Farmers running small holdings will be encouraged to remain in the agricultural sector in order to receive their payments, thus limiting the intersectoral and intrasectoral labor mobility.
4. Farmers are continually uncertain of their future payments. This could encourage them to take a conservative approach in making structural improvements and induce them to spend time and money convincing the political sector to guarantee their compensation.
5. Employment in farming will decrease less and some extra employment will be created in the public sector in order to implement the new administrative practices and controls. However, the marginal contribution of this extra employment to social welfare is likely to be negative.

The newly born reform of the CAP is likely to show its advantages in the upcoming years, but its intrinsic contradictions will be more apparent as well.

Long-term Benefits of a More Decoupled CAP Reform

Society may be justified in granting direct payments to farmers for the conservation of natural resources and other environmentally beneficial practices. Positive externalities are currently produced by agriculture, but, as they are public goods, they are not valued by market prices. On the other hand, compensations for income losses due to reduced price support after the CAP reform may be paid as a lump sum, allowing farmers to cumulate future payments for a number of years.[13] In order to avoid sudden budgetary problems, lump-sum payments could be financed by the

E.C. budget in form of bonds, salable on the financial market, as recently proposed by the Land Use and Food Policy Inter Group (LUFPIG) of the European Parliament (Marsh, *et al.* 1991).

If a lump-sum compensation for the reduction in incomes is computed for a number of years and, for example, offered to farmers as bonds salable on the financial market, farmers would have the choice to cash the payment annually or to sell the bonds and cash at any time their discounted cumulated compensation for future payments.

The long-term effects on structural adjustment of this more decoupled feature of the CAP reform are quite interesting; they include the following:

1. Bureaucratic costs would be reduced and the possibility of fraud decreased as the administrative work of calculating and analyzing payments would only have to be done once.
2. Compensation could be modulated according to farm size, or to other parameters, without generating inefficient resource allocation in the future. Investment decisions could then be based mainly on market conditions and there will be less public incentive for owning a smaller farm instead of a more efficient and viable one.
3. Proper environmental standards could be targeted by means of regulation, incentives for positive externalities and disincentives on negative externalities, without directly hindering a more efficient allocation of resources. Land set aside could be encouraged on the basis of conservation objectives, and not to manage supply control for reason of complacency towards foreign competitors.
4. Labor mobility out of agriculture would not be hindered.
5. Farmers' incomes would not be tied directly to policymakers. The spending for lobbying would be reduced and farmers would be more reliant on actual market prices.

Although accepting its economic advantages, these decoupled aspects of a bolder CAP reform may be considered too risky by policymakers whose concerns are focused on possible demographic and territorial problems. Lump-sum compensations could then be tested on a specific section of the agricultural sector, e.g., providing this extra choice only to smaller, economically nonviable farms, or limiting lump sum compensations to specific E.C. regions where agricultural employment is clearly excessive. Such a scheme would favor the needed structural adjustment. Complementary measures for restructuring farms in these areas and fostering economic development in other economic sectors are also clearly necessary to promote regional and rural development on a wider economic basis than the sole agricultural sector.

Conclusion

The reform of the Common Agricultural Policy has amounted to the substitution of new income support instruments for the usual price policy, essentially in the cash crop sector. Our first point is that the domestic political balance was unable to generate such a large change in policy design, in spite of inefficiencies and imbalances due to the traditional CAP. The pressure of the United States has been a major factor in the evolution of the reform. We argue that trade interests have been crucial to catalyze international collective action in order to countervail domestic pressure groups. Apparently, the reform satisfies the U.S. objectives as well as the GATT compromise. The U.S. gains from the CAP reform are noticeable, but we do not foresee the disappearance of sources of tension between the two countries, as E.C. animal products become more competitive and as the working for the CAP in the vicinity of world prices will make trade flows sensitive to agricultural and macroeconomics shocks.

According to some quantitative estimates,[14] which are consistent with ours, the expected effect of a decoupled CAP reform on trade flows between the E.C. and the United States should not be too dramatic as a whole. The increased extensification related to a larger number of economically viable farms will likely be balanced by reduced land set-aside, improving the allocation of resources.

The most interesting effects should be apparent in the changing perspectives for further trade liberalization, as intersectoral labor mobility and lower farm production costs are essential conditions for allowing a further reduction in farm support and for developing a freer international trade for agricultural products without excessive burden on consumers and taxpayers. Improved structural adjustment, generating lower production costs and lower demand for protection, is likely to be the best safeguard against continuing requests for protectionist measures both in the E.C. and the United States. A less interventionist policy by the E.C. and the United States is likely to be followed by other developed countries and favor a more efficient international allocation of resources.

The CAP could then concentrate more on providing incentives for environmental conservation and improvement, subsidizing farmers in less-developed regions where depopulation could occur and favoring a better income distribution through decoupled policy instruments. However, as domestic special interests, both in the E.C. and the United States, are still very strong, such a completion of the CAP reform is likely to be possible only if external pressures for reform are joined by domestic political pressures from consumers and by a more socially oriented attitude of policymakers (Tarditi, 1993).

The pursuit of an agreement in the GATT is therefore a means to keep further developments in the CAP under control and to promote the positive externalities from multilateral reform. Hence the search for a package dressed up along the principles of the GATT and based on trade barriers rather than on effective support reduction. This package has the further benefits of fostering the capability of the proponents of action to actually reform their most protected sectors, like sugar and dairy, which they were unable to adjust in isolation. The magnitude of changes in these sectors will be limited, but the GATT will put a cap not only on the CAP but also on the support of the protected industries in otherwise agricultural export-oriented countries.

It appears that the Uruguay Round will succeed in placing agriculture partly under the GATT. This success is not satisfactory, however, and the long-run objective of further decoupling payments from production incentives should be pursued in order to promote agricultural trade on a more competitive basis and to reserve intervention of the state to the promotion of public goods.

Notes

1. The prospect for increased feed demand in the E.C. did however help the Commission in reaching an agreement among members for a more market-oriented approach to the 1992 reform of the CAP.

2. Petit (1985) provides an insightful discussion of some of the earlier determinants of agricultural policies in the United States and the E.C. while Josling *et al.* (1990), discuss some of the more current factors influencing the direction of policy.

3. See Munk (1990) for a further discussion of the public finance pressures for reform in the context of the current GATT round of negotiations.

4. See Goodwin and Ortalo-Magne (1992) for a recent empirical study of the influence of commodity programs on the prices of land in Canada, France, and the United States.

5. This scenario is run assuming that acreage and headage payments introduced by the reform are granted in a fully decoupled way, e.g., on the basis of past criteria only. Furthermore, there is no set-aside in this scenario.

6. An alternative solution could be to peg the loan rates according to the principle of marketing loans, but the loan rates themselves may be adjusted by policy makers.

7. This is also a debatable representation as there is an extensive discretionary power given to the administration to adjust the policies if program costs increase. The cost associated with dairy policy must be considered as "potential" rather than automatic.

8. The U.S. income indicator mainly reacts to world prices of grains, oilseeds, and pork and poultry. There is no distinction between participants and nonparticipants in the U.S. grain program and, therefore, no benefit from higher world prices on U.S. grain producers is represented in the model. Incomes are nega-

tively affected by higher world grain prices. Thus, the positive effect of the CAP reform on U.S. incomes is probably underestimated.

9. Another reason includes the attempt to minimize adjustment in the protected sectors (CARD, 1991).

10. Respectively 5 percent of domestic consumption of the reference and 24 percent of subsidized exports in the reference.

11. There is ample evidence that most delegations have followed that route. Canada was an example when it strove to get production quotas treated in a more lenient fashion than other price support policies without supply control. The United States is another case in point when the choice of the reference period for the AMS reduction is clearly designed to minimize support cut under this rule. Japan is the extreme case in that respect, but the E.C.'s reluctance to accept specific commitments on subsidized exports is an other example of this general attitude.

12. Social security invisible transfers were substantial, accounting for more than 50 percent of public expenditure in agriculture in early 1980s. Altogether, income transfer to agriculture was approximately equal to the sectoral value added (Tarditi and Croci-Angelini, 1988, pp. 28 and 70). Unfortunately, the survey on national expenditure in agriculture (CEC, 1982) decided by the E.C. Commission in the early 1980s and providing extremely interesting information was never updated.

13. The LUFPIG proposal at the European Parliament was envisaging a 15-year period. The same period has been assumed for a simulation of the impact of a decoupled CAP reform on markets and prices (Folmer et al., 1993).

14. For example, Folmer et al., 1993.

References

CARD. 1991. "Determining Winners and Losers From a GATT Agreement: The Importance of Base Period Rules." GATT Research Paper 91-GATT, Ames, Iowa.

Commission of the European Communities. 1982. "Public Expenditure in Agriculture." pp.229.

———. 1991. "The Development and Future of the Common Agricultural Policy." COM(91) 258.

E. C. Commission. Various years. *Agricultural Situation in the Community*. Brussels.

Folmer C., M. D. Keyzer, M. D. Merbis, H. J. J. Solwijk, and P. J. J. Veenendaal. 1993. "CAP Reform and its Differential Impact on Member States." Research Memorandum, Center for World Food Studies, Amsterdam, the Netherlands.

Goodwin, B. K., and F. Ortalo-Magne. 1992. "The Capitalization of Wheat Subsidies into Agricultural Land Values." *Canadian Journal of Agricultural Economics* 40:37-54.

Guyomard H., and L. P. Mahé. 1991. "Agriculture in the GATT: An Assessment of the USA's 1989 Proposal." *Food Policy*, 16 : 330-341.

———. 1993. "GATT Negotiations, CAP Reforms and E.C.-U.S. Relationships." Working Paper, ENSAR INRA-ESR-PAM, Rennes, France. (Report for the Commission to appear in *European Economy*).

ISTA. Various years. *Oil World Annual*. ISTA, Hamburg, Germany.

Johnson M., L. P. Mahé, T. L. Roe. 1993. "Trade Compromises Between the European Community and the United States: An Interest Group-Game Theory Approach." *Journal of Policy Modelling* 15: 199-222.

Josling, T. E., F. H. Sanderson, and T. K. Warley. 1990. "The Future of International Relations: Issues in the GATT Negotiations." In *Agricultural Protectionism in the Industrial World,* edited by F. H. Sanderson. Washington D.C: Resources for the Future.

Mahé, L.P., and T. L. Roe. 1993. "Political Economy of Trade Negotiations: An Empirical Game Theory Analysis." In *Issues in Agricultural Development: Sustainability and Cooperation,* edited by M. Bellamy and B. Greenshields. IAAE Occasional Paper No. 6:330-337.

Marsh J., B. Green, B. Kearney, L. Mahé, S. Tangermann, and S. Tarditi. 1991. *The Changing Role of Common Agricultural Policy.* London: Belhaven Press.

Munk, K. J. 1990. "Price Support to the E.C. Agricultural Sector. An Optimal Policy?" *Oxford Review of Economic Policy* 5: 76-89.

OECD. 1987. Echanges et politiques agricoles. OCDE, Paris, France.

Olson, M. 1965. *The Logic of Collective Action.* Cambridge, MA.: Harvard Univ. Press.

Orden, D. 1990. "International Capital Markets and Structural Adjustment in U.S. Agriculture." *Amer. J. of Agric. Econ.* 72: 745-54.

Paarlberg, R. 1987. "Political Markets for Agricultural Protection: Understanding and Improving Their Function." Paper presented to the annual meeting of the IATRC, Airlie House, 3-16 December.

———. 1989. "The Political Economy of American AgriculturalPolicy: Three Approaches." *Amer. J. of Agric. Econ.* 71: 1157-1164.

Petit, M. 1985. "Determinants of Agricultural Policies in the U.S. and the E.C." *International Food Policy Research Institute.* Research Report No. 51, IFPRI, Wash., D.C.

Surry, Y. 1992. "Un Modèle de Transmission des Prix Garanties des Cèrèales dans la Communautè Economique Européenne. *Cahiers d'Economie et Sociologoie Rurales* 22: 9-35.

Tarditi, S., and E. Croci-Angelini. 1988. "Aspetti metodologici e criteri di valutazione della politica economica nel settore agricolo". In Società Italiana di Economia Agraria, *La Politica Economica nel Settore Agricolo,* Il Mulino, Bologna: INEA. pp. 18-30.

Tarditi, S. 1993. "Perspectives in the European Community." In *Agriculture in the Uruguay Round: Reform Objectives and Outcomes,* edited by K. A. Ingersent. Univ. of Nottingham: Macmillian.

U. S. Dept. of Agriculture. Various years. *Agricultural Statistics.* USDA ERS, Washington, D.C.

———. 1993. *World Agriculture: Trends and Indicators, 1970-91.* Statistical Bulletin, 861, USDA ERS, Washington, D. C.

———. Economic Research Service. 1992. *Foreign Agricultural Trade of the United States.* USDA ERS, Washington, D. C.

Discussion

Walter H. Gardiner

The chapter by Guyomard, Mahé, Roe, and Tarditi represents a truly transatlantic effort and a very ambitious attempt to address a wide range of topics related to the past, present, and future of E.C.-U.S. trade relations in agriculture. The chapter focuses on the interpretation of the recent CAP reform in the context of the Uruguay Round and in the perspective of the traditional E.C.-U.S. agricultural trade conflict.

In the introduction to their chapter, the authors claim that the history and role of the GATT were dominated by E.C.-U.S. disputes and that recent bilateral developments were at the heart of the present round. While the headlines have certainly focused on E.C.-U.S. trade disputes in the course of reporting on the progress (or lack) in the Uruguay round, it is important to recognize the critical role played by the Cairns Group in this process. The Cairns group elevated agriculture to center stage and was instrumental at the showdown during the final week of the originally scheduled deadline in December 1990. Furthermore, while the E.C.'s Common Agricultural Policy (CAP) has been "the familiar target for attacks," the U.S. Export Enhancement Program and Japanese rice import policy have not been overlooked in the debate.

The second part of the chapter provides a useful background for interpreting the CAP reform by tracing the E.C.-U.S. trade conflict since the early 1960s with supporting facts and figures. The major source of E.C.-U.S. trade tensions is effectively illustrated in a figure of bilateral agricultural trade, which shows U.S. exports falling from a high of more than $10 billion in 1980 to nearly $6 billion in 1985 while E.C. exports to the United States rose steadily over this period. In terms of net trade, however, U.S. net exports to the E.C. of around $2.5 billion in the early 1990s hardly represent a "recovery" from more than $7.6 billion in net exports in 1980 (Organization for Economic Cooperation and Development [hereafter OECD], 1993a). A similar pattern has developed for the E.C.'s other trade partners. The rest of this section is devoted to more specific trade issues ranging from the age-old dispute over the E.C. variable levy system to the more recent procymidone (wine) case brought by the United States against the E.C.

The third section of the chapter evaluates the E.C.-U.S. trade conflict using game theory and draws on recent empirical work to support their thesis. They begin with the all-too-familiar domestic pressures for reform (growing surpluses, rising budget costs, and income distribution problems), which they contend were incapable of generating the type of reforms to the CAP that materialized in May 1992. This, along with the lack of reforms to the dairy and sugar sectors where there has not been large-country trade pressure, lead the authors to conclude that the final package of CAP reforms was more the result of external rather than domestic pressures. While the authors provide some convincing evidence and arguments to support this claim, the role of certain E.C. domestic interests such as the feed manufacturers, livestock producers, environmentalists, consumers, and nonagricultural concerns are not discussed as part of the reform process.

In the section on special interests in agriculture, the authors provide a useful review of past and recent studies on the nature of special interests in the economic policy process. The OECD's current report on agricultural policies (1993b) lends support to the statement that farmers' small number relative to a country's population cause their benefits to be much higher than the per capita costs incurred by consumers and taxpayers (Table 6.3). The benefit/cost ratio for 1992 ranged from a low of 48 in Australia to 100 in the United States and averaged 50 for OECD countries. The authors also note that agricultural support to producers is easily confused with support for other aspects of agriculture including environmental amenities, rural development, and natural resources. The OECD's agriculture ministers at their March 1992 meeting acknowledged this multidimensional aspect of agricultural support and called for an examination of this relationship and measures used to address them.

Citing a recent study by Johnson *et al.* (1993) using 1986 data, the authors state that the culmination of various factors provides some sectors with more political influence than others. In both the E.C. and the United States, sugar and dairy interests exhibit the most influence followed by producers of animal feeds and grains. This is also supported using 1992 data on Producer Subsidy Equivalents and Nominal Assistance Coefficients from the recent OECD report (1993b).

TABLE 6.3 Total Transfers Associated with Agricultural Policies, 1992 (US$)

Country	Per Fulltime Farmer Equivalent	Per Head of Population	Benefit/Cost Ratio
Australia	4,200	89	47
Canada	20,400	330	62
E.C.	17,700	450	39
Japan	24,000	600	40
U.S.	36,100	360	100
OECD average	21,900	440	50

Source: OECD, *Agricultural Policies, Markets and Trade*, 1993.

The results of the authors' own work on the nature of the interdependent effects of E.C.-U.S. agricultural policies reveal that the own effects of policy reform are greater than the indirect effects of unilateral reform of one country on another. This conclusion is in general agreement with other studies not mentioned here, including those by the Commission of the European Communities (1988), Tyers and Anderson (1986), and Roningen and Dixit (1989).

In the fourth section of the chapter, the authors analyze three E.C. reform scenarios (CAP reform, fully decoupled CAP reform, and Blair House) against a base-run (continuation of pre-reform CAP) using "MISS," a three-region (E.C., United States, and rest-of-world) price-equilibrium model. The scenarios are evaluated in terms of their effects on world commodity prices and selected U.S. indicators (farm income, budget outlays, and trade balances). It is difficult to critically evaluate the results provided in the two summary tables as few details are provided on the model structure or the mechanics of implementing the various scenarios. Furthermore, no results are provided on the effects of the various scenarios on key E.C. variables, nor is there a discussion of key uncertainties like the effectiveness of the set-aside program (Herlihy, 1993). However, the authors have used the model extensively in past work, so those familiar with the literature should have little difficulty here.

The main results of the reform scenarios are assessed against other recent studies (Folmer *et al.* 1993; Goldin *et al.* 1993; and Hart *et al.* 1993). The slight increase in world grain prices appears reasonable and is consistent with other studies, given the reduced supply of E.C. grains as a result of the set-aside program and the increased demand stemming from cuts in support prices. Oilseed prices decline in the CAP reform and Blair House scenarios, which implies that the substitution effect (lower meal demand as a result of lower E.C. grain prices offsets the reduction in oilseed supplies). The result is consistent with Folmer *et al.* but is opposite that obtained in three studies reviewed in Hart *et al.* However, the authors in this study obtained a world price increase for oilseeds under the decoupled CAP reform, which imposes a stronger oilseed supply cut that dominates the demand effect.

The price of corn gluten feed declines sharply in all scenarios while other feeds like manioc and so-called "grain substitutes" remain virtually unchanged. (See Schmidt and Gardiner for a discussion of the "grain substitute" issue). The only other study which addresses other feeds is Folmer *et al.* which shows carbohydrates as well as protein feeds declining moderately under the reform scenarios. The degree to which secondary or by-product feeds follow the cuts in E.C. cereal and oilseed prices is a critical issue and cause for much debate in determining feed composition in the E.C. and the export consequences for suppliers of these feeds.

In the case of world prices for meat and dairy products, this study shows price increases in all scenarios, led by beef, then dairy, and finally pork and poultry. These results are consistent with most other studies except in Folmer *et al.* where pork and poultry prices remain unchanged. The issue here is whether the increased E.C. production of pork and poultry resulting from lower E.C. feed costs under reform is sufficient to offset higher-cost meat production in the rest of the world from higher grain prices. A more detailed analysis is needed.

The final point with regard to world price impacts is that decoupled CAP reform has the largest price impacts and Blair House the least, which implies that CAP reform is more binding on E.C. producers than the Blair House Agreement. If true, the issue of CAP-Blair House compatibility is a moot one and, instead of rejecting Blair House, reluctant E.C. member states might want to sign on and seek some easing of CAP restrictions. Other ongoing work in the E.C. Commission, the OECD, and at the Economic Research Service of USDA, which has not yet been made available to the public, should contribute to the debate on the global effects of CAP reform.

The impacts of the E.C. reform scenarios on the United States are presented for farm income, budget costs, and trade balances. The results show little impact on farm income as the benefits to higher grain prices are virtually offset by higher feed costs. The authors acknowledge that, because of inadequate representation of nonparticipants in U.S. crop programs, the income results might be understated. The benefits of lower budget costs and higher trade balances are the largest for decoupled reform and the smallest for "Dunkel," which is consistent with higher world prices in the former case. (Authors have labeled results under "Dunkel" instead of "Blair House," though no explanation is given.) The authors also make the important point that future E.C.-U.S. trade conflicts may shift from grains and feeds to livestock products (particularly pork and poultry) as price ratios between grain-fed animals and grains narrow between the two regions. Lower opportunity costs of land together with lower feed costs in the E.C. are likely to make E.C. dairy products more competitive as well.

In the final section of part four, the authors make the case that the introduction of the concepts of tariffication, minimum import access, and quantitative cuts in subsidized exports reflect an attempt by the United States and the Cairns group to use the GATT to put limits on the CAP, which the E.C. in and of itself could not do. They also make the point that the GATT could also be a means of helping other countries, particularly the United States and Japan, overcome domestic pressures to obtain much-needed reforms in agriculture.

The final section of the chapter is devoted to longer-term issues related to CAP reform and its implications for future E.C.-U.S. trade. The authors note that the CAP has traditionally concentrated more on price support without developing an effective strategy for structural adjustment, leaving this to individual member states. This has contributed to: unbalanced adjustments across sectors and countries; inefficiencies and inequities with respect to producers, consumers, and taxpayers; and rigidities that prevent the mobility of resources within the E.C. The authors rightly call for a proper long-term policy that increases the transparency of public support for agriculture and improves intersectoral mobility of resources favoring structural adjustment, which should in turn reduce the future justified claims for public support. This will allow the CAP to concentrate more on environmental goals, improve resource allocation, and better target support to farmers in less-developed areas. The success of CAP reform in improving E.C. farm structures will largely determine the future of E.C.-U.S. trade relations and will be the focus of many research efforts and conferences to come.

References

Commission of the European Communities. 1988. "Disharmonies in E.C. and U.S. Agricultural Policy Measures." Luxembourg.

Folmer, C., M. A. Keyzer, M. D. Merbis, H. J. J. Stolwijk, and P. J. J. Veenendaal. 1993. "CAP Reform and Its Differential Impact on Member States." Research Memorandum, Centre for World Food Studies, Amsterdam, the Netherlands, April.

Goldin, I., D. van de Menbrugghe, and A. Cordella. 1993. "The Consequences of CAP Reform for Developing Countries." Background paper for report on reform of the E.C. Common Agricultural Policy, Paris, April.

Hart, C., M. D. Helmar, D. J. Hayes, and W. H. Meyers. 1993, "A Comparison of Analyses of CAP Reform." Paper presented at World Outlook Project Meeting, Joint Research Centre, Ispra, Varese, Italy, May 17-18.

Herlihy, M. T. 1993. "Effectiveness of Acreage Control Programs in the United States: Implications for the European Community." Paper presented at the conference *New Dimensions in North-American-European Agricultural Trade Relations*, Calabria, Italy, June.

Organization for Economic Cooperation and Development. 1993a. *Agricultural Data Base*. Directorate for Food, Agriculture and Fisheries. July.

_____. 1993b. *Agricultural Policies, Markets and Trade* Paris, 1993.

Roningen, V. O., and P. Dixit. 1989. "How Level is the Playing Field?: An Economic Analysis of Agricultural Policy Reforms in Industrial Market economies." FAER No. 239, USDA ERS, Washington, D.C., Dec.

Schmidt, S., and W. H. Gardiner. 1988. "Nongrain Feeds: E.C. Trade and Policy Issues." FAER No. 234, USDA ERS, Washington, DC, Jan.

Tyers, R., and K. Anderson. 1986. "Distortions in World Food Markets: A Quantitative Assessment." Background paper for the World Bank's *World Development Report*.

7

The CAP in a Growing E.C. and in a Rapidly Changing European Political Scenario: Its Implications for U.S.-E.C. Agricultural Trade Relations

Stefan Tangermann

Introduction

"A far away country of which we know nothing." Thus the Czech president of the Central European Union, refusing to commit peacekeeping troops to England in the wake of nationalist riots that followed Scotland's secession from the United Kingdom. It is 2038. A century earlier the invasion of Czechoslovakia had led within months to the second world war. Now, the Central European Union—Germany, the Czech republic, Slovakia, Slovenia, Austria, Hungary, Poland, Benelux, and the Venetian republic—is making the foreign policy of the European Community (E.C.). Nominally the Central European Union is an E.C. sub-group. But since the expansion of the Community at the start of the 21st century, French and British inability to fulfill the economic requirements of a common currency, plus the failure of Europe's southern countries to compete with the miracle economies of central Europe, has meant that the 24-member E.C. has turned into a stable hub with wobbly spokes. Increasingly, to the rest of the world, "Europe" is synonymous with the economic powerhouse of the German hinterland.

Is this vision, spelled out in *The Economist* (March 13, 1993), exciting, frightening, reassuring, realistic, complete nonsense, or all of this at the same time? One thing is certain—the European Community is in a process of fundamental change. Thirty-five years after its creation, at a time when it could also have entered into a phase of stagnation, senescence, gradual decay, and final dissolution, the European Community is moving rapidly ahead, at an even accelerating speed. The creation of a Single Market was not even completed when the E.C. Heads of State and Government got together in Maastricht to initial a treaty on the European Union, which would make a large step forward in the process of European integration. While the Maastricht Treaty has not yet been ratified by all E.C. member states, enlargement of the Community to include (some) EFTA (European Free Trade Area) countries is being prepared. Also, in the countries of Central Europe, much noise is made about their urgent will to become members of the Community. In other words, rather than being stagnant, the E.C. is moving ahead in many different directions at the same time.

As all these grand plans for the future are being designed, and in part already implemented, the European Community also has all sorts of day-to-day difficulties. The Community is proud of its European Cooperation in Foreign Policy, and it looks forward to ever-improving foreign policy co-ordination and even joint defense policies as agreed in the Maastricht Treaty on the European Union—but E.C. member states cannot agree on how to behave in the former Yugoslavia. In the Maastricht Treaty, initialed in February 1992, E.C. Heads of State and Government agreed that the second stage of the European Monetary Union (EMU) shall begin on January 1, 1994—but in September 1992 exchange rates among currencies of E.C. member states began to move all over the place and some member countries have left the Exchange Rate Mechanism of the European Monetary System. The Single European Act has confirmed and widened the applicability of majority voting in the Council of Ministers—but now France threatens to rejuvenate the supposedly defunct 1966 Luxembourg compromise (allowing member states to veto even those Community decisions which should be taken by majority voting), because it cannot agree with other member states on accepting an agricultural deal in the General Agreement on Tariffs and Trade (GATT) negotiations. The Maastricht Treaty has set strict macroeconomic criteria for member countries before they are allowed into European Monetary Union, but for the time being no more than two member states meet these criteria. In its association agreements with Central Europe, the E.C. has promised to open up its markets (partially) to exports from Central Europe—but shortly before Easter 1993 (when demand for "Easter lamb" is traditionally high in Western Europe) the E.C. banned all live animal, meat, and dairy product imports from all countries in Central Europe.

What is, then, the state of affairs in Europe? Is Europe bound to become the big, unified political and economic superpower? Or is it all grand talk, but little substance, and will Europe continue to grapple laboriously with the nitty-gritty of its many cumbersome problems? And what will the implications of either future be for trans-Atlantic agricultural trade relations? I certainly do not have all the answers to such questions. The best I can offer is my personal speculation on some of the issues involved. In the first section I shall begin by making some observations on the political economy of European integration, illustrated largely by some elements of the process of creating the Single Market. In the following section, I shall comment on what is supposed to be a key factor in Europe's political and economic future, i.e., the Maastricht Treaty. After that I shall turn to the future enlargement of the European Community. In the final two sections I will discuss whether all this may, or may not, have implications for the future of the Common Agricultural Policy and for future agricultural trade relations between Europe and the United States.

The Political Economy of Europe Integration: A Simplistic View

European integration is a long and complex process. It is driven by many forces, ranging all the way from common cultural and historical roots to commercial considerations. An analysis of all these various facets is far beyond the scope of this chapter, and certainly beyond my competence. Instead, let me expose my simplistic view of some political economy aspects of European integration. My layman's hypotheses about how the European Community operates, and in particular how political and economic processes interact in Europe, are the following:

1. It all begins with high-flying political ideas and pretentious plans.
2. In many cases, the driving forces are (foreign) policy considerations, but the vehicles used are economic policies.
3. Once political decisions have been taken, the economic plans are implemented, but the political cosmetic is often more important than the economic substance.
4. As soon as put in motion, plans develop their own dynamics, and more may be achieved than was considered likely in the first place.
5. The economic outcome may differ significantly from what was expected—to the better or the worse.
6. Whatever is practically achieved through any particular plan, Europe is growing together in the process.
7. Contrary to intentions, economic integration proceeds faster than political cohesion.
8. As one result of this dialectic process of economic and political transformation, the power of the central bureaucracy grows fast.
9. As a consequence, Europe's economic policies become occasionally (but not necessarily) more rational.
10. In spite of all its deficiencies, the European Community has a strong attraction for other countries in Europe.

These are my very personal views, and I shall not be able to substantiate all these hypotheses fully in this chapter (nor anywhere else, because I am not a political scientist). I shall rather offer some scattered observations, illustrating some of these aspects by selected examples, and not attempting to construct anything like a comprehensive proof.

A good starting point is the process of creating the Single Market ("Europe 1992"). Around the mid-1980s, there was a widespread feeling in the Community that Europe was falling behind other parts of the world, in both political and economic terms. Economic growth slowed down in Europe; unemployment was high. No major progress towards a united Europe had been made since the establishment of the EMU in 1979. One began to speak of "Eurosclerosis" (Giersch, 1985) and "Europessimism," and some went as far as suggesting that the Community had entered into its "dark age" (Hoffman, 1989).

At this stage, the newly appointed Commission of the European Community, very much under the influence of its strong president Jacques Delors, took the political decision that a new push had to be made. The simple but powerful concept behind this decision was the "bicycle theory," according to which Europe had to move ahead because otherwise it was to fall. The Commission cranked up the stuttering engine of Europe by producing its famous White Paper on "Completing the Internal Market." At face value, this paper was a technical document dealing with purely economic measures. However, in reality the White Paper and the process following from it was a highly political instrument, born out of the political visions of people who wanted to foster Europe's political strength, and targeted masterly at the imagination of the general public, which had begun to lose faith in Europe's political future.

The Single Market project indeed turned out to become a prime example of an ingenious political campaign. An important element in the eventual political success of this project was setting 1992 as the deadline for completing the Internal Market, a date far enough in the future that the enormous legislative and political task did not appear completely unfeasible but sufficiently close so everybody could see how it might affect his or her own life. Another important step the Commission took was to sponsor a study that estimated the economic benefits of completing the Single Market, the Cecchini report (1988). The estimates produced in that report were viewed with much skepticism by many economists (Siebert, 1990), but independently of its academic merits the report fulfilled well its purpose of promoting the idea of the Single Market.

So inspiring was the idea of a Single Market that people and institutions at all levels began to be fiercely active. The Councils of Ministers worked on the huge amount of legislation envisaged in the White Book. Member state parliaments and governments adopted the required national legislation, at least to a large extent. The general public got excited about the new prospects, and, rather than asking why it was only now, some twenty years after the creation of a customs union in the Community, that remaining trade barriers were abolished, everybody behaved as if there had not yet been anything like free trade among E.C. member countries. Companies reconsidered their strategies and established subsidiaries in other member states; business consultants organized well-attended (and highly paying) seminars on Europe 1992 and what it meant for industry; governments reorganized ministries and created branches dealing exclusively with measures helping domestic business to survive intensified competition in the Single Market; newspapers ran whole series of articles on how one should best prepare for 1992; universities reconsidered their curricula to make sure their students could compete with those from other member countries; and village schools improved their foreign language teaching because it was felt everybody in the new Europe needed to be better able to communicate across former cultural barriers. In other words, the Single Market began to exist in people's minds long before it was put into practice.

In a way, even now in 1993, after so much has been done to implement the Single Market, it is still more real in people's minds than it is in practice. True, much has been achieved in terms of pulling down the various barriers to free movement in the Community, and all this is extremely good. Indeed, even border controls have been abandoned, at least for goods, though not yet for people. However, in some important regards the Single Market is still an optical illusion, created for its own sake, rather than for the economic benefits it is supposed to achieve. One important case in point is the treatment of indirect taxes. With the elimination of border controls, differences in indirect tax rates among member countries can no longer be compensated at the border, as used to be the case before 1993. Member states should therefore have harmonized all indirect taxes. However, they could not (yet) agree on full tax harmonization, and important differences in tax rates remain, in particular in VAT rates. Hence, an alternative mechanism needed to be installed as the optical effect of a border-free Europe was considered indispensable. Differences in VAT rates on intra-E.C. trade are now compensated at the level of the individual companies engaged in that trade, through a rather cumbersome procedure. One of the major arguments for the Single Market was that the elimination of border controls would lead to major cost savings and more intensive competition. However, rather than having to bear the costs of border formalities, companies engaged in across member country trade now have to bear the costs of the new formalities for compensating VAT rate differences through the tax system, and it is not at all certain that these costs are not higher than the costs of previous border formalities. Indeed, companies and their tax consultants now have significant difficulties implementing the new system (*Frankfurter Allgemeine Zeitung*, May 12, 1993), and there are reports about cases where companies prefer to buy domestically rather than in other member countries, simply because they want to avoid the difficult tax formalities.

More generally, in spite of all the progress made in creating the Single Market, it is still far from completion in many regards. Not only have some of the legislative changes envisaged by the E.C. Commission not yet been implemented; there are also other elements, never mentioned in the Commission's White Book, that are still preventing a truly free market for all goods, services, and factors of production in Europe.[1] In agriculture, there is still a long way to go before a Single Market in the true sense of the term is implemented (Swinbank, 1990). For example, sugar and milk quotas are still not tradable across member countries; Spain, which has not yet reached the end of the transition period following its accession in 1986, still cannot export its strawberries (and some other products falling under the extended transition regime) freely to other member countries, and like in the case of indirect taxes, compensatory amounts are now levied at the level of companies rather than at national borders; the Green Money system has not been abolished altogether but has been replaced by a new mechanism largely protecting farmers in countries with appreciating currencies through upward adjustments of common support prices.

In spite of such deficiencies, the Single Market process must be considered a major success. Goods, services, capital, and people can now move more freely among E.C. member states than a few years ago, and more freely than would be the case had the Commission not launched the Single Market process. Member state governments are much more aware of the need to create legislation and institutions that improve, rather than hinder, free trade and factor movements across borders. Thinking in terms of international economic linkages has generally been enhanced in Europe. Companies and people make more of an effort now to be internationally competitive. Fears of a "fortress Europe" have not really materialized in any substantial form (GATT, 1993).[2] Indeed, the rest of the world has watched the Single Market process very carefully, and, it appears, with a bit of admiration for what Europe has been able to achieve. Politically, the idea of a united Europe has been rejuvenated among the general public in Europe, and this has contributed significantly to making institutional progress, in the form of the 1987 Single Act and the 1992 Maastricht Treaty.

In terms of the ten hypotheses I have advanced above, it appears to me that experiences made with the Single Market process suggest that:

1. This process has been inspired mainly by political concerns about a lack of dynamics in Europe;
2. the vehicle chosen to deal with these political concerns was closer economic integration;
3. the optical effect of eliminating borders in the E.C. was more important than the resulting economic benefits;
4. most people (including myself) did not anticipate both the enormous impact that the Single Market had on peoples' minds and the fact that most of the proposed legislative changes were indeed achieved;
5. the microeconomic effects of the Single Market on company behavior and so forth have exceeded expectations, while in macroeconomic terms completion of the Single Market has not prevented Europe from falling into a recession and major currency crises in 1992 and 1993;
6. governments, companies, and people in the individual member states are now much better aware of each others problems and aspirations, and Europe has made a big leap forward towards dealing with different institutions and (technical) standards in different member states, without letting them get into the way of freer trade;
7. in spite of closer economic integration, political cooperation among member states has not advanced significantly;
8. because of its leading political role in the Single Market process, and because of the large amount of legislative activities related to it (which in the E.C. can still be triggered only by the Commission), the Commission has gained even more influence, relative to the Council of Ministers (and, hence, relative to member country governments).

Below I shall come back to the latter hypothesis, as well as to:

9. a possible gain in rationality and
10. attractiveness for other countries.

One additional comment is appropriate with regard to hypothesis (7) concerning the lag between economic integration and political cohesion in Europe. As a matter of fact, the lack of political integration becomes more obvious the more progress is made towards an economically integrated Europe. The Community's inability to create better political understanding and more effective political cooperation among member states has surfaced on many occasions, but it has been most visibly demonstrated by its failure to agree on, and implement, a proper and timely response to the cruel developments in the former Yugoslavia. Indeed, Europe could not have exposed its political weakness more obviously than by waiting for the United States to take the lead in the international efforts to deal with this genuinely European affair (and then not following the United States when the President of the United States had made up his mind as to how to proceed in this matter). For Europeans, it is painful, but probably necessary to listen to statements as the following one by William Pfaff in the Los Angeles Times.

"In Western Europe a kind of frozen fascination exists before the spectacle of Europe plunging back into the worst of its 20th century past—a paralyzed willingness to let anything happen, so long as it happens to others. This European debacle validates every one of the perceptions of Europe that lay behind American isolationism in the 19th century, and in the 1920s and 1930s, and which motivated the American hegemony politely but firmly imposed upon Western Europe in the 1950s, in the circumstance of the Cold War. Today such an American hegemony is no longer feasible. The Cold War is finished. The Europeans must be held responsible for themselves. Yet, they give every evidence of unwillingness or incapacity to assume that responsibility. Can they really expect the United States to save Europe from itself a third time in the 20th century? Do they not understand this might not happen?" (Baccigaluppi, 1993)

The feeling of political weakness is now spreading fast in Europe, and it has led some to diagnose a "new Eurosclerosis," after everybody believed the "old" Eurosclerosis of the mid-1980s had been overcome (Frankenberger, 1993). Paradoxical as it may appear, another factor in that new depression of the mood in Europe is related to what is supposed to be the next major, and indeed critical, step forward, i.e., the Maastricht Treaty.

Economic, Monetary, and Political Union: Will the Maastricht Treaty Work?

In theory, the new developments triggered by the Maastricht Treaty should dwarf the Single Market process. In a way, the creation of a Single Market was nothing more than completing what the E.C. had embarked upon right from the beginning, i.e., free trade among member states. This was not a small task, but it was little compared to what the establishment of a full Economic, Monetary and Political Union will require. And it appears that this is exactly what many people in Europe sense, and why they feel somewhat uneasy, to say the least, about this new effort. Contrary to the basically enthusiastic excitement about the Single Market, there are many doubts, in the general public, about the Maastricht Treaty, and to some extent there is a split between the political class (which signed the Maastricht Treaty), and the general public's feelings about it.[3] This has become rather obvious in the process of ratification. Where the Treaty could be ratified by parliaments (i.e., by politicians), ratification went relatively smoothly, except in the United Kingdom. Where the general public had the say in a referendum, ratification was achieved, after much struggling, by only a minute majority, as in France and, only at second attempt, in Denmark.

What is the problem with the Maastricht Treaty? To my mind, the Maastricht Treaty is likely to provide yet another proof of some of the ten hypotheses I have suggested in the previous section, but this time the more problematic elements of these hypotheses may prevail. Again I cannot deal with the many details but shall constrain myself to a few comments, some of which will be deliberately one-sided.

Though the Maastricht Treaty on a European Union is, also, supposed to create a political union, its provisions regarding Union citizenship, changes in legislative procedures, and a Common Foreign and Defense Policy are relatively weak and/or vague. The more fundamental and important issues of a true political union, such as its constitutional nature (a central European state, a European Federation, or a union of nation states?) and the possible need for new supranational institutions and what their powers should be, are not even touched in the Treaty. In other words, the main elements of the Maastricht Treaty are those relating to the Economic and Monetary Union, i.e., the economic provisions. Among those economic provisions, the establishment of a Monetary Union is by far the most significant and important element, as far as departures from the current state of affairs in the Community are concerned. Provisions for common economic policies in other areas are rather limited. In short, to a large extent the Maastricht Treaty boils down to an agreement to establish a Monetary Union.

Yet the driving forces behind this largely economic/monetary treaty are, again, political concerns. Without too much exaggeration, and with due respect for other member countries' role in the Maastricht process, it can probably be said that the Treaty to a large extent reflects France's and Germany's (or, probably more exactly, President Mitterand's and Chancellor Kohl's) desire to move ahead towards more intensive political cohesion in Europe, and towards a stronger position of Europe in world affairs.[4] There is again something like the "bicycle theory" behind the Maastricht Treaty, plus the theory that a common currency will promote policy coordination in other areas and that it will generally create a common political attitude in Europe. Thus it is my impression that an economic device, i.e., the EMU, is again used for political purposes.

In the case of the Single Market, this utilization of economic measures for political objectives may have worked to some extent. I doubt whether it will do so in the case of the EMU. There is much less appreciation in Europe's general public that a common currency[5] is really so important and beneficial than there was the feeling that more open competition is a good thing to have. Much more so than in the case of the Single Market, the EMU will affect all private individuals in Europe, because it will alter the type of money they have in their purses. Indeed, people understand or feel that the EMU is a much more fundamental departure from the past than the Single Market. Besides the various hopes attached to the EMU, there are therefore also deep-rooted anxieties in peoples' minds when it comes to considering the pros and cons of an EMU. It is for that reason that the Monetary Union has not found the same type of general political support as the Single Market. As a consequence, it is not at all clear that the Maastricht Treaty will have the positive political effects in Europe (and elsewhere) that its creators hoped for. Indeed, it may well turn out that the Maastricht Treaty backfires in these political terms. To an extent this has already happened, as evidenced by the difficult process of getting it ratified in some member countries and the resulting depressed European mood, reflected in the diagnosis of a "new Eurosclerosis."

Moreover, the uneasy feeling of the general public about the Monetary Union is probably (implicitly) based on sound economics. Free trade is undoubtedly good economics, and once you have it, free trade usually works. On the other hand, it is far less clear that a common currency for the E.C. is good economics and that the Monetary Union will really work.

The economic benefits resulting from a Monetary Union can come in various forms. As in the case of the Single Market, the E.C. Commission has made sure that a quantitative estimate of these benefits is produced and published. According to this estimate (E.C. Commission, 1990; Emerson and Huhne, 1991) the benefits of creating an EMU may be as high as a one-time gain of 10 percent of GNP in the E.C., plus possibly a lasting increase in the rate of economic growth in the Union. A gain of this magnitude would be very high, indeed, and it could justify all sorts of costs. However, there are reasons to doubt whether the Commission estimate is really plausible (Minford, 1993). The largest part of the gain estimated in that study comes from the assumed reduction in overall uncertainty for investors in the E.C., and from the resulting increase in the productivity of capital. Whether the EMU will indeed reduce the risk premium on capital so much is, however, a matter for conjecture. The more immediate and certain benefits of a common currency, on the other hand, come in the form of an elimination of the transaction costs related to the exchange of currencies and measures dealing with currency uncertainty. According to the Commission estimate, these direct benefits are no more than 0.4 percent of Community GNP, and even that may be on the high side.

Compared with such more moderate economic benefits, the potential costs of establishing an EMU in the near future may be relatively high. Four types of costs appear to me to require particular attention.

First, it is not clear whether an EMU will achieve a sufficient degree of price stability in the Union. True, the institutional provisions for the

European Central Bank foreseen in the Maastricht Treaty, in particular regarding independence of the members of its Council and prohibition of providing credit to the E.C. and member states, appear to provide an optimal basis for a tight monetary policy. Indeed, on paper they are even better than the sometimes highly praised institutional foundations of the German Bundesbank (Sachverständigenrat, 1992). However, whether they will guarantee a policy geared to price stability in practice is not really certain. After all, President Mitterand is already on record as having said that the European Central Bank would merely implement European Council decisions. More fundamentally, if E.C. member countries really wanted more price stability, they could well have it individually, by pursuing appropriate policies at the national level. The theory that an EMU would create more price stability must logically be based on the assumption that member states of the Union can achieve more jointly than what they manage to do individually. To a large extent, it appears, this assumption is based on the hope that in an EMU the prior role of the Deutschmark as an anchor currency is converted into stability for the common currency. If this assumption were justified, then it would be difficult to understand why the Bundesbank and German monetary policy, in particular the current high interest rates in Germany, are so strongly criticized in other member states (Jochimsen, 1993).

Second, monetary policy needs to be consistent with fiscal policy. However, under the Maastricht Treaty, national member states of the Union retain authority over their fiscal policies. There are provisions (in Article 104c) that call for member states to avoid excessive budget deficits, and, if a member state government does not honor these provisions, the Council of Ministers can impose various types of pressure on that member state and can even fine it. However, it is difficult to believe that these fiscal disciplines will work. Fundamentally, true fiscal harmonization would require a real political union. As noted above, the Maastricht Treaty is far from establishing a political union with common democratic institutions having full supranational powers, and the time is probably not really ripe for having such a full political union in Europe. However, with anything less than that, it will always remain difficult to enforce international sanctions on individual nations, and the history of international institutions provides ample evidence of the difficulty to establish functioning sanction mechanisms. The temptation for individual member states of the EMU will be strong to use fiscal policies (and in practice this means deficit spending) freely as the only remaining instrument of national economic policy. In effect this would undermine monetary policies of the European Central Bank. It would also force transfers from other member states, either through direct budgetary mechanisms (such as the E.C. cohesion fund or other structural funds) or through the market by contributing to higher overall inflation in the whole Union.

Third, larger transfers across member states may also result from the fact that a Monetary Union eliminates exchange rate changes as a mechanism for macroeconomic adjustments. For example, if wages in a given member state increase more than in line with productivity gains, that member state can now regain its international competitiveness through devaluing its currency. In a Monetary Union, that adjustment mechanism no longer exists, and rising unemployment in the member state concerned will be the likely consequence. With some degree of real wage inflexibility and limited labor mobility, the rise in unemployment may be quasi-permanent. The deteriorating economic performance of that member country will then call for more transfers from other member states, to be channeled conveniently through the Union's various structural funds. An increase in the volume of these funds is a deliberate and accepted element of future E.C. policies. However, large transfers among member states require a degree of solidarity in the better-off member states, which probably does not yet exist in Europe (Jochimsen, 1993).

Fourth, with rapid structural changes in Europe and with the imminent enlargement of the Community and the impact it will have on intra-Community trade flows, there may be the need for significant adjustments in real exchange rates. Of course, a common currency does not exclude changes of real exchange rates, through adjustments in prices of nontradables, among participating countries. However, the possibility of adjusting nominal exchange rates would make the necessary real exchange rate changes much easier. In other words, enlargement of the Community and establishment of an EMU, though pursued simultaneously, may not fit very well together. I shall come back to this point below.

There is one aspect that could potentially reduce the significance of at least the first two of these four categories of costs. The Maastricht Treaty specifies convergence criteria to be met by those member states that are allowed into the Monetary Union. These criteria relate to the convergence of inflation and interest rates among member states, to stability of exchange rates and to the size of budget deficits and public debts. In 1992, only France and Luxembourg met all criteria (Sachverständigenrat, 1992). Even Germany has not met the budget deficit criterion since 1991 (essentially because of large public spending related to German unification). Depending on how one looks at it, the existence of these convergence criteria, and the fact that so few member states meet them, can justify fears or hopes.

Fears are justified if one assumes that the convergence criteria will eventually be weakened, or disregarded, when it comes to the actual decision on which member states can join the Monetary Union. If that happens, the EMU may not really become a stable union, and the problem of inconsistency between (joint) monetary and (national) fiscal policies may become very real. The probability of that outcome is not small. It appears rather unlikely that more than very few member countries will meet the convergence criteria even by 1997, i.e., at the time when the Maastricht Treaty calls for the final check on who can join the Monetary Union to be automatically established in 1999. In particular, with current convergence criteria for budget deficits and public debt, one would have to make rather heroic assumptions on economic growth and public spending restraint for the next years to come if one wanted to assume that countries such as Italy and Belgium, not to speak of Spain and Portugal, will manage to meet these criteria by 1997 (Sachverständigenrat, 1992). It is not unlikely that the Council of Ministers will find it politically impossible to stick to the criteria as currently defined if it turns out that only a small minority of member states can join the Monetary Union and that important founding members of the Community (such as Italy and Belgium) would remain excluded.[6] Indeed, the Belgian Minister of Finance has already suggested that the convergence criterion on budget deficits should be revised.

Hopes are justified if one assumes that the convergence criteria as defined now are strictly adhered to, or even strengthened. Indeed, strengthening them would appear advisable in the sense that the inflation criterion is now defined only in relative terms, i.e., in terms of the difference among inflation rates across member states, rather than in terms of a given absolute maximum rate of inflation. Moreover, convergence should be defined over a number of years, rather than only in the last year before the decision on entering into the EMU is taken. If the convergence criteria are indeed not weakened, or even strengthened, this would have two types of positive effects.

First, these criteria would continue to have a healthy impact on economic policy making in E.C. member states for the years to come. Indeed, the mere existence of these criteria, even if the Monetary Union were not to come soon, provides a strong incentive for policy makers to improve on their performance, because they begin to be judged by the general public on how well they do relative to these criteria. It appears that this has already had a healthy effect on economic policies in some member countries.

Second, strict adherence to the existing (or strengthened) criteria may eventually postpone the date at which the Monetary Union becomes reality. Postponement would provide more time for economic policies and developments in E.C. member states to converge through active policymaking and the corresponding behavior of private economic agents, rather than forcing (some degree of) convergence on EMU economies through the artificial permanent fixing of exchange rates. If a number of countries have indeed achieved a track record of parallel economic developments over a number of years, then there may be some point in arguing that they are unlikely to need the exchange rate mechanism for making economic adjustments among each other. An EMU among such countries could then naturally come as a result of past economic developments. However, using the EMU to force convergence is a much less convincing proposition.

Whatever the future of the Maastricht Treaty may be, it has already contributed significantly to strengthening and making more acceptable one particular principle of European integration that was long debated and often held in disdain. It is the principle of "variable geometry," which allows different member states to proceed with different speeds and intensities towards European integration. The Maastricht Treaty explicitly foresees that some member states may join EMU later than others.[7] Moreover, in the Protocols attached to the Treaty, Denmark and the United Kingdom have been granted special status, and following the first negative referendum in Denmark even more special conditions for Denmark have been accepted by the European Council during its December 1992 session in Edinburgh. As a result there is now the clear recognition that there will be two, or even more, tiers of member countries when it (ever) comes to establishing an EMU. So far, not much political noise has been made about this principle of variable geometry, and it still remains to be seen how it will be applied in practice when it comes to important issues. However, it would not be surprising, and in my personal view it would not be bad, if that principle were more widely used in the future of European integration. Obviously the relevance of that principle is growing as the Community grows, through accession of more and more countries in Europe.

Enlargement of the Community

Given all the uncertainties arising out of the Maastricht Treaty, it is reassuring that there is at least one certainty about the future structure of the European Community—the Community will continue to grow. For the time being, eight new countries have officially applied for membership (Austria, Cyprus, Finland, Malta, Norway, Sweden, Switzerland, and Turkey). With four of the EFTA countries among them (Austria, Finland, Norway, and Sweden), the Community is now actively negotiating the conditions for accession.[8] The countries of Central Europe are already on the doorstep. With five of them (Bulgaria, [former] Czechoslovakia, Hungary, Poland, and Romania), the E.C. has already signed Association Agreements (still awaiting ratification) that explicitly recognize their objective to join the Community. If all of these 13 countries become members of the Community, membership more than doubles from the current 12 to 25 member states.

But even more countries may come. Two more EFTA countries (Iceland and Liechtenstein), already included in the EEA (European Economic Area), may at some stage want to apply for membership. The three Baltic republics, with whom the E.C. has so far "only" concluded Trade and Cooperation Agreements, are likely to get Association ("Europe") Agreements in the not too distant future, preparing them for later membership. The countries emerging from the former Yugoslavia will certainly, when peace has finally been achieved, be candidates for closer relationships with the E.C. It would then be only natural to include Albania, which already has a Trade and Cooperation Agreement with the E.C., in the network of European integration.

What is the timetable for enlargement of the Community? Originally, the plan was not to begin accession negotiations before the Maastricht Treaty was ratified and the Community had decided on its future budget regime and structural policies (the "Delors II" package). However, after the negative outcome of the first Danish referendum this plan was silently dropped, and negotiations with the four EFTA countries have now been pursued since early 1993. Officially, the Commission still maintains that these negotiations should be finished before the end of 1993, such that these countries could accede to the Community in 1995. It appears that this timetable is overly ambitious. In practical terms, accession negotiations to a large extent mean going through the whole body of existing legislation in the Community (the *"acquis communautaire"*) with the applicant countries, to see where they may have difficulties adopting E.C. legislation right from the start, such that temporary derogations may be necessary. Because of the enormous amount of existing E.C. legislation, this is a rather time-consuming process.[9] Moreover, where difficulties arise, political solutions have to be found, both in negotiations with the E.C. Council of Ministers and in the applicant countries, and this process, too, takes time. In other words, it appears unlikely that negotiations with the four EFTA countries will be over before the end of 1993. However, their accession in 1996 may well be feasible. For institutional and political reasons, it appears likely that all acceding EFTA countries will join the E.C. on the same date.

Accession of the four EFTA countries currently negotiating with the E.C. is likely to be a relatively smooth process. In terms of their overall economic situation, they fit well into the spectrum of current E.C. members. Indeed, in terms of the EMU convergence criteria set in the Maastricht Treaty, these countries now perform better than most current member states of the Community (Sachverständigenrat, 1992). Negotiations on their free trade in industrial products with the E.C. have already been successfully concluded in the framework of the EEA. For some of the EFTA countries, however, problems remain in agriculture. This is least the case for Sweden, which has recently reformed its agricultural policy fundamentally, such that Swedish prices for many agricultural products are now indeed below their current level in the E.C.[10] Austria will have to achieve downward adjustment of some of its farm product prices and will need to seek agreement on how to make its milk quotas, direct payments, regional subsidies and a couple of other special measures consistent with E.C. rules. However, no insurmountable problems are envisaged.

More significant problems are faced by Finland, whose support prices are significantly above the E.C. level and where a number of special support policies do not fit easily with the E.C. regime. However, the government of Finland is determined to conclude the accession negotiations successfully, and by making the former President of its farmers' union the Foreign Minister it has indicated that it seeks to use all possible strategic and tactical means in order to achieve that success. Norway is the most problematic case, and membership may eventually not be achieved (in this round of negotiations). Agriculture is an important factor in the Norwegian equation. Norway's policy of regionally differentiated agricultural price support, with rather high prices in the more remote northern regions, does not at all fit with the E.C. regime, and it appears that Norway is not prepared to give up on its current system, not even by switching from price support to (regionally differentiated) direct payments. However, even if some type of "technical" solution to that problem could be found in the current talks between Norwegian and E.C. negotiators (which for the time being does not appear very likely), it is far from certain that Norway would indeed enter the E.C. In opinion polls a large majority of the Norwegian population speaks against E.C. membership, and the referendum that will finally need to be held in Norway may, therefore, decide against joining the Community. In other words, of the four EFTA countries currently negotiating access, only three may actually join the E.C. in this round of enlargement.

The prospects and a timetable for accession by the countries in Central Europe are more difficult to assess. In Central Europe, membership of the E.C. is seen as one of the most important aims to be pursued in the years to come. These countries regard themselves, quite rightly, as integral parts of Europe, in geographical, cultural, historical, and political terms. Indeed, for long periods in the history of Europe, the region that we are now again calling Central Europe was in fact the center of Europe, not only in a geographical but also in a cultural and political sense. Most people in Central Europe regard their separation from the West under Soviet rule after the second World War as an aberration of history that should never have happened. For them, having overthrown the communist regime does not only mean to have freed themselves from a totalitarian political system and a centrally planned economic mess but also to have returned to Europe, where they belonged in the first place.

It is difficult to exaggerate the intensity of the desire to be a fully accepted part of a united Europe which is now prevalent in Central Europe. Everybody dreams and speaks about this theme. As the European Community is now seen as the epitome of Europe, E.C. membership is regarded as the symbol of having returned to Europe. In a way, it seems, many people in Central Europe would regard the process of political and economic transformation on which they have embarked in 1989 as incomplete if it did not eventually lead to membership of the E.C. And all this is not just vague feeling and political rhetoric; it is reflected in many practical day-to-day activities. In several policy areas, the countries of Central Europe are beginning to emulate E.C. policies. In agriculture, for example, there is now a tendency to adopt what are called "CAP-like" policies. Analyses are being made, in government and academia, of what E.C. membership would mean to various economic sectors. There is an endless stream of conferences and papers on various implications of E.C. membership. In other words, it often appears that accession to the E.C. is seen as an acute and immediate prospect, in a way as the light at the end of the dark tunnel through which these countries now go in their difficult transformation process.

However, this does not mean that the E.C. is already prepared to accept accession of the countries in Central Europe in the near future. Indeed, there is not yet even anything like an agreed perspective on the process that may one day lead to accession. The four Visegrad countries (Czech Republic, Slovak Republic, Poland, and Hungary) are pressing the E.C. strongly to agree soon to a definite timetable. The Czech government has said its aim is to join the E.C. by 1998, independently of what happens to the other Visegrad countries (*East Europe Agriculture and Food*, 1993). The Polish government wants to commence official talks on E.C. membership in 1996, with a view to full accession in the year 2000 (*East Europe Agriculture and Food*, 1993).

The E.C. Commission proposed, in a Communication to the Council, that the European Council should, at its meeting in Copenhagen on June 21-22, 1993, "confirm, in a clear political message, its commitment to membership of the Union for Europe agreements signatories when they are able to satisfy the conditions required. The message would further reflect the need for political decisions at the appropriate time which take into account the particular situation of each applicant ..." (E.C. Commission, 1993). Though the European Council may well decide, at its

Copenhagen meeting, to send a message of that general nature to Central Europe, it appears unlikely that this message will provide any specific timetable.[11] It may, however, be the case that formal accession negotiations with the Visegrad countries will be initiated some time after accession of the EFTA countries, say in 1997 or 1998. These negotiations may turn out to be even more complicated than any earlier negotiations with accession candidates, and for that reason, but also because the Community may want to delay the date of entry, actual full membership of any Visegrad country may not occur before the turn of the century. Membership of other countries in Central Europe may, then, not be achieved before well into the 21st century.

However, the Community may create, for the countries in Central Europe, a new type of institutional status vis-à-vis the E.C., halfway between association and full membership. Pursuing further its corresponding suggestion to the European Council in Edinburgh (December 1992), in its recent Communication to the Council (E.C. Commission, 1993), the Commission has suggested to establish a European Political Area (EPA) "through which the countries of Central Europe would participate progressively in the political work of the European Union." The EPA would essentially have the form of regular joint meetings of the European Council, the E.C. Council of Ministers and its subordinate bodies with corresponding representatives from the associated countries in Central Europe. These joint meetings would discuss issues of common interest and thereby enhance the political dialogue between the Community and Central Europe. "In addition, consultations should be held between diplomatic missions in third countries and in advance of important meetings of international organizations." Also, the Commission suggests special extended sessions be held of the European Council and the Council of Ministers "of a consultative nature on specific predetermined issues of common European interest,"[12] with the participation of representatives of partner countries. Finally, the Commission suggests cooperation in the fields of justice and home affairs (e.g., immigration and drugs).[13]

While the countries in Central Europe may find an EPA better than nothing, they are unlikely to be enthusiastic about it. After all, an EPA would largely remain a cosmetic exercise, giving, in the Commission's word, the countries of Central Europe "a greater sense of participating in the process of integration" and fulfilling "their aspirations of being involved in regular consultations on matters concerning the Europe Agreements and beyond," while (in my words) keeping them at arm's length as far as actual membership is concerned. The countries of Central Europe will want more, and anything short of a definite timetable for negotiations on their accession to the E.C. will not really satisfy them. However, it appears unlikely that they will get that very soon.

Given the large gap between Western Europe on the one hand and Central Europe on the other, in economic terms but also in many other dimensions, and considering the still rather fluent nature of the transformation process in Central Europe, it is not exactly easy to imagine that these countries could soon become full members of the Community, with all rights and obligations. However, personally I think that the E.C. has no choice but to work very rapidly towards their integration into the Community. Indeed, I am convinced that broadening the Community to the East is now much more important than deepening integration among existing members, through mechanisms such as those envisaged in the Maastricht Treaty. The world has just passed a historical junction, of a nature that does not happen more often than a couple of times in a century. The wall has come down in Europe, and there is now the chance of making good what has gone so badly wrong in earlier parts of this century. West Europeans, who have lived so well in the last four decades or so, now have the obligation to share their wealth and their institutions with their neighbors in the East who have suffered all that time under a cruel regime. Moreover, and much more selfishly, Western Europe must make sure that political and economic stability among its eastern neighbors is enhanced if it wants to continue living a prosperous and safe life.

In a situation such as this, strenuous efforts to push forward with more and more sophisticated (and anyhow not fully convincing) forms of integration among the existing members of the Community appear to me much less advisable than preparing actively for membership of the countries in Central Europe. Moreover, contrary to what the Commission and some politicians say, I feel that the two approaches of deepening and of broadening integration in Europe are not mutually reinforcing, but that the process of deepening integration among existing members tends to make accession by new members, in particular those from Central Europe, more difficult. At the institutional level, the difficulties of coping with accession to the E.C. will be greater the more sophisticated the institutional framework of the E.C. In economic terms, a European Union with (some members having joined) a Monetary Union will appear even more out of reach for Central Europe. Moreover, accession by countries from Central Europe would, and should, result in significant economic adjustments among existing E.C. member countries, and this might well require real exchange rate changes that go beyond those achievable with fixed nominal exchange rates (see above). Would it, then, not be better to delay the creation of a Monetary Union and to agree that January 1, 1999, rather than being the latest date for entering into the EMU, is the date on which the Visegrad countries are expected to join the Community?

The Future of the Common Agricultural Policy

How will the fundamental changes that the Community now faces, both because of its internal developments and as a result of enlargement, affect the Common Agricultural Policy (CAP)? Again this is a matter for speculation, and I can only offer my personal views. In a way these views may be disappointing—because I do not expect that the CAP will change a lot in response to the overall changes going on in the Community.

After all, the Maastricht Treaty does not (directly) affect any of the fundamental principles on which the CAP is based, nor the mechanisms through which it is pursued. Of course, introduction of a common currency (among some member countries) would eliminate the need for the Green Money system (among those countries). This may lead to a somewhat lower level of price support under the CAP. However, E.C. agricultural policy makers may now have lost most of their earlier money illusion, and elimination of Green Money may therefore not make much of an impact on the actual level of price support in the Community. Another effect that the Maastricht Treaty may have on the CAP could come through the budget. As a result of the Maastricht Treaty, the Community will increase spending on structural measures, including spending under the new Cohesion Fund. As a result, less money could be available for the CAP. However, in its decision on the Delors II financial package during the Edinburgh meeting, the European Council has determined that the "budget guideline" for the CAP, introduced in 1988, will not be changed, at least for the time being.

Enlargement of the Community, first to include EFTA countries, and later possibly countries from Central Europe, is also unlikely to affect the CAP very fundamentally. The newcomers will have to accept the *acquis communautaire* of the CAP, rather than bringing agricultural policy changes to the Community. Individually, and even on aggregate, the accession candidates are small relative to the Community of twelve as far as their net trade position in agriculture is concerned. The Community's market balance in agriculture will, therefore, not change significantly when they accede. Gradual adjustment of their agricultural policies to the CAP in the acceding countries may, however, somewhat change that picture. As Austria and Finland have to bring down their levels of price support, their levels of self-sufficiency may decline. On the other hand, once Central Europe joins the Community, its farm support is likely to go up, and that would have an expansionary effect on agricultural production in the countries concerned. On aggregate these market changes in Central Europe may be more significant than those in the EFTA countries, and as a result, the overall level of self-sufficiency in an enlarged Community may increase somewhat. However, relative to the market balance in the existing E.C. these changes may be small.

Other effects that overall change and growth of the Community may have on the CAP may be of a more subtle and indirect nature. Three factors of this nature are treatment of agricultural policies as a more "normal" activity in the E.C.; a growing weight of the E.C. Commission in the internal power balance of the Community; and the move towards a "variable geometry."

In the past, the CAP was the epitome of a common policy in the E.C. By far the largest share of the E.C. budget was spent on agricultural policies; a predominant part of day-to-day activities in the Commission was related to agriculture; a far more than proportional share of Commission staff was engaged in agricultural matters; a large number of Council meetings was held among ministers of agriculture; the preparation of these agricultural Councils took a large part of the member country representatives in Brussels; at the European Council meetings, Heads of State and Government often had to deal with agricultural issues that farm ministers were unable to settle among themselves. In other words, the Community was, to a significant extent, an agricultural community.

With the ongoing political and economic changes in the E.C., and with E.C. enlargement, it appears that other issues are becoming increasingly important, such that agricultural policies fall back to where they belong, i.e., to being just one of the many issues a modern government has to deal with. More attention will, in future, be required by issues of overall economic and monetary policy, by the political implications of enlargement (in particular to include countries in Central Europe), and by the implications that these wider developments have. Agricultural policy would, then, be a more "normal" activity of the Community, rather than being one of the most important things the E.C. is dealing with. This development may have a similar effect, such as the likely increase in the political weight of the Commission.

In the past decade or so, the political weight of the Commission appears to have increased considerably in the power balance among Community institutions, in particular relative to that of the Council of Ministers. Among the many reasons, the two quantifiable ones are the growing complexity of E.C. legislation and policies, which is difficult to cope with from anywhere else than Brussels; and the increasing number of E.C. member states which has tended to weaken each individual country's power and, by implication, the aggregate power of all member states vis-à-vis the central institution, i.e., the Commission (Meester and van der Zee, 1993). Among the qualitative factors in the changing power balance, the most important one is probably the fact that the Commission has skillfully played the role of promoting most actively the idea of a united Europe. The invention and creation of the Single Market is the most outstanding example. Another factor is the increasing importance of international interdependence, and the growing weight of the Community in international economic relations. It is effectively the Commission that represents the Community at the international level, and this also provides it with more weight within the Community. Two examples are the GATT negotiations, where the Commission's role is much stronger than that of the member states (except for a possible veto by France), and negotiations with Central Europe where the Commission has very much adopted a leading role.

With ever-growing complexity of Community policies under the Maastricht Treaty, and with expanding membership of the Community, the Commission is likely to gain further weight. The Commission is not at all immune from political influences, and individual Commissioners may well act as representatives of interests in their home countries (Moyer and Josling, 1990). However, compared with Ministers in the Council, the Commission is more independent and less susceptible to political lobbying. Hence it can, at least potentially, act more on the basis of rational economic considerations than most governments of individual member states would tend to do.

For the future of the CAP, both the treatment of agricultural policy as a more "normal" activity and a growing weight of the Commission may mean that the process of reform will continue. The recent MacSharry reform was already an interesting example of how powerful the Commission now is in the CAP, and probably also of how the importance of agricultural policies is diminishing in the E.C. This reform was, indeed, a significant departure from past policies. When the Commission first tabled its proposals, most member states were strongly opposed. However, in the end the Commission essentially won the game, with only minor modifications to its original proposals. One reason probably was the fact that in the E.C. this reform was debated in parallel with the ongoing GATT negotiations and that most governments began to understand that for the E.C. there are more important things than to maintain traditional forms of agricultural support. The Commission will want to continue this process of reforming the CAP. The sugar regime, which was not included in the MacSharry reform, is the next candidate. Reform endeavors in the milk and beef sector may be strengthened. Other products not so far included in the reform, such as olive oil, wine, fruits, and vegetables, may come further down the line.

The third potentially important factor, the variable geometry of the Community, will mean that in future there may be more differentiation among member countries, under the roof of common policies. The Maastricht Treaty explicitly provides for variable geometry in the area of monetary policy, by suggesting that only a subset of member countries may join the Monetary Union. The principle of subsidiarity, also enshrined in the Maastricht Treaty, is another dimension of variable geometry. Expansion of the Community to include more member countries will, also, enhance the tendency to provide more room for nationally differentiated approaches, as long as fundamental Community principles, such as free trade among member states, are not violated.

In agricultural policy terms, variable geometry may mean that less emphasis is placed on price support at the Community level and more scope is left for national policies, such as direct payments and regional as well as structural measures. One approach that would fit well into that picture would be to make more determined progress towards decoupling. In particular, compensation payments under the MacSharry reform, which now come in the form of acreage and headage payments, could one day be completely decoupled. If that is achieved, member countries could be left to make nationally differentiated payments, possibly on top of some lower jointly financed Community payment. An approach like that would, also, make it easier to deal with some of the problems originating from the different agricultural policies which the accession candidates have had in the past. Moreover, full decoupling of compensation payments from current acreages and herd sizes would greatly reduce the enormous administrative efforts that the Community, and E.C. farmers, now have to make in order to cope with the new MacSharry payments.

However, this latter comment takes us back to where this discussion on the future of the CAP started. In spite of all the fundamental changes that the Community faces in the years to come, it is not clear that the CAP will be very much affected by these changes. The more important factors for the future of the CAP will probably remain those which are internal to agricultural policy, i.e., the changing market balance, the budget implications of the policy, and the problems of implementing a highly interventionist set of policy measures. In addition, and probably more important than any other single factor, a successful conclusion of the Uruguay Round negotiations would have a significant impact on what the CAP can, and cannot, do in the future. A GATT deal on agriculture would in fact speed up a development that begins to be conceivable in Europe, also because of the domestic implications of future political and economic developments in the Community—the gradual demise of a century of agricultural protectionism.

Implications for North-Atlantic Agricultural Trade Relations

If all this is true, then the implications that the changing political picture in the E.C. and growth of the Community will have for North-Atlantic agricultural trade relations may be rather limited, at least on aggregate. If my assumption is valid that there may be an increasing tendency to go for decoupling in the CAP, that the level of price support may be further reduced, and that CAP reform will be extended to other commodity sectors, then there is the chance that surplus production in the E.C. will diminish and more room may be created for imports. On the other hand, expansion of the Community to the East may, when it happens, result in an expansion of agricultural production in Central Europe. Both factors taken together may mean little overall change in Europe's market balance and, hence, little aggregate change in agricultural trade across the North Atlantic. However, this does not mean that there will not be changes in individual trade flows, and hence new types of difficulties among the United States and the E.C.

In the E.C., an increasing share of total agricultural and food trade has been trade among the member states. While in 1973 less than 40 percent of total agricultural and food imports was intra-trade, the share of intra-trade in total agricultural and food imports had grown to more than 60 percent by 1990 (see Figure 7.1). In part the fact that intra-Community agricultural and food trade has grown more rapidly than trade with third countries is due to the successive enlargements of the Community. However, it is interesting to note that even in periods when the size of the Community did not change, the share of intra-trade in total trade continued to grow.

FIGURE 7.1 Share of Intra-trade in E.C. Agricultural and Food Imports.

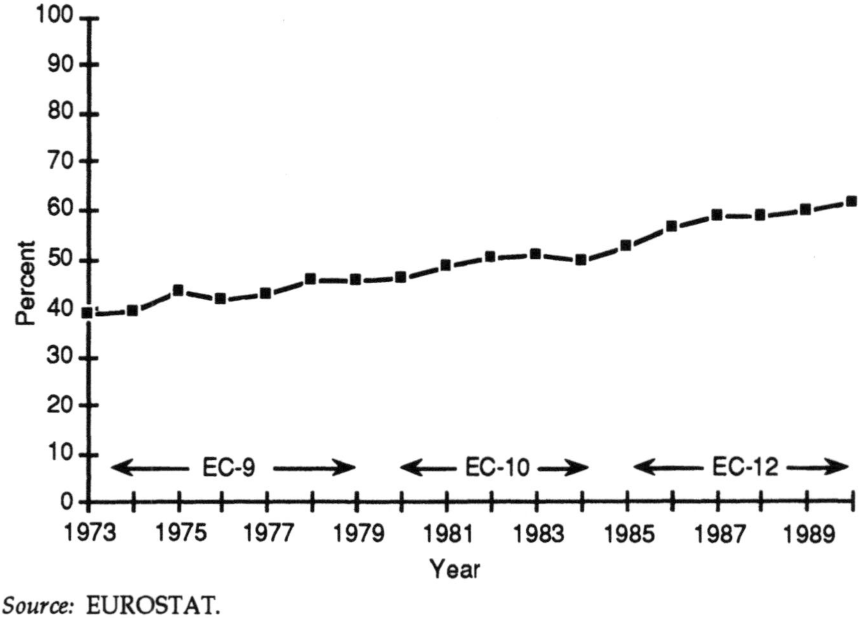

Source: EUROSTAT.

One could hypothesize that the rapidly growing importance of intra-E.C. trade in food and agriculture is mainly a result of the CAP and the high protection it provides to E.C. markets vis-à-vis the rest of the world. However, strong relative expansion of intra-trade in the E.C. is not limited to agriculture and food. For all merchandise trade on aggregate there is the same tendency towards more and more intra-E.C. trade. Indeed, the share of intra-trade in total merchandise trade is nearly the same (close to 60 percent) as in agricultural and food trade of the Community.

Clearly one would expect neighboring countries to have more trade with each other than countries located in different parts of the world. However, on a worldwide scale the relative growth of intra-trade has been a rather specific development in the European Community. On the American continent (North America, Central America and South America), intra-trade (all merchandise goods) among the countries of that continent has, during the 1980s, not grown much more than trade with other regions of the world (see Figure 7.2). Trade within the region of South and East Asia, on the other hand, has even grown less than trade of that region with other parts of the world. Again, the growth of total merchandise intra-trade in the Community is unlikely to be the result of protectionist policies in the E.C. After all, total E.C. trade with third countries has not grown less than total trade of the American continent with other parts of the world,

FIGURE 7.2 Growth of GDP, Extra-trade, and Intra-trade in Blocs, 1980-89.

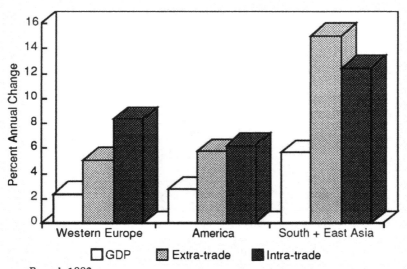

Source: Brand, 1992.

relative to GDP growth in the two regions (Figure 7.2). Hence, growth of intra-E.C. trade may be due more to trade expansion than to trade diversion.

The relative growth of intra-E.C. trade has, then, probably to do with intensifying integration among the member states. To some extent, this closer and closer integration may have resulted in increasing specialization among E.C. countries, and some part of the growing intra-E.C. trade may reflect that tendency. However, in agriculture and food (and probably also in other sectors) this appears not to have been the major factor. Growth rates of production of individual products have not differed very much among E.C. member countries, and therefore specialization does not appear to have increased very much. A more important factor appears to have been the rapidly growing intra-industrial trade in food. Indeed, it appears that there is a positive correlation between the degree of processing on the one hand and the share of intra-trade in total trade on the other hand. Moreover, intra-E.C. trade in processed foods has grown more rapidly than intra-E.C. trade in agricultural raw materials, such that the share of processed products in intra-E.C. agricultural trade has increased considerably (see Figure 7.3).

FIGURE 7.3 Share of Processed Products in E.C. Agricultural Trade.

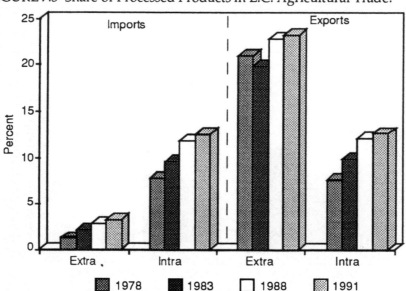

Source: EUROSTAT. *Note:* Non-annex II products.

In other words, with more and more integration in Europe, the importance of trade in processed foods is growing rapidly. The resulting competitive pressure should strengthen the efficiency and sophistication of Europe's food industry. Moreover, as Europe expands through the accession of new member states, there is a growing internal market for the food industry, providing for opportunities to exploit economies of size. As a result, the international competitiveness of Europe's food industry should grow even more. The share of processed products in extra-E.C. agricultural exports is already significantly higher than it is in extra-E.C. imports (Figure 7.3). In future the E.C. may become an even larger net exporter of processed food, independent of what happens to raw material surpluses.

For North-Atlantic trade in the food and agricultural sector this may mean that new types of conflicts can arise. Traditionally, conflicts between the United States and Europe in that sector had mainly to do with agricultural trade and market policies and with trade in agricultural raw materials. If my hypotheses are valid, the ongoing changes in Europe are unlikely to result in an intensification of these conflicts. However, an increasingly competitive European food industry may be looking for wider markets in other parts of the world. With lower levels of price support for agriculture in Europe after reform of the CAP, exports of Europe's food industry may be less dependent on subsidization of the raw material content. Hence competition among U.S. and European food industries can no longer, in the future, be said to be distorted by government policies to the same extent as in the past. The increasing share of the world market for high-value agricultural products that E.C. suppliers have gained in the past (Elleson, 1990) may increase even further in future, based purely on the growing competitive strength of Europe's food industry.

The commercial conflicts that could potentially arise out of that development would not have much to do with traditional fights among agricultural policy makers. They would be more similar to some of the problems Europeans and Americans have with the strong export performance of industry in Japan and East Asia.

Notes

1. For example, some member states still implement national import quotas for some "sensitive" products, as originally regulated under Article 115 of the Treaty of Rome. With the elimination of border controls, implementation of these national quotas now comes in the form of sanctions imposed, by member state governments, on those companies whose imports exceed the national quotas. Other areas where more needs to be done in order to create a truly open internal market are the energy sector (Matthies, 1993), the transport sector, and public procurement.

2. The only major exception is the new EC banana market regime.

3. For the case of Germany, the divergence between deeply rooted scepticism in the general public and the rather lax way in which the Federal Parliament has ratified the Maastricht Treaty with suspicious haste has been described by Steuer (1993), who also points to the lack of democratic content in the Maastricht process. While the Treaty as such is ratified through traditional democratic processes in E.C. member states, the final decisions on entering into actual Monetary Union will be taken by the Council of Ministers, without parliaments having a word on those decisions.

4. In very much the same way, the creation of the European Monetary System in 1979 has been said to have been based largely on political motivations, and, in particular, those of President Giscard d'Estaing and Chancellor Schmidt (Spaventa, 1990).

5. According to the Maastricht Treaty (Article 109 l), on the first day of the third and final stage of the Monetary Union (i.e., on January 1, 1999 at the latest), exchange rates between participating currencies would be irrevocably frozen, and the ECU (European Currency Unit) would be introduced as an autonomous currency. However, actual replacement of (participating) national currencies by the ECU can come later.

6. The quantitative definition of the convergence criteria is contained in Protocols attached to the Maastricht Treaty. However, these Protocols can be changed, presumably without ratification by member states. Moreover, the Treaty (Article 109 j) does not say that the criteria must be fulfilled, but that the Commission must report on member states' performance in relation to these criteria before the Council decides on membership of the Monetary Union.

7. To some extent, the principle of "subsidiarity," also established (though not well defined) in the Maastricht Treaty, also points in the same direction because it would tend to allow member states to deal (in nationally different ways) with those issues that do not need to be tackled at the Community level. A discussion about the interesting implications of the subsidiarity principle is beyond the scope of this chapter.

8. After the negative outcome of the Swiss referendum on the EEA, Switzerland's application for membership is not being pursued for the time being.

9. Physically the stacks of documents to go through in these negotiations are several meters high. In agriculture alone the acquis comprises 20,000 pages.

10. Devaluation of Sweden's currency in the fall of 1992 has, also, contributed to making Swedish farm prices low relative to those in the EC.

11. Since this chapter was written, the Copenhagen European Council has, indeed, accepted these Commission proposals and decided that the associated countries of Central Europe can become members of the European Union. However, a timetable was not set.

12. Areas named by the Commission are energy, the environment, transport, telecommunications, science, and research.

13. The Copenhagen European Council has essentially accepted these Commission proposals.

References

Frankfurter Allgemeine Zeitung. 1993. "Schwierigkeiten mit der neuen Umsatzsteuer." May 12:15.

The Economist. 1993. "The Old World's New World. Survey Eastern Europe." March 13.

Baccigaluppi, R. J. 1993. "How Global Conditions Affect Food and Agriculture in the U.S. and Around the World—Overview." Paper presented at the 11th Plenary Meeting of the International Policy Council on Agriculture, Food, and Trade. Chicago, May 6-8.

Brand, D. 1992. "Konsequenzen der regionalen Blockbildung für die Welthandelsentwicklung." *IFO Schnelldienst* No. 12:10-23.

Cecchini, P., *et al.* 1988. *The European Challenge 1992: The Benefits of a Single Market.* Aldershot.

East Europe Agriculture and Food. 1993. No. 128, May, p. 3.

Elleson, R. 1990. "High-Value Products. Growing U.S. and E.C. Competition in World Markets." *USDA, ERS Staff Reports No. AGES 9022.* Washington (April).

Emerson, M., and C. Huhne. 1991. *The ECU-Report.* German translation: *Der ECU-Report. Die einheitliche europäische Währung und was sie für uns bedeutet.* Bonn, Heidelberg, Brussels.

E.C. Commission. 1990. "One Market, One Money—An Evaluation of the Potential Benefits and Costs of Forming an Economic and Monetary Union." *European Economy* 44(October).

————. 1993. "Towards a Closer Association with the Countries of Central and Eastern Europe." Communication by the Commission to the Council, in view of the meeting of the European Council in Copenhagen, 21-22 June 1993. Brussels, May 3.

EUROSTAT. *External Trade Statistics,* CD-ROM, var. issues.

Frankenberger, K.-D. 1993. "Die neue Eurosklerose." *Frankfurter Allgemeine Zeitung,* April 26:1.

GATT. 1993. *Trade Policy Review: The European Communities 1993.* Geneva.

Giersch, H. 1985. "Eurosclerosis." *Institut für Weltwirtschaft, Kieler Diskussionsbeiträge Nr. 112.* Kiel (Oktober).

Hoffman, S. 1989. "The European Community and 1992." *Foreign Affairs* 68:27-47.

Jochimsen, R. 1993. "Die Rollenverteilung in der Wirtschaftspolitik nach den Beschlüssen von Maastricht." *List Forum* 19:8-23.

Matthies, K. 1993. "Hindernisse auf dem Weg zum Energie-Binnenmarkt." *Wirtschaftsdienst* 73:143-146.

Meester, G., and F.A. van der Zee. 1993. "E.C. Decision Making, Institutions and the Common Agricultural Policy." *European Review of Agricultural Economics* 20:131-150.

Minford, P. 1993. "The Path to Monetary Union in Europe." *World Economy* 16:17-27.

Moyer, H.W., and T.E. Josling. 1990. *Agricultural Policy Reform—Politics and Process in the E.C. and the USA.* Ames, IA: Iowa State Univ. Press.

Sachverständigenrat zur Begutachtung der gesamtwirtschaftlichen Entwicklung.
    1992. "Jahresgutachten 1992/93." Deutscher Bundestag, 12. Wahlperiode,
    Drucksache 12/3774. Bonn, November 19.
Siebert, H., ed. 1990. *The Completion of the Internal Market.* Tübingen.
Spaventa, L. 1990. "The Political Economy of European Monetary Integration."
    Banca Nazionale del Lavoro Quarterly Review No. 172 (March):3-20.
Steuer, W. 1993. "Maastricht und der Deutsche Bundestag." *Wirtschaftsdienst*
    73:138-142.
Swinbank, A. 1990. "Implications of 1992 for EEC Farm and Food Policies." *Food
    Policy* No. 2, 15:102-110.

Discussion

Spiro E. Stefanou

Professor Tangermann provides an interesting and wide-ranging discussion of the issues that must be addressed as the CAP and E.C. evolve over the next two decades. One of the chapter's main themes is that European political and economic integration are not separable processes. One need only look at the evolution of the labels European economic integration have assumed over the decades. The evolution from integrating an industry to many sectors of an economy and beyond is reflected in the labels the European integration movement has taken on over the last four decades. Initially the European Coal and Steel Community, the Community evolved to the broader label of European Economic Community to the Economic Community. The political integration implications of recent and future initiatives cannot be ignored.

The economic and political arguments act on one another. The evolution of economic union places pressure on political union. A prime example addressed in the chapter is monetary union. Does a lack of currency sovereignty lead to a loss of political sovereignty? Probably not. Many nations (even some in the E.C.) have little control over their own currencies. But the illusion of currency sovereignty has important domestic political value. Professor Tangermann notes that monetary union eliminates exchange rate changes as a macroeconomic adjustment mechanism if wages tend to be inflexible and labor tends to be immobile. As a result the rise in unemployment may be inflexible. Furthermore, the harmonization of monetary policy will encourage harmonization of fiscal policy, requiring a deepening of the political harmonization.

But does economic harmonization preclude significant domestic action? Individual nations cannot fully devalue currency to attract investment and increase employment. Other incentives exist to address employment issues such as tax breaks or investment in industry-specific (or even firm-specific) infrastructure. This is frequently an issue for economic development of rural communities and provides an example of how agricultural policies are linked to employment policies via rural development initiatives. Unfortunately, many of these initiatives are of a beggar-thy-neighbor variety or may even cost local communities and nations more than they gained. Consequently, we cannot really expect the indirect approach of using economic instruments and their associated incentives to guide us to specific political objectives.

Developing policy in an evolving world is the challenge. The difficulty, in part, arises from chasing a moving target. The policy mechanism in such an environment can be endogenous (encouraged by Professor Tangermann) or one that is periodically revised where revision can be anticipated or not anticipated. The endogenous policy instrument may be politically naive. We must necessarily assume that all players (present and potential entrants) are fully aware of the endogenous policy rules. Policy discussion and formation is a very public activity. Furthermore, no one player is dominant and the institutional setting may be evolving as well. The periodical revision of policy requires us to amend an assumption that the current players are aware of the rules for policy revision; however, the principal decision makers and the perspectives they bring to the table change in the intermediate term. Consequently, future and potential entrants are not operating with full information regarding the policy revision process. Seeing revision can occur leads to the problems of time inconsistency in policy making. In addition, the evolving institutional setting suggests that we are not dealing with a stationary process.

Professor Tangermann observes that the fixed goals of unification laid out by the E.C. has set a firm long-run target that necessitates an attitude adjustment that has largely come about. Enlargement is coming on two fronts—the developed economies of former EFTA nations and others, and the emerging market economies of Central and East Europe (CEE). Professor Tangermann forcefully promotes that the E.C.'s political obligations are stronger towards the latter nations, recognizing that the political and economic stability among CEE nations is at risk. Such a policy serves both the E.C. and the CEE nations. The first, ostensible, purpose is the same for both the E.C. and CEE: to alleviate suffering and lessen the risk of turmoil. This aid also has a less benign purpose for each party: to economically and politically support the E.C. stakeholders (e.g., policymakers, producers, and marketing agents) and to control stakeholders in the East. There are trade-offs between short- and long-run political and economic stability in the CEE. Many of the short-run measures toward political stability may involve softening the adjustment process to the extent future economic stability is delayed.

In addressing the future of the CAP, Professor Tangermann poses the heretical question: Why is agriculture special? He suggests agricultural policies be treated as a more normal economic policy. Certainly, general trade issues do not provide grounds for a specific agricultural policy. Treating any sector as special can lead to complications as the E.C. enlarges. Agricultural production and pricing policies are invariably linked to rural economic development objectives. As time goes on it can be difficult to assess if the rural development component is a principal or secondary objective.

Professor Tangermann projects that there will be fewer conflicts between the United States and Europe as the E.C. focuses more on the higher value-added food processing activities. He notes that conflicts between the United States and Europe in agricultural trade and marketing policies have focused traditionally on raw materials. The extent to which conflicts will not arise will depend on the degree of protection and subsidization accorded to the food processing sector. On the one hand, it may be easier to resist directing subsidies to relatively few firms (compared to numerous farms) engaged in food manufacturing. However, the potential for lobbying activity is intensified and there are no limits to the emotional appeal of subsidies as a means of offsetting disadvantages or supporting other objectives such as promoting employment and industrial development in a deserving region.

The leadership the member nations can offer as the E.C. moves into the Twenty-first Century is not clear. The key here is mentioned by Professor Tangermann when he contrasts the role of the Commission against that of the member states. The Commission in Brussels is a large bureaucracy about as focused as one can expect of any large bureaucracy. Once charged with a task, the bureaucracy attempts to meet the challenge. The conflict arises in seeing the 12 member nations as a consistently aggregated entity. As others mention in this book, the members nations are also pursuing separate agendas. These agendas can involve promoting domestic interests by supporting domestic clients, supporting other nations' clients via vote trading with other members, or hiding abuses of E.C. policies purported by domestic interests. Consequently, the agendas and missions to be executed by the Commission are muddled by a leadership entity suffering from a multiple personality disorder.

An important conclusion merging from Professor Tangermann's chapter is that political factors force economic integration and economic pressures force political action. Alas, the complex set of issues that are poised to emerge in the next few decades suggest that economic policy is too important to be left to economists!

As Professor Tangermann opens his chapter with a glimpse of future history he intends to demonstrate that future change is inevitable and not likely predictable. I will offer an alternative future history scenario that may illustrate the inseparable nature of economic and political forces. This scenario may also be exciting, frightening, not reassuring, complete nonsense, or all of these at the same time:

> The lands of the former Soviet empire are starting to rebound. Reduced to wastelands, the causalities of deteriorating and unstable nuclear power plants and weapon stockpiles, these republics are now creating a growth industry of accepting the mounting nuclear waste from others—

and at handsome storage fees! The year is 2010. Nations like Ukraine, Russia, and Kazakhstan are finding themselves treated as lepers by the world community. Their populations fleeing for nearly the last two decades for economic and intergenerational survival, these nations found the strategy of disabling and cleaning up nuclear facilities and starting over to be prohibitively expensive. Seeing the money to be made, chronically poor nations in other parts of the world are considering development of their own nuclear dumping sites. Economists have rediscovered the remarks of Larry Summers and his followers are in high demand. The possibility now exists for a mutation to a three-handed economist.

Fortress Europe has remained intact—and has promoted the development of other fortresses in the Western Hemisphere and East Asia. It took off with the advent of the increasing trend towards conservatism and cultural isolation worldwide starting with the European anti-immigration initiatives emerging in the early 1990s and their codification in the mid-1990s. Breaking into Fortress Europe has been difficult. The most successful strategy has been to play the Green Card. Seeing themselves being relegated to less-developed-country status, the Slovaks attack on two fronts. The Chernobyl-vintage nuclear power plant outside Bratislava is operated at peak levels threatening a nuclear disaster. The second front is played on the Slovak-Hungarian frontier. Given the inability of the World Court at The Hague to enforce its ruling on the Slovak operation of the dam along the Danube, the Slovaks manipulate operations to reduce the Danube flowing into Hungary's Sziegetkoz marsh—one of Europe's last wetlands— to a trickle. The Slovak's goal is to enter the E.C.. Recognizing that a reconciliation with the Czech Republic is too expensive given the still lingering pain of the German experience initiated earlier in the decade, the Slovaks feel they must resort to more extreme measures. Pressured by Austria, Hungary, and Poland, in particular, the E.C. offers Slovakia entry within the variable geometry formulation. Thus, Green Money has re-emerged—this time as the currency of environmental extortion. Not surprising, with six power plants less stable than the Chernobyl vintage, Bulgaria accedes to the E.C. six months later under the same terms the Slovak received—well ahead of the 2010 projected accession date. Power politics has taken on a frightfully new meaning.

PART FOUR

GATT Negotiations and North American-European Agricultural Trade Relations

8

The U.S.-E.C. Confrontation in the GATT from a U.S. Perspective: What Did We Learn?

Lisa Hardy-Bass

What have we learned from the agricultural trade confrontations that have taken place between the United States and the E.C.? I will try to answer this question by focusing on the period during which we have been negotiating the Uruguay Round. I have a particular bias on this question that may differ slightly from the perspective of my colleagues in Washington and Geneva. Since I have spent the past four years in Brussels at the U.S. Mission to the E.C., I have been closer to U.S.-E.C. bilateral trade conflicts than to the General Agreement on Tariffs and Trade (GATT) negotiating table. With that small caveat, let me begin.

Lesson No. 1: We're Not as Different as We Think

I am struck by the depth of our common values and objectives with respect to agriculture between the United States and the E.C. Trade conflicts invariably stem from national decisions to pursue what we think is in the best interest of our farmers and agribusinesses. We each seek to ensure a safe, adequate food supply at reasonable prices and to protect and maintain the long-term viability of our rural communities and the vitality of our economies.

It is also true that the internal pressures that motivate our agricultural and trade policy decisions are very similar. Both of us are concerned by the unprecedented contraction in our farm populations since the 1950s. These demographic changes threaten to destabilize rural communities that have no alternative employment opportunities and further weaken the link between a population and its agrarian roots.

More recently, it has been government budgets that have dictated both

U.S. and E.C. agricultural policies. The U.S. 1985 and 1990 Farm Bills sought to redress the damage done to our farmers by completely isolating them from market forces. In the late 1970s to early 1980s U.S. farmers made their planting decisions based on government set target prices regardless of market conditions. As a result, the United States priced itself out of the export market and saw its best customers lost to competitors. All the while, the government spent more while farmers earned less.

CAP reform was also driven by the unsustainable and inequitable burden of the CAP budget. Commissioner MacSharry often spoke of how 20 percent of E.C. farmers received 80 percent of the support payments. More importantly, over the last few years, while the CAP budget grew to more than 35 billion ECU per year, E.C. farm income declined. It is no coincidence that the Uruguay Round came on the heels of the 1985 Farm Bill; and that a major breakthrough had to wait for the E.C. to adopt CAP reform.

While it is clear that we have common values and common problems, from time to time we have different, even conflicting approaches to them, hence our trade conflicts. To my mind, multilateral trade negotiations are about finding compromise among our differences.

Lesson No. 2: The United States Is a Different Negotiating Partner

The second point I want to make is not so much a lesson learned as it is a confirmation of what has happened in the last decade or so. In these negotiations we are seeing the effects of a changed United States and of a changed European Community—changes that have occurred because of the successful economic strategies we have followed since World War II. Today the economic prosperity of the United States is equaled, and in some cases surpassed, by our allies and like-minded market economies.

On the flip side, this success story means that, for the first time, our negotiating partners entered these negotiations on an equal footing. The days of U.S. economic dominance and its ability to make unilateral concessions are gone. In its place, we are now seeing a more assertive posture by the United States to defend its own economic interests. The United States cannot afford to be as generous with its trading partners.

We in U.S. agriculture are particularly sensitive to this change of attitude. In every previous round of multilateral trade negotiations, agriculture was isolated from the trade liberalizing benefits of the negotiations because it was different, because it was too sensitive, because of food security concerns, because, because, because... Most of all, because it was too difficult and because the United States and Europe could afford to not reform agricultural trade. Those days are also gone.

Quite frankly, the United States can no longer afford not to reform agricultural trade. As the U.S. government is unable to provide a comprehensive safety net, the export market has become critical to the livelihoods of our farmers and to our rural communities. This change, I believe, has made the U.S. government more resolute and result-oriented than ever before. This might also explain why the Uruguay Round has dragged on for so long. We have not been willing to, and indeed are unable to, sacrifice our own economic interests to the same degree as in the past in order to bring the Round to a close.

Lesson No. 3: The GATT Has Served Us Well but Needs Strengthening

During these seven years, the existing GATT system has been pushed to the absolute limit. I do not mean to imply that the GATT does not work. Quite the contrary. The GATT has proven that it can work—but there are limits to its effectiveness. This is particularly true with respect to its ability to resolve trade disputes definitively.

The U.S.-E.C. oilseed dispute is a good example of this. The United States initiated this case in 1988, in the middle of what was to have been a four-year multilateral trade negotiation. In my view, it is no small achievement that the GATT provided us with a dispute-settlement mechanism to address this agricultural trade dispute of unprecedented economic value and political sensitivity without derailing the multilateral trade negotiations. It was slow going, with lots of high drama; not just one but two GATT panels were necessary. Four years and six months later, the GATT dispute settlement process produced what the United States believes was a fair judgment of the E.C.'s oilseed regime and the E.C.'s GATT obligations.

The oilseed case, however, also points out why we need a stronger and binding dispute settlement mechanism under the GATT. At the end of the day, with two panel rulings clearly in favor of the U.S. position, the GATT mechanism was unable to deliver a final solution that would redress the injury and impairment to U.S. oilseed producers. The United States and E.C. instead had to resort to bilateral negotiations to achieve results. In the meantime, other oilseed-exporting countries are still waiting for negotiations under the GATT to address their concerns.

This brings me to my fourth, and final, lesson from these negotiations—the nature of our bilateral relationship.

Lesson No. 4: U.S.-E.C. Relations Are Like a Marriage— We Bring Out the Best and the Worst in Each Other

Taking our best side first, it is relevant to put into perspective the breadth and depth of U.S.-E.C. relations. With the headlines full of stories about trade wars, demonstrations by farmers, and failed negotiations, we tend to take for granted how well the relationship does work. We tend to forget about NATO, the Gulf War, and coordinated aid to the former Soviet Union. This gets back to my first point—we tend to take for granted what we have in common.

Let me give you an example of the durability of U.S.-E.C. relations that is closer to all of our hearts. Do you realize that, in 1992, between the oilseed and corn gluten feed disputes, more than 35 percent of all U.S. agricultural exports to the E.C. were the subject of a trade dispute? It is utterly ironic that these products already receive duty-free treatment into the E.C. And yet, here we were embroiled in defending GATT rights the United States has had for more than 25 years.

It should come as no surprise that as a result of these bilateral trade disputes we also had to combat considerable cynicism towards the GATT in the United States. There were, and still are, a lot of people in the United States asking the U.S. government why we need an Uruguay Round agreement when the E.C. does not live up to the agreements we have already negotiated.

You may be asking yourselves, how is this a demonstration of the durability of U.S.-E.C. relations? In my view, it is a testament to our shared economic objectives and the depth of U.S.-E.C. relations that neither side gave up and sought out the comfort of domestic protectionism. Moreover, it is to the credit of negotiators on both sides that we managed to make our way through last year's mine field without sparking a trade war. We had a few close calls along the way, such as the threat of U.S. retaliation over oilseeds and the brief resignation of E.C. Agriculture Commissioner MacSharry. By and large, though, the U.S.-E.C. relations weathered the storm and we were able to conclude the Blair House Agreement.

We can all find shortcomings with Blair House. However, to criticize Blair House without appreciating the atmosphere in which it was negotiated is not only a disservice to U.S.-E.C. negotiators: it is naive. There are those who would like to read each component of Blair House as a separate entity and take what they like and leave the rest, but the Blair House Agreement is bigger than the sum of its individual parts. U.S. and E.C. negotiators, thankfully, understand this.

Now for our worst side: my colleagues at the Mission responsible for U.S.-E.C. political relations like to talk about the need for an "early warning system" so that we can resolve brewing irritants before they get out of hand. I think this is a good idea, but it is too early for agriculture. We are too busy solving all of today's problems; we do not have time to try to avoid tomorrow's potential pitfalls. Moreover, in my experience, the U.S. and E.C. tend to resolve their differences only after they move to a crisis point. I sometimes wonder if we are not inherently unable to resolve a mole-hill-size problem before it grows into a mountain.

Why do we manage by crisis? Part of the blame certainly lies with the strength of our respective constituencies back home and the inherent weakness in international trade rules. I also believe that part of the problem lies with the decision-making structure of the Community. In my time in Brussels, I have been amazed by the minute detail that often crowds the agenda of the Agricultural Council because member states were unable to reach a compromise at a level below ministers. If relatively minor concerns can not be resolved at lower levels, such as an appropriate definition for "light butter," the difficulty grows exponentially when fundamental aspects of trade with the United States are concerned.

The corn gluten feed dispute is a good case study in E.C. decision making. For background, the current corn gluten feed dispute has its roots in a legitimate concern on the part of the Community three years ago about fraud in another corn by-product, corn germ meal. The United States took the E.C. concerns very seriously and worked with the Commission to define more precisely the production practice that has corn germ meal as its by-product.

This should have been a success story under an early warning type system. Instead, it marked the point where our problems began. Some in the Community assumed that if there was fraud in one corn by-product, there must be fraud in corn gluten feed too. The United States has been trying to assure the Community of the legitimacy of our corn gluten feed shipments ever since. We have negotiated two agreements of corn gluten feed—one in October 1991, and the other at Blair House. To date, the E.C. has implemented neither of these agreements. And yet, through this period, we have been given no evidence to demonstrate that the composition of U.S. corn gluten feed is any different from what it was 10 to 15 years ago. One has the sneaking suspicion that there is more at issue here than what meets the eye.

I think it is fair to say that, because of the political sensitivity of corn gluten feed and the strong support for rebalancing in the Community, technical experts have understandably been hesitant to implement a solution to this problem without the consent of their political masters. Politicians, on the other hand, have not wanted to be seen as conceding anything to the United States concerning cereal substitutes and have chosen, conveniently, to consider the matter a technical issue that does not require their involvement. We have gone around and around on this issue for more than two years, all because no one wants to take responsibility for a solution because is bad politics.

It is a sorry state of affairs when resolution of a U.S.-E.C. trade dispute is bad politics. Unfortunately, that is precisely the situation we face when it comes to the Uruguay Round, oilseeds and corn gluten feed.

U.S.-E.C. trade relations have also experienced the effects of the ongoing evolution of E.C. institutions. While the United States wholeheartedly supports European unity and recognizes there will be ups and downs as the E.C. becomes a more sophisticated partner, this evolution is at times frustrating for us. For example, the Commission's competence in trade matters is clear. It is with the Commission that we have negotiated the Uruguay Round. There are times, however, when the E.C. appears to us as a 13-headed dragon with 26 arms and 26 legs. (Mind you, I don't envy the Commission either, whose job it is to slay the 13-headed dragon and replace it with one beast with all 26 legs moving in the same direction.) I don't need to tell you that it is difficult to talk to a 12- or 13-headed dragon, let alone negotiate with it.

The dragon has a tendency to appear when negotiations get tough. Most recently it has reared its head after the United States and the Commission negotiated the Blair House Agreement. Each thought the agreement would satisfy themselves and the 12-headed dragon. However, as we all know, not all 12 heads of the dragon were satisfied. So I ask you, how do you deal with a 12 or 13-headed dragon that represents the root of much of your own culture, is one of your closest allies, and one of your largest trading partners?

It is troubling to the United States when we hear member states suggest that parts of the Blair House text should be renegotiated. What kind of a relationship can the United States and European Community have if each is not confident that the other will live up to its agreements?

In agricultural trade, I think we have another particularly troubling phenomenon on our hands that has contributed to this perennial state of crisis we have experienced in the last 6 to 7 years. That is, many in the Community perceive the Uruguay Round as a negative, or at best a zero, sum game. They believe there can only be one winner and one loser. Many Europeans are surprised to learn that certain sectors of U.S. agriculture would also have to adjust to an Uruguay Round result and that there are benefits for the E.C. to gain from an Uruguay Round agreement.

The conclusion to my comments is perhaps more important than the topic itself. That is, can we learn from these lessons in the next six months and bring the Uruguay Round to a mutually satisfactory conclusion? I believe the answer is yes, provided that we, the United States and the E.C., can negotiate based on the strength of our common interests.

I have been surprised by the lack of attention many have given to the market access component of an Uruguay Round agreement. The lack of attention to market access gives the impression that the Blair House text represents the end of the agricultural negotiations under the Uruguay Round. This is not true. Blair House does very little to create new trade opportunities. The United States and the E.C. have a shared interest as the world's two largest agricultural exporters in accomplishing a large market access package on a global scale. We need to capitalize on these common interests for all of us to be winners.

Discussion

Luca Salvatici

Lisa Hardy-Bass made a commendable effort by summing up in four lessons several years of complex trade negotiations and I am going to use her scheme as a framework for my comments.

Lesson No. 1: We're Not as Different as We Think

Usually, the more distant we are from two objects, the less we are able to notice the differences between them: it is a question of evaluation scale. Once I asked a taxi driver if a certain address was very far away: "On a continental scale it is very close," he answered, "nevertheless, it is at the other side of the city!"

At a very broad level, it is not difficult to find similarities in the way the E.C. and the United States handle agricultural problems. First of all, both of them seem to follow the same *coupled* model of agricultural policy, granting support to the farmers in exchange for food production (i.e., the principal parameter for distributing the benefits of public intervention is the amount of production). Secondly, the driving forces that pushed the process of reform during the 1980s are the same in both countries (even if the relative weights may be quite different): budget costs, instability of international markets, equity concerns, and environmental sustainability. Thirdly, both the E.C. Commission and the U.S. Government seem to use the Uruguay Round as a way to put pressure on domestic interests represented in the Council of Ministers and in the Congress.

Anyway, if we look a bit closer, structural and political differences between the United States and the E.C. become apparent and help to explain the difficulty of agricultural trade negotiations. As far as farm structure is concerned, there are important differences in the average farm size and in the number of workers involved in agriculture. Such differences in structure imply that while the United States considers agriculture (at least for some products) a performing and exporting sector, most of the Community policymakers justify public intervention in agriculture from a social rather than from an economic point of view. In addition to this general attitude towards agriculture, there are also big differences in the choice of policy instruments. Even if both E.C. and U.S. agricultural policies are coupled, the U.S. deficiency payments and the E.C. price support have very different implications in terms of trade policy instruments (e.g., the implementation of a deficiency payment scheme does not require the imposition of variable levies). Obviously differences in policy instruments wreak havoc on trade negotiations, as it is difficult to evaluate the reciprocity of concessions when the commitments undertaken concern different trade measures.

In this perspective some optimism could be drawn from the recent developments of the CAP, as it seems to have undertaken a process of progressive *"americanization"*: direct per hectare payments based on past yields, compulsory set-aside as a condition for benefiting of income aids, and so forth. I do not know if "we are not as different as we think," but I am sure that by the end of the Uruguay Round—whatever the results will be—"we will be less different than before."

Lesson No. 2: The United States is a Different Negotiating Partner

It is quite well known that one of the most compelling reasons why President Reagan launched a new round of trade negotiations was the huge U.S. trade deficit. The growing deficit was a sign of the declining competitiveness of U.S. products on world markets and I would not dare to provide here an explanation of such a complex phenomenon that seems to characterize a long-term trend of the U.S. economy. What I want to underscore is that U.S. policy makers have underestimated all the *internal* causes for the worsening of the trade accounts—i.e., lack of investment, overvaluation of the dollar, excessive internal demand, and so on— preferring to put the blame on foreign governments that would have distorted competition mechanisms through unfair support policies for national producers. This kind of attitude could also help to explain the success of the so-called *new international economics*, that in a sense has provided a "scientific" basis for such a benign explanation of the U.S. industries' crisis.

As far as agriculture is concerned, the CAP was the most suitable candidate to become the scapegoat for the problems of U.S. agriculture, even if it is misleading to explain the reduction of U.S. agricultural exports only as a consequence of the existence of the CAP. What is more important is that in the case of agriculture the emphasis was put on "fair trade" rather than "free trade" and on the setting of a "level playing field" has drastically broadened the scope of GATT negotiations, bringing into consideration internal support policies as well as traditional trade measures as the object of negotiations.

In conclusion it is certainly true that the United States is in a different position than in previous rounds, but it should be stressed that the consequence for the E.C. (as well as for the other members of the GATT) is the necessity to face a weaker (at least in economic terms) and more motivated negotiating partner.

Lesson No. 3: The GATT Has Served Us Well, but Needs Strengthening

Those who ask for a strengthening of the GATT are not satisfied with the present (and in some cases even with the past) functioning of the Agreement and argue that "GATT failures" are mainly due to the weakness of an institution with an uncertain juridical status (as it is well known that the GATT is not a true international organization like the United Nations or the International Monetary Fund and was created only on a temporary basis), including provisions full of vague statements (such as "equitable share of the world market") according to which almost anything can be allowed (as in the case of the "waivers") and nothing is ultimately forbidden (e.g., the widening "gray area" of nontariff barriers).

On the other hand there are those who highlight the results obtained by the GATT in terms of tariff reduction and avoidance of disruptive trade wars, pointing out that such results were made possible not in spite of, but as a consequence of, GATT flexibility. Agreements between sovereign states, as a matter of fact, can only be based on mutual consensus and not on an external imposition.

Even if these two positions are at odds in terms of suggestions for the future of the GATT, they share two common assumptions:

- We are no longer in a *hegemonic country scenario*, where the United States can assure an adequate supply of the public good "free trade," and
- We are in an *oligopolistic interdependence scenario*, where the crux of the matter is to enhance the performance of international institutions in terms of monitoring and punishing defections, so as to reduce the incentive for free riding by single countries.

I'd like to add just a brief comment on these two assumptions. As far as the second is concerned, my point is that considering problems of collective action only in terms of free riding is misleading, as equity concerns about the distribution of benefits stemming from free(r) trade do play a crucial role within the bargaining process.

Regarding the lack of a hegemonic country, the major problem is the U.S. uncertainty about their present role: sometimes they claim that the GATT should be strengthened and multilateral solutions are needed; sometimes they consider themselves strong enough to do this by themselves through unilateral actions. Such a schizophrenic attitude has led to inconsistent strategic behavior by the United States, which perhaps has not managed to renovate its reputation as a hegemonic country but has certainly succeeded in undermining the credibility of the GATT as the multilateral forum where trade problems are dealt with. If this is true, it may be that the GATT needs strengthening, but at present it is certainly weakened by the inconsistencies of U.S. behavior.

Lesson No. 4: U.S.-E.C. Relations Are Like a Marriage— We Bring Out the Best and the Worst in Each Other

Beginning with the best side, I am slightly puzzled by the enthusiasm shown by Lisa Hardy-Bass about the Blair House Agreement. I am ready to believe that it is a good agreement and that sagacious negotiators on both sides did their best; however I cannot avoid noticing that it is miles away from the initial U.S. position (the so-called "Zero Option"). Perhaps I am a bit *naive*, but the present satisfaction with the Blair House Agreement confirms the impression that the initial U.S. goals in the Round were excessive and were stated especially for domestic purposes (i.e., putting pressure on Congress in order to pass the 1985 Farm Bill). If this is true, the Zero Option was nothing more than a bluff that, in any case, blocked any real progress in the negotiations for at least two years.

Coming to the worst side, I think that the picture of the Community as a 13-headed dragon is really well chosen. Nevertheless, it should not be forgotten that the United States is far from being a single actor. Since the beginning of the Uruguay Round the confrontation between the President and the Congress of the United States has been a crucial feature of the negotiations and it is presently going to define the final deadline for the Round, as at the end of this year the Trade Mandate—which allows for a "fast track" procedure of adoption of any eventual agreement by the Congress—will expire.

On the other hand, my impression is that contrasts between the "liberal" President and the "protectionist" Congress are largely overstated and are only functional to the U.S. negotiation strategy. In fact, present trade policies are largely composed of nontariff barriers administered by the executive branch, while a picture of the Congress as only concerned with parochial interests is a caricature hardly believable. What is certainly true is that protectionist measures adopted by the Congress and "vetoed" by the President are powerful bargaining weapons, consistent with the old maxim: speak gently, but handle a big stick behind your back!

9

The U.S.-E.C. Confrontation in the GATT from an E.C. Perspective: What Did We Learn?

Eckart Guth and Tonia Pankopf

Introduction

There is a good chance that the Uruguay Round will be successfully concluded by the end of 1993. Negotiations on agriculture have for a long time been the centerpiece and the stumbling block of the whole Round. With the breakthrough achieved by the Blair House agreement, the prospects are good for the process of bringing agriculture fully into the General Agreement on Tariffs and Trade (GATT). This could herald the end of a period during which agriculture and its trade were not considered suitable for GATT rules and disciplines applicable to other goods.

Although the Uruguay Round negotiations are about the future, it is worthwhile to look into the past and to analyze what has brought the E.C. and the United States to its present-day situation. One should not throw stones if sitting in a glass house; therefore, some windows in the E.C. glass house should be opened by admitting that things have gone wrong in the Common Agricultural Policy (CAP) as well as in U.S. agricultural policy. Six theses describe from an E.C. perspective the role that the United States has played in international agricultural trade.

1. The overall trade relationship between the E.C. and the United States has always been prosperous and balanced.

Traditionally, the E.C. and the United States have been each other's largest trading partner. Last year, the overall bilateral trade flow was substantial, amounting to approximately $200 billion dollars, with $95.9

billion of exports to the United States and $102.8 billion of U.S. exports to the E.C. With respect to agricultural trade, U.S. farm exports to the E.C. amounted to $6.9 billion while E.C. farm exports to the United States totaled $4.7 billion. Agriculture is a relatively small amount of trade, and yet, unfortunately, it constitutes a large percentage of trade disputes between the E.C. and the United States.

For the past forty years, the trans-Atlantic partnership has been based upon mutual interdependence. Europe recognized the role that the United States played in its security. In the U.S. view, the economic well-being and security of Western Europe was intertwined with and could not be divorced from its own security. This led to a large degree of similarity in U.S. and European security and economic agendas. The United States was convinced that the economic health of the Community was an essential component in the struggle against communism. With the Marshall Plan, the United States undertook a long-term program to assist economic recovery and political integration in Europe. As the creation of a common market for industrial goods in the Community was not possible without at the same time creating a common market for agricultural goods, the United States had also to accept the establishment of a common agricultural policy.

Thanks to the fast-growing demand and some basic inconsistencies (disharmonies) in the Community's external and internal protection (zero protection for oilseeds and cereal substitutes and high internal prices for competing products such as cereal and butter), the Community remained a net importer for two decades. As a result, the full extent of the basic inconsistencies of the CAP were neither seen nor felt by the United States for a long time.

On the contrary, the United States benefited to a large extent from the CAP, exporting more cereals and cereal substitutes than a more market-oriented CAP would have allowed. At the same time, the more negative aspects of the CAP, in the form of a growing export potential and the Community's increasing share of world markets for major agricultural products, materialized only at a later stage in the early 1980s. It was then that the Community changed from a net importer into a net exporter, becoming the second largest exporter of food after the United States.

With both partners together occupying one half or more of the world market for major agricultural products, it is evident that the respective agricultural policies affect one another considerably. It is not surprising that on occasion agricultural trade disputes overshadow to a large extent the good political relationship between the E.C. and the United States, starting with the so-called "chicken war" in the 1960s and culminating in the recently resolved oilseed dispute.

2. *The United States (and others) have carried out an agricultural policy that best suited the development of its agriculture.*

In the early 1930s after the Great Depression, the United States introduced internal price support mechanisms and the concept of an equitable income for the family farm to restore the farm economy and discourage migration. At that time, it was clearly felt that the prevailing world market prices were not sufficient to maintain adequate internal farm incomes. The concepts of price support and equitable income later served as a model, in particular in Europe for the CAP, as a means to support farm incomes.

After the Second World War, U.S. farm policy started to become export-oriented for the first time by introducing "food for the hungry world" policies. This phase went along with the introduction of further instruments of internal and external price stabilization. By the middle of the 1970s, the arsenal of instruments was nearly complete, with the existence of target prices, loan rates, deficiency payments, export credits, and food aid. These instruments were mainly deployed for products for which the United States thought it had a certain comparative advantage (cereals, oilseed, poultry, and citrus fruit). Not surprisingly, this "arms race" resulted in rapidly expanding U.S. agricultural exports. The United States thus became acquainted with the idea that they alone were responsible for feeding the world and tried to instill in their farmers and the world the belief that their export performance in agriculture was solely the product of their higher productivity and competitiveness.

The United States also introduced export promotion programs, subsidizing the disposal of its surplus production with aid/assistance programs and credit guarantee programs, then later introducing such programs as the Export Enhancement Program (EEP) and the Targeted Export Assistance Program (TEA). Unlike the direct export subsidies in the E.C., U.S. export subsidies are concealed and more difficult to quantify. Soon after World War II, when production controls failed to hold supplies in balance with demand, the U.S. Congress passed the Agriculture and Trade Development and Assistance Act, Public Law 480, or Food for Peace. Conceived for altruistic purposes, P.L. 480 also served to increase foreign demand and dispose of surplus commodity stocks. During the late 1950s and early 1960s, food aid under P.L. 480 accounted for between one quarter and one half the value of all agricultural exports. The credit programs, Export Credit Guarantee program (GSM-102), one of the largest U.S. export promotion programs, and the Intermediate Export Credit Guarantee program (GSM-103), have allowed countries to repay loans at subsidized rates. In 1983, for example, the United States sold one mmt of subsidized wheat to Egypt under a credit guarantee program.

The Food Security Act of 1985 introduced an export subsidy program to recapture lost markets. The Export Enhancement Program required the USDA to use Commodity Credit Corporation stocks to subsidize exports of U.S. wheat to a number of countries, targeting in particular Mediterranean rim markets (Algeria and Egypt) that were traditional E.C. markets. Such a program, however, hurts not only the E.C. but other cereal exporters, such as Canada, Australia, and Argentina. In order to capture market shares, the United States not only targeted their exports at specific markets but also pursued a policy of price undercutting. As the Community responded to this policy by matching U.S. prices, the other wheat exporting countries were most concerned by the downward spiral that this "catch-as-catch-can" policy caused.

In parallel to export-oriented policy instruments, in the early 1950s the United States developed the necessary protectionist tools to insulate certain agricultural sectors against imported products by applying quantitative import restrictions (Section 22 products). Against this historical background, the United States should not be surprised when other countries, in the face of similar economic and social problems, have been inspired to some extent by American agricultural and trade policy to develop similar agricultural instruments and policies.

In fact, state intervention in agriculture is nothing new or novel. As Socrates, the Greek philosopher, observed: "Nobody is qualified to become a statesman who is entirely ignorant of wheat." The United States, together with other industrialized countries, have developed during this century a panoply of government intervention mechanisms bringing politicians more than ever into agricultural trade. Unfortunately, most of the agricultural policy devices try to externalize internal problems, in other words, to off-load domestic surplus problems onto world markets.

3. The failure of the GATT to deal effectively with agricultural trade stems to a large extent from the exceptions requested by and granted to the United States.

Professor Gale Johnson said in this respect:

> The unwillingness of the United States in the late 1940s and early 1950s to subject its domestic farm programs to the disciplines of international trade resulted in the inclusion in GATT of exemptions for agriculture with respect to subsidies, including export subsidies.

Unlike the trade in textiles, which for the time being is still exempted from the GATT rules, agriculture forms part of the GATT. Thirty-eight articles of the GATT apply to agriculture; only four GATT articles (VI, XI, XVI, and XX) specifically mention agricultural products.

In general terms, the problem of agricultural trade is therefore not that it is excluded from the GATT but rather that the rules are often:

- not applied because derogations have been asked for by contracting parties (waivers, protocols of accession),
- not operational, lacking clear guidelines for dispute settlement (export subsidization, import restrictions), and
- circumvented by state trading (boards) and grey area measures (such as self-restraint agreements).

GATT's leading player did not resist the temptation to secure special privileges. Fearing free trade might interfere with its domestic price support programs, the United States insisted on exemptions to the absolute prohibition of quantitative restrictions and subsidies, including export subsidies. The United States received exemptions on export subsidies for primary products under Article XVI.

Article XI, designed by the United States, exempted import restrictions on agricultural products under certain specified conditions. It took several GATT panels to demonstrate that Article XI left too much room for interpretation and was therefore not operationally effective in practice. However, the United States was unwilling to abide even by this exemption. In 1951 the contracting parties found U.S. import restrictions on dairy products an infringement of Article XI since the United States had not restricted its domestic production. In addition, the United States had enacted legislation inconsistent with Article XI. Section 22 of the Agricultural Adjustment Act of 1933 authorized the United States to impose quantitative restrictions or special fees whenever a foreign import substantially hindered the implementation of a U.S. farm program. This required the United States in 1955 to obtain a waiver concerning Article XI 2.c for their quantitative restrictions on agricultural products. Interestingly enough this waiver is still in force today.

The short-sightedness of U.S. agricultural trade policy in the early 1950s clearly enabled the proliferation of export subsidies and quantitative restrictions in other industrialized countries (E.C., Scandinavia, Japan, Canada, Austria, and Switzerland). A close look at the agricultural trade policies applied by most industrialized countries clearly shows that the United States is not solely responsible for today's situation. The least one can say, however, is that the United States underestimated the long-term negative impact of the protectionist instruments of their agricultural policy (Waiver, Article XI) on the development of agricultural trade policies in third countries. The same holds true for the ambiguities that were allowed to slip into the formulation of Articles XI and XVI. It took years and several Panels to demonstrate that Article XVI is not operational for dispute settlement and therefore needs to be reviewed or replaced by other disciplines. In this context, it is worth noting that the United States was not prepared to pursue an offer tabled by the Community in the early 1980s to restrict its wheat exports to a world market share of 14 percent in exchange for a commitment by the United States not to increase exports of corn gluten feed (CGF). Interestingly, CGF exports thereafter did not increase very much, while the E.C. substantially gained world market shares in wheat, up to 20 percent.

The countries hit hardest by the world agricultural market situation have been thinly populated industrial and agricultural countries where domestic demand is low and dependence on exports accordingly high. Australia may serve as an example: it exports 60 percent of its wheat, 50 percent of its beef, and 90 percent of its sugar output. Although countries such as Australia, New Zealand, Canada and Argentina do not entirely renounce the provision of state support, the farmers in these countries do have to rely more on their own competitiveness as regards the major export products, which they have to be able to offer at prices close to world market levels.

Contrary to the view expressed by the former U.S. Secretary of Agriculture Block: "What went wrong in the 1980s?" things were already starting to go awry in the 1950s and 1960s. However, the negative fallout for the United States really came to the forefront in the 1980s, when the Community changed from a net importer to a net exporter in the absence of international rules and disciplines obliging the Community to adapt its export policy instruments to this fundamental change.

4. The United States settles agricultural disputes outside the bounds of the GATT rules.

Neither unilateral interpretation of rights and obligations nor unilateral action by one party to coerce another to comply with the rules is permitted in the GATT. Through dispute settlement procedures, GATT aims to preserve the balance of concessions and obligations between contracting parties and not to resort to unilateral sanctions against a party in breach of the rules. In contradiction of these GATT tenets, the United States employs Section 301 of the 1974 Trade Act to enforce rights under international trade agreements and to counteract foreign trade practices that burden or restrict U.S. trade. The former Super 301 of 1988 Omnibus Trade and Competitiveness Act included stricter time limits to the Section 301 process making retaliation mandatory when U.S. trade was adversely affected by a policy or alleged trade agreement violation. Today legislation is pending in the U.S. Congress to reactivate Super 301.

The so-called "chicken war" in 1962-63 represents an exception insofar as it was possible in this case to resolve the dispute fully within the framework of the dispute settlement procedures of the GATT. It is worth noting that, to offset the losses the United States incurred as a result of the Common Customs Tariff, the GATT authorized the United States in this case to withdraw tariff concessions. The United States thereafter increased tariffs for trucks to 25 percent. The implication of this decision is still being felt today, in the dispute over attempts by the U.S. government to reclassify multipurpose passenger vehicles (minivans and sport-utility vehicles) as trucks in order to secure a higher degree of protection for respective U.S. automobile makers.

In most later agricultural trade disputes, the United States either referred to or threatened to use trade sanctions against the Community in order to make its view prevail. One such example was the dispute on E.C. tariff preferences on imports of lemons and oranges from Mediterranean countries. The pasta-citrus war escalated in November 1985, when the United States threatened to apply a 40 percent ad valorem duty on pasta products not containing egg and a 25 percent *ad valorem* duty on pasta products containing egg; Community pasta trade worth $29 million was concerned. Thus the United States clearly breached the GATT dispute settlement procedure and weakened the credibility of the GATT. Only when the Community drew up a list of counter-retaliation measures worth an equivalent value of trade by increasing duties on U.S. imports of lemons and walnuts into the E.C. did a negotiated settlement become possible.

It is worth noting that the Community was confident of its ground in the citrus as well as in the pasta case, not so much because the relevant GATT rules left enough room for interpretation but more so because the Community relied on two political agreements with the United States. After resolving a previous disagreement on citrus products, the United States and the E.C. had reached an understanding in the Casey-Soames agreement of 1973. The United States would not challenge the Community preferential agreements as long as they were nonreciprocal and did not extend further concessions. Moreover, the United States agreed in an exchange of letters between USTR Strauss and Commissioner Gundelach during the Tokyo Round not to undermine the basic instruments of the CAP, among which the right to provide export refunds for agricultural raw materials was of primary importance for the Community.

Later on there were three other agricultural disputes in which the United States deliberately departed from the normal GATT dispute settlement procedures. Following the accession of Spain and Portugal, the Community negotiated with the United States and other contracting parties under Article XXIV §6 to compensate for any overall trade loss resulting from the enlargement of the customs union. Because of differences over the interpretation of Article XXIV §6 and exaggerated requests from the United States for tariff compensation, mainly for losses of corn and sorghum exports to Spain and Portugal, neither side could agree on a mutually satisfactory solution. The main area of disagreement concerned the unwillingness of the United States to recognize the benefits resulting from the reduction in industrial tariffs from an average of 15 percent to 5 percent as compensation for losses in the agriculture sector. In this situation, the United States relied again on unilateral trade measures and threatened to invoke retaliatory measures by applying 200 percent duties on such products as white wine, brandy, and gin, approximately $400 million worth of E.C. exports.

Only afterwards, when the United States reduced considerably its compensation request under Article XXIV §6, was a temporary arrangement achieved between the United States and the E.C. The main component of this agreement was the commitment by the Community to import annually up to 2.0 mmt of maize and 300,000 mmt of sorghum into Spain until 1990. Thereafter the arrangement has regularly been rolled over and may finally be settled within the framework of the Uruguay Round.

The most recent case of U.S. unilateralism concerns the oilseed dispute where the United States threatened to introduce trade sanctions against the Community three times, initially after the first GATT panel report in January 1990. More recently, after the GATT panel's second report in June 1992, the United States threatened to retaliate by imposing punitive levies on approximately $1 billion dollars worth of E.C. imports. The third time occurred last November during negotiations to compensate the United States for the negative consequences of the E.C. oilseed regime. Unsatisfied with the progress of negotiations, the United States announced its intention to impose 200 percent punitive levies on white wine, wheat, gluten, and rapeseed oil, amounting to $300 million worth of E.C. imports. Finally a solution was reached in the so-called Blair House agreement.

The hormone dispute represents the most serious infringement of GATT rules in that it has been the only time the United States has carried through the Section 301 process to implementation. In 1989 the United States imposed 100 percent tariffs on E.C. agricultural imports totaling $97 million dollars after neither side could agree on the legal basis for the dispute settlement procedure concerning the E.C. prohibition of artificial hormones in beef production.

The U.S. approach of employing unilateral measures whenever it considers its rights to be infringed by a third country is in line with its reluctance when it comes to the implementation of GATT panels that ruled against it (tuna panel, sugar-Nicaragua, Section 337).

It appears obvious that U.S. unilateralism against other contracting parties and the pick-and-choose approach toward unfavorable GATT panel rulings damage the GATT dispute settlement procedure considerably and explain why substantial progress in this domain is essential for many contracting parties in the Uruguay Round negotiations.

5. The United States employs agricultural trade instruments to pursue other political objectives.

Another characteristic of U.S. agricultural trade policy is that its instruments have, on a number of occasions, been used for reasons other than agriculture. The most striking examples are the U.S. export embargo on oilseeds following a production shortfall in the United States in the mid 1970s and the export embargo for cereals to the former Soviet Union, following the invasion of Afghanistan by Soviet troops. The first case was used by the Community as an example that the United States is not a reliable supplier and that it would therefore be better to build up its own oilseed production. As explained earlier, the shock waves of this decision were felt until very recently in the form of the oilseed dispute. The second embargo led to considerable losses of market shares of wheat and coarse grain in the former Soviet Union and allowed the Community to gain correspondingly on this market. Later on, it took the United States the conclusion of rather favorable long term contracts with the Soviet Union and an aggressive price policy to recuperate lost terrain.

The combined effects of the above-mentioned politically motivated decisions, the volatility of the U.S. dollar, and the rigidity of the internal agricultural price support in the United States explain to a large extent why in the 1980s the United States lost world market shares for cereals, oilseed, poultry, and eggs, not only to the Community, but also to more competitive and commercially more reliable trading partners like Brazil and Argentina.

Nevertheless, for a long time the United States used the CAP as the major scapegoat to explain all their agricultural trade problems. To a certain extent, this attitude may also have distracted the United States for quite some time from an in-depth analysis of the major flaws inherent in the GATT rules and disciplines on agricultural trade, and even more so of the inconsistencies in U.S. agricultural policy.

6. The United States is willing to learn from the past and is prepared to accept compromises in order to enable progress in the Uruguay Round.

Due to its hypocrisy in the early years of the GATT, the United States is to some degree responsible for the disarray prevailing in today's agricultural trade situation. To its credit, the United States has tried hard to rectify earlier mistakes by bringing agriculture fully into the GATT. The first serious attempt in the Kennedy Round failed, however, because the United States was not satisfied with the Community's offer to bind its degree of self-sufficiency at 90 percent. With hindsight, such a compromise, it appears, would have eliminated much of the potential for later trade disputes, in light of the fact that today E.C. self-sufficiency is significantly higher.

This "all or nothing" attitude reappeared when the United States made its first proposal in the Uruguay Round to eliminate all subsidies and non-tariff barriers by the year 2000, allowing only decoupled income support and tariff protection. The prolonged insistence of the United States on this negotiating stance was partly responsible for the lack of overall progress in the initial stage. Other contracting parties argued rightly that the United States was overkilling and not even capable of delivering at home what it was proposing within the GATT.

The fact that other contracting parties, including the Community, did not call their bluff shows the risk involved in accepting such a strategy was rather greater than other contracting parties could accept. In retrospect, the initial U.S. proposal was nevertheless beneficial to some extent, for it set the tone for the whole Uruguay Round negotiations by making it clearly understood that the objective was the liberalization of agricultural trade and the integration of agriculture into the general GATT rules. The United States supported mainly by the Cairns Group counterbalanced all attempts to build the negotiations on the idea of the "specificity" of agricultural trade.

The willingness of the major protagonists to negotiate mutually acceptable solutions in the framework of the objectives set by the Punta del Este declaration can best be illustrated by a review of their negotiating positions since 1986. At the Ministerial meeting of Punta del Este in September 1986, all participants agreed to embark on the challenging process of bringing agriculture into the GATT.

Ministers agreed that there is an urgent need to bring more discipline and predictability to world agricultural trade by correcting and preventing restrictions and distortions including those related to structural surpluses so as to reduce the uncertainty, imbalances, and instability on world agricultural markets. It was agreed that negotiations should aim to achieve greater liberalization of trade in agriculture and bring all measures affecting import access and export competition under strengthened and more operationally effective GATT rules and disciplines.

While the United States proposed the elimination of all subsidies and access restrictions by the year 2000 allowing provisions only for direct income aid (decoupled from production) and food aid, other countries and groups of countries were less rigorous and more realistic on the formulation of a long-term objective. The Community proposed reducing government support for agriculture in a progressive and substantial way. The Community's proposal supported the use of a PSE (Producer Subsidy

Equivalent)-based measurement tool for negotiating a concerted reduction in support and protection (Aggregate Measure of Support, or AMS). The Community's approach was centered very much on reducing internal support and improving disciplines on export subsidies and market access concomitantly. The more the Community weakened the AMS approach, however, the more obvious the need became to take specific binding commitments on market access and export subsidization.

The initial Cairns Group proposal was viewed by many observers as a compromise between the U.S. and E.C. proposals in addressing both the long-term concerns of the United States and the short-term concerns of the Community. Other industrial countries such as European Free Trade Agreement (EFTA) countries and Japan made efforts to contribute to the liberalization of agricultural trade; however, they did so by proposing better disciplines in areas such as export subsidization, which, as net importing countries, would not affect them much.

At the Mid-Term Review of the GATT in Montreal, the United States had given up its extremist and unrealistic position; the deadlock ended and the path cleared to find a reasonable compromise for a framework agreement to guide the agricultural trade negotiations. All participants agreed on an overall objective: substantial progressive reductions in agricultural support and protection over an agreed period of time. In order to realize this objective, strengthened and more operationally effective GATT rules and disciplines should be negotiated, encompassing all measures directly and indirectly affecting import access and export competition.

Thereafter it took the failure of the Brussels Conference and a long period of technical and political discussions on the bilateral and multilateral level to allow the Director General of GATT, Mr. Dunkel, to come forward with his Final Draft Agreement (FDA) on 20 December 1991.

The Dunkel Paper

The Dunkel paper was not acceptable to the Community and some other contracting parties. It was, however, accepted as a basis mainly for bilateral negotiations between the E.C. and the United States The Dunkel paper made specific proposals in four areas, which can be summarized as follows.

Domestic Support

The disciplines on internal support are based on the AMS, which is a figure that allows one to express and compare different kinds of support policies (price support, deficiency payments, input subsidies, etc., considered as having an effect on production and trade). The Dunkel compromise suggested the following:

- base year 1986-88
- credit from 1986 for reduction of AMS
- 20 percent reduction commitment
- duration 1993-1999

Although the Community endorsed the general idea concerning internal support, it was unable to accept that the income compensation introduced under the CAP reform should be subject to a reduction commitment.

Market Access

The discipline on market access is mainly based on the concept of tariffication. All non-tariff barriers (quotas, waivers, variable levies, etc.) on agricultural products should be transformed into a tariff equivalent (TE) and be reduced over time:

- base year 1986-1988
- average 36 percent reduction for each tariff line with a minimum of 15 percent
- duration 1993-1999

On insistence from the Community, special safeguard mechanisms form an integral part of tariffication. Furthermore, the following is proposed:

- current access is maintained; and
- in cases where imports are less than 3 percent of domestic consumption in the base period 1986-1988 in the first year of implementation and less than 5 percent in the last year of implementation, steps shall be taken to allow imports up to the minimum access level.

Although the Community could accept the overall orientation of tariffication, it was unacceptable that the Dunkel paper contained no provisions concerning rebalancing (i.e., measures necessary to stabilize E.C. imports of cereal substitutes).

Export Competition

The discipline on export competition is composed of two commitments, one concerning budgetary outlays, the other concerning subsidized export quantities:

- base period average 1986-90
- duration 1993-1999
- 36 percent reduction budget
- 24 percent reduction quantities

The Community was ready to make a specific commitment on subsidized exports but considered the reduction figure of 24 percent as too high.

Sanitary and Phytosanitary Measures

An integral part of the Dunkel text concerns sanitary and phytosanitary measures. It endorses the principle that sanitary and phytosanitary measures should be based on scientific evidence, and it recognizes the principle of equivalence and regionalization.

Furthermore, the Community considered it necessary to take up the following points that were not dealt with in the FDA:

Peace Clause. For the Community it is essential that the use of the different instruments of the CAP cannot be challenged under the GATT once an agreement on the three agricultural negotiating areas has been achieved. This assurance was not given under the Dunkel proposal.

Oilseed Dispute. The Community considered it essential that the dispute over the Community's oilseed regime should be settled in the framework of the bilateral discussions between the United States and the Community in the Uruguay Round.

The oilseed dispute started in 1988 when the United States challenged the Community's aid for oilseeds in a GATT Panel on the grounds that the production aid granted to E.C. oilseed producers nullified and impaired the tariff concessions (zero tariff for oilseeds) that the Community had agreed upon in 1962 (Dillon Round). Because the United States considered the subsequent reform of the Community's oilseed regime in 1991 as being insufficient to remove the nullification and impairment, the United States asked to reconvene the same Panel in order to re-examine the oilseed issue. The reconvened Panel recommended that the Community remove the nullification and impairment by either further modifying the oilseed regime or entering into negotiations under Article XXVIII of the GATT (renegotiation of tariff binding).

In June 1992 the GATT Council authorized the Community to enter into negotiations with all interested countries on the basis of GATT Article XXVIII §4. The United States also agreed to this approach but insisted that, from its point of view, some modifications in the existing oilseed regime would be needed to find a mutually satisfactory solution to the dispute.

The Agreement between the Community and the United States reached on 20 November 1992 allows for the continuation of multilateral trade negotiations in the Uruguay Round and thus paves the way for a possible conclusion of the Round. The substance of the agreement can be summarized as follows:

1. *Internal Support.* It has been agreed to exempt the type of income payments that the Community applies under the reformed CAP from the reduction commitment under the AMS. It is thus possible to compensate E.C. farmers fully for the income losses resulting from price reductions.
2. *Market Access* (rebalancing). Both sides agreed to enter into consultations if the imports of cereal substitutes increase to such an extent that they undermine the results of the reform of the cereals market.
3. *Export Competition.* It was agreed to apply a figure of 21 percent for the quantitative export commitments instead of the 24 percent foreseen in the Dunkel paper. The figure of 36 percent for budget reduction was confirmed. It will thus be possible to respect commitments resulting from a possible conclusion of the Uruguay Round within the framework of the agreed CAP reform. It was further agreed to confirm the commitment made by the Community in 1985 not to subsidize beef exports to the Far Eastern market (Japan, Taiwan, Malaysia, Singapore, and South Korea).
4. *Peace Clause.* Both sides agreed on a text that ensures that the agricultural policy instruments applied will not be challenged under Articles XVI and XI (nullification and impairment) of the GATT, as long as the disciplines resulting from the Uruguay Round in the three negotiating areas are fully respected. This implies that the instruments of the CAP, including internal aid measures and export refunds, are for the first time fully recognized in the GATT.
5. *Oilseeds.* In the light of the conclusions of the two Panels in the oilseed dispute, it was agreed that the Community shall apply the set-aside level resulting from the annual decision of the Community in this respect on a base acreage limited to 5,128,000 hectares. The set-aside for oil seeds can, however, in no case be less than 10 percent. Contrary to the initial U.S. request, there will be no supplementary ceiling in terms of tonnage on total production. The Community will provide a tariff concession for the import of 500,000 mmt of maize. The production of oilseeds for non-food production (bio-ethanol, for example) on set-aside land will be possible up to a certain level corresponding to a maximum by-product level of oilseed meal (one mmt of meal expressed in terms of soy meal equivalents, which is the traditional formula used to compare the fodder resulting from different oilseeds).

It was thus possible to terminate a dispute that overshadowed the Uruguay Round for four years and in its last phase brought the United States and the E.C. to the brink of a trade war.

The Agreement reached in the bilateral discussions between the United

States and the Community on several outstanding negotiating issues, including the settlement of the oilseed dispute, made it possible to resume the multilateral negotiations of the Uruguay Round in Geneva. The Agreement now needs to be discussed further with all other participants in the Uruguay Round negotiations. If it is finally accepted along the agreed lines, it will impose concrete disciplines on the use of agricultural trade policy instruments in all countries of the world and make sure that all participants contribute in a balanced way to the improvement of trade in agricultural products.

Conclusion

The process of the Uruguay Round negotiations as described above underlines the thesis that the United States (as well as the Community) were willing to learn from the past and to make compromises to achieve the long-term objective of liberalization of agricultural trade. It is, however, a great success for the GATT in general, and agricultural trade in particular. The E.C. and the United States have agreed for the first time on a process that over time should lead to less and less state intervention in agricultural trade, allowing Heads of State to concentrate on other even more important issues of world politics than agriculture. It appears as if the negotiators have combined the wisdom of two great U.S. statesmen, John F. Kennedy and Benjamin Franklin: "Never fear to negotiate" because "no nation was ever ruined by trade."

Notes

The views expressed in this chapter do not represent the official position of the E.C. Commission but are the personal opinions of the authors.

Discussion

George E. Rossmiller

The chapter by Eckart Guth and Tonia Pankopf takes an admittedly European Community (E.C.) view of the historical evolution of U.S. agriculture and agricultural trade policy and the impacts of interactions of those policies with those of the E.C., which have given rise to trade tensions and disputes, starting with the infamous Chicken War of the early 1960s. The authors have a disclaimer, up front, that indicates that they could tell as many bad stories and lay out as many of the mistakes that the E.C. has made as they do in the chapter with regard to the United States. However, being critical of the E.C. was not their mandate or purpose. In any case, I had to keep reminding myself that the charge to the authors was to set down the E.C. perspective on U.S. policy and behavior—not to write a balanced chapter. Presumably, the balance comes when this chapter and that of Lisa Hardy-Bass (Ch. 8) are read back to back.

The Guth and Pankopf chapter is organized under six theses about U.S. policy and U.S.-E.C. agricultural trade relations. The authors have presented an interesting contribution that gets it mostly right most of the time. Let me make some brief comments on each of the six theses they present.

On the first thesis, that of balanced and prosperous trade, I will only make two points. First, it is true that the U.S. tolerated the CAP as a necessary irritant in achieving the larger political objective of a strong and unified Europe. This is one instance where the E.C. gained from the U.S. use of agricultural policy (Thesis No. 5) to achieve political objectives. Otherwise the CAP would have had a much harder time of it, if the United States had not had to hold its agricultural interests in check.

Second, the CAP was designed for an area in substantial food deficit. By the mid-1970s commodity after commodity—dairy earlier, wheat then grains, sugar, and beef—were produced in surplus to domestic needs and were subsidized into world markets. One wonders why it took fifteen or more years for the E.C. to recognize that a food deficit policy simply does not fit a food surplus community of countries. One further wonders how much harmony might have been gained if CAP reform had taken place when it could first have been prescribed.

With regard to the second thesis, that the United States has carried out its agricultural policy in its own best interest, three points might be relevant. First, during the 1970s, through no particular policy actions on the part of agriculture, the United States rapidly gained market share in a burgeoning agricultural export market. The reasons for the rapid increase in agricultural trade in general during the 1970s are well known. In addition, the United States had an advantage over other exporting countries in that, with large stocks of commodities and idle land that could be brought quickly into production, the United States was able to respond more rapidly than others to the growing demand. And, during that period the value of the U.S. dollar in foreign exchange markets was extremely low, giving the United States a certain price advantage. Of course in the early 1980s, both the general and the specific conditions relative to U.S. agriculture reversed dramatically and the United States experienced a rapidly declining market share in a deteriorating international market.

Second, since the Export Enhancement Program (EEP) was initiated in the 1985 Farm Bill it has had many, many critics, including myself. There has been plenty of evidence indicating that the EEP has been much less effective than expected by U.S. policy makers in helping the United States recapture market share from the Community. On the other hand, the Export Enhancement Program should not detract from the fact that in the 1985 and the 1990 Farm Bills provisions were put in place that effectively decoupled U.S. agriculture programs at the margin.

Third, I have often argued, or maybe I should say hypothesized, since it would take counterfactual analysis, which is rather hard to do, that the CAP was the best thing that ever happened to U.S. agriculture. I have argued this on the assumption that if there had been a policy in the European Community that subjected European agriculture to world market forces, agricultural structural adjustment would have taken place in the Community to the extent that they would have become much more efficient producers, able to compete in world markets with the best the United States, Canada, Australia, and others could offer. Were it possible to do, this would be a very interesting piece of analysis.

With regard to the third thesis, laying the failure of the GATT at the feet of the United States, it is true that the United States, pursuing what it thought at the time to be its self-interest, weakened the GATT with regard to agriculture, right from the beginning. But since then as other countries became more powerful and could have initiated changes to strengthen the GATT on agriculture, they did not. The blame for the initial weakening of the GATT was with the United States. Blame for keeping it weak must be shouldered much more broadly.

On the fourth thesis, that of the United States settling its disputes outside of the GATT, I believe this says much more about the inadequacy of the GATT dispute settlement process than it does about the United States, *per se.* The GATT has been likened to a court with no bailiff. Once a guilty party stands condemned, there is no bailiff to enforce the sentence. Moreover, the guilty party can avoid sentencing simply by rejecting the verdict. If a panel decision is not adopted (which takes a consensus) it has no status—and thus can be ignored. Small wonder then that the United States and others have looked outside of the GATT for satisfaction. It is the GATT that needs fixing—and the Uruguay Round is a step towards trying to do so.

With regard to the fifth thesis, that the United States uses agricultural trade policy for political purposes, the authors choose the 1973 soybean embargo and the 1980 Soviet grain embargo as illustrative examples. These two embargoes were the subject of an exhausting, if not exhaustive, study several years ago (USDA, 1986). If I recall the conclusions correctly, it was the economics of the oilseed markets in 1973 that was responsible for the increase in production in Latin America and, I believe, in Europe, not the embargo, which lasted only four days in any case. The 1980 Soviet grain embargo succeeded mainly in pushing trade flows around. The reduction in U.S. share of grain exports came later and was attributable to domestic policy and a strong dollar. Nevertheless, the United States does seek unrelated political objectives through the use of trade policy, always with the potential of loss by the economic interests involved.

Finally, the authors suggest that the United States has learned from past mistakes and is willing to compromise to reach an Uruguay Round agreement. I think this is true. I also think that the E.C. is ready to consummate an agreement, despite the last minute French pandering to its farmers, which is very unfortunate now and may have set a very bad precedent for the future. French farmers seem to have learned that all they need to do is disrupt the countryside and storm Paris and they will be bribed to stop—until the next time. The last bribe cost $1.3 billion. What is a final GATT agreement likely to cost?

The Uruguay Round will eventually end in agreement, but the outcome will not be startling. Most countries have adjusted their agricultural policies enough to be in conformance, or near conformance, with the likely Uruguay Round result. The two important things the end of the Uruguay Round will accomplish at this point are to consolidate and lock in the gains already made and to establish the base and point of departure for the next round.

The question we should be addressing is what lessons have we learned that might be useful in the next round. Unfortunately, the answer is probably "not much." The Uruguay Round has been difficult because the negotiation was on a totally different basis than in the past and the objective was actually to bring agriculture fully under GATT rules. The next round is likely to be, at least, equally difficult since it will be dealing with other first time-issues such as the environment and how to deal with regional trading arrangements of a variety of kinds. It is also likely that the United States and the E.C. will not be allowed to turn the next round into a bilateral negotiation. The developing countries found separate voices this time from the G7, in part, through the Cairns Group and in part through the food importers group. These separate voices are likely to regroup in the next round around different individual issues and to show greater strength than they have in this round.

Finally, it is time for us as professionals to look towards the next round and begin elaborating the issues as we see them.

References

United States Department of Agriculture. 1986. *Embargoes, Surplus Disposal, and U.S. Agriculture.* USDA ERS, Agricultural Economic Report No. 564, Dec.

10

U.S.-E.C. Farm Trade Confrontation: An Outsider's View

Kym Anderson

To people who have not been involved in agricultural policy debates it seems incredible that the Uruguay Round of the GATT (General Agreement on Tariffs and Trade)—by far the most ambitious set of multilateral trade negotiations ever undertaken—could have been held up for so long by a farm trade dispute affecting products that account for less than one-tenth of world trade and less than one-twentieth of employment in the main countries involved in the dispute. It seems all the more incredible given that the economies hurt most by these policies are the United States and the E.C. themselves, and even more so now than a few years ago because of the recession in these and other industrial economies that a successful Uruguay Round conclusion would help ease.

Of course the farm trade issue is not all that has held up the Uruguay Round. To some extent that dispute has served as a convenient smoke screen for disagreements in some of the other 13 areas under negotiation in the Round. Had these other, nonagricultural, parts of the negotiations been settled, more pressure would have been applied from the top to resolve the dispute over agricultural policy reform earlier.

But the fact remains that agriculture has been a major stumbling block throughout the Round. This raises numerous questions, four of which are the focus of the present chapter:

1) Why has the U.S.-E.C. farm trade dispute been so difficult to resolve?
2) What will it take to bring about a resolution? In particular, is the Blair House accord of November 1992 likely to suffice?
3) Will third countries be sufficiently satisfied with a resolution based on that accord as to enable the Uruguay Round to be brought to a conclusion?
4) What lies ahead with or without a successful conclusion to the Round?

Why Has the U.S.-E.C. Farm Trade Dispute
Been So Difficult to Resolve?

Why has it been so difficult to agree on reforming what are, after all, extremely and increasingly wasteful farm policies in the United States and the E.C.? They are wasteful in terms of raising consumer prices for food; requiring ever-larger treasury outlays to farmers; redistributing welfare with increasing inefficiency (not only because it costs consumers and taxpayers much more than one dollar for every dollar received by farmers, but also because the largest producers receive the lion's share of the benefits, and there is considerable corruption in the administration of some of the programs); making non-agricultural producers less competitive insofar as farm programs retain resources in agriculture; and damaging the natural environment, not least because these price-support policies encourage excessive use of farm chemicals.[1]

In answering this question, it needs to be understood that this is not just a dispute between the United States and France, as some media commentators would have us believe. Those countries just happen to be the most vocal representatives of two groups of countries. On the one hand, there are the traditionally lightly protected, food-exporting contracting parties to the GATT, involving not only the 14 members of the Cairns Group[2] but also numerous other developing countries. And on the other hand, there are the highly protected industrial countries other than North America and Australasia, namely the European Free Trade Agreement (EFTA) members, Japan, and Korea, as well as most E.C. members.

It also needs to be understood that it is not only recently that farm policy has become a contentious issue in trade negotiations. Indeed it is because those policies are so contentious that (a) the first four rounds of GATT negotiations virtually ignored them and the next three eventually had to drop them, and that (b) many preferential trade agreements excluded farm products. We should therefore not be surprised that the inclusion of them in the Uruguay Round is causing problems. The inclusion of farm policies was considered necessary, however, because they had become so distortionary both absolutely and relative to non-farm trade policies. More than that, there was a growing awareness that, in the process of economic development, governments tend to gradually change from taxing to subsidizing agriculture relative to industry.

The Extent of Past Agricultural Protection Growth

Governments have been intervening in agricultural trade for centuries (McCalla, 1969; Tracy, 1989; Lindert, 1991). While much of that intervention has been aimed at stabilizing domestic food prices and supplies, there is a general tendency for such policy interventions to change gradually in the course of a country's development from effectively taxing agriculture relative to other tradable sectors to effectively subsidizing farmers. From the late 1100s to the 1660s, prior to the first industrial revolution, Britain used export taxes and licenses to prevent domestic food prices from rising excessively. An Act was introduced in 1463 to restrict food imports when prices were low, but food export restrictions continued to bite in high-priced years. Then in the 1660s to 1680s a series of Acts gradually raised food import duties (making imports prohibitive under most circumstances) and reduced the export restrictions on grain, and these provisions were made even more protective by the corn law of 1815. The famous repeal of the corn laws in the mid-1840s heralded a period of relatively unrestricted food trade for Britain, but agricultural protection returned in the 1930s and has been increasing since then.

In many other West European countries similar tendencies have been observed, although on the Continent the period of free trade in th last century was considerably shorter, and agricultural protection levels during the past century were somewhat higher than in Britain.[3] Gulbrandsen and Lindbeck (1973) estimate that the average nominal rate of agricultural protection in Western Europe increased from less than 30 percent in the 1930s and early 1950s to 38 percent in 1956-7, 47 percent in 1963-4, and 62 percent in 1968-9. Meanwhile, tariffs on West European imports of manufactures have been progressively reduced since the late 1940s.

Japan provides an even more striking example of the tendency to increasingly assist agriculture relative to other industries. There industrialization began later, after the opening up of the economy following the Meiji Restoration in 1868. By the turn of the century Japan had switched from being a small net exporter of food to becoming increasingly dependent on rice imports. This was followed by calls from farmers and their supporters for rice import controls. Their calls were matched by equally vigorous calls from manufacturing and commercial groups for unrestricted food trade, since the price of rice at that time was a major determinant of real wages in the nonfarm sector. The heated debates were not unlike those that led to the repeal of the corn laws in Britain six decades earlier. In Japan, however, the forces of protection triumphed, and a tariff was imposed on rice imports from 1904. That tariff then gradually rose over time, providing a nominal rate of protection for rice of more than 30 percent during World War I. Even when there were food riots because of shortages and high prices just after that war, the Japanese government's response was not to reduce protection but instead to extend it to its colonies and to shift from a national to an imperial rice self-sufficiency policy. That involved accelerated investments in agricultural development in the colonies of Korea and Taiwan behind an ever-higher external tariff wall that by the latter 1930s provided a nominal rate of rice protection for the empire of more than 60 percent (Anderson, 1983; Anderson and Tyers, 1992). After postwar reconstruction Japan continued to raise its agricultural protection, just as had been happening in Western Europe, but to even higher levels: from an average nominal rate for grains and meats of around 50 percent in the late 1950s to around 100 percent by the early 1970s and to more than 200 percent by the late 1980s (Tyers and Anderson, 1992).

An import-substituting industrialization strategy was adopted in the 1950s in liberated South Korea and Taiwan, which harmed agriculture, but that was replaced in the early 1960s with a more neutral trade policy that resulted in very rapid export-oriented industrialization in those densely populated economies. That development strategy imposed competitive pressure on the farm sector, which, just as in Japan in earlier decades, prompted farmers to lobby (successfully, as it happened) for ever-higher levels of protection from import protection in those newly industrialized economies as well (Anderson, *et al.*, 1986).

The net effect on domestic-to-border price ratios of these demands for increasing agricultural protection in the relatively land-scarce economies of Western Europe and Northeast Asia, in combination with multilateral agreements among industrial countries to lower tariffs on manufactures under the GATT,[4] is clear from Table 10.1. By the mid-1980s, agricultural prices in international markets (measured relative to industrial product prices) were 30 percent below the level of the early 1960s. Agricultural relative to industrial prices also fell by 30 percent in Australasia and North America during that 25-year period, reflecting the fact that domestic prices in these traditional food-exporting countries followed closely the changes in export prices. In Western Europe and Northeast Asia, by contrast, domestic agricultural prices relative to industrial prices changed little over this period of declining international terms of trade for agriculture. That is, compared with Australasia and North America, the domestic terms of trade for agriculture in Western Europe and Northeast Asia improved by more than one-third.

Effects of Agricultural Protection Growth

The long-term growth of agricultural protectionism in industrializing countries has added to the tendency for agriculture's share of world merchandise trade to keep dropping (it fell from 27 to 13 percent between 1965 and 1990), and for the trend in the international price of farm products relative to that for industrial products to decline (shown from 1900 in Figure 10.1). But what is striking about Figure 10.1 is the extent and speed of that relative price decline during the 1980s. That, together with the fact that the E.C. from the latter 1970s was providing export subsidies to dispose of its induced surpluses, stimulated the United States to defend

TABLE 10.1 Agricultural Relative to Industrial Product Prices in Industrial Countries and in International Markets, 1961-1987ª (1961-64=100)

	Domestic Prices					International Prices	Column 1 / Column 6	Column 5 / Column 6
	Australasia and N. America	European Community-10	European Free Trade Assoc.	Japan	All W. Europe and N.E. Asiaᵇ			
	(1)	(2)	(3)	(4)	(5)	(6)	(7)	(8)
1961-64	100	100	100	100	100	100	100	100
1965-69	100	101	105	124	104	99	101	105
1970-74	109	99	104	128	104	100	109	104
1975-79	95	106	102	131	110	89	108	124
1980-84	80	97	96	114	100	83	98	121
1985-87	70	90	98	122	96	70	99	136

ªThe "domestic prices" columns show the changes in the prices received by farmers in each country group relative to the price received by producers of other tradables (as reflected in the industrial wholesale price index in those countries). The "international prices" column shows the changes in the index of prices of agricultural exports from industrial market economies relative to the index of prices of manufactured exports from industrial market economies.
ᵇThe EC-10, EFTA, and Japan, plus Spain and Portugal and the newly industrializing economies of Korea and Taiwan.

Source: Tyers and Anderson, (1992, p. 49).

FIGURE 10.1 Real International Food Prices, 1900 to 1992.

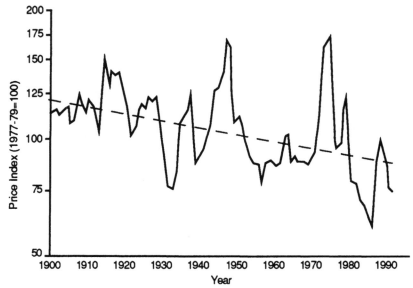

Note: Prices are an index of export prices in $U.S. for cereals, meats, dairy products, and sugar, deflated by the U.S. producer price index (primarily for industrial products), with weights based on the importance of each product in global exports, 1977-79.
Source: Author's calculations based mainly on price series made available by the World Bank Economic Analysis and Projections Department (see Grilli and Yang, 1988).

its export markets by subsidizing its farm exports as well—a move that contributed to international food prices falling to their lowest level this century in real terms. As a result there was an increase in the latter 1980s in the gap between domestic and international prices not only for Western Europe and Japan but also for North America (Table 10.2). This meant that the deadweight welfare losses in those protecting countries from distorting their food markets more than doubled over the 1980s, and the benefits to farmers increased by about 50 percent (Tyers and Anderson, 1992). In particular, the export subsidies under the U.S. Export Enhancement Program (EEP) have been very costly to the United States, have added only very modestly in proportional terms to the cost of the E.C.'s Common Agricultural Policy (CAP), and have imposed large costs on other actual or would-be agricultural-exporting countries (Anania, Bohman, and Carter, 1992).

The rapidity and depth of the international food price decline, and the associated growth in assistance to northern hemisphere farmers who were

TABLE 10.2 Nominal Rates of Assistance to Agriculture in Industrial Countries, 1979-1991 (Percent based on producer subsidy equivalents)[a]

	1979-81	1982-84	1985-87	1988-91
EC-12	58[b]	50[b]	85	84
EFTA	N/A	113[c]	180	176
Japan	133	170	250	190
United States	19	28	56	33
Canada	32	41	79	48
Australia	10	16	16	13
New Zealand	22	37	28	6
All OECD	41	45	79	73

[a]The border price plus the per unit producer subsidy equivalent, expressed as a percentage of the border price for each commodity, and averaged across commodities using production valued at border prices as weights. The E.C. rates include national government assistance as well as that provided by the Community's CAP.
[b]E.C.-10; [c]1979-85
Source: OECD, 1992.

to a considerable extent insulated from that price fall during the first half of the 1980s, gave birth to the Cairns Group. The farm income of that group of 14 countries in 1990 is estimated to have been reduced by at least one-sixth, and their farm exports by one-half, because of agricultural protection in other industrial countries (Tyers, 1993), so it is not surprising that they insisted that the Uruguay Round of multilateral trade negotiations (MTN) could not proceed without agriculture high on the agenda. In taking that stand the Cairns Group was quietly supported by many other developing countries, including some net importers of food who would be significant food exporters in the absence of agricultural protection in the industrial countries and/or in the absence of their own anti-agricultural policies.[5]

Reasons for Agricultural Protection Growth

Empirical estimates of the trade and welfare effects of agricultural protection are helpful, but less than adequate, for shedding light on the reasons for governments' choices of domestic agricultural policies and of trade negotiating tactics. This is because governments choose policies not only with overall efficiency and aggregate national economic welfare in mind but also in response to noneconomic concerns and to concentrated political pressures from vested interest groups. It is understandable that nonfarmers in countries with a weaker comparative advantage in agriculture (the densely populated economies of Western Europe and Northeast Asia) are more sympathetic in supporting agriculture, for example, partly because they are more concerned about security of food supplied from abroad, partly because their farmers have come under stronger pressure to decline and from a base of smaller-scale agriculture than is the case in the more sparsely settled areas of North America and Australasia, and partly because—unlike the food-exporting countries—food-importing countries (which included much of Western Europe until half a generation ago) could assist farmers without budgetary outlays simply by imposing import taxes.

But leaving aside these points that are helpful in understanding the differences between industrial countries' levels of support to farmers at a point in time, why do we observe over time the tendency for distortions to incentives to gradually move from taxing to favoring farmers relative to industrialists in the course of economic development? After all, this seems counterintuitive, given that the farmers' share of national wealth and votes declines with development. A key explanation is to be found by examining the domestic distributional effects of policy interventions. Those effects can be summarized as follows.

Consider first a small country facing exogenously given international prices, a country whose polity cannot influence or be influenced by other countries. Assume the economy has three sectors (agriculture, industry, and nontradables) with sector-specific capital and intersectorally mobile labor. If it is a poor agrarian country with the majority of its workforce involved in semisubsistence farming, a policy-induced increase in the price of food would have a large impact on the demand for labor, thereby substantially raising wage rates. Yet this wage hike could be insufficient to offset the increase in the cost of living for laborers, who spend a large proportion of their income on food and nontradables (the price of which also would rise). Even more importantly, the rise in wages reduces very substantially the income of industrial capitalists. The latter therefore have an incentive to incite (particularly urban) laborers to oppose farm assistance policies and instead support a policy regime favoring industry ("urban jobs") over agriculture. Furthermore, the magnitude of the gain per farmer, following an increase in the relative price of farm products, would be small compared with the loss for industrial capital owners. The net gain to landholders would be small because of a rise not only in the cost of their consumption of food (in opportunity cost terms if they are self-sufficient) and nontradables, but also in their wage payments insofar as they are net buyers of farm labor services. Together these would erode much of the increased return to farm assets.

A recent simulation study suggests raising the price of industrial relative to farm products in such a poor agrarian economy could result in the proportional loss to farmers being only one-tenth the proportional gain to industrial capitalists (Anderson, 1993a). Add to that the fact that in such an economy the cost of collective lobbying action by a small group of urban capitalists is far smaller than those costs for peasant farmers who are poorly served with transport and communications infrastructure, plus the superficial appeal of the arguments for infant industry protection, and it is not surprising that we observe policies in poor countries favoring industry over agriculture.

In rich industrial countries where agriculture accounts for a very small share of production, employment, and consumptive expenditure, by contrast, the skew in the income distributional effects of distorting the relative price of farm products is the reverse. Raising farm product prices has little effect on wages, on the price of nontradables, on returns to industrial capital, or on household expenditure. Hence nonfarm groups, including industrial capitalists, have little incentive to oppose farm-support policies in advanced industrial economies. With the farmer's inputs receiving only a small fraction of the farm's sales revenue, however (most of it being absorbed by purchased intermediate inputs, unlike in poor countries), his net farm income and asset values are boosted very considerably in percentage terms by agricultural price support policies. The above-mentioned simulation study suggests that the proportional gain to farmers from a policy-induced increase in the relative price of farm products could be seven times the loss to industrial capitalists in such an economy, and more than five times the proportional gain to farmers in the poor agrarian country. And the difference between costs of collective action for farmers and those for industrialists also are much lower in rich than in poor countries, not least because the commercialization of agriculture breeds farmer cooperatives, thereby reducing the free-rider problem for farmers seeking to lobby collectively (Olson, 1965, 1986).

Given these vast differences between rich and poor countries in the incentives for producers to lobby for policies that favor their sector, the tendency for governments to alter their country's policy regimes gradually in the course of their economic development, away from disfavoring to favoring farmers, is understandable.

This could lead one to be pessimistic about the prospects for reforming farm protection policies, particularly when market supply and demand conditions are such that the real price of agricultural products is likely to continue to gyrate around a declining long-run trend and cause the agricultural sector's employment share to decline.[6] In this environment, politicians are reluctant to withdraw support: after all, that can always be done after the next election when the economic costs of present policies will be even more obvious!

There is, however, the possibility that the increase in the *aggregate* (as distinct from *per farmer*) demand for farm-support policies will slow down, given the continuing decline in the proportion of employment and

GDP from farming. Hillman (1982) and Long and Vousden (1991) show that government assistance to a declining industry is likely only to slow rather than prevent that decline. Furthermore, Cassing and Hillman (1986) demonstrate that once the industry shrinks sufficiently, the aggregate political contributions its producers are able to make in return for continued government support can become less than the political cost of opposition to that policy, at which point protection is withdrawn. That has already happened to some manufacturing industries (e.g., Swedish shipbuilding, U.S. footwear), but not so far to highly protected agriculture. Perhaps the farm sector's contribution has to become much less than the current 2 or 3 percent of Gross Domestic Product (GDP) and 4 or 5 percent of employment before this threshold point is reached in domestic political markets.

Or, is it possible that outside influences could reverse or at least slow the upward trend in the domestic political equilibrium level of agricultural protection? The next subsection focuses on that question.

The Role of Other Countries and of Multilateral Trade Negotiations in Affecting Agricultural Protection Growth[7]

Pressures on a country's domestic political markets from abroad, which were ignored in the previous subsection, can take several forms. Historically, many developing countries' policies were influenced (or dictated) by an imperial power. This often had a feedback effect on the imperial nation's own policies. Farmers in Britain, for example, were less able than their counterparts in some continental European countries to argue that agricultural protection was necessary to ensure security of supply, because Britain's colonies in the southern hemisphere offered ample sources of food and fiber. During the first half of this century, Japan's rice producers also were less successful in seeking protection from import competition than they would have been if the country had not been able to secure access to rice supplies from its colonies of Korea and Taiwan (Anderson and Tyers, 1992). The lower protection in the imperial country results not only because sympathy for higher farm prices is correlated with food security concerns. Possibly more important is the fact that, since much of the funding for agricultural investment in the colonies came from the imperial country, those landed capitalists had a strong vested interest in open trade within the empire.

More recently, and especially during the past decade, we have seen several other ways in which one or more countries influence—or try to influence—another country's policy regime. When this happens benignly, as it can with an adverse change in the international prices faced by an industry (especially if the change is unexpected, large, and/or because of a foreign government's policy change), the response is usually (a) an increase in that industry's demand for assistance and (b) a decrease in the political cost of supplying it more assistance (the sympathy or social insurance factor—see for example Eaton and Grossman, 1985). In some cases a mechanism to cope with such situations is built into policy, as with the E.C.'s variable import levies/export restitutions, such that only a fraction (perhaps close to zero) of the international price change is transmitted to the domestic market in the short run at least. In the case of the United States, its government's response to the rapid decline in international food prices in the early 1980s—with U.S. elections scheduled for November 1984—was to boost assistance to its own farmers (see Table 10.2 above). The marginal political cost of this extra assistance had fallen because it was argued in the United States that the drop in farmers' returns was in large part due to E.C. farm policies and would be remedied by retaliating in kind and thereby raising the budgetary, and hence political, cost in the E.C. of continuing its export subsidies. Even though the E.C. showed no sign of reducing its subsidies during the latter 1980s, the greater U.S. export subsidies continued for at least three reasons: in part to keep pressure on E.C. policy makers, in part to win political support in the November 1988 elections, and in part to have a higher base level of support from which to reduce assistance in the event of an Uruguay Round agreement to liberalize subsequently.

The U.S. subsidy increase put even more downward pressure on international food prices. Canadian farmers responded by successfully demanding an assistance boost also (see Table 10.2). That option would, however, have been a more costly political option for the smaller and poorer agricultural-exporting countries, including those in the Cairns Group, where manufacturers tended to hold the upper hand politically. Instead, all the governments of those countries could do was to try to ensure agriculture remained high on the Uruguay Round agenda, and to encourage the United States and E.C. to find a compromise between their extreme positions in the Round. Presumably those extreme positions were adopted because neither the U.S. government nor the E.C. leadership was convinced they would gain politically from an Uruguay Round agreement in the early 1990s. (The situation in the E.C. is simply that politicians have wanted to reduce agricultural protection as little as possible. In the United States the situation is more complex: low-cost, export-oriented farmers stand to gain considerably, but U.S. farmers on average have much less to gain than Cairns Group farmers from a multilateral liberalization of farm policies,[8] and many of the more-assisted farm and non-farm U.S. interests have remained unconvinced they would benefit from a Round agreement.)

Does the Blair House Accord Provide a Basis For
Resolving the U.S.-E.C. Dispute?

The meeting of U.S. and E.C. negotiators at Blair House in November 1992 resulted in an accord that seemed to provide an acceptable compromise to the two parties in dispute. The French government initially took exception to the agreement, but in June 1993 it too seemed prepared to accept the accord as a basis for returning to the Uruguay Round of multilateral trade negotiations. The extent of liberalization implied by the accord will not be known precisely until the Round is concluded and we see the nature of the policy re-instrumentation that occurs, but the orders of magnitude involved are clear. In particular, it is clear that the accord is a long way from the initial U.S. demand of the latter 1980s of complete liberalization of all agricultural protection. It is even a long way from people's expectations of mid-1990, when the United States was talking of a 75 percent liberalization and the E.C. was vaguely suggesting perhaps a 25 percent reform, which led to the guess that a 50 percent liberalization, phased over several years, might be the compromise in the Uruguay Round agreement that was scheduled to be completed in Brussels in December 1990. Nor is the Blair House accord to involve as much reform as was in the Dunkel Draft Final Act of December 1991, which would have averaged a cut of about one quarter in the levels of protection in force in the late 1980s. The accord will require an average cut in producer price supports of less than one-sixth phased over six years, or less than 3 percent per year. This would comprise reductions of 15 percent in the tariff equivalent of import controls and 21 percent in the volume of subsidized exports.[9] Moreover, since the accord is based on the MacSharry proposal for CAP reform issued in May 1992, it is likely to reflect the commodity bias in that proposal. In particular, grain and oilseed policies are likely to be reformed most, meat policies only moderately, and dairy and sugar programs least of all (despite the fact that they are the most protected commodities).

The scope for the latter commodity bias in the Blair House accord, together with the resolution of the United States' long-standing dispute over E.C. assistance to oilseed producers, helps explain the preparedness of the United States to use the accord as a basis for an Uruguay Round agreement. This is because it would mean relatively little pain for U.S. dairy and sugar producers relative to the large gains for their producers of grains and soybean and would involve little discipline on domestic support for those commodities with supply constraints in place.

For the E.C. too the effective absence of discipline on its supply-constrained dairy and sugar programs, and the much smaller degree of reduction required of border measures compared with the initial U.S.

demands, will make it relatively easy to sell an agreement on this basis within the E.C., particularly now that the MacSharry proposal for CAP reform has been widely accepted. But there are two other reasons to expect the E.C. to find this more acceptable as part of an Uruguay Round agreement now than a couple of years ago. The first is simply that the recession has deepened considerably in the E.C., so there is more urgency to conclude the Round to help jump-start the European economies.

The second reason to expect the E.C. to be more amenable now than two years ago to agreeing to CAP reform has to do with the process of widening the E.C. There are two aspects of this process to consider: the absorption of EFTA member countries into the E.C., and the accommodation of the aspirations of the Central and East Europeans. The absorption of EFTA countries into the E.C. would make it easier for the E.C. to meet its requirements under the Blair House accord, for the following reasons. The joining EFTA members would be required to lower their domestic food prices from their current very high levels to CAP levels (see Table 10.2). If the common CAP prices were to be those resulting from the MacSharry proposals, a recent empirical study suggests that by the year 2000 if all EFTA countries were to join the E.C. then as a group they would become net food importers and absorb about one-seventh of the volume of EC-12 exports (Anderson and Tyers, 1993b). That is, more than the full amount of adjustment that would be required of Western Europe by a Blair House-type agreement would be undertaken anyway not only as a result of implementing the MacSharry proposals but also as a consequence of reforms EFTA countries would have to undertake to join the E.C. That is, EFTA countries would bear much of the brunt of the farm adjustment on behalf of all Western European countries.

It is conceivable that the common CAP prices in an enlarged E.C. of 15 or more members would be higher than those suggested by the MacSharry proposal/Blair House accord—and without contravening that accord, given the large reduction in protection in the EFTA countries. They could be higher for a combination of several reasons. First, a considerable proportion of the EC-12's export surplus would be sold to the former EFTA countries at internal CAP prices instead of being sold on the open market at the ruling international prices. This would reduce substantially (by nearly one-third) the budgetary cost of the export subsidies necessary to dispose of the CAP-induced surpluses, and so reduce opposition to the CAP in EC-12 countries. At the same time (a) the agricultural ministers of the former EFTA countries would be joining the E.C.'s annual price-setting committee with a more protectionist leaning on average than the EC-12 ministers; (b) the high-income EFTA countries would be required to make significant net contributions to the E.C.'s budget; and (c) the cheap-rider problem in restraining CAP expenditure would worsen because of the additional number of E.C. member countries.[10] Together these changes would tend to cause the average level of agricultural protection in the enlarged E.C. to settle above what it otherwise would have been in an E.C. of just 12 member countries, notwithstanding any Blair House-type accord. In that event, it is conceivable that agricultural exporters elsewhere could be worse off rather than better off from E.C. enlargement to include some or all of the EFTA countries. This rather sobering conclusion adds a premium to the value of reaching an Uruguay Round conclusion that puts a cap on the CAP's agricultural protection level (to borrow from the title of Chapter 6 by Guyomard et al.). Moreover, it demonstrates that restrictions on the quantity and value of subsidized farm exports from Western Europe that might be agreed to in the Uruguay Round are no guarantee that EC-12 domestic farm prices and protection levels will not rise.

EFTA countries are not alone in wanting to join the E.C. of course. Many of the former communist countries of Central and Eastern Europe are among those lining up. While their full membership is inconceivable until well into next century, the most advanced of them (the Central European countries of the Czech Republic, Hungary, Poland, and Slovakia) have already begun a form of associate membership involving some preferential access to E.C. markets. Since the usable industrial capital stock per worker in those countries is very low relative to the stock of agricultural land and other farm capital per worker, their comparative advantages during the next decade or so are likely to be in primary products (and standard-technology manufactures—see Hamilton and Winters (1992) and Anderson (1992c, 1993b)). So it is in these product areas that access to E.C. markets is most sought after. While to date the E.C. has been resisting, at the behest of its domestic interest groups, there are serious concerns about immigration from, and/or political upheavals in, the transforming economies should they not begin to prosper soon.

Completely free access for Central and Eastern European farmers to E.C. food markets seems unlikely in the foreseeable future, if only because of its impact on the CAP budget. According to another recent simulation exercise, if just the four Central European countries were given free access to E.C. markets by the end of the decade at CAP prices, this would cause the budgetary cost of the CAP in the year 2000 to be enlarged by one-third (Anderson and Tyers, 1993b). A more likely development is that Central European farmers will gradually be given more preferential access to West European markets over time (from the current very low base), perhaps just enough to make them prefer to support rather than oppose the E.C.'s agricultural protection policy—as has been the case for the African, Caribbean, and Pacific island signatories to the Lome Convention.

Even so, insofar as the former centrally planned economies expand their net exports of farm products, along with the reforming developing countries of Latin America and elsewhere, they will add to the downward trend in real international food prices. This also will raise the budgetary cost of the CAP. That is, whether the Central and East Europeans are given access to E.C. food markets or not, those economies will be imposing increasing budgetary pressure on the E.C. to reduce its domestic farm prices. To put the point another way, the domestic political cost of CAP reform will be offset somewhat by the fact that the reform would lower the incentive for the transforming economies of Central and Eastern Europe to seek preferential access to Western Europe's food markets.

For all these reasons, and especially because the United States has lowered enormously its expectations concerning the agricultural part of the Uruguay Round, it would now seem that at least that part of an agreement involving the United States and E.C. is within reach. The next question is: would such an accord satisfy the other contracting parties to the GATT?

The Acceptability of a Blair House-Type Accord to Third Countries

There are several advantages of accepting a Blair House-type accord, as part of an Uruguay Round agreement, that apply to all countries. The first is that it involves the tariffication of all trade restrictions, which, together with the decreased probability of future U.S.-E.C. farm export subsidy wars, would ensure that international food prices would fluctuate less in future. Second, insofar as it allowed a conclusion to the Uruguay Round, that would be a major boon in at least four respects: through the boost it would give to world GDP; through improvements in the trade dispute settlement procedures as part of the GATT; through restoring confidence in the GATT rules-based multilateral trading system generally, which, among other things, would further encourage the former centrally planned economies to clean up their trade policy act so they can join the GATT; and through reducing the discrimination of the preferential trading blocs (by lowering their external trade barriers) and thereby reducing the incentives for excluded countries to join existing blocs or form new ones.[11]

But what about the features of the Blair House accord itself from the viewpoint of countries other than the United States and members of EC-12? Consider the following groups of countries.

EFTA Member Countries

Those joining the E.C. later this decade would be virtually unaffected, because they will be lowering their internal prices down to CAP levels anyway, and the gap between EFTA prices in 1986-88 and the CAP prices expected in the late 1990s under the MacSharry plan is considerably more than the extent of reduction required under the Blair House accord. Those EFTA countries not joining the E.C. in the next few years, however, will have to reform somewhat. In the case of Switzerland this process has already begun, with the switching from price-support measures to more direct forms of farm income support. As a net food importer at these lowered domestic prices, economic welfare in Switzerland would be reduced by the rise in international food prices,[12] but this effect would be far more than offset by the economic welfare gains from the country's own liberalization.

Japan and Korea

As net food importers these economies too would be adversely affected by the rise in international food prices, *ceteris paribus*. Of course that would be far more than offset by the economic benefits from liberalizing their own agricultural policies, but, assuming current policies represent a political equilibrium situation, such a forced liberalization would be considered a political cost. Even so, these countries ultimately are likely to agree to reform their farm policies (possibly in the last hours of the negotiations) because they have so much to gain potentially from the nonagricultural parts of an Uruguay Round agreement, and because the alternative of no Uruguay Round agreement for them is far worse, since it would probably involve much more aggressive unilateral pressure from the United States to provide greater market access.

Europe's Economies in Transition

Since most of the economies of Eastern Europe and the former Soviet Union are not GATT contracting parties, their views are not directly relevant for concluding the Uruguay Round. They are of interest indirectly, though, because their incentives to integrate with Western Europe are affected. Those heavily dependent on food imports (most notably Russia) would be a little worse off partly because of higher international food prices and partly because there would be less embarrassing surplus food stocks in Western Europe and North America to be given away to them at a low or zero price. However, most of these economies in transition are now, or may well soon become, net exporters of temperate foods (Anderson, 1992c, 1993b; Hamilton and Winters, 1992). In that case they would benefit from the increase in international food prices. Furthermore, as mentioned above, CAP reform would lower the incentive for the transforming economies of Central and Eastern Europe to seek preferential access to Western Europe's food markets.

Food-Deficit Developing Countries

Those heavily dependent on food imports would, like Russia, face higher prices for their imports and receive less food aid. Some people have argued against CAP reform for this reason, but of course it would be far cheaper to give larger aid grants to Sahelian countries, for example, than not to reform the CAP. Furthermore, most people in such developing countries benefit from higher food prices, because farm households typically make up the bulk of the population—and they tend to be much poorer on average than their city cousins as well (otherwise their cousins would not have moved to the city). Moreover, other aspects of the Uruguay Round, such as liberalization of the Multifiber Arrangement, would benefit such countries, quite possibly by more than they would lose from higher food prices.

The Cairns Group and Other Developing Countries

The Cairns Group includes middle-sized players such as Brazil and Argentina that are particularly significant because it was their dissatisfaction that led to the failure to conclude the Uruguay Round as scheduled in December 1990. But this set of countries is much broader than just the 14 Cairns Group members and includes numerous developing countries that are currently net importers of food but would be net food exporters at higher post-Uruguay Round prices or will become so as their own unilateral liberalizations to reduce their anti-agricultural bias proceed. One might expect these countries, and especially the Cairns Group members who have lobbied so hard to keep agriculture high on the Round's agenda, to be dissatisfied with the Blair House accord, for several reasons:

- the very small degree of liberalization, relative to earlier hopes, and particularly in dairy, sugar, and to a lesser extent meat products;
- the fact that much of the liberalization now seems inevitable anyway, particularly because of the MacSharry-inspired CAP reform in the E.C. and the protection cuts required of those EFTA members who intend to join the E.C. later this decade;
- the lack of effective discipline on internal support measures; and
- the effective legitimization the accord gives to policies such as export subsidies, including the U.S.' Export Enhancement Program.

But these disappointing features are likely to be perceived as being more than offset by the following positive features of an Uruguay Round agreement based on that accord:

- it would slow and hopefully reverse the long-run upward trend in agricultural protection rates in advanced industrial countries and lock in the reforms to prevent backsliding (which makes it more significant than just the MacSharry proposed CAP reforms, not least because the latter might otherwise be less than fully implemented);

- it would make it more difficult for middle-income countries and the former centrally planned economies to follow the advanced industrial countries' example of increasing agricultural protection as economic development proceeds;
- it would ensure the United States' EEP payments are lowered and reduce the probability of further farm export subsidy wars, which with tariffication would, as mentioned above, reduce fluctuations in international food prices;
- it would raise the average level of food prices in international markets by around 3 percent compared with no reform;
- it would bring stronger GATT rules on the use of sanitary and phytosanitary provisions as substitute trade barriers and for settling trade disputes in the GATT; and
- even though the reforms would be phased in over six years, the increased certainty of higher and more stable prices in the years ahead would encourage greater farm investment in the expanding farm sectors immediately.

What Lies Ahead?

The long history of agricultural protection growth in industrializing countries, and the more recent history of failure even to get agriculture on the agenda of multilateral trade negotiations prior to the Uruguay Round, provided ample evidence that it would not be easy to conclude this Round if agriculture remained prominently on its agenda. As well as that difficulty has been Western Europe's preoccupation with major developments within its own region, which in the 1980s had (a) reduced its governments' preparedness to contemplate adding the further shock of agricultural policy reform and (b) caused the attention of trade negotiators in North America and other regions to be diverted from the Round and towards forming regional integration agreements of their own (Anderson and Blackhurst, 1993).

Given that background, getting an agreement to "merely" slow or slightly reverse that agricultural protection growth and bring agriculture back into the GATT mainstream, ready for future MTN rounds, would be judged by history to be very significant progress. And the above assessment suggests the Blair House accord may well be an acceptable basis for settling the agricultural part of the Round. It would be even more acceptable to many participants if it included a commitment to liberalize further after the first six years and if it had incentives to liberalize more than the minimum amount during those first six years (e.g., by ensuring "credit" be given in subsequent rounds for any additional reform during the first six years).

Returning to a point made at the outset, however, it needs to be recognized that, having got to this point in the agricultural part of the negotiations, there may still not be the political will to bring the Round to a successful conclusion, because of remaining disputes in nonagricultural areas. In that unfortunate event, would that mean agricultural protection growth would continue rather than be halted? The answer is probably yes for those middle-income countries that are rapidly industrializing (for the political economy reasons mentioned in the section titled "Reasons for Agricultural Protection Growth")—except where the United States adopts aggressive unilateral tactics, as it is likely to continue doing in East Asia. An offsetting influence on international food prices will be the recent and ongoing unilateral reforms to the trade policies of numerous developing countries that in the past have discriminated against agriculture. It is possible that enthusiasm for such reforms may be lessened if the industrial economies fail to agree to liberalize farm trade, however. An alternative or additional possibility is that a weak or aborted Round outcome may encourage some developing countries to seek the safe haven of a regional integration agreement (Baldwin, 1993). In that event their farm policies may become more or less liberal. Certainly Mexico's reform have been bolstered by the move towards a North American Free Trade Agreement (NAFTA) agreement.

And what about in Europe? Pressure within the E.C. to reduce food prices unilaterally is without doubt considerably greater now than prior to the Uruguay Round. This is partly because consumers, taxpayers, environmentalists, and nonagricultural exporters are now much better informed about the enormous economic and environmental[13] costs of the CAP than was the case a decade ago, and partly because those costs—and especially the budgetary outlays—have grown so much in recent years. The unilateral reform of the CAP agreed to by E.C. ministers in mid-1992 (the so-called MacSharry proposal) is a sign of these changes in the climate of public opinion within the E.C., notwithstanding the fact that they were agreed to with half an eye on the nonfarm benefits expected from an Uruguay Round agreement once farm reform was achieved.

Similar domestic pressures have grown in the other countries of Western Europe as well (the EFTA members), but in addition most of those countries are aspiring to be full members of the E.C. Since their agricultural protection levels are well above those of the E.C. (see Table 10.2), they will need to be brought down substantially during this decade—as Sweden has already begun to do—for membership to proceed.[14]

What will the common level of prices be in an enlarged E.C. involving these additional Alpine and Nordic countries of Western Europe in the absence of Uruguay Round discipline? As mentioned above, there would be several reasons to expect CAP prices to be higher as a consequence of E.C. enlargement to include some EFTA countries, not the least being the substantial reduction in budgetary outlays because the new members would absorb a considerable share of the EC-12 surplus and would pay CAP instead of international prices for those imports. As well, the East European economies would have more incentive in this situation to seek preferential access to E.C. food markets. If sufficient access were to be granted, that would make these economies in transition supporters rather than opponents of the CAP.

For Japan and South Korea, the absence of an agricultural accord as part of an Uruguay Round agreement would not put an end to external pressure on their protectionist farm policies. On the contrary, they would be likely to face a sharp increase in aggressive unilateral pressure from the United States. Even if this resulted in a significant opening up of Northeast Asian food markets, however, it would be very much a second-best outcome from the viewpoint of other agricultural exporters, in two respects. First, the selection of products targeted by the United States would be ones aimed at appeasing U.S. farmers' demands for access. Specifically, feedgrain and oilseeds are more likely to be stressed than livestock products. And secondly, a greater degree of "managed" trade is likely to result, involving source-specific import targets for particular commodities. Not only would that favor the United States over other exporters but it would undermine the GATT rules-based, nondiscriminatory multilateral trading system on which the prosperity of smaller economies depends heavily.

In short, the prospects ahead in the absence of a successful conclusion to the Uruguay Round are for more uncertain, less stable agricultural trade relations: more-managed bilateral trades, more focus on discriminatory regional integration arrangements, further U.S.-E.C. farm export subsidy wars, and a smaller unmanaged international market that would be less capable of absorbing gyrations in excess demand by some of the former communist countries (of the sort that developments in China caused to fiber markets in the mid-1980s). Certainly it would not be all smooth sailing if something like the Blair House accord were to be adopted as part of an Uruguay Round agreement, for there is a considerable degree of quantitative management of farm trade in that accord. But a successful Uruguay Round agreement would boost trade in all sectors and thereby improve investor confidence and help bring the world economy out of recession.

For trade economists, the difficulty in concluding the Uruguay Round, and in particular the difficulties the United States and E.C. have had in reaching a compromise on agricultural policy reform, point to an obvious area requiring further research. The study of the political economy of trade policy has made great progress during the past two decades, but primarily from the viewpoint of an individual country whose polity is unaffected by overseas interest groups. Only recently have a few analyses begun to appear that model explicitly the general equilibrium trade policy interactions that take place between governments responsive to domestic interest groups (e.g., Grossman and Helpman, 1992; Hillman and Moser, 1992). The task ahead is to develop such models further so that they can capture the reality of more than two country groups (to help understand the role that can be played by the Cairns Group, for example), and so they can go beyond just two sectors and focus on the impact of adding "difficult" sectors such as agriculture to a multiproduct, multilateral trade negotiating process as was done for the Uruguay Round.

Notes

The author is grateful for helpful comments from Brian Fisher, Stefan Tangermann, and other participants at the conference in Calabria, Italy and at a CEPR/European Centre for Advanced Research in Economics seminar in Brussels on 24 June, 1993. Thanks are also due to the Australian Research Council, London's CEPR, and the RAISA project of the Italian National Research Council for financial assistance.

1. For one set of estimates of the extent of these adverse effects, and references to related studies, see Tyers and Anderson (1992) and Anderson (1992b).

2. The 14 countries in the Cairns Group are Argentina, Australia, Brazil, Canada, Chile, Columbia, Fiji, Hungary, Indonesia, Malaysia, the Philippines, New Zealand, Thailand, and Uruguay. The group is named after the Australian city where they first met in the mid-1980s. The Group's sole purpose to date has been to ensure that agricultural trade liberalization remains high on the agenda of the Uruguay Round. While none of these countries is very large on its own in terms of trade-bargaining power, as a group the value of their agricultural output exceeds that of either the United States or the E.C., and their farm exports exceed the United States and E.C. combined. They are also responsible for more than one tenth of the world's imports of manufactures (Tyers 1993). For some details of their activities see, for example, Higgott and Cooper (1990) and Oxley (1990).

3. For more on this history, see also Kindleberger (1975) and Stuart (1992).

4. It is true nontariff barriers to trade in some manufactures have grown as tariffs on imports of manufactures have come down, but evidently these have been insufficient to prevent rapid growth in manufactures trade. Indeed the global trade-to-GDP ratio has risen from less than one-fifth in the late 1930s to more than one-third today (Anderson and Blackhurst, 1993, Appendix), only a part of which would be due to the drop in international transport and communications costs and in the value-added share of output.

5. The analysis showing why even net food importing developing countries can lose from agricultural protection in industrial countries is spelled out in, for example, Anderson and Tyers (1993a), along with one set of estimates of the

losses involved. The estimates of the number of such developing countries and the extent of their losses vary according to the model used and assumptions made, however, as the studies reported in Goldin and Knudsen (1990) testify.

6. For an explanation of why agriculture declines in the course of economic growth, see Anderson (1987).

7. This subsection draws on Anderson (1992a).

8. See, for example, Tyers and Anderson (1992, Table 7.7).

9. All import restrictions are to be converted to bound tariffs equivalent to the restrictions in place in 1986-88, and the unweighted average of those tariffs is to be lowered by 36 percent, but each tariff item need be reduced by no more than 15 percent. Since many items had a zero tariff equivalent in the base period of 1986-88, this effectively allows countries to limit their actual tariff reductions to 15 percent. In the case of export subsidies, their value is to be reduced by 36 percent and their volume by 21 percent for each commodity, from a 1986-90 base. But because of the drop in international food prices since that base period, only the volume limit will be binding. If the excess supply elasticity was 0.8, this would represent a reduction in the export subsidy rate of one-sixth. Internal price supports also are to be reduced by an average of 20 percent from a 1986-88 base, but in most cases that has already been met because international prices have risen since that base period. In any case the use of an averaging criterion would make it easy to meet such a target. Moreover, since programs that have supply constraints such as acreage set-aside provisions are not counted in the calculation of the aggregate measure of internal support, there is virtually no requirement in the accord for countries to reduce internal supports (Sumner, Ch. 4).

10. Each EC member country would have more incentive to seek price increases for the products for which its excess supply is relatively large, and to cooperate less in policing farm supply constraints such as land set-asides.

11. On the safe-haven motive for wanting to join preferential trading blocs, see Baldwin (1993).

12. According to recent estimates by Helmar et al. (Ch. 12) and Vanzetti et al. (Ch. 13), a liberalization along the lines of the Blair House accord would raise the level of international food prices by around 3 percent on average, *ceteris paribus*.

13. For a discussion of the environmental consequences of agricultural protection policies, see, for example, Anderson (1992b) and Lutz (1992).

14. However, some EFTA farmers are arguing that, since some CAP payments are tied to acreage set-asides or production quotas, it is in their national interest to expand farm output now so as to have a larger base at the time of joining the EC later this decade, to which output-reducing measures would apply.

References

Anania, G., M. Bohman, and C. Carter. 1992. "United States Export Subsidies in Wheat: Strategic Trade Policy or Expensive Beggar-Thy-Neighbor Tactic?" *American Journal of Agricultural Economics* 74: 534-45.

Anderson, K. 1983. "Growth of Agricultural Protection in East Asia." *Food Policy* 8: 327-36.

———. 1987. "On Why Agriculture Declines With Economic Growth." *Agricultural Economics* 1: 195-207.

———. 1992a. "International Dimensions of the Political Economy of Distortionary Price and Trade Policies." In *Open Economies: Structural Adjustment and Agriculture*, edited by I. Goldin and L.A.Winters. Cambridge: Cambridge Univ. Press.

———. 1992b. "Agricultural Trade Liberalization and the Environment: A Global Perspective." *The World Economy* 15: 153-71.

———. 1992c. "Will Eastern Europe and the Former Soviet Union Become Major Agricultural Exporters?" In *Improving Agricultural Trade Performance Under the Uruguay Round*, edited by T. Becker, R. Gray, and A. Schmitz, Kiel: Wissenschaftverlag Vauk.

———. 1993a. "Lobbying Incentives and the Pattern of Protection in Rich and Poor Countries." *Economic Development and Cultural Change.* Forthcoming.

———. 1993b. "Intersectoral Changes in Transforming Socialist Countries: Distinguishing Initial From Longer Term Responses." In *Economic Growth and Agriculture*, edited by I. Goldin. London: Macmillan. Forthcoming.

Anderson, K., and R. Blackhurst, eds. 1993. *Regional Integration and the Global Trading System*. London: Harvester Wheatsheaf and New York: St Martin's Press.

Anderson, K., *et al.* 1986. *The Political Economy of Agricultural Protection*. Boston, London, and Sydney: Allen and Unwin.

Anderson, K., and R. Tyers. 1992. "Japanese Rice Policy in the Interwar Period: Some Consequences of Imperial Self Sufficiency." *Japan and the World Economy* 4: 103-27.

———. 1993a. "More on Welfare Gains from Liberalizing World Food Trade." *Journal of Agricultural Economics* 44: 189-204.

———. 1993b. "Implications of E.C. Expansion for European Agricultural Policies, Trade and Welfare." Paper presented to a CEPR conference, *EC's New Entrants: Shifting Weights in Europe*, held near Helsinki, May 13-15.

Baldwin, R. 1993. "A Domino Theory of Regionalism." Paper presented at CEPR conference, *EC's New Entrants: Shifting Weights in Europe*, 13-15 May, held near Helsinki.

Cassing, J.H., and A.L. Hillman. 1986. "Shifting Comparative Advantage and Senescent Industry Collapse." *American Economic Review* 76 (June): 516-23.

Eaton, J., and G. M. Grossman. 1985. "Tariffs as Insurance: Optimal Commercial Policy When Domestic Markets are Incomplete." *Canadian Journal of Economics* 18: 258-72.

Goldin, I., and O. Knudsen. 1990. *Agricultural Trade Liberalization: Implications for Developing Countries*. Paris: OECD.

Grilli, E. R., and M. C. Yang. 1988. "Primary Commodity Prices, Manufactured Goods Prices, and the Terms of Trade of Developing Countries: What the Long Run Shows." *World Bank Economic Review* 2 (January): 1-48.

Grossman, G. M., and E. Helpman. 1992. "Trade Wars and Trade Talks." Princeton University. Mimeo.

Gulbrandsen, O., and A. Lindbeck. 1973. *The Economics of the Agricultural Sector*. Stockholm: Almqvist and Wicksell.

Hamilton, C., and L. A. Winters. 1992. "Opening Up International Trade in Eastern Europe." *Economic Policy* 7: 78-116.

Higgott, R. A. and A. F. Cooper. 1990. "Middle Power Leadership and Coalition Building: Australia, the Cairns Group, and the Uruguay Round of Trade Negotiations." *International Organisation* 44: 589-632.

Hillman, A. L. 1982. "Declining Industries and Political-Support Protectionist Motives." *American Economic Review* 72 (December): 1180-87.

Hillman, A. L., and P. Moser. 1992. "Trade Liberalization as Politically Optimal Exchange of Market Access." Paper presented to the fifth ERWIT Conference,24-28 June, at Lisbon.

Kindleberger, C. P. 1975. "The Rise of Free Trade in Western Europe, 1820-75." *Journal of Economic History* 35(March): 20-55.

Lindert, P. H. 1991. "Historical Patterns of Agricultural Policy." In *Agriculture and the State: Growth, Employment and Poverty*, edited by C. P. Timmer. Ithaca: Cornell Univ. Press.

Long, N. V., and N. Vousden. 1991. "Protectionist Response and Declining Industries." *Journal of International Economics* 30: 87-103.

Lutz, E. 1992. "Agricultural Trade Liberalization, Price Changes and Environmental Effects." *Environmental and Resource Economics* 2: 79-89.

McCalla, A. 1969. "Protectionism in International Agricultural Trade." *Agricultural History* 43: 329-44.

Organization for Economic Cooperation and Development. 1992. *Monitoring and Outlook of Agricultural Policies, Markets and Trade*. Paris: OECD.

Olson, M. 1965. *The Logic of Collective Action*. Cambridge: Harvard Univ. Press.

———. 1986. "The Exploitation and Subsidization of Agriculture in Developed and Developing Countries." In *Agriculture in a Turbulent World Economy*, edited by A. Maunder and U. Renborg. London: Dartmouth for the IAAE.

Oxley, A. 1990. *The Challenge of Free Trade*. London: Harvester Wheatsheaf.

Stuart, C. 1992. "Corn Laws and Modern Agricultural Trade Policy." Seminar Paper No. 524, Institute for International Economic Studies, Stockholm.

Tracy, M. 1989. *Agriculture in Western Europe:1880-1988*. London: Harvester Wheatsheaf.

Tyers, R. 1993. "The Cairns Group and the Uruguay Round of International Trade Negotiations." In *Agriculture in the Uruguay Round: Reform Objectives and Assessment*, edited by R. C. Hine, K. A. Ingersent, and A. J. Rayner. London: Macmillan.

Tyers, R., and K. Anderson. 1992. *Disarray in World Food Markets: A Quantitative Assessment*. Cambridge: Cambridge Univ. Press.

Discussion

Brian S. Fisher

In his chapter Professor Anderson has highlighted the tendency for the rate of agricultural protection to rise as industrialization proceeds. The general pattern is that developing countries tax their agriculture while industrial countries assist farmers in many ways. It can be readily demonstrated that unilateral reform of such distortions is in the overall interests of such countries. However, for the political reasons outlined by Professor Anderson, reform tends to be slow in coming.

It is worth noting however, that some countries have embarked on unilateral microeconomic reform programs, including in some instances for their agricultural sectors. Such programs may have been put in place because of a recognition of the need to deal with problems of growth and external imbalance (A case in point is the reform of the New Zealand economy that occurred in the 1980s). Less well documented are those instances where reform has been motivated, at least in part, by the coincidence of the development of a peculiar set of institutions and the staffing of those organizations and policy departments in government by individuals with a strong reform agenda. These factors, together with strong political leadership, play an important part in the reform process. The work of the then Australian Industries Assistance Commission in the 1970s and 1980s, the growing strength of a reformist National Farmers Federation and the vision of the then Minister for Primary Industries and Energy, John Kerin, led to some major changes in agricultural policy in Australia in the 1980s.

From the perspective of the traditional agricultural exporters (and those that would be efficient exporters if it were not for the current corruption of world markets) the important thing about agricultural protection is not the effects on economic welfare within the countries who practice it, but the effect it has on world markets and trade. The shrinking size of the international food and fiber markets caused by the erection of tariff and non-tariff barriers and the growing exports of subsidized agricultural products has not only led to a fall in world prices but has also led to an increase in the variability of those prices. This has lowered farm incomes in traditional exporting countries and has also increased the risk faced by farmers. In his chapter Professor Anderson has highlighted the long term downward trend in real food prices over this century but, more importantly, has drawn our attention to the major dip in real prices during the mid 1980s, a time when there was a significant increase in the disposal of subsidized agricultural commodities on world markets by both the United States and the European Community.

There are few countries that are blameless in the distortion of agricultural commodity markets. Even those schemes designed to stabilize agricultural prices which have little or no effect on the effective rate of protection can fail, with substantial short and medium term impact on world markets for the particular commodity. A case in point is the failure in 1991 of the Australian wool buffer stock scheme (Gunasekera and Fisher, 1992). It is fair to say, however, that the major source of distortion in international agricultural markets in the 1980s and the early 1990s has been the Common Agricultural Policy of the European Community. There is some evidence that for the major cereals the various U.S. Farm Bills have had a neutral impact on production and trade (Roberts et al., 1989). In other words, over the long term the production enhancing effects of U.S. farm policy has been largely offset by set-aside and other arrangements that have reduced aggregate output. The same cannot be said for the European Community which has been transformed from a net grain importer to a major net gain exporter with the help of subsidies over the last 20 years.

The trends in agricultural protection and the consequent effects on international food and fiber markets during the mid 1980s largely explain the approach taken to the Uruguay Round by the Cairns Group. The Group has striven for a better outcome than that represented by one based on the Blair House Accord (for the estimated effect on world prices of a Blair House Accord style outcome compared with that of complete liberalization or an outcome based on the Dunkel Text see Table 10.3). Professor Anderson has outlined some of the reasons for dissatisfaction with a Blair House Accord style arrangement among the Cairns Group. In particular he has highlighted the small degree of likely liberalization, particularly for dairy products and sugar. The difference in export mix and the projected likely changes in international prices across products explain the difference in the relative gains from an agreement based on the Blair House Accord across Cairns Group countries (see Table 10.4).

The other major concerns are the effective legitimization of export subsidies (albeit at a lower level) and the lack of strong discipline on internal support measures. The compensation payment associated with the MacSharry inspired CAP reforms of 1992 cannot be considered to be fully decoupled (Roberts, Andrews, and Rees, 1992).

These concerns aside, Professor Anderson has set down a number of reasons in support of locking in a Blair House style agreement on agriculture in the Uruguay Round. Perhaps the most important of these is that such an agreement would "slow or slightly reverse" the long term trend toward more agricultural protection in industrialized countries. While the

TABLE 10.3 Projected Changes in World Prices as a Consequence of Global Complete Liberalization and the Adoption of the Dunkel Text and the Blair House Accord (Percent)

	Global Complete Liberalization[a]	Dunkel Package[b]	Blair House Accord[b]
Beef[c]	11	9	6
Pork	11	7	7
Sheep Meat	21	5	2
Poultry Meat	16	4	4
Butter	85	10	10
Cheese	38	20	17
Milk Powder	81	15	10
Wheat	20	7	6
Corn	23	7	6
Other Coarse Grains	16	7	6
Rice	15	7	7
Soybeans	-3	2	1
Other Oilseeds	8	7	6
Cotton	4	3	3
Sugar	40	3	3

[a] Based on 1986 data.
[b] Based on 1989 data.
[c] Under the Dunkel and Blair House Scenarios beef is free of foot and mouth disease whereas for global liberalization no distinction has been made between the two types of beef.
Source: Krissoff, Sullivan, Wainio, and Johnston (1990); Vanzetti, Andrews, Hester, and Fisher (1993).

overall gains in world agricultural prices would be modest, gains in economic welfare around the world would still be substantial (Table 10.5). An agreement would also bring stronger GATT rules on the use of sanitary and phytosanitary regulations as a substitute for other trade barriers. Even so, there is a continued need to carefully monitor the introduction of various new forms of non-tariff barriers. In the coming decade there is likely to be growing pressure to use environment-related issues as the excuse for imposing new trade restrictions.

In his chapter Professor Anderson has advanced a plausible hypothesis that internal prices could be higher with the possible entry of EFTA countries into the E.C. later this decade. This, together with the U.S. response to any increase in the levels of agricultural protection in Europe are strong reasons to press hard for progress on agriculture in this Round. It is indisputable that the interests of the traditional agricultural exporters and the many small developing nations around the world are best served by reform of multilateral trading arrangements and a strong and workable GATT.

TABLE 10.4 Change in Producer Welfare (as a proportion of the value of exports) in Cairns Group Countries with Implementation of the Blair House Accord[a] (Percent)

	Beef	Pork	Poultry Meat	Milk and Dairy Products	Wheat	Coarse Grains	Rice	Oilseeds and Oilseed Products	Sugar	Total
Australia	8			29	10	12	1		2	11
New Zealand	3			12						8
Canada		8		-258	13	38		-2		11
Argentina	9			124	8	7	19	5	13	9
Brazil	32		24					2	16	16
Chile								23		17
Colombia									12	195
Uruguay	3						11			8
Hungary	-1	13	2	47	5					14
Indonesia						270		14		84
Malaysia								4		5
Philippines								12	20	45
Thailand			16			21	10		4	11
Cairns Group Total	11	45	22	34	6	40	64	5	3	14

[a] Based on a SWOPSIM model simulation using 1989 as the base year.

TABLE 10.5 Estimated Changes in Annual Total Welfare as a Result of the Blair House Accord (US$m)

	Producer Welfare	Consumer Welfare	Government Savings	Total Welfare
United States	5,644	−5,842	408	210
European Community	−1,961	8,198	−5,527	710
Cairns Group[a]	4,856	−3,956	319	1,219
Japan	−3,232	4,268	86	1,121
North Asia	−3,571	9,732	−2,618	3,543
Rest of the World[b]	7,389	−10,100	−108	−2,819
World Total	8,587	2,300	−7,415	3,471

[a]Excludes Fiji.
[b]Rest of the World includes non-EC Western European countries, a number of food importing developing countries, and the former centrally planned economies.

Source: Vanzetti, Andrews, Hester, and Fisher (Ch. 13,).

References

Gunasekera, H. D. B. H., and B. S. Fisher. 1992. "Australia's Recent Experience with the Collapse of its Wool Buffer Stock Scheme" *The World Economy*, 15: 251-69.

Krissof, B., J. Sullivan, J. Wainio, and B. Johnston. 1990. *Agricultural Trade Liberalization and Developing Countries*, Economic Research Service Staff Report AGES 9042, USDA, Washington DC.

Roberts, I., G. Love, H. Field, and N. Klijn. 1989. *U.S. Grain Policies and the World Market*, ABARE Policy Monograph No. 4, AGPS, Canberra.

Roberts, I., N. Andrews, and R. Rees. 1992. "Market Effects of the 1992 EC Reforms for Cereals and Beef" *Agriculture and Resources Quarterly*, (December) 4: 584—602.

PART FIVE

U.S.-E.C. Agricultural Trade Relations: Where Do We Go from Here?

11

U.S.-E.C. Agricultural Trade Relations: Where Do We Go from Here?

Tim Josling and Michel Petit

For seven years the United States and the E.C., along with their trading partners, had been engaged in negotiations within the General Agreement on Tariffs and Trade (GATT). These talks had, among other objectives, the need to define the framework for improved trade relations in agricultural markets. Had the Uruguay Round been completed at the time of writing, the title of the chapter would reflect a bold look forward to a new era. What follows the Uruguay Round? Further steps towards the reduction of protection? New areas of trade conflict to be tackled? It would indeed be interesting to be able to draw a line under the Round, and turn to pastures new.

However, it is possible to analyze the main avenues open to policy makers even though the Uruguay Round was not completed. Though the completion of the Round will influence the pace of developments, underlying trends are likely to continue. This is because the trade relations between the United States and the E.C. are largely determined by major economic and political forces that exist independently of the stage of negotiations in the GATT. The GATT is in fact only one of the avenues for resolution of the trade conflicts that arise between the United States and the E.C.[1]

In this chapter, we will review briefly both the economic and political forces shaping European and U.S. domestic agricultural and trade policies. Long-term developments in E.C. trade relations, for instance, will go far to determining agricultural trade policies. These include those pressures that stem from the need to extend a welcome to the former Soviet bloc countries of Central and Eastern Europe, as they attempt to become more integrated with the West; the more immediate task of incorporating the European Free Trade Agreement (EFTA) countries into the Community; and the E.C.'s increasing involvement in environmental matters. In the United States, the evolution of domestic agricultural policies over time will help to determine the climate for agricultural trade relations. The pressures on agricultural policy in the United States include the need to stay competitive, the need to reduce government spending on price support programs, the pressure to target payments to the family farmer, and the growing emphasis on rural development. Trade conflicts are, however, likely to persist, in spite of the evolution of farm policies as a result of these economic and political forces. This leads us to speculate on the possible avenues for conflict resolution.

Evolution of European Agriculture and Agricultural Policies

It is likely, as argued by De Benedictis *et al.* (Ch. 5), that the MacSharry reform constituted a turning point in the evolution of the European Community's agricultural policy. This does not, however, mean clear sailing for the Common Agricultural Policy (CAP). Even the reformed CAP will be under constant pressure: its future will be shaped by pressures for enlargement of the Community, by alternative demands on the Community's budget, and by the concerns for the environment arising from the intensification of agriculture in Western Europe.

As discussed by Tangermann (Ch. 7), the enlargement pressures are of a geopolitical nature and dictated by the general benefits to be derived from closer economic integration with European countries that are not currently members of the Community. But enlargement beyond 12 members will entail more complex policy packages, involving many contradictory interests and imposing changes in the Community's traditional way of reaching policy decisions (Petit *et al.* 1987). This contradiction is particularly visible today in the case of "sensitive trade" in textiles, steel, and agriculture with European countries such as Poland and Hungary, which could become significant exporters of these products to the E.C. Agriculture is thus at the front line in this potentially tense struggle between domestic and foreign policies. The need to protect domestic agricultural markets has already led to actions that are in complete contradiction with the political desire to promote reforms in those countries and integrate them within the Western European economy.

Budget pressures have traditionally been the most powerful force bringing about change in the CAP, as illustrated for instance in the case of the adoption of milk quotas in 1984 and of budget stabilizers in 1988. Budget pressures arose because of the increasing cost of subsidizing a growing volume of exports. Admittedly, the recent MacSharry reform of the CAP was not driven by such pressures. It owed more to the desire to move away from the excessive use of price supports. One consequence of such a move is that the cost of direct payments to farmers will be high. Thus, as discussed by De Benedictis et al. (Ch. 5), budget pressures will continue to be very strong, in particular given the many other demands on the budget for regional, environmental, and industrial programs.

Environmental concerns have in previous decades played only a minor role in shaping the evolution of the CAP. But the political significance of the environmental movement in several countries of the European Community has given such concerns more and more weight. Enlargement to include the countries of EFTA will accentuate this trend, as will the movement into positions of responsibility of politicians raised in the era of environmental awareness. Farm groups will have to form alliances with such politicians, out of survival if not conviction. As a result, the non-commodity contributions of the agricultural sector will play a more and more important role in shaping farm policy instruments. This also points to the use of payments and taxes geared to something other than the output of commodities.

The impact of these various pressures and of their interaction varies, of course, by country and by region within each country. This leads to a set of political forces the resolution of which is difficult to forecast. Yet one may predict that several issues, which have come to the fore in the policy debate in the E.C. in recent months, are likely to play a significant role in shaping the policy debate and its outcome in future years.

The most significant of such issues is the regional dimension of the European economic policy debate. Traditionally the differentiation between Northern and Southern Europe has played an important role in the shaping of economic policy, leading to the adoption of various programs for the development of Mediterranean areas, including investments in agriculture. The importance of this regional divide has been reflected within the Council of Ministers, where decisions ultimately are made. It was clear that the primary objective of several countries has been to secure the largest volume of budget transfer to their own country that would result from the package being adopted. Chapter 5 by De Benedictis et al. suggests that the importance of this North-South differentiation may become yet more important in the future.

Cutting across this issue is another that could be called the center-periphery relationship. This shows up as a gap between the centers of economic development, enjoying a high level of prosperity and where agriculture is also often quite prosperous, and periphery regions, less successful in terms of their economic development and where agriculture is also poor. Examples of periphery regions include much of the south of Italy, Scotland, northern parts of Germany, and the central mountains of France. This disparity is likely to become more important in the agricultural policy debate. In this respect, it is significant that in the Maastricht referendum in France all the peripheral regions voted "no" on the question of the Economic Union, whereas the central regions voted "yes." As a result of this outcome, the issues of land use and rural development have come back to the fore of the policy debate in France. The current political debate in Italy may also be interpreted, in part, in terms of this differentiation between center and periphery, and one would expect that the issue would have significant political weight in the future.

Related to the geographic differentiation issue is a more general equity issue that, though it has always been part of the policy debate, has never played a dominant role in shaping the CAP. One can argue that the protection of agricultural markets, the main source of international trade tensions, has mainly benefited large farmers who are often located in centers of economic development. The decoupling of support to agriculture involved in the reform of the CAP will undoubtedly lead to issues being raised about the equity of such direct budget transfers. Large payments to wealthy farmers will be questioned. As a result, one can expect that those farmers will put pressure on public authorities to be compensated through some form of protection. In addition, with the enlargement of the Community, the environmental concerns and the equity issues—themselves perceived in different ways in the various countries of the Community—will intensify the pressures for a less common policy and for the renationalization of policy instruments. This trend has already been seen to have some impact. Such renationalization will lead to complicated, partially offsetting, effects of domestic agricultural policies on trade. Generally speaking, however, the aggregate impact will probably be less pressure for overall protection than within a more uniform "fortress Europe."

Foreign policy pressures also deserve a mention. Pressures will come from the desire to assist with the process of reform in Eastern European countries, as already discussed above. But this process also extends to relations with the former Soviet Union. Discussions with Russia on trade liberalization will inevitably involve agricultural goods. Pressures will also arise from the desire to accommodate the interests of developing countries. In the past, such pressures led to a compromise solution for their access to the European markets for such products as beef and sugar, as reflected in the successive Lomé agreements with the ACP (African, Caribbean, and Pacific) countries and the bilateral access arrangements for bananas. It is not clear at this stage what the pressures from developing countries will be in the future and what their impact on the policy outcome will be. But there is no doubt that these foreign policy pressures will influence the positions taken by the European Community in international fora dealing with agricultural trade, particularly in GATT.

The set of forces and trends will together lead to irresistible internal pressures within the Community for the farming sector to become more competitive. The level of support will diminish. Even if no agreement is reached in GATT, the budget pressure will be such that the open-ended commitment on export subsidies will be removed. By contrast, however, the scope for import growth within the Community for bulk agricultural commodities will continue to be very limited. Some differentiated products will have access to specific market niches, and this may represent the best hope for the trading partners of the Community.

This discussion also suggests that agricultural trade will be involved in a much more complex set of trade interests, leading to more convoluted internal negotiations. As the Community is enlarged, the process of decision making will also become much more complex. The flexibility of the European Community in agricultural trade negotiations, which was never very great, will be further diminished. There is no reason to believe that the pressures to solve internal problems at the border will be diminished. The Blair House agreement in November 1992, though not as yet fully accepted by France, may serve to define the outcome of the agricultural trade negotiations in the GATT round. But even if this happens, such an outcome is unlikely to lead to a reduction of pressures for agricultural protection and active trade intervention. The current internal debate on the Blair House agreement within the Community and within France should be interpreted in this light. On the whole, therefore, the potential for continuing conflict with the United States on international trade matters will remain very great.

Evolution of U.S. Agriculture and Agricultural Policies

In spite of obvious and major geographic, historical, and institutional differences with the European Community, the current economic and political pressures and trends in the United States have striking similarities with those of Europe. This similarity strengthens the conclusion of a continued potential for conflicts. The budget pressures on U.S. commodity programs can be expected to increase. The magnitude of the overall budget deficit and the desire to increase spending for "investments" will undoubtedly put pressure on the budget for all traditional agricultural programs. The new emphasis on, and renewed interest in, rural development programs will continue to put pressure on commodity programs, which have already been subjected to budget cuts. This means in turn that the large producers of these commodities, the main beneficiaries of those programs, will feel the pinch. Commodity price supports could give way to programs designed to make agriculture more competitive. This implies a change in the conventional wisdom in the United States, that American agriculture is already very competitive and only needs a "level playing field" on the international scene to expand its exports.

By contrast, the extent to which equity issues and concerns will play a role in the policy debate is difficult to predict. Gardner (Ch. 3) argues convincingly that the amount of political pressure exerted by farmers' organizations is closely linked to variations in farm income. Intersectoral distribution issues however have not traditionally had a large impact on the outcome of the policy debate, even if they were present in the debate itself. President Clinton's appointment of a Secretary for Agriculture from a poor district of the South may be a sign of a renewed emphasis on rural development, as alluded to above; and this may indeed signal a greater concern for equity issues in agricultural policymaking. This is already reflected in shifts in budget allocations and other priorities within USDA. But whether payment limits and other equity mechanisms become more effective is not easy to tell.

Food safety and environmental concerns have now come to the fore in the agricultural policy debate in the United States, and these concerns will continue to play a very important role. Their influence on the outcome of the policy process, particularly regarding trade issues and trade postures, is not clear. For the moment, the main outcome has been a greater degree of protectionism through nontariff barriers. It may turn out that the concerns for pollution, particularly water pollution, will lead to a reduced level of production and, therefore, to less pressure for aggressive trade postures on international commodity markets.

Besides those pressures internal to the agricultural sector, long-term developments in the trade policy environment will certainly affect the position of the U.S. government in agricultural trade negotiations. One global issue will be the general attitude vis-à-vis GATT. At this stage, one can only note the ambivalence of the new administration. On the one hand, it has repeatedly emphasized its commitment to a successful completion of the Uruguay Round of trade negotiations, and it has pursued the same regional trade strategy as the previous administration through a qualified endorsement of the North American Free Trade Agreement (NAFTA) proposal. By contrast, various spokespersons for the administration have made strong public statements threatening unilateral action, particularly against Japan and the European Community accused of unfair trade practices. This attitude reflects strong pressures within the American economy and political establishments for "fair trade" legislation, and "results-oriented" agreements. The outcome for agricultural trade of this current general trade policy debate has so far been a strong statement of the importance of solving the market access issue as a condition for the successful settlement of the Uruguay Round. For this to happen, the final package, which must be presented to Congress for approval, will undoubtedly include specific market access measures. It will also contain import barrier reductions that will hurt some U.S. agricultural interests. It is not possible to predict at this stage whether or not the affected agricultural groups will oppose a GATT package and how successful they will be if they do.

Different commodity groups will be differentially affected. Bulk commodities such as grain will clearly continue to play an important role in U.S. trade, but the growth market is for high-value products. One can expect that issues will arise of market access abroad and access to the U.S. markets for imports from other countries for those products. This will increase the potential for trade skirmishes and trade wars. Disputes over wine and processed fruit products will probably be even more numerous than in the past.

Possible Avenues for Conflict Resolution

The conflicts between the United States and the E.C. in agricultural trade go back thirty years, to the founding of the CAP in the early 1960s. The sharpness of the conflict however has increased in the past decade. Is the prospect for a continuing deterioration in the trade relations in the area of agriculture between the United States and the E.C.? Or is there the possibility of an amelioration of the conflicts, either as a result of the Uruguay Round or through other mechanisms?

What should one make of the combined effect of these changes? Will internal policy developments and external trade policies make relations between the E.C. and the United States easier in the future? The policy changes seem to be in the direction of easing the trade disputes. Emphasis on better targeted policies and a reduction in market intervention should help to defuse tensions. It seems unlikely that trade policy will be dominated by a clash of rival rural development policies. But, as already indicated, opportunities for open conflict will continue to exist in large number. In addition, protection can always be cloaked in the guise of rural development and investment strategies. This is particularly likely in the case of investment-intensive specialty crops, where aggressive subsidies to set up industries could be challenged by those already in the market. Compensation payments to producers can also be misused, if not strictly linked to a price reduction. Environmental policies can easily collide, as domestic interest groups seek to influence and define the trade agenda to reinforce domestic control of agricultural practices.

The question therefore arises as to how to encourage the drift to less trade-distorting policies. There are several multilateral instruments, through the GATT and other plurilateral bodies, such as the firming up of international rules on agricultural trade, the strengthening of GATT dispute settlement, and the negotiation of specific codes of conduct for agricultural trade. In addition there are bilateral and regional instruments of trade tension reduction, such as the development of specific U.S.-E.C. codes of conduct, and the possibility of interbloc (E.C.-NAFTA) negotiations. One should not forget the possibility of commodity-specific instruments of trade policy, including not only the traditional commodity agreements (which involve a degree of "managed" trade) but also the negotiation of "free trade" commodity sectors.

Multilateral Avenues

Of these options the path towards the agreement on a new framework of trade rules in the Uruguay Round is the one that has been emphasized during the past decade. It remains too early to tell whether this path will attain the goal. Indeed, the attempt to bring agriculture into line with other products as far as trade rules are concerned may have become part of the problem as well as part of the solution. What started as a genuine multilateral discussion on trade rules for agriculture had degenerated by the end of 1992 into a strictly E.C.-U.S. deal, which had then to be ratified by other countries. The deal is not unimportant if it provides the basis for the conclusion of the Round, but it offers little in the way of immediate liberalization of agricultural markets.

A conclusion of the GATT Round along the lines of the Blair House accord would however provide for some significant changes in trade rules. These include the conversion of nontariff import barriers into tariffs, the control on both quantity and expenditure on export subsidies, the categorization of policies into those deemed to be minimally trade-distorting ("green box" policies), and those that are subject to international monitoring and control.

These rule changes would represent a clear advance on the situation before 1986, and a major turning point in the regulation of international trade in agriculture. However, they do not remotely represent a situation of free trade in agricultural products: the cost of changing the rules has been to give up some degree of liberalization. The elimination of nontariff import barriers would be of considerable value, and should make trade much more transparent, but reducing by 36 percent tariff rates that were very high in 1986-88 still leaves a considerable amount of protection. Reducing export subsidies by 36 percent in expenditure and 21 percent in volume would not end such subsidies. The reduction of overall support by 20 percent, designed to constrain domestic (nonborder) measures, is also not very tough.

The danger lies in the possibility that countries will interpret these new rules loosely. One could end up with tariffication with numerous loopholes and exceptions; export subsidies paid under another heading; and a plethora of domestic subsidies conveniently devised to take advantage of green-box ambiguities. It is, in fact, a selling point of the agreement that few changes will be needed in domestic policy. The Commission has argued strenuously that the reform of the CAP already imposes constraints on E.C. agriculture that will make it possible to live within new GATT rules. The U.S. Congress is in no mood to write too many restraints on U.S. farm policy, which is after all considered domestically to be more liberal than that of trading partners. The GATT agreement would actually be most useful as a backstop, to prevent backsliding of policies that are undergoing reluctant reform.

The failure to reach a GATT agreement would send E.C.-U.S. trade relations into somewhat of a limbo. One would expect a certain amount of blame attribution, and some saber-rattling. The issue is what would follow the initial disappointment. The GATT would still exist, shaken but intact. One would actually expect an increased use of the existing trade dispute settlement channels to attack aspects of domestic agricultural policy. The United States has had a "temporary" waiver of its Article XI obligations since 1955. When the United States was the dominant force in the GATT, it was difficult to challenge such a position. With many more GATT members, and their economic weight more evenly distributed, it is not clear how long others will continue to allow such derogations. The E.C. might also not be immune to further challenges. The Uruguay Round agreement would in part build the (reformed) CAP into the GATT: but lack of such an agreement could reopen the extent to which the E.C. has managed to avoid normal GATT disciplines. A period of tough panel decisions could cause as many "problems" for the CAP as the Blair House accord. In addition, as indicated above, the number of limited trade wars or trade skirmishes on specific products would likely increase.

Bilateral and Regional Avenues

Bilateral trade talks have always had an appeal, at least to the big countries, as a way of resolving disputes. The United States has entered into "successful" discussions with Japan on agricultural trade issues for many years, culminating in the opening up of markets for beef and citrus. Those who champion reciprocity in trade talks find the bilateral format attractive. It is also popular with those who argue for "results-oriented" policies, which set targets for market access. The GATT provides a mechanism for "multilateralizing" bilaterally-negotiated market access. In that sense the world has a stake in such talks. But the scope for trade liberalization is inherently limited by the bilateral nature of such talks. No one pays much attention, for example, to the trade interests of the small and the weak. Moreover, such bilaterals can easily form the basis for selective liberalization, leading to distortions among products.

The growth of regional trade blocs has broadened the options for framing trade rules and thus multiplied the number of possible scenarios for the future of U.S.-E.C. agricultural trade relations. In the past, agricultural trade relations have not been much-affected by free trade areas (FTAs) and other trading blocs: agriculture has in fact often been left out of FTAs. This may change in the future, particularly if these arrangements take on greater significance in national trade policies.

Domestic agricultural policies are likely to cause problems for agriculture trade within FTAs, just as they do for the GATT. The obligation to ease market access within FTAs will put pressure on protectionist policies. The realities of arbitrage in an FTA imply one of three outcomes: the exclusion of agriculture from the FTA provisions; the movement toward uniform bloc policies (common policies); or a change to policies relying on decoupled payments (Josling, 1993). In this light, the further development of trade blocs could therefore have both a positive and a negative impact on trade relations. Insofar as trade blocs tackle internally the trade and policy problem, the situation will be improved. If they merely add to the defensive nature of domestic policy, their effect is likely to be less benign.

Is it likely that future trade discussions will occur between the E.C. and the NAFTA countries as trade blocs? This is on *prima facie* grounds improbable, as the NAFTA countries will not soon have a coordinated policy-making structure along the lines of that of the E.C. However we could see *de facto* policy-making arising from, say, joint working groups on environmental standards or animal health practices. This could easily lead to joint E.C.-NAFTA working groups on such issues. If trade tensions from health, safety, and environmental conflicts increase, as expected, this type of collaborative mechanism could be used to contain such tendencies. Negotiations on support reduction between E.C. and NAFTA seem less likely at the bloc level, in part because the main problems of farm commodity trade involve parties from many different regions and trade blocs.

Sectoral Avenues

Also possible as an approach to conflict resolution is a reversion to the notion that different commodities may require different treatment. Commodity-based international trade policy has a long history, and no one would argue for the repeat of past mistakes. But it is possible to think of other commodity-specific attempts at liberalization and conflict resolution. Sector free-trade plans have appeared in other areas and indeed form the basis for the U.S. approach to tariff reductions in the GATT Round.

The argument against sector-level trade agreements is that excluded sectors get "off the hook" and the chance of making a deal is reduced by the narrower focus. In that sense agriculture has itself suffered by being dealt with as a separate "sensitive" sector. But one could imagine certain sectors within agriculture (horticultural products, tree fruits, and oilseeds might qualify) where a free-trade pact could be negotiable, leaving other sectors (such as sugar, dairy, and grains) subject to lesser degrees of liberalization.

Conclusion

The tone of this chapter is wary but not pessimistic. Trade relations could improve significantly with changes in support policies. The GATT Round would give such policies a push. On balance it seems worthwhile to conclude the GATT Round, even if the outcome is not ideal. The alternatives are not attractive. There is the possibility of the outbreak of a trade war between the United States and the E.C. over export competition and market access. Such a confrontation would likely derail domestic reform efforts in Europe and budget-control objectives in the United States. The numerous small and medium-sized countries that have reformed their agricultural and trade policies in advance of a GATT agreement may also have difficulty making those reforms stick.

However, the issue may not only be one of policy changes. The importance of market conditions cannot be overemphasized. The exacerbation of agricultural trade tensions since 1980 coincides with the emergence of E.C. agriculture as a major exporter in temperate-zone markets. The United States has seen its exports to the E.C. diminish over the last decade, and has faced increasing competition in third-country markets. The trend in overall exports sets the tone for U.S. farm policy. The budget cost largely reflects the balance between domestic production and export demand. Escalation of budget costs over the 1980s was a major policy concern in the E.C. The E.C. budget is also impacted by world market conditions. Export subsidy costs are the most volatile part of FEOGA (Fonds Européan d'orientation et de garantie agricole) expenditure on market support. When FEOGA costs increase, so do tensions between member states, and between the E.C. and the United States.

This dependence on world markets for peaceful relations emphasizes the importance of other factors, such as the speed of development of the vast agricultural potential of the former Soviet Union and the countries of Eastern and Central Europe. If these countries become major exporters of grain and livestock products, in particular if they resort to the price-support policies of the Organization for Economic Cooperation and Development (OECD) countries, the tensions between the United States and the E.C. will be exacerbated. If the trade is not absorbed into European markets it will spill over onto world markets and depress prices. If it does stay within Europe, there will be even less access opportunities for U.S. exports to E.C. markets.

Many see another factor on the horizon that could lead to firmer markets. This is the possible emergence of the People's Republic of China (PRC) as a major importer of foodstuffs and animal feeds. A decade of growth in the PRC at current levels would create a massive demand for foods from an increasingly prosperous urban population. For that to translate into imports, China would have to find export markets for manufactured goods. So the prospect for peace in agricultural trade relations may hinge on whether Eastern Europe develops its agricultural export markets faster than a growing China can absorb surplus production from the West. This in turn depends on maintaining an open trading system for nonfarm commodities and discouraging noneconomic food production in the eastern part of Europe.

Notes

1. A similar set of issues is addressed in a special issue of *Agricultural Economics* (8)4, June 1993, edited by Brandao and Petit, devoted to a new assessment of agricultural trade and development relationships. A similar conclusion of the major influence of economic and political trends, beyond GATT, arises from these essays.

References

Josling, T. 1993. "Agriculture in a World of Trade Blocs." *Australian Journal of Agricultural Economics*. Forthcoming.
Petit, M., et al. 1987. *Agricultural Policy Formation in the European Community: The Birth of Milk Quotas and CAP Reform*. Amsterdam: Elsevier.

PART SIX

Additional Dimensions in Agricultural Policy Changes and North American-European Agricultural Trade Relations

12

GATT and CAP Reform: Different, Similar, or Redundant?

Michael D. Helmar, William H. Meyers, and Dermot J. Hayes

Introduction

Many of the economic and political changes that have been occurring around the world in the early 1990s have had and will continue to have major impacts on agricultural production, consumption, and trade patterns. Among the most important of these are reform of the Common Agricultural Policy (CAP) of the European Community (E.C.) and the proposed changes to world trade that would result from a successful conclusion to the Uruguay Round of the General Agreement on Tariffs and Trade (GATT) negotiations.

In February 1991, then-E.C. Agricultural Commissioner Ray MacSharry submitted a proposal for CAP reform. This proposal was controversial, setting the stage for more than a year of negotiations and adjustments before it was approved in May 1992. Implementation began in 1993, and the effects of this reform could have substantial impacts on production and exports of agricultural commodities by the E.C., and, to a lesser extent, on consumption of these products.

In December 1991, the GATT Secretariat proposed a draft final agreement (the Dunkel text) to renew stalled negotiations on reducing trade barriers. Since that time, it has been widely adopted as the basis of further negotiations on reducing trade-distorting policies in agriculture. In November 1992, the United States and E.C. reached agreement on several modifications to the Dunkel text, as well as on their bilateral oilseeds dispute. These agreements have become known as the Blair House agreements, and have been generally accepted as modifications to the Dunkel text. The Dunkel text and Blair House agreements would effectively bind countries such as the E.C. and United States to maintain reductions in commodity support levels and trade barriers that have been achieved since 1986. There would be reductions required in other, mostly developed, countries as well, with effects being felt by world agricultural markets and trade in general.

These changes include many important direct and indirect impacts on North American and European trade and world agricultural markets. This study evaluates prospects for agricultural trade and prices under a baseline scenario and alternative scenario assumptions about agriculture without a CAP reform agreement and with a GATT agreement.

Analytical System and Procedures for Quantitative Analysis

To assess the impacts of a Dunkel-Blair House agreement and CAP reform, results for agriculture are compared under three alternative scenarios:

1. A baseline scenario that incorporates CAP reform, the Blair House oilseed agreement, and existing policies in other major trading countries;
2. a GATT scenario that incorporates proposed changes in the agricultural policies of major trading countries as per the Dunkel text and Blair House agreement;
3. a scenario in which CAP reform is not implemented, but E.C. policies that existed in 1992 are continued, with the exception of the oilseed sector in which the Blair House oilseed agreement is implemented.

To get a better perspective on the impacts of GATT, the no-CAP reform scenario is compared to both the baseline and GATT scenarios. In this way, the "pure" effects of GATT are assessed and the impacts of CAP reform are compared with the impacts of GATT. Using this perspective, a greater appreciation for the impacts of GATT is obtained, especially if such an agreement would bind countries such as the E.C. to unilateral reforms already adopted.

This analysis is conducted by utilizing the agricultural commodity models of the Food and Agricultural Policy Research Institute (FAPRI). For major trading countries, the FAPRI models are econometric models that estimate the supply, utilization, net trade, and prices of wheat, feed grains, rice, and soybeans (Devadoss *et al.*, 1993). Models have also been developed for beef, pork, poultry meat, and dairy markets. All the components of the modeling system used in this analysis are dynamic, meaning that both short- and long-term effects of policy changes can be identified. Policy instruments are explicit in these models so import, export, and domestic support policies can be modified as required by proposed GATT provisions. The models are calibrated to reproduce recent historical data as closely as possible and to generate projections for the next ten years.

Baseline Scenario

FAPRI baseline projections are based on assumptions about the general economy, agricultural policies, technological change, and the weather. The baseline scenario includes the CAP reform already implemented by the E.C. and the Blair House oilseed agreement. The policy regimes in the United States and other developed market economies are assumed to continue according to the provisions of current law. The macroeconomic outlook assumed for this baseline is the one published in November 1992 by the WEFA Group for the United States and in October 1992 by Project LINK for other countries of the world. A detailed description of the baseline scenario is in FAPRI 1993a and FAPRI 1993b.

GATT Scenario

The GATT scenario assumptions are based on current expectations about the provisions of the agriculture agreement in the Uruguay Round. These assumptions are based on the Dunkel text with revisions and adjustments as specified in the Blair House agreement of November 1992. Proposed changes to trade-distorting policies as outlined in the Dunkel text are aimed at three areas: internal support, export subsidies, and market access. The Blair House agreement modified internal support and export subsidy restrictions.

Internal support, as measured by an aggregate measure of support (AMS) using fixed reference prices, is reduced by 20 percent from the 1986 level. According to the Dunkel text, the AMS reductions were to be commodity specific, that is, each commodity was subject to AMS reductions. With the Blair House agreement, this was changed to an agricultural sector-wide AMS, allowing the AMS for some commodities, such as U.S. sugar, to avoid reduction as long as the aggregate AMS reduction is at least 20 percent. The Blair House agreement also put U.S. deficiency payments and compensatory payments of the reformed CAP into a special "blue box" category, exempting them from inclusion in AMS calculations. The AMS is reduced evenly over a period of six years from the 1986 level. According to Dunkel, this period was to be from 1993 to 1998, but because the GATT negotiations are not completed, it is assumed that the implementation period is delayed one year. If obligations under export competition or import access require that internal prices be less than the support price calculated under the internal support rules, the support price is allowed to be maintained at a level greater than the internal price through mechanisms such as deficiency payments so long as the AMS reduction requirements are met. Credit is allowed for reductions in AMS undertaken since 1986.

Under Dunkel, export subsidies are to be reduced in two ways. Expenditures are to be reduced 36 percent from the 1986-90 average level, and quantities exported with subsidies are to be reduced 24 percent from the 1986-90 average level. These reductions are made from 1994 to 1999 in equal increments. Export subsidies under a bona fide food aid program are not subject to reduction. Deficiency payments on the quantities exported are not considered export subsidies. The Blair House agreement changed the subsidized export quantity reduction to 21 percent from the 1986-90 average level.

Market access is to be achieved in various ways. Nontariff barriers are converted into tariff equivalents and reduced over six years by a simple average over all agricultural goods of 36 percent from the 1986-88 average tariff equivalent. Tariffs are required to be reduced by a minimum of 15 percent over six years for individual commodities. Any tariff reduction of more than 15 percent that would result in increased imports of that commodity is assumed to revert to the 15 percent minimum. It is further assumed that the simple average reduction of 36 percent will be met through higher tariff reductions on minor commodities. Where nontariff import barriers are in place, minimum access to the domestic market is required to be the greater of 3 percent of domestic consumption in 1994, increasing to 5 percent by 1999, or minimum access of 1986-88 average import levels. However, it is possible that current and minimum access commitments will be negotiated and not calculated as proposed by Dunkel, and that some alteration of rules for market access might be made for net exporting countries. What these negotiated changes will be is unknown. For this reason, the Dunkel text was followed with respect to market access.

Results of the GATT Scenario

Based on the Dunkel text and the Blair House agreement, FAPRI models of world agriculture are solved to obtain results for the GATT scenario. This section reports results for major country net trade and world prices. Because the Blair House agreement changed AMS calculations to agricultural sectorwide and not commodity specific, most countries are expected to be GATT-legal in this respect by the beginning of implementation of new GATT rules. Because of this, there will be little change in production of major producing countries, except as would be necessary to reduce excess supplies to meet export quantity and import access restrictions.

Wheat and Feed Grains

Results for trade and world prices for wheat and feed grains are reported in Table 12.1 for 1991, 1994, and 1999. GATT implementation is assumed to begin in 1994 and the final year of implementation is assumed to be 1999. Changes in trade levels are primarily the result of export subsidy and market access restrictions. For wheat, the E.C. more than meets the export subsidy expenditure and quantity commitments of 36 percent and 21 percent, respectively, as a result of set-aside requirements under CAP reform. Wheat net exports from the E.C. are actually marginally higher under the GATT scenario as increased barley feeding offsets some wheat use in livestock rations, making more wheat available for export. Canada and Australia are both the beneficiaries of the higher world prices induced by the reduction in Export Enhancement Program (EEP) expenditures by the United States and respond with increased wheat production and exports. The former Soviet Union (FSU) also reacts to higher world prices, resulting in reduced net imports. Because of increased exports by exporting countries and reduced imports by importers, U.S. wheat exports grow more slowly than in the baseline. Because of the weaker world market, U.S. export prices decline. However, this decline is less than the reduction necessary in per-unit EEP subsidies, so the Rotterdam wheat price increases.

In respect to feed-grain trade, GATT primarily affects exports of barley and imports of corn by the E.C. Export quantity restrictions for barley become binding for the E.C. in 1997, and market access requirements force an increase in corn imports by this region. Downward pressure is put on barley and corn prices in the domestic E.C. market, and increased set-asides and feeding are necessary in order to equalize these prices with the feed-quality wheat prices. The result is a decrease in feed-grains net exports by the E.C. and an increase (decrease) in exports (imports) by other regions of the world. The United States picks up the majority of the feed-grain market vacated by the E.C. because it has excess capacity and a comparative advantage in corn production. There are also no corn EEP subsidies, so the United States will be able to take full advantage of any gaps in world feed-grain markets. Because of the large excess capacity in the United States and little export subsidy expenditure adjustment necessary, most of the increase in exports is absorbed with relatively little price rise for corn, barley, and sorghum under this scenario, as compared with wheat.

TABLE 12.1 World Grain Trade Under the Baseline and GATT Scenarios

	1991	1994		2000	
	Baseline Level	Baseline Level	GATT (Change)	Baseline Level	GATT (Change)
Net Wheat Exports		(1,000 Metric Tons)			
United States	33,760	31,990	-290	38,300	-1,920
European Community	19,610	13,010	80	11,270	700
Japan	-5,790	-5,750	-40	-6,060	0
Canada	25,330	21,450	90	21,810	720
Australia	7,110	11,170	300	12,790	360
Developing	-64,980	-68,270	50	-82,580	-220
Former USSR	-21,550	-9,010	70	-3,450	420
Rest of World	6,510	5,410	-260	7,920	-60
Net Feed-Grain Exports		(1,000 Metric Tons)			
United States	47,579	47,596	379	59,471	1,272
European Community	6,154	2,286	-672	2,402	-2,211
Japan	-21,281	-21,352	5	-22,891	24
Canada	3,885	4,633	50	6,196	158
Australia	2,363	3,479	25	3,555	11
Developing	-36,847	-40,431	54	-50,242	223
Former USSR	-18,001	-7,753	73	-4,475	52
Rest of World	16,148	11,542	86	5,983	472

Net Rice Exports (1,000 Metric Tons)

United States	1921	2,174	167	2,078	177
European Community	-197	-313	-18	-311	-168
Japan	0	0	-280	0	-466
Thailand	4780	4,838	42	5,587	53
Pakistan	1199	1,005	25	1,097	82
India	430	193	5	193	84
Indonesia	-551	-21	11	-155	-67
Vietnam	1870	2,046	31	2,531	87
Rest of World	-9452	-9,922	17	-11,020	218

World Prices (U.S. Dollars per Metric Ton)

Wheat (FOB Gulf)	135.35	131.38	-1.04	150.33	-6.21
Wheat (CIF Rott)	159.37	154.74	2.24	176.86	9.08
Corn (FOB Gulf)	107.28	95.93	3.43	104.04	2.99
Barley (FOB N Pac)	122.00	118.90	2.00	121.35	3.30
Sorghum (FOB Gulf)	110.00	94.28	2.86	101.04	1.85
Rice (FOB Bangkok)	329.37	289.75	6.97	331.29	10.71

Soybeans and Soybean Products

The results of GATT on soybeans and soybean products are presented in Table 12.2. Oilseeds tend to be relatively free of trade barriers in most countries and the baseline already included the Blair House agreement for adjustment in E.C. oilseed policies. These two factors translate into little direct impact of GATT restrictions on oilseed markets. However, there will likely be some indirect impacts resulting from demand for protein meals and the effect these demand changes have on the oilseed complex as a whole. GATT restrictions on meat exports and requirements for market access result in reduced meat trade by the E.C., causing reduced prices and production in the pork and poultry sectors. Reduced poultry production and lower hog inventories lead to decreased demand for soybean meal resulting in lower meal imports and world prices. The soybean complex adjusts to lower meal prices through reduced crush and production of meal and oil. The reduction in production of oil without a reduction in demand leads to an increase in soybean oil price. The net effect is no significant change in soybean prices relative to the baseline. Most of the reduction in soybean meal trade is expected to be absorbed by the United States, but there will likely be some impact felt by South American exporters.

Beef, Pork, and Poultry

The effects of GATT on world trade and prices of meat is presented in Table 12.3. The E.C. and Japan are the two countries that historically have had the most trade-distorting policies for meat. However, under the baseline, Japan is assumed to complete the 1988 beef liberalization agreement by tariffying import quotas and reducing the tariff equivalents to 50 percent by 1993. The E.C. is assumed to reduce beef intervention prices as a result of CAP reform, resulting in decreases in production and exports of beef. Because of these policy changes in the baseline, Japan and the E.C. have more than met the trade commitments specified under GATT and it is expected that GATT will have little direct effect on the world beef market. However, because of the impacts on the pork market, the E.C. is projected to export slightly more beef under GATT than in the baseline, lowering the world beef price, and inducing slightly higher imports by the United States and Japan, among other countries.

Unlike beef, CAP reform does not directly address pork production leaving this sector exposed to direct impacts from GATT. Under GATT, the E.C. would be bound to decrease subsidized exports and increase market access for pork. In this analysis, it is assumed that 50 percent of E.C. pork exports are without subsidies. Specialty pork products such as high-quality hams from Denmark are currently exported without subsi-

TABLE 12.2 World Soybean and Soybean Product Trade Under the Baseline and GATT Scenarios

	—1991—	—1994—		—2000—	
	Baseline Level	Baseline Level	GATT (Change)	Baseline Level	GATT (Change)
Net Soybean Exports		(1,000 Metric Tons)			
United States	18,558	20,747	0	23,151	42
European Community	-13,741	-14,309	-1	-14,654	25
Japan	-4,670	-5,036	0	-5,259	0
Argentina	3,199	3,079	0	3,406	-1
Brazil	3,399	3,399	0	3,507	10
Developing	-6,706	-7,501	0	-9,577	0
Former USSR	-800	-854	0	-820	0
Rest of World	761	475	1	246	8
Net Soymeal Exports		(1,000 Metric Tons)			
United States	6,149	5,249	-173	6,033	-399
European Community	-9,578	-9,002	178	-9,880	432
Japan	-691	-766	2	-916	1
Argentina	5,743	5,973	0	7,117	-3
Brazil	8,500	8,337	4	9,420	-17
Developing	-6,127	-6,355	2	-7,493	-14
Former USSR	-2,946	-2,722	-50	-2,626	0
Rest of World	-1,050	-714	45	-1,655	0

(continues)

TABLE 12.2 (continued)

	1991	1994		2000	
	Baseline Level	Baseline Level	GATT (Change)	Baseline Level	GATT (Change)
Net Soyoil Exports					
	(1,000 Metric Tons)				
United States	750	762	-1	1,039	5
European Community	668	575	0	525	-8
Japan	15	5	0	-1	0
Argentina	1,141	1,168	0	1,401	-1
Brazil	650	635	0	753	-2
Developing	-2,301	-2,684	1	-3,171	2
Former USSR	-241	-177	0	-260	4
Rest of World	-682	-284	0	-286	0
World Prices					
	(U.S. Dollars per Metric Ton)				
Soybeans (FOB Gulf)	222.96	237.90	0.27	232.76	-0.19
Meal (FOB Decatur)	208.56	196.91	0.38	211.32	-5.08
Oil (FOB Decatur)	421.08	531.98	-0.34	477.45	18.28

TABLE 12.3 World Meat Trade Under the Baseline and GATT Scenarios

	1991	1994		2000	
	Baseline Level	Baseline Level	GATT (Change)	Baseline Level	GATT (Change)
Net Beef Exports		(1,000 Metric Tons)			
United States	-518	-384	0	-19	-38
European Community	805	501	81	221	183
Japan	-515	-707	-52	-938	-66
Canada	-108	-62	2	-111	0
Australia	1,080	1,012	-2	1,054	12
Brazil	165	380	5	387	-2
Eastern Europe	71	11	6	68	-4
Rest of World	-980	-751	-40	-662	-85
Net Pork Exports		(1,000 Metric Tons)			
United States	-223	-80	340	-67	627
European Community	567	749	-552	778	-884
Japan	-587	-743	9	-885	7
Canada	251	279	12	278	11
Eastern Europe	202	240	40	449	11
Taiwan	324	322	3	336	2
Mexico	-39	-106	9	-175	2
Rest of World	-495	-661	139	-714	224

(*continues*)

TABLE 12.3 (continued)

	1991	1994		2000	
	Baseline Level	Baseline Level	GATT (Change)	Baseline Level	GATT (Change)
Net Broiler Exports		(1,000 Metric Tons)			
United States	572	652	74	704	292
European Community	300	309	-105	328	-284
Japan	-347	-486	6	-628	-1
Canada	-46	-50	-13	-65	-77
Brazil	322	342	5	437	0
Thailand	164	184	1	247	0
Eastern Europe	21	74	2	131	0
Saudi Arabia	-199	-226	1	-253	0
Rest of World	-787	-799	29	-901	70
U.S. Market Prices		(Dollars per Hundredweight)			
Omaha Steers	74.28	71.40	1.39	81.75	-1.26
Barrows & Gilts	46.69	45.84	3.64	55.25	1.04
12-City Broilers	52.00	54.37	0.89	57.20	0.10

dies, therefore requiring no limitations on trade. However, a strict interpretation of the Dunkel text would require increased imports in some areas of the E.C. in order to comply with minimum access commitments. The subsidized export quantity restrictions combined with the requirement for market access results in the E.C. actually becoming a net importer of pork by the end of the century. Some beef consumption is offset by pork consumption, making more beef available for export, but the total effect is lower meat exports from the E.C. The decrease in pork exports by the E.C. leads to higher world pork prices and decreased consumption and increased exports from other countries. The United States is expected to pick up much of the market lost by the E.C., but many other countries will increase pork exports, including Asian countries that have the ability to increase pork production.

As with pork, GATT requires some restrictions on E.C. poultry meat trade. However, other countries such as Canada will also be required to meet commitments on trade. The reduction in exports by the E.C. and increase in imports by Canada contribute to slightly higher world prices. Other countries increase imports in the medium- to long-term, due mainly to import access requirements. The United States increases poultry meat exports under the GATT scenario.

Dairy Products

The results for dairy products are presented in Table 12.4. The largest adjustment to the dairy product sector under GATT comes from trade restrictions on the E.C. Since the AMS is not binding, the dairy quota in the E.C. is assumed to be the same as under the baseline. Minimum access requirements result in more cheese imports, and subsidized export quantity reductions further erode the E.C.'s net export position for cheese. In order to meet these trade commitments, the E.C. is projected to produce more butter and nonfat dry milk (NFD). The trade commitments for both butter and NFD are not expected to be binding for the E.C.; therefore, exports of these products are expected to increase somewhat under GATT, although not enough to completely offset reduced cheese exports. World cheese prices are expected to rise, and Australia and New Zealand will likely respond by increasing production and exports of cheese, and reducing production and exports of butter and NFD. The response from the United States is projected to be limited to reduced butter exports. Cheese prices are projected to rise substantially on the world market as E.C. net exports are reduced. The butter price rise is expected to be partially offset by the declining NFD price.

The changes in trade resulting from GATT are smaller than the corresponding trade changes due to CAP reform for grains, oilseeds, and beef, but generally larger for pork, poultry, and dairy products. CAP reform

TABLE 12.4 World Dairy Trade Under the Baseline and GATT Scenarios

	1991 Baseline Level	1994 Baseline Level	1994 GATT (Change)	2000 Baseline Level	2000 GATT (Change)
Net Butter Exports		(1,000 Metric Tons)			
United States	64	113	-89	113	-37
European Community	214	135	46	111	62
Japan	-21	-6	7	-8	-7
Canada	12	6	-9	6	-10
Australia	55	56	0	52	-3
New Zealand	176	205	1	257	-6
Rest of World	-500	-509	44	-531	1
Net Cheese Exports		(1,000 Metric Tons)			
United States	-126	-127	0	-145	0
European Community	341	381	-98	409	-277
Japan	-122	-125	5	-144	1
Canada	-9	-7	-1	-9	24
Australia	40	46	25	35	60
New Zealand	100	90	27	108	70
Rest of World	-224	-258	42	-254	122
Net NFD Milk Exports		(1,000 Metric Tons)			
United States	67	67	0	49	0
European Community	214	268	14	270	54
Japan	-117	-110	17	-122	-16
Canada	35	23	2	24	-5
Australia	126	99	-6	101	-6
New Zealand	171	124	-5	164	4
Rest of World	-496	-471	-22	-486	-23
FOB Prices, N. Europe		(U.S. Dollars per Metric Ton)			
Butter	1,409	1,564	192	1,612	115
Cheese	1,733	1,538	267	2,006	910
Nonfat Dry Milk	1,367	1,970	-74	2,095	-64

meets many of the required reductions in trade barriers for the commodities that it directly addresses. The implication of relatively small effects of GATT on world markets in grains, oilseeds, and beef is that, like the E.C., most other countries have already made the necessary reductions in trade-distorting policies. However, a GATT agreement would at least bind the policy changes that have been made.

No-CAP Reform Scenario

In order to fully appreciate the impacts of the alternative scenarios, it is necessary to be cognizant of the implications of the baseline. This may be more important in evaluating the GATT scenario than in any other impact analysis. Because the baseline contains implementation of CAP reform with substantial effects, the impacts of a GATT agreement on the E.C. will be relatively small. However, in the absence of CAP reform, the impacts from a GATT agreement would likely be large. Viewing the baseline from this perspective allows a greater appreciation for the impacts of a GATT agreement.

The no-CAP reform scenario assumes that the reform package of May 1992 is never adopted and that its provisions are not implemented either individually or as a whole. The assumptions about agricultural policies in the E.C. are the same for the projection period as for 1992 with two notable exceptions. The first is the inclusion of the Blair House oilseed agreement beginning in the 1993-94 marketing year. This agreement is a result of a GATT panel ruling against the E.C., upholding the U.S. contention that the oilseed regime in the E.C. was trade-distorting and not (directly) a result of the CAP reform or Uruguay Round processes. The second change is the inclusion of coresponsibility levies in 1992-93 that were eliminated in the CAP reform deal. Agricultural policies in all other countries and regions, economic assumptions for all countries and regions, the rate of technological change, and weather assumptions are the same as in the baseline.

Table 12.5 presents a comparison of E.C. policy instruments under the baseline and no-CAP reform scenario. In some instances, such as intervention prices for grains, the change from one scenario to the other is in the level of the instrument. In other cases, such as in the use of set-asides or coresponsibility levies, the instrument is part of the CAP in only one scenario.

Set-aside requirements are eliminated for crops with the exception of oilseeds, which remain subject to the Blair House oilseed agreement in the no-CAP reform scenario. Grain target, threshold, and intervention prices are consistent with the CAP as it existed in 1992, except that co-responsibility levies are reinstated for 1992. This means that the grain stabilizer

TABLE 12.5 E.C.-12 Agricultural Policy Assumptions in the Baseline and No-CAP Reform Scenarios

		1991	1992	1993	1994	1995	2000
		(ECUs per metric ton)					
Durum Intervention Price	Baseline	228	221	117	108	100	100
	Scenario	228	221	221	214	208	178
Wheat, Corn Intervention Price	Baseline	169	163	117	108	100	100
	Scenario	169	163	163	159	154	132
Wheat, Corn Net Producer Support[a]	Baseline	155	163	142	143	145	145
	Scenario	155	156	150	146	142	122
Barley Intervention Price	Baseline	160	155	117	108	100	100
	Scenario	160	155	155	150	145	124
Barley Net Producer Support[a]	Baseline	147	155	142	143	145	145
	Scenario	147	147	142	138	133	113
Grain Compensatory Payment	Baseline	—	—	25	35	45	45
	Scenario	—	—	—	—	—	—
		(ECUs per hectare)					
Rapeseed Reference Price[b]	Baseline	401	163	163	163	163	163
	Scenario	401	163	163	163	163	163
Soybean Reference Prices[b]	Baseline	481	163	163	163	163	163
	Scenario	481	163	163	163	163	163
Durum Production Aid	Baseline	182	182	279	279	279	279
	Scenario	182	182	182	182	182	182
Oilseed Production Aid	Baseline	—	384	359	359	359	359
	Scenario	—	384	359	359	359	359

		(Percent)					
Grain Set-aside Rates	Baseline[c]	—	—	15	11	11	11
	Scenario[d]	—	—	—	—	—	—
Oilseed Set-aside Rates	Baseline[d]	—	—	15	10	10	10
	Scenario	—	—	10	10	10	10
Basic Coresponsibility Levy	Baseline	5	—	—	—	—	—
	Scenario	5	5	5	5	5	5
Additional Coresponsibility Levy	Baseline	3	—	—	—	—	—
	Scenario	3	3	3	3	3	3
		(ECUs per metric ton)					
Beef Intervention Price	Baseline	3,430	3,430	3,259	3,087	2,916	2,916
	Scenario	3,430	3,430	3,430	3,430	3,430	3,430
Pork Basic Price	Baseline	1,900	1,900	1,805	1,710	1,615	1,615
	Scenario	1,900	1,900	1,854	1,825	1,793	1,647
Milk Target Price	Baseline	268	268	267	265	265	265
	Scenario	268	268	268	268	268	268
Butter Intervention Price	Baseline	2,928	2,928	2,855	2,781	2,781	2,781
	Scenario	2,928	2,928	2,928	2,928	2,928	2,928
		(ECUs per head)					
Male Bovine Premium	Baseline[e]	90	90	90	90	90	90
	Scenario	40	40	40	40	40	40

a Guaranteed producer price, minus effects of stabilizers, plus government payments.
b In 1991, intervention price for rapeseed, minimum price for soybeans.
c Average set-aside prior to exemption for small producers.
d Same as "c" for 1993/94, actual rate thereafter.
e Two payments of 90 ECU per animal, one at 10 months, one at 22 months of age.

system remains in place throughout the time period covered by this scenario.

Beef intervention prices are held at 1992 levels instead of being reduced by 5 percent in 1993, 1994, and 1995, as in the baseline. Suckler cow premiums are eliminated and male bovine premiums are reduced to be consistent with beef policy as it existed before 1992. Basic pork and poultry sluicegate prices are assumed to decline over time to reflect the costs of production, which decrease as the grain stabilizer results in declining feed prices in the no-CAP reform scenario. Butter intervention prices are increased by 2.5 percent in 1993 and 1994, reversing the reductions that were stipulated by CAP reform. The effects of not reforming the CAP are presented in Table 12.6.

No-CAP Reform vs. CAP Reform and GATT:
A Clearer Picture of Uruguay Round Impacts

In comparing the GATT scenario to the baseline, the direction and magnitude of impacts depends not only on assumptions about the implementation of a GATT agreement but perhaps more so on the baseline itself. Since the baseline used in this study already contained CAP reform, which takes the E.C. a long way toward meeting many of the possible GATT requirements, the impacts of GATT might seem small. In some cases, such as wheat and beef, for example, the direction of the impacts is the opposite of what many previous studies have indicated. While the no-CAP reform scenario is still only one possible view of agriculture without the E.C. reforms, it is a familiar perspective, particularly since CAP reform is only in its beginning stages of implementation. The E.C. portion of the baseline will change considerably over the next few years as the E.C. policies begin to shape reality and not just conjecture. This fluid, conjectural view of E.C. agriculture under CAP reform makes it difficult to gain a solid appreciation of the effects of any policy change that includes the E.C. To get a clearer picture of what GATT would mean to world agriculture, the differences between the GATT and no-CAP reform scenarios are viewed in a side-by-side comparison to the differences between the baseline (CAP reform) and no-CAP reform scenario. In this perspective, the differences between CAP reform and GATT impacts can be viewed as the changes attributable to GATT beyond the effects of CAP reform.

The European Community

The impacts of CAP reform and GATT and the contribution of CAP reform towards GATT impacts for the E.C. are presented in Table 12.7. The contribution column is the percentage of the GATT impact that is attributed to CAP reform. For grains, the reductions in production and net

TABLE 12.6 Impacts on E.C. Agricultural Products Under The Baseline and No-CAP Reform Scenarios

	1991	1995		2000	
	Baseline Level	Baseline Level	Scenario (Change)	Baseline Level	Scenario (Change)
Wheat		(1,000 Metric Tons)			
Production	90,050	79,430	6,870	81,410	8,370
Domestic Use	64,890	68,650	-2,360	70,160	-1,360
Net Exports	19,610	11,750	8,590	11,270	9,680
Barley					
Production	51,649	47,000	3,440	49,220	3,700
Domestic Use	42,400	43,050	-2,280	44,398	-1,208
Net Exports	8,500	4,050	5,600	4,835	4,885
Corn					
Production	26,721	22,950	2,840	24,161	1,279
Domestic Use	27,761	25,520	1,390	26,417	603
Net Exports	2,196	2,770	-1,630	2,283	-703
Soybeans					
Production	1,509	1,464	0	1,539	-3
Domestic Use	15,150	15,826	52	16,191	30
Net Exports	13,741	14,366	52	14,654	32
Rapeseed					
Production	7,341	5,537	0	5,823	0
Domestic Use	7,322	6,066	-36	6,241	-26
Net Exports	72	529	-36	418	-26
Protein Meals[a]					
Production	16,886	17,196	12	17,873	4
Domestic Use	28,527	27,874	274	29,108	71
Net Exports	11,298	10,689	260	11,242	68
Support Prices		(ECUs per Metric Ton)			
Wheat, Corn	155	100	42	100	22
Barley	147	100	33	100	13
Soybeans	288	163	0	163	0
Rapeseed	307	163	0	163	0
Beef		(1,000 Metric Tons)			
Production	8,678	8,184	-34	8,105	-38
Domestic Use	7,627	7,729	-326	7,894	-671
Net Exports	805	480	312	221	627

(continues)

332

TABLE 12.6 (continued)

	1991 Baseline Level	1995 Baseline Level	1995 Scenario (Change)	2000 Baseline Level	2000 Scenario (Change)
Pork					
Production	13,754	14,245	-27	14,458	-81
Domestic Use	13,187	13,487	-105	13,681	-106
Net Exports	567	758	78	778	24
Poultry					
Production	6,847	7,277	-33	7,556	-29
Domestic Use	6,539	6,928	-59	7,186	51
Net Exports	308	349	25	370	-80
Milk					
Production	113,880	111,180	-62	111,240	40
Fluid Use	32,380	31,910	-41	30,860	-32
Cheese					
Production	4,892	5,154	-32	5,385	-29
Domestic Use	4,494	4,768	-1	4,974	0
Net Exports	341	392	-28	409	-29
Butter					
Production	1,801	1,574	15	1,514	18
Domestic Use	1,580	1,463	-8	1,399	-5
Net Exports	214	124	21	111	23
Prices		(ECUs per Metric Ton)			
Beef Producer	2,651	2,210	390	2,210	390
Pork Producer	1,656	1,360	150	1,360	27
Poultry Producer	1,466	1,233	148	1,233	47
Milk Farm Price	296	299	3	305	2
Meat Consumption		(Kilograms per Capita, Retail Weight)			
Beef	15.52	15.58	-0.66	15.76	-1.34
Pork	26.83	27.18	-0.21	27.32	-0.21
Poultry	19.00	19.95	-0.17	20.50	0.14
Lamb and Mutton	3.65	3.31	0.04	3.03	-0.14
Total	65.00	66.02	-1.00	66.61	-1.55
Per Capita Meat Expenditures at Producer Prices	164.91	(ECUs) 139.80	14.52	140.21	5.06

^aAggregate of soybean, rapeseed, and sunflower meals

TABLE 12.7 Impacts on E.C. Agricultural Products Under the CAP Reform and GATT Scenarios in 2000

	No-CAP Reform Level	CAP Reform (Change)	GATT (Change)	Contribution of CAP Reform to GATT (Percent)
Wheat		(1,000 Metric Tons)		
Production	89,780	-8,370	-8,370	100
Domestic Use	68,800	1,360	653	208
Net Exports	20,950	-9,680	-8,977	108
Barley				
Production	52,920	-3,792	-5,054	75
Domestic Use	43,190	1,208	1,367	88
Net Exports	9,720	-4,885	-6,415	76
Corn				
Production	25,440	-1,279	-1,411	91
Domestic Use	27,020	-603	-65	928
Net Imports	1,580	703	1,384	51
Soybeans				
Production	1,536	3	2	150
Domestic Use	16,221	-30	-56	54
Net Imports	14,686	-32	-57	56
Rapeseed				
Production	5,823	0	0	100
Domestic Use	6,215	26	46	57
Net Imports	392	26	46	56
Protein Meals[a]				
Production	17,877	-4	-9	44
Domestic Use	29,179	-71	-483	15
Net Imports	11,310	-68	475	14
Support Prices		(ECUs per Metric Ton)		
Wheat, Corn	122	-22	-22	100
Barley	113	-13	-13	100
Soybeans	163	0	0	—
Rapeseed	163	0	0	—
Beef		(1,000 Metric Tons)		
Production	8,067	38	48	79
Domestic Use	7,223	671	495	136
Net Exports	848	-627	-444	141
Pork				
Production	14,377	81	-176	-46
Domestic Use	13,575	106	732	14
Net Exports	802	-24	-908	3
Poultry				
Production	7,527	29	-94	-31
Domestic Use	7,237	-51	151	-34
Net Exports	290	80	-246	-33
Milk				
Production	111,280	-40	-360	11
Fluid Use	30,828	32	392	8
Cheese				
Production	5,356	29	-170	-17
Domestic Use	4,974	0	107	0
Net Exports	380	29	-248	-12

(continues)

TABLE 12.7 *(continued)*

	No-CAP Reform Level	CAP Reform (Change)	GATT (Change)	Contribution of CAP Reform to GATT (Percent)
Butter				
Production	1,532	-18	47	-38
Domestic Use	1,394	5	5	100
Net Exports	134	-23	39	-59
Prices		(ECUs per Metric Ton)		
Beef Producer	2,600	-390	-213	183
Pork Producer	1,387	-27	-119	23
Poultry Producer	1,280	-47	-108	44
Milk Farm Price	307	-2	-30	7
Meat Consumption		(Kilograms per Capita, Retail Weight)		
Beef	14.42	1.34	0.99	135
Pork	27.11	0.21	1.46	14
Poultry	20.64	-0.14	0.44	-32
Lamb and Mutton	2.89	0.14	0.07	200
Total	65.06	1.55	2.96	52
Per Capita Meat Expenditures		(ECUs)		
at Producer Prices	145.27	-5.06	-4.9	102

[a]Aggregate of soybean, rapeseed and sunflower meals.

exports are large for both the CAP reform and GATT scenarios. This means that, in the absence of CAP reform, GATT would have a substantial impact on the E.C. grains sector. Compared to no-CAP reform, in the year 2000, the aggregate of wheat, barley, and corn production and exports are reduced 14.8 mmt and 16.8 mmt, respectively, in the GATT scenario, and 13.4 mmt and 15.3 mmt, respectively, under CAP reform. The contribution of CAP reform to the total GATT impacts is large for grains. In some cases, such as for wheat net exports, CAP reform, as implemented in the baseline, goes beyond cuts that would be required under GATT. For barley, further cuts in exports would be required under GATT, likewise increased market access for corn. Grain utilization relative to no-CAP reform is increased approximately 2 mmt in both scenarios in 2000. These changes are the result of changing market prices of grains and other feeds within the E.C. and are not required changes under CAP reform or GATT. In general, CAP reform meets a large proportion of the expected GATT commitments for grains.

Oilseed production is virtually unchanged between the three scenarios because of the Blair House oilseed agreement that is incorporated in each. Because trade in oilseeds and products is not restricted, GATT market access requirements do not force increased imports of oilseeds and products. Reductions in crush are marginal and are the result of changing prices of oilseeds and products. Even though CAP reform seems to contribute the major proportion of changes in oilseeds, most impacts of both

CAP reform and GATT are so small that they are insignificant. The most notable impacts in the oilseed complexes are the changing meal prices relative to feed grains and changes in livestock, poultry, and dairy production. These changes result in small decreases in meal use under CAP reform leading to lower net import levels. Under GATT, the combination of changes in livestock production and substitution of grains, especially corn, for protein meals results in a much larger decrease in meal utilization than under CAP reform.

Beef trade impacts are actually smaller under GATT than under CAP reform, implying that CAP reform effects on beef in the baseline are more than adequate to meet GATT export quantity restrictions. This is reflected in the contribution of CAP reform of more than 100 percent in Table 12.7. Compared to the no-CAP reform scenario, however, GATT effects on subsidized beef exports by the E.C. would be substantial. The net export reductions would be primarily the result of subsidized export restrictions.

GATT and CAP reform have generally opposite impacts on the pork and poultry sectors. Since CAP reform does not address pork and poultry directly, impacts are almost completely attributable to GATT provisions. Because of lower feed prices without any trade restrictions under CAP reform, pork and poultry production increase. In the GATT scenario, subsidized export reductions make it necessary to reduce production of both meats, overcoming the slight production-enhancing effects of CAP reform. These changes also result in consumption increases for both pork and poultry.

Because butter is addressed in CAP reform, there are some minor milk production impacts in that scenario. With the exception of the 5 percent reduction in butter intervention price, however, no dairy policies are affected by CAP reform. Under GATT, substantial reductions in subsidized cheese exports would be required, resulting in lower domestic cheese prices. The lower cheese prices would lead to lower milk producer prices, and milk production would be reduced beyond reductions attributable to CAP reform. There would be an increase in butter and NFD production because domestic cheese prices decline relative to butter price, thereby shifting milk to butter production. Butter exports increase under GATT because of the restrictions on cheese and because subsidized export constraints are not binding. Because CAP reform has little direct effect on dairy, GATT is responsible for nearly all impacts on this sector.

In general, CAP reform impacts are a large percentage of total GATT impacts for grains and beef, and relatively small compared to GATT for pork, poultry, and dairy. For oilseeds, the impacts of either CAP reform or GATT are insignificant, except for protein meals which are affected by GATT much more than by CAP reform. CAP reform meets many but not all of the requirements of GATT on E.C. agriculture as proposed by

Dunkel and the Blair House agreement. However, GATT would be significant in further reducing trade distortions due to E.C. agricultural policies in some important sectors.

World Prices

Impacts on world prices under GATT and CAP reform are presented in Table 12.8. Most of the changes from no-CAP reform are larger for the GATT scenario than for CAP reform. In most cases, the contribution of CAP reform is more than 50 percent, implying that the additional effects of GATT on world agricultural markets are smaller than the effects of CAP reform as implemented in this particular baseline. Some exceptions are dairy products and protein meals. Both of these categories are areas to which CAP reform gave little or no attention.

Wheat price changes at the gulf are larger under CAP reform than under GATT because CAP reform as implemented in the baseline restricts E.C. wheat imports more than required by GATT commitments. The reduction in subsidized EEP exports also forces more wheat back on the U.S. market, which absorbs the grain through lower prices leading to increased consumption and higher stock levels. The lower domestic prices lead to lower prices at the gulf. Rotterdam prices, on the other hand, increase more under GATT than under CAP reform. The reduction in EEP subsidies increases the wedge between the gulf price and Rotterdam price. Since this wedge effectively reduces world prices, the net effect of reducing it is an increase in the Rotterdam price of wheat. Barley and corn world price impacts under CAP reform are smaller than GATT impacts. However, like the Rotterdam wheat price impacts, additional GATT effects on world markets are less than effects from CAP reform. Nearly all rice price impacts are due to GATT.

GATT will have little effect on oilseeds because the Blair House oilseed agreement is already incorporated into all three scenarios. There is a small effect from the reduction of EEP subsidies on soybean oil, but the largest impact is from substitution of grains for protein meals due to relative price changes. The additional GATT effects will be larger than CAP reform effects for meals and smaller than CAP reform effects for vegetable oils. The larger impact on oilseeds from CAP reform than from additional GATT effects implies that the combination of impacts on meals and oils is larger for CAP reform.

Most of the impacts on dairy product prices are due to GATT, and a relatively small portion are due to CAP reform. Only the E.C. butter price is changed for dairy under CAP reform, and this change is relatively small. Therefore, the impacts on world dairy prices are small. Substantial changes to E.C. cheese trade are required in the GATT scenario. Because of

TABLE 12.8 Impacts on World Agricultural Prices Under the CAP Reform and GATT Scenarios in 2000

	No-CAP Reform Level	CAP Reform (Change)	GATT (Change)	Contribution of CAP Reform to GATT (Percent)
	————Dollars per Metric Ton————			
Wheat				
FOB U.S. Gulf	133.38	16.97	10.72	158
CIF Rotterdam	157.06	19.80	28.88	69
Barley				
FOB Pacific NW	114.63	6.72	10.02	67
Corn				
FOB U.S. Gulf	98.02	6.01	9.02	67
CIF Rotterdam	109.84	6.76	10.13	67
Rice				
FOB Bangkok	330.91	0.38	11.02	3
Soybeans				
FOB U.S. Gulf	229.70	3.06	2.88	106
CIF Rotterdam	245.32	3.01	2.83	106
Soybean Meal				
FOB Decatur	214.05	-2.73	-7.81	35
CIF Rotterdam	228.01	-2.77	-7.93	35
Soybean Oil				
FOB Decatur	450.81	26.64	44.92	59
CIF Rotterdam	469.03	27.52	46.38	59
Canola/Rapeseed				
Western Canada	216.55	5.70	7.33	78
CIF Rotterdam	215.32	3.01	2.83	106
Rapeseed Meal				
FOB Hamburg	161.50	-2.57	-7.36	35
Rapeseed Oil				
CIF Rotterdam	439.94	27.40	46.19	59
Cheese				
FOB N. Europe	2,083.00	-77.00	833.00	-9
Butter				
FOB N. Europe	1,575.00	37.00	152.00	24
Nonfat Dry Milk				
FOB N. Europe	2,065.00	30.00	-34.00	-88
Beef				
(Nebraska Direct Fed Steers)	1,758.63	43.37	14.55	298
Pork				
(Iowa-Southern Minnesota Barrows and Gilts)	1,175.28	42.72	64.37	66
Poultry				
(12-City Wholesale)	1,256.41	4.59	5.51	83

the magnitude of the cuts in cheese exports by the E.C., the effects on all dairy products are larger in the GATT scenario than under CAP reform.

Beef results are peculiar because the beef export level for the E.C. under CAP reform is lower than maximum allowable levels under GATT. For this reason, GATT price impacts on beef are smaller than those for CAP reform. Beef prices might be distorted by changes in the U.S. cattle cycle resulting from changing market signals and the amount of time it takes for these market signals to impact production. Comparing the magnitudes of the impacts under these conditions for a specific year must be done with care. However, it appears that the directions of the price changes are as expected, and it is fair to say that both CAP reform and GATT will have significant impacts on world beef markets. Pork and poultry prices are affected more by CAP reform than by additional GATT commitments.

Summary and Conclusions

This chapter presents the effects of a GATT scenario and compares these changes to the impacts of CAP reform. The GATT scenario is presented in a framework which already includes CAP reform. To get a clearer picture of GATT, the effects of not reforming the CAP are also presented. Under a GATT agreement consistent with the Dunkel text as amended by the Blair House agreement, world grain, oilseed, and beef markets would be subject to relatively little adjustment. Particularly for grains, groups such as the United States and the E.C. have unilaterally reduced support levels since 1986. For the E.C., any remaining support reductions necessary to meet GATT restrictions are projected to be made under CAP reform. These reductions in support levels enable the E.C. to meet most of the export subsidy quantity and expenditure restrictions that would apply under GATT.

However, for pork, poultry, and dairy products, export restrictions and market access requirements would still have to be met to be in compliance with a GATT agreement for several countries. Since the E.C. is a major exporter of many agricultural commodities and has been among the countries with the highest levels of agricultural protection, the steps taken unilaterally under CAP reform have a larger impact on world agricultural markets than implementing a GATT agreement. On the other hand, if CAP reform were to be implemented in a manner different from that which is assumed here, or if there are changes that would render it ineffective, then a GATT agreement might have a substantially larger impact than this analysis implies. At the very least, it would bind the E.C. to changes it has already made unilaterally.

Comparing the impacts from GATT to the impacts from CAP reform implies that much of the expected outcome of GATT has been obtained through unilateral reform by the E.C. However, not only would GATT reach beyond CAP reform and further affect the E.C., but it would force other countries to shoulder some of the responsibility for trade barrier reduction. Furthermore, it should not be implied that the additional impacts of GATT would not be significant. GATT would be significant from the standpoint of further reducing trade distortions beyond gains made through CAP reform. But perhaps the Uruguay Round's most significant contribution will be to create the framework in which real agricultural trade liberalization negotiations can be carried on in future GATT rounds.

References

Devadoss, S. D., P. C. Westhoff, M. D. Helmar, E. Grundmeier, K. Skold, W. H. Meyers, and S. R. Johnson. 1993. "The FAPRI Modeling System: A Documentation Summary." In *Agricultural Sector Models for the United States: Descriptions and Selected Policy Applications* edited by C. Robert Taylor, Katherine H. Reicheldterfer, and Stanley R. Johnson. Ames: Iowa State Univ. Press.

Dunkel, A. 1991. "Text on Agriculture." Submitted to the General Agreement on Tariffs and Trade.

FAPRI. 1993a. "FAPRI 1993 U.S. Agricultural Outlook." Staff Report #1-93. Iowa State University, Ames, IA.

FAPRI. 1993b. "FAPRI 1993 World Agricultural Outlook." Staff Report #2-93. Iowa State University, Ames, IA.

Helmar, M. D., D. L. Stephens, K. Eswaramoorthy, D. S. Brown, D. J. Hayes, R. Young, and W. H. Meyers. 1992. "An Analysis of Reform of the CAP." FAPRI Staff Report #4-92. Center for Agricultural and Rural Development, Iowa State University, Ames, IA.

Project LINK. 1992. "Project LINK World Outlook: Post Meeting Forecast." Project LINK, Department of Economic and Social Information and Policy Analysis, United Nations, New York, NY.

The WEFA Group. 1992. *World Economic Outlook, Volume 1, Developed Economies, Post-Meeting Forecast.* The WEFA Group: Bala Cynwyd, PA.

13

U.S.-E.C. Agricultural Trade Relations and the Uruguay Round: A Cairns Group Perspective

David Vanzetti, Neil Andrews, Susan Hester, and Brian S. Fisher

As the Uruguay Round of GATT negotiations moves, somewhat hesitantly, toward a conclusion, it is clear that, as in previous Rounds, the United States and the European Community have played dominant roles in the negotiations. If the Round is concluded, success may be attributed largely to the influence of these two main parties. Similarly, if the Round fails the European Community and the United States will be largely responsible for its failure. Whatever the eventual outcome, the influence of U.S.-E.C. trade relations on other GATT members is undoubtedly extremely significant. By contrast, it may appear that the influence of third parties on the United States and the European Community is small.

It can be argued, however, that this view of the negotiations is incomplete. As a group of agricultural exporting countries, acting cohesively, the Cairns Group has played a significant role in having agriculture placed on the agenda for negotiation at the Uruguay Round, in contrast with earlier GATT rounds. The emergence of the Cairns Group has added a new dimension to the bargaining process in the GATT trade negotiations (Higgott and Cooper, 1990).

The purpose in this chapter is twofold: within the context of U.S.-E.C. trade relations, to examine the role of the Cairns Group of countries in the GATT negotiations, and to make a preliminary assessment of the potential effects of likely outcomes in the Round on the major trading regions and on Cairns Group member countries.

U.S.-E.C. Agricultural Trade Relations: A Historical Perspective

A key feature of U.S.-E.C. agricultural trade relations in recent decades has been the discrepancy between ideology and behavior. The United States, for example, has persistently argued for reductions in barriers to trade since the GATT was founded and has been the driving force behind nearly every round of GATT negotiations (Oxley, 1990), yet it has also initiated many GATT exemptions that are contrary to the principles of fostering freer trade. Previous rounds of multilateral trade negotiations have failed to achieve any significant change to protectionist agricultural policies. The Dillon (1960-62), Kennedy (1964), and Tokyo (1974-79) Rounds failed to bring about any changes to domestic agricultural price and income support programs because of the unwillingness of the two major participants, the United States and the European Community, to agree upon the inclusion of agricultural trade reform on the agenda for negotiation.

Willingness to negotiate on agriculture increased in the mid-1980s as levels of protection and surpluses in both the United States and the European Community rose. There was also the recognition that there are potential gains from opening up domestic markets to international trade, and that multilateral trade liberalization is likely to result in significant benefits even after accounting for domestic adjustment costs. The willingness to negotiate has been partly due to the decline of the United States as the dominant trading power. The U.S. share of world trade has fallen while its dependence on trade and therefore its sensitivity to trade issues has increased. It now shares the dominance of world trade with the European Community and Japan, resulting in increased competition or threat of retaliation from these and other countries. It is for these reasons that the Uruguay Round represents a first step toward serious negotiations on agricultural policies.

The success of international agreements, such as the GATT, depends fundamentally on the extent to which the most powerful signatories to those agreements are prepared to support them. Since the inception of the GATT in 1947, the most powerful industrialized countries, which founded the agreement, have been responsible for the increased restriction and management of competition in agricultural trade, contrary to the market liberalizing principles contained in the agreement.

A number of years after the establishment of the GATT, the United States set a precedent for the major industrialized countries: that GATT rules must accommodate domestic policy requirements. The United States refused to bring its farm programs under the discipline of international trade, instead insisting on a waiver from the general trade rules, allowing it to restrict the import of agricultural products (under Section 22 of the

U.S. Agricultural Adjustment Act, 1955) and generally insulate its markets from foreign competition (Avery, 1992). The development of the Common Agricultural Policy (CAP) by the European Community, in which export subsidies and quantitative import restrictions play an important role, was made easier by the existence of the Section 22 waiver. In addition, as the United States became progressively more dependent on world export markets, it became more sensitive to restrictions in international competition, such as those emanating from the CAP, making freer trade appear more attractive to it. Competitive export subsidies and quantitative restrictions on imports are examples of policies that may be considered politically desirable by individual nations but are clearly suboptimal in terms of economic efficiency, especially when other traders impose similar restraints on trade in retaliation. Unfortunately, with the legitimacy of subsidies and quotas that has arisen largely from the Section 22 waiver, it became impossible for the GATT contracting parties to effectively oppose the protectionist aspects of the CAP. The number of exceptions to the GATT rules continued to increase to such an extent that levels of protection on agricultural products at the start of the Uruguay Round in 1986 were greater than those at the start of the Dillon Round in 1960 (Johnson, 1991).

Both the Kennedy and the Tokyo Rounds failed to result in any significant liberalization of agricultural trade. However, in the lead-up to the Uruguay Round negotiations, proposals for reform of agriculture were put forward by Argentina, Australia, Canada, New Zealand, and the United States. The European Community was still divided as to whether the Uruguay Round negotiations should include agriculture. It was evident that there would never be agreement on an agricultural agenda unless the stalemate was broken at the political level. As a consequence, the strategy developed by Australia was to build significant political leverage by bringing together a large number of countries whose credible threat of withdrawal from the negotiations would cause the European Community and the United States to make concessions and start a process of meaningful change (Gallagher, 1988).

The Cairns Group's Role in the Uruguay Round Negotiations

The Cairns Group of 14 agricultural exporters (Argentina, Australia, Brazil, Canada, Chile, Colombia, Fiji, Hungary, Indonesia, Malaysia, New Zealand, Philippines, Thailand, and Uruguay) was formed in 1986. While the diverse political systems and trading interests of the member countries at times conflict with Cairns Group aims, the common interest of the Group is the single issue of reforming global agricultural trade. In addition to playing an important role in a large proportion of the world's agricultural markets, the Cairns Group members have competitive export-oriented agricultural sectors with only low levels of support in some member countries. In contrast, the major markets for the Cairns Group agricultural products, in the European Community, the United States, and Japan, are heavily protected or feature highly supported export industries. Because of their dependence on agricultural exports, many of the Cairns Group countries would gain little from the Uruguay Round if liberalization of agricultural markets did not occur.

Prior to the Uruguay Round, the Cairns Group had met several times to establish proposals for agriculture to be fully integrated into the GATT process, as well as for a longer-term reform package for agriculture. At the GATT ministerial meeting in Punta del Este, Uruguay, in September 1986 to launch the Round, efforts by the Cairns Group ensured that the agricultural mandate that did finally emerge met the Group's demands. The support of the United States, despite its own subsidy program and high levels of support for import-competing industries, was important in obtaining E.C. agreement to a text on agricultural subsidies for the GATT agenda. However, there is no doubt that the fundamental groundwork for the negotiating mandate that emerged, including the terms of the text, had been laid down by the Cairns Group (Gallagher, 1988). The Cairns Group proposed a plan, based on an Australian proposal (see Miller, 1986; Australian Government, 1987) for the scaling down of agricultural protection when an impasse between the United States and the European Community seemed likely. Furthermore, the notion that effective reform required improvements in three areas—domestic support, market access, and export subsidies—was put forward in a Cairns Group negotiating proposal.

At the Mid-Term Review held in Montreal in December 1988, tentative agreement was achieved in eleven of the fifteen negotiating groups on specific aspects of the GATT, with agriculture as one of the exceptions due to the marked divergence between the U.S. and E.C. negotiating positions. At the risk of bringing the Uruguay Round to a halt, the Latin American members of the Cairns Group threatened to refuse the ratification of the agreements reached in the eleven negotiating groups unless the stalemate in agricultural negotiations was broken. This proved a credible threat, and talks continued in Geneva during April 1989. There is little doubt that, had the Latin American members of the Cairns Group not made the stand they did, the stalled Mid-Term Review "would have sounded the death knell of the Uruguay Round" (Oxley, 1990).

Cohesion has been maintained within the Cairns Group, in spite of a divergence of interests. In particular, Canada had problems with the Group's proposal for comprehensive tariffication without exceptions, especially in regard to its dairy industry. Also of concern to Group members was the free trade agreement that Canada signed with the United States and the subsequent preferential access to U.S. markets of Canadian goods and services. Other problems in the Cairns Group have arisen from concerns raised by food importing developing countries outside the Group who argued that the policies of the Group would result in an increase in world food prices and hence would disadvantage such countries in the short run.

Despite the risks that Canada, particularly in mid-1988, and Hungary in 1991, might leave the Group—events that would have damaged the Group's effectiveness—the Group has maintained a high degree of unity overall, driven by the single issue of agricultural trade liberalization, and despite differing priorities among member countries, it is well understood by all members that there are substantial global gains from liberalization of agricultural markets. The Group continues to provide leadership in agricultural trade reform for many agricultural exporting countries.

Current Situation in the Uruguay Round

The Uruguay Round was initially scheduled to conclude at the end of 1990. However, agreement, particularly for agriculture, could not be reached by then, and the negotiations were extended. In December 1991 Arthur Dunkel, then Director-General of the GATT, advanced a package of reform proposals that might be used as a basis for concluding the negotiations (GATT, 1991). Many participating countries agreed that these proposals provided a suitable basis. However, a number of countries could not agree to the agricultural component of the Dunkel proposals. The European Community opposed the provisions concerning reductions in export subsidies and domestic support, while Japan opposed proposals for comprehensive tariffication. The focus for agriculture then shifted to bilateral negotiations between the United States and the European Community in an attempt to narrow the differences between these two countries. A bilateral agreement on agriculture was finally reached in November 1992. This is the so-called "Blair House Accord," which appears to provide the best indication so far of the nature of any eventual agreement for agriculture. The May 1992 reforms to the Common Agricultural Policy were a major influence on the E.C. approach to these bilateral discussions. It appears that a number of elements of the Blair House Accord have been designed specifically to accommodate these reform measures. The Dunkel package, otherwise known as the Draft Final Act, the Blair House proposals and the 1992 CAP reforms are described briefly below.

The Dunkel Package for Agriculture

The Dunkel package contains support reduction commitments in the three areas of market access, internal support, and export subsidies, with reductions in support to be implemented over the six years from 1993 to 1999 (GATT, 1991). The key elements of the proposals are set out below.

- Nontariff barriers would be converted to tariff equivalents. These tariff equivalents, and the tariffs that actually applied in the base period (1986-88), would be reduced by an average of 36 percent for agricultural products as a whole for each country, with a minimum reduction for each tariff line of 15 percent.
- Minimum access opportunities would be established. The minimum would initially be 3 percent of domestic consumption in the importing country in the 1986-88 base period and would be expanded to reach 5 percent by the end of the implementation period.
- The total value of domestic support provided by measures that are regarded as trade distorting would be reduced by 20 percent from its 1986-88 base level. This reduction would apply to each commodity individually. Domestic support payments would be exempt from this discipline only if they were strongly decoupled from production decisions.
- Budget outlays on export subsidies would be reduced by 36 percent and volumes of subsidized exports by 24 percent, from their 1986-90 averages.
- Special and differential provisions would be available to developing countries. These countries would be able to reduce support over a period of up to 10 years, while the minimum reductions would be two-thirds of those specified above. The least developed countries would be exempted from reduction commitments.

The provisions of the Dunkel text are discussed in Andrews, *et al.* (1992).

The Blair House Accord

The Blair House Accord is a bilateral agreement between the United States and the European Community on those aspects of the negotiations on which these countries had differing views. While this agreement maintains the basic framework of the Dunkel proposals, certain aspects have been modified. The main differences are set out below.

- The 20 percent reduction in domestic support would apply to the aggregate value of support for agriculture as a whole, rather than for individual commodities.

- Certain forms of direct payments (see below) would be excluded from reduction commitments for domestic support, despite the fact that these payments would be only weakly "decoupled" from production decisions.
- The reduction in the volume of subsidized exports would be 21 percent rather than the 24 percent under the Dunkel proposals.

Reforms to the Common Agricultural Policy

In mid-1992, the European Community reformed its Common Agricultural Policy. The principal feature of the reforms is that internal support prices are to be reduced for some major temperate zone agricultural products, notably grains and beef. These reductions are to be counterbalanced by compensatory direct payments to cereal and beef producers, with the payments being linked, in part at least, to actual areas planted to crops and to cattle numbers. Changes for other commodities such as dairy products and sheep meat are only minor. The reforms for grains and beef are discussed in more detail in Roberts, *et al.* (1992).

In the case of grains, unit levels of support to producers are being maintained. However, the support is now being provided more through direct compensatory payments and less through internal price support than was previously the case. In addition, a land set-aside scheme is to apply for grains, oilseeds, and protein crops (peas, field beans, and lupins). The use of area reduction programs, together with partial decoupling of support, is expected to restrain surplus cereal production, while lower internal prices are expected to increase domestic grain consumption. Distortions to world trade and prices are likely to be reduced significantly by the stimulus to E.C. grain consumption as a result of the reduction in internal price support. However, the extent to which any reduction in distortions are reflected in higher world prices will depend on the reactions of other producing countries, such as the United States, to the reforms (Roberts *et al.*, 1992).

The reforms appear likely to have relatively little impact on E.C. beef production, as the reduction in price support is to be replaced by the use of direct "headage" payments. However, the reduction in price supports may result in some increase in domestic consumption. Even with the reforms, E.C. beef exports will still need to be highly subsidized in order to be competitive internationally. However, should the reforms fail to result in a significant reduction in E.C. beef surpluses, there is likely to be continued and perhaps increased pressure within the Community to export subsidized beef to as many markets as possible.

Despite the uncertainties, however, it appears that the CAP reforms would enable the European Community to go a considerable way toward meeting the disciplines implied by a GATT agreement along the lines of the Blair House Accord. Indeed, it appears that a number of the changes to the Dunkel package that were incorporated into the Accord were made in order to accommodate this new set of Community policies, such as the agreement to exclude the direct compensatory payments from disciplines that would arise from a Uruguay Round agreement.

Implementation Issues

The Blair House Accord—at present only a bilateral agreement between the United States and the European Community on the measures that would be mutually acceptable to them should the Round be finalized—is likely to provide the basis for any changes that are made to the Dunkel package. However, it will be necessary to obtain multilateral agreement on such changes in order for the negotiations on agriculture to be finalized and for the proposed reforms to become binding. While the Dunkel text, combined with the Blair House Accord, provides the best indication to date of the most likely outcome of the Uruguay Round, a number of issues regarding implementation remain unresolved.

Aggregation of Domestic Support. Under the Dunkel package, the value of domestic support would be calculated for each individual product and commitments would be made to reduce domestic support for each product by 20 percent during the implementation period. Under the Blair House Accord, the value of domestic support would be aggregated across the whole of agriculture, and it is this aggregate level of support that would be reduced. Reductions in support for individual products in excess of 20 percent could be used to allow smaller reductions for other products. As a result, some products that have high levels of support or are politically sensitive in particular countries could be subject to little or no reduction in domestic support—indeed, it is possible that domestic support could be increased for some products.

Exemption of Compensation Payments. A central feature of the 1992 reforms to the CAP of the European Community was the reduction of internal support prices, a corresponding increase in direct "compensation" payments and an increased emphasis on supply controls (see Roberts, *et al.*, 1992, for a detailed analysis of the CAP reforms). The status of the E.C. compensation payments in the Round has been a significant issue since these payments were first proposed. Rather than being based on output, these compensation payments are to be based on inputs used in a particular year—for example, for grains the payments will be made per hectare of land used for production, while for beef they will be made per animal. The European Community has argued that these payments do not encourage production and therefore should be exempt from reduction commitments for domestic support under the Round (Agra Europe, 1992b). However, while payments for both grains and beef are subject to certain limits, these payments would provide an incentive to increase the use of land or animals up to those limits (Roberts *et al.*, 1992).

Under the Dunkel text, in order for E.C. compensation payments to qualify as being exempt from reduction commitments they would need to satisfy the criteria relating to decoupling. To be classed as decoupled under this text, payments cannot be related to the type or volume of production, to international or domestic prices, or to the amounts of factors of production used in any year since the base period (GATT, 1991). As E.C. compensation payments are to be based (up to specified limits) on the current area planted or the current number of animals in a herd, they do not meet these requirements and so would not be exempt from reduction commitments under the Dunkel text. However, under the terms of the Blair House Accord, these payments would be exempt from reduction commitments.

Given the size of the planned phased reductions in direct price support for grains under the 1992 CAP reforms (about 30 percent by 1995-96) it is probable that under the Blair House Accord, although the corresponding direct compensation payments to E.C. grain growers would not be subject to disciplines, the value of grain support as defined in the Accord would decline by more than 20 percent from the 1986-88 base period level. As the value of domestic support would be aggregated across the whole of agriculture under the Blair House Accord, the excess reduction in the grain component of aggregate support could be used to allow support reductions of less than 20 percent for other products.

While the European Community might be able to avoid making substantial reductions to total domestic support for grains, under the Blair House Accord, it would still have to meet commitments on reductions in the volume of subsidized exports. The increase in domestic grain consumption that results from lower grain prices, and any reductions in domestic production that results from the operation of the land set-aside component of the CAP reforms, would assist the European Community in meeting these commitments. However, whether or not the 1992 CAP reforms will enable the European Community to fully meet its obligations regarding reductions in the volumes of subsidized exports (under either proposal) remains unclear at this stage.

If the 1992 CAP reforms are not sufficient to deliver the 21 percent reduction in the volume of subsidized grain exports required by the Blair House Accord, the European Community could replace its remaining price support, including export subsidies, with increased direct compensation payments. If it adopted this approach, all support for grain would be provided through direct compensation payments, which, as discussed above, are exempt from disciplines under the Blair House Accord (though not under the Dunkel text). This would further increase the "credits" that the European Community would have available for reducing the extent of the actual reduction in support for other products. Furthermore, as E.C. exports would no longer be regarded as being subsidized in this situation, the European Community would not be required to reduce the actual volume of its grain exports by 21 percent.

The European Community's ability to totally replace price support with direct compensation payments would be constrained by the budgetary cost of this option. If price support for grains were not totally eliminated and the European Community continued to be an exporter of grains, some degree of export subsidization would remain. If existing reforms are not sufficient to reduce the volume of subsidized exports by the required 21 percent, the European Community might need to adopt other strategies, such as the use of more stringent set-asides.

Comprehensive Tariffication. A key objective of both the United States and the Cairns Group is the conversion of all nontariff barriers to tariff equivalents and the subsequent reduction of these tariff equivalents. Both Japan and South Korea have strongly opposed comprehensive tariffication, particularly for their rice industries. If exceptions to comprehensive tariffication are permitted, it is likely that the benefits of liberalization would be eroded across a wide range of commodities.

Excessive Tariff Equivalents. The extent of liberalization that can be achieved through the reduction of tariff equivalents could be eroded if these equivalents are set excessively high. The European Community has unilaterally defined tariff equivalents to include a Community preference of 10 percent on top of E.C. intervention prices (Agra Europe, 1992a). This would build considerable unused "fat" into the base tariffs, with the effect that those tariffs could be reduced considerably before having an impact on import levels and internal prices. This approach by the European Community could set a precedent for other countries.

Regardless of how these various issues are resolved, it is likely that implementation of any agreement will be open to interpretation, with each country having an incentive to interpret the provisions in a manner that suits itself. There will be a role for the Cairns Group and others in monitoring the implementation of whatever agreement is adopted and in bringing infringements to the attention of international fora such as a GATT panel or of national political groups that may be adversely affected by the policies.

Potential Impacts of the Uruguay Round

In the following analysis the SWOPSIM (Static WOrld Policy SImulation Model) world agricultural trade model is used to make a preliminary assessment of the possible implications for the major developed economies and Cairns Group countries of likely changes in market access, domestic support, and export subsidies under the Uruguay Round of agricultural trade negotiations. SWOPSIM is a static, non-spatial, partial equilibrium world trade model. In the SWOPSIM modeling framework, responses to policy changes are assumed to take place over the medium term, which is considered to be about five years. A detailed description of the SWOPSIM framework is presented by Roningen (1986) and Roningen, *et al.* (1991). The intention here is to provide an indication of the broad directions and magnitudes of the effects of likely changes resulting from a possible Uruguay Round outcome.

The version of the model used in this study is based on 1989 production, consumption, trade, and price data and estimates of agricultural support (or taxation—whether explicit or implicit) in each country included in the model. The model used in this study includes all the individual Cairns Group countries except Fiji, in addition to the United States, the European Community, Japan, North Asia (South Korea and Taiwan) and a group of developing food-importing countries.

The standard 22 commodity coverage in SWOPSIM has been expanded to differentiate between beef from foot-and-mouth-free and -affected areas and also to include manioc. It is important to distinguish between beef produced in foot-and-mouth-free areas and beef that is not, so as to correctly identify impacts on those countries that will trade in each of these markets following the liberalization of beef trade. Manioc is an important component of feedgrain substitutes in the European Community and is a major agricultural export commodity of Thailand and, to a lesser extent, Indonesia. Changes in the E.C. grain market as a result of liberalization under the Uruguay Round is likely to affect E.C. import demand for manioc and is therefore likely to have implications for manioc producers in Thailand and Indonesia. The model does not include tropical products, such as coffee, rubber, and forest products, which contribute significantly to exports in many developing countries.

The 18 regions in the current version of the model, together with the countries or regions from the SWOPSIM database that have been included in each of these regions, and the 24 commodities in the model, are listed in Table 13.1.

The results from this version of SWOPSIM are not strictly comparable with those from earlier versions. The base year in this version, 1989 (the most recent year for which full data were available), was characterized by

TABLE 13.1 Regions and Commodity Groupings in the SWOPSIM Model

Regions	Commodity groups
United States	Beef (FMD*-free)
European Community	Beef (FMD*-affected)[a]
Australia	Pork
New Zealand	Sheep meat
Canada	Poultry meat
Indonesia	Wheat
Malaysia	Corn
Philippines	Other coarse grains[b]
Thailand	Rice
Argentina	Poultry eggs
Brazil	Dairy fresh milk
Chile	Dairy butter
Colombia	Dairy cheese
Uruguay	Dairy powder
Hungary	Soybeans
Japan	Soybean meal
North Asia: South Korea and Taiwan	Soybean oil
Rest of the world	Other oilseeds[c]
	Other meals[d]
	Other oils[e]
	Cotton
	Sugar
	Tobacco
	Manioc[a]

[a] Additional product in the model used for this study.
[b] Barley, millet, mixed grains, oats, rye, and sorghum.
[c] Copra, cottonseed, flaxseed, palm kernels, peanuts, rapeseed, safflower, and sesame.
[d] Meals produced from copra, cottonseed, linseed, palm kernels, peanuts, rapeseed, safflower, and sesame.
[e] Vegetable oils produced from copra, cottonseed, palm, olive, palm kernels, peanuts, rapeseed, safflower, and sesame.
*FMD = foot-and-mouth disease.

high world agricultural prices, particularly for grains and dairy products, due to a drought in North America and a return to relatively low stocks of dairy products in the European Community. As a result, world prices for grains were much closer to targeted domestic prices in the United States, the European Community, and Canada, and hence levels of grains protection were unusually low in that year. Thus, any trade liberalization scenario would appear to have a much smaller impact on world prices than would be the case had a 1986 data base been used, as in earlier SWOPSIM studies. This has a significant effect on the estimates of welfare changes. While, for many products, protection levels have risen since 1989 for the above reason, for some, such as Japanese beef, a significant degree of liberalization has already occurred.

Two policy scenarios are analyzed:

- Scenario 1—adoption of the Dunkel text, as proposed in December 1991; and
- Scenario 2—adoption of the Blair House Accord, as outlined above.

In the modeling of both the Dunkel package and the Blair House Accord it is assumed that the parties ensure that any obligations to reduce the volume of subsidized exports are met with production restraints if necessary. It is also assumed that policy makers take advantage of the flexibility provided in both the Dunkel package and the Blair House Accord by reducing support for politically sensitive products to the minimum extent permitted. Examples of such products are rice in Japan and North Asia and dairy and poultry products in Canada. It is assumed that under the Dunkel package, where base period support comprises both nontariff barriers and direct payments, the associated tariff equivalents for these politically sensitive products are reduced by the minimum 15 percent, with reductions in direct payments making up the remainder to ensure that the required 20 percent reduction in total domestic support for each product is achieved. Where the product does not receive any direct payments, the full adjustment is assumed to occur in the tariff equivalent. Under the Blair House Accord, the minimum reduction in the tariff equivalents for the sensitive products are assumed to be the minimum 15 percent permitted, while greater reductions in support are made for other products to ensure that the required 20 percent reduction in domestic support for agriculture in aggregate is met.

Furthermore, it is assumed that there is no re-instrumentation of policy (such as the replacement of export subsidies with direct income support) except where policy changes are considered very likely. However, the policy re-instrumentation resulting from the CAP reforms announced in May 1992 have been incorporated into the analysis of both the Dunkel package and the Blair House Accord. The effects on world prices and economic welfare reported in this study therefore include the effects of the 1992 CAP reforms.

Model Results

Impacts on World Markets. Reform of agricultural policies that results in greater market access, reduced internal support, and curtailment of subsidized exports would have a marked positive impact on prices of agricultural commodities entering world markets. The modeled impacts of the adoption of the Dunkel package and the Blair House Accord on world prices of agricultural products are shown in Table 13.2.

The largest increases in world prices, under both liberalization proposals, relate to dairy products. World prices of FMD-free beef, cereals, and "other" oilseeds also show considerable increases. In general, price changes are broadly similar under the two scenarios. However, largely because of the less significant reductions in domestic support for livestock products in the European Community under the Blair House Accord, the adoption of the Accord results in price increases of around 3 percentage points less for beef and sheep meat than under the Dunkel package. Cheese and milk powder price increases are less under the Blair House Accord, mainly because of lesser reductions in support for dairy products in Canada and the United States.

Impact on Welfare. Liberalization of agricultural policies will have an important impact on producers, consumers, and taxpayers through changes in domestic support and world prices. Unilateral removal of protection and domestic producer support in a country that cannot influence world prices can be expected to lower domestic prices, resulting in an income transfer from producers to consumers and taxpayers, but with the economy as a whole gaining from a more efficient allocation of resources. If all or a number of countries liberalize simultaneously, and world prices rise as a result, net exporting countries will gain further from this world price

TABLE 13.2 Changes in World Prices from 1989 Base (percent)

	Dunkel Package	Blair House Accord
Beef (FMD*-free)	9	6
Beef (FMD*-affected)	3	1
Pork	7	7
Sheep meat	5	2
Poultry meat	4	4
Butter	10	10
Cheese	20	17
Milk powder	15	10
Wheat	7	6
Corn	7	6
Other coarse grains	7	6
Rice	7	7
Soybeans	2	1
Other oilseeds	7	6
Cotton	3	3
Sugar	3	3
Manioc	2	2

*FMD = foot-and-mouth disease.

effect. On the other hand, in the short run at least, net importing countries will lose from the higher world prices, at least partially offsetting the benefits to them flowing from their own domestic policies. In the longer term net importing countries may gain from the greater price stability and the development of a stronger agricultural sector. Within each country, taxpayers generally benefit from trade reform, although they may be worse off if reforms involve the reduction or removal of tariffs (which generate revenue), or the relaxation or elimination of import quotas in those cases where the quota rents accrue to the government of the country concerned. The net effect of reform on producers, consumers, and taxpayers depends on the relative impacts on producer and consumer prices of domestic reform and world price changes.

Modeled changes in annual total welfare in key countries and regions, and for major sectors within these countries, are shown in Table 13.3. Clearly, there are substantial global gains from liberalization under both scenarios, as modeled. Perhaps of greater note is how small the difference is, around 15 percent, in global welfare effects between the two liberalization packages. However, this is not so for the major participants in the

TABLE 13.3 Modelled Changes in Annual Total Welfare (U.S. $m)

	Producer Welfare	Consumer Welfare	Government Savings	Total Welfare
United States				
Dunkel	6,180	−6,492	448	137
Blair House	5,644	−5,842	408	210
European Community				
Dunkel	−5,398	7,097	−200	1,500
Blair House	−1,961	8,198	−5,527	710
Cairns Group[a]				
Dunkel	5,817	−4,771	249	1,295
Blair House	4,856	−3,956	319	1,219
Japan				
Dunkel	−3,108	3,939	28	860
Blair House	−3,232	4,268	86	1,121
NorthAsia				
Dunkel	−4,060	11,207	−3,108	4,040
Blair House	−3,571	9,732	−2,618	3,543
Rest of the World[b]				
Dunkel	8,867	−11,995	−115	−3,213
Blair House	7,389	−10,100	−108	−2,819
World Total				
Dunkel	7,804	−985	−2,672	4,147
Blair House	8,587	2,300	−7,415	3,471

[a] Excludes Fiji.
[b] Rest of the World includes non-E.C. Western European countries, a number of food importing developing countries, and the former centrally-planned economies.

negotiations. In terms of total welfare, the United States benefits more from the Blair House package, although the absolute difference (U.S. $70 million) between the welfare changes under the two scenarios is small. The European Community is calculated to be significantly better off under the Dunkel package than the Blair House Accord, due to lower government costs. The Cairns Group, as a coalition, appears to gain significantly from the higher world prices under both proposals. Gains in total welfare for Japan are estimated as relatively similar under both packages. North Asia gains more from the Dunkel package, whereas the Rest of the World incurs smaller losses under the Blair House Accord.

The modeled changes in welfare among the producers, consumers and taxpayers in the European Community may provide a clue as to why, in negotiations to date, the European Community favors the less liberal Blair House Accord over the Dunkel package, despite the fact that the latter would provide greater welfare gains to the European Community as a whole. European producers lose only U.S. $2 billion a year from the Blair House Accord, compared with over U.S. $5 billion under the Dunkel package. The E.C. preference for the Blair House Accord therefore may reflect the evident political strength of the farm lobby in Europe. Nevertheless, E.C. taxpayers would pay dearly for the significant compensation payments, which are exempt from reduction commitments, provided to European producers under the Blair House Accord provisions.

In comparison with a continuation of existing policies, both the Dunkel package and the Blair House Accord would result in substantial distributional changes between producers, consumers, and taxpayers. Substantial transfers from producers to consumers would occur in the European Community, Japan, and North Asia as a result of lower domestic prices following liberalization. In North Asia consumers are calculated to gain around U.S. $10-11 billion following liberalization under either scenario.

Higher world and domestic prices under both scenarios result in substantial transfers from consumers to producers in the United States (around U.S. $6 billion), the Cairns Group (U.S. $4-5 billion) and the Rest of the World (U.S. $7-8 billion). Due to the large number of food-importing countries included in the Rest of the World, total welfare falls in this group under both scenarios because the losses that accrue to consumers, U.S. $10-12 billion, far outweigh the gains that producers experience as a result of higher world prices. However, the welfare measures used do not include the benefits that could be expected to flow from the increase in stability in world prices likely to result from liberalized trade. Tyers and Anderson (1992), for example, note that a 50 percent reduction in industrial country agricultural protection rates alone would reduce international food price fluctuations by about half. The benefits of price stability are particularly important to low-income food-importing developing countries.

Similarly, liberalization as modeled in both the Dunkel and Blair House scenarios has different effects on government savings in different countries. Taxpayers gain from either of the two proposed reform packages in each region with the exception of the European Community, North Asia, and the Rest of the World. Taxpayers in the United States are better off by at least U.S. $400 million following trade liberalization in both scenarios because of increased tariff revenue. In Japan and North Asia, conversion of import quotas to tariffs for products such as grains, sugar, and dairy products results in no additional gains to the taxpayer, because in this model quota rents prior to tariffication, of U.S. $3 billion and U.S. $19 billion for Japan and North Asia respectively, were assumed to accrue to the government. However, taxpayer gains may be understated here, to the extent that quota rents have in fact not been substantially captured by the government. E.C. taxpayers lose because of the switch from assisting farmers via consumer-funded price support to government-funded compensation payments.

Impact on Producer Welfare in Cairns Group Countries. In all Cairns Group countries, producers gain under both scenarios as a result of increased world and domestic prices. However, producers in every Cairns Group country would gain less from the lesser liberalization contained in the Blair House Accord than from the Dunkel package (see Table 13.4).

To provide a better understanding of the possible impact for Cairns Group producers from a Uruguay Round outcome, modeled changes in

TABLE 13.4 Modelled Changes in Annual Producer Welfare in Cairns Group Countries (U.S. $m)

	Dunkel Package	Blair House
Australia	761	629
New Zealand	260	206
Canada	733	609
Indonesia	831	774
Malaysia	291	247
Philippines	414	370
Thailand	269	251
Argentina	794	628
Brazil	955	732
Chile	60	35
Colombia	268	225
Uruguay	43	26
Hungary	139	124

producer surplus under the Blair House Accord on a country-by-commodity basis are shown in Table 13.5. Producers of most products within the Cairns Group gain. The largest gains to grain producers in Cairns Group countries occur in Canada (U.S. $390 million for wheat and U.S. $175 million for coarse grains other than corn), Australia (U.S. $180 million for wheat), and Brazil (U.S. $170 million for corn). These gains arise primarily as a result of the required 21 percent reduction in the volume of E.C.-subsidized exports and the winding back of export subsidies under the U.S. Export Enhancement Program. It should be noted however that, because U.S. grain production is supported largely through the use of deficiency payments, it is possible to make export sales without resorting to the use of direct export subsidies. Therefore, it is likely that subsidized U.S. exports will be replaced, to a large degree, by exports without export subsidies.

The overall gains to Canadian grain producers arise because the benefits to them from increased world prices outweigh the losses resulting from reductions in grain support. However, the net gains to Canadian grain producers reported here are likely to be overstated as a result of the use of 1989 as the base year for the model. World grain prices in 1989 were higher than in most other recent years, mainly due to a major drought in North America. As a result, the unit value of support for grains in Canada was abnormally low in 1989. Consequently, the reduction in support that has been modeled in this study would be less than the required reduction in Canadian grain support under a Uruguay Round agreement based on either the Dunkel package or the Blair House Accord. It is likely that this underestimation of the reduction in Canadian grain support would lead to an overestimation of the net gains to Canadian grain producers.

For rice, the largest gains in the Cairns Group accrue to producers in Indonesia (U.S. $620 million), Malaysia and the Philippines (both U.S. $120 million). These potential gains illustrate the importance to these countries of effective rice liberalization in both Japan and in newly industrializing countries (particularly South Korea).

Oilseed producers in a number of Cairns Group countries also receive significant gains. The largest gains go to producers in Argentina and Malaysia (both U.S. $220 million), Indonesia (U.S. $125 million), the Philippines (U.S. $95 million), and Brazil (U.S. $85 million). These gains are largely the result of the oilseed component of the Blair House Accord, where the European Community agreed to limit oilseed production through the use of land set-asides as part of the settlement of the U.S.-E.C. oilseed dispute (Agra Europe, 1992c). A further contributing factor is a reduction in soybean output in both the United States and Brazil. These reductions occur as a result of smaller price increases for soybeans than competing crops in these countries and the subsequent movement of

TABLE 13.5 Changes in Producer Welfare in Cairns Group Countries with Implementation of the Blair House Accord ($ million)

	Australia	New Zealand	Canada	Indonesia	Malaysia	Philippines	Thailand
Beef (FMD*-free)	173	33	128			17	
Beef (FMD*-affected)							
Pork	39	6	54			84	
Sheep meat	2						
Poultry meat	12	2	-3			8	18
Eggs	15		52				
Milk and dairy products	125	159	-168				
Wheat	176	1	389				
Corn	1	1	14	30		28	26
Other coarse grains	36	2	173				1
Rice	1			620	25	121	121
Oilseed and oilseed products	25		-37	124	220	93	18
Cotton	3						1
Sugar	20			-29		11	33
Tobacco	1		5	10	1	5	5
Manioc				19		2	28
Total	629	206	609	774	247	370	251

(continues)

TABLE 13.5 *(cont.)*

	Argentina	Brazil	Chile	Colombia	Uruguay	Hungary	Cairns Group Total
Beef (FMD*-free)							352
Beef (FMD*-affected)	45	73	4	13	7	-1	141
Pork	33	135	8	22	2	39	424
Sheep meat	4	2	1	1	3		14
Poultry meat	11	61		11		4	125
Eggs	18	63		27		5	180
Milk and dairy products	155	275	20	86		27	678
Wheat	77	-312	6	-1	4	13	355
Corn	22	168	2	7		20	320
Other coarse grains	10	5	2	5	1	5	240
Rice	4	37	2	25	6		962
Oilseed and oilseed products	221	84	49	12	1	10	819
Cotton	12	20		5			41
Sugar	10	64	-59	11	1	1	63
Tobacco	5	29	1	2			65
Manioc		27		2			78
Total	628	732	35	225	26	124	4,856

*Foot-and-Mouth Disease

resources from soybean production to the production of other crops. The smaller price increase for soybeans in the United States and Brazil reflects the much smaller increase in world prices for soybeans (1 percent) than grains and other oilseeds (all about 6 percent).

Substantial gains also accrue to beef producers in both Australia (U.S. $175 million) and Canada (U.S. $130 million). These gains are greater than the gains to beef producers in Brazil (U.S. $75 million) and Argentina (U.S. $45 million). The distinction between beef produced in regions that have been deemed to be free of foot-and-mouth disease and beef produced in areas that are affected by the disease is an important factor in these results. As Australia and Canada are free of foot-and-mouth disease, producers in these countries stand to gain more as a result of the greater increases in the world price for beef produced in areas that are free of foot-and-mouth disease. However, a large part of this increase is due to an increase in Japanese imports that result from the assumed 36 percent reduction in the Japanese tariff equivalent. This reduction is only part of the liberalization of the Japanese beef market. As such, it is likely that this increase in Japanese imports and the associated increase in the world price would occur even without a successful conclusion to the Uruguay Round.

Notable losers from liberalization, as modeled, are Brazilian wheat growers (U.S. $310 million) and Canadian dairy producers (U.S. $170 million). In both cases, the reduction in support under the Blair House Accord is estimated to more than offset the benefits to these industries of higher world prices. The losses to Canadian dairy producers arise as a result of the assumed tariffication of import controls for dairy products and the subsequent reduction of the relevant tariff equivalents. However, the actual impact of the implementation of a final Uruguay Round outcome on Canadian dairy producers will depend largely on the way in which tariffication is actually implemented.

Some Qualifications

A number of points need to be borne in mind when interpreting the results presented in this chapter. First, because the base period, 1989, was a year in which levels of protection, for grain and dairy products in particular, were unusually low, the price and welfare changes in response to policy reform estimated in the analysis were lower than they would have been had a more representative year been used as a base. However, this source of underestimation will be counteracted to the extent that some liberalization has occurred since 1989, as is the case with Japanese beef.

Second, because of the flexibility allowed in aggregating domestic support, it is not possible to ascertain the schedule of reductions for each commodity. Assumptions here have had to be made concerning policy changes, and they may not be those that would actually be implemented.

Third, because of its static nature, the model does not explicitly account for the benefits of, for example, technological change that liberalization is likely to encourage, the ensuing economies of size, and the efficiency gains from improved resource allocation.

Fourth, the analysis is based on a partial equilibrium framework and covers predominantly the temperate zone farm products. Important gains from trade liberalization likely to accrue to producers of tropical agricultural products are not analyzed. In the medium to longer term, developing countries would also be likely to benefit from improved access to industrial country markets for tropical and other primary and processed products and for textiles and clothing, following a successful outcome of the Uruguay Round of trade negotiations.

Finally, the major trading countries stand to gain substantially from trade liberalization in sectors other than agriculture. No account is taken here of likely gains from the removal of barriers to trade in services, such as banking and insurance, and the improved enforcement of intellectual property rights. In addition, the boost to world economic growth from trade liberalization in these areas is likely to increase demand for and prices of most agricultural products.

Concluding Comments

A notable feature of the Uruguay Round is the role of a coalition of middle-power countries in setting the agenda. In previous negotiations the United States, as the dominant world trading power, had a strong influence on the activity and direction of the GATT. However, in recent years the European Community and Japan have increased their shares of world trade, resulting in an increasingly complex agenda setting process in the GATT. The consensus of a larger number of countries is now necessary for agreement on any major issue in the GATT. This has enabled the Cairns Group, as the major coalition concerned with agriculture, to play a significant role in placing agriculture on the GATT agenda. Its actions have increased the likelihood that meaningful reform of agricultural trade will be implemented.

The Cairns Group has a continuing role in ensuring that the final agreement is implemented as intended. Attention will be needed to ensure that the pressures for weakening the agreement are resisted. Cairns Group members are likely to have greater influence as part of a cohesive group than as individual countries. This influence will help to provide assurance that a successful implementation of an outcome in the Uruguay Round is forthcoming. The political importance of the Cairns Group in the negotiations, and the potential economic gains, are likely to provide the Group with a degree of cohesion in opposing any weakening of the agreement, and this is likely to outweigh the reduced flexibility and the need for compromise that comes from membership of such a group.

Nevertheless, U.S.-E.C. trade relations will have a major influence on the final outcome of the Round and on the implications of any negotiated agreement for other countries. Some version of the Blair House Accord appears, at the time of writing this chapter, to be the most likely outcome. The analysis presented in this chapter suggests that global gains from the Blair House Accord are likely to be similar to those under the Dunkel package. From a global perspective, that an agreement similar to one of these packages be implemented is more important than the precise nature of the agreement. The major differences between the Dunkel package and the Blair House Accord are that the latter allows the aggregation across all commodities of reductions in domestic support and the exemption of E.C. compensation payments from reduction commitments. Both of these measures permit lesser reductions in support for some commodities. Although some contentious implementation issues remain to be resolved, it appears that E.C. producers and taxpayers are likely to be affected very differently under the two proposals. U.S. producers would be expected to prefer the more trade liberalizing Dunkel package. As most of the pressure for reform comes from producers in countries with relatively low protection and support and, to a lesser extent, taxpayers in countries with high support (through pressure on government deficits), results reported in this chapter indicate that the United States has an incentive to hold a firm line against efforts by some interests within the European Community to weaken the Blair House Accord in reaching a final agreement.

Australian producers, along with producers in most other Cairns Group countries, would gain more from implementation of the Dunkel package than the Blair House Accord due to the higher prices that would result from the implementation of the more liberal Dunkel package.

Notes

The authors wish to acknowledge helpful comments provided by Don Gunasekera, Paul O'Mara, Ivan Roberts, Lawrie Stanford, and Vivek Tulpulé.

References

Agra Europe. 1992a. "EC Maintaining Its Own Version of Tariffication." *Agra Europe*. Tunbridge Wells, England, No. 1486, April 10: P/2.
———. 1992b. "GATT: Little Progress in Phantom Negotiations." *Agra Europe* Tunbridge Wells, England, No. 1507, September 4.

————. 1992c. "Commission Text of the E.C.—U.S. Agreement on Agriculture." *Agra Europe.* Tunbridge Wells, England, No. 1519, November 27: E/1-E/4.

Andrews, N., I. Roberts, and G. Love. 1992. "Recent Developments in the Uruguay Round for Agriculture." *Agriculture and Resources Quarterly* 4: 196-208 (June).

Australian Government. 1987. *Resolving the World Agricultural Crisis: An Australian Proposal* (January).

Avery, W. P. 1992. "Agriculture and Free Trade." In *World Agriculture and The GATT,* edited by W. P. Avery. Boulder, CO: Lynne Rienner Publishers.

Gallagher, P. W. 1988. "Setting the Agenda for Trade Negotiations: Australia and the Cairns Group." *Australian Outlook: Journal of the Australian Institute of International Affairs* (April).

GATT. 1991. *Draft Final Act Embodying the Results of the Uruguay Round of Multilateral Trade Negotiations.* Trade Negotiations Committee, MTN.TNC/W/FA, GATT Secretariat, Geneva.

Higgott, R. A. and A. F. Cooper. 1990. "Middle Power Leadership and Coalition Building: Australia, the Cairns Group, and the Uruguay Round of Trade Negotiations." *International Organisation* 44.

Johnson, D. G. 1991. *World Agriculture in Disarray.* 2d ed. London: Macmillan.

Miller, G. 1986. *The Political Economy of International Agricultural Policy Reform.* Canberra: AGPS.

Oxley, A. 1990. *The Challenge of Free Trade.* London: Harvester Wheatsheaf.

Roberts, I., N. Andrews, and R. Rees. 1992. "Market Effects of the 1992 EC Reforms for Cereals and Beef. *Agriculture and Resources Quarterly* 4: 584-602.

Roningen, V. O. 1986. "A Static World Policy Simulation (SWOPSIM) Framework." Washington D.C.: USDA ERS Staff Report No. AGES860625.

Roningen, V. O., J. Sullivan, and P. Dixit. 1991. "Documentation of the Static World Policy Simulation (SWOPSIM) Modeling Framework." Washington D.C.: USDA ERS Staff Report No. AGES9151.

Tyers, R. and K. Anderson. 1992. *Disarray in World Food Markets: a Quantitative Assessment.* Cambridge, U.K.: Cambridge Univ. Press.

14

Agricultural Trade and Policy for Central and East Europe

Larry Karp and Spiro E. Stefanou

The importance of agricultural trade, and the direction of trade flows, varies across Central and Eastern Europe (CEE). For example, agriculture constitutes over a fifth of Hungarian exports and a twentieth of Czechoslovakian exports. As a basis for discussion of CEE agricultural trade in the 1990s, we provide an overview of this trade during the 1980s. Statistics are presented on the share of agriculture in total trade and the relative importance of different markets. During the 1980s CEE became increasingly reliant on Western agricultural markets. Although CEE had a large market share of some (former) USSR (FSU) imports, its market share for grain, the most important import, declined during the 1980s.

We calculate statistics for the similarity of the composition of agricultural exports to the West and to former centrally planned economies (the "East"), and compare these to analogous measures for total exports. This comparison measures the extent to which agriculture, relative to other sectors, needs to adjust in response to the collapse of trading arrangements in the East. We find that the composition of CEE agricultural exports to the East and the West was more similar than was the composition of exports in general. This undercuts the claim that agricultural sectors in CEE need special adjustment assistance because of the loss of Eastern markets. However, the fact that agricultural markets in the West are more highly protected than other commodity markets continues to be a rationale for special treatment of agriculture by CEE policymakers.

There has been a tendency in CEE to move away from the free trade policies adopted immediately after liberalization. The ambition to join the European Community (E.C.) is frequently cited as a justification for implementing policies that resemble the CAP. In our view, neither the restrictive policies in the West, nor the ambition to join the E.C., warrant

restrictions on agricultural trade in CEE. These restrictions are an inefficient way of supporting CEE agriculture, and they are unlikely to make
accession to the E.C. easier.

The likely effects of CEE reform on world agricultural markets has been
estimated using quantitative models. There appears to be a broad consensus that unilateral reform will have a small effect on world markets. Reform in the FSU, on the other hand, is likely to result in major changes, especially for the world grain market. Reform of Western policies, such as
those currently under consideration as part of GATT negotiations, have the
potential to benefit CEE agriculture. Existing restrictions in the West, particularly in the E.C., have hampered attempts to reform CEE agriculture.

Section I provides an overview of agricultural trade during the 1980s.
Section II discusses CEE trade policy and its relation to the goal of E.C.
accession. Sections III and IV review quantitative models used to estimate
the effects on world agricultural markets of reform in CEE and the FSU,
and in the West.

Agricultural Trading Relationships

Agricultural trade has been a significant part of total trade in CEE.
Agricultural exports as a percentage of total CEE exports increased in 1990
over the 1987-89 level, while the share of imports decreased (Table 14.1).
Within CEE and FSU, agriculture as a share of total exports is largest for
Hungary and smallest for FSU and Czechoslovakia. Agriculture as a share
of total imports is largest for FSU and also important for Czechoslovakia
and Poland but much smaller for Bulgaria and Hungary. Combined CEE

TABLE 14.1 Agricultural Trade as Percentage of Total Trade

	1987-1989	1990
Imports		
Bulgaria	7.1	6.9
Hungary	8.8	8.5
Poland	14.3	13.2
Czechoslovakia	14.3	12.0
USSR	17.3	16.2
Exports		
Bulgaria	10.5	12.1
Hungary	21.3	24.3
Poland	10.0	14.6
Czechoslovakia	4.9	6.2
USSR	2.7	2.3

Source: UN, ECE, Agricultural Review for Europe No. 34, Vol. I, 1992.

and FSU agricultural exports to Western Europe exceeded imports in 1990 (Table 14.2). Bulgaria, Hungary, Poland, and Czechoslovakia ran trade surpluses, while the FSU, Romania, and Albania ran deficits with the E.C. and other European nations.

The economic liberalization in CEE coincided with the dissolution of the CMEA (Countries for Mutual Economic Assistance) leading to the interruption of the traditional trading relationships within CEE and between CEE and FSU. This reinforced a tendency, which had already been apparent, of increased importance of Western agricultural trade. Barter exchanges between CEE and FSU republics have been widely reported but are difficult to quantify. With 17 percent of total FSU imports consisting of agricultural products during the 1980s, the FSU was a major market for CEE products. CEE had large market shares of FSU imports of eggs, vegetables, and fruit (Table 14.3). It had a small market share for cereal, the single most important agricultural import for FSU (25 percent of their total). FSU grain imports increased at an annual rate of 3.7 percent between 1986 and 1990, but grain imports from North America increased at an annual rate of 9 percent, and in 1988-90 accounted for two-thirds of the

TABLE 14.2 Balance of Trade of Western Europe from Central and Eastern European Countries in 1990 (1990 $U.S. mill.)

	Albania	Bulgaria	Hungary	Poland	Romania	CS	USSR	Total
EC	-20	76	808	692	-311	33	-946	332
EFTA	12	72	188	-21	-4	8	-140	115
Others	-19	8	249	211	-30	25	-179	265
Total	*-27*	*156*	*1245*	*882*	*-345*	*66*	*-1265*	*712*

Source: UN,ECE, Agricultural Review for Europe, No. 34, Vol II. (A positive entry indicates that the country at the top of the table had a surplus with the region on the left of the table.)

TABLE 14.3 USSR Agricultural Imports from Central Eastern Europe as a Percentage of Total Volume

	1985	1986	1987	1988	1989	1990
Cereals	NA	5.1	3.6	3.2	3.2	3.4
Eggs	55.3	55.5	89.8	85.7	80.0	38.0
Fresh Vegetables	74.7	69.7	78.3	76.4	67	80.6
Preserved Vegetables	99.2	99.1	99.0	99.7	97.7	94.0
Fresh Fruit	37.8	26.1	37.9	36.8	32.3	29.1

Source: UN, ECE, Agricultural Review for Europe, No. 34,Table XX.
NA = Not applicable.

market. France, the major E.C. grain exporter, supplied 10 percent of the FSU grain imports by the late 1980s. Hungary, the dominant CEE exporter, lost market share over the decade, and had less than 3 percent of the market by 1990 (Table 14.4).

Hungary has maintained a positive agricultural trade balance with CEE, Western Europe, and in aggregate (Table 14.5). Bulgaria is the only European country with which Hungary has consistently been a net agricultural importer. The FSU and Western Europe account for 30 and 50 percent of Hungarian agricultural exports, respectively, in 1989-90. In the mid-1980s Hungarian agricultural exports to CEE and FSU exceeded exports to Western Europe, but this was reversed by 1987. By 1990, agricultural exports to Western Europe were nearly twice the level of exports to the East. Time-series data on Hungarian agricultural exports (Table 14.6) show that the increased importance of the West relative to the East is due to increasing meat and dairy exports to Western Europe and decreasing cereal exports to CEE and FSU.

Poland's agricultural trade balance fluctuated over 1985-90, but except for 1990, remained small and positive (in comparison, say, to Hungary's balance). Poland maintained a positive balance with both Western Europe and the East over 1987-90. Over the last two years of the decade, exports to Western Europe were more than ten times as large as exports to the FSU (Table 14.7).

Czechoslovakia was a net agricultural importer from formerly planned economies between 1980 and 1990, but became a net exporter in 1991 (Table 14.8). Agricultural exports to formerly planned economies accounted for over 30 percent of all agricultural exports from 1980 to 1988. Agricultural imports from these economies accounted for approximately 65 percent of all agricultural imports in the mid-1980s but dropped by more than half during 1989-91.

Table 14.9 indicates that agricultural exports for Czechoslovakia, Hun-

TABLE 14.4 USSR Cereal Imports by Volume (000 mt)

	1986	1987	1988	1989	1990
Argentina	602	1,993	1,760	866	859
Australia	3,348	781	312	249	74
Canada	7,314	6,127	5,049	2,587	5,064
United States	3,968	9,050	17,056	22,805	15,697
France	4,225	3,971	3,400	3,397	4,174
Hungary	1,354	1,107	1,111	1,192	1,075
Other Countries	5,946	7,356	5,904	5,873	5,089
Total	26,757	30,385	35,042	36,969	32,032

Source: UN, ECE, Agricultural Review for Europe, No. 34, Vol. II, Table XX.

TABLE 14.5 Hungarian Agricultural Trade, 1985-90 (in nominal million $US)

	1985	1986	1987	1988	1989	1990
Agricultural Exports To:						
Western Europe	708	775	813	977	1027	1136
European Community	487	529	593	697	757	854
Eastern Europe*	864	846	801	809	634	682
Bulgaria	5	6	7	19	3	1
Poland	67	54	22	43	53	32
Romania	15	20	25	14	10	109
Czechoslovakia	102	94	79	116	73	60
USSR	675	672	668	617	495	480
TOTAL (All Countries)	1895	1923	1926	2151	2171	2308
Agricultural Imports From:						
Western Europe	181	236	240	254	290	245
European Community	102	129	149	128	124	150
Eastern Europe*	64	94	116	91	72	115
Bulgaria	13	11	14	6	6	4
Poland	20	24	19	24	9	27
Romania	1	2	7	1	1	1
Czechoslovakia	17	29	34	26	24	36
USSR	13	28	42	34	32	47
TOTAL (All Countries)	632	773	800	766	682	700
Agricultural Balance:						
Western Europe	527	539	573	723	737	891
European Community	385	400	444	569	633	704
Eastern Europe*	800	752	685	718	562	567
Bulgaria	-8	-5	-7	13	-3	-3
Poland	47	30	3	19	44	5
Romania	14	18	8	13	9	108
Czechoslovakia	85	65	45	90	49	24
USSR	662	644	626	583	463	433
TOTAL (All Countries)	1263	1150	1126	1385	1489	1608

Sources: UN, ECE, Agricultural Review for Europe, Vol. II, Tables XXIV, XXV, 1992; SITC 0, 1, 21, 22, 29,4
*Includes USSR.

gary, and Poland have retained a constant to increasing share of total merchandise exports. In addition, Tables 14.6-8 suggest the composition of agricultural exports from Czechoslovakia, Hungary, and Poland started a redirection from formerly planned economies to market-oriented economies. Consequently, there is no reason to single out agriculture as one of the sectors which have been most severely hurt by the disintegration of FSU and the resulting loss of markets. Of course, there are other factors

TABLE 14.6 Hungarian Exports to Western Europe and CEE and FSU, 1985-90 (in million $US)

	1985	1986	1987	1988	1989	1990
Meat and Meat Products to:						
All Countries	471	502	553	604	608	835
Western Europe	226	233	247	327	402	545
CEE and FSU	176	196	234	214	131	227
Dairy Products & Eggs to:						
All Countries	37	39	31	32	68	100
Western Europe	11	18	17	19	39	68
CEE and FSU	NA	NA	NA	NA	NA	NA
Cereals to:						
All Countries	309	281	198	296	269	194
Western Europe	30	31	29	43	42	21
CEE and FSU	275	247	166	250	220	162
Oilseeds to:						
All Countries	44	39	54	62	41	38
Western Europe	33	31	33	35	34	31
CEE and FSU	11	8	19	20	5	6
Oils and Fats to:						
All Countries	111	79	80	101	100	114
Western Europe	59	51	49	73	75	80
CEE and FSU	28	20	28	25	23	31

Sources: FAO Trade Yearbook, 1990; UN, ECE, Agricultural Review for Europe, No. 34, Vol. II, Tables XXVI, XXVII.
NA = Not applicable.

pointing to a different conclusion. The most important of these is that in Western markets, agricultural trade is more restricted than manufacturing trade.

CEE Trade Policy and the Accession to the E.C.

Although a liberal trade policy does not guarantee a rational agricultural policy, the type of agricultural policy found in many Western countries does rely on trade protection. The potential advantages of liberal trade are widely recognized: It allows consumers access to low cost and high quality goods; it encourages efficient allocation of productive resources; it disciplines domestic monopolists; it fosters progress by promoting the spread of new technology. To these four benefits, which are certainly important for CEE agriculture, there is the added fifth benefit that a commitment to liberal trade makes it impossible to contemplate a Western-style agricultural policy.

Agriculture will not enjoy the full benefits of an anticipated general

TABLE 14.7 Agricultural Trade in Poland, 1985-90 (in current million $US)

	1985	1986	1987	1988	1989	1990
Agricultural Exports To:						
Western Europe	589	671	829	914	1150	
European Community	470	561	699	760	978	1227
Eastern Europe*	194	215	194	183	149	132
Bulgaria	13	7	8	11	5	
Poland	11	14	8	8	8	
Romania	21	20	2	6	2	
Czechoslovakia	19	26	27	25	15	
USSR	130	148	149	133	119	73
TOTAL *(All Countries)*	1124	1257	1484	1582	1771	1903
Agricultural Imports From:						
Western Europe	625	682	535	873	849	
European Community	403	392	335	552	576	331
Eastern Europe*	235	198	100	97	56	36
Bulgaria	21	27	37	34	18	
Poland	57	34	13	11	14	
Romania	18	14	10	6	--	
Czechoslovakia	3	3	2	4	9	
USSR	136	120	38	42	15	9
TOTAL *(All Countries)*	1476	1453	1310	1640	1392	666
Agricultural Balance:						
Western Europe	-36	-11	294	41	309	
European Community	67	169	364	208	402	896
Eastern Europe*	-41	17	94	86	93	96
Bulgaria	-7	-20	-29	-23	-13	
Poland	-46	-20	-5	-3	-6	
Romania	3	6	-8	0	2	
Czechoslovakia	16	23	25	21	6	
USSR	-6	28	111	91	104	64
TOTAL *(All Countries)*	-352	-196	174	-58	379	1237

Sources: UN Agricultural Review, Vol II, Tables XXIX, XXX, 1992; Karp and Stefanou (1992), Table 18, for 1990 data; SITC: 0,1,21,22,29,4.
*Includes USSR.

liberalization in trade. In the case of the Association Agreements with the E.C., the special treatment of agriculture was externally imposed on CEE. The December 1992 agreement on the Central European Free Trade Area, comprising Poland, Hungary, Slovakia, and the Czech Republic, demonstrates the strength of agricultural protectionist tendencies within CEE. The agreement allows the signatories the right to protect their agricultural sectors. Tariffs will be reduced for certain agricultural products, but quantitative restrictions and other domestic policies will remain.

Current CEE agricultural trade policy is described as an attempt to

TABLE 14.8 Agricultural Trade in Czechoslovakia, 1980-91 (in million korunas, nominal)

	1980	1985	1987	1988	1989	1990	1991
Agricultural Exports to:							
Market Economies	4,288	4,079	4,484	5,059	9,136	18,232	18,615
Formerly Planned Economies	1,998	2,874	2,553	2,646	2,005	3,767	9,343
All Countries	6,286	6,953	7,037	7,705	11,141	21,999	27,958
Agricultural Imports From:							
Market Economies	5,232	3,821	3,595	4,080	10,843	19,476	17,983
Formerly Planned Economies	5,317	7,814	7,158	7,651	6,368	7,875	3,414
All Countries	10,549	11,635	10,753	11,731	17,211	27,351	21,401
Agricultural Balance:							
Market Economies	-944	258	889	979	-1707	-1,244	632
Formerly Planned Economies	-3,319	-4,940	-4,605	-5,005	-4363	-4,108	5,929
All Countries	-4,263	-4,682	-3,716	-4,026	-6070	-5,352	6,557

Sources: Czechoslovak Chamber of Commerce and Industry, 1989 and 1990; Federal Office of Statistics, Czechoslovakia, June 1992, Table 28.

TABLE 14.9 Agriculture as a Percentage of Total Merchandise Exports (percent)

	1985	1986	1987	1988	1989	1990
CSFR	4.4	4.7	4.8	5.1	4.8	6.2
Hungary	21.8	20.6	19.9	21.4	22.7	24.3
Poland	8.3	8.9	9.8	9.2	11.1	14.6

Source: FAO Trade Yearbook, 1990.

strike a balance that provides the benefits of liberal trade while still protecting domestic producers (Csaki and Varga, 1992). During the beginning of the transition, Czechoslovakia, Hungary, and Poland (EE-3) were remarkable for their freedom from trade restraints. For example, the average import tariff on agricultural and food products in Czechoslovakia in 1991 was 5 percent (Czech Institute of Agricultural Economics, 1992). Pressure from domestic importers led to the adoption of greater protection in 1992. Table 14.10 shows tariff rates for EE-3. If, as is frequently asserted, processors have significant monopsony power, then they, rather than primary producers, are likely to be the major beneficiaries of this protection.

Czechoslovakia, Hungary, and Poland have also subsidized agricultural exports. Czechoslovakia and Poland subsidized exports of grain and livestock to FSU in 1991 and 1992 (Czech Institute of Agricultural Eco-

TABLE 14.10 Selected CEE Agricultural Import Duties, 1992 (percent)

	Czechoslovakia	Hungary	Poland
Live Beef and Pork	25-30	0	35-40
Meat Products	30	15-20	30
Butter	30	60	40
Milk and Cream	30	30	35
Eggs	NA	30	25
Sugar	60	0	40

Sources: Kabat (1993), Tomczak (1992), USDA, FAS.

nomics, 1992). Hungary has maintained a long-standing policy of subsidizing exports; nearly 80 percent of the 1993 Hungarian agricultural budget is allocated to measures such as export subsidies (Agra Europe, 1993). The 80 percent growth of Hungarian agricultural output between 1960 and 1990 was largely achieved by subsidies and state trading, which insulated Hungary from world prices. Hungarian export subsidies amounted to 12 percent of the value of agricultural exports (24.5 billion forints) in 1991 and are estimated to be 13 percent in 1992 (USDA, FAS; and PlanEcon). Livestock and meat products are the most heavily supported, ranging from 20-30 percent of Hungarian agricultural export receipts in 1992 (USDA, FAS, 1992). Hungary's agricultural export success in the last decade may come to haunt it as the necessary restructuring to achieve competitiveness is postponed in favor of maintaining current export earnings.

The brief period of liberal agricultural trade following reform is in danger of being replaced by a protectionist policy typical of developed economies. In this sense, reform appears to be moving in the wrong direction. The optimal staging of reform in general, and the role of trade liberalization in particular, have recently been discussed by Dornbusch (1992), Falvey and Kim (1992), and Rodrik (1992) among others. Because of the need to raise public finance,[1] the opposition by producer groups, and balance of payments problems, it may not be possible to remove all trade restrictions in the short term. In that case, the consensus is that quantitative restrictions should be replaced by tariffs, which should be reduced according to an announced and sustainable plan. The same advice is appropriate for the agricultural sector. This does not provide an argument for an "agricultural policy"—any more than does the need to privatize and demonopolize the economy.

However, public finance and the balance of payments are sometimes put forward as justifications for agricultural subsidies and tariffs. For example, despite their admitted inefficiency as a method of transfers, these policies are defended on the grounds that direct transfers are impractical because of their costs to the treasury. The exigencies of public finance may justify a general level of trade protection, but they do not provide a basis for special protection of a particular sector. To believe otherwise is to accept the proposition that policies for every sector should be self-financing, a position that tolerates the most inefficient programs. Similarly, the idea that a balance of agricultural trade is an intrinsically worthwhile policy goal is as narrow as the notion that a balance of chicken trade would serve the national interest.

We alluded above to the argument for agricultural protection based on the disintegration of the Soviet Union and the resulting loss of markets. Since liberalization, agricultural export subsidies have been used to maintain sales to that region. If these subsidies delay production and marketing changes needed to re-orient trade, they do not serve the long run interests of the agricultural sector. They merely provide an inefficient means of making transfers to producers and distributors. In addition, it is not clear that the agricultural sector has been hurt worse than other sectors by the loss of Eastern markets.[2] The evidence that we described indicates: (1) CEE economies had already begun to redirect agricultural exports toward the West, even before the liberalization of the early 1990s, and (2) the composition of CEE agricultural exports to the West and to the former CMEA was more similar than was the case for nonagricultural exports. These observations suggest that the loss in Soviet markets would result in a more severe adjustment problem for manufacturing than for agriculture.

One of the principal justifications for special support to CEE agriculture is the fact that Western nations heavily subsidize their agricultural sectors. Conceivably, this provides a reason for an interventionist approach in the CEE. We will consider two aspects of this issue. The first is the vague but politically compelling idea that policies in the West invite a policy response from CEE. The second is a more focused argument that CEE policies are needed to set the stage for integration into the E.C.

There are no limits to the emotional appeal of subsidies as a means of offsetting disadvantages. For example, socialist agricultural policy in Czechoslovakia highly subsidized those farms with poor soil or poor access to transport. If these natural and accidental features are considered a legitimate reason for government favor, how much more persuasive is the fact that foreign competitors are receiving subsidies? As a statement about fairness, this can only be an argument for income transfers, not for an agricultural policy that promotes production. Two types of beliefs might still rationalize invoking Western subsidies as a reason for CEE agricultural protection.

The first is the implausible notion that CEE policy provides a means of exerting leverage over Western policy. Western trade restrictions and agricultural subsidies make it harder to sustain economic liberalism (or democracy or the willingness not to migrate) in CEE. However, enlightened self-interest has proven to be a poor match against sectoral interests in the West. Only optimists will think that concern for agriculture in CEE, or fear of retaliatory measures by CEE, will hasten reform of Western agricultural policies.

Second, it might be believed that agricultural reform will quicken in the West, and that CEE agriculture will then be able to compete without subsidies, providing that it has not been allowed to decay in the meantime. This argument relies on asymmetric information (between farmers and policymakers) or imperfect capital markets. In either case, it may offer a justification of broad support for agriculture, such as that provided by credit subsidies, as discussed in Karp and Stefanou (1994), but it does not justify an attempt to manage agriculture by means of commodity-specific policies. The level of agricultural protection in the West does not make commodity-specific interventionist policy in CEE a rational response.

We now turn to the issue of whether an interventionist CEE agricultural policy should be used to prepare for accession to the E.C. (e.g., Munk, 1992). The logic behind this position is as follows: CEE would benefit from joining the E.C.; it would be too costly for the E.C. to allow CEE into CAP if they were to arrive as net agricultural exporters; therefore CEE should adopt an agricultural policy that aims at an approximate balance of agricultural trade as a means of paving their way into the E.C. We disagree with this argument on a number of grounds.

First, suppose that CAP continues to protect E.C. agricultural producers primarily through price support programs, as is currently the case. If accession means that CEE producers face the same prices as producers in other member countries, then in order for accession not to be costly to the E.C., it has to be the case that CEE is not a net exporter at those prices. That is, it is not enough for the CEE to have a zero balance of agricultural trade; it has to be the case that this trade is balanced at the prices that will prevail after accession. Even if one knew what those prices were, there is no reason to believe that their adoption would result in balanced trade, since this depends on technology, factor endowments, and consumer tastes. Clearly, CEE agricultural policy should not be designed to modify these factors in such a way that they are consistent with trade balance at prices that will be revealed some time in the future.

Second, suppose as above that the basis for CAP remains price policies, but that now accession means CEE faces quotas to insure that their exports do not flood the (old) E.C. market. This would be a retrograde policy, since the Association Agreements negotiated in 1992 incorporate a gradual elimination of quotas. In this scenario, CEE is exchanging liberal entry (under the Association Agreements) for quotas and higher prices. There is no reason to suppose that CEE negotiators would accept a deal that makes them worse off. The CEE negotiating position would only be weakened if they already had balanced trade; they would effectively have conceded everything before the negotiations.

Third, and more plausibly, suppose that the projected reforms of CAP get underway so that price policies are increasingly replaced by direct income support. This support could be justified as compensation to producers for having accepted the capital loss resulting from the diminished price support. There is no reason why it would also be given to CEE producers after accession, since, not having been protected by the original measures, they had not suffered the capital loss following their removal. To the extent that income support does replace price support, the costs to CAP and the benefits to CEE producers of accession diminish, whatever the agricultural balance of trade; to the extent that price supports remain the cornerstone of CAP, our arguments above apply.

Finally, the idea of designing an agricultural policy to somehow track a large trading partner assumes an unrealistic level of knowledge about the shape that the partner's policy will take in the future, and it also assumes an unrealistic ability to manage domestic events. Aspirations to join the E.C. do not provide a rationale for a sector-specific agricultural policy.

Reform Within the CEE and FSU

There have been a number of attempts to measure the effects on agriculture of liberalization within the East and West. This and the following section summarize and compare these estimates and draw conclusions from them. Market liberalization is defined as the partial or wholesale removal of Producer and Consumer Subsidy Equivalents (PSEs and CSEs). To the extent that PSEs exaggerate the true extent of the subsidy to producers, the model's predictions exaggerate the effect of liberalization. Agricultural policies in Western countries are treated as tariff equivalents, whereas in fact many are quotas or a combination of tariffs and quotas. This means that the models are likely to exaggerate the trade effects when unilateral CEE liberalization leads to increased output. If excess supply increases and the exporters face quotas, the result is a deterioration in their terms of trade and a decline in export revenue, rather than an increase in the volume of exports. Thus, the predictions may be too optimistic, since they are based on models that tend to overstate the degree of flexibility in agricultural markets.

There is widespread belief, based on statistics of factor productivity (e.g., output per hectare), that CEE agriculture is inefficient. Several of the models described below assume that the gap between Western and CEE productivity will narrow as a result of privatization and the reliance on price signals rather than central planning. This effect of reform is modeled by shifting out the supply functions by amounts that are consistent with the projected increase in efficiency. A simple comparison between CEE and Western levels of average factor productivity probably exaggerates the extent of technical inefficiency in the CEE. Technical efficiency means that production is maximized for given inputs. In a recent survey, Murrell (1992) concludes that CEE and FSU agriculture was largely technically efficient. There is stronger evidence of allocative inefficiency (the wrong inputs are being used, or are being used in the wrong mixes); in Poland, for example, state farms are oversupplied with fertilizer and machinery. Appropriate prices should improve allocative efficiency, which will shift out the supply functions. However, statistics on average factor productivity may be poor indicators of the extent of this improvement.

Cochrane (1990) estimates the production and trade effects of reform in Poland and Yugoslavia first under the assumption that the removal of price policies (the elimination of PSEs and CSEs) is not accompanied by efficiency gains. Since the net effect of these policies is to support producers (the PSEs are mostly positive), their removal leads to a large fall in production and an increase in imports. Price liberalization, without accompanying gains in efficiency, causes the agricultural sector to contract.

Price liberalization and efficiency gains together result in a large increase in pork production and decrease in consumption. The resulting increase in pork exports is sufficient to cause Poland to become a net agricultural exporter. Poland's comparative advantage within the agricultural sector is in pork production. However, this conclusion is based on PSEs that show that the pork sector was taxed in the late 1980s; updated calculations by the same author show a revised PSE for pork that is positive (although small). Had this revised data been used, the projected output increase in the pork sector would have been smaller. Other implications of the model are that Poland switches from exporting to importing beef and increases imports of wheat, corn, and oilmeal.

The removal of the price policies and the concomitant improvements in efficiency lead to aggregate welfare gains. This is mainly due to the decline in government expenditures, although consumers also gain. Despite the fact that the agricultural sector expands, producer welfare falls, as a result of the removal of transfers. An expanding agricultural sector does not necessarily imply an increase in returns to labor and capital employed there. The model results are also consistent with the widely held view that reform of the agricultural sector will contribute to CEE's balance of payments.

Liefert, *et al.* (undated) carry out a similar modeling exercise for the FSU. Their results are interesting both because of the importance of the FSU in agricultural trade and as a source of comparison with CEE. Estimates of CSEs and PSEs indicate that consumers are subsidized; producers are slightly subsidized, although alternate assumptions about the exchange rate change those subsidies to small taxes.[3] Under the assumption of a relatively high exchange rate, liberalization leads to an increase in the agricultural trade deficit of over 50 percent, whereas with a lower rate the predicted deficit falls by 90 percent; in either case, the FSU remains an agricultural importer.

Corn imports remain high, but the region changes from an importer to an exporter of wheat. Aggregate grain imports decrease, and under some scenarios the FSU becomes a grain exporter. Aggregate grain production either falls or increases only slightly, depending on the assumed exchange rate. The change in trade flows is chiefly due to a fall in consumption caused by lower demand from a smaller livestock sector and a more efficient mix of feed. In the 1980s the FSU accounted for slightly less than a fifth of world grain trade; grain imports accounted for roughly a fifth of total grain consumption, and nearly a third of the FSU expenditures on agricultural imports. The potentially dramatic change in the grain sector would be important both for the world grain market and the FSU economy. The model predicts a rise in imports of soybean products, leading to a more efficient mixture of livestock feed. The authors estimate that meat production falls and consumption rises, leading to an increase in imports.

Leifert's, *et al.* and Johnson's (1992) analyses imply that reform in the FSU will lead to a large decline in grain imports and possibly cause the region to become a grain exporter. In Johnson's view this change is attributed in roughly equal parts to increased availability due to less waste and reduced demand due to a fall in livestock consumption. In Liefert, *et al.* the second cause is dominant, since increased efficiency and lower subsidies have an offsetting effect on production levels. Liefert, *et al.*'s high estimate for trade changes is of the same order of magnitude as a conservative interpretation of Johnson's data.[4]

Within the agricultural sector, the FSU has a comparative advantage in grains relative to livestock; the opposite holds in Poland. In both countries, reform is likely to decrease the deficit in the agricultural balance of trade. Although the relative change in trade flows may be larger in Poland, the absolute change will be much larger in the FSU. The reduction in FSU grain imports is likely to swamp whatever increase in demand may arise from reform in CEE.

These efforts to quantify the trade effects of economic reform imply an important policy message for the West and particularly the E.C. Reform in the CEE is seen as threatening Western agricultural interests; this has led to continued restrictions on agricultural trade. The magnitude of this threat, and even its existence, is uncertain and is probably marginal compared to the adjustments that will be required by changes within the FSU. The potential for CEE agricultural reform to contribute to the economic development and political stability requires accommodation by the West, which to date has been tentative. For example, Winters (1992) notes that the Association Agreements between the E.C. and CEE seem designed as much to ease the adjustment needed in the E.C. as to exploit new trading opportunities. The West may be able to protect its agricultural markets from changes in the CEE, but not from changes in the FSU. A large importer like the FSU is able to act unilaterally by restricting imports; the expansion of CEE exports requires Western acquiescence. Since the West cannot avoid large adjustments to agricultural trade resulting from changes in the FSU, it has little to gain from avoiding the smaller adjustments caused by changes in CEE. The political costs of attempting to avoid or delay those changes, by means of a restrictive trade policy, may be very great.

Effects of External Reform on CEE Agriculture

Models attempting to quantify the effects of Western reform on CEE agriculture assume the West is willing to modify its trade flows, but without changing its domestic nominal rates of protection (the gap between domestic and world prices). This section describes the effects on CEE of liberalization of Western agricultural policies. The discussion includes the effects of the Association Agreements, general lowering of price distortions in the West, current proposals before GATT, and bringing the EE-3 into CAP.

The structure of agricultural production and trade that existed before World War II is evidence of the extent to which post-War policies have influenced the evolution of the agricultural sector. Changing these policies should have a large effect on future development. Because of the importance of the E.C. as both an export and import market for CEE agriculture (discussed in Section I), changes in the CAP are particularly relevant. During the 1920s and early 1930s the combined region of CEE and the FSU was a net agricultural exporter, supplying approximately 20 percent of Western European imports. In the post-World War II years the region was a net exporter of meat and live animals until the implementation of CAP. The FSU became an importer of both grains and meat, and CEE was a net exporter of meat and importer of grains. Through the 1970s CEE was a net agricultural importer from E.C. and switched to being a net exporter during the 1980s. By the late 1980s the E.C. accounted for approximately 30 percent of Hungarian and Czechoslovakian agricultural exports and approximately 60 percent of Polish and Yugoslavian exports.

Tangermann (1992) estimates the short-term effect of the E.C. Association Agreements on agricultural trade for Poland, Czechoslovakia, and Hungary. The calculated value of the Agreements, as a percentage of the value of total agricultural exports to the E.C. in 1990, is in the region of 3-5 percent in 1992. Since the quotas are scheduled to increase over time, this value should also increase. By 1996 it reaches 7 percent for Poland, 14 percent for Hungary, and 22 percent for CSFR (Czech and Slovak Federal Republic). Tangermann notes that these estimates exaggerate the probable benefits to EE-3 for two reasons. First, the numbers above involve the potential rent resulting from the Agreements, but a substantial percentage of that may be captured by the distributors in the E.C. rather than exporters in EE-3. Second, the calculations are based on E.C. support policies prior to the CAP reform announced in May 1992. That reform will reduce E.C. prices, causing the value of the preference margin to fall. This could reduce by more than half the value of preferential access. Thus, it seems unlikely that the Association Agreements will provide a major impetus to CEE agricultural development.

Koopman and Cochrane (1991) estimate the trade effects of a more ambitious reform in the West combined with reform in the East. As in the models described above, liberalization in the East is represented by removing domestic price supports and shifting out supply curves by an amount consistent with closing one-third of the estimated gap between Western and Eastern productivity. If Western markets adjust, but price distortions are not changed, there is a negligible rise in net meat exports from the East, and a 25 percent decrease in Eastern grain imports. If, in addition to reform in the East, the E.C. removes its domestic distortions, this causes Eastern meat exports to increase by 75 percent and grain imports to fall by a further 25 percent. The incremental effect of liberalization in the rest of the world has a small effect on meat exports and causes Eastern grain imports to fall to a third of the base level.

These relative magnitudes seem plausible. As described above, unilateral reform in the East would have a large effect on the grain market because of the importance of the FSU as an importer. A significant expansion of meat exports requires that the principal market, the E.C., reduce its distortions. Since North America is a major grain exporter to the East but is not a large import market for meat, its liberalization chiefly affects the grain market, but by a smaller amount than E.C. reform. Using a gravity model (in which trade flows are related to population, prosperity, and propinquity) Wang and Winters (1991) estimate that liberalization in the East leads to aggregate increases in trade. The effect of this on non-E.C. regions is more pronounced than in other models. Despite this difference, the results of the various models are consistent with the view that liberalization in the E.C. is more critical to the development of Eastern agriculture than is liberalization in other OECD (Organization for Economic Cooperation and Development) nations.

Liberalization of Western agricultural policies will not result in the elimination of price distortions. The eventual GATT agreement, if it occurs, is likely to resemble the more modest set of suggestions contained in the Blair House Accord. The main features of the Accord are that it decreases E.C. expenditures on export subsidies by a third and decreases the volume of exports that benefit from those subsidies by a quarter. Internal support prices are to be reduced by a fifth. Quotas are to be converted to tariff equivalents and the average tariff reduced by a third, with tariffs for individual commodities reduced by at least 15 percent. Remaining import barriers are to allow a minimum access of 3 percent of consumption in 1993, increasing to 5 percent in 1999. Roningen's (1992) analysis of the Blair House Accord and complete removal of E.C. agricultural support estimates the Accord has roughly one-quarter the effect on world prices and E.C. supply as would complete liberalization.

CARD (1992) estimates that the Accord causes E.C. exports of wheat and feed grains to fall by 6 million metric tons in 1993 and 13 million tons in 1998. Liefert, *et al.*'s conservative estimate of the decrease in FSU import demand for grains is approximately 25 million tons; their high estimate is 40 million tons, which is of a similar order of magnitude to the changes implied by Johnson's calculations. The comparison therefore suggests that, at least for the grains market, the type of reforms currently under consideration in the West will not be sufficient to offset the likely effects of liberalization in the East. CARD also predicts that the Blair House Accord would have substantial effects of the pork market, with price rising 6 percent over the no-reform scenario and world exports doubling. The CEE is a major beneficiary of reforms for this commodity, since its pork exports increase by more than 10 percent even without domestic reform.

The Association Agreements and the type of Western reform currently discussed at the GATT negotiations are at best a partial response to changes taking place in the East. A more ambitious proposal considers integration of EE-3 (including their agricultural sectors) into the E.C. If this does occur, it would almost surely not happen in this decade, and it would only take place after the CAP had been reformed.

In a recent study Tyers (1992) uses a dynamic multi-country model to estimate the effects of a combination of several types of changes: unilateral reform of the CAP, productivity growth in the East, and gradual accession of EE-3 to CAP. A reference scenario, which assumes that none of these changes take place, shows the ratio of production to consumption increasing in the OECD and decreasing in the East and developing nations. Unilateral reform of CAP, without productivity growth in the East or integration of EE-3, moderates this trend, but does not change its direction. World prices for most commodities rise (10 percent for wheat and 7 percent for ruminant meat); however, the price of non-ruminant meat (which includes pork) falls, as the decline in protection of other sectors causes producers to shift resources. Since pork is a crucial sector for EE-3 agriculture, this fall in price diminishes the net benefits EE-3 producers receive from unilateral E.C. reform.

The phased extension of CAP to EE-3 moderates or reverses the price rises that result from unilateral reform. In particular, by the midpoint of the integration process (the year 2000), the price of dairy products falls by more than 10 percent. This is due to an increase in dairy production in EE-3 resulting from an increase in the protection of that sector. Tyers estimates that unilateral reform of the CAP would reduce costs by $23 billion per year, but inclusion of EE-3 would lead to an increase in budget costs of about half that amount. (These amounts include only the costs of price support programs.)

Liberalization in the FSU partially offsets the decline in world dairy price, since dairy production in that region falls and imports increase. There are substantial declines in cereal consumption; wheat production increases by more than a quarter. The aggregate effect is to increase net exports from the East. These results reinforce the conclusion that the net effects of reforms in the East and West are likely to be lower world prices for major commodities, and for grains a reduction or even reversal of trade flows.

Concluding Comments

Agricultural trade is important, but to varying degrees for CEE countries. The importance of Western markets began to increase during the 1980s. The composition of CEE agricultural exports is more similar in Eastern and Western markets than is the case for general commodity trade. These two factors tend to diminish the (considerable) damage to CEE agriculture caused by the disruption of Eastern trading relations.

Although the potential changes in levels of production and trade due to reform are considerable, these changes have not yet occurred. Western reluctance to liberalize agricultural trade could become a major impediment to the success of CEE reforms. There is also the danger that an interventionist agricultural policy will be adopted in CEE; this could hinder growth in CEE and ultimately damage their agricultural sectors. These two dangers are related. Western reform is more useful to CEE agriculture than is Western advice.

Notes

The research assistance of Kate DeRemer and Jana Hranaiova is greatly appreciated. Larry Karp would like to acknowledge financial support from The Centre for Economic Policy Research and the hospitality of the Department of Economics at the University of Southampton. Spiro Stefanou gratefully acknowledges support of the Economic Research Service, U.S. Department of Agriculture, and a grant from the International Research and Educational Exchanges Board, with funds provided by the Andrew W. Mellon Foundation, the National Endowment for the Humanities, and the U.S. Department of State. None of these organizations is responsible for the views expressed.

1. Poland, the Czech Republic and the Slovak Republic have instituted a value-added tax (VAT) in early 1993, weakening the public finance argument for tariffs.

2. This issue is discussed in Section III of Karp and Stefanou (1992).

3. In this context "the exchange rate" refers to the number of dollars per unit of domestic currency during the time at which the PSEs and CSEs were calculated; it does not refer to the current or future exchange rate.

4. Johnson's estimates of amount of waste and of the potential for productivity increases may be high. Barkema, *et al.* (1992) report that Russian crop yields are comparable to those in the West and state that the main potential for improvement in the agricultural sector lies with improving marketing.

References

Agra Europe. 1993. *East Europe Agriculture and Food Monthly*. No. 124, January.

Barkema, A., M. Drabenstott, and K. Skold. 1992. "Agriculture in the Former Soviet Union: The Long Road Ahead." *Economic Review, Federal Reserve Bank of Kansas City*. Vol 77: 79-85.

CARD. 1992. "Implication of a GATT Agreement for World Commodity Markets, 1993-98: An Analysis of the Dunkel Text on Agriculture." GATT Research Paper 93-GATT 1, Iowa State University, Ames, Iowa.

Cochrane, N. 1990. "Trade Liberalization in Yugoslavia and Poland." Agriculture and Trade Analysis Division, USDA.

Csaki, C., and G. Varga. 1992. "Economic Dimensions of Transformation in Hungarian Agriculture." Paper presented at the 9th Plenary Meeting of the International Policy Council on Agriculture and Trade, Frankfurt, Germany, April 29-May 2.

Czechoslovak Chamber of Commerce and Industry. 1989. *Facts on Czechoslovak Foreign Trade: 1989* (translation from German), Prague.

———. 1990. *Facts on Czechoslovak Foreign Trade: 1990*, Prague.

Czech Institute of Agricultural Economics. 1992. "Report on the Evaluation of the Agricultural Policy in 1991" (translation from Czech). Ministry of Agriculture of the Czech Republic, issued March 1992, Prague, 56 pp. + appendix.

Dornbusch, R. 1992. "The Case for Trade Liberalization in Developing Countries." *Journal of Economic Perspectives* 6: 69-85.

Falvey, R., and C. D. Kim. 1992. "Timing and Sequencing Issues in Trade Liberalization." *The Economic Journal* 102: 908-924.

Federal Office of Statistics, Czechoslovakia. 1992. *Statisticke Prehledy (Monthly Statistics of Czechoslovakia)*, Prague.

Johnson, D. G. 1992. "World Trade Effects of the Dismantling of Socialized Agriculture in the Former Soviet Union." Paper presented at IATRC conference, St. Petersburg Beach, Florida, December 13-15.

Kabat, L. 1993. "Agricultural Policy and Trade Developments in 1992-93: The case of Czechoslovakia/Slovakia." Paper prepared for an ad hoc group on East/West Economic Relations, OECD.

Karp, L., and S. Stefanou. 1992. "Polish Agriculture in Transition: Does it Hurt to be Slapped by an Invisible Hand?" Centre for Economic Policy Research Discussion Paper No. 622.

————. 1993. "Prospects and Policy for Central and Eastern European Agriculture." Working Paper.

————. 1994. "Using Credit Subsidies to Support Central and East European Agriculture." In *The Economic Transformation of Agriculture in Central and Eastern Europe,* edited by A. Buckewell, S. Davidova, K. Moulton, and A. Schmitz. Norwell, MA.: Kluwer Academic Publishers.

Koopman, R. B., and N. J. Cochrane. 1991. "Trade Implications of E.C. 1992 for a Reforming Eastern Europe and Soviet Union." In *EC 1992 Implications for World Food and Agricultural Trade,* proceedings.

Liefert, W., R. Koopman, and E. Cook. Undated. "The Effect of Soviet Agricultural Liberalization on the USSR." Trade Analysis Division, USDA ERS.

Murrell, P. 1992. "Can Neoclassical Economics Underpin Reform of Centrally Planned Economies?" *Journal of Economic Perspectives* 5(4): 59-76.

Munk, K. J. 1992. "The Development of Agricultural Policies and Trade Relations in Response to the Transformation in Central and Eastern Europe." Paper presented at IATRC annual meeting, St. Petersburg Beach, Florida, December 13-15.

PlanEcon Report: Developments in the Economies of Eastern Europe and the Former USSR (various issues 1990-92), Washington, DC.

Rodrik, D. 1992. "The Limits of Trade Policy Reform in Developing Countries." *Journal of Economic Perspectives* 6: 87-105.

Centre for Economic Policy Research, Discussion Paper No. 676.

Roningen, V. 1992. "Whither European Community Common Agricultural Policy." IATRC Working Paper 92-3.

Tangermann, S. 1992. "Central and Eastern European Reform, Issues and Implications for World Agricultural Markets." Paper presented at IATRC annual meeting, St. Petersburg Beach, Florida, December 13-15.

Tomczak, F. 1992. "Developments in the Agri-Food System of Poland since the Reforms." Paper presented at the 9th Plenary Meeting of the International Policy Council on Agriculture and Trade, Frankfurt (Germany), April 29-May 2.

Tyers, R. 1992. "Food Trade Following Economic Reform in Greater Europe and the Former Soviet Union." Paper presented at 31st European Seminar for the European Association of Agricultural Economics, Frankfurt, Germany, December 7-9.

United Nations, Economic Commission on Europe. 1992. *Agricultural Review for Europe,* No. 34, Volumes I-IV, Geneva.

United Nations, Food and Agricultural Organization (various issues). *Trade Yearbook,* Rome.

United States Department of Agriculture, Foreign Agricultural Service. 1992. Agricultural Situation, Annual Report: Hungary.

Wang, Z. K., and L A. Winters. 1991. "The Trading Potential of Eastern Europe." CEPR Working Paper No. 610.

Winters, L. A. 1992. "The Europe Agreements: With a Little Help From Our Friends." In *The Association Process: Making it Work*, CEPR Occasional Paper No. 11.

World Economy Research Institute. 1992. *Poland International Economic Report: 1991-92*. Warsaw School of Economics, Warsaw.

15

Set-aside Policy and Programs in the EEC

Giuseppe Barbero and Annalisa Zezza

Introduction

The idea of a set-aside program gained increasing acceptance in European Economic Community (EEC) circles in the mid-eighties, under the pressure of a mounting crisis of the Common Agricultural Policy (CAP), which had been unable to reduce or even contain production surpluses and budget deficits. A set-aside program was finally adopted at the end of 1988 (Regulation 1765/88) alongside with potentially more powerful supply-restrictive measures such as "maximum guaranteed quantities" (MGQ) for the surplus commodities (with automatic price reduction in case of production exceeding the allowed quantity) and budget stabilizers. The EEC set-aside regulation provided for voluntary participation by grain producers and also left it to some regions to decide whether to participate at all. While it can be suspected that the policymakers were not very confident that the set-aside program would make a substantial contribution toward solving the surplus problem, the E.C. Regulation may be more fairly interpreted *a posteriori* as a "trial balloon" for determining the farmer reactions towards such a policy innovation. Being paid for not producing was a total novelty among European farmers, who, for a long time, had been stimulated by the CAP to do exactly the opposite, i.e., enlarge the production capacity and increase land productivity. This sort of encouragement was implicit in the special features of the price support system, which meant an almost total elimination of uncertainty as to market outlets, together with relatively high and stable prices. The simple fact that farmers were often producing for waste (as in the case of fruits) or for dumping (as in the case of cereals and dairy products) generally did not undermine their belief that they were producing food commodities for a market. Understandably, therefore, it could only be guessed how farmers would react to a set-aside program. As we shall see, the response from farmers of the member countries and regions has been highly uneven.

That the 1988 regulation may have been exploratory rather than a definitive attempt at supply and budget control is perhaps also suggested by the offer, in the program, of a broad spectrum of possible choices for alternative uses of the retired land, including less intensive form of land use (afforestation, extensive pastures), supply of nonfood commodities (energy products), the cultivation of traditional Mediterranean legumes, and nonagricultural utilizations. This latter alternative, in turn, was in line with the analysis and policy options put forward in a well-known 1988 document issued by the E.C. Commission (a communication to the Council and the Parliament) on the "Future of Rural Society." The document marked a substantial departure of the E.C. approach to the low income problem of family farmers and the underdevelopment of marginal rural areas. A number of programs have since then been put into operation to promote the recovery and modernization of the poorer rural areas through less reliance on agriculture, whose development possibilities are often severely constrained by soil and topographic conditions, than on nonagricultural activities, including rural tourism, with the assistance of the combined resources of the several structural funds available.

With the 1992 CAP reform the approach to retiring land from production of surplus commodities, reducing the intensity of land use, and explicitly catering for environmental objectives in the utilization of natural resources, has been considerably changed and directed to more specific targets. The new multi-annual set-aside, which is now compulsory for the so-called large producers unless they renounce the per hectare compensation, is now better targeted to reduce cereal and oilseed production, and perhaps, in a medium-long term, budget expenditures. A long-term (20 year) set-aside, addressed to environmental objectives, has also been introduced as part of a package of "accompanying policy measures." Finally, a renewed effort to encourage early retirement of farmers and farm workers, and thus speed up structural adjustment, is the object of a separate EEC Regulation

The new set-aside programs, then, appear to be similar to what the United States has experienced with the Acreage Reduction Program (ARP) and the Conservation Reserve Program (CRP).[1] Similarity of programs and the relevance of the U.S. experience in the field of supply control should make EEC policymakers and analysts very attentive to overseas procedures and performances in order to minimize errors in the implementation of set-aside programs.

In the rest of this chapter we shall, first, review the application of the 1988 set-aside regulation in the various E.C. member countries and give a summary description of the 1992 set-aside program and of its potential impact; the new, long-term set-aside program will also be briefly considered. There follows a summary of an EEC study to analyze causes of slippage and to investigate the relationships between rotational and non-rotational set-aside. The latter analysis will be substantially restricted to the Italian case although similar exercises have been carried out for all member countries.

Implementation of EEC Set-aside Programs
(Regulations 1094/88 and 2096/91)

Up to the crop year 1992 about 1,766,000 hectares, i.e., about 2.6 percent of the total arable land and 5.1 percent of the cereal area, had been retired from production in the European Community under the multi-annual program of 1988 (Table 15.1). Another 803,000 hectares have been set aside under the annual program, which was applied for the first time in the crop year 1991-92; the latter figure represents about 1.2 percent of arable land and 2.3 percent of cereal area. In the same period cereal production has continued to increase, repeatedly exceeding the MGQ. The annual agricultural reports of the E.C. attribute this production performance to the persistent trend of yield improvements.

The degree of farmers' participation in the set-aside programs has varied greatly among member countries. Italy and Germany alone cover 71 percent (Italy 44 percent) of the land retired under the multi-annual program, whereas France and Spain, which together have about 50 percent of the Community cereal area, account for only 18.4 percent of the total set-aside land. These two countries, however, have shown a greater interest in the annual program, which has been practically neglected (except in Germany) by the other countries. The set-aside requirement in the latter case is only 15 percent, as against 20 percent in the older scheme, and the premium is lower but fully financed by EEC. The Fonds Européan d'orientation et de Garantie Agricole (FEOGA) expenditure for the set-aside program was 360 million ECUs in 1992, barely one percent of the total outlay for price support and structural change (about 34,000 million ECU). If national co-financing is added, total direct payments to producers for the same year should be approximately doubled.

The application of the programs also shows substantial variations among regions, farm sizes, and farming types. A brief review of the literature illustrating national participation is given below.

In Great Britain (Ansell, 1992) the program has enlisted mainly larger farms and the highly urbanized south-eastern region, probably because of

TABLE 15.1 Set-aside in EEC (Regulations 1094/88 and 2096/91)

Country	Idled Land (hectares)				Total Multi-annual	Annual	Total	Percent of Cereal Area[a]	Cereal Production Variation 1989-92
	1988-89	1989-90	1990-91	1991-92					
Belgium & Luxembourg	386	149	270	98	903	1,077	1,980	0.52	-1.69
Denmark	0	0	4,596	3,545	8,141	1,379	9,520	0.60	16.04
Germany[b]	167,775	52,208	79,854	179,433	479,270	314,875	794,145	16.78	6.01
Greece	0	250	250	213	713	1,470	2,183	0.16	39.79
Spain	25,047	13,858	28,264	22,774	89,943	250,000	339,943	4.41	-9.09
France	14,220	39,702	112,653	68,917	235,492	203,000	438,492	4.75	8.17
Netherlands	2,535	5,919	6,667	252	15,373	45	15,418	7.79	12.05
Ireland	1,141	486	52	71	1,750	2,500	4,250	1.23	-0.53
Italy	93,756	234,972	242,761	207,487	778,976	11,603	790,579	18.55	6.71
United Kingdom	52,090	48,810	28,594	25,628	155,122	12,977	168,099	4.31	0.63
Portugal	-	-	-	-	-	4,415	4,415	0.47	0.98
Total	356,950	396,354	503,961	508,418	1,765,683	803,341	2,569,024	7.42	5.39

Source: E.C. Commission (1992).
[a] Referred to 1988-89.
[b] Additional 599,243 hectares were set-aside in the new Landers of the former Eastern Germany.

better incomes and employment in the non-agricultural sectors. With regard to land use 95 percent of the set-aside land went to fallow, 75 percent of which is permanent. Set-aside has also been used to experiment with measures capable of producing environmental benefits. Farmers enrolling in the Countryside Premium Scheme would receive an extra compensation, from 45 pounds for bird reproduction sites up to 110 pounds in case of grass courts for recreation purposes. According to the Countryside Commission, one of the reasons for the program's success was the farmers' motivation for doing something useful on their set-aside land (Ewins and Roberts, 1992).

In Germany (Fasterding, Plankl, and Jones 1992), with the help of high national contributions, the program has had the function of keeping people in agriculture and preventing marginal farms from being pulled off the market. Mainly full-time and owner-operated crop farms have participated in the program.

In France, set-aside was not well received initially, but in the last two years about 450,000 hectares have been enrolled, almost half of which fell under the annual program. Apparently farmers were afraid of losing their land base for future direct compensation (Agra Europe, 1992).

In Spain, enrollment was even lower than in France; about 200,000 hectares were enrolled, but only by the annual program. Up to 1992, interest was restricted to large farms with an average size of 207 hectares, up to 467 hectares in the Toledo region. A relatively high percentage of farms have set aside all their land (Merino Pacheco and Escribano, 1992).

In Italy, on the other hand, the multi-annual program has had a large response, reaching almost 780,000 hectares at the end of the fourth year (1992), about 13 percent of the cereal area; more than half of the retired land is concentrated in the southern regions (Sicily and Sardinia accounting for about 80 percent) and over one-third in the central regions (mainly Tuscany). Northern producers, which contribute over 50 percent of cereal production (soft wheat and maize), have substantially kept out of the program, probably because the premium foreseen for the North was not attractive enough. Permanent fallow is the main alternative land use (about two-thirds) in Italy, followed by rotational fallow and extensive pasture. Afforestation is found in some regions, while the area allocated to the remaining uses is negligible everywhere. Small and large farms have joined in the program; about 20 percent of the retired area comes from farms that have given up all their arable land, but the bulk comes from farms that have set aside from 30 to less than 100 percent of their arable land. It is hard to estimate, at present, the direct production impact of the introduction of set-aside in Italy. The prevalence of permanent fallow, indicative of poorer parcels or marginal land, and the geographical concentration in the less productive regions, which incidentally exhibit great yield fluctuations from year to year, suggest that the slippage effect was rather high. Soft wheat and maize production shows slightly decreasing trends, much less pronounced than the decline of the sown areas. On the other hand, the production of durum wheat of 1991 and 1992 is higher than in the three years preceding the introduction of the program. Available information does not allow discrimination among the following possible causes of the durum wheat performance: the exceptional yields in 1991 due to favorable climatic conditions, the long-term trend in yield improvements, or the intensification process on the remaining arable land.

Set-aside Under CAP Reform

Rotational and Nonrotational Set-aside (Regulation 1765/92)

With the adoption of an income support system for producers of certain arable crops (cereals, oilseeds, and protein crops), according to EEC Council Regulation No 1765/92, to be eligible for a compensatory payment, farmers have to fulfill a set-aside requirement (15 percent) when they choose (or fall under) the "general scheme" as against the "simplified scheme," which is open to small producers only and which does not entail any obligation. Large producers are those whose land base in the years 1989 and 1991 was such to produce, on the basis of the average yield of the region concerned, a total of 92 tons or more of cereal equivalents. The land set aside shall be subject to rotation, but a plot cannot be reused for set-aside for a five year period. Nonrotational set-aside shall also be permitted, but in return for a higher set-aside percentage rate. The latter clause implicitly assumes that producers who opt for the non-rotational form of set-aside will generally idle lands of lesser productive capacity; it aims, therefore, to offset any potential difference, in terms of output reduction, between the two forms of set-aside. The percentage rate for nonrotational set-aside was fixed by the E.C. Council of Ministers, in a proposal by the Commission, at 20 percent (except for 18 percent in the United Kingdom). The 15 percent requirement for rotational set-aside may be changed in the future in accordance with supply and market conditions. This will automatically call for a change of the equivalent percentage for nonrotational set-aside.

A special feature of the program is that the set-aside obligation refers to seven months only (in Italy, from mid-December to mid-July) in order to allow normal cultivation in the remaining months. This means that, in most cases, producing a fodder crop should be possible.

The new set-aside regulation requires the member states to submit to the Commission a regionalization plan for the program application, but it allows the countries a certain amount of flexibility in adapting some of the provisions to national or regional needs and preferences, especially with regard to environmental goals.[2] Assessment of the probable production impact of the new program must consider that set-aside is now an obligation for the so-called large or professional producers. It is estimated that there are about 550,000 large producers in the 12 member states (Table 15.2). Since they control over 28 million hectares of arable land eligible for set-aside, the area under set-aside should amount to approximately 4,300,000 hectares. Large producers represent a large proportion of cereals growers in countries such as France, Denmark, and the United Kingdom (from 40 to 60 percent). Hence the greatest contributors at the EEC level in terms of set-aside hectares are expected to be France (almost 1.5 million hectares), Spain (0.8 million), Germany, and the United Kingdom (approximately 650,000 each). Denmark shall have to set aside, in principle, an area almost as large as that of Italy (about 220 to 250 thousand hectares). The impact in terms of output reduction should therefore be much larger than previously. Under the 15 percent rotational set-aside, slippage effects are also expected to be relatively small, as we shall show later on.

In Italy there are only about 40,000 large producers as defined by the EEC Regulation, or about 3 percent of the farms producing cereals and

TABLE 15.2 Potential Set-aside in EEC (Regulation 1765/92)

	Belgium/ Luxembourg	Denmark	Germany	Greece	Spain	France
Number of cereal producers (000)	42	71	562	387	740	590
Area under cereals (000 ha)	334	1574	6788	1260	3372	9228
Number of professional producers (000)	3	33	96	7	45	228
Cereal area eligible for set aside (000 ha)	123	1020	2905	233	3757	7400
Set aside area (000 ha)	20	226	671	41	1006	1485
Set aside area as share of total cereals area (%)	5.4	9.7	6.4	2.8	6	12
	Ireland	Italy	Netherlands	Portugal	U.K.	EEC-12
Number of cereals producers (000)	25	1351	56	408	80	3646
Area under cereals (000 ha)	337	4807	178	872	3483	32233
Number of professional producers (000)	5	41	6	10	50	524
Cereal area eligible for set aside (000 ha)	233	1695	158	432	3383	21032
Set aside area (000 ha)	35	254	24	65	634	4461
Set aside area as share of total cereals area (%)	10.4	4.5	9.6	7.4	14.6	9.8

Source: Post and Blom., 1993.

oilseeds. Since they are largely concentrated in the northern regions, where yields of cereals are well above national averages, the new geographical distribution of idled lands will reverse the pattern of the 1988 scheme. This also means that there will be an additional production impact of the two programs, at least until the 1988 program is in force.

Long-term Set-aside (EEC Regulation 2078/92)

The long-term set-aside (20 years) is part of a package of measures, defined by EEC Regulation 2078/92, which pursue environmental objectives through a variety of programs co-financed by the EEC. They include: (a) reduction of chemical inputs; (b) biological production; (c) extensification through appropriate choice of crops and of production techniques; (d) reduction of the number of animals per unit of fodder area; (e) other methods of environment-friendly production; (f) rearing of local animal breeds and of vegetable species at risk; (g) management of abandoned agricultural and forest plots; (h) long-term set-aside; (i) enjoyment by the public (including organized recreational facilities) of the abandoned lands, of set-aside lands, and of protected areas. Farmers committing themselves to one or more programs for at least five years (except for the long-term set-aside, which requires a 20-year commitment) shall be compensated for their income loss and the production of positive externalities. Thus, the programs also serve the purpose of keeping active a larger number of farmers than would be the case in the absence of income support.

These measures, in principle, should be applied in all regions although not necessarily in the entire regional territory. Some of the measures can be combined, but the compensation established for each one of them is not, or only partially, cumulative. Member states and regional governments must submit specific programs by the end of July 1993. In so doing they must specify the criteria for eligibility, the type of zoning for each program with priority indications, the value of unit compensation, the conditions to be observed by the beneficiaries, and the information and extension activities foreseen. The long-term set-aside is strictly oriented towards protection of natural resources (soil, water, biotypes), to re-create wetlands, to reconstruct the landscape along traditional lines, and to create new parks and natural reserves. It is anticipated, in Italy at least, that this type of engagement will likely give rise to a practically irreversible land-use destination, because present institutional constraints will make it very difficult to repossess the land for private use.

It is anticipated that the implementation of the above programs, especially in the southern countries, will involve a substantial administrative effort, a partial restructuring and strengthening of existing agricultural, rural and environment protection services, and increased administrative costs, the volume of which, for the time being, is not yet known.

An Estimate of Slippage Effects Under Alternative Set-aside Options

As it was mentioned earlier, with the application of CAP reform, large producers fall under the set-aside obligation and have to opt for rotational (RSA) or nonrotational (NRSA) set-aside. The requirement for RSA was fixed at 15 percent by the E.C. Regulation, while the Council has recently set NRSA at 20 percent (18 percent for the UK) following a study in all EEC member countries.[3] In the rest of the chapter we shall draw largely from that study, taking the Italian case as an example.

Farmer Choices and Causes of Slippage

It is expected that farmers will decide between rotational and nonrotational set-aside on the basis of their intrafarm variability of land quality and on the relative profitability (market prices plus compensation) of the relevant crops after the application of the CAP reform. The choice, furthermore, will be influenced by the consideration of the range of possible crops, including those that do not come under the set-aside obligation, such as fodder, sugar beets, and horticultural crops. For example, sugar beets yield benefit from a previous wheat crop; this means that wheat may remain in rotation even if its relative profitability is reduced by the CAP reform.

Estimation of the various forms of slippage, therefore, must consider that, in their choice of the production mix, farmers are guided largely by short/medium term profit-maximizing criteria, where what matters is total net revenue (in our case, gross revenue minus variable costs). Obviously, in the longer run, farmers will adjust to external shocks or to internal structural changes (family life cycle, for instance) by varying the extent of fixed costs. Since the scope of the study was to estimate the possible slippage effects of two set-aside options in terms of equivalent reduction of the cereals output only, attention was concentrated on the slippage causes more relevant for this purpose.[4]

As a general proposition, it is assumed that farmers will tend to choose rotational set-aside when the land quality of the various parcels composing the farm land base is homogeneous. Conversely, they will prefer nonrotational set-aside when the land base is made up of parcels showing substantial productivity differences. With cropping pattern unchanged, the more uniform the land quality within a given farm, the more the reduction of total production, due to set-aside, will simply be a function of average crop yields because, by definition, the average yields of any given crop obtainable throughout the farm land base are very similar to one another. It may be noted that in this situation average and marginal land productivity tend to coincide. However, one must account for at least three possible slippage effects that may also occur under NRSA. First, there may be a partial change of the cropping pattern, with a shift from less profitable to more profitable crops, which may result in a more than proportional reduction in the production of the discarded crop and in a lesser reduction or even an increase in the production of another crop. Second, it is expected that, under certain conditions, yields on parcels left idle for a year might be higher than without fallow. Intensification of production due to greater application of available labor and other factors on the diminished cultivated land is a third possible cause of slippage; however, whether it will actually occur and be of significant magnitude it is hard to say at present because the CAP reform is changing the absolute and relative levels of crop profitability. Obviously, it is to be expected that, in the first two years of the application of RSA, the slippage effects will be of greater magnitude because farmers most likely will set aside first the parcels of lower quality. This negative effect, under the hypothesis of a rigorous observance of the rotational scheme, will be upset almost entirely in the subsequent years because the more productive parcels also have to be left idle.

Another interesting question, which is not dealt with here, is to what extent the introduction of readily available, more efficient technologies will upset or more than upset the announced gradual, but substantial, reduction of price support.

In case of nonrotational set-aside it can be assumed that the guiding principle will be the marginal land productivity and that the slippage effect will also vary with the marginal productivity. However, in areas of high land fragmentation, in order to reduce costs, farmers may choose to set aside distant parcels even if they are not necessarily the poorest ones. This circumstance will tend to reduce the slippage effect. Also, in the case of irrigated crops (maize, soya, sunflowers) farmers may prefer to keep the parcels where water is more abundant or easier to apply, due to location, topography, or the availability of fixed irrigation devices. In this case it is more difficult to anticipate the resulting slippage effect, because the result may either be in the direction of higher output or of lower costs without relevant output effects.

If the dispersion of the farm yields around the mean for the region concerned is low, indicating a high homogeneity of conditions, then such regions can be taken as emblematic of areas where a large percentage of producers will be primarily interested in rotational set-aside. Conversely, regions with a high dispersion of yields around the mean will more likely include a relatively larger number of producers interested in nonrotational set-aside.

The heavy reliance, in the context of this study, on the analysis of yield variability makes it necessary to clarify the relationship between yields and land quality. Yields are indeed imperfect indicators of land quality;

ceteris paribus, capital and labor inputs, and management capacity are other important factors in explaining yield variations for any given crop. In general, and even in the most homogeneous regions, we found low or modest correlation coefficients between yields and gross margins and also a wide range of variation of the ratio of variable costs to gross output. As a consequence, when, as it is done below, we speak of hypothetical parcels characterized by given yield ranges and averages, it must be clear that such figures are not necessarily indicators of land quality alone but rather the resultant of a larger set of variables, including the cereal mix, the type and volume of variable costs, and the type of management practices. The estimated slippage effects are then to be considered as the composite effects of a number of variables and not only of land quality.

Methodological Approach

In the absence of any relevant and systematic survey of soil qualities by region and by farm, the Italian set-aside study has essentially relied on data obtainable from the Farm Account Data Network (FADN) database (RICA is the corresponding Italian and French acronym), which covers the entire national territory and a large variety of farming types and farm sizes. Unfortunately, the FADN data supply average crop yields and gross margins for individual farms but do not incorporate any information with regard to the intrafarm variability due to differences in land quality. As illustrated below, we have overcome this obstacle by using information on interfarm variability to derive estimates of intrafarm variability.

The sample drawn from the RICA database and utilized for the study refers to the year 1990 and includes arable farms of more than four ESU (European Size Units). Farms without grain production have been ignored. In total, the overall sample utilized for our purposes comprises 11,000 farms, stratified by macroregions (north, center, and south), administrative regions and altitude (mountains, hills, and plains), with further subdivision, when possible, into homogeneous groups (for example, small and large producers). This stratification makes it possible to take into consideration the main structural variables that determine cropping patterns and influence crop yields under Italian conditions.

As indicated earlier, the estimating method rests on the assumption that knowledge of interfarm variability of yields and gross margins, which can be computed from the RICA sample for each "region" and for "homogeneous" groups of farms (for example, small and large producers), is a useful starting point to approximate the intrafarm variability for the same variables. As it is generally held that the interfarm variability overstates the extent of intrafarm variability, a choice had to be made with regard to most appropriate quantitative relationships between the two forms of variability. We have discarded the hypothesis of equality (intrafarm variability = interfarm variability) because even a simple inspection of interfarm statistics for the various subsamples indicates that the range of variation displayed is very unlikely to be true for any single farm. As a first approximation we have, therefore, assumed that a truncated distribution defined by the interval "average regional yield (M) +/– standard deviation (SD)" could be an acceptable proxy of the average intrafarm variability within each farm group. In the absence of any empirical evidence, the plausibility of this assumption was checked by means of a simulation exercise finalized to reproduce, through random numbers and a set of different constraints, the range, the SD, and the coefficient of variation of farm average yields. The results produced by repeated iterations have confirmed that the truncated distribution of regional yields can be considered as a reasonable proxy of the intrafarm variability. It is important to stress this point because, as a consequence of the estimating procedures outlined below, the higher the coefficient of variation of yields, the higher will be the slippage of NRSA and the equivalence point between RSA and NRSA.

Considering that in the case of 15 percent RSA, after a period of five years, a parcel, corresponding to 15 percent of the relevant acreage, can again be selected for set-aside, the length of the rotation will be 6 years only; thus, only 90 percent of the eligible arable land will be involved in RSA. It is expected that farmers will begin by setting aside parcels of lowest quality (i.e., lowest yields) and move gradually, year after year, to parcels of higher yields; however, after the sixth year the poorest parcel(s) can again be selected and the remaining 10 percent of the eligible acreage (presumably characterized by the highest yield) will never fall under set-aside. In the logic of our method, this is the source of the average RSA slippage over a period of six years. For analytical purposes, we are concerned with a fraction only of the relevant area under the normal curve, i.e., that defined by the intervals M–SD and M+0.75 SD. In order to simulate farmers' behavior in the yearly choice of the 15 percent to be set-aside, this 90 percent of the relevant area can be partitioned into six equal yield intervals (or hypothetical parcels) by using a standard table showing the area under the normal probability curve.[5]

For each interval an average cereal yield can be computed from the sample farms falling in the same interval. Therefore, an interval can be assimilated to a land "parcel" with the qualifications previously illustrated, i.e., a "parcel" characterized by a specific combination of land quality, crop mix, and input use. Of special significance for this study is the average yield of the first interval, which is here designated as X'. To calculate the slippage effects and the equivalent percentage rate one also needs: the average yield of the six intervals taken together (X*); and the average yield of the relevant area (X), which does not necessarily coincide with M since the two tails of the distribution are disregarded.

The percentage production reduction (or slippage effect) of RSA and NRSA and the equivalence percentage rate are given by:

$$SLrsa = (X - X^*)/X$$

$$SLnrsa = (X - X')/X$$

$$E = PRnrsa = (1-SLrsa)/(1-SLnrsa) *15 .$$

As it is anticipated that in the future the percentage rates for rotational set-aside might be changed, we have also considered two other alternatives, with PRrsa=20 percent and 25 percent. The rotation period is assumed to be five years for PRrsa=20 percent and four years for PRrsa=25 percent. In both cases X=X* and therefore SLrsa=0, for the purpose of estimating the equivalent point E.

Summary Results and Conclusions

Reference will be made only to summary results, because space does not permit a detailed discussion of the full set of estimated values. Table 15.3 reports average equivalence percentage rates of non-rotational set-aside for Italy as a whole and for the three macroregions (north, center, south). These aggregated values have been arrived at by weighing the regional E's with the total cereal acreage (or cereal and oilseed acreage) of large producers in each region.[6] Percentage rates for NRSA, i.e., those corresponding to a 15 percent RSA in terms of output reduction, vary from 18 percent in Northern Italy to about 22 percent in the south. These results are in line with the expectations based on the analysis of crop yield variability, which is, on average, considerably higher in the South on account of less favorable climatic and soil conditions. The expected slip-

TABLE 15.3 Slippage (SL) and Equivalent Rate (PR) for Rotational (rsa) and Nonrotational (nrsa) Set-aside in Italy

	Rsa = 15%			Rsa = 20%[1]		Rsa = 25%[1]	
	SLrsa	SLnrsa	PRnrsa	SLnrsa	PRnrsa	SLnrsa	PRnrsa
North	0.02	0.19	18.04	0.17	24.06	0.11	27.88
Center	0.01	0.23	19.26	0.21	25.39	0.09	27.64
South	0.03	0.32	21.70	0.29	28.50	0.17	30.28
Total	0.02	0.23	19.12	0.21	25.39	0.12	28.35

[1]SLrsa = 0 for PRrsa = 20% and 25%.
Source: Estimates by the authors.

page of RSA is low, *ceteris paribus,* because over a period of six years 90 percent of the affected arable land must fall under the set-aside obligation. On the contrary, the slippage of NRSA rises to about one-third because of the assumption that producers choosing this option will only idle less productive lands.

In general terms, when discussing and assessing these results, one should keep in mind that they stem from a static analysis that takes as given the CAP prereform situation. This entails a high chance of underestimating RSA slippage with producers bound by set-aside obligations and, of facing a new set of prices plus set-aside compensations. For example, the likelihood of further yield improvements has not been taken into account. On the other hand, because of rotational needs, as well as cautionary measures against uncertainty, especially under conditions of erratic climate and simple rotations (wheat-barley, for instance), not all lower gross-margin crops will necessarily be abandoned. It is nonetheless reasonable to expect, as our analysis has indicated, that SLrsa might be a substantial one in several regions in the first two years of the program application.

Keeping in mind the objective of the study and the methodology used for the purpose, there is reason to believe that the values obtained for the equivalent percentages are relatively stable, because, for instance, an underestimation of SLrsa is likely to be compensated by an underestimation of SLnrsa. Finally, it is interesting to note that the results for the other E.C. countries, in many cases arrived at through different methods, fall into a rather narrow range: national averages for E's vary from 16 to 22 percent.

From an environmental viewpoint is it justified to raise the question whether, and under what circumstances, promotion of nonrotational set-aside should be an explicit policy goal for specific areas. Under the former CAP, high and stable prices for cereals have stimulated repeated cultivation of steep slopes subject to water erosion and fertility depletion. This is especially true of volcanic and clayish soils in Central and Southern Italy. For soil and water conservation purposes and also for landscape improvement, a permanent cover would have a beneficial effect in these environments. There is, thus, the possibility of a trade-off between supply control and environmental objectives. At present, the latter objectives are supposed to be taken care of by the accompanying measures of the CAP reform, in particular by the 20 years set-aside, but the time commitment and the constraints that this involves are probably too binding and might severely limit farmers' and landowners' participation. Undoubtedly, the EEC measures will need some further fine-tuning for a more effective conciliation of supply control and protection of the environment.

Notes

1. The first is an annual program with the objective of reducing production and acreage base relevant for price policy. Set-aside acreage varies from year to year according to market conditions: Farmers are obliged to comply in order to benefit from price support but do not get any compensation for the set-aside land. They must keep land in good physical condition and agronomic shape. The CRP, which lasts ten years, in turn aims at preserving land from erosion. With the 1991 U.S. Farm Bill, objectives and conditions have been increasingly targeted (identification of sensitive areas, further constraints for farmers) in order to maximize program benefits. Increased attention has also been given to cost reduction (Erwin, 1992).

2. For example, the Italian version indicates the agronomic practices to be observed on the set aside lands. A cover crop obtained through seeding is allowed, with the exclusion of crops indicated by the EEC Regulation, but must be plowed under. Finally, under certain conditions, which are specified in detail, set-aside lands can be used for the production of nonfood commodities.

3. The study, involving experts from all E.C. countries, was commissioned in the second half of 1992 to guide the Commission in proposing the percentage requirement when farmers choose non-rotational set-aside. The aim was to estimate an empirical quantitative relationship, in terms of anticipated production reduction, between rotational and non-rotational set-aside. Within the framework of common objectives and definitions, each national research group endeavored to utilize the information available at the national level (farm accounts, soil surveys, panel data, experimental research results, etc.). In some cases more than one approach was followed.

4. The following definitions were retained:
   a. Slippage effect (SL):
   $$SL = (A-P)/A$$
where A = % decrease of the area of a given crop (or crop mix); P = % related decrease of production of that crop (or crop mix).
   b. Equivalent percentage of nonrotational set-aside (E):
   $$E = PRnrsa = (1-SLrsa) / (1-SLnrsa) * PRrsa$$
where: PR = percentage rate; rsa = rotational set-aside; nrsa = non-rotational set-aside.

5. The resulting intervals are as follows:

M – SD;	M – 0.64 SD
M – 0.64 SD;	M – 0.35 SD
M – 0.35 SD;	M – 0.085 SD
M – 0.085 SD;	M + 0.17 SD
M + 0.17 SD;	M + 0.44 SD
M + 0.44 SD;	M + 0.75 SD

6. If one considers that the estimated regional E's are affected by a sampling error, the magnitude of which is unknown, aggregation of results at the level of macroregions seems to be justified. This also has the advantage of offering more compact final results applicable to standard geographical subdivisions that have a long-standing tradition in Italy.

References

Ansell, D. J. 1992. "The Economics of Set Aside in England and Wales in Theory and Practice." In *Set Aside*, edited by J. Clarke. British Crop Protection Council.

Barbero, G., A. Bartola, L. Cesaro, C. Giacomini, R. Zanoli, and A. Zezza. 1993. *Rotational Versus Non-rotational Set Aside in Italy.* Final report of a study on request of the Commission of European Community, INEA, Rome, March.

E.C. Commission. 1992. "The Agricultural Situation in the Community." Bruxelles.

Erwin, D. E., R. E. Heimlich, C. T. Osborn. 1992. "Environmental Set Aside Compliance Programmes: Preliminary Lessons from the US Experience." In *The Implementation of Agri-Environmental Policies in the E.C.* Workshop Proceedings, Brussels.

Ewins, A. E., and R. J. Roberts 1992. "The Countryside Premium Scheme for Set Aside Land." In *Set Aside*, edited by J. Clarke. British Crop Protection Council.

Fasterding, F., R. Plankl, and A. Jones. 1992. "The Impact of E.C. Set Aside Policy in Germany. In *Set Aside*, edited by J. Clarke. British Crop Protection Council.

Merino Pacheco, M., and J. Briz Escribano. 1992. "Institutional Aspects of the Land Set Aside Experience in Spain. In *Set Aside*, edited by J. Clarke. British Crop Protection Council.

Post, J., and J. Blom. 1993. *The Slippage Effects of Rotational and Non-rotational Set-aside of Land in the E.C. Countries.* Final report of a study on request of the Commission of European Community, Brussels, April.

Zezza, A. 1992. *Set aside: controllo della produzione vs. protezione dell'ambiente,* Urbino, CNR-Raisa Workshop proceedings, November.

16

The Effectiveness of the E.C.'s New Set-aside Program: An Assessment Based on U.S. Experience and Interviews with E.C. Farmers

Michael T. Herlihy and Mary Lisa Madell

Introduction

Agricultural programs in the United States and the European Community (E.C.) share many common goals. These include supporting farm incomes, ensuring adequate supplies of food, and protecting the rural environment. Although many of the goals are the same, the policies used to achieve them and the reasons they were adopted are often quite different. However, with the recent reform of the Common Agricultural Policy (CAP), the E.C. adopted policies to control surplus production and support farm income that contain elements very similar to those found in U.S. commodity programs. The set-aside program that is part of the E.C.'s new arable crops regime is a prime example of this convergence in agricultural policy mechanisms.

Surplus production has been a critical problem for U.S. agriculture since the 1920s. Continuous improvements in technology and management practices kept production well ahead of demand except for wartime and a few short periods such as the mid-1970s. As a result, acreage reduction programs have been included in every major U.S. law for agricultural price support and adjustment since 1933 (Bowers, unpub.).

Surplus production, especially of arable crops, has become a critical problem for the E.C. In response to mounting surpluses, the E.C. instituted a reform of its Common Agricultural Policy that includes a set-aside program. Two methods are used in this chapter to assess the effectiveness of the new E.C. set-aside in controlling production. U.S. experience with acreage reduction programs provides historical perspective on factors contributing to slippage and the magnitude of acreage, yield, and production slippage. Interviews with E.C. farmers reveal the likely producer response to the new set-aside rules.

U.S. Policies for Program Commodities

U.S. policies for program commodities are characterized by two essential features: participation in the programs is voluntary, and program benefits are linked to program obligations. As a result, the level of program participation depends on a weighing of expected program benefits and obligations.

The primary benefit to participants is the deficiency payment. It is a direct payment to the producer equal to the difference between the target price and the higher of either the loan rate or the average market price during a period established by law (currently the average for the full marketing year). Participating producers receive deficiency payments based on their base acreage and farm program payment yield. Under the Food, Agriculture, Conservation, and Trade Act of 1990, the farm program payment yield was frozen at 1990 payment levels. The acreage base was set at the average number of acres planted and considered planted for harvest over the preceding 5 years for wheat or feed grains and the preceding 3 years for cotton or rice. Acreage considered planted includes land idled under the acreage reduction or paid diversion programs as well as land not planted due to weather-related factors. However, the base on land enrolled in the Conservation Reserve Program (CRP) is excluded from the crop acreage base for the duration of the contract.

Price supports are provided through nonrecourse loan programs by the Commodity Credit Corporation (CCC) available to participating producers. The crop serves as collateral and the per unit value is the loan rate. If the market price falls below the loan rate, the producer may settle the loan by forfeiting the crop to the CCC in lieu of paying principle and interest. The nonrecourse loan program supports production by providing market stability through an effective price floor. The loan rate is currently determined as 85 percent of the average of market prices for the last 5 years (excluding the highest and lowest).

The primary obligation of program participants is that they idle part of their crop acreage under an annual program that is designed to control the supply of program commodities. The percentage of acreage that must be idled is announced by the Secretary of Agriculture prior to the start of the marketing year, along with target prices and loan rates. Farmers are required to maintain idled land with specified minimum conservation practices and weed control.

U.S. Acreage Reduction Programs

Acreage reduction programs (ARPs) are the most common type of annual acreage control programs for U.S. field crops (Langley and Newman, 1987). ARPs are voluntary land retirement programs in which participating farmers idle a prescribed portion of their specific crop acreage base of wheat, feed grains, cotton, or rice. The United States usually implements an ARP when stocks are high and prices are low. Under the Food, Agriculture, Conservation, and Trade Act of 1990, minimum ARP levels are based on stocks-to-use ratios. Farmers do not receive payments for land idled under ARPs, but they must participate (idle land) to be eligible for deficiency payments, loan programs, and other USDA farm program benefits.

Participating producers are sometimes given the option of idling additional acreage under a paid land diversion (PLD) program if the Secretary determines that acreage should be further reduced. A PLD program gives farmers a specific payment per acre to idle a percentage of their crop acreage base. The idled acreage is in addition to that required under an ARP.

Set-aside is another type of annual supply control program that has been used in the United States. There is a fundamental difference between set-asides and ARPs. ARP programs are crop-base specific, that is, producers are required to idle acreage from a specific crop base. Set-asides, in contrast, are not crop-specific. Under a set-aside program, producers are only required to idle acreage equal to a specific percentage of planted acreage. Thus while an ARP for corn would idle corn-base acreage, a set-aside program would idle total cropland on the farm as a unit based on the amount of program crops planted.

The acreage reduction, set-aside, and paid land diversion programs are annual programs designed to help control the supply of program commodities. The CRP, on the other hand, is a multiyear land retirement program with the primary objective of removing environmentally fragile land from production. Under the CRP, farmers who sign contracts agree to convert eligible cropland to approved conservation uses for a period of 10 years. In return, participating farmers receive annual rental payments and a one-time reimbursement of up to one half of the cost of establishing permanent vegetative cover on the land.

Effectiveness of Acreage Reduction Programs

Limits in the effectiveness of acreage reduction programs in reducing supply have been encapsulated in the term "slippage." Slippage describes the situation where the effectiveness of acreage reduction programs is less than the number of idled acres would suggest because of a variety of actions taken by farmers that offset the effect of acreage restrictions on the quantity of the commodity supplied.

Slippage can arise from a number of sources. One type of slippage, referred to as acreage slippage, occurs when harvested acres change by less than the change in acres diverted under the programs (Ericksen and Collins, 1985). Acreage slippage arises in the United States in part because not all farmers participate in the programs. Farmers operating outside the commodity programs are able to sow as much land as they wish to program crops. As program participants cut back on acreage sown to comply with acreage restrictions and, thus, retain eligibility for program payments, nonparticipants often expand acreage in anticipation of higher prices.

For participating farmers as well, program provisions may have a number of incentives that diminish the effectiveness of the acreage restrictions over time and, thus, contribute to acreage slippage. For example, the relative price stability of U.S. program provisions may have encouraged risk-averse farmers to bring additional land into production above what would have been used in the absence of the programs. In addition, some discretion in area eligibility under the programs may have allowed farmers to declare fallow and other nonproductive land as program acreage, so when land needs to be withdrawn under an acreage restriction provision, farmers are able to comply with little effective reduction in acreage planted. Noncompliance on the part of participating farmers also can lead to acreage slippage.

Another type of slippage associated with commodity programs is yield slippage. Yield slippage occurs when acreage reduction programs lead to an increase in average yields, thereby reducing the effectiveness of the programs. Yield slippage can arise from three sources. Because farmers rationally choose to withdraw their least productive land from production first, average reported yields can be expected to rise. Secondly, farmers may substitute other inputs (such as fertilizer, chemicals, water, labor, or capital) for land, thereby increasing yields on the land remaining in production. And finally, withdrawing land from production one year may boost yields on that same land in the following year because of the retention of higher levels of soil moisture and nutrients.

Approaches to Quantifying Slippage

Various approaches have been used to quantify the impact of slippage on the effectiveness of acreage reduction programs. Research on slippage associated with U.S. commodity programs is reviewed below and quantitative estimates are summarized in Tables 16.1-16.3. This section draws on literature identified by Norton (1985) and reviewed by Herlihy, Haley, and Johnston (1992), supplemented with a number of more recent studies.

Acreage Slippage

One of the seminal pieces of work on acreage response to farm program variables was that of Houck and Ryan (1972). They estimated acreage supply equations for corn using weighted corn prices and acreage diversion payments for corn as the main explanatory variables. Houck and Ryan also estimated an equation for corn acres diverted, with weighted acreage diversion payments for corn as the only explanatory variable. In the corn acres diverted equation, the coefficient on diversion payments was double the absolute value of the coefficient for the variable in the acreage supply equation. This indicates that, for a given increase in the acreage diversion variable, corn acres planted decreased by only half the amount by which acreage diverted from corn increased. The results obtained by Houck and Ryan imply an acreage slippage coefficient of 0.50 for corn over the time period covered in this study, 1949-69 (Table 16.1).

Sharples and Walker (1974) estimated the effect of acreage diverted from crop production by wheat and feed grain programs on the planted acreage of row crops (corn and soybeans) in the North Central region of the United States. Planted acreage of row crops was estimated as a function of the acreage diverted under the wheat, feed grain, and cotton programs, a time trend, and a dummy variable representing changes in program rules for diverting cropland for 1971-72. They found that, for each acre increase in diversion or set-aside over 1961-72, total acres planted in row crops declined by only 0.621 acres. This implies that, for every acre diverted from production under these programs, 0.379 (1 − 0.621) of an acre is effectively retained in production of row crops due to actions taken by participating and nonparticipating farmers (the model cannot determine which).

Ericksen (1976) defined acreage slippage (AS) in the following terms:

$$AS_1 = 1 - [(AH_{1*} - AH_1) / AD_1] \tag{1}$$

where:

AS_1 = acreage slippage for crop 1,

AH_{1*} = acreage of crop 1 that farmers would harvest under program provisions without acreage diversion requirements,

AH_1 = actual acreage of crop 1 harvested under the same program provisions with acreage diversion requirements, and

AD_1 = acreage of crop 1 diverted.

The acreage slippage coefficient defined by Ericksen can range between 0 and 1. A coefficient of 0 means that the land diversion requirement is 100 percent effective in reducing acreage harvested; that is, acreage harvested falls by the full amount of acreage idled under the program. A coefficient of 1, on the other hand, indicates that the land diversion requirement has had no effect on acreage harvested.

TABLE 16.1 Acreage Slippage Coefficients for the United States

Study	Period	Wheat	Corn	Barley	Oats	Sorghum	Rice	Cotton	Total Cropland Acreage
Houck and Ryan (1972)	1949-69	—	0.500	—	—	—	—	—	—
Sharples and Walker (1974)	1961-72	—	0.379[a]	—	—	—	—	—	—
Ericksen and Richardson (1975)	1937-73	—	—	—	—	—	—	—	0.400
Garst and Miller (1975)	1961-70	0.390[b]	—	—	—	—	—	—	—
	1971-74	0.590[c]	—	—	—	—	—	—	—
	1961-70	0.700[d]	—	—	—	—	—	—	—
	1971-74	0.720[e]	—	—	—	—	—	—	—
	1971-74	0.250[f]	—	—	—	—	—	—	—
	1971-74	0.380[g]	—	—	—	—	—	—	—
Tweeten (1979)	1959-75	—	—	—	—	—	—	—	0.350[h]
	1959-75	—	—	—	—	—	—	—	0.260[i]
	1959-75	—	—	—	—	—	—	—	0.430[j]
	1959-75	—	—	—	—	—	—	—	0.360[k]
Bancroft (1981)	1959-79	0.210	0.360	0.610	—	0.520	—	—	—
Gadson, Price, and Salathe (1982)	1959-79	0.328	0.399	0.646	—	0.646	—	—	—
Evans (1984)	1962-83	0.350	—	—	—	—	—	—	—
Norton (1985)	1948-82[l]	-0.080	0.343	—	—	—	—	0.215	—
	1948-82[m]	0.339	0.258	—	—	—	—	0.267	—
Dvoskin (1988)	1956-85	0.250	0.390	—	0.380	0.420	0.240	0.370	—
Jung-Sup (1991)	1961-88	0.493	0.260	—	—	—	—	—	0.340

"—" = Not available.

[a]Corn and soybeans combined; [b]For total wheat under diversion programs; [c]For total wheat under diversion programs; [d]For winter wheat under diversion programs; [e]For winter wheat under set-aside programs; [f]For spring wheat under diversion programs; [g]For spring wheat under set-aside programs; [h]Short-run estimate for short-term acreage diversion programs; [i]Long-run estimate for short-term acreage diversion programs; [j]Short-run estimate for long-term land retirement programs; [k]Long-run estimate for long-term land retirement programs; [l]Calculated from coefficients estimated using seemingly unrelated regression (SUR); [m]Calculated from coefficients estimated using ordinary least squares (OLS).

Ericksen reported the results of some unpublished research undertaken with Richardson in which they analyze factors affecting total cropland use over 1937-73. In their model, a lagged parity ratio was used to capture farmers' expectations of net returns for the current year. A second variable, land idled in the acreage reduction programs (annual and long term) was used to estimate the effect of diverted acreage on total cropland use independent of net returns expectations. The acreage slippage coefficient implied by their results is 0.40 (1 – 0.6, where 0.6 is the estimated coefficient for the acreage reduction variable).

Garst and Miller (1975) estimated the effect of the acreage diversion and set-aside programs on U.S. wheat acreage over 1961-74. They attempted to isolate the effects of policy and price variables. Total acreage planted to all wheat, spring wheat, and winter wheat were estimated separately as a function of acreage allotments, additional paid diversion acres for wheat, wheat acres set-aside, lagged real producer prices for wheat, and dummy variables representing changes in policy instruments at discrete times.

To eliminate problems of multicollinearity between the price variable and the set-aside variable, the price term was dropped. With this formulation, Garst and Miller estimated coefficients for both the diversion and set-aside programs. Their estimates imply an acreage slippage coefficient for all wheat of 0.39 for the diversion programs. Under the set-aside program, their estimates imply a slippage coefficient of 0.59 for total wheat, about one third more than that for the diversion program. For the winter wheat region, the implied acreage slippage coefficients are 0.70 for diversion and 0.72 for set-aside, implying that diversion was only slightly more effective for winter wheat. The implied slippage coefficients for spring wheat are 0.25 for diversion and 0.38 for set-aside. The analysis showed that diversion programs were more effective than set-aside programs in reducing wheat area. Garst and Miller expected, and found, that slippage would be smaller under the diversion programs because the acreage requirements were more restrictive than those of the set-aside programs.

Tweeten (1979) estimated an acreage response equation for total cropland harvested as part of an analysis of the social cost of government production controls. Cropland harvested was specified as a function of lagged cropland harvested, acres diverted by short-term acreage-diversion programs, acres in long-term land retirement programs, the ratio of crop prices to prices paid by farmers, and a time trend. He estimated the equation using annual data for 1959-75. His results indicate that each acre increase in short-term diversion programs decreased cropland harvested by 0.65 acre in the short run and by 0.74 acre in the long run. Each acre increase in long-term land retirement programs is estimated to decrease cropland harvested by 0.57 acre in the short run and by 0.64 acre in the long run. The implied acreage slippage coefficients for short-term diversion programs are 0.35 in the short run and 0.26 in the long run. For long-term land retirement programs, the implied slippage coefficients are 0.43 for the short run and 0.36 for the long run.

Recognizing that participating and nonparticipating farmers may respond differently to changes in farm policies and market conditions, Bancroft (1981) estimated separate acreage response equations for each group of producers for the model he developed for his Ph.D. dissertation. The response of participating farmers was captured in two equations, one that estimated total program participation (acres planted and idled by participants) and a second that explained additional land diverted beyond minimum diversion or set-aside requirements. A third equation explained the response of nonparticipants. In this last equation, acres planted by nonparticipants to a particular crop were estimated as a function of acres diverted or set-aside in the program for that crop, acres planted in the program for that crop, the average of market and program real expected net returns per acre for competing crops, real expected market net returns per acre for that crop, a time trend, and selected dummy variables.

Bancroft estimated equations for wheat, corn, barley, and sorghum using annual data for 1959-79. His results indicate that the net effect of a 1-acre increase in wheat diversion or set-aside was to decrease plantings of wheat by 0.79 of an acre. This implies an acreage slippage coefficient of 0.21 (1 – 0.79) for wheat. Bancroft's estimates of acreage slippage for corn (0.36), sorghum (0.52), and barley (0.61) suggest that the wheat programs were the most effective in terms of withdrawing land from production.

The approach used by Bancroft was subsequently incorporated into the Food and Agricultural Policy Simulator (FAPSIM) model of USDA (Gadson, Price, and Salathe, 1982). Although Bancroft's equations were revised slightly and reestimated for the FAPSIM model, the implied acreage slippage coefficients from Gadson, Price, and Salathe (1982) are very close to those reported by Bancroft (Table 16.2).

Evans (1984) calculated the effectiveness of diversion, set-aside, and acreage reduction programs for wheat using year-to-year changes in wheat area harvested and in acres diverted under wheat programs. Using data for 1962-83, he calculated the ratio of total changes in harvested acres to total changes in diverted acres. His results indicate that acreage reduction programs for wheat were 65 percent effective on average in reducing harvested acreage. Put another way, this implies that a 1-million-acre increase in diversion resulted in only a 650,000-acre reduction in area harvested. Evans' calculations imply an acreage slippage coefficient of 0.35 for wheat.

In her work on slippage, Norton (1985) used a profit function approach to estimate the effect of set-aside, acreage reduction, and diversion pro-

TABLE 16.2 Yield Slippage Coefficients for the United States[a]

Study	Period	Wheat	Corn	Barley	Oats	Sorghum	Rice	Cotton
Gadson, Price, and Salathe (1982)	1951-79	0.131	0.473	0.344	—	1.33	—	—
Price (1988)[b]	1961-87	0.151	0.245	0.575	—	1.18	540	5.39
Price (1993)[b]	1965-90	0.113	—	—	—	—	—	—
Herlihy (1993)	1986	0.123	0.419	0.389	0.250	—	456	—

"—" = Not available.

[a]Yield slippage coefficients are defined as the increase in national average yield per million acres diverted from production under program provisions. Units are bushels per acre for wheat, corn, barley, oats, and sorghum; pounds per acre for rice and cotton.
[b]Obtained from unpublished research by Mike Price.

grams on acreage harvested and production using annual data for 1948-82. The study covered wheat, corn, and cotton. The model developed by Norton contained six product supply equations that were estimated using the restrictions usually imposed on an aggregate profit function model (Norton, 1985). The model was estimated with production and acreage harvested as dependent variables in two separate estimations. Norton used Zellner's seemingly unrelated regression (SUR) method because it provides more efficient estimates than OLS and allows behavioral restrictions to be imposed on the equations. For comparison, the model was also estimated without any restrictions using ordinary least squares (OLS).

Unfortunately, the results were not entirely consistent between the two approaches, suggesting specification problems. The acreage slippage coefficient reported for wheat from the SUR model is negative (-0.08), indicating that acreage harvested decreased by an amount greater than acreage diverted. This is not consistent with published data, nor does it agree with results from other studies. In contrast, the estimates of acreage slippage obtained from the OLS model are positive for all three crops (Table 16.2).

Dvoskin (1988) analyzed the effectiveness of set-aside, acreage reduction, and diversion programs using an approach similar to the one employed by Ericksen and Richardson. Using annual data for 1956-85, he estimated acreage slippage for a wide range of commodities including wheat, corn, barley, oats, sorghum, rice, and cotton. The method used by Dvoskin estimated changes in acreage harvested as a function of changes in program acres idled. The acreage slippage coefficients implied by Dvoskin's results are very similar to those of the other studies.

Jung-Sup (1991) used an allocable fixed-input model to specify acreage response functions for wheat, corn, and soybeans under voluntary land diversion programs. Acreage planted was specified as a function of lagged crop prices (proxies for expected prices), lagged total supply (an indicator of future supply conditions), crop specific exchange rates (included as foreign demand shifters), a time trend or a moving average yield (to represent technological change), and variables representing government programs.

Jung-Sup used three different approaches to model government support programs. In the first set of equations, he included government program variables such as land diversion requirements, loan rates, and target prices. In the second set of equations, a binary dummy variable was used to distinguish between free market and government program regimes while the third approach used diverted acres directly as a measure of government intervention.

The estimated coefficients for diverted acreage from the third set of equations (-0.743 for corn and -0.507 for wheat) reflect the magnitude of slippage under U.S. commodity programs. His results suggest that each additional acre diverted under acreage programs for corn-reduced area planted by only 0.74 acres, implying a slippage coefficient of 0.26. For wheat the implied slippage coefficient was 0.49.

Yield Slippage

In contrast to the considerable amount of work done on acreage slippage, relatively few studies have been undertaken on yield slippage. However, the research has shown that program participation and land diversions are positively correlated with increases in per acre yields. As noted earlier, the potential for yield slippage arises from program participants withdrawing their least productive land from production first, the substitution of other inputs for land, and improved soil moisture and nutrient levels on idled acreage.

On the land productivity issue, Weisgerber (1969) estimated the relative productivity of U.S. cropland diverted under both annual and long-term retirement programs during 1966 based on county-level productivity indices. His results indicated that the average productivity of diverted cropland was 80 to 90 percent of cropland remaining in production. Weisgerber estimated the relative productivity of diverted cropland at 90 percent for wheat, 85 percent for grain sorghum, 83 percent for barley, 82 percent for corn, and 80 percent for cotton.

Weisgerber identified two sources of variation in productivity, an intrafarm differential due to differences in productivity of different fields within a farm, and an interlocational differential resulting from differences in the productivity of land from one region to the next. Weisgerber found that the interlocation effect accounted for a substantially larger share of the total differential for all commodities in the study, with the exception of wheat. He reported that regions having below average yields accounted for a larger proportion of the acreage diverted.

A farmer's decision of what land to divert was not determined by the marginal acre of cropland according to Weisgerber but rather by the marginal field eligible for diversion since regulations limited the diversion of fields below a minimum size. Other things being equal, the acreage diverted was the field with the least net return per unit of land. Weisgerber argued that, although some land would be diverted because it was the lowest yielding, other land would be diverted due to high production costs resulting from such things as small, steep, or irregularly shaped fields, distance from the rest of the farm, or high input requirements.

In *Foundations of Farm Policy,* Tweeten (1979) describes Weisgerber's estimates of the productivity of diverted cropland as "probably high." Tweeten assumes that diverted cropland was three-fourths as productive as that of cropland remaining in production.

More recently, Hoag, Babcock, and Foster (1993) measured the significance of heterogeneous land quality on yield slippage for corn in six North Carolina counties during 1985-88. They used a field-level analysis to isolate the impact of land productivity to determine the importance of land allocation decisions on yield slippage. Their results support those reported by Weisgerber.

Hoag, Babcock, and Foster found that the diverted acreage was 95 percent as productive as the acreage that remained in production. The authors reported that, while farm-level yield slippage does occur in North Carolina, participating farmers do not make land allocation decisions based on maximizing slippage. In fact, their findings indicate that the diversion of low-quality land (measured by yield potential) contributes relatively little to yield increases under acreage reduction programs. Their results support the contention of Weisgerber that characteristics other then land productivity, including minimum size requirements and the shape, location, and accessibility of fields, play an important role in the diversion decision.

Ericksen defined acreage slippage in terms of the difference between what farmers would harvest under commodity programs with and without acreage diversion provisions. Herlihy (1993) specified the effect of acreage reduction programs on yields in similar terms. He defined the yield slippage coefficient (YSC) as:

$$YSC_1 = [(YD_1 - YD_{1*}) / AD_1] \qquad (2)$$

where:

YSC_1 = yield slippage for crop 1,

YD_1 = actual yield for crop 1 under program provisions with acreage diversion requirements,

YD_{1*} = yield for crop 1 under program provisions without acreage diversion requirements, and

AD_1 = acreage of crop 1 diverted.

Lin and Davenport (1982) examined factors affecting corn yields in the major corn-producing regions of the United States over the period 1955-80. The yield of corn harvested for grain was estimated as a function of acreage planted to corn, nitrogen application, precipitation, temperature, dummy variables for corn blight and frost conditions, and time as a proxy for technology. Their results indicated that, as acreage planted to corn increased, yields declined.

The effect of acreage reduction programs on yields was estimated indirectly by Ash and Lin (1987). They applied the specification developed by Lin and Davenport to a wider range of crops and regions. The yield response equations were estimated using data for 1956-84. Ash and Lin also found that, as planted acreage expands, average yields fall.

Ash and Lin calculated elasticities of yield and production with respect to acreage changes using the estimated coefficients on the acreage planted variable and the following identity.

$$E_q:A = 1 + E_y:A \tag{3}$$

where:

$E_q:A$ = elasticity of production with respect to a change in planted acreage, and

$E_y:A$ = elasticity of yield with respect to a change in planted acreage.

The elasticity of yield calculated for wheat in the Northern Plains is -0.41. The authors conclude that a 10 percent reduction in acreage planted to wheat in the Northern Plains would raise average wheat yields by 4.1 percent. Assuming 100 percent compliance, they estimate that this would reduce wheat production by only 5.9 percent.

Ash and Lin also estimated the yield effect of farmers diverting less productive cropland. Compared with no acreage reduction programs, they estimated that in 1986 national average yields per acre were higher by 2.5 bushels for wheat, 5.7 bushels for corn, 0.7 bushel for barley, 0.1 bushel for oats, and 580 pounds for rice.

Using the results from Ash and Lin and equation (2), Herlihy calculated yield slippage coefficients, that is how much national average yields per acre increased on average for each million acres diverted under the programs in 1986. For wheat, the results imply an average yield effect or slippage coefficient of 0.123 bushel per acre. The implied yield slippage coefficients he calculated for other commodities are listed in Table 16.2.

The yield equations that were incorporated into the FAPSIM model developed at the Economic Research Service (ERS) of USDA (Gadson, Price, and Salathe, 1982) explicitly quantify the relationship between diverted acreage and yields. Yields are estimated as a function of acreage set-aside and diverted, the ratio of crop prices to the price of fertilizer, weather, a time trend to reflect changes in technology, and selected dummy variables. Yield equations were estimated for wheat, corn, barley, and sorghum using data from 1950-79.

The results from this specification indicate that yields per acre harvested rise as the acreage diverted by program participants increases. For example, the coefficient on the diversion variable for wheat implies that, for every million acres diverted from production under program provisions, the national average wheat yield increased by 0.131 bushels. Yield slippage coefficients estimated by Gadson, Price, and Salathe for the other crops in the FAPSIM model can be found in Table 16.2. For most commodities, these estimated slippage coefficients are very close to those calculated by Herlihy.

Price, in unpublished research undertaken at ERS in 1988, used the specification developed by Gadson, Price, and Salathe and data for 1961-87 to update the yield equations used in the FAPSIM model and recently he reestimated the yield equation for wheat using data through 1990. The updated estimate for corn is significantly lower while that for barley is considerably higher than those estimated earlier by Gadson, Price, and Salathe or those calculated by Herlihy. The yield slippage coefficients for wheat and sorghum vary by less. Yield slippage coefficients are unlikely to remain constant over time given changes in program provisions, participation rates, cropping patterns, and the introduction of new varieties and programs like the CRP.

Love and Foster (1990) developed a method to directly estimate yield slippage rates from aggregate per acre production functions. They defined the yield slippage rate (S) as:

$$S = -(\Delta Y / Y)^*(II / \Delta II) \tag{4}$$

where:

Y = aggregate per acre yield,
ΔY = year-to-year change in aggregate yield,
II = ratio of land planted with a crop to total land, planted and diverted, for that crop,
ΔII = change in proportion planted from year to year, and

$$II = A / (A + D) \tag{5}$$

where:

A = acreage planted,
D = acreage diverted for government programs, and
$1 - II$ = the proportion of land diverted.

Love and Foster presented a methodology for estimating the yield slippage rate as the elasticity of per acre yield with respect to changes in the proportion of land diverted. They estimated yield slippage rates for corn, wheat, and soybeans using a simultaneous system of eight equations that consisted of three production functions (per acre), three fertilizer demand equations (per acre), and two equations explaining the proportion of planted acreage to total acreage (the sum of planted and diverted acreage). Soybeans were included in the analysis (although they were not a program commodity and were not subject to acreage diversions) because cross-compliance requirements dictate that diverted land cannot be used for other commodities and because corn and soybeans are close substitutes in production.

In addition to allowing for the direct estimation of yield slippage rates, the aggregate production function specification used by Love and Foster also allows for nonconstant slippage that varies with the proportion-planted variable (II). The authors argue that yield slippage is likely to vary inversely with the level of acreage diversion. The expectation is that slippage is greatest at low levels of land diversion and that the effectiveness of acreage reduction programs increases with higher levels of compliance. Their results support this hypothesis, that is, slippage rates are higher for the first acre taken out of production (II = 1) and then decline as more acres are diverted under commodity programs. Their estimated yield slippage rates range from 29 to 37 percent for wheat, from 48 to 58 percent for corn, and from 30 to 38 percent for soybeans (due to land diverted under the corn program).

Production Slippage

Another type of slippage discussed in the economics literature is production slippage. Production slippage refers to the situation where production of a crop changes by less than the amount implied by the acreage reduction programs. The coefficient of production slippage is a more comprehensive measure of the slippage effect in that it attempts to capture the combined effect of acreage reduction programs on both area harvested and yield.

Ericksen (1976) defined production slippage (PS) in the following terms:

$$PS_1 = 1 - [\,[\,(AH_{1*} \times YH_{1*}) - (AH_1 \times YH_1)\,]\,/\,[AD_1 \times YH_{1*}]\,] \quad (6)$$

where:

$AH_{1*}=$ acreage of crop 1 that farmers would harvest under program provisions without acreage diversion requirements,

$YH_{1*} =$ yield for crop 1 given AH_1^* acres harvested,

$AH_1 =$ actual acreage of crop 1 harvested under the same program provisions with acreage diversion requirements,

$YH_1 =$ actual yield for crop 1 with AH_1 acres harvested, and

AD_1 = acreage of crop 1 diverted.

Two different approaches have been used to estimate the magnitude of production slippage for U.S. crops. Norton (1985) estimated the effects of acreage reduction programs on the area harvested and production of wheat, corn, and cotton. She used the estimated coefficients from a system of product supply equations to calculate production slippage coefficients directly. The production slippage coefficients were calculated as follows:

$$SC_p = 1 - (EDC \times 10 / AYD) \tag{7}$$

where:

SC_p = slippage coefficient for production,
EDC = estimated coefficient on the acreage diversion variable in the product supply equation with production as the dependent variable, and
AYD = average yield per acre for 1956-82.

The coefficient on the acreage diversion variable (EDC) is an estimate of the production effect of the acreage reduction programs per acre increase in diversion. In terms of Ericksen's formula, this coefficient represents an estimate of $[(AH_{1*} \times YH_{1*}) - (AH_1 \times YH_1)] / AD_1$.

The estimate of production slippage for wheat from the SUR equation (0.343) indicates that, for every million acres idled under the program provisions for wheat, production of wheat declined by the equivalent of 657,000 harvested acres. This result implies production slippage of about 34 percent for wheat; that is, acreage reduction programs for wheat were about 66 percent effective in reducing production. Results from the other equations estimated with SUR suggest that production slippage is over 30 percent for corn and is just slightly less than 50 percent for cotton. For wheat and corn, the OLS estimates reported by Norton are considerably different. They imply that production slippage for wheat is almost 70 percent, while for corn it is close to zero.

Herlihy, Haley, and Johnston (1992) calculated production slippage coefficients using the formula developed by Ericksen. Acreage and yield slippage coefficients obtained from the literature and 1986 data were used to estimate area harvested and yield in the absence of acreage reduction programs (AH_{1*} and YH_{1*}). Their results indicate that production slippage for wheat, barley, rice, and cotton was between 35 and 45 percent, while for corn and sorghum it is closer to 55 percent (Table 16.3).

E.C. Acreage Reduction Programs

Whereas acreage reduction programs have been a part of U.S. agricultural policy for 6 decades, the E.C. has had only limited experience prior to CAP Reform. In contrast to the set-aside program implemented under CAP

TABLE 16.3 Production Slippage Coefficients for the United States

Study	Period	Wheat	Corn	Barley	Oats	Sorghum	Rice	Cotton
Norton (1985)	1948-82[a]	0.343	0.312	—	—	—	—	0.496
	1948-82[b]	0.692	0.067	—	—	—	—	0.606
Herlihy, Haley, and Johnston (1992)	1986	0.434	0.563	0.394	0.380	0.582	0.429	0.423

"—" = Not available.
[a] Calculated from coefficients estimated using seemingly unrelated regression (SUR).
[b] Calculated from coefficients estimated using ordinary least squares (OLS).

Reform, participation in the E.C.'s two prior programs was not tied to receiving program benefits. A voluntary 5-year set-aside program, designed to reduce production of surplus commodities, provided annual per hectare payments to farmers who withdrew at least 20 percent of their arable land from production. Under this program, begun in 1988, payments and program guidelines varied by member state. In addition, a 1-year set-aside program was instituted for 1992 specifically to reduce area planted to cereals. The program offered farmers the opportunity to withdraw land for just one year in exchange for per hectare set-aside payments.

The new set-aside program is a key element in the E.C.'s attempt to reform the CAP. CAP Reform significantly changes the market organizations for cereals, oilseeds, and protein crops (feed peas, beans, and sweet lupines). High administered prices are being cut, with the average support price for grains reduced 33 percent over three years beginning in 1993-94. For protein crops and oilseeds, guaranteed minimum prices are eliminated. To make up for the price cuts, farmers will receive compensation payments based on historic regional average yields. Farmers must continue to plant to receive the compensation payments. Payments are limited to eligible base area, defined as the average of area planted to arable crops in 1989, 1990, and 1991, plus any area enrolled in the 5- or 1-year set-aside programs during those years.

For professional farmers (those applying for compensation payments on arable crops area sufficient to produce 92 tons of grains at average regional yields), eligibility for compensation payments is linked to a requirement to set aside a specified percentage of their arable crops area. In the first year of the program, the basic set-aside requirement was set at 15 percent of arable base area, and farmers were required to rotate the set-aside land throughout their area. Beginning in the second year, farmers will have the option of a nonrotational set-aside but will have to withdraw additional land from production (either 3 or 5 percentage points above the basic set-aside rate).

Effectiveness of E.C. Acreage Reduction Programs

Some elements of the E.C.'s new set-aside program are very similar to those of U.S. acreage reduction programs. Thus, many of the same factors that have limited the effectiveness of U.S. programs will likely contribute to slippage in the E.C. There are also a number of important differences between the United States and the E.C. programs:

1. *Participation.* Participation in U.S. and E.C. acreage reduction programs is voluntary. However, all U.S. farmers wishing to receive program benefits must participate. In the United States, only about 75 to 85 percent of base acres are generally enrolled in programs for the major grains. In the E.C., participation rates should be much higher, since participation is the only way to receive compensation for the large price cuts. In addition, E.C. farmers receive set-aside payments for the land they idle, whereas U.S. farmers do not receive specific set-aside payments under the ARP. Under CAP Reform, the combination of set-aside and compensation payments is a strong incentive for E.C. farmers to participate.

2. *Crop Coverage.* The United States sets ARP rates by crop, so that the set-aside obligation applies to a specific crop. The E.C.'s set-aside requirement applies to all crops covered by the reformed arable crops regime and thus is not crop-specific. E.C. farmers have more freedom to alter their crop mix, and therefore the effective set-aside rate by crop could vary significantly from one year to the next.

3. *Prices.* In the United States, the ARP has operated in an environment of relative price stability. Under CAP Reform, the E.C. is introducing the new set-aside program at the same time it is substantially reducing prices for arable crops. In addition to the 33 percent cut in the average grains price, producer prices for oilseeds fell 50 percent in 1992, while protein crop prices are expected to fall sharply in 1993.

4. *Base Areas.* Base areas in U.S. acreage reduction programs are applied at the individual farm level. Therefore individual farmers are held accountable for their actions. While CAP Reform offers the option of individual base areas, all member states have elected to rely upon regional base areas. An E.C. farmer who does not comply could avoid being penalized if the regional base area does not exceed the limit. In addition, a farmer who complies could be penalized for the action of his neighbor.

The E.C.'s experience with acreage reduction programs is very limited. As a result, it is not possible to obtain quantitative estimates of the effectiveness of the new E.C. program. However, U.S. experience with acreage reduction programs and the response of E.C. farmers participating in the new program do provide a basis for a preliminary assessment of the effectiveness of the program.

Lessons From U.S. Experience

Acreage Slippage

The most significant source of acreage slippage under the E.C. program will result from the provision allowing small farmers to receive program benefits without having to meet any set-aside obligation. In the United States, all farmers must participate in acreage reduction programs to qualify for program benefits. Given the large number of small farmers in the E.C., an important part of eligible arable area is not subject to the set-aside requirement. The net impact of this provision is to reduce arable area set aside by participants from 15 percent (the nominal rate) to less than 10 percent.

Base area inflation is also an important source of acreage slippage. All E.C. member states have chosen to use regional rather than individual base areas to establish the area eligible for compensation payments. The program relies on overall compliance in a region, rather than on individual farms. This will provide an incentive for individual farmers to bring additional area into production and claim compensation for it as arable crop base area. Because penalties for claiming compensation on area above the base area are enforced on a regional rather than individual level, it is in each farmer's interest to inflate his base area as much as possible, especially if he believes his neighbors will do the same thing.

The use of nonproductive area to fulfill the set-aside requirement is another potential source of slippage. The E.C. Commission had wanted to require farmers to rotate their set-aside through their arable crop base, to limit farmers' ability to idle nonproductive land (such as stream banks and field borders) with little effective reduction in arable crop area. Under pressure from member-state governments, a nonrotational option was adopted, which requires a higher set-aside rate. For most areas, the rate is set 5 percentage points above the basic rotational rate, but in declared nitrate-sensitive areas and in countries where more than 13 percent of the base area is set aside (e.g., the United Kingdom) the nonrotational rate is only 3 percentage points above the rotational rate.

Noncompliance is also a potential source of acreage slippage: participating farmers could simply continue to plant on set-aside hectares. In the United States, noncompliance has been reduced to minimum levels through strict monitoring and severe penalties. Each year, a random sample of at least 5 percent of all farms is taken. Farmers found not in compliance suffer the loss of payments for one year, plus penalties, and in cases involving fraud, a farmer can be excluded from participating in the program in the future. E.C. regulations call for on-site checks on a similar percentage of participating farms (only 3 percent need to be inspected in member states where more than 700,000 applications have been submitted). Penalties will be assessed depending on the magnitude of the error. Only producers whose applications contain errors of 20 percent or more receive no compensation. In cases of fraud, producers face the loss of compensation in both the year of the application and the following year.

The relatively small size and large number of farms will make it difficult to control noncompliance. The E.C. has proposed using aerial photography and remote sensing to make sure that the required amount of area is being set aside. However, program provisions that allow producers to grow industrial crops on set-aside land, or to combine the rotational and nonrotational set-aside on the same farm, will make limiting acreage slippage difficult. The E.C.'s lack of experience with administering and enforcing the set-aside program could encourage producers to evade program guidelines.

U.S. experience has shown that some producers split their farms into smaller operations run by family members (title splitting) to avoid payment limits. The small-farmer exemption from the set-aside requirement could lead to similar actions by E.C. farmers that would limit the effectiveness of the program. Farmers could restructure or reorganize their farms into smaller entities to avoid the set-aside requirement. Farmers with area just above the limit for small producers could simply not claim compensation on some of their arable crops area. These "false" small producers would then escape the set-aside requirement all together.

Yield Slippage

The same factors that lead to yield slippage in the United States will influence the effectiveness of the E.C.'s set-aside program. Because participating farmers will tend to idle their least productive land, average yields will be higher on the land remaining in production. The introduction of a nonrotational set-aside option will likewise contribute to yield slippage. The rotational program precludes set-aside land from being entered in the program again for the 5 subsequent years. At a 15 percent set-aside rate, 90 percent of the eligible area would be idled at one time during the 6-year period. The nonrotational set-aside will allow producers to plant their most productive area every year.

A second source of yield slippage results from intensification of production. The U.S. experience has shown that, when the land input is restricted, farmers increase the use of other inputs (capital, labor, chemicals, etc.) on the land remaining in production. The price cuts that accompany the set-aside requirement make it unclear to what extent this will occur in the E.C. In the short run, however, other inputs (labor and capital) are likely to be applied more intensively on the remaining land. This would allow the farmer to maintain or increase yields, even if chemical input use is adjusted in response to lower prices.

Finally, the set-aside itself has yield-increasing effects. Idling land for one year under the rotational set-aside increases the productivity of the land through retention of higher levels of soil moisture and nutrients. A study done at Reading University (Ansell and Tranter, 1992) reported that the average increase in wheat yields from fallowing was expected to be 13 percent.

Lessons From Farm Interviews

Table 16.4 summarizes sources of acreage and yield slippage found in the United States. The results of a survey of E.C. producers are then used to identify similar potential occurrences in the E.C. The survey consisted of a series of farmer interviews conducted in Belgium, France, Germany, and the United Kingdom in 1992 and 1993 and provided important insights into the response of E.C. producers to the new set-aside program. All of the farmers interviewed were classed as professional producers, and all intended to participate in the professional producer scheme. The discussions about the set-aside attempted to gauge the effectiveness of the set-aside requirement in four areas: impact on crop mix, impact on yields, impact on area, and noncompliance.

Impact on Crop Mix

The E.C.'s new arable crops regime is significantly different from the U.S. ARP in that the set-aside requirement is not crop-specific. The farmer's eligible base area consists of area planted to grains, oilseeds, and protein crops. The requirement to set aside is tied to the total eligible area and can be fulfilled by reducing area to one or all program crops.

The effective set-aside rate can therefore be expected to vary by crop. In deciding which crop to reduce to accommodate the set-aside, farmers must weigh differing price reductions, differing payments, and differing yields. For example, the price reduction for oilseeds that occurred in 1992 is considerably greater than that for grains in 1993. Since payments are based on average historical regional yields for all grains, producers of higher-yielding grains on better land are not fully compensated by direct payments.

Most farmers relied on estimates of gross margins to determine which crop would be reduced. In the first set of interviews, farmers were asked which crop they intended to reduce because of the set-aside. Barley, which is lower-yielding than wheat, was most frequently mentioned by the farmers interviewed. Rapeseed was likewise considered less attractive,

TABLE 16.4 Sources of Slippage in the United States and European Community

Source	United States	European Community
Acreage Slippage		
Program participation and requirements	Voluntary participation means not all farmers participate and nonparticipants often expand acreage in anticipation of higher prices. Lack of a set-aside leads some farmers to not participate.	Small farmers receive program benefits without having to set aside. Exemption reduces the effective set-aside rate from 15 to under 10 percent. Professional producers can escape the set-aside as "false" small producers.
Base Area Inflation	Farmers declare nonproductive land as program acreage. Price stability of commodity programs encourages producers to bring additional land into production.	Farmers declare nonproductive land as program acreage. Regional base areas provide incentive for farmers to bring additional area into production. Nonrotational set-aside increases incentive to bring additional area into production.
Noncompliance	Noncompliance in the United States has been reduced to negligible levels because of strict monitoring, enforcement, and penalties.	The E.C.'s lack of experience in administering or enforcing a large-scale set-aside program could encourage farmers to plant on set-aside land. Program provisions allowing industrial crops on idled land, or combinations of rotational and nonrotational set-aside, could make enforcement difficult.
Yield Slippage		
Intrafarm differences in land quality	Participating farmers idle their least productive land, increasing average yields on the remaining area.	Participating farmers idle their least productive land, increasing average yields on the remaining area. Provisions allowing nonrotational set-aside would concentrate set-aside on a farm's marginal land.
Inter-regional differences in land quality	Regions with lower-quality land have higher participation rates.	
Intensification of production	Farmers increase the use of non-land inputs (labor, capital, chemicals, etc.) on the lan remaining in production.	Provisions allowing transfer of set-aside obligations or additional voluntary set-aside would concentrate set-aside in regions with more marginal land.
Yield-enhancing effects of set-aside	Removing land from production can lead to retention of soil moisture and nutrients, increasing yields in the following year.	Farmers increase the use of labor and, in the short-run, capital on the land remaining in production. Price cuts accompanying the set-aside encourage farmers to reduce chemical inputs and conserve capital inputs such as machinery.
Noncompliance	Noncompliance in the United States has been reduced to negligible levels because of strict monitoring, enforcement, and penalties.	Removing land from production can lead to retention of soil moisture and nutrients, increasing yields in the following year.
		Mixing of industrial crops grown on set-aside land with rest of harvest could increase reported average yields on non-set-aside land.

because the market price—essentially the world price—is uncertain. The second series of interviews confirmed that farmers had largely followed up on the intentions they indicated in the first year.

The most significant consequence for the E.C. of varying effective set-aside rates is the continued overproduction of common wheat, where the E.C. faces its greatest problems in the arable crops sector. Large intervention stocks and substantial subsidized exports are necessary to absorb the quantities produced. Common wheat was considered by E.C. farmers interviewed to be their traditional crop and the one that provided the greatest yield certainty. Producers felt that they knew how to grow wheat and could be assured of attaining good yields. The per hectare supplementary payment for producers of durum wheat will be limited to specified traditional areas under CAP reform, excluding some areas where durum was being grown. Producers in these areas, mostly northern France, will switch into production of common wheat.

E.C. producers are re-evaluating their choices of crop varieties. Prior to CAP reform, producers sought varieties that would produce the highest yield. They were willing to try new varieties frequently, keeping them for three or four years. Producers indicated that they would begin to consider more than just the yield potential in selecting a variety. Resistance to disease and low input requirements would be as important as good yields. Moving to varieties with lower input requirements and less yield potential would reduce the effects of yield slippage.

Yield Slippage

A lower effective set-aside rate for wheat than for other arable crops should result in higher average grains yields, as common wheat makes up an increased part of total grains. Average wheat yields themselves can be expected to increase, as producers will grow fewer lower-yielding second and third wheats. Trial results published in Farmers Weekly (Skinner, 1991) show that wheat yields fall on average by 11 percent for second-year wheats and by 15 percent for third-year wheats. In the United States, yield slippage for wheat reflects the fact that much of the crop is grown on less productive land. In the E.C., by contrast, wheat is grown on the best area. Therefore, the yield slippage for wheat in the E.C. can be expected to be more significant than in the United States.

As should be expected, farmers set aside their worst land in the first year of the program. The land they decided to enter into the set-aside was on stream banks or on the edges of wooded areas or roads. In addition to being lower-yielding, this land tends to be difficult to farm. Many indicated that they would be able to find other parcels of marginal land to set aside in the following year, but in the third year it would become more difficult. Member states have pressured the Commission to reduce the 5-year rotation to 3 years, which would obviously reduce the effectiveness of the rotational set-aside.

The farmer interviews revealed that producers are already using labor more intensively in their farm management, although total labor on the farm may be reduced. The set-aside allows farmers to use their labor much more intensively on their remaining planted area, particularly during peak planting and harvesting times. The increased intensity of farmers' or farm managers' labor may be offset in part by reductions in the labor force. Many operators of larger farms visited for the survey mentioned that they planned to reduce hired labor, either by letting workers go or by not replacing workers who retire.

Management of the set-aside constrains the transfer of labor to land remaining in production. The labor required to maintain the set-aside area varied considerably. Specific rules governing the management of the set-aside are determined by the member states. They establish exactly when and for how long area will be set aside, specify what can be used as a green cover, and can impose rules and penalties for environmental protection. In the United Kingdom and Germany, farmers had the option of planting a green cover or of letting volunteers emerge. French farmers also had the option of a bare set-aside. Some farmers did very little work on their set-aside area, while a few managed it quite intensively. No fertilizers or chemical inputs may be used on the area during the set-aside period in Germany or France, but manure can be spread on set-aside land in the United Kingdom.

The reduction in area may not result in more intensive use of nonlabor inputs because of the concurrent reduction in prices for arable crops. Producers had begun to adapt their chemical input usage in response to lower prices even before CAP reform. With the reform, many have moved away from a prophylactic approach to treating fields, instead using a more hands-on approach, applying plant protection materials as needed. Machinery usage was likewise expected to decline, as farmers try to make their machines last longer.

The nonrotational option will contribute to yield slippage by concentrating the set-aside on marginal land. In many areas, a 20 percent nonrotational set-aside is unlikely to achieve the same production control as the 15 percent rotational set-aside. A majority of the farmers in the survey indicated that the nonrotational option might be interesting at a 19 to 21 percent set-aside rate. Farmers' decisions of which set-aside program to adopt depends on their ability to find enough land that is lower-yielding or difficult to farm. A number of farmers indicated that they would indeed be able to find 20 percent of less good area to enter into the nonrotational set-aside. Farmers who were not interested in the nonrotational option either had insufficient marginal land or felt that their crop rotation could not accommodate the nonrotational set-aside.

Acreage Slippage

Anecdotal evidence indicates that some producers who would be classed as professional producers did not participate in the scheme in the first year. Some were unfamiliar with the regulations and therefore did not submit application forms, but others decided not to participate. The latter group farm very large areas and attain yields significantly above the regional average. They expected it to be more profitable to plant their entire area although they had to forego compensation payments. Some producers just above the professional farmer limit applied for payments on just part of their arable crops area, declaring themselves as small producers and not setting aside. This type of nonparticipation, "false" small producers, is likely to be greatest in member states with large numbers of farms just above the limit, especially Germany, Belgium, and the Netherlands. Prohibitions of manure-spreading on set-aside land in some countries may also result in some producers opting not to set aside.

A number of farmers in the survey had expanded their arable area or planned to do so, in order to spread out their fixed costs. Some had brought additional areas under program crops, by reducing nonprogram crop area or temporary grassland. None of the farmers interviewed believed that it would be worthwhile for producers to divide professional-sized holdings into smaller farms exempt from the set-aside requirement. There are incentives for some type of title splitting in the livestock sector, where limitations on per head payments apply.

The nonrotational set-aside option is likely to encourage increased acreage slippage, because it increases the incentive to farmers to bring nonprogram crop area or temporary grassland into their arable crops area. Farmers can bring lower-yielding land into their arable crops base for the nonrotational set-aside, knowing that they will not be required to farm it in subsequent years. One farmer planned to participate in the nonrotational program, setting aside on his current farm and planting all the better land on a farm he had just acquired.

Noncompliance

Noncompliance with the set-aside requirement, namely planting land enrolled in the set-aside, will compound problems of acreage slippage. The interviews revealed only one report of an instance of noncompliance but demonstrated that limited enforcement will be a problem. The first year of CAP reform implementation placed significant administrative burdens on the national ministries of agriculture responsible for processing applications for payments and ensuring compliance with program provisions. At the time of the second interviews in 1993, the enforcement measures had largely been confined to checking the application forms for errors.

Another kind of noncompliance could increase yield slippage. Producers are allowed to grow crops for industrial uses on their set-aside land. They must contract with an industrial processor for the crop, but they may grow the same crops on the industrial set-aside as they are growing on the rest of their area. If prices for industrial crops are lower than for crops for feed or food use, producers would have an incentive to mix some of their harvested industrial crop with the rest of their production. Yields on the set-aside area would be artificially low, while those on the remaining area would be inflated. One of the farmers interviewed indicated that he would experience this kind of yield effect.

On-site inspections of farms participating in the set-aside program will be necessary to avoid noncompliance. The E.C. Commission has mandated that member states conduct inspections of a minimum percentage of the farms for which arable aid applications were submitted. The farm interviews indicate that fewer farms will actually be inspected, at least in the first year of implementation. The new administrative systems of national governments were probably not well enough established to process all the applications and conduct inspections between May 15 (when the forms are submitted by producers) and July 15 (the earliest date for the end of the set-aside). Limited enforcement in the initial year of the transition may encourage producers to evade the rules.

Conclusions

The E.C.'s chief aim in instituting a set-aside requirement was to control overproduction of arable crops, especially grains. U.S. experience under similar acreage reduction programs has indicated that their effectiveness is limited by slippage. The effects of slippage on the set-aside program have important implications for the E.C. Controlling production of grains and other arable crops is necessary to containing the growth of E.C. agricultural spending. The E.C.'s budget is in danger of breaching the statutory spending cap (the guideline) in 1994. In addition, the E.C. is under international pressure to reach a GATT agreement that would limit agricultural support and reduce the quantity of subsidized exports.

Based on U.S. experience, a number of factors that will contribute to slippage under the E.C. program can be identified. These include program provisions affecting participation, base area inflation, intensification of production, intrafarm and interregional differences in land quality, noncompliance, and administration and enforcement difficulties. The response of E.C. farmers to the set-aside program, as gauged in discussions with farmers in Germany, France, Belgium, and the United Kingdom, points to levels of slippage that will limit significantly the effectiveness of the program.

The small-farmer provision, which exempts an estimated 35 percent of E.C. base area from the set-aside requirement, reduces the effective set-aside rate from the nominal 15 percent rate to less than 10 percent. Acreage and yield slippage will further reduce the effectiveness of the program. The largest problems will result from base area inflation, from yield slippage associated with the nonrotational set-aside option, and from noncompliance.

The effectiveness of the set-aside in controlling production is likely to be further eroded by modifications that permit more flexibility. The introduction of a nonrotational option will contribute to both acreage and yield slippage. Other proposed modifications include reducing the rotation period to only 3 years, allowing farmers to transfer their set-aside obligation to other farmers, providing compensation for additional set-aside, and expanding eligibility to area not now covered by the arable crops regime. The shorter rotation period would allow farmers to plant their best land every year. Allowing producers to transfer their set-aside obligation, or to set aside beyond the established rates, would both work to concentrate the set-aside on marginal land. Expanding the area eligible for payments would compound problems of base area inflation. Overall, an effective set-aside rate close to 7 percent can be expected, implying production slippage of approximately 50 percent.

Notes

The authors thank Daniel Plunkett, Harry Baumes, Milton Ericksen, David Kelch, and Bob Koopman of the Economic Research Service, U.S. Department of Agriculture, and Richard G. Mook of the University of Kentucky for their comments on this chapter. The authors also recognize the invaluable contribution of Brian Johnston to earlier work on slippage in the United States and Ann Hillberg Seitzinger in conducting the first set of farmer interviews.

References

Ansell, D. J., and R. B. Tranter. 1992. *Set-Aside: In Theory and Practice.* University of Reading, October.

Ash, M., and W. Lin. 1987. "Regional Crop Yield Response for U.S. Grains." AER-577. USDA ERS, Sept.

Bancroft, R. L. 1981. "An Econometric Analysis of Aggregate Acreage Response, Program Participation, and Land Retirement." Unpublished Ph.D. dissertation. Purdue University, West Lafayette, IN.

Bowers, D. E. "U.S. Acreage Reduction Programs, 1933-1987." Unpublished paper. USDA ERS.

Dvoskin, D. 1988. Excess Capacity in U.S. Agriculture: An Economic Approach to Measurement. AER-580. USDA ERS, Feb.

Ericksen, M. H. 1976. "Use of Land Reserves to Control Agricultural Production." Policy Issue Paper No. 635. USDA ERS, Sept.

Ericksen, M. H., and K. Collins. 1985. "Effectiveness of Acreage Reduction Programs," in Agricultural Food Policy Review: Commodity Program Perspectives. AER-530. USDA ERS, July.

Ericksen, M. H., and J. W. Richardson. 1975. Unpublished research. Oklahoma State Univ., Stillwater and USDA ERS.

Evans, S. 1984. "Wheat: Background for 1985 Farm Legislation." AIB-467. USDA ERS, Sept.

Gadson, K. E., J. M. Price, and L. E. Salathe. 1982. "Food and Agricultural Policy Simulator (FAPSIM): Structural Equations and Variable Definitions." ERS Staff Report No. AGES-820506. USDA ERS, May.

Garst, G. D., and T. A. Miller. 1975. "Impact of the Set-Aside Program on U.S. Wheat Acreage." *Agricultural Economic Research*, Vol. 27, No. 2, Apr., pp. 30-37.

Haley, S. L., M. T. Herlihy, and B. Johnston. 1991. "Estimating Trade Liberalization Effects for U.S. Grains and Cotton." *Review of Agricultural Economics*, Vol. 13, No. 1, Jan.

Herlihy, M. T. 1993. "Effectiveness of Acreage Control Programs in the United States: Implications for the European Community." Conference paper, June.

Herlihy, M. T., S. L. Haley, and B. Johnston. 1992. "Assessing Model Assumptions in Trade Liberalization Modeling: An Application to SWOPSIM." IATRC Working Paper, No. 92-2, Apr.

Hoag, D. L., B. A. Babcock, and W. E. Foster. 1993. "Field Level Measurement of Land Productivity and Program Slippage." *American Journal of Agricultural Economics*, Vol. 75, Feb., pp. 181-189.

Houck, J. P., and M. E. Ryan, 1972. "Supply Analysis for Corn in the United States: The Impact of Changing Government Programs." *American Journal of Agricultural Economics*, Vol. 54, No. 2, May.

Jung-Sup, C. 1991. "Acreage Supply Response Under U.S. Land Diversion Programs." *Journal of Rural Development*, Vol. 14, pp. 37-56.

Langley, J., and M. Newman. 1987. "The Role Of Acreage Control Programs in U.S. Agricultural Policy." Policy Research Notes No. 39, USDA ERS.

Lin, W., and G. Davenport. 1982. "Analysis of Factors Affecting Corn Yields: Projections to 1985." Feed Outlook and Situation. FDS-285, USDA ERS, May.

Love, A. H., and W. E. Foster. 1990. "Commodity Program Slippage Rates for Corn and Wheat." *Western Journal of Agricultural Economics*, Vol. 15, No. 2, Dec., pp. 272-81.

Norton, N. A. 1985. "The Effect of Acreage Reduction Programs on the Production of Corn, Wheat, and Cotton: A Profit Function Approach." M.S. thesis, University of Maryland, College Park.

Seitzinger, A. H., and M. L. Madell. 1992. "Producer Response to CAP Reform." Unpublished paper. USDA ERS, Jul.

Sharples, J. A., and R. Walker. 1974. "Shifts in Cropland Use in the North Central Region." *Agricultural Economics Research*, Vol. 26, No. 4, Oct., pp. 106-111.

Skinner, M. 1991. "A Computer Aid to Set-Aside Decisions." *Farmers Weekly*, 16 Aug.

Tweeten, L. G. 1979. *Foundations of Farm Policy*. 2d ed., Lincoln: Univ. of Nebraska Press.

Weisgerber, P. 1969. "Productivity of Diverted Cropland." AER-398. USDA ERS, Apr.

17

Dairy Policy Choice in the United States and the European Community

Mary A. Marchant, Steven A. Neff, and Mei Xiao

Politics is not the art of the possible. It consists in choosing between the disastrous and the unpalatable.　　　　　*John Kenneth Galbraith*

Introduction

As two leading players in international dairy markets, and agricultural markets more generally, potential benefits exist to both the United States and the European Community (E.C.) in attempting to understand the other region's policy goals and constraints. Clearer understanding why the United States and the E.C. have chosen their respective dairy policies gives indications of why each has followed its particular course in the General Agreement on Tariffs and Trade (GATT) Uruguay Round negotiations, as well as implications for European integration and reforms within the former Soviet bloc countries.

Through more than six years of negotiation in the GATT Uruguay Round, the United States and the E.C. have locked horns over agricultural policy differences, including methods of domestic support and export competition. Dairy product markets are among the most distorted agricultural markets in the world, as evidenced by high ratios of domestic prices to international prices in many countries. In the decade 1982-1991, U.S. support prices averaged 1.85 times the international milk price equivalent, as composed from international prices for butter and nonfat dry milk. For the E.C. during the same time, the intervention milk price equivalent was more than twice the international milk price equivalent. Resistance to reform in several countries, including the United States and the E.C., is partially responsible for preventing a GATT Uruguay Round agreement.

By understanding why regions choose the policies they do, the relative importance of key variables affecting policy choice are identified and can be used to anticipate policy responses to major developments such as GATT. With an increased concern about budget costs of agricultural programs, it is important to understand how domestic policy choices affect dairy program costs.

In this chapter, we examine the systematic elements in U.S. and E.C. dairy policy choice and estimate the influence of key domestic variables. First, this chapter describes U.S. and E.C. dairy policies as background to empirical research on dairy policy choice. Next, domestic dairy policy instruments are identified for each region, (e.g., internal price supports, quotas, export subsidies). The different policies used in the United States and E.C., along with the different institutional settings, necessarily require that somewhat separate cases be built for each as appropriate, e.g., the E.C. time series are shorter because the E.C. did not exist when U.S. dairy support policies began. Once policy instruments are identified, policy equations for each instrument are specified as functions of other domestic variables and estimated econometrically. Finally, an assessment of the implications of research results is examined for important agricultural policy challenges.

Why Dairy?

The United States is second only to the E.C. in world milk production. In the United States, milk sales constitute 12 percent of all farm sales receipts, ranking second behind cattle. Dairy is even more important in the E.C., where dairy ranks first, at 18 percent of all farm sales receipts, while beef (two-thirds of which comes from the dairy herd) ranks second at 13 percent.

Dairy policy is important in the agricultural support budgets of both the United States and the E.C. As an example of the large and variable government expenditures, U.S. dairy program costs ranged from $700 million to $2.6 billion in the 1980s (USDA, 1991). Dairy averaged 7 percent of U.S. farm support costs in the late 1980s, with an average annual expenditure of $1.6 billion. The budget problem is even more severe in the E.C., where dairy has historically received the greatest amount of government support, averaging 18 percent of E.C. agricultural spending at $6 billion annually, with the largest portion used for export subsidies. The importance of the E.C. dairy industry was exemplified in the recent GATT negotiations, where dairy farmers along with other protesting farmers throughout Europe protested cuts in their production quotas and reduction in export subsidies.

Government domestic and trade policies play a significant role in U.S. and E.C. dairy markets, unlike other important commodities (e.g., pork) with much less policy direction. Also, significant dairy policy changes took place in both the United States and E.C. during the 1980s. By contrast, the sugar markets in the United States and the E.C. also have heavy policy involvement, but there have been no significant policy changes in sugar since 1982.[1]

The U.S. dairy industry has traditionally adopted a defensive posture toward the international market due to subsidized exports from European countries and countries with lower milk production costs, primarily New Zealand and Australia. In a highly regulated industry, in which domestic policy intervention is the rule rather than the exception, world market equilibrium is determined by the interaction of domestic policy residuals. In other words, world market exports (imports) are surplus (shortfall) of domestic supplies at domestic prices, influenced by domestic policies.

This analysis may not extend to other subsectors of the agricultural economy or to political forces that affect policy decisions. This research does contribute to gaining an understanding of the factors that influence U.S. and E.C. dairy policy choice, which can be used in the broader context of trade negotiations.

U.S. and E.C. Dairy Policies

Dairy policies in both the E.C. and the United States have similar goals of improving farm income and use similar price support policies to achieve these goals. U.S. and E.C. domestic prices have historically been two to three times greater than the world price (USDA, *World Dairy Situation, ASCS Commodity Fact Sheet; CAP Monitor*). These domestic policies have historically encouraged overproduction, generated surpluses and government stocks, and resulted in large government expenditures. Both have followed a mixed surplus disposal strategy (subsidized exports, food aid, and subsidized domestic consumption, with considerable building and depleting of stocks [Marchant, *et al.*, 1991, 1992]).

Both the United States and the E.C. use price support programs to directly support manufactured dairy products (butter, cheese and powder) and indirectly support fluid milk prices. The guaranteed minimum price in the United States is called the support price, while in the E.C. it is called the intervention price. Both regions took strong domestic action in the mid-1980s. In 1984, the E.C. instituted a marketing quota, reinforced with a superlevy penalty for its violation (Oskam, 1985; Burrell, 1989). In 1987, the quotas were further reduced and the E.C. made an extraordinary appropriation of funds to dispose of its butter and powder stocks. Concurrent with E.C. policy setting, the United States sought to reduce its surplus through strong action in the 1985 Food Security Act by instituting (1) the Dairy Termination Program (also known as the Whole Herd Buy-Out Program), which paid dairy farmers to leave the industry for five years and (2) the supply-demand adjuster (trigger mechanism), which for the first time related changes in the support price to government stock levels. U.S. dairy markets were in surplus at the time this policy was created. As a result, during the 1980s, the support price dropped 20 percent from $12.60 when the 1985 Farm Bill passed to the 1990 level of $10.10 per cwt of grade B milk, testing 3.67 percent butterfat (USDA, *Dairy Situation and Outlook Report*, Oct. 1990).

Both the United States and the E.C. reinforce domestic support programs with restrictive border policies. The United States restricts the amount of imports primarily by imposing an import quota supplemented with small tariffs, while the E.C. imposes a variable import levy, which serves more to exclude imports than to generate government revenue. In addition, both the E.C. and the United States subsidize exports in one form or another, making them competitive on the world market by paying a subsidy that ensures they meet the prevailing international price. The E.C. uses export subsidies more extensively than the United States.

The surplus generated from the above domestic policies are purchased by each respective government and stored or directly subsidized into markets to avoid government acquisition, storage, and disposition costs. The surplus can be dealt with in several ways: (1) it can be donated via domestic and international donations, (2) it can be purchased to store in domestic stockpiles, or (3) it can be sold at market prices or at concessional prices in domestic or international markets. A more direct way to handle surplus is to control its volume via production controls, buy-out schemes, or a reduction in the price support level.

Historically, the United States primarily used donations to dispose of its surplus manufactured dairy products (butter, cheese, and nonfat dry milk). Domestic donations were the dominant disposal method for butter and cheese and international donations were the dominant disposal method for powder between 1955 and 1989 (Fallert, *et al.*, 1990; Marchant, 1989, 1993). Beginning with the 1985 Farm Bill, the United States explicitly subsidized exports through the Dairy Export Incentive Program (DEIP) in the form of dairy products from Commodity Credit Corporation (CCC) stockpiles (Newman and Gardiner, 1988), although the DEIP was little used until 1991. The United States implicitly subsidizes exports through its international donation programs, e.g., P.L. 480–Title II and Section 416.

The E.C. has historically used export subsidies to sell surplus manufactured dairy products (MDP) on the world market at world prices. From 1974 to 1983, the dominant disposal method for E.C. butter was the world market using export subsidies; since 1984, a combination of domestic and international strategies has been used. For E.C. powder, between 1974 and 1986, the dominant disposal method has been subsidized domestic consumption, with a primary outlet being animal feed for calves. The use of export subsidies dramatically increased between 1985 and 1988 as a method of surplus disposal for both E.C. butter and powder due to the E.C.'s extraordinary appropriation of funds to reduce its stocks (Commission of the European Communities, *The Agricultural Situation in the Community*, 1990; USDA, *Western Europe Agriculture and Trade Report*, 1989). In summary, the United States has historically disposed of surplus dairy products using domestic and international donations along with stockpiling, whereas the E.C. has historically used domestic subsidized consumption, stockpiling, and export subsidies.

Policy Choice Modeling

The goal of this chapter is to understand and explain policy choices for dairy, a key agricultural subsector in the United States and the E.C. We examine dairy policy choice functions for the United States and E.C. to find the systematic components behind U.S. and E.C. dairy policy choices, compare the findings, and draw implications for U.S. and E.C. dairy policies.

Unfortunately for researchers of policy choice, many policies do not continue for extended periods of time. The result is a limited time series with few observations for estimation purposes, as in the case of the E.C. marketing quota. In the case of dairy policies, only a few of the main policy instruments have existed over a long time period compared to other short-lived policies, e.g., the U.S. Dairy Termination Program. Not only are the policies changeable and sometimes brief, but social priorities change. An example is budget expenditure for dairy programs, which is far more important in the United States in 1993 than it was in the 1970s and the early 1980s. Econometrically, these changes in social priorities mean that variables used to explain policy choices can have changing coefficients.

U.S. Dairy Policy Choice

The support price is the primary U.S. dairy policy instrument, which was permanently enacted by Congress with the Agricultural Act of 1949 with the following goals: (1) To assure an adequate supply of milk, (2) to reflect changes in production costs, and (3) to assure a level of farm income to maintain productive capacity to meet future needs. To achieve the above goals, the price support program established minimum and maximum price levels for manufacturing grade milk. Original legislation and subsequent amendments through 1980 specified the price support level be set by the Secretary of Agriculture between 75 and 90 percent of parity. Beginning with the Agriculture and Food Act of 1981, the relationship between the price support level and parity was severed, and Congress set the support price. The original legislation also specified that price would be supported through purchases of manufactured dairy products (MDP) by the Commodity Credit Corporation (CCC). The CCC offers to purchase MDP from handlers at the support purchase price, equaling the price support level plus a make allowance (processing margin).

Theoretical Model of U.S. Dairy Policy Choice. Since this chapter is limited to an analysis of factors that influence dairy policy choice, only dairy policy choice equations are estimated, as opposed to a structural model of the dairy industry. A general form for policymakers' choice of the U.S. support price (P^{Spt}) for MDP follows.[2]

$$P_t^{Spt} = f\left[P_{t-1}^{Spt};Stocks^{us};GC^{US};Y^{Farm};Z\right] \tag{1}$$

Equation (1) describes the support price and is a function of five general groups of variables based on economic and political economic theory: (1) **Institutional inertia,** following the hypothesis that, once a policy is in place, it does not dramatically change (Allison, 1971; Lavergne, 1983; Von Witzke, 1990; Young, 1987); thus, we expect a positive relationship between the support price in the current year and the support price in the previous year. (2) **Stocks:** We expect stocks to be negatively related to the price support level; that is, as stocks rise, policymakers should lower the guaranteed minimum support price level in an effort to reduce overproduction and the buildup of costly stockpiles of MDP. (3) **Government costs** (GC^{US}), accounting for budgetary concerns (Infanger, *et al.*, 1983; De Gorter, 1983; Von Witzke, 1990). A negative relationship is expected; that is, as the budgetary costs rise, the price support level should fall. (4) **Domestic farm income** (Y^{Farm}), following the hypothesis that one means to achieve the domestic goal of raising farm incomes is to increase the support price (Dixit and Martin, 1986; Gardner, 1987). Again, a negative relationship is expected; that is, as farm income level falls, policymakers may attempt to improve farm incomes by raising the price support level. (5) A vector of other applicable variables (Z). For example, international variables following the hypothesis that policymakers consider the international market when choosing domestic policy instruments (Lattimore and Schuh, 1979; Sarris and Freebairn, 1983; Paarlberg, 1983; Paarlberg and Abbott, 1986; Von Witzke, 1990); or a variable representing special interest groups, following the hypothesis that political influence, as measured by campaign contributions or economic rent can influence policymakers' decisions (Welch, 1974; Caves, 1976; Sarris and Freebairn, 1983; Krueger, 1974).

Empirical Estimation of the U.S. Policy Choice Model. Data were obtained from the U.S. Department of Agriculture, the Bureau of Labor Statistics (BLS), and the Federal Election Commission (FEC). A dummy

variable was included for years in which Congress enacted farm legislation. Ordinary least squares (OLS) estimations used annual time series
data, beginning in 1951, depending on data availability for specific variables. Presented below are empirical estimation results for U.S. dairy
policy choice of the price support level for MDP (standard errors and "t"
statistics are listed below estimated coefficients).

$$\hat{P}_t^{Spt} = .391 + 1.13\,P_{t-1}^{Spt} - 0.043Exp(Stk_t) - 0.022Y_{t-1}^{farm} + 0.008(GR - GC)_{t-1}^{US} \quad (2)$$

(0.17)	(0.026)	(0.008)	(0.009)	(0.002)
2.3	42.8	-5.3	-2.2	3.7

$R^2 = 0.99 \qquad F = 1152 \qquad h = 0.4547 \qquad n = 31$

$$\hat{P}_t^{Spt} = .005 + 1.31\,P_{t-1}^{Spt} + 0.005(GR - GC)_{t-1}^{US} - 0.053\left(\frac{GC^{MDP}}{GC^{Ag}}\right)_{t-1} - 0.62(P^{Spt} - P^{Wld}) \quad (3)$$

(0.19)	(0.04)	(0.002)	(0.009)	(0.11)
0.03	32.6	2.87	-6.0	-5.8

$R^2 = 0.99 \qquad F = 815 \qquad h = -0.299 \qquad n = 15$

Equation (2) was estimated at an aggregate level using nominal prices,
where expected stocks were measured as actual additions to government
stocks, assuming perfect foresight, and farm income was measured as the
change in net farm income. The difference between equations (2) and (3)
was that equation (3) has fewer observations but includes two more
independent variables, both of which were significant: (1) The ratio of the
government costs of the dairy program relative to government costs of
total agricultural programs and (2) the difference between the support
price and the world price for MDP.

Empirical results indicated a common set of explanatory variables
which appeared to affect policymakers' choice of the support price. Estimations indicated that policymakers appear to be influenced by the following: (1) The support price in the previous year, supporting the hypothesis that institutional inertia is important, (2) the cost share of government
expenditures on the dairy program, as measured by the ratio of government costs of the dairy program relative to government costs of the entire
agricultural sector (GC^{MDP}/GC^{Ag}), where, as the cost share increased in
the previous period, the support price fell, (3) the difference between the
support price and the world price, where a positive price distortion
resulted in lowering the support price, (4) expected additions to CCC
stocks, that is, as stocks increased, the support price fell, (5) change in net
farm income, that is, as farm income fell, support prices rose, and (6) U.S.

Federal Government deficit where as the deficit increased, the support price fell.[3] Empirical results were good in terms of statistical significance and properties, and reinforced empirical results of others, described above.

E.C. Dairy Policy Choice

E.C. dairy policy was created in 1962, upon adoption of the Common Agricultural Policy (CAP). At that time, the E.C. was a net importer of dairy products (Trostle, *et al.*, 1986). CAP goals included a fair return to farmers, reasonable consumer prices, and introduction of policies designed to increase yield and labor productivity. Because the E.C. was a net importer, the creation and use of export subsidies to make E.C. products competitive on the world market was not a costly budget item. E.C. domestic policies resulted in the E.C. obtaining self-sufficiency in 1972. Since then, exports have dramatically increased and, along with domestic subsidies, have become a dominant surplus disposal method.

In regards to E.C. domestic dairy policies, they are targeted at two different levels: production and surplus disposal. The E.C. supports minimum producer prices through support purchases (called intervention in the E.C.) of butter and powder, similar to the support purchase prices used in the United States. The other key production policy variable is the marketing quota, a supply control measure instituted in 1984 by the E.C. Council of Ministers in an effort to decrease costly surpluses generated by the intervention price policy. As discussed in the introductory section, U.S. and E.C. domestic policies that guarantee producer prices have historically resulted in surpluses. This surplus disposal problem has been more severe in the E.C. than in the United States. The E.C. disposes of stocks and other surpluses using a variety of methods that fall into two categories: subsidized domestic consumption and export subsidies. Domestic use of nonfat solids is subsidized in feeding liquid skim milk to calves, incorporating skim milk powder (SMP) into calf feed, and manufacturing casein. In this chapter, we estimate the policy choice function for the subsidy rate for SMP use in calf feed, which is the largest use of E.C. powder. Subsidized butter consumption is also handled through several programs, whereby E.C. food manufacturers and final consumers purchase butter at reduced prices. We estimate the policy choice function for the subsidy rate for butter use by food manufacturers, the largest category of subsidized domestic consumption.

Theoretical Model and Empirical Results for E.C. Dairy Policy Choice. Described below are both the theoretical policy equations and empirical estimation results for four key E.C. dairy policies: (1) Intervention price (P_t^{intv}), (2) marketing quota (M_t^q), (3) E.C. domestic subsidized consumption rate (SEC$_t$), and (4) subsidized export rate (SX_t^{ec}). Data used for estimation came from a variety of sources including Commission of the

European Communities' *The Agricultural Situation in the Community, Agra Europe,* and USDA's *Western Europe Agriculture and Trade Report.* Annual time series data ranging from 1978 through 1992 (depending on the variable) were used for estimation ("t" statistics are listed below estimated coefficients). Previous variable definitions hold.

Intervention Price

$$P_t^{intv} = f\left(P_{t-1}^{intv} ; Y_{t-1}^{farm} ; Stock_{t-1}^{ec} ; GC^{ec} ; Z\right) \tag{4}$$

This equation is similar to the U.S. price support equation presented above. Thus, similar independent variables are included. In the case of the E.C., the Z vector represents, in addition to the considerations mentioned for the United States, the presence of the milk marketing quota and the particular interests of member states, where individual members may have more or less than equal influence on E.C. policy choice based on their political power (comparable to political influence by special interest groups). The only variable that proved quantifiable was the marketing quota, which is included as a dummy independent variable set equal to one for the years since it was implemented in 1984 and equal to zero before 1984. Comparable to the U.S. theoretical model, we expect the current intervention price to be (1) positively related to the intervention price in the previous year, based on the institutional inertia hypothesis; and (2) negatively related to previous stock levels ($Stock_{t-1}$), government expenditures (GC), and E.C. farm income levels (Y^{farm}). Empirical results for powder and butter are presented below, both with and without the marketing quota dummy variable (M^q).

For powder:

$$\hat{P}_t^{intv} = 168. + 0.6\ P_{t-1}^{intv} + 0.02\ Y_{t-1}^{farm} + 0.08\ Stock_{t-1}^{ec} - 0.006\ GC_t^{CAP}$$

$$\quad\quad\quad 1.8 \quad\quad 4.6 \quad\quad\quad\quad 2.8 \quad\quad\quad\quad 2.1 \quad\quad\quad\quad\quad -1.8$$

$$R^2 = 0.98 \quad\quad Adj\ R^2 = 0.97 \quad\quad F = 104 \quad\quad\quad n = 15 \tag{5}$$

$$\hat{P}_t^{intv} = 223 + 0.6\ P_{t-1}^{intv} + 0.02\ Y_{t-1}^{farm} + 0.07\ Stock_{t-1}^{ec} - 0.006\ GC^{CAP} + 27\ M_t^q$$

$$\quad\quad 1.6 \quad 4.0 \quad\quad\quad\quad 2.2 \quad\quad\quad\quad 1.5 \quad\quad\quad\quad\quad -1.7 \quad\quad\quad\quad 0.4$$

$$R^2 = 0.98 \quad\quad Adj\ R^2 = 0.96 \quad\quad F = 76 \quad\quad\quad n = 15 \tag{6}$$

For butter:

$$\hat{P}_t^{intv} = 1456. + 0.6\ P_{t-1}^{intv} + 0.002\ Y_{t-1}^{farm} - 0.03\ Stock_{t-1}^{ec} - 0.01\ GC_t^{CAP}$$

$$\quad\quad\quad 3.0 \quad\quad 3.0 \quad\quad\quad\quad 0.1 \quad\quad\quad\quad -0.8 \quad\quad\quad\quad\quad 0.07$$

$$R^2 = 0.65 \quad\quad Adj\ R^2 = 0.51 \quad\quad F = 5 \quad\quad\quad n = 15 \tag{7}$$

$$\hat{P}_t^{intv} = 1089. + 0.4 \ P_{t-1}^{intv} + 0.04 \ Y_{t-1}^{farm} - 0.1 \ Stock_{t-1}^{ec} - 0.01 \ GC_t^{CAP} - 495 \ M_t^q$$

$$\quad\quad 2.6 \quad 2.6 \quad\quad\quad 1.7 \quad\quad\quad 1.2 \quad\quad\quad -0.81 \quad\quad\quad -2.5$$

$$R^2 = 0.79 \quad\quad Adj \ R^2 = 0.68 \quad F = 7 \quad\quad n = 15 \quad\quad\quad (8)$$

For E.C. intervention prices, estimation results show that the overall model is significant at the 1 percent level for both powder models and for the butter model that included the marketing quota dummy variable, while equation (7) was significant at the 2 percent level. The previous intervention price is highly significant at the 1 percent level in virtually all cases, with the exception of equation (8), where it was significant at the 3 percent level. For the stock variable, we expected a negative sign. Although most of the estimated results had a positive sign, the stock variable was insignificant in most cases. The government cost variable had the correct sign and had the highest level of significance in equation (5). The marketing quota appeared to affect the butter intervention price but not the nonfat powder intervention price. The farm income variable had a positive sign in all of the above estimated equations and its level of significance varied, but was most significant for the powder models. Our original hypothesis was that, if farm incomes fell in the previous year, the E.C. would raise the intervention price in an effort to achieve the domestic goal of raising farm incomes. When looking at the data on E.C. farm incomes, farm incomes were rising in 11 of 15 observations, while in the United States the change in farm incomes were equally split between rising and falling observations.

One possible explanation is asymmetric decision making by policymakers, where if the change in farm incomes is falling, policymakers strive to improve farm incomes by increasing the support price (a negative relationship), but if the change in farm income is rising, policymakers may wish to continue this trend by further increasing the intervention price (a positive relationship). Support price increases are always politically popular with farmers, especially so in the E.C. because it was an explicit policy to bring farm incomes up to nonfarm incomes. The political counterweights to farmers are consumers and the budget. Unless consumers are mobilized (not the case) or there is a binding budget constraint (only occasionally the case), higher support prices are popular.

Milk Marketing Quota

$$M_t^q = f\left(Stock_t^{ec}, GC_t^{CAP}, SX_{t-1}\right) \quad\quad\quad (9)$$

The goal of the marketing quota is to decrease both government stocks acquisition and government expenditures by restricting milk production without having to reduce intervention prices. We expect that the marketing quota will be negatively related to E.C. government expenditures, stock levels, and subsidized export rates (SX). If CAP costs or stocks are high, quotas are reduced as a correction. Similarly, high export subsidy rates indicate both an oversupplied international market and surplus disposal problems, which may be avoided by reducing the quota. Although the marketing quota is for milk, rather than for butter and skim milk powder, variables for stocks and export subsidies are in terms of products. We accordingly specified the marketing equation twice, using the milk marketing quota as the dependent variable in both and the cost of the CAP as an independent variable in both but with butter stocks and the butter export subsidy in equation (10) and powder stocks and the powder export subsidy in equation (11). This was both practical and also served as a test to determine if one product dominated the choice of the marketing quota level.

$$M_t^q = 121093 - 0.8 \ GC^{CAP} + 0.8 \ Stock_t^{ec} - 4.6 \ SX_{t-1}^{ec} \quad (10)$$

$$ 24 -4.4 0.2 -1.1$$

$$R^2 = 0.86 \text{Adj } R^2 = 0.75 F = 8 n = 8$$

$$M_t^q = 117799 - 0.65 \ GC_t^{CAP} - 2.9 \ Stock_t^{ec} - 2.0 \ SX_{t-1}^{ec} \quad (11)$$

$$ 26 -4 -1.4 -0.8$$

$$R^2 = 0.91 \text{Adj } R^2 = 0.85 F = 14 n = 8$$

Both marketing quota equations, while admittedly limited to a short series by the fact that quotas were only instituted in 1984, were nevertheless significant at the 5 percent level and virtually all variables exhibited the correct sign. The government cost variable was significant at the 1 percent level for powder and at the 5 percent level for butter. Although the result was slightly stronger for the equation using butter variables, neither formulation showed stocks or export subsidies to be significant.

Subsidized E.C. Consumption Rates

$$SEC_t = f\left(Stock_{t-1}^{ec}, GC_t^{ec}, P_{t-1}^{int}\right) \quad (12)$$

Subsidized domestic consumption is a surplus disposal strategy (as is subsidized exports), in contrast to the above production policy instruments. We expect that the rate of subsidized consumption is negatively related to government expenditures. If government costs are high, then policymakers may seek to reduce government costs by decreasing the subsidy rate. Domestic consumption subsidy rates should be positively related to stocks as policymakers strive to reduce stockpiles and avoid further intervention buying by more intensive use of subsidies. Internal E.C. subsidies are primarily in the form of animal feed for powder and discount prices to bakeries for butter. Butter data were not sufficiently available for proper specification. Empirical results for subsidized powder consumption are presented below.

For powder:

$$SEC_t = -19.7 - .01 \ GC_t^{CAP} + 0.1 \ Stock_{t-1} + 0.5 \ P_{t-1}^{intv} \tag{13}$$

$$(-0.3) \quad (-3.6) \qquad\qquad (+3.9) \qquad\qquad (7.0)$$

$$R^2 = 0.88 \qquad Adj \ R^2 = 0.85 \qquad F = 27 \qquad n = 15$$

For E.C. domestic subsidies of powder, of which a large proportion is used for animal feed, the estimated equation is significant at the 1 percent level. The government cost variable, the lagged stock variable, and the lagged intervention price were all significant at the 1 percent level and had the correct signs. If CAP costs are relatively high, the Commission may opt for a low subsidy to defer some expense until budgetary slack returns. If stocks are already high, a higher subsidy will help to reduce the stocks. If the intervention price in the previous year was high, a high export refund may be desirable to prevent additional surpluses from depressing the E.C. market.

Subsidized E.C. Export Rates

$$SX_t^{ec} = f\left(Stock_{t-1}^{ec}, GC_t^{ec}, ER_t, P_{t-1}^{intv}\right) \tag{14}$$

Export subsidies are another surplus disposal strategy that dispose of large E.C. surpluses on the world market at the world price using export restitution payments. The estimated equation includes independent variables similar to the E.C. domestic subsidy equation, and we expect the same sign for explanatory variables. In addition, exchange rates ($/ECU) are now included, where we expect a positive relationship between the exchange rate and the export subsidy rate because a weakening U.S. dollar results in lower international prices as reflected in European currencies, thus requiring higher E.C. export subsidies. Empirical results for powder and butter are presented below.

For powder:

$$SX_t^{ec} = -1139. + 0.6 \ Stock_{t-1}^{ec} + 0.1 \ GC_t^{dairy} - 0.03 \ GC_t^{CAP} + 1138 \ ER_t + 0.3 \ P_{t-1}^{intv}$$

$$\quad -4.8 \qquad 5.3 \qquad\qquad 2.1 \qquad\qquad -4.2 \qquad\qquad 2.9 \qquad\quad 0.9$$

$$R^2 = 0.94 \qquad Adj \ R^2 = 0.88 \qquad F = 15 \qquad n = 11 \tag{15}$$

For butter:

$$SX_t^{ec} = 5937 + 0.6 \ Stock_{t-1}^{ec} + 0.16 \ GC_t^{dairy} - 0.02 \ GC_t^{CAP} + 190 \ ER_t - 1.6 \ P_{t-1}^{intv}$$

   2 3.4   1.5   -1.5   0.2 -2.2

  $R^2 = 0.88$ Adj $R^2 = 0.76$ $F = 7$ $n = 11$ (16)

Overall significance of estimation results for the export subsidy rate for powder were significant at the 1 percent level, and at the 2 percent level for butter. In terms of signs, the stock variable was positively correlated with export subsidy rates, as expected; thus, as stocks increased, export subsidies were used for surplus disposal. The stock variable was highly significant in both equations, at the 1 percent level for powder and at the 2 percent level for butter. Government costs had different signs depending on its origin—dairy program costs (GC_t^{dairy}) were positively correlated with subsidized exports, as expected, since subsidized exports are a large component of program costs. Alternatively, government costs for CAP (GC_t^{CAP}) were negatively correlated with dairy export subsidies. This makes sense from the viewpoint that, if CAP costs are high and the Ministers do not want them to increase, they may choose a less expensive form of surplus disposal than subsidized exports; thus, they are negatively correlated. Government cost variables were significant in the powder equation but insignificant in the butter equation. As expected, the $/ECU exchange rate is positively correlated with subsidized exports. It was significant in the powder equation at the 3 percent level but insignificant for butter. The lagged intervention price was significant at the 8 percent level for butter but insignificant for powder. The intervention price was expected to carry a positive sign because a high intervention price in the previous year would tend to produce a greater need for surplus disposal through a higher export refund rate. The mixed signs and mixed significance of the intervention price lead us to discount the importance of the prior year's intervention price.

Summary of E.C. Estimates. The previous year's support price had a dominant influence on both production support policies (intervention price and marketing quota) and surplus disposal policies (both domestic and external). To a lesser extent, the overall cost of CAP—not just the dairy portion—also proved important in selecting both production support and surplus disposal policies. In the case of powder production support policies, the CAP cost was significant, affecting both the intervention price and the quota policy instruments. It appears that the Community will raise the quota if affordable and cut the quota if the CAP budget needs to be cut.

Farm income did not add significantly to the explanation of E.C. butter intervention prices but was significant for the skim milk powder intervention price. This was somewhat surprising; we expected farm incomes to affect both butter and powder intervention prices. One explanation is that the influence of the farm income variable was captured in the previous year's intervention price. An alternative explanation is that the E.C. Commission considers its own budgetary interests first, ahead of farmers' interests. The weakness of this explanation is that it explains the large E.C. dairy budgets only in terms of bureaucratic aggrandizement, i.e., with the Commission acting to increase its own control in the market and its command of financial resources.

For E.C. powder, both the subsidized domestic consumption rate and the subsidized export rate were influenced by stock levels and government costs. The exchange rate significantly influenced the export subsidy rate for powder but not for butter, perhaps because butter surplus disposal was influenced more by export donations than by subsidized exports. For E.C. butter, the stock variable, but not the cost variable, affected the export subsidy rate. Stocks significantly influenced surplus disposal policies but generally had little influence in choosing production policies.

Assessment and Implications of Results

To assess the importance of variables that influence domestic dairy policy in the United States and the E.C., empirical results (Table 17.1) of the U.S. price support and the E.C. intervention price equations can be compared. Both show a dominant influence of the support (intervention) price in the previous year, which supports the institutional inertia hypothesis discussed above. U.S. farm income, stocks, and government costs also appeared to influence U.S. policymakers' choice of the price support level.

In the E.C., additional policy instruments are used. Government costs appear to influence both production and surplus disposal policies. Public stocks significantly influence E.C. surplus disposal policies. From a dairy policy perspective, which may be applicable to other commodities, the E.C. appears to choose policies sequentially—first choosing farm level support policies and then choosing surplus disposal policies. If the farm policies produce a large surplus, the surplus disposal policy instruments are then changed accordingly to minimize the consequent budget costs and stocks. While the limited number of observations may hinder statistical analysis, we were able to establish a connection between budget costs and the marketing quota decisions.

The tenuous state of the GATT Uruguay Round negotiations complicates and confuses attempts to predict future policy decisions based on past behavior. The statistical results in combination with recent events may, however, point toward likely policy approaches to current and future challenges. For the United States and the European Community in

TABLE 17.1 Summary of Empirical Results

	Production Policies								EC Disposal Policies		
	United States		European Community (EC)						SEC	Subsidized Exports	
	p^{Spt}		p^{intv}				Quota		Powder	Powder	Butter
Variable	MDP (2)	MDP (3)	Powder (5)	Powder (6)	Butter (7)	Butter (8)	Powder (10)	Butter (11)	(13)	(15)	(16)
P_{t-1}	X	X	X	X	X	X			X	NS	X
Y^{farm}	X		X	X	NS	NS					
Stocks	X		X	NS	NS	NS	NS	NS	X	X	X
GC^{US}	X	X									
GC^{Ag}	X	X	X	NS	NS	NS	X	X	X	X	NS
GC^{Dairy}		X								X	NS
Quota				NS		X	NS	NS			
SX_{t-1}											
ER										X	NS
p^{wld}		X									

Note: Numbers in parentheses refer to equations in the text.
NS = Nonsignificant variable.
SEC = Subsidized E.C domestic consumption.
P^{intv} = E.C. Intervention Price.
P^{Spt} = U.S. Support Price.

the Uruguay Round, an understanding of each other's agricultural policies is not sufficient to assure that an agreement will be reached, but such an understanding may be necessary for each to propose solutions that are acceptable to both parties so that the proposals can be offered for general consideration by all the contracting parties of the GATT. To paraphrase Galbraith's insight to the policy process, perhaps the United States and the E.C., by understanding each other's policies better, will discover trade rules that are merely unpalatable rather than disastrous.

Notes

The authors express their appreciation to Giovanni Anania, Alex F. McCalla, Colin Carter, Timothy E. Josling, and Fred J. Ruppel for constructive comments.

1. U.S. sugar allotments were announced in summer 1993. Their effect, duration, and legality are in question at the time of writing.

2. The functional form for this model also describes the E.C. intervention prices, as shown below.

3. Estimations using real prices indicated that the first three variables were significant.

References

Agra Europe. London, UK: AGRA EUROPE, Ltd., various issues.

Allison, G. 1971. *The Essence of Decision: Explaining the Cuban Missile Crisis.* Boston: Little, Brown and Co.

Burrell, A. M., ed. 1989. *Milk Quotas in the European Community.* Oxon, U.K.: CAB International.

CAP Monitor. London, UK: AGRA EUROPE, Ltd., various issues.

Caves, R. E. 1976. "Economic Models of Political Choice: Canada's Tariff Structure." *Canadian Journal of Economics* 2: 278-300.

Commission of the European Communities. *The Agricultural Situation in the Community.* Various issues.

De Gorter, H. 1983. "Agricultural Policies: A Study in Political Economy." Ph. D. thesis. University of California, Berkeley.

Dixit, P. M., and M. A. Martin. 1986. *Policymaking for U.S. Commodity Programs: A Case Study of the Coarse Grains Sector.* FAER-219. USDA ERS.

Fallert, R. F., D. P. Blayney, and J. J. Miller. 1990. *Dairy: Background for 1990 Farm Legislation.* Washington, D.C.: USDA ERS Staff Report No. AGES9020 (March).

Gardner, B. L. 1987. "Causes of U.S. Farm Commodity Programs." *Journal of Political Economy* 95: 290-310.

Infanger, C. L., W. C. Bailey, and D. R. Dyer. 1983. "Agricultural Policy in Austerity: The Making of the 1981 Farm Bill." *American J. of Agricultural Economics* 65: 1-9.

Krueger, A. 1974. "The Political Economy of the Rent Seeking Economy." *American Econ. Review* 64: 291-303.

Lattimore, R. G., and G. E. Schuh. 1979. "Endogenous Policy Determination: The Case of the Brazilian Beef Sector." *Canadian Journal of Agricultural Economics* 27: 1-16.

Lavergne, R. P. 1983. *The Political Economy of U.S. Tariffs: An Empirical Analysis.* New York: Harcourt-Brace-Jovanovich Academic Press.

Marchant, M. A. 1989. "Political Economic Analysis of Dairy Policies in the United States." Ph. D. thesis. University of California, Davis.

———. 1993. *Political Economic Analysis of U.S. Dairy Policies and European Community Dairy Policy Comparisons.* New York.: Garland Publishing, Inc.

Marchant, M. A., S. A. Neff, and A. F. McCalla. 1991. "Domestic Policy Interdependence: Analysis of Dairy Policies in the United States and the European Community in the 1980s." Dept. of Ag. Econ. Staff Paper No. 300, University of Kentucky (Oct.).

———. 1992. "Domestic Policy Interdependence: Analysis of Dairy Policies in the USA and the EC." In *Issues in Agricultural Development: Sustainability and Cooperation.* International Association of Agricultural Economists Occasional Paper No. 6, in Margot Bellamy and Bruce Greenshields, eds. pp. 339-343. Brookfield, VT.

Newman, M. D. and W. H. Gardiner. 1988. "Impacts of 1988 EC Budget: Stabilizers, and Set-Aside Decisions on EC Wheat Surpluses." *Western Europe Agriculture and Trade Report Situation and Outlook Series,* pp. 13-22. Washington, D.C.: USDA ERS RS88-1 (June).

Oskam, A. J. 1985. "A Superlevy System for the Dairy Sector—Consequences and Alternatives." *European Review of Agricultural Economics* 12: 431-48.

Paarlberg, P. L. 1983. "Endogenous Policy Formation in the Imperfect World Wheat Market." Ph. D. thesis. Purdue University.

Paarlberg, P. L., and P. C. Abbott. 1986. "Oligopolistic Behavior by Public Agencies in International Trade: The World Wheat Market." *American Journal of Agricultural Economics* 68: 528-42.

Sarris, A., and J. Freebairn. 1983. "Endogenous Price Policies and Wheat Prices." *American Journal of Agricultural Economics* 65: 214-24.

Trostle, R., M. Lambert, S. Sposato, J. Lopes, and M. Cohen. 1986. *European Community Dairy Sector: Policies, Problems, and Prospects.* Washington, D.C.: USDA ERS Staff Report No. AGES860316 (Oct.).

U.S. Department of Agriculture. *Western Europe Agriculture and Trade Report.* Washington, D.C.: ERS ATAD, various issues.

———. *Dairy Situation and Outlook Report.* Washington, D.C.: ERS, various issues.

———. 1991. *ASCS Commodity Fact Sheet: 1990-91 Dairy Price Support Program.* Washington, D.C.: ASCS. (May).

———. *World Dairy Situation.* Washington, D.C.: FAS, various issues.

Von Witzke, H. 1990. "Determinants of the U.S. Wheat Producer Support Price: Do Presidential Elections Matter?" *Public Choice,* 64: 155-65.

Welch, W. P. 1974. "The Economics of Campaign Funds." *Public Choice* 20: 83-97.

Young, L. 1987. "The Formation of Wheat Policies in the U.S., Canada and Japan: Case Studies of Endogenizing Policy Behavior." Ph. D. thesis. University of California, Davis.

18

Agribusiness and U.S.-E.C. Agricultural Trade Policy

Marina Mastrostefano

Introduction

The degree of integration between the United States and the E.C. in terms of intra-industry trade and reciprocal foreign investment has grown enormously in the last decade. This is particularly true for the food and agricultural sector. This chapter explores the implications of these structural changes for international trade and trade liberalization.

Traditional approaches to trade policy analysis focus on producers and consumers and assume a benevolent government that tries to maximize national social welfare. They therefore concentrate on the international implications of domestic policies at home and abroad as they affect domestic producers.

This bias towards producers has two serious limitations in the context of the real world. First, in the Heckscher-Ohlin tradition, it focuses on differences in factor endowments as a basis for trade. This leads to a bias toward primary products and a concern with interindustry trade. However, the reality is that international trade is growing most rapidly between major developed countries that are both importing and exporting similar products to each other, i.e., intra-industry trade. The second limitation is that traditional trade policy analysis basically ignores the role of firms that are intermediaries between domestic producers and domestic and foreign consumers. These firms perform the classic marketing functions of space, form, and time transformation of products. Observation of the international environment suggests that it is becoming increasingly international and integrated on a global scale. Firms are becoming larger (and therefore fewer in number), multiproduct, and multinational.

Even political issues of agricultural trade should no longer be considered a matter of individual domestic concern, especially between developed countries like the United States and the E.C., where the economic size and importance of traders and processors of agricultural commodities is becoming increasingly multinational. As the industrial part of the agri-food sector increases, the role of agents such as processors becomes more important. Thus the food industry has to be considered a third group with its claims and interests that could well be more influential than the farmers themselves. Applied work to date, as indicated in the literature, has mostly considered farmers and consumers only, probably on the assumption that processors and farmers have the same interests. This may not be generally true. There is also another group of protagonists in the determination of commercial policy, namely international commodity traders. World agricultural trade often has large marketing institutions and global giants—such as Cargill, Continental, Ferruzzi—that are prevalent in many markets that have the capability to move commodity supplies worldwide. Moreover, in contrast with the production sector of agriculture, both processors and traders have an increasing tendency to be highly integrated and assume international dimensions: Hence, a mixture of domestic and foreign economic interests leads to domestic policy outcomes.

If these are the realities of the global food and agricultural sector, what do we know about how these large and potentially politically powerful firms behave in the formulation of trade policy? Do they favor freer trade or are they for the continuation of protectionism? Does the nature of the product make a difference? Multinational processing firms tend to expand more frequently by direct foreign investments than by expanding exports. Why?

This chapter attempts to begin to address some of these issues. It has the following objectives: First, to provide an overview of developments in the multinational structure of agribusinesses with particular focus on the United States and the E.C.; second, to explore the question of whether direct foreign investment (FDI) and expanded exports complement or substitute each other; third, to develop a framework for exploring the question of whether multinational agribusiness firms prefer freer trade or protectionism; fourth, to suggest that including multinational behavior in our international trade policy analysis should improve our understanding of why agricultural trade liberalization is so difficult.

Profile of the International Structure of E.C.-U.S. Agribusiness

The aim of this section is to briefly discuss the recent evolution of the international structure of E.C. and U.S. agribusiness, which reflects the strategic mechanisms used by food manufacturers in the global rivalry between firms of many nations.

The agri-food sector shows some special features in the international market. Food manufacturers do relatively little exporting compared to all the other manufacturing sectors but have extensive overseas interest in direct investments.

In the case of multinational enterprises, previous work has shown that trade with affiliates is more important for nonfood multinational export and import than for food multinationals. Food multinationals focus on sales by foreign affiliates, which account for more than 25 percent of the worldwide sales (domestic sales, foreign sales, and exports), and 82 percent of food affiliate sales are in the country in which the affiliate is located (Handy and McDonald, 1989). Results derived from a survey of 57 of the largest U.S. food processing firms show, that only 2 of them export more than 15 percent of their sales of domestic processed food, 3 companies have exports that exceed 5 percent, and 4 of them report no export at all. On the other hand, 36 of the 57 firms in the sample own food processing plants in a foreign country and, taking an average of the whole sample, about 30 percent of all processing plants are located abroad (Handy and Siegle, 1989).

Nevertheless, both the United States and the E.C. are major importers and exporters of manufactured food. In 1989 the E.C. was the second largest U.S. export market for processed food as well as a major supplier of U.S. imports. E.C. countries accounted for about 23 percent of all U.S. imports and 17 percent of U.S. exports.

In particular, it is possible to underline certain differences in the behavior of agri-food industries. First, and most important, trade varies widely among different processing industries ranging, for example, from more than 70 percent for wet milling and starch to less than 1 percent for soft drinks (Handy and Henderson, 1990). In other words, exports are concentrated in firms whose products are relatively homogenous and subject to an initial stage of processing: meats, oils, rice, flour, and coffee.[1]

However, both in the case of international trading companies of commodities and in the case of highly processed food industries, integration, market power, and the multinational structure are evolving very fast. The international environment is increasingly dominated by the "triad" of economic power formed by the United States, Japan, and the European Community. Therefore, competitive strategies have to be formulated within the context of the interplay between these three economic blocks. Growing interdependence presents new profit opportunities for agricultural and food firms that can transfer and exploit competitive advantages into the international market.

In the case of commodities, a few multinationals account, both in the E.C. and in the United States, for almost all international trade, while domestic trade is mainly handled by national firms. Over the last ten years, the same 5 or 6 biggest transnational companies realized large cross-investments in the United States and the E.C. in first-processing industries such as crushing, starch, and milling. Generally speaking, international trade and investments in raw agricultural commodities seem to be driven by financial and international market capital variables and to be sensitive to macroeconomic variables such as exchange rates. The primary economic functions of big trading companies are short-term financing, transportation, and storage. They are able to forecast—and possibly influence—prices in a worldwide context and react quickly. Yet trade and FDI are also influenced by other elements. The concentration of the international trade in the hands of a few companies has given these firms the opportunity to exploit the political measures enacted for agricultural protection. For example, handling large quantities of commodities, they are able to influence price determination and, with that, may gain substantial profits from "playing" with the mechanisms of variable levies and export restitution in use in the E.C. At the same time, investments in first-processing industries were probably influenced by the possibility of capturing both domestic support and the border protection for processed products.[2]

In other words, the strategies of firms involved in the commodities trade and in first processing are mainly based on the market conditions of those countries where they can better exploit the public resources available for protection of the agricultural sector.

The case of highly processed food, on the other hand, that is typically heavily advertised and distributed through grocery chains is entirely different. In these industries, decisions of investing in food processing, grocery retailing, and food services are mainly oriented by consumer market strategies. According to data of the U.S. Bureau of Economic Analysis (1985) firm size, processing level of products, and ratio of advertising to sales account for a large percentage of the variation in foreign involvement. In particular: (a) Exports are a foreign sales strategy for firms with small foreign sales but less important for the largest firms with the greatest foreign exposure; (b) the ratio of advertising to sales has a large, positive and statistically significant impact on FDI and on the local sales of a foreign affiliate: advertising-intensive firms are more likely to affect sales to foreign countries through direct investment rather than exports. In other words, the more the product is consumer and market oriented—that is, more processed and more advertised—the greater the importance of direct investments and local sales (Martinez, 1989).

During the last decades, both the elements indicated as driving forces for increased FDI—that is, agricultural protection and highly developed consumer markets—were concentrated in the E.C. and the United States. One of the main consequences has been the big change in the geographic location of the food industry's foreign direct investment and the growth of

E.C. and U.S. cross-investment. The United States has shifted in the last twenty years from Canadian and Latin American sales (50 percent in 1966, 30 percent in 1986) to European sales (from 40 percent to 61 percent). The same occurred for E.C. firms, which have sharply increased investment in U.S. food manufactures (McDonald and Weimer, 1985).[3] The U.K. is clearly the dominant base country for foreign investment in U.S. food manufacturing. Furthermore, the British share may be understated, because several Canadian parent companies are themselves controlled by British firms.[4]

In terms of value of sales, the U.S. and E.C. food sectors are very similar in size. In 1989, the total sales value of the food processing sector was $289.7 billion in the European Community and $315.2 billion in the United States (Handy and Henderson, 1990). Both countries are dominated by a relatively small number of large, multiproduct firms that operate at home and abroad, competing among themselves regardless of nationality.

A more general international perspective confirms these characteristics. The largest 500 companies that qualified as multinationals have 90 percent of the world's FDI. About 100 of those are extensively involved in trading, processing, and distributing food and beverages. Their home country is usually advanced and industrial; on the average about 50 percent is from the United States and 50 percent from Western Europe and Japan. Generally speaking, U.S. and European multinationals have a preference for ownership of their subsidiaries while Japanese companies tend to set up joint ventures and local participation. Yet industrialized and advanced countries also received most FDI. The United States, Canada, and the U.K. are the three largest host-countries for international investments. In fact, as a rule, multinationals invest in basic sectors—such as extractive—in less developed countries, but have larger cross-investments in manufacturing and business in industrialized countries. Thus, for the most part, foreign investments in food processing sectors are geographic extensions of home-country activities rather than the result of seeking new sources of raw materials.[5]

A closer examination at the firm level confirms the framework presented above. In Table 18.1 the world's 20 largest firms in terms of sales of processed food are shown. With the exception of three Japanese companies, they are all from the United States or European countries, mainly with very large cross-investments both in the United States and in the E.C. The United States dominates the list with 12 firms, while 5 are from Europe. Several firms are not only involved in food processing but also in other agricultural activities such as commodity trade—in the food service sector (restaurants, fast food chains, and so on) as well as in different industries. For example, 50 percent of Unilever's income derives from the soap industry, while for one of the biggest grain companies like Cargill, less than 20 percent of sales comes from processed food.

TABLE 18.1 World's Largest Food Processing Firms

Company	Headquarter	Worldwide Processed Food Sales (U.S. $billions)	Share of Processed Food Sales Out of Total Sales	Major Product
1) Nestlé S.A.	Swiss	31.0	96.9%	Diversified food, restaurants
2) Philip Morris/ Kraft Gen. Foods	USA	29.8	63.4%	Foodstuffs, tobacco, beer
3) Unilever	UK/N	17.2	50.0%	Diversied food, soap
4) Conagra	USA	15.3	77.3%	Foodstuffs, meats, poultry
5) Kirin Brewery	Japan	11.2	98.2%	Beer, soft drinks
6) RJR Nabisco	USA	9.9	58.6%	Foodstuffs, tobacco
7) IBP	USA	9.5	100.0%	Meats
8) Anheuser-Bush	USA	9.3	95.9%	Beer, snacks
9) Pepsico	USA	9.0	59.2%	Soft drinks, snacks
10) Grand Metropolitan	UK	8.8	60.7%	Diversified food, restaurants
11) Coca-Cola	USA	8.5	95.5%	Soft drinks, fruit juices
12) Taiyo Fisher	Japan	8.1	90.0%	Seafood products
13) Cargill (estimated)	USA	7.9	18.4%	Meats, grains
14) Allied Lyons	UK	7.6	100.0%	Beverages, restaurants
15) BSN	France	7.5	93.8%	Snacks, bakery, beverages
16) Archer Daniels Midland	USA	7.3	92.4%	Food products, grains
17) Sara Lee	USA	7.1	60.7%	Frozen food, meals
18) Mars	USA	7.0	87.5%	Confectionery, pet food
19) Snow Brand Milk Products	Japan	6.6	100.0%	Dairy products
20) Borden	USA	6.5	85.5%	Dairy, pasta, adhesives

Source: Calculated from data collected from Handy and Henderson (1990).

Foreign Investment and Exports: Complement or Substitutes?

The rapid internationalization of the food economy forces renewed attention to the rules affecting the global market. While everyone seems to be in favor of improving international competitiveness, no one really knows how to define and measure it. As long as trade is not necessary for the international involvement of food marketing firms, competitiveness and trade are not synonymous.

There are many alternative strategies for managing foreign markets, each one involving different degrees of investment in time, money, risk, expertise, and so on. However, the conduct of firms on the international market could be described as follows:

1. Entry into the foreign market via foreign agents or brokers;
2. setting up a separate domestic export office within their company;
3. having their products packaged by a foreign firm;
4. producing and marketing their products in a foreign country under a licensing agreement;
5. making a joint venture with sharing of all expenses excluding the cost of acquiring their own subsidiary;
6. operating independently by acquiring facilities—from production assets to distribution chains—in the foreign country.[6]

The first three options relate mainly to export of domestic production while the last three need appropriate production and market procedures and involve varying degrees of direct investment. In practice, firms can use any one or all of these strategies at the same time. In the agri-business sector it is possible to recognize, once again, two different cases.

Firms involved in commodities trade and first processing are not likely to substitute their trading activities with FDI. They increased their profits during the seventies when world trade and prices were growing very fast. Consequently, they restructured in order to maximize their advantages. On the one hand, they invested in trading facilities in all major European ports in order to concentrate exports in their hands and capture most public resources allocated for export refunds. On the other hand, they reinvested profits in storage capacity and transportation facilities in the United States, in order to meet export demand on the international market.[7] In other words, one of the leading reasons for their investments in foreign business and manufactures has been simply to maximize profits deriving from their trading activities and exploit trade policies implemented by national governments. Thus, for firms with these activities, trade and FDI are not substitutes but complements.

The situation in the highly processed food industry is quite different. There, exports often seem to be a first step in foreign activity. In many cases, the degree of trade openness decreases when firm size and foreign involvement increase. Sometimes firms prefer to produce consumer food products in foreign plants rather than to export. There are several reasons accounting for this choice. Setting up production facilities in foreign countries avoids trade barriers. But even where trade barriers are minor there is a tendency to move to foreign production and local sales. For example, transportation costs are especially important for ready-for-final-consumer products. Furthermore, producing highly processed and advertised consumer products in the foreign markets makes it easier to keep up on local tastes and opportunities for product development. Finally, being in the country also serves to ease dealings with local governments and regulatory agencies. Sometimes, when FDI are large enough, firms cut their exports and focus their strategy only on local sales. Therefore, in these cases, FDI and trade do not complement, but seem to substitute each other.

The empirical situations confirm that different strategies and degrees of substitution between exporting and FDI are associated with different levels of product processing and trade openness.

Tables 18.2 and 18.3 give a breakdown of the situation within the United States and the E.C., listing the top 20 food processing firms of both ranked according to their food-processing sales. In both cases home-firms are dominant, and only two companies in the United States—namely Nestlé and Unilever—and two in the E.C.—Nestlé and Philip Morris—are foreign owned. Nevertheless, there are important differences between the multinational structure of the E.C. and the U.S. food-processing sector.

In the 5 largest U.S. firms, the share of processed food sold by foreign affiliates is very small with the only exception of Kraft General Foods, which reinforced its presence enormously in the E.C. market when it acquired the European giant Jacob Suchard in 1990. The share of sales derived from foreign affiliates of the other companies in the list is definitely greater, ranging from 30-40 percent of the sales of total processed food. The 20 largest E.C. food processing companies show less variation in food sales by their foreign affiliates.

In any case, the average share of sales by foreign affiliates is exactly the same for both the largest 20 U.S. and the 20 E.C. food firms (i.e., 70.5 percent). On the other hand, the degree of market concentration is definitely greater in the United States than in the E.C. In the United States, in fact, the top 10 firms control about 30 percent of market sales, and the largest 20 about 40 percent. In the E.C. market the same number of firms have smaller shares—that is, 20 and 30 percent respectively.

In conclusion, it is important to point out the recent rapid evolution of these firms toward a multinational structure and head-to-head competition.[8] A result of the global orientation of the food industry is the growing

TABLE 18.2 Largest Food-Processing Firms in the United States

Company	Head-quarters	Processed Food Sales in the U.S. Market (U.S. $billions)	Processed Food Sales by Foreign Affiliates (% of total sales)	U.S. Market Concentration (Σ of Market Share)
1) Philip Morris/Kraft Gen. Foods	USA	17.3	41.9%	5.5%
2) Conagra	USA	14.7	3.9%	10.1%
3) IBP	USA	9.5	0.0%	13.2%
4) Anheuser-Busch	USA	8.7	6.5%	15.9%
5) Cargill	USA	7.9	0.0%	18.4%
6) Nestlé S.A.	Switzerland	7.2	76.8%	20.7%
7) RJR Nabisco	USA	6.9	30.3%	22.9%
8) Pepsico	USA	6.8	24.4%	25.1%
9) Archer Daniels Midland	USA	5.9	19.2%	26.9%
10) Sara Lee	USA	5.5	22.5%	28.7%
11) Mars	USA	4.5	35.7%	30.1%
12) Campbell Soup	USA	4.1	29.3%	31.4%
13) General Mills	USA	4.1	8.9%	32.7%
14) Borden	USA	3.9	40.0%	33.9%
15) Coca-Cola	USA	3.9	54.1%	35.2%
16) Coca-Cola Enterprises	USA	3.9	0.0%	36.4%
17) H. J. Heinz	USA	3.7	37.3%	37.6%
18) Ralston Purina	USA	3.5	42.6%	38.7%
19) Unilever	UK/N	3.5	79.7%	39.8%
20) Quaker Oats	USA	3.4	39.3%	40.9%

Source: Calculated from data collected from Handy and Henderson (1990).

number of plants each firm owns in a foreign country. For example, Heinz operates 63 food-processing plants, 25 in the United States, 30 in the E.C. and 8 in other countries and derives more than 50 percent of its sales from foreign operations. The same goes for Campbell, which has 87 plants: 57 in the United States and 31 in the E.C. The CPC International Company has 112 plants: 29 in the United States, 29 in Europe, and 54 in other countries, and the same is true for many other of the largest international food processing firms (Handy and Siegle, 1989).

The Interests of International Agents in Trade Issues

From the preceding presentation of the international economic structure of E.C. and U.S. agribusiness sectors, it is now possible to outline and clarify the principal political issues that are involved.

TABLE 18.3 Largest Food-Processing Firms in the European Community

Company	Head-quarters	Processed Food Sales in the E.C. Market (U.S. $billion)	Processed Food Sales by Foreign Affiliates (% of total sales)	E.C. Market Concentration (Σ of Market Share)
1) Unilever	UK/N	10.9	36.7%	3.8%
2) Nestlé S.A.	Switzerland	10.8	65.2%	7.5%
3) Philip Morris	USA	7.7	74.2%	10.1%
4) BSN Groupe	France	6.2	17.3%	12.3%
5) Allied Lyons	UK	5.8	23.7%	14.3%
6) Gruppo Ferruzzi	Italy	4.9	23.4%	16.0%
7) Grand Metropolitan	UK	4.7	46.6%	17.6%
8) Bass PLC	UK	4.5	26.2%	19.2%
9) Hillsdown Holdings PLC	UK	3.5	46.2%	20.4%
10) Booker PLC	UK	3.2	8.6%	21.5%
11) Cadbury Schweppes PLC	UK	3.1	35.4%	22.5%
12) Guiness	UK	3.0	41.2%	23.6%
13) United Biscuit	UK	3.0	31.8%	24.6%
14) Associated British Food	UK	2.9	27.5%	25.6%
15) Pernod Richard Groupe	France	2.6	0.0%	26.5%
16) Heineken N.V.	Netherlands	2.6	27.8%	27.4%
17) Unigate PLC	UK	2.5	32.4%	28.3%
18) Ranks Hovis McDougall	UK	2.4	17.2%	29.1%
19) Coop Melkprod. Noord	Netherlands	2.3	0.0%	29.9%
20) Sudflesiah	Germany	2.0	0.0%	30.6%

Source: Calculated from data collected from Handy and Henderson (1990).

The interest of traders and processors in commercial policies—that is, free trade or protection—is related to the effects and consequences that any policy has on their income. From a political economy point of view, each group seeks, in various ways, a redistribution of income through tariffs and other trade barriers; on the other hand, policymakers are expected to meet these domestic expectations in order to maximize their own objective-function.

The political economy literature has until now been mainly concerned with domestic lobbies—namely, producers and consumers—without taking into account the existence of international groups that are differently affected by commercial policies. Yet, in the world economy, there is a growing role of groups with multinational features. They can transfer capital internationally in order to influence trade policy decisions in an external political arena. Despite the importance of investigating these foreign lobbies, few works in the new political economy literature deal with their political interest and not one of these refers to agriculture.

The following discussion addresses the interests, in terms of free-trade or protection, of "international agents" involved in the agribusiness sector. Let us assume that multinational companies implement a symmetrical lobbying activity both at home and abroad. With this in mind, a general pattern of economic and policy determination regarding trade can be drawn, as in Figure 18.1.[9] The traditional theory of trade is concerned with the relationship represented by link 1. The inquiry is conducted using well-known neoclassical assumptions about factor endowment and mobility, domestic and international competition, and technology. To the extent that the government is included—that is, only in the case of market failure—it is expected to maximize a social welfare function. Link 1 could also represent the field of interest of imperfect competition in international trade. In fact, introducing an imperfect competition approach along with the agents operating in different countries allows the analysis to probe the effects of different kinds of trade restrictions on international strategic interaction and therefore, on new equilibrium prices.

On the other hand, links 2 and 3 represent a more comprehensive field of investigation for new political economy analyses. In the new framework, the lobbies are assumed to act in each country (link 2) and across

FIGURE 18.1 Trade Policy Determination with Foreign Lobbies.

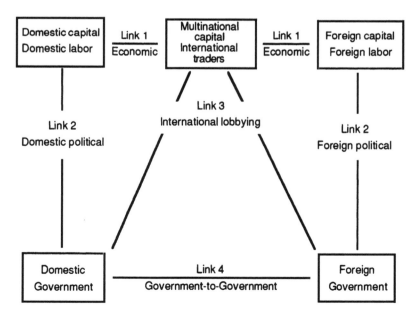

borders (link 3) through the efforts of those agents who can influence a foreign government. Finally, the direct relationships between domestic and foreign governments are represented by link 4. The General Agreement on Tariffs and Trade (GATT) is a major example of the attempt to approach these issues by multilateral negotiations. But there could be bilateral arrangements between the most important developed countries that are not neutral with respect to the protection of their assets abroad. Sometimes diplomatic channels are used to influence policymakers of other countries. However, economist have rarely considered such interactions and have left this field of interest to political scientists.[10]

With regard to agriculture and to the E.C.-U.S. agricultural trade relationship, the question is which elements must be utilized for analyzing the political interests of traders and processors. The political antagonism that emerged between the E.C. and the United States with regard to agricultural trade and processing was reflected mainly on third markets by the use of export subsidies. The Export Enhancement Program (EEP) implemented by the United States in 1985 is an example of an export policy that was designed in retaliation to E.C. export restitutions. Several works present models of the interactions of these policies involving governments, marketing boards, and private firms, in an oligo-polistic approach in order to analyze the effects of various indirect policy instruments—i.e., tax and/or subsidies—that affect the production and exchange of imperfectly substitutive goods.[11] Yet, the interests and the role of the multinational firms affecting trade policies at home and abroad may in this case be ambiguous since in order to meet export commitments they buy grain from various sources and are involved in different level of processing activities.

As has been noted previously, the importance and the characteristics of intra-industry sale—by trade and foreign direct investments—yields remarkable differences in the strategies adopted in the agri-business sectors. Looking at the U.S. market we can assume that the decisions of firms with regard to production and sales will depend on:

1. The state of the U.S. domestic market;
2. the possibilities of exporting to the E.C. market and to third markets;
3. the ability to produce in the E.C. using foreign assets;
4. the share of European exports to third markets that U.S. multinationals can manage by their E.C.-based foreign subsidiaries.

A symmetrical pattern applies, of course, to the E.C. market. Each one of these elements is an outcome of the interactions between market structure and policies implemented inside and outside the two countries.

In the E.C., for instance, domestic production and sales depend on the internal degree of competition in the commodities and food industries as well as on feasible export and processing subsidies implemented to compensate for high domestic support prices of basic commodities. Furthermore, both processing and export subsidies (restitutions) influence flows directed from the E.C. to the United States and to third markets. The actual calculation of export subsidies for E.C.-processed food can be extremely complicated, especially for those products containing many basic commodities involved in the CAP's export restitutions. From the point of view of firms, these internal and external subsidies—in addition to others paid on certain products according to destination—benefit all producers located in Europe. In fact, these measures affect the performance of both E.C. firms and U.S. assets located abroad. Furthermore, E.C. food processors, along with U.S. multinational firms producing in the E.C., have a competitive advantage for products shipped to third markets over similar products shipped from the U.S. mainland.

The same situation applies to the agents—domestic and international—located in the United States. The United States does not have an internal policy for subsidizing processors, but the U.S. Food Security Act of 1985 authorized several export promotion programs designed to increase U.S. exports of agri-food products. Several European exporting firms are participating in the U.S. EEP. The British Pillsbury Company, for instance, ranks as the seventh firm in total value of EEP bonuses received as of February 1989 (General Accounting Office, 1990). Furthermore, the EEP includes—in addition to agricultural commodities—initiatives for processed foods such as flour or frozen poultry.[12] In addition, the Target Export Assistance (TEA) uses surplus stocks from the Commodity Credit Corporation (CCC) to reimburse U.S. exporters. 80 percent of the $110 million of TEA allocations in 1986 went to support specific processed exports such as fruit cocktail, frozen vegetables, California wine, and others. TEA was also used to expand the export of processed food in general, by subsidizing a variety of activities including advertising, point of sales materials, and restaurant promotions. A Dairy Export Incentive Program (DEIP) also exists, which enables U.S. exporters to meet prevailing world prices for targeted dairy products to specific destinations. This program offers U.S. exporters subsidies in the form of dairy products in the CCC stockpile. In addition, the United States has several export credit guarantee programs to increase or maintain U.S. exports to foreign markets.

As in the E.C. case previously shown, these U.S. external subsidies may represent part of the interest of E.C. producers in foreign trade policies by affecting the amount of competition on third markets and the performance of exports of U.S.-based E.C. multinationals.

Figure 18.2 sketches a rough idea of the several elements that have been

FIGURE 18.2 U.S. and E.C. Market Flows and Policies in the Food Sector.

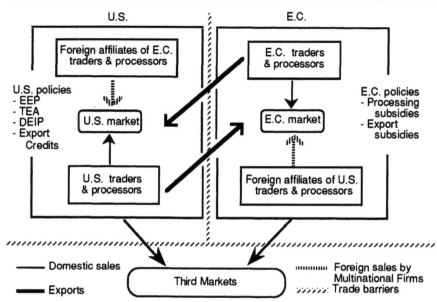

considered in the previous discussion. The chart shows the different flows of domestic sales and exports in the U.S. and the E.C. markets and the most important policies implemented in the two countries. On the one hand, multinational groups can benefit from domestic subsidies in each country and, at the same time, avoid tariffs and trade barriers by managing their intrafirm trade. On the other hand, even if they receive export subsidies in both countries where they operate, the price war decreases the terms of trade for their commodities.

However, the price war is not likely to end merely because export subsidies are cut off. It has been shown in fact how the emerging strategies are no longer based on geographical borders, but on head-to-head global competition in a worldwide oligopolistic environment. Thus, unless firms turn to a strategy of collusive behavior not solely across borders but also among themselves, they are going to keep competing for market shares in third markets.

Generally speaking, the possibility that a second-best policy, like subsidies, is in the interest of firms depends on the existence of some distortion, which, in the case of agricultural trade, is the imperfectly competitive market structure (Brander and Spencer, 1985). On the one hand, the case of international grain companies has shown that they gained advantage from existing agricultural protection that, in the course of the last two decades, has guaranteed growing trading profits. They have also made foreign investments in order to increase their commercial activity. In other words, agricultural subsidies could have encouraged a kind of rent-seeking activity. On the other hand, it has been demonstrated that interest in international trade issues diminishes along the value-added chain of the agri-business sector. The more highly processed the products are, the greater the role of consumer market variables and the FDI then turns into a substitute for trading activity. Yet even in this case, there are no special reasons why multinational firms should prefer free trade. Instead, they could derive advantage from the oligopolistic environment created by trade restrictions. As a result, international agents in agri-business probably will not lobby for free trade either at home or—as usually postulated in the theory of international trade for the foreign export industry—abroad.

Concluding Remarks

The previous discussion highlighted the growing economic and political power of multinationals and their interests in international trade. Although for different reasons, neither commodity traders nor food processors seem to be really advantaged by trade liberalization. Instead, it has been shown how they can very often benefit from trade protection. The effort that those agents made to adjust to new conditions of the international market suggests that, at least in the short run, they are not going to be interested in lobbying for free trade as suggested in the traditional literature on multinationals.

Furthermore, trade restrictions can be very advantageous for large firms from another point of view. It can be shown, in fact, how trade restrictions, when firms compete in an oligopolistic environment, alter the nature of interaction in a collusive direction—even if the export is set at the free-trade level, thereby raising the equilibrium price and the profits.[13] Thus, as long as a few firms are powerful enough, they could try to set up special arrangements—such as orderly-marketing arrangements (OMAs), voluntary export restraints (VERs), and so on—in order to increase their profits and, at the same time, to be sheltered from the competition of fringe firms.

Since international trade relations in recent years have seen the emergence and the enormous increase in number of such measures, VERs have often been explored as a political remedy for import disruption. Crisis conditions in the international markets of a large number of manufactured goods have created pressure for protectionism, causing U.S. and E.C. trade authorities in particular to look to VERs as an alternative to the traditional instruments of trade control whose use is severely restricted by international trade agreements. But one of the main features of such arrangements—euphemistically called "gray-area measures"—is that no legislative struggle is needed, and government involvement in them is often ambiguous and limited to administrative and bureaucratic levels. Sometimes nongovernment measures could include agreements, whether explicit or implicit, between industrial groups in the exporting and importing countries (Finger, 1989; Krishna, 1989; Harris, 1985).

In conclusion, it is important to stress how the rapid internationalization of the food economy, as well as of other sectors, needs renewed attention to the rules affecting the global market. In particular, there could be the actual risk that, as a consequence of the enlargement and the growing power of private industrial groups in international markets, firm sovereignty could replace national sovereignty in matters of international policy (Handy and Henderson, 1990). The main result of this would be the replacement of a trade policy with a business policy and the shift from the goal of public welfare maximization to the goal of maximizing the private profits function. In some cases, negotiated export agreements have been an example of such negative policies (Feenstra and Lewis, 1987). In fact, by raising prices, they favor the few agents allowed into trade, while they hurt consumers and others who are excluded from the negotiating process.

The policy question here becomes how it is possible to defend international markets not just from traditional protectionism but also from this new protectionism that is very difficult to identify and that sometimes almost looks like a sort of perverse form of international cooperation. But there is another issue even more important in terms of policy recommendation. It has been mentioned how lobbying for protection could be seen as a device for obtaining higher profits, competing—at the international level—in a subsidized, oligopolistic market structure. Thus, the most important political action would be not just to pursue generic free trade, but also to control and regulate the existing and growing degree of monopoly in international markets. In other words, two main courses of action should be pursued in order to obtain freer trade. On the one hand, prevent the possibility of increasing cartellizations in the world commodity market (Pindyck, 1979). On the other hand, prevent just a few multinational firms from dominating the entire agribusiness sector in the future.

Despite their importance, these issues have been completely absent from the agenda of the GATT. In essence, there are two new challenges emerging in the international framework: The first one is related to the so-called new protectionism, which is fundamentally at variance with the principle of nondiscrimination, as expressed in Article I and XIII of the GATT, and with the multilateralism of the international trading system. The second one is improving the regulation of international policies so that it will be possible to have better control over the concentration of international markets.

Notes

The research for this chapter was supported by the National Research Council of Italy (CNR-NATO Fellowship Programme). I am also grateful to "The Arkleton Trust International Rural Exchange Fellowship Pro-gramme" for financial support and to the Department of Agricultural Economics, University of California, Davis, where I was visiting scholar during the time this chapter was written. A very special thanks to Alex McCalla for his valuable help and encouragement.

1. A consequence of this situation is the difference of export share in bulk and processed agricultural products. The United States, for instance, exports 21 percent of world bulk agriculture but only 5 percent of world processed food.

2. An interesting analysis of these problems is developed in Scoppola (1993).

3. In 1984, for the first time, foreign companies owned a greater amount of equity in the U.S. food sector than the reverse. Around 70 percent was in the food-processing sector and 30 percent in wholesaling and retailing (Institute of Food Technologists, 1988).

4. There are several reasons for the high British share of FDI mainly related to similarities in the United States and the U.K. The language especially may give British firms an advantage over other foreign entrants in the marketing and development of branded consumer products. British firms are especially active in preserved food and vegetables, beverages, tobacco, and pet food, all industries in which advertising and marketing play important roles. The principal exception to this rule is brewing. Special reasons account for the absence of foreign investment in brewing. American tastes differ considerably from European tastes in beer, and modern beer production is subject to considerable economies of scale. Therefore foreign markets are still too small to allow the construction of breweries. As a result, breweries tend to license the use of their brands rather than invest overseas.

5. Investing in advanced countries, multinationals are more likely to get their foreign activities financed through national savings of the host-country. Previous work has shown that about 30 percent of multinational financing derives from the host country's financial institutions and 50 percent from undistributed profits (Connor, 1984).

6. It is important to emphasize that licensing and joint venture are not included in trade and investment statistics and are also omitted in the company annual reports. This makes it more difficult to evaluate competitiveness.

7. Important business is done in the United States by private traders with storage activities for the Commodity Credit Corporation (CCC).

8. For example, Nestlé acquired the leading Italian pasta firm Buitoni in 1988 and became a European leader in the pasta sector. After a short while, the same company also acquired a small U.S. pasta firm specifically to obtain its technology for preserving and packaging fresh pasta. At the same time, Borden—the U.S. pasta leader—bought two regional Italian pasta firms in 1989 and 1990 and is now consolidating pasta production into large hyper-plants both in the United States and the E.C. A parallel integration is going on in the input industries. Large food manufacturers are looking for "one-stop shopping" in their ingredient suppliers who are consolidating to meet this need. (Handy and Henderson, 1990).

9. The original idea of this chart is drawn from a recent contribution concerning the political economy literature (Moore, 1990). However, in that paper policy determination was related only to domestic issues.

10. For example, in the United States, the Departments of State and Commerce have policies and programs to facilitate foreign investment by U.S. companies (Connor, 1984). In 1976 Mexico changed its law on trademarks and patents subsequent to a strong note of protest from the U.S. Department of State.

11. Literature on these topics studies the nature of competition in the export market and interprets policy analysis. The majority of studies abstract from behavior of firms and focus on countries as agents with market power. More recent studies have investigated an imperfectly competitive agricultural market in the presence of marketing boards and large exporting firms (Alouze, *et al.*, 1978; Gruenspecht, 1988; Just, *et al.*, 1979; Karp and McCalla, 1983; Kolstad and Burris, 1986; Krishna and Thursby, 1988; 1990; Markusen, 1984; McCalla, 1966; Mc Nally, 1990; Paarlberg and Abbott, 1984; Pindyck, 1979; Schmitz, *et al.*, 1981; Thursby, 1988; Thursby and Thursby, 1990).

12. The EEP mechnism for processed food is the same as for commodities. Exporters submit bids to the USDA and when bids are approved a bonus is paid in generic certificates that can be exchanged for commodities from the CCC.

13. There is an increasing amount of literature on the subject of international trade under imperfect competition and trade restriction (Pindyck, 1979; Kent, 1984; Wolf, 1989; Krishna, 1989; Brecher and Bhagwati, 1987; Harris, 1985). Furthermore, profit increases obtained by export restriction mean, on the positive side, that there could be a specific interest collusion even in supporting these types of trade policies. It has been shown how, in a framework where foreign interests have a role in the determination of domestic trade policy, voluntary export restraints (VERs) are consistent with conciliatory positions, while tariffs are divisive (Hillman and Ursprung, 1988). This model basically offers a positive interpretation of the strategic collusive features of a VER versus a tariff.

References

Alouze, C., A. Watson, and N. Sturgess. 1978. "Oligopoly Pricing in the World Wheat Market." *American Journal of Agricultural Economics* 60: 173-85.

Becker, G. 1983. "A Theory of Competition Among Pressure Groups for Political Influence." *The Quarterly Journal of Economics* 98: 371-401.

Bureau of Economic Analysis. 1985. "U.S. Direct Investment Abroad." Benchmark Survey.

Brander, J., and B. Spencer. 1985. "Export Subsidies and International Markets Share Rivalry." *Journal of International Economics* 18: 83-100.

Brecher, A., and J. Bhagwati. 1987. "Voluntary Export Restrictions Versus Import Restrictions: A Welfare-theoretic Comparison." In *Protection and Competition in International Trade*, edited by H. Kiezkowski. Oxford, U.K.: Basil Blackwell, pp. 41-55.

Carter, C., A. McCalla, and J. Sharples, eds. 1990. *Imperfect Competition and Political Economy: The New Trade Theory in Agricultural Trade Research.* Boulder, CO: Westview Press.

Caves, R. 1982. *Multinational Enterprise and Economic Analysis.* Cambridge, MA: Cambridge Univ. Press.

Connor, J. 1984. *Multinational Firms In the World Food Marketing System.* Cooperative Extension Service, Michigan State University, East Lansing, MI.

Das, S. 1986. "Foreign Lobbying and the Political Economy of Protection." Working Paper, Indiana University, Bloomington, IN.

Elleson, R. 1990. *High-Value Products: Growing U.S. and E.C. Competition in World Markets.* USDA ERS Agricultural Trade Analysis Division.

Ethier, W. 1986. "The Multinational Firm." *The Quarterly Journal of Economics* Vol. CI: 805-33.

Feenstra, R., and T. Lewis. 1987. "Negotiated Trade Restrictions With Private Political Pressure." National Bureau of Economic Research. Working Paper No. 2374, Cambridge, MA. September.

Finger, M. 1989. "Protectionist Rules and International Discretion in the Making of National Trade Policy." In *New Institutional Arrangments for the World Economy,* edited by Hans Jurgen Vorsgeran. Berlin: Springer-Verlag.

General Accounting Office. 1990. "International Trade: Activity Under the Export Enhancement Program." Fact Sheet for Congressional Requesters No. 1.

Gruenspecht, H. 1988. "Export Subsidies for Differentiated Products." *Journal of International Economics* 24: 331-44.

Handy, C., and D. Henderson. 1990. "Implications of a Single E.C. Market for the U.S. Food Manufactures Sector." In *Impacts of Europe 1992 on the Processed Food Industries.* Dept. of Agricultural Economics, Ohio State Univ., Columbus. NC-194 Economic Studies, Report No. 1.

Handy, C., and M. McDonald. 1989. "Multinational Structures and Strategies of U.S. Food Firms." *American Journal of Agricultural Economics* 71: 1246-254.

Handy, C., and N. Siegle. 1989. "International Profile of US Food Processors." *Journal of Food and Distribution Research* 1: 5-11.

Harris, C. 1985. "Why Voluntary Export Restraints Are Voluntary." *Canadian Journal of Economics* 18: 799-809.

Helpman, E. 1984. "A Simple Theory of International Trade with Multinational Corporations." *Journal of Political Economy* 92: 451-71.

Hillman, A. 1989. *The Political Economy of Protection.* Chur-London-Paris: Harwood Academic Publishers.

Hillman, A., and W. Ursprung. 1988. "Domestic Politics, Foreign Interest, and International Trade Policy." *American Economic Review* 78: 729-745.

Husted, S. 1986. "Foreign Lobbying: A Theoretical Analysis." Paper presented at *Western Economic Association Meetings* at San Francisco, July.

Institute of Food Technologists. 1988. "The Growth and Economic Impact of the Food Processing Industry." Summary Report, Chicago, May.

Just, R., A. Schmitz, and D. Zilberman. 1979. "Price Controls and Optimal Export Policies Under Alternative Market Structures." *American Economic Review* 69: 706-15.

Karp, L., and A. McCalla. 1983. "Dynamic Games and International Trade: An Application to the World Corn Market." *American Journal of Agricultural Economics* 65: 641-56.

Kent, J. 1984. "The Political Economy of Voluntary Export Restraint Agreements." *Kyklos* 37; 1: 82-101.

Kolstad, C., and A. Burris. 1986. "Imperfectly Competitive Equilibria in International Commodity Markets." *American Journal of Agricultural Economics* 68: 25-36.

Krishna, K. 1989. "Trade Restrictions as Facilitating Practices." *Journal of International Economics* 26: 251-70.

Krishna, K., and M. Thursby. 1988. "Optimal Policies With Strategic Distortions." *National Bureau of Economic Research*, Working Paper No. 2527, Cambridge, MA.

———. 1990. "Trade Policy With Imperfect Competition: A Selective Survey." In *Imperfect Competition and Political Economy: The New Trade Theory in Agricultural Trade Research*, edited by C. Carter, A. McCalla, and J. Sharples. Boulder, CO: Westview Press, pp. 9-35.

Krueger, A. 1974. "The Political Economy of the Rent Seeking Society." *American Economic Review* 64: 291-303.

Magee, S. 1984. "Endogenous Tariff Theory: A Survey." In *Neoclassical Political Economy: The Analysis of Rent-Seeking and DUP Activities*, edited by D. Colander. New York: Ballinger Publishing Company.

Markusen, J. 1984. "The Welfare and Allocative Effects of Export Taxes Versus Marketing Board." *Journal of Development Economics* 14: 19-36.

Martinez, A. 1989. "US Food Processors Expanding Overseas." *Farmline*, June, pp. 4-7.

McCalla, A. 1966. "A Duopoly Model of World Wheat Pricing." *Journal of Farm Economics* 48: 711-27.

McDonald, M., and S. Weimer. 1985. "Increased Foreign Investments in U.S. Food Industries." ERS USDA, Report No. 540, Washington, D.C.

McNally, M. 1990. *Strategic Interactions in the International Wheat Market*. Dissertation Research Prospectus. Department of Agricultural Economics, University of California, Davis.

Moore, M. 1990. "New Developments in the Political Economy of Protectionism." In *Imperfect Competition and Political Economy: The New Trade Theory in Agricultural Trade Research*, edited by C. Carter, A. McCalla, and J. Sharples. Boulder, CO: Westview Press, pp. 143-167.

Ohmae, K. 1987. *Beyond National Border*. Homewood, IL: Dow Jones-Irwin.

Olson, M. 1965. *The Logic of Collective Action and the Theory of Groups*. Cambridge: Harvard Univ. Press.

Paarlberg, P., and P. Abbott. 1984. "Towards a Countervailing Power Theory of World Wheat Trade." In *International Agricultural Trade*, edited by G. Storey, A. Schmitz and A. Sarris. London: Westview Press.

Peltzman, S. 1976. "Towards a More General Theory of Regulation." *Journal of Law and Economics* 19: 211-240.

Pindyck, R. 1979. "The Cartelization of World Commodity Markets." *American Economic Review*. May, 69: 154-158.

Ray, E. 1990. "Empirical Research on the Political Economy of Trade." In *Imperfect Competition and Political Economy: The New Trade Theory in Agricultural Trade*

Research, edited by C. Carter, A. McCalla, and J. Sharples. Boulder, CO: Westview Press, pp. 175-214.

Rugman, A., and A. Verbeke. 1990. *Global Corporate Strategy and Trade Policy.* London and New York: Routledge.

Schmitz, A., A. McCalla, D. Mitchell, and C. Carter. 1981. *Grain Export Cartels.* Cambridge, MA: Ballinger.

Scoppola, M. 1993. "La riforma della Pac e gli interessi delle multinazionali." *La Questione Agraria* 52. Forthcoming.

Stolper, W., and P. Samuelson. 1941. "Protection and Real Wage." *Review of Economic Studies* 9: 58-73.

Thursby, M. 1988. "Strategic Models, Market Structure, and State Trading: An Application to Agriculture." *Trade Policy Issues and Empirical Analysis,* edited by R. Baldwin. Chicago: Univ. of Chicago Press.

Thursby, M., and J. Thursby. 1990. "Strategic Trade Theory and Agricultural Markets: An Application to Canadian and U.S. Wheat Export to Japan." In *Imperfect Competition and Political Economy: The New Trade Theory in Agricultural Trade Research,* edited by C. Carter, A. McCalla, and J. Sharples. Boulder, CO: Westview Press, pp. 87-106.

Wolf, M. 1989. "Why Voluntary Export Restraints? An Historical Analysis." *World Economy,* September, pp. 273-291.

19

Bringing U. S. Sugar Policy into the GATT

Jonathan Brooks

Introduction

The success of the U.S. sugar industry in securing a high degree of protection is commonly attributed to political factors. Important among these are the commanding role that congressional committees and sub-committees play in the legislative process; the practice of vote-trading among commodity interests; the nature of the omnibus farm bill process; and sugar's status as a net import, which means that protection can be afforded without the need for transparent government outlays. Underlying such explanations is the presumption that government policy, rather than being exogenous, is endogenously "captured" according to the interactions of interest groups. This rationale for government action has been portrayed in economic theories of political behavior, first by Stigler (1971) and subsequently by Peltzman (1976) and Becker (1983). These theories model a political marketplace in which policies respond to a balance of competing political pressures. Gardner (1987) has found this approach to be broadly successful in explaining the causes of U.S. commodity programs.

The manner in which interest groups seek input into the policy process is complex and frequently unquantifiable. However, by considering congressional amendments to sugar legislation it is possible to gauge the effect that pro- and anti-sugar lobbying has had on the voting decisions of legislators. In particular, it is possible to measure the extent to which campaign contributions from interest groups have influenced voting outcomes. Such an approach can be framed implicitly in the context of "capture" theories of government by making voting decisions contingent upon pressures exerted from different interest-group sources.

A simultaneous relationship between votes and money is specified in this study, where a congressman's propensity to vote in favor of pro-sugar legislation depends on political action committee (PAC)[1] contributions received from pro- and anti-sugar interest coalitions (as well as other size-related measures of interest group pressure), while the propensity of each of these coalitions to contribute to a particular congressman depends on the likelihood of that congressman voting in their favor. The effect of vote-trading is captured by considering the effect that campaign contributions from non-sugar groups have on sugar votes. This approach differs from that adopted in single-equation studies (Welch, 1982; Turner, 1986) and from simultaneous models that ignore the role of competing campaign contributions (Abler, 1991). By quantifying the effectiveness of pro- and anti-sugar lobbying, it should be possible to gauge the sources and amount of political pressure necessary to reverse the observed voting outcomes and bring U.S. sugar policy more into line with GATT stipulations.

Policy Background

The sugar policy of the United States supports returns to domestic producers and processors, while providing limited access for sugar imports. The main policy instruments are a "tariff-rate" quota on imports, which is set at a level that ensures the policies do not result in budgetary costs, and the provision of support through a loan rate. Since 1985, the loan rate has stood at 18 cents per pound. This supported domestic raw cane prices at an average of 21.8 cents per pound over the period 1985-92, while world raw cane prices averaged 8.8 cents per pound over the same period. Under this price umbrella (and further fueled by reductions in grain price supports), total U.S. sugar production increased by 33 percent between 1985 and 1992, from 5.42 to 7.23 million short tons per year.[2] The size of tariff-rate quota necessary to maintain domestic prices above the loan rate has varied with fluctuations in the world sugar price, but there has been a general tightening of the quota in line with domestic production increases. The tariff-rate quota for 1993 is set at 1.36 million short tons, compared with a 1985 import quota of 2.68 million short tons (the 1990 farm bill guarantees minimum import access of 1.25 million short tons per year).

Winners and Losers from U.S. Policy

Isolation from the world market has clearly benefited domestic sugar producers. In addition, high support prices have fostered the use of alternative sweeteners, such as high fructose corn syrup (HFCS), which has almost completely replaced sugar in the soft drinks market. Artificial sweeteners now account for about one-half of all U.S. sweetener consumption. Protection of the U.S. sugar market has cost domestic consumers an estimated \$2.3-\$2.9 billion per year in the form of higher prices and imposed net costs on the U.S. economy of around \$780 million per year (Sturgiss, 1990).[3] Consumers pay approximately \$2.60 for every dollar transferred to producers—the cost being so high because consumers pay more for all sweeteners, not just sugar.

Higher U.S. production of sugar and other sweeteners and lower U.S. consumption of sugar has been associated with a reduced demand for imports. This is estimated to have depressed world sugar prices by 21-33 percent over the period 1982-88 (ABARE).[4] Lower world sugar prices have imposed major costs on sugar-exporting countries. Although quota recipients have gained from sales to the high-priced U.S. market, U.S. policies have imposed net costs on these countries, as the size of the quota has contracted and nonquota exports have fetched lower prices. Despite receiving a portion of the U.S. quota, ABARE estimate that U.S. policies cost Australia between \$90 million and \$230 million a year from 1982 to 1988. The Caribbean countries (ostensibly favored by the quota arrangements) gained at the beginning of this period but lost an estimated \$110 million in 1988. By contrast, major beneficiaries have been the world's sugar importers, principally, Japan, China, and the former Soviet Union. The net cost to the world economy (excluding the United States) is estimated at between \$310 million and \$490 million a year over the period 1982-88. This estimate excludes costs to sweetener-using industries, such as confectionery.

The GATT Ruling

In 1988, Australia complained to the GATT that U.S. sugar import quotas were in violation of GATT Article XI, which broadly prohibits quantitative import restrictions.[5] In June 1989, a panel appointed by the GATT council ruled against the United States. The U.S. Administration agreed to accept this ruling and implement the changes necessary to bring U.S. sugar policy into compliance with GATT obligations. However, when U.S. sugar policy provisions were next considered at the time of the 1990 farm bill, Congress failed to abide by the Administration's commitment and approved what was essentially an extension of existing policy. Although the President signed into law a policy known to be in violation of the GATT injunction, attempts to fashion a GATT-consistent policy failed to muster the necessary political support in Congress. An understanding of the determinants of congressional behavior is thus central to an assessment of why Congress has failed to approve a GATT-consistent policy and what political changes would be necessary to reverse this position.[6]

Congressional Votes on U.S. Sugar Legislation

Three sugar-related amendments to the 1990 and 1985 farm bills are considered in this chapter. The first, a 1990 House amendment to lower the loan rate for sugar from 18 cents per pound to 16 cents per pound through fiscal 1995 was defeated 150 to 271. The second, a Senate motion to kill an amendment containing the same loan rate reduction was agreed upon 54 to 44. The third, a 1985 House amendment to lower the loan rate by 1 cent per year until it reached 15 cents per pound (and to eliminate the cost of transportation as one of the factors used in setting the market stabilization price of sugar), considered for purposes of historical comparison, was defeated 142 to 263.

None of these motions would, by themselves, have been sufficient to bring U.S. sugar policy in line with GATT stipulations. But their adoption would have signaled an important defeat for sugar interests and a first step toward GATT consistency. Measuring the determinants of voting decisions on these pieces of legislation gives some measure of the pro- and anti-GATT forces at work in Congress.

The Relevance of Floor Votes

Empirical analysis of the impact that campaign contributions have on voting behavior captures just one link in the chain of legislative policy formation. The comprehensive nature of farm bill legislation makes for frantic "behind the scenes" activity in the development phase, as interest groups seek to ensure that their own interests are represented in the final legislation. Roll-call votes are of diminished significance to the extent that controversies are discussed and compromised on before the issue ever comes to a vote (the committees and subcommittees of Congress play a vital role in this regard).

Yet whilst studies of floor votes are incapable of capturing the process of issue selection, agenda setting, amendment introduction, or the politics of compromise generally, they are uniquely informative. In the first place, they provide information on an important aspect of the legislative process. Even though floor votes represent just part of the story, consideration of these votes provides important insights into how legislators respond to different modes of political pressure. Moreover, roll-call votes represent the best empirical measure available. Tying these to measures of political pressure provides at least some way of quantifying the effectiveness of interest group lobbying. Other facets of the policy process are difficult to assess, except in descriptive terms. It also seems reasonable to believe that the pattern of political pressure manifested on the floor of Congress may bear some relation to the pattern of political pressure exerted at other stages of the policy process.

Notwithstanding these arguments, the complexity of the policy process and the leeway afforded to the Administration in the implementation of policy mean that care must be taken not to overdraw the conclusions from studies of voting behavior. The effect of political pressure on legislators' votes may differ from its impact on enacted policy.

The Model

A simultaneous probit-tobit system is specified such that the propensity of congressman i to vote in favor of pro-sugar legislation depends on the propensity of both sugar and (opposing) sweetener-user interests to contribute campaign funds, while the propensity of each of these interests to contribute also depends on the likelihood of the congressman voting in their favor. The structural equations are given by:

$$Y_{1i}^* = \gamma_{12}Y_{2i}^* + \gamma_{13}Y_{3i}^* + X_{1i}'\beta_1 + \varepsilon_{1i} \tag{1}$$

$$Y_{2i}^* = \gamma_{21}Y_{1i}^* + \gamma_{23}Y_{3i}^* + X_{2i}'\beta_2 + \varepsilon_{2i} \tag{2}$$

$$Y_{3i}^* = \gamma_{31}Y_{1i}^* + \gamma_{32}Y_{2i}^* + X_{2i}'\beta_3 + \varepsilon_{3i} , \tag{3}$$

where Y_{1i}^* is a latent variable indicating the propensity of the ith congressman to vote in favor of the pro-sugar amendment, and Y_{2i}^* and Y_{3i}^* measure the propensity of sugar and sweetener-user interests respectively to contribute to congressman i. The observed counterpart of Y_{1i}^* is given by:

$$Y_{1i} = \begin{cases} 1 & if \ Y_{1i}^* > 0 \\ 0 & if \ Y_{1i}^* \leq 0 , \end{cases} \tag{4}$$

where $Y_{1i} = 1$ for a "yes" vote and $Y_{1i} = 0$ for a "no" vote. Thus, a congressman votes "yes" if the propensity to do so is greater than zero and "no" if the propensity is less than or equal to zero. The observed counterparts of Y_{2i}^* and Y_{3i}^* are defined such that:

$$Y_{2i} = \begin{cases} Y_{2i}^* & if \ Y_{2i}^* > 0 \\ 0 & if \ Y_{1i}^* \leq 0 \end{cases} \tag{5}$$

$$Y_{3i} = \begin{cases} Y_{3i}^* & if \ Y_{3i}^* > 0 \\ 0 & if \ Y_{1i}^* \leq 0 , \end{cases} \tag{6}$$

where Y_{2i} represents campaign contributions from sugar interests and Y_{3i} represents contributions from sweetener-user interests. In each case, contributions are equal to the propensity to contribute, unless the propensity to contribute is less than or equal to zero, in which case contributions are zero. For the 1990 House and Senate votes, campaign contributions in the

1989-90 election cycle are considered, while for the 1985 House vote, contributions made in the 1985-86 election cycle are used.[7] The political action committees that comprise "sugar" and "sweetener-user" interests are listed in the appendix.

The symbols γ_{12}, γ_{13}, γ_{21}, γ_{23}, γ_{31}, and γ_{32} are parameters, while β_1, β_2, and β_3 are vectors of coefficients of the exogenous variables, all to be estimated. The disturbance term ε_i is a random drawing from the $N(0,\Omega)$ distribution. Since equation (1) is of the probit form, the underlying parameters of interest are $\partial E[Y_1]/\partial Y_2^*$ and $\partial E[Y_1]/\partial Y_3^*$. Since $E[Y_{1i}] = \Phi(\gamma_{12}Y_{2i}^* + \gamma_{13}Y_{3i}^* + X_{1i}'\beta_1)$, by the chain rule $\partial E[Y_{1i}]/\partial Y_j^* = \phi(\gamma_{12}Y_{2i}^* + \gamma_{13}Y_{3i}^* + X_{1i}'\beta_1) \bullet \gamma_{1j}$, $j=2,3$. These show how the expected probability of a favorable vote increases with the propensity to contribute more money. In each case, the expectations are evaluated at the sample means of the explanatory variables. The parameters γ_{21} and γ_{31} measure the extent to which changes in a congressman's likelihood of voting in favor of the contributing coalition's position is likely to elicit more money.

The vector of variables X_{1i} captures the exogenous determinants of the congressman's voting decision. Contributions from corn; cotton and rice; peanuts and tobacco; and dairy PACs over the same period are included to gauge the extent of vote-trading among commodity coalitions. This captures the effect whereby coalitions of commodity interests work together to defend individual programs (in this case sugar) against attacks during the development of omnibus farm bill legislation. In addition, corn interests gain from higher sugar support prices since this fosters the use of corn-based sweeteners, while cotton and rice policy is covered by the same House subcommittee as sugar. The incorporation of peanut and tobacco, and dairy interests extends coverage to the traditional "farm bloc." Inclusion of the total number of sugar farms in the congressman's constituency controls for the influence that sugar farms exert on congressmen by virtue of their presence in the constituency and independent of financial lobbying. The number of non-sugar farms is included to control for support provided by other farming interests (that is, vote-trading).[8] A dummy for committee membership measures the extent to which agriculture committee members are more likely to vote in favor of sugar interests. There are 45 House committee members (out of a total of 435 members) and 19 Senate committee members (out of 100), so even if all support the sugar program, one would not expect this variable to be important in explaining the defeat of an anti-sugar amendment. The percentage of the congressman's constituency voting for George Bush in the 1988 presidential election is incorporated to capture the "ideology" of the congressman's electing constituents (for the 1985 vote, the proportion voting for Reagan in 1984 is used). This gauges the extent to which their conservatism may make the congressman less (or more) inclined to support the provisions of the sugar program. The congressman's rating according to the American Federation of Labor (between 1 and 100) is also incorporated to control for the congressman's record on existing economic legislation. This may give some indication of his/her predisposition toward U.S. sugar policy. Cane-state and beet-state dummies are included to control for the effect that the presence of a sugar industry in the state has on voting behavior, while regional dummies are also included.

Equations (2) and (3) capture the determinants of the sugar and sweet-ener-user coalitions' propensities to contribute to congressman i. Contri-butions from the opposing coalition are included endogenously (in latent form) to capture the possibility of a bidding war between the competing coalitions, while the vector of variables X_{2i} captures the exogenous deter-minants of contribution levels (with these variables the same for either coalition). The inclusion of total contributions received by the congressman's opponent at the last election controls for the fact that more money may be solicited from both sides when the congressman faces a well-financed opponent. The congressman's margin of victory in the most recent (general) election is included directly and also in squared form to control for a dual motive for making contributions. On the one hand, contributors prefer to pay to congressmen who are more likely to win, since they are more likely to be in a position to return favorable votes. On the other hand, the returns may be higher to contributions made in a tight race to the extent that congressmen are more appreciative. There are thus incentives to contribute both the larger the congressman's share of the vote *and* the closer the share to 50 percent (assuming a two-horse race). The congressman's seniority, as measured by his or her rank within the party, is included to capture the possibility that senior members may receive more money because of the influence they hold over junior mem-bers' votes. A committee membership dummy is included for the same reason, and also because of the important role that committee members play in the development of policy. The American Federation of Labor rating measures the extent to which the sugar and sweetener coalitions bear in mind the congressman's position on previous economic legislation before making a donation (the inclusion of this variable in the vote equation captures whether or not their assessment is correct).

Estimation follows the two-stage procedure advocated by Nelson and Olson (1978). First, the reduced-form equations are estimated by applying probit maximum likelihood to equation (7) and tobit maximum likelihood to equations (8) and (9):

$$Y_{1i}{}^* = \Pi_1 X_i + v_{1i} \tag{7}$$

$$Y_{2i}{}^* = \Pi_2 X_i + v_{2i} \tag{8}$$

$$Y_{3i}{}^* = \Pi_3 X_i + v_{3i} \, , \tag{9}$$

where X_i is the union of exogenous variables in X_{1i} and X_{2i}. The instruments $\hat{Y}_{gi}{}^* = \hat{\Pi}_g X_i$ are then replaced on the right-hand side of equations (1)-(3) and treated as fixed regressors. The structural equations are then estimated by applying probit maximum likelihood to the voting equation (1) and tobit maximum likelihood to the contributions equations, (2) and (3). Estimates of the structural parameters are consistent and asymptotically normal.

Results

The simultaneous-equation results for the 1990 and 1985 House votes, and the 1990 Senate vote, are reported in Tables 19.1, 19.2, and 19.3 respectively. For purposes of comparison, the single-equation results are reported in Tables 19.4, 19.5, and 19.6. A value of "1" is assigned to pro-sugar votes cast at each amendment.

1990 House Vote

With the simultaneous system, the 1990 House vote exhibited a significant two-way relationship between money and votes. Although the effect of money on votes was smaller than with the single-equation specification, contributions from sugar interests still appeared to have a significant effect on the congressman's voting decision. The coefficient on sugar contributions (that is, $\partial E[Y_1]/\partial Y_2{}^*$) shows that an extra \$1,000 typically elicited an 8 percent change in the probability of the congressman voting in favor of the pro-sugar position. Contributions from sweetener-users were statistically insignificant (and had the "wrong" sign), while contributions from other commodity interests were also insignificant.

The insignificance of sweetener contributions would appear to result from the fact that their monies were spread more evenly throughout the House of Representatives. In particular, sweetener-users showed a tendency to target committee members, even though all voted in favor of the sugar lobby (presumably to temper their opposition at other stages of the policy process). By contrast, the sugar coalition tended to pay more to congressmen likely to vote in their favor, with a one percent improvement in the probability of a favorable vote typically eliciting an additional \$750. The targeting of contributions by sugar and sweetener coalitions to House members in 1990 is shown in Table 19.7. It is notable that sweetener-user PACs paid almost the same to pro-sugar as anti-sugar voters, whereas sugar PACs virtually ignored anti-sugar voters, paying them an average of \$236 (compared with an average \$2,750 to pro-sugar voters, and an average \$5,540 to committee members).

TABLE 19.1 1990 House Vote. Simultaneous Equation Results

Variable	Vote $(\partial E[Y_1]/\partial X)$	Sugar Contributions	Sweetener Contributions
Propensity to vote pro-sugar		752.4 (8.42)	-16.60 (0.20)
Propensity of sugar PACs to contribute	0.815E-04 (2.88)		-0.593E-01 (0.84)
Propensity of sweetener PACs to contribute	0.450E-04 (0.70)	-0.435 (1.56)	
Corn PAC contributions	0.174E-03 (1.08)		
Cotton and rice PAC contributions	-0.362E-04 (1.25)		
Peanuts and tobacco PAC contributions	-0.367E-04 (0.55)		
Dairy PAC contributions	-0.443E-05 (0.35)		
Number of sugar farms	-0.534E-05 (0.10)		
Number of other farms	0.259E-05 (0.85)		
Committee dummy	0.769 (0.00)	-273.5 (0.38)	712.6 (1.51)
AFL-rating	0.170E-03 (0.45)	1.318 (0.14)	-13.35 (2.62)
Presidential vote	0.532E-04 (0.04)		
1/Seniority		0.232 (0.10)	-0.503 (0.37)
Cane state dummy	0.125E-01 (0.23)		
Beet state dummy	-0.321E-01 (0.43)		
Margin		-227.4 (2.19)	-53.90 (0.84)
Margin-squared		1.336 (1.99)	0.330 (0.80)
Challenger receipts		-0.310E-03 (1.58)	-0.146E-03 (1.16)
Party (Democrat=1)		137.6 (0.21)	736.6 (1.94)
North central dummy	0.456E-01 (0.67)	1126 (2.45)	541.9 (2.00)
South dummy	0.797E-01 (0.14)	1157 (2.34)	810.4 (2.93)
West dummy	-0.744E-02 (0.11)	1402 (2.94)	401.0 (1.37)
Constant	0.390E-01 (0.36)	8216 (2.10)	1741 (0.72)

Note: Absolute values of asymptotic t-ratios are given in parentheses. For probit: 79 percent correct predictions; Maddala $R^2 = 0.33$; Cragg-Uhler $R^2 = 0.45$.

TABLE 19.2 1985 House Vote. Simultaneous Equation Results

Variable	Vote $(\partial E[Y_1]/\partial X)$	Sugar Contributions	Sweetener Contributions
Propensity to vote pro-sugar		955.5	192.6
		(9.77)	(1.32)
Propensity of sugar PACs to contribute	-0.412E-04		0.157E-01
	(0.59)		(0.12)
Propensity of sweetener PACs to contribute	-0.194E-04	0.611E-02	
	(0.18)	(0.05)	
Corn PAC contributions	0.211E-03		
	(1.04)		
Cotton and rice PAC contributions	0.770E-04		
	(0.93)		
Peanuts and tobacco PAC contributions	0.350E-04		
	(1.45)		
Dairy PAC contributions	0.246E-05		
	(1.79)		
Number of sugar farms	0.875E-04		
	(0.87)		
Number of other farms	0.133E-04		
	(1.82)		
Committee dummy	1.092	-4229	-346.7
	(0.01)	(6.09)	(0.40)
AFL-rating	0.116E-03	0.990	-6.273
	(0.98)	(0.18)	(1.16)
Presidential Vote	-0.175E-04		
	(0.97)		
1/Seniority		1.705	0.215
		(1.12)	(0.14)
Cane state dummy	0.225		
	(2.24)		
Beet state dummy	0.950E-01		
	(0.84)		
Margin		-108.5	-32.42
		(1.65)	(0.48)
Margin-squared		0.642	0.194
		(1.43)	(0.44)
Challenger receipts		-0.982E-04	-0.111E-03
		(1.16)	(1.20)
Party (Democrat=1)		-543.4	-74.01
		(1.53)	(0.20)
North central dummy	0.184	174.8	-900.5
	(1.95)	(0.52)	(2.91)
South dummy	0.231	-174.85	-446.8
	(3.19)	(0.51)	(1.38)
West dummy	0.329	-334.5	-726.8
	(3.73)	(0.95)	(2.15)
Constant	-0.299	4406	1733
	(1.69)	(1.77)	(0.68)

Note: Absolute values of asymptotic t-ratios are given in parentheses. For probit: 79 percent correct predictions; Maddala $R^2 = 0.36$; Cragg-Uhler $R^2 = 0.50$.

TABLE 19.3 1990 Senate Vote. Simultaneous Equation Results

Variable	Vote $(\partial E[Y_1]/\partial X)$	Sugar Contributions	Sweetener Contributions
Propensity to vote pro-sugar		738.6 (2.45)	-381.5 (1.36)
Propensity of sugar PACs to contribute	-0.111E-04 (0.09)		0.537 (4.79)
Propensity of sweetener PACs to contribute	-0.127E-03 (1.73)	1.363 (5.89)	
Corn PAC contributions	0.623E-04 (0.65)		
Cotton and rice PAC contributions	0.115E-04 (0.25)		
Peanuts and tobacco PAC contributions	0.527E-05 (0.29)		
Dairy PAC contributions	0.415E-04 (0.68)		
Number of sugar farms	-0.417E-05 (0.08)		
Number of other farms	0.652E-05 (1.37)		
Committee dummy	0.297 (1.01)	1211 (1.04)	279.0 (0.29)
AFL-rating	0.219E-02 (0.41)	3.524 (0.12)	-2.178 (0.10)
Presidential Vote	0.314E-01 (1.27)		
1/Seniority		-100.1 (2.67)	65.70 (2.13)
Cane state dummy	1.981 (0.26)		
Beet state dummy	0.276 (0.87)		
Margin		-1160 (1.69)	327.2 (0.56)
Margin-squared		8.029 (1.53)	-1.740 (0.39)
Total receipts		-0.206E-03 (1.11)	0.201E-03 (1.38)
Party (Democrat=1)		3779 (2.24)	-2662 (2.24)
North central dummy	-0.292 (1.12)	3589 (2.63)	-977.2 (0.84)
South dummy	0.339 (1.29)	-445.5 (0.30)	1427 (1.30)
West dummy	0.283 (0.81)	1562 (1.03)	-199.8 (0.17)
Constant	-2.503 (1.27)	40590 (1.81)	-15120 (0.80)

Note: Absolute values of asymptotic t-ratios are given in parentheses. For probit: 73 percent correct predictions; Maddala $R^2 = 0.39$; Cragg-Uhler $R^2 = 0.52$.

TABLE 19.4 1990 House Sugar Vote. Single Equation Results

Variable	Vote	Sugar Contributions	Sweetener Contributions
Pro-sugar vote		3694 (10.08)	-132.1 (0.65)
Sugar PAC contributions	0.821E-03 (7.41)		-0.715E-01 (1.88)
Sweetener PAC contributions	-0.814E-04 (0.79)	-0.107 (0.64)	
Corn PAC contributions	0.122E-02 (0.97)		
Cotton and rice PAC contributions	-0.146E-03 (0.65)		
Peanuts and tobacco PAC contributions	0.258E-04 (1.02)		
Dairy PAC contributions	0.352E-04 (0.71)		
Number of sugar farms	0.531E-03 (1.33)		
Number of other farms	0.161E-04 (0.63)		
Committee dummy	5.279 (0.00)	3594 (7.53)	655.8 (2.23)
AFL-rating	0.936E-02 (0.30)	3.971 (0.46)	-13.33 (2.64)
Presidential vote	-0.463E-02 (0.53)		
1/Seniority		-0.360E-01 (0.02)	-0.533 (0.39)
Cane state dummy	0.481 (1.32)		
Beet state dummy	0.333 (1.30)		
Margin		-289.5 (2.19)	-52.67 (0.86)
Margin-squared		1.730 (1.99)	0.319 (0.81)
Challenger receipts		-0.404E-03 (1.99)	-0.138E-03 (1.11)
Party (Democrat=1)		226.5 (0.34)	733.3 (1.95)
North central dummy	0.234 (0.84)	1279 (2.71)	531.5 (2.02)
South dummy	0.908 (3.45)	692.5 (1.43)	791.6 (2.87)
West dummy	0.413 (1.26)	1132 (2.26)	384.9 (1.35)
Constant	-1.087 (1.77)	8687 (2.14)	1863 (0.79)

Note: Absolute values of asymptotic t-ratios are given in parentheses. For probit: 86 percent correct predictions; Maddala $R^2 = 0.44$; Cragg-Uhler $R^2 = 0.62$.

TABLE 19.5 1985 House Sugar Vote. Single Equation Results

Variable	Vote	Sugar Contributions	Sweetener Contributions
Pro-sugar vote		2323	-249.2
		(9.41)	(1.08)
Sugar PAC contributions	0.192E-02		0.962E-01
	(7.04)		(1.47)
Sweetener PAC contributions	-0.183E-03	0.189	
	(1.16)	(2.20)	
Corn PAC contributions	-0.487E-04		
	(0.05)		
Cotton and rice PAC contributions	-0.912E-03		
	(2.66)		
Peanuts and tobacco PAC contributions	0.877E-04		
	(1.15)		
Dairy PAC contributions	-0.524E-05		
	(0.11)		
Number of sugar farms	-0.310E-05		
	(0.01)		
Number of other farms	0.708E-04		
	(2.17)		
Committee dummy	5.676	1880	923.7
	(0.00)	(6.10)	(2.94)
AFL-rating	0.162E-02	0.211	-6.625
	(0.39)	(0.04)	(1.22)
Presidential vote	-0.176E-01		
	(1.85)		
1/Seniority		1.104	-0.207
		(0.68)	(0.13)
Cane state dummy	0.837		
	(2.09)		
Beet state dummy	0.305		
	(1.01)		
Margin		-146.1	-35.38
		(2.05)	(0.53)
Margin-squared		0.894	0.227
		(1.90)	(0.51)
Challenger receipts		-0.509E-04	-0.103E-03
		(0.58)	(1.11)
Party (Democrat=1)		-396.1	49.49
		(1.04)	(0.14)
North central dummy	0.450	994.0	-512.6
	(1.36)	(3.11)	(1.78)
South dummy	1.106	397.4	-58.44
	(3.72)	(1.12)	(0.19)
West dummy	1.401	390.3	-260.0
	(3.63)	(1.13)	(0.83)
Constant	-0.758	3939	1620
	(1.02)	(1.47)	(0.64)

Note: Absolute values of asymptotic t-ratios are given in parentheses. For probit: 86 percent correct predictions; Maddala $R^2 = 0.51$; Cragg-Uhler $R^2 = 0.70$.

TABLE 19.6 1990 Senate Sugar Vote. Single Equation Results

Variable	Vote	Sugar Contributions	Sweetener Contributions
Pro-sugar vote	·	6362 (5.00)	-465.3 (0.48)
Sugar PAC contributions	0.109E-02 (3.41)		0.336 (3.02)
Sweetener PAC contributions	-0.717E-03 (2.34)	0.801 (3.52)	
Corn PAC contributions	-0.190E-03 (0.66)		
Cotton and rice PAC contributions	0.984E-04 (0.70)		
Peanuts and tobacco PAC contributions	0.509E-05 (0.08)		
Dairy PAC contributions	-0.103E-04 (0.06)		
Number of sugar farms	-0.926E-04 (0.66)		
Number of other farms	0.207E-04 (1.87)		
Committee dummy		3517 (2.80)	1736 (1.70)
AFL-rating	0.953E-02 (1.07)	43.62 (1.28)	4.388 (0.18)
Presidential vote	0.467E-01 (1.07)		
1/Seniority		-5.359 (0.13)	56.40 (1.65)
Cane state dummy	6.159 (0.06)		
Beet state dummy	0.765 (1.26)		
Margin		-1798 (2.29)	-194.6 (0.31)
Margin-squared		14.32 (2.39)	2.427 (0.50)
Total Receipts		0.291E-04 (0.14)	0.204E-03 (1.25)
Party (Democrat=1)		-814.0 (0.45)	-2802 (2.12)
North central dummy	-1.236 (1.51)	4818 (3.08)	762.1 (0.63)
South dummy	0.641 (1.18)	1128 (0.72)	2406 (2.08)
West dummy	-0.149E-01 (0.02)	1890 (1.09)	826.3 (0.66)
Constant	-4.089E-01 (1.57)	46340 (1.81)	-721.5 (0.35)

Note: Absolute values of asymptotic t-ratios are given in parentheses. For probit: 87 percent correct predictions; Maddala $R^2 = 0.51$; Cragg-Uhler $R^2 = 0.69$.

TABLE 19.7 Average Payments, Sugar Legislation, 1989-90

Payment	Sugar PACs (House)	Sweetener PACs (House)	Sugar PACs (Senate)	Sweetener PACs (Senate)
To committee members	$5,535	$698	$5,509	$2,596
To pro-sugar voters	$2,751	$477	$4,870	$1,407
To pro-sugar voters not on committee	$2,196	$432	$3,087	$759
To anti-sugar voters	$236	$422	$488	$1,205
Overall	$1,855	$458	$2,406	$1,317

Note: Of the 45 committee members in the House, none voted against the sugar program in 1990. In the Senate, one of 19 commitee members voted against the program.

Source: National Library on Money and Politics.

Even though all committee members voted in favor of the sugar program, committee membership was unable to explain votes because there were too many noncommittee members also voting the same way. Moreover, whereas with the single-equation estimation committee members received significantly more money from sugar PACs, this effect was not significant after controlling for their greater tendency to vote in favor of sugar policy. In other words, there is no evidence that sugar PACs paid committee members extra money for reasons other than their ability to provide favorable votes.

Ideology, as measured by the presidential vote and the AFL rating, appeared to have no measurable effect on the voting decision. But whilst sugar contributions did not depend on the AFL rating, sweetener-users tended to target congressmen of whom the AFL disapproved. A misperception of the importance of being "liberal" may also account for the sweetener-users' lack of effectiveness.

The southern regional dummy had a significant effect on votes in the single equation case but no effect in the simultaneous model (i.e., after controlling for the fact that these congressmen received more money). Nor did simply being from a beet- or cane-producing state have a significant effect on the voting decision. However, both sugar and sweetener-user PACs tended to target congressmen outside the control region (the Northeast), which covers nine states where no sugar is grown.

As anticipated, margin had a dual effect on contributions. Other things equal, Representatives elected with 87 percent of the vote received the lowest contributions from sugar PACs.[9]

1985-90 Differences

The principal differences between the House votes in 1990 and 1985 were that sugar money did not appear to have a significant effect on votes in 1985, while regional effects were important. The rising scale of PAC contributions may partially account for this difference. Payments by sugar PACs increased by 80 percent between 1985-86 and 1989-90 (while sweetener-user payments rose by just 4 percent). In contrast to 1990, sweetener-users tended to target the control region (their natural base of support) in 1985. Committee membership had a significantly negative effect on sugar contributions, suggesting that committee members were paid relatively less, given their overwhelming tendency to support the sugar program.

House-Senate Differences[10]

In the Senate, sugar contributions appeared to have no effect on voting outcomes, whereas sweetener contributions were significant at the 95 percent level. In this case, an additional $1,000 translated into a one percent improvement in the probability of a Senator casting an anti-sugar vote. The relatively strong Senate opposition to the sugar program was reflected in the fact that, of the 54 votes cast in favor of the pro-sugar position, 18 came from committee members. Thus, 36 noncommittee members voted for the program, compared with 43 against (one committee member voted against). Although sugar money appeared to be ineffective, contributions from corn and cotton and rice interests did appear to be effective in garnering pro-sugar votes.

The most striking difference in the activities of sugar and sweetener PACs in the Senate was that each spent more when the other group spent more (sugar interests spent $1,400 for every extra $1,000 spent by sweetener-users, while sweetener-users spent $540 for an additional $1,000 spent by sugar PACs). Since sweetener-users appeared to be effective in the Senate, the bidding up of PAC expenditures may have been counterproductive for the sugar lobby. The sweetener-users exhibited a greater propensity to target (minority) Republicans and junior Senators, whereas sugar PACs favored senior members. These differences may have accounted for the failure of the sugar lobby to receive a majority of non-committee support, despite outspending sweetener-users by two to one.

The number of farms in the state was significant in explaining pro-sugar votes, while regional effects were also more important than in the House. Support for President Bush in 1988 was associated with votes for the sugar program, though this connection could be spurious since Michael Dukakis' natural base of support was in New England where no sugar is grown.

Conclusions

This study provides limited evidence that PAC contributions by sugar and sweetener coalitions have been effective in influencing votes on House and Senate sugar amendments and some evidence that vote-trading with corn and cotton and rice interests has been effective in the Senate. However, the dominant linkage appears to run the other way, with favorable votes attracting more money from either coalition.

These results are strong enough to overturn the conclusions drawn in single-equation studies, notably those by Turner and Welch, which ignore the two-way relationship between money and votes. Turner found that Senate voting on tobacco, peanut, and sugar bills in 1981 was better explained by the inclusion of PACs but that "ideology" was the single most important characteristic, while Welch found that money was the least significant variable in explaining House votes on dairy price supports in 1975.

The results also qualify the conclusions drawn by Abler, who found that for House votes on sugar and dairy legislation in 1985 (the first of which is considered in this study) the association between votes and money was due entirely to the second linkage; that is, PAC money did not appear to be able to buy the congressman's vote, though PACs tended to contribute more to congressmen who were likely to vote in their favor.[11]

Abler concluded that PACs give money to help elect congressmen predisposed to support their programs rather than to buy votes. His policy conclusion was that limits on PAC contributions would have little short-run impact, but in the long-run might lead to congressional representation that is less supportive of PAC interests. This inference—which has also been made by Chappell (1982), who looked at several issues including dairy supports—is inconsistent with the observation that 95 percent of all campaign contributions from agricultural political action committees are made to incumbents.

The fact that contributions are geared almost exclusively to incumbents provides overwhelming evidence that PACs are not in fact trying to determine electoral outcomes. A more likely cause of the observed relationship is that PACs frequently contribute to congressmen whose vote is more or less guaranteed, in the hope that they will promote the interest group's cause and seek to win the votes of other legislators. Thus, for example, sugar producers support agriculture committee chairman "Kika" de la Garza, from Texas, not to win his vote (which is already guaranteed) nor to ensure his re-election (which is a near certainty), but to entice him to be proactive in support of sugar growers' interests (which he is).[12]

The questionable impact of money on voting behavior may also reflect the fact that money is seldom sufficient to buy a congressman's vote but is often necessary. Campaign funds are of singular importance to congressmen, and a donation may be the vital first step to gaining a congressman's ear. All sides may give to a congressman, but only those who supplement this with additional lobbying are likely to see their cause advanced. PACs as a whole may thus be influencing voting decisions only to the extent that their donations reflect more assiduous lobbying than is conducted by non-PAC interests.

Indeed, the salient point arising from these results does not really concern the effect of money per se. Rather, to the extent that PAC contributions proxy for a range of (mostly unmeasurable) lobbying activity, this measure is sufficient to negate most group-size related characteristics. In other words, active (rather than passive) lobbying is integral to the outcome of U.S. sugar legislation.

A rigid interpretation of the results would hold that a strategic cut of about $200,000 in pro-sugar contributions could reverse the 1990 House vote. Few observers would expect reform to come so cheaply. Perhaps they would acknowledge, however, that a few more "Chinese walls" between congressmen and lobbyists would provide a first step toward GATT consistency.

Notes

I am grateful to Colin Cameron, Garth Holloway, Alex McCalla, and Colin Carter for helpful suggestions.

1. PAC is the campaign fund of a sponsoring interest group, formed for the purpose of giving money to candidates.

2. The USDA anticipates production reaching a record 7.70 million short tons in fiscal 1993.

3. These costs include efficiency losses and the transfer of rents to import quota holders.

4. ABARE also estimate that the stimulus to sugar production provided by lower grain support prices had reduced the world sugar price a further 9 percent by 1988.

5. The E.C. submitted a document in support of the Australian case. This document maintained that the U.S. sugar program had "...encouraged the growth of isoglucose (HFSS), and its by-product corn gluten feed, which was produced almost exclusively for export to the EEC. The distorting effects of these exports were serious in that they constituted a very cheap substitute for EEC cereals for animal feed and thus tended to encourage the growth of EEC milk and beef production." That is, U.S. sugar policies were held to be partially responsible for E.C. dairy and beef surpluses.

6. In 1991, as a minor concession to the GATT ruling, the United States replaced its import quota with a tariff-rate quota. The tariff-rate quota is fixed in the same manner as a conventional quota, with quota holders charged a nominal duty of

0.625 cents per pound, except for the Caribbean Basin Initiative and Generalized System of Preferences countries, whose sugar enters duty-free. Any sugar exceeding the tariff-rate quota is charged a high and generally prohibitive tariff of 16 cents per pound. The change in policy is largely a matter of semantics.

7. Some of these contributions will have been made after the vote. However, it seems more reasonable to include 1985-86 contributions than 1983-84 contributions, given the importance of capturing donations made in 1985 and the model's assumption that congressmen and contributors make their decisions simultaneously.

8. The proportion of the constituent population engaged in rural occupations was also tried but found to be statistically insignificant in both single- and simultaneous-equation models.

9. The 1985 estimate was 85 percent. Payments were smallest to senators elected with 72 percent of the vote.

10. Some measurement problems are encountered due to the fact that senators serve six-year terms. Senators up for re-election in 1989-90 tended to receive more contributions in the 1989-90 election cycle. Turnover in the Senate makes it difficult to accommodate this with lags, while estimation using contributions received by each senator during the election cycle in which they were elected yielded a slightly lower number of correct predictions.

11. The dairy amendment considered by Abler would have deleted the farm bill's dairy provisions and substituted provisions that reduced the dairy price support in the event of government purchases exceeding specified levels. It would also have eliminated the bill's increases in the minimum federal marketing order milk prices. Since these changes would have affected surplus and deficit regions differently, the aggregation of dairy PACs adopted by Abler assumes a false harmony of interests. The results on sugar legislation, however, compare roughly with the findings of this study.

12. On behalf of south Texas growers, de la Garza urged members to vote "no" on the sugar amendment. He proclaimed on the House floor, "It is jobs U.S.A., jobs U.S.A., jobs U.S.A.! You cannot cut it anymore. You cannot hide it anymore," *Congressional Quarterly, 1990 Almanac*, p. 332.

References

Abler, D. G. 1991. "Campaign Contributions and House Voting on Sugar and Dairy Legislation." *American Journal of Agricultural Economics* Feb: 11-17.

Becker, G. S. 1983. "A Theory of Competition Among Pressure Groups for Political Influence." *Quarterly Journal of Economics* Aug: 371-400.

Chappell, H. W. 1982. "Campaign Contributions and Congressional Voting: A Simultaneous Probit-Tobit Model." *Review of Economics and Statistics* 64: 77-83.

Congressional Quarterly. 1990. *1990 Almanac*, Washington D.C.

Gardner, B. L. 1987. "Causes of U.S. Farm Commodity Programs." *Journal of Political Economy* 95: 2.

National Journal. 1986. *The Almanac of American Politics*, Washington D.C.

———. 1990. *The Almanac of American Politics*, Washington DC.

Nelson, F., and L. Olson. 1978. "Specification and Estimation of a Simultaneous-Equation Model With Limited Dependent Variables." *International Economic Review* 19: 695-705.

Peltzman, S. 1976. "Toward a More General Theory of Regulation." *Journal of Law and Economics* 19: 211-40.

Stigler, G. 1971. "The Theory of Economic Regulation." *Bell Journal of Economics* 2: 3-21.

Sturgiss, R. 1990. *1990 and U.S. Sugar Policy Reform.* ABARE Discussion Paper, No. 8025, ABARE, Canberra, Australia.

Turner, M. H. V. 1986. "V.I.C.E. and Votes: Determinants of the U.S. Senate's Voting Behavior on National Agricultural Legislation." Ph.D. Dissertation, University of Hawaii, Dec.

United States Department of Agriculture. 1993. *Sugar and Sweetener: Situation and Outlook Report.* USDA ERS, Washington D.C., Mar.

United States Department of Commerce. 1989. *1987 Census of Agriculture.* Washington D.C.

Welch, W. P. 1982. "Campaign Contributions and Legislative Voting: Milk Money and Dairy Price Supports." *West. Polit. Quart.* 35: 478-95.

Appendix

Data and Variables

Vote: The votes considered are House amendment 285 (1990), House amendment 289 (1985), and Senate amendment 166 (1990). Only "yae" and "nay" votes are considered. Paired votes, publicly announced positions, and abstentions are all excluded from the sample. *Source: Congressional Quarterly Almanac, 1985* and *1990.*

PAC Contributions: Contributions made in the 1989-90 election cycle are considered for the 1990 votes, while those made in 1985-86 are used for the 1985 vote. The aggregated coalitions comprise PACs of the following organizations:

Sugar: Amalgamated Sugar Company, American Crystal Sugar Corporation, American Sugarbeet Growers' Association, American Sugar Cane League, California Beet Growers' Association, Florida Sugar Cane League, Great Lakes Sugar Beet Growers, Hawaiian Sugar Planters' Association, Michigan Sugar Company, Rio Grande Valley Sugar Growers, Savannah Foods and Industries, South Minnesota Beet Sugar Cooperative, Spreckels Industries, Texas Sugarbeet Growers Association, United States Sugar Corporation, U.S. Beet Sugar Association.

Sweetener-Users: The Milk Industry Foundation (International Association of Ice Cream Manufacturers), National Soft Drinks Association, National Food Processors Association, Peanut Butter and Nut

Processors Association, Dr Pepper, Coca Cola, Pepsi-Cola Bottlers Association, Pepsi-Cola General Bottlers, Johnston.

Corn: AG Processing Inc., American Maize Products Company, Cargill Inc., Continental Grain, Farmers Grain Terminal Inc., Harvest States Cooperatives, Scoular Company, Archer-Daniels-Midland.

Cotton and Rice: American Cotton Shippers Association, American Rice Inc., Arizona Cotton Growers, Calcot, Cotton Warehouse Association of America, National Cotton Council, Plains Cotton Cooperative Association, Rice and Soybean PAC, Rice Growers' Association of America, Riceland Foods, Supina Association of America, Producers Cotton Oil Company.

Peanuts and Tobacco: Brown and Williamson Tobacco, Cigar Association of America, Georgia Peanut Producers' Association, National Association of Tobacco Distributors, Peanut Butter and Nut Processors' Association, Alabama Peanut Producers' Association, Philip Morris, Pinkerton Tobacco Company, RJR Nabisco, Southeastern Peanut Association, Southwestern Peanut Membership Organization, Tobacco Institute, U.S. Tobacco Company (U.S. Tobacco Executives Association), U.S. Burley Producers' Association, Universal Leaf Tobacco Company, Virginia-Carolina's Peanut Membership Organization, Virginia-Carolina Peanut Association Inc.

Dairy: Agri-Mark Inc., Arizona Dairymen, Associated Milk Producers, Blue Bell Creameries, Borden Inc., Coble Dairy Products Corporation, Dairylea Cooperative, Dairyman's Cooperative Creamery Association, Dairymen Inc. (also state PACs in Georgia, Kentucky, Louisiana, Mississippi, North Carolina, Pennsylvania, Tennessee, Virginia), Dairymen's Mountain Association, Darigold/North-West Dairymen's Association, Dean Foods Company, Michigan Milk Producers' Association, Mid-America Dairymen, Milk Industry Foundation, Milk Marketing Inc., Western United Dairymen's Association.

Source: National Library on Money and Politics.

Number of Sugar Farms: Farms falling within SIC 02078. County-level data is aggregated to the congressional district level, by including all counties falling wholly or partially into a congressman's district. *Source: 1987 Census of Agriculture.*

Number of Other Farms: Measured as the total number of farms (SIC 01001) minus those falling within SIC 02078. *Source: 1987 Census of Agriculture.*

Committee Membership Dummy: A value of 1 is assigned to committee members; other congressmen receive zeros. *Source: Congressional Quarterly Almanac, 1986* and *1990.*

Constituent Ideology: The proportion of the constituency voting for George Bush in the 1988 presidential election (1990 vote); the proportion voting for Ronald Reagan in the 1984 presidential election (1985 vote). *Source: Almanac of American Politics, 1986* and *1990.*

AFL Rating: The AFL-CIO publishes a rating of congressmen according to their votes on key economic issues. Its chief concern is with the economic interests of the American worker and, unlike other groups' ratings, its index avoids noneconomic issues such as abortion and foreign policy. *Source: Almanac of American Politics.*

Cane and Beet State Dummies: The cane state dummy is set to one for Florida, Hawaii, Louisiana, and Texas, and zero for all other states. The beet state dummy is set to one for the thirteen beet-producing states and zero for the rest. The thirteen states are: California, Colorado, Idaho, Michigan, Minnesota, Montana, Nebraska, New Mexico, North Dakota, Ohio, Oregon, Texas, Wyoming. *Source: USDA Sugar and Sweetener, Situation and Outlook Report, March 1993.*

Total Losers' Contributions: This measures the contributions received by opponents to the incumbent congressman in the 1989-90 and 1985-86 election cycles. Because only one-third of the Senate is up for re-election every two years, this is replaced by the incumbent Senator's contributions in the Senate specification. *Source: National Library on Money and Politics.*

Regional Dummies: The Census Regions are used. The control region is the North East.

20

The Relationship Between Selected Agricultural and Environmental Policies in the European Community

Dale Leuck, Stephen Haley, and Peter Liapis

Introduction

Efforts in the European Community (E.C.) to reduce agriculturally based pollution have underscored the relationships between agricultural and environmental policies. For example, the E.C. Nitrate Directive was passed in 1991 for the purpose of reducing nitrate levels in water supplies.[1] Nitrate levels have increased in the last several decades because of increased use of nitrogen fertilizers and disposal of livestock manure, activities that have been influenced by the E.C.'s Common Agricultural Policy (CAP). Nitrate may cause metabolic disorders in humans and livestock.

The Nitrate Directive establishes a standard by which to compare the effect of other policies in reducing nitrate levels because it sets annual limits on residual nitrogen from livestock manure and fertilizer in excess of crop uptake. By so doing, it implies reductions in livestock production and fertilizer use. Another proposed policy is to reduce fertilizer use by taxing fertilizer. Reductions in fertilizer may reduce crop production. Therefore, both policies may also affect world prices and trade.

Reform of the CAP may also reduce agricultural production and affect world prices and trade (Roningen and Dixit, 1989; Tyers and Anderson, 1986). However, limited research has been done on how CAP reform and environmental policies may affect nitrate levels and agricultural activities (Abler and Shortle, 1992). The objective of this chapter is therefore to assess how the Nitrate Directive, a possible 50 percent tax on nitrogen fertilizer, and the package of CAP reforms adopted by the E.C. Agricultural Ministers on May 21, 1992 (known as the MacSharry plan), may affect residual nitrogen levels, E.C. agricultural production and input use, and world prices and trade.

The Nitrate Directive and any possible fertilizer tax will be implemented within the context of CAP reform. Three scenarios are first run to compare the separate effects of these three policies on residual nitrogen levels and agricultural activities. Two additional scenarios then show the effect of combining CAP reform and the Nitrate Directive, and CAP reform and a fertilizer tax on the same variables.

The chapter is divided into five parts. Nitrate pollution and policies to reduce it are described in the next section. These policies are a 50 percent tax on nitrogen fertilizer and the E.C. Nitrate Directive. The possible impact of the Nitrate Directive on production is assessed in the next section. Residual amounts of nitrogen are calculated on a per hectare basis for each country and those countries that exceed the MAR are identified. The reductions in livestock numbers and fertilizer use to reduce residual nitrogen levels to the MAR are calculated. The following section describes the 1992 proposal for CAP reform. The 1986 version of the static world policy simulation model (SWOPSIM) used to evaluate these policies is described in the fourth section. In the last section, the effects of the Nitrate Directive, nitrogen tax, and CAP reform on nitrate levels, agricultural production, input use, trade, and world prices are described.

Nitrate Pollution in the E.C. and Possible Solutions

Nitrate pollution in the E.C. has increased because agriculture became more intensive after World War II as demand increased and the CAP provided high price supports (Commission of the European Communities, 1991). The production of milk, beef, and veal has more than doubled between 1950 and the present; while pork and poultry production have more than tripled. Grain production doubled and fertilizer use tripled between 1960 and 1990 because higher-yielding grain varieties requiring larger amount of fertilizers were adopted (Figure 20.1).

The E.C. Nitrate Problem

Excessive amounts of nitrate in surface water precipitate algae blooms, which, in turn, take oxygen out of the water. The algae blooms smell bad and may be toxic if ingested. The decreased oxygen content of the water destroys aquatic life.

Nitrate may also adversely affect both livestock and human health. High levels of nitrate may reduce feed efficiency in livestock and cause stomach cancer in humans. In concentrations exceeding 100 parts per million (ppm), nitrate may cause respiratory failure in infants, although this is quite rare.

FIGURE 20.1 E.C.-10: Fertilizer Nitrogen Rate and Total Grain Yield.

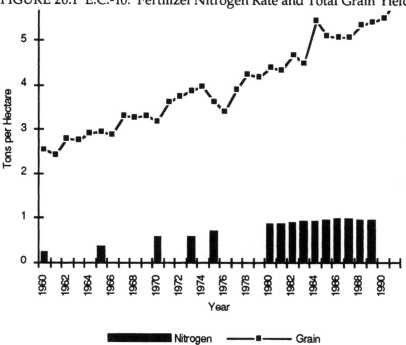

Source: E.C. Commission and International Fertilizer Statistics, selected issues.

Nitrate is derived from nitrogen. Livestock manure and the commercial fertilizer industry are the two main sources of nitrate. Much smaller amounts come from industrial sources, automobile exhausts, and electrical storms and enter the ground in the form of acid rain. Some nitrate also has its source in plant wastes and sewage sludge.

The amount of nitrate absorbed by plants is influenced by the structure of the soil, its content of organic matter, the amount of rainfall, and the density of the plants. Up to 50 percent of soil nitrate may leach rapidly into water supplies in regions having light, sandy soils; heavy rainfall; and/or a high water table. Leaching may take up to several decades under other circumstances.

A maximum allowable concentration (MAC) of 50 ppm of nitrate was established as safe by the E.C. Commission (1980). About 2 percent of French drinking water is in excess of the MAC; and in the Netherlands the average nitrate concentration found in ground water 30 meters below sandy soils is 106 ppm (Manale, 1991). In Germany, the residual amount of nitrate left in the soil after plant uptake is accounted for has increased from 10 kilograms (kg) per hectare (ha) to more than 100 kg/ha in the last twenty years (Agra Europe, 1991).

Both fertilizer and manure satisfy the nitrogen needs of crops. Fertilizer is the more practical nitrogen source because it may be economically pelleted, transported, and applied at optimum times of the year. Manure is generally viewed as a costly waste in need of being disposed of, instead of as an economic source of nutrients.

Agra Europe (1992) describes current nitrate problems as being located in the low-lying areas of Belgium, France, the Netherlands, the north of Italy, part of Germany, and parts of southern England (Figure 20.2). The countries with nitrate pollution extending over large regions have relatively high densities of cattle and pig production. For example, Belgium, the Netherlands, Denmark, and Germany have more cattle and pigs per ha of utilized agricultural area (UAA) than other E.C. countries (Table 20.1).

Social efficiency in resource allocation may best be achieved by making the polluter pay for the costs that pollution imposes on society. Desired behavior may be induced by strict requirements such as those included in the Nitrate Directive. Polluters may also by encouraged to adopt environmentally sound production practices by means of a tax. The former approach is more likely to reduce residual nitrogen levels to desired levels, while the latter allows farmers greater flexibility in choosing production practices.

The E.C. Nitrate Directive

The E.C. Nitrate Directive was passed on June 14, 1991 (E.C. Commission, 1991). Its intent is to maintain nitrate levels in groundwater below the MAC.

The specific details and requirements of the Directive are to be decided upon and implemented over eight years. Regions having excess amounts of nitrate are to be designated as "vulnerable zones" by the member countries within two years. Countries must draw up "codes of good practice," required in the vulnerable zones and voluntary elsewhere. Countries have an additional two years in which to design specific programs to reduce nitrate levels to the MAC and four years in which to implement them.

The Directive attempts to reduce the leaching and runoff of nitrate from manure by regulating periods when manure may be applied, and its application to waterlogged, sloping, flooded, frozen, or snow-covered ground. The amount of rainfall is to be accounted for and manure storage encouraged.

The Directive states that nitrogen disposal from livestock manure not exceed 170 kg/ha after the transition period, but it allows that consider-

FIGURE 20.2 Areas of Surplus Animal Manure.

TABLE 20.1 Cattle and Pigs for Selected E.C. Countries, 1989 (Head per hectare of UAA)

	Belgium	The Netherlands	Denmark	Germany	France	Italy	United Kingdom
Cattle	2.29	2.36	0.79	1.23	0.7	0.51	0.65
Pigs	4.75	6.80	3.27	1.90	.45	.54	.40

Source: E.C. Commission, various issues.

ation be taken of the use of nitrogen by crops, the amount of nitrogen from inorganic fertilizer, and the amount of nitrogen in the soil. Therefore, the 170 kg/ha may be viewed as the maximum annual residual (MAR) of nitrogen, inclusive of nitrogen from both manure and inorganic fertilizer, less uptake by crops.

Fertilizer Tax

The imposition of a tax on fertilizer may reduce nitrate pollution at its source and provide revenue to reduce its effects. Conceptually, such a tax could be set at a rate equal to the monetary value of the environmental damage being caused, leaving farmers to decide how to modify their practices. However, agricultural pollution originates from nonpoint sources, which are difficult to accurately monitor and measure. It is also often difficult to measure the monetary value of the damage.

Although no specific proposal for a tax exists, a tax of 50 percent is modeled as a standard for comparison.

Possible Implications of the Nitrate Directive for Production

The implications of the Nitrate Directive for agricultural production are calculated using data from Koopmans (1987) and Leuck (1993). Nitrogen balance tables relating the amount of nitrogen applied to the amount taken up by crops for each E.C. country are calculated for 1986. These balances are used to calculate reductions in livestock numbers and fertilizer use needed to reduce residual nitrate levels to the MAR.

The estimated amounts of nitrogen from inorganic fertilizer and the uptake by crops are presented in Table 3 of Leuck (1993). For the E.C., nearly 10 percent of the 8.7 million tons of nitrogen from inorganic fertilizer use is residual (that is, exceeds crop uptake). For Denmark and the Netherlands, residual nitrogen is 25 and 44 percent, respectively. Belgium, Ireland, and Italy all have a small deficit.

The application of organic nitrogen by country is presented in Table 4 of Leuck (1993). About one-half of organic nitrogen is from cattle, although this varies from 10 percent in Greece to 69 percent in Ireland. Pigs are a major source of organic nitrogen in Denmark, Belgium, and the Netherlands. Sheep are a significant source of nitrogen in the United Kingdom and Greece.

The amount of nitrogen from livestock manure is estimated to be 9.6 million tons for the E.C. (Table 20.2). This is on top of the 8.7 million tons of inorganic nitrogen, from which the E.C. is 10 percent residual. Some countries with residual nitrogen from fertilizer also use large amounts of manure. For example, the Netherlands must accommodate an amount of organic nitrogen that is 1.5 times the amount from fertilizer.

TABLE 20.2 Nitrogen Applied, Uptake, and Residual, EC-10, 1986

	Livestock	Inorganic	Total	– Uptake	= Total	Residual	
	1,000 Metric tons					Percent	Kg per ha
Belgium/ Luxembourg	382	199	580	211	369	64	240
Denmark	434	381	816	287	529	65	187
Germany	1,717	1,578	3,295	1,314	1,981	60	165
Greece	455	432	887	403	484	55	84
France	2,393	2,568	4,961	2,406	2,555	52	81
Ireland	536	343	879	407	473	54	83
Italy	1,157	1,011	2,167	1,027	1,140	53	65
Netherlands	752	504	1,255	284	972	77	480
United Kingdom	1,819	1,671	3,490	1,521	1,969	56	106
Total	9,645	8,688	18,333	7,860	10,473	57	108

Source: Leuck, 1993.

Of the total nitrogen applied in the E.C., 57 percent is residual (Table 20.2). The residual amount of nitrogen varies from 52 percent in France to 77 percent in the Netherlands. Nearly two-thirds of the 10.5 million tons of residual nitrogen is located in Germany, France, and the United Kingdom. Only 18 percent of the residual nitrogen is found in Belgium, Denmark, and the Netherlands, which exceed the 170 kg/ha MAR. The Netherlands has residual nitrogen equal to 480 kg/ha; Belgium has a residual of 240 kg/ha; and Denmark has a residual of 187 kg/ha.

The reduction of residual nitrate to the MAR would require significant reductions in livestock numbers for crops in these three countries (Table 20.3). For Belgium, Denmark, and the Netherlands, nitrate levels exceed the MAR by 29 percent, 9 percent, and 65 percent, respectively. Without reduced fertilizer use, livestock numbers would have to be reduced by 28 percent, 11 percent, and 84 percent, respectively. Such reductions are clearly not politically possible.

The Directive allows the MAR to be achieved by reducing both fertilizer and manure. For the purpose of analysis, the present study assumes that the percentage declines in livestock numbers not exceed the required percentage decline in residual nitrogen (Table 20.3). Any further reduction in residual nitrogen is assumed to be brought about by relatively small reductions in fertilizer use (Table 20.3). Such reductions may not affect yields in these three countries because sufficient manure exists for use as a substitute. These assumptions provides a benchmark by which to evaluate the Directive.

TABLE 20.3 Reductions in Livestock Numbers and Fertilizer Use to Achieve the MAR (Percent)

	Belgium	Denmark	Netherlands
Livestock	28	11	84
Livestock & Fertilizer			
Livestock	28	9	65
Fertilizer	0	2	28

Source: Leuck, 1993.

Although the reductions in livestock numbers in these countries are significant, they are more moderate when viewed on an E.C.-wide basis (Table 20.4). Pig numbers are reduced the most, by 11.7 percent, followed by a 10 percent reduction in eggs and broilers. Dairy and beef numbers are reduced by 7.8 and 4.8 percent, respectively. Sheep numbers are reduced by less than 1 percent.

The May 1992 CAP Reform Package

The CAP reform package passed in May 1992 by the E.C. Council of Agricultural Commissioners contains significant changes in E.C. agricultural policy (Madell, 1992). The reform package is based on proposals submitted to the E.C. Commission in June 1991 by E.C. Agricultural Commissioner Ray MacSharry. Although MacSharry's proposals were modified in subsequent debate, the resulting reform package of May 1992 is nevertheless sometimes referred to as the MacSharry plan. The reform package is planned for implementation over three years starting in 1993/94. Its main features are:

- Price supports are reduced:
  - grains intervention prices cut 30 percent
  - oilseed support prices cut 50 percent
  - beef intervention price cut 15 percent
  - butter intervention price cut equivalent to a 3 percent cut in the price of milk
- Compensation for price cuts made with direct payments:
  - 45 ECU (European Currency Unit) per ton for grains
  - 152 ECU per ton for oilseeds
- Payment based on historic yields or herd size
- Larger farmers required to set aside 15 percent of crop base. For this study, estimates made (but not published) by the European Branch of the Economic Research Service were used. These estimates of individual commodity land area reductions are as follows: wheat—7

TABLE 20.4 Reduction in E.C. Livestock to Achieve MAR (Percent)

	Dairy	Beef	Pigs	Layers	Broilers	Sheep
E.C.-10	7.8	4.8	11.7	10.1	10.1	.91

Source: Leuck, 1993.

percent; corn—9 percent; other coarse grains, soybeans, and other oilseeds—12 percent.

The direct payments made to farmers are assumed not to influence their production decisions. That is, direct payments are assumed to be totally "decoupled" from production.

The Model Used to Analyze Policy Alternatives

ST86 SWOPSIM Model

The trade liberalization model, ST86, used to analyze policy alternatives for 1986, is a static, partial equilibrium representation of world agricultural trade. ST86 is constructed in the static world policy simulation (SWOPSIM) framework (Roningen, 1986), using the ST86 database (Sullivan *et.al.*, 1989) and includes 22 agricultural commodities and 11 countries/regions. It has been used to analyze the economic effects of agricultural trade liberalization by the industrial market economies (Roningen and Dixit, 1989).

Inclusion of Nitrogen Fertilizer in ST86

The standard SWOPSIM modeling framework does not explicitly include a fertilizer sector. In order to introduce a fertilizer tax into ST86, Gunasekera *et al.* (1992) adjusted the producer subsidy wedge by calculating the output tax equivalent of the tax. This method of introducing a fertilizer tax does not allow for any structural reaction of fertilizer demand to the tax.

An alternative is to directly model fertilizer demand. This approach allows both the tax to affect output through an explicit model structure and the effects of policy changes on fertilizer use and the delivery of nitrates into the soil to be tracked.

The structure is similar to the way feedgrain demand is modeled. The quantity supplied of crops using fertilizer enter into the fertilizer demand equation and are exponentially weighted by their proportion of total nitrogen fertilizer use. An E.C.-wide own-price elasticity of demand for fertilizer is based on a study by Burrell (1989). For the United Kingdom, Burrell's estimate ranges between .4 and .6. For this study, an elasticity equal to the average (-.5) is used in the fertilizer demand equation. A perfectly elastic supply of fertilizer is assumed, although some sensitivity analysis is performed.

Haley (1993) discusses the specific form of the fertilizer demand function, including how cross-price elasticities are calculated.

The Joint Production Approach Using Duality Theory

One of the limitations of ST86 is that it is a synthetic model, in that elasticities are not estimated but obtained from a variety of published sources using different estimation techniques or based on expert opinion (see Sullivan *et al.*, 1989). Such a method may result in a system characterized by regional supply elasticities that are theoretically inconsistent with behavioral or technological relationships. Input demand elasticities are also not included in the standard model.

A more structured approach is based on duality theory (Ball, 1988). Also known as the joint products approach, it provides theoretical restrictions on the behavior of both output supply and input demand equations that can be econometrically tested. The joint products approach also explicitly incorporates technology in determining the degree of substitutability among inputs and the joint production of multiple outputs using multiple inputs that characterizes agriculture at the aggregate level.

This approach also allows the effects of policy on multiple inputs to be measured. These inputs include fertilizer, real estate, two types of capital, machinery, hired labor, energy, and other inputs. Details of the joint production approach to model building using duality theory can be found in Ball (1988) and Liapis (1990). This approach is still at a preliminary stage of development for the E.C., in that direct estimation of a profit function using E.C. data is only presently being done. The elasticities that are used to modify ST86 to account for joint production are calculated by applying E.C. production shares to elasticities from production functions estimated for the United States.

The Effects of Selected Policies on Nitrate Levels, Production, Trade, and World Prices

The assumption about technology does affect the amount by which policy changes affect production and input use. Therefore, it appears promising to continue research on this topic. Since the application of the joint production approach to E.C. agriculture is still at a formative stage, only its impact on supply and input use is discussed.

The Effect of Selected Policy Options on Agricultural Supply

The Nitrate Directive has more significant effects on supply than does the fertilizer tax (Figure 20.3). Livestock production declines by the magnitudes specified in the Directive, 5 percent for beef and about 8 to 12 percent for other livestock products. Crop production increases by insignificant amounts only under the assumption of joint production (not shown). A 50 percent tax on nitrogen fertilizer only reduces crop production, and by no more than 2 percent. The supply response to the fertilizer tax is greater and is spread over all commodities if joint production is assumed (Figure 20.4). Grain production is decreased slightly more than 4 percent, while oilseed and livestock products decrease about 2 percent.

Other assumptions regarding a fertilizer tax lead only to slightly larger declines in production (not shown). A 75 percent fertilizer tax leads to incremental decreases of about one-half percent in production. The imposition of an elasticity of fertilizer supply of 0.5 also leads to incremental decreases of about one-half percentage point in production. While some level of tax would lead to large reductions in production, the levels of fertilizer taxes that have been suggested do not appear to give the production responses that may occur under CAP reform.

The effects of CAP reform on supply are more varied and significant

FIGURE 20.3 E.C. Supply Changes Under Selected Policy Options.

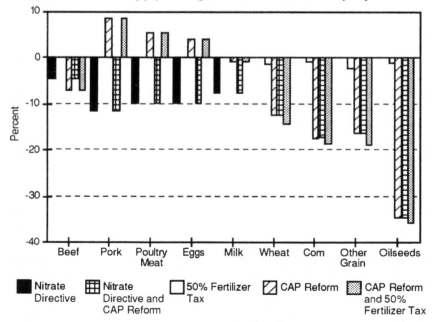

FIGURE 20.4 E.C. Supply Changes With and Without Joint Production Technology.

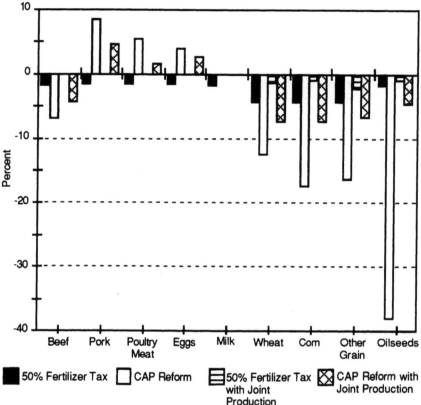

than those of the environmental policies. Commodities for which price reductions under CAP reform are greater tend to decline the most. Oilseed production declines about 38 percent. Corn and other coarse grains (mainly barley) decline about 18 percent. The decline in wheat production is about 13 percent.

The product-to-feed price ratio is increased for livestock. Nevertheless, beef production declines about 7 percent. The production of pork increases about 8 percent, and the supply of poultry products increases by about 5 percent. Dairy production does not increase because it is bound by the dairy quota.

Joint production technology limits the changes in crop and pork production under CAP reform (Figure 20.4). The increase in pork production is limited to 5 percent. The production of oilseeds declines less than 5 percent, and grains decline about 7 percent. The assumption of technology does not affect beef, eggs, or dairy, however.

Under the combination of the Nitrate Directive and CAP reform, live-stock production declines by the amounts implied by the Nitrate Direc-tive, while crop production declines by the amounts implied by CAP reform (Figure 20.3). This asymmetry of response occurs, in part, because the increase in the livestock-to-feed price ratio under CAP reform keeps livestock production bound against the constraint implied by the Nitrate Directive. Furthermore, the Nitrate Directive has no independent effect on crop production, leaving it to decline in response to CAP reform.

The implication of this scenario is that the amount of residual nitrogen declines by a greater amount than in the case of the Nitrate Directive alone. This would seem to suggest that it is possible to substitute the reduction in residual nitrogen from reduced cropping for the increased residual from increased livestock production. However, livestock and crop production do not have the same geographic distributions. The reductions in livestock production calculated above as implied by the Nitrate Directive are located in Denmark, Belgium, and the Netherlands. The reductions in crops indicated by ST86 for CAP reform include crops throughout the E.C.

The addition of a 50 percent fertilizer tax to CAP reform has only small marginal effects on crops (Figure 20.3).

Changes in Nutrient Balance and Resource Use

The Nitrate Directive and CAP reform reduce the total residual nitro-gen about 4 percent and 5 percent, respectively (Figure 20.5). In the case of the Nitrate Directive, residual nitrogen declines because of reduced live-stock numbers. Under CAP reform, the decline in residual nitrogen occurs because of reduced crop production and is offset somewhat by general increases in livestock production. Indeed, beef is the only livestock com-modity for which production declines. Therefore, there are likely to be regional differences in the decline of residual nitrogen between the two scenarios.

The 50 percent nitrogen tax reduces residual nitrogen by about 8 percent, twice the amount targeted by the Nitrate Directive. This is a rather significant reduction in residual nitrogen levels in view of the small reduction in grain production of about 2 percent. At the high levels of nitrogen used, the use of nitrogen fertilizer declines about 10 percent in response to the tax, and the response of crop production to fertilizer use is quite small. The effects of the fertilizer tax are spread throughout the E.C. and do not have offsetting increases in livestock numbers.

The resource effects of various scenarios can only be calculated using the joint products approach. In the case of the Nitrate Directive, the use of all inputs increases less than 1 percent (Figure 20.6). With the fertilizer tax, the use of fertilizer declines by 20 percent and the other inputs decline by

FIGURE 20.5 Changes in Nutrient Balance Due to Selected Policies.

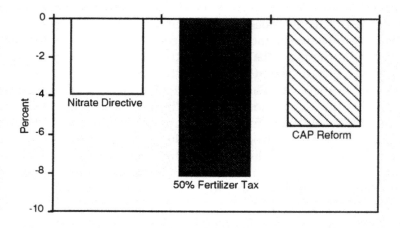

FIGURE 20.6 Changes in the Levels of Resource Use Due to Selected Policies (Joint production).

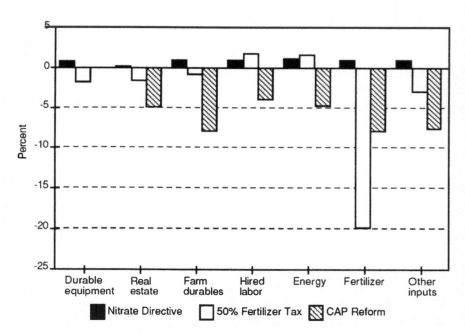

less than 3 percent. Under CAP reform, all inputs except durable equipment decline. The declines are much greater than in the case of the fertilizer tax, with the exception of fertilizer itself.

Trade and World Price Effects

The net trade and world price effects are significant for most commodities in all scenarios except the fertilizer tax. The Nitrate Directive reduces net E.C. exports of livestock products, and increases net exports of wheat and other coarse grains (Figures 20.7-8). The E.C. shifts from being a net exporter to a net importer of all livestock products except beef, the net exports of which decline about 50 percent. Net exports of wheat and other coarse grains increase about 10 percent and 50 percent, respectively, because feed demand for these grains declines against unchanged production. Net imports of corn and oilseeds decline because less of these are used as livestock feed. Net imports of corn drop by nearly 100 percent and net imports of oilseeds decline about 20 percent.

As a result of the trade effects under the Nitrate Directive, world prices increase for all livestock products and decrease for all crops except corn

FIGURE 20.7 Net Trade Effects for Livestock: European Community, Selected Policies.

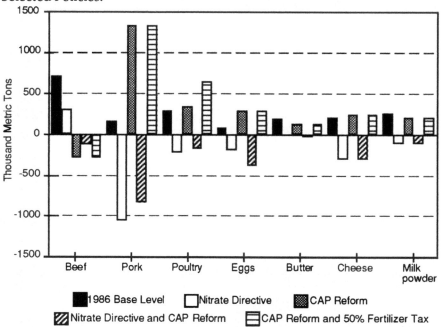

FIGURE 20.8 New Trade Effects for Grain, Selected Policies, European Community.

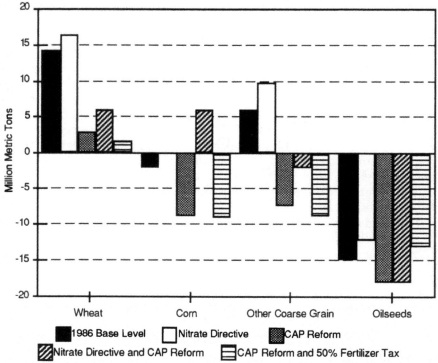

(Figure 20.9).[2] The largest increases are for butter (9 percent), eggs (8 percent), and pork (6 percent). Net trade for the United States declines for beef, increases for pork and poultry products, and does not change for the other products (Figures 20.10-11). Beef and pork are the only commodities for which the United States is a net importer. Net imports of beef decline about 75 percent and net imports of pork increase about 10 percent.

The trade and world price effects are less consistent under CAP reform. Net E.C. exports of pork and poultry products increase, while the E.C. becomes a net importer of beef. Net trade in dairy products does not change significantly. The decline in crop production and increase in livestock production and feed demand significantly affects trade in grains and oilseeds. The net exports of wheat decline about 80 percent, while net imports of corn increase by about 300 percent. The E.C. shifts from exporting 5 million tons of other coarse grains to importing about 8 million tons. The net imports of oilseeds increase about 20 percent.

World prices increase for all products except pork, poultry products,

FIGURE20.9 World Price Effects, Selected Policies.

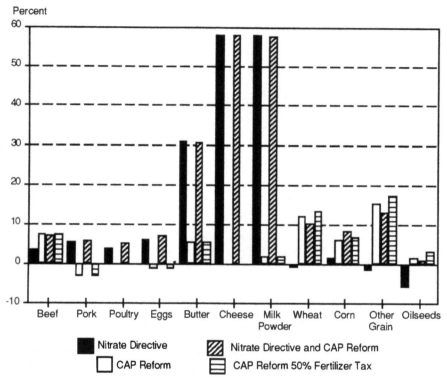

and cheese (Figure 20.9). Price increases are more modest for livestock products, ranging from about 2 percent for powdered milk to about 8 percent for beef. Price increases exceed 10 percent and 15 percent, respectively, for wheat and other coarse grain, and are about 8 percent for corn. Oilseed prices only increase about 1 percent.

CAP reform affects the net trade in livestock products for the United States differently than does the Nitrate Directive. Net beef imports decline by one-half, but this is not as much as they decline under the Nitrate Directive. Net imports of pork increase more under CAP reform than under the Nitrate Directive, or double in magnitude from the base. Exports of poultry meat decline and the United States shifts from being a net exporter of eggs and cheese to a net importer. Other dairy products are not affected. The net exports of all grains and oilseeds increase more under CAP reform than they do under the Nitrate Directive.

The net trade effects arising from the combination of the Nitrate Directive and CAP reform are not dominated by one policy or the other, as the

FIGURE 20.10 Net Trade Effects for Livestock, Selected Policies, United States.

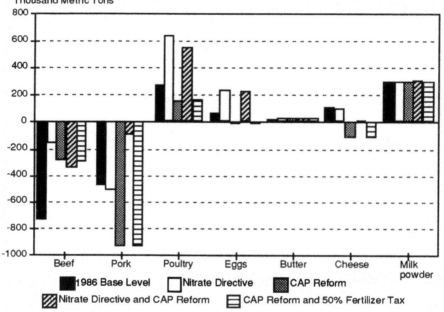

FIGURE 20.11 Net Trade Effects for Grain, Selected Policies, United States.

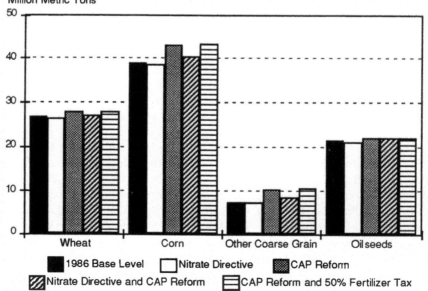

supply changes were. This is because lower livestock prices under CAP reform affect consumer demand for livestock products. However, livestock production is constrained to declines implied by the Nitrate Directive. As a result of reduced livestock production and increased demand, the E.C. becomes a net importer of all livestock products (Figure 20.7).

The net exports of wheat and other coarse grains decline under the combination of policies, but not by as much as under CAP reform alone (Figure 20.8). This is because livestock feed demand also declines under the combination of CAP reform and the Nitrate Directive, leaving more wheat and coarse grains to be exported. The E.C. still becomes a net importer of coarse grains under the combination of the two policies, but not by as much as under CAP reform alone. The E.C. also becomes a net exporter of corn because overall feed demand declines under the combination of policies. Oilseed imports increase to the same level as in the CAP reform scenario.

World prices for all products increase under the combination of the Nitrate Directive and CAP reform. Prices increase about the same amount for beef and crops, as with CAP reform alone. For pork and poultry products, they increase about as much as under the Nitrate Directive. Prices increase the most for dairy products (30 to 60 percent). Price increases for dairy products are similar to the increases under the Nitrate Directive because dairy production declines by the same amount under both scenarios, but E.C. demand does not increase significantly when CAP reform is added.

The addition of the Nitrate Directive to CAP reform increases the level of U.S. beef imports slightly and reduces pork imports by about 90 percent. The export of poultry products increases, but dairy products do not change much. Net exports of corn and other coarse grains decrease slightly but remain above the base level. Wheat and oilseed exports decrease slightly but also remain above the base level. The addition of a 50 percent fertilizer tax to CAP reform does not significantly affect world prices or trade.

Conclusions and Limitations

E.C. production is more widely and significantly affected by CAP reform than by either the Nitrate Directive or the fertilizer tax. Livestock production declines under the Nitrate Directive, while the nitrogen tax reduces crop production only slightly.

Under the Nitrate Directive, the E.C. becomes a net importer of livestock products, exports more wheat and coarse grains, and imports less corn and oilseeds. World livestock and corn prices increase, but U.S. oilseed producers export less at lower prices.

Under CAP reform, pork and poultry production increase and crop production decreases. Exports of pork, poultry, and wheat increase and imports of feedgrain and oilseeds increase. World prices increase for all products except pork, poultry products, and wheat, and the United States exports more of the higher-priced products.

The combination of the Nitrate Directive and CAP reform reduces both livestock and crop production in the E.C. World livestock prices generally increase the most in this scenario, but world crop prices increase less than under CAP reform alone because of lower E.C. feed demand. The combined policies affect U.S. livestock trade in ways similar to the Nitrate Directive, with the exception of pork. U.S. grain exports increase to levels between the Nitrate Directive and CAP reform.

A fertilizer tax reduces residual nitrogen the most but not sufficiently in regions of intensive livestock production. CAP reform reduces residual nitrogen less in intensive livestock areas because pork and poultry production increase and dairy remains stable. Only the Nitrate Directive reduces residual nitrogen to desired levels where needed.

The use of aggregate data conceals known nitrate problems in areas of The United Kingdom, France, and Germany. A more detailed analysis of how the nitrogen cycle operates under varying soil and environmental conditions is lacking in the present study. Some work of this type has been done by Veenendaal and Brouwer (1991).

Notes

1. This chapter only covers the E.C.-10: Belgium, Luxembourg, Denmark, Germany, France, Ireland, Italy, the Netherlands, and the United Kingdom. Although agriculturally induced water pollution is increasing in Spain and Portugal, the problem in these countries is relatively moderate.

2. Increased livestock production in the United Sates causes demand for corn to expand sufficiently to result in a higher world corn price.

References

Abler, D., and J. Shortle. 1992. "Environmental and Farm Commodity Policy Linkages in the U.S. and the EC." *Eur. R. Agr. Econ.* 19: 197-217.

Agra Europe. 1991. "Agriculture and the Environment: How Will the EC Resolve the Conflict?" July.

Ball, V. E. 1988. "Modeling Supply Response in a Multiproduct Framework." *Amer. J. Agr. Econ.* 70: 813-825.

Burrell, A. 1989. "The Demand for Fertilizer in the United Kingdom." *J. Agr. Econ.* 40: 1-20.

Commission of the European Communities. Agricultural Situation in the Community, Brussels, selected issues.

————. 1980. *Official Journal of the European Communities.* No. 229. Aug., pp. 11.

————. 1991. *Official Journal of the European Communities.* No. 375. Brussels, Dec.

Gunasekera, G. Rodriguez, and N. Andrews. 1992. "Taxing Fertiliser Use in E.C. Farm Production: Implications for Agricultural Trade." ABARE Conference Paper 92.20, May.

Haley, S. 1993. "Assessing Environmental and Agricultural Policy Linkages in the European Community: A Trade Modeling Perspective." International Agricultural Trade Research Consortium, Working Paper No. 93-3, Apr.

International Fertilizer Statistics. UN, FAO, International Fertilizer Association. Rome, Italy, selected issues.

Koopmans, T. 1987. "An Application of an Agro-Economic Model to Environmental Issues in the E.C.: A Case Study." *Eur. R. Agr. Econ.* 14.

Leuck, D. J. 1993. "Policies to Reduce Nitrate Pollution in the European Community and Possible Effects on Livestock Production." Staff Report No. AGES 9310, USDA ERS, Sept.

Liapis, P. 1990. "Incorporating Inputs in the Static World Policy Simulation Model (SWOPSIM)." USDA ERS Technical Bulletin No. 1780. Washington, D.C. June.

Madell, M. L. 1992. "CAP Reform." *Western Europe Agriculture and Trade Report: Situation and Outlook Series.* USDA ERS Dec.

Manale, A. 1991. "European Community Programs to Control Nitrate Emissions From Agriculture." *International Environment Reporter.* The Bureau of National Affairs, June 19.

Roningen, V. A. 1986. "Static World Policy Simulation (SWOPSIM) Modeling Framework." Staff Report No. AGES860625, USDA ERS.

Roningen, V., and P. Dixit. 1989. "How Level is the Playing Field? An Economic Analysis of Agricultural Policy Reforms in Industrialized Market Economies." FAER No. 239, USDA ERS.

Sullivan, J. 1990. "Price Transmission Elasticities in the Trade Liberalization (TLIB) Database." Staff Report No. AGES9034, USDA ERS.

Sullivan, J., J. Wainio, and V. Roningen. 1989. "A Database for Trade Liberalization Studies." Staff Report No. AGES89-12, USDA ERS.

Tyers, R., and K. Anderson. 1986. "Distortions in World Food Markets: A Quantitative Assessment." World Development Report 1986. World Bank.

Veenendaal, P., and F. Brouwer. 1991. "Consequences of Ammonia Emission Abatement Policies For Agricultural Practices in the Netherlands." *Environmental Policy and the Economy.* Elsevier Science Publishers B.B.: The Hague, Netherlands.

21

New Dimensions in World Fisheries: Implications for U.S. and E.C. Trade in Seafood

Cathy Roheim Wessells and Petter Wallström

Many international trade issues facing seafood markets today result from policies similar to those that affect agricultural markets. Yet some trade issues are unique to seafood markets because of policies that attempt to manage and protect marine resources. There are several reasons why policies affecting international trade in seafood merit further examination. First, seafood plays a vital role in feeding the world's population. Worldwide, over 16 percent of total animal protein in the diet is supplied by fish (Food and Agriculture Organization [hereafter FAO], 1992a). Domestic production plays an important part in this supply, in addition to the U.S. $38 billion of edible seafood which is traded globally (FAO, 1990b). Second, there have been several recent conflicts between international and domestic policies of natural resource management and international free trade agreements that affect seafood markets. The resolution of these conflicts often have implications for agriculture. Clearly, environmental policies have established themselves as an important component of international free trade agreements, as evidenced by the current debate over the North American Free Trade Agreement (NAFTA). Third, as examples of how important seafood trade is for the United States and the European Community (E.C.), total trade between these two regions is as valuable as trade in products such as nuts, vegetables, and meats; and more valuable than trade in fruit and cheese products. For these reasons and many others, it is important to examine more closely the implications of trade and environmental policies for international seafood markets.

Several events have occurred in the past 15 years that have helped to create the complex trade conflicts facing seafood markets. One of the most important of these was the expansion by coastal nations to a 200-nautical mile jurisdiction over coastal waters and resources during 1976-78. In the United States, the Magnuson Fishery Conservation and Management Act provided regional fisheries management councils with the authority to adopt policies to manage fishing effort and preserve stocks. One method of management is to exclude foreign fleets from harvesting fisheries resources within that zone. While fisheries remain a common property resource, this limited privatization by nations allows for some control over the harvest and maintenance of fish stocks. However, the effect was, in the simplest terms, to create an international trade in seafood. Nations that had previously harvested their own supply of fish were now, in some cases, forced to become importers. Other nations that found themselves with a surplus of fish became exporters. With increasing trade during the past 15 years, conflicts between nations involving tariff and nontariff barriers have repeatedly occurred, as have conflicts between fisheries management and international trade policies.

Another event that has had a significant impact on international trade in seafood is the tremendous growth in worldwide aquacultural production of several species of finfish, shellfish, and crustaceans. This has generated a growth in supply of several species that has outpaced the growth in demand. In the salmon market, this led to imposition of anti-dumping duties and countervailing duties on fresh Norwegian salmon by the United States, threatened imposition of such duties by the E.C., and imposition of minimum import prices for Norwegian salmon by the E.C. In the United States, the similarity of production of farmed seafood to other agricultural food production has led the U.S. Department of Agriculture to increase its involvement in and jurisdiction over the industry. Indeed, both President Clinton and Secretary of Agriculture Espy are from the South where catfish farming has a high profile. A pertinent question becomes, will aquaculture follow the path of agriculture with the latter's contentious trade issues?

This chapter presents a survey of four current issues in U.S. and E.C. trade in seafood products. First, domestic fisheries policy of the United States and E.C. that relate specifically to seafood markets are examined. This includes a discussion of the E.C.'s Common Fisheries Policy (CFP), which was patterned after the Common Agricultural Policy (CAP). Second, a growth in concern over food product quality and safety is leading nations to become more active in product standards regulations. New directives passed by the E.C. specifying more rigorous seafood standards have created new uncertainty in worldwide seafood trade as exporting nations are also forced to comply. Third, a summary of the U.S. International Trade Commission (USITC) investigation of Norwegian dumping of aquacultured salmon will be presented to illustrate the effects of increasing worldwide aquacultured production on trade relations. Finally, fisheries management policies have conflicted with international free trade policies such as the U.S.-Canada Free Trade Agreement (USCFTA) and the GATT. These policies include management of fisheries within the protected jurisdiction of individual nations as well as management of high seas fisheries. This chapter will discuss the growing uncertainty regarding reconciliation of management of fisheries and other marine resources with free trade agreements. The chapter closes with a discussion of the implications of these issues for the future of trade relations between the E.C. and United States.

Background on Seafood Production and Trade

Before beginning the discussion of seafood trade issues, it is useful to present a few facts regarding the level and characteristics of current worldwide seafood production and trade, with a specific focus on North America and Europe. As Figure 21.1 shows, North American and European landings (including aquaculture production) were only 20 percent of

FIGURE 21.1 Regional Proportion of World Catch of Fish and Shellfish, 1990.

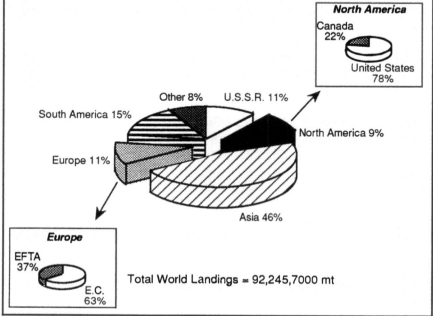

Source: FAO, 1990a.

world production in 1990 (FAO, 1990a). However, North America and Europe are among the most important participants in international seafood trade (FAO, 1990b). The United States is the second largest importer of fish products in the world, after Japan. In 1990, U.S. imports of fishery commodities were worth nearly $5.6 billion. This was about twice the value of the third leading importer, France. U.S. imports of seafood are steadily growing; during the 1980s, the nominal value of seafood imported into the United States nearly doubled.

Although Asia is the largest producer of fish in the world, the United States is the largest exporter of seafood, by value, in the world. In 1990, the United States exported over $3 billion in edible fish products.[1] This is nearly a three-fold nominal increase in exports since 1981. Canada is the world's second largest exporter. In 1990, Canada exported seafood worth over $2.2 billion, nearly twice what it exported in 1981.

There are only two E.C. members among the top ten exporters: Denmark fourth and the Netherlands ninth. The E.C. does, however, boast seven of the top ten seafood importers in the world. France is the third largest importer; Italy and Spain fourth and fifth, respectively. When taken as a single unit, however, the E.C. becomes the world's leading importer. In fact, the E.C. imported more than $13 billion worth of seafood in 1990. By comparison, Japan imported slightly less than $11 billion worth of seafood in 1990. Imports of fishery products have increased sharply for all members of the E.C. since the early 1980s.

Table 21.1 shows that, on net, both the North American countries and the E.C. have trade deficits with respect to edible fishery commodities. The E.C. deficit has been growing steadily. In 1981, the E.C.'s seafood trade deficit was approximately $2 billion, growing to over $7 billion in 1990. Italy is the main contributor to the E.C. seafood trade deficit. In 1990, Italy's trade deficit reached $2.2 billion. If Norway joins the E.C., its seafood trade balance would improve since Norway's net exports are greater than any of the other nations in North America, the E.C., and the European Free Trade Association (EFTA). Figure 21.2 shows the trade balance between the United States and E.C. While the trade balance has fluctuated, the United States currently has a trade surplus with the E.C.

To provide some perspective on the size of seafood trade between the United States and E.C., Table 21.2 presents the value of edible seafood trade in 1990 relative to the two-way trade of other agricultural products, excluding grains. U.S. exports of edible seafood to the E.C. are second only to exports of nuts, while the value of total trade compares favorably with trade in vegetables and meat. The majority of seafood imports by the E.C. and United States come from other regions, particularly the EFTA nations of Norway and Iceland, South America, Asia, and Africa. Developing nations supply an estimated $4 billion of seafood to the E.C. each year.

TABLE 21.1 Trade Balance for Fishery Commodities by Country and Region (US$ 1,000)

Country	1981	1982	1983	1984	1985	1986	1987	1988	1989	1990
USA	-1,846,169	-2,142,385	-2,624,729	-2,699,558	-2,889,422	-3,267,702	-3,837,541	-2,948,169	-3,224,248	-2,553,364
Canada	962,128	1,018,245	942,019	898,793	1,003,309	1,318,722	1,580,269	1,613,112	1,391,328	1,649,493
Mexico	0	0	0	0	0	451,327	563,362	401,280	448,328	319,269
NAFTA	-884,041	-1,124,140	-1,682,710	-1,800,765	-1,886,113	-1,497,653	-1,693,910	-933,777	-1,384,592	-584,602
France	-738,749	-743,222	-734,039	-682,010	-680,848	-1,009,198	-1,367,404	-1,512,898	-1,420,663	-1,877,840
Italy	-613,502	-651,329	-630,852	-637,123	-844,070	-1,096,919	-1,597,956	-1,713,670	-1,779,034	-2,219,562
Spain	-41,045	-237,063	-110,409	-82,766	-631,223	-323,274	-847,019	-1,075,337	-1,040,853	-1,617,147
UK	-686,846	-595,839	-599,276	-572,390	-578,302	-704,923	-669,400	-875,913	-833,499	-949,179
Germany FR	-539,598	-507,311	-525,603	-502,223	-533,752	-754,320	-831,031	-934,712	-926,679	-1,234,225
Denmark	635,642	603,414	619,152	572,175	582,270	785,400	908,176	1,000,225	880,635	1,049,389
Netherlands	181,175	193,832	238,544	212,325	235,217	378,444	443,747	370,261	390,144	489,390
Belgium	-274,584	-254,015	-231,796	-211,310	-219,782	126,192	-362,936	-408,992	-418,446	-524,737
Portugal	-68,732	-90,877	-50,671	-48,800	-97,844	-113,528	-270,963	-280,093	-166,877	-326,117
Greece	-65,094	-69,246	-52,571	-54,194	-49,909	-60,846	-64,264	-80,266	-83,121	-107,138
Ireland	41,326	56,991	68,758	61,155	69,213	89,655	137,545	147,252	156,025	168,607
EC	-2,170,007	-2,294,665	-2,008,763	-1,945,161	-2,749,030	-2,683,317	-4,521,505	-5,364,143	-5,242,368	-7,148,559
Norway	942,814	839,905	929,596	856,532	851,589	1,065,953	1,354,182	1,450,489	1,385,647	1,822,408
Iceland	711,905	536,822	525,171	505,534	612,657	856,387	1,067,688	1,050,360	1,013,308	1,223,243
Finland	-93,273	-89,632	-86,755	-77,244	-68,966	-99,653	-121,546	-116,877	-132,511	-116,566
Austria	-77,016	-70,931	-73,546	-67,228	-66,102	-90,725	-115,760	-116,282	-119,559	-145,857
Sweden	-174,485	-182,072	-172,788	-170,876	-164,393	-237,082	-287,105	-263,734	-280,461	-275,000
Switzerland	-203,238	-189,717	-191,306	-184,525	-189,171	-259,275	-324,927	-352,883	-334,092	-379,217
EFTA	1,106,707	844,375	930,372	862,193	975,614	1,235,605	1,572,532	1,651,073	1,532,332	2,129,011

Source: FAO (1990b).

FIGURE 21.2 Real Value of U.S.-E.C. Trade in Edible Fishery Products.

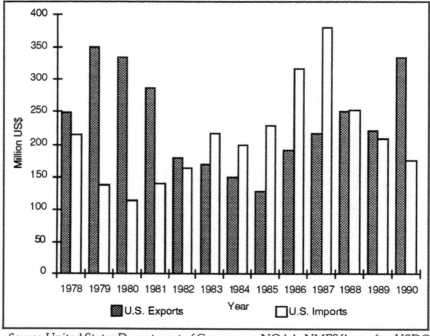

Source: United States Department of Commerc e, NOAA, NMFS [hereafter USDC], *Fisheries Statistics of the U.S.* various years.

Domestic Fisheries Policies

United States

The United States, for the most part, practices a policy of relatively free seafood trade. Tariffs on most unprocessed fish and shellfish are zero, while processed product tariffs are generally low. There are no policies of price support or price stabilization, nor are there highly structured policies of sustained subsidization of fishermen.[2] The focus of the U.S. government with regard to the fishing sector has been almost exclusively one of imposing regulations on fishing effort.

Recently, however, there has been more emphasis placed on product promotion. For example, the Federal government provides the Alaska Seafood Marketing Institute with several million dollars per year to assist in marketing Alaskan seafood products overseas. The Foreign Agricultural Service of the U.S. Department of Agriculture recently added seafood to its agenda, adding canned pink salmon to its PL 480 list in 1991. There has been little success with this program because, while prices of canned pink salmon have dropped, it remains an expensive product

TABLE 21.2 U.S.-E.C. Trade in Seafood Relative to Other Food Products, 1990 ($1,000)

Product	U.S. Exports to the E.C.	U.S. Imports from the E.C.
All Edible Seafood	350,294	183,938
Vegetables and Preparations	250,091	408,498
Nuts and Preparations	520,045	23,015
Fruits and Preparations	309,781	72,963
Meat and Meat Products	169,598	368,335
Cheese	1,090	251,244
Wine	38,453	858,277

Sources: USDA, 1991. USDC, *Fisheries Statistics of the United States*, 1990.

relative to other items on the PL 480 list. Atlantic mackerel has been on the PL 480 list for two years.

European Community

The European Community has a more comprehensive program for the fisheries sector. The Treaty of Rome in 1957 envisaged the development of a common European fisheries policy as part of the Common Agricultural Policy. As a result, the Common Fisheries Policy (CFP) was instituted in 1970 and has been modified with the joining of Denmark, Ireland, and the UK in 1973 and again in 1986 with the expansion of the E.C. to include Spain and Portugal. The addition of Spain and Portugal doubled the number of fishermen, increased the tonnage of the Community fishing fleet by about 50 percent, and doubled the average per capita consumption of fish in the Community, from 14 to 27 kg per annum (Commission of the European Communities [hereafter E.C. Commission], 1991b).

The cost of the CFP is relatively low. Although the Community funds allocated to it have increased from ECU 190 million in 1986 to 450 million in 1990, this still accounts for only 0.9 percent of the Community budget (E.C. Commission, 1991b). The policy relates to four main areas: access to waters and the conservation and management of stocks; organization of the market; structural changes and research; and international relations. It is the policy regarding the organization of the market that has the greatest impact on seafood trade with the E.C.

The common organization of markets for fish was introduced in 1970 in order to stabilize producers' incomes and guarantee an adequate supply of high-quality fish. Its main provisions are: (1) Marketing standards that define quality specifications (size, weight, freshness) for seafood, which has been subject to increasingly strict inspection over the years; (2) Community support for producer organizations (POs) in the form of start-up aid for those POs whose members apply common rules in the area of production and marketing; (3) a complex pricing system designed to stabilize prices and market fluctuations, administered through the producers' organizations; and (4) an external trade policy which sets a "reference" price to ensure the stability of the market by protecting E.C. fishermen from large increases in low-priced imports.

It is the latter two functions of the CFP that the United States has long argued against. A guide price serves as the target price for fisheries products for sale in the E.C. It is the basic element of the E.C. price system and represents the Council's judgment on the price that will ensure an "equitable" rate of return to the fishermen. The withdrawal price serves as the minimum price below which the price of seafood for sale by the producers' organizations is not allowed to drop. If the price of certain imported fishery products falls below a reference price, set by the E.C. as a minimum import price, the E.C. can institute various measures to curb or completely halt the importation of the product. For example, variable levies or import quotas may be used.

Another aspect of the E.C. price support system is a carryover premium, which pays producers' organizations for storage until their fish is processed, returned to the market, or destroyed. It works as a complimentary program to reference and withdrawal price programs in that its purpose is to encourage producers organizations not to withdraw seafood from the market. Since the premiums cover processing and storage costs, the program enables producers' organizations to process and hold fish rather than lose money as a result of withdrawing fish from the market. Premiums under this program are available only for certain species, including most groundfish and pelagic species and shrimp. Groundfish and shrimp compose a substantial volume of U.S. exports to the E.C. U.S. exports of squid to the E.C. are affected by another related program, a private storage aid program. Squid is an important export to the E.C. from the eastern United States, but these imports compete with an important domestic fishery in Italy.

Product Quality Standards

A recent event with major implications for trade between the E.C. and third countries is the passage of E.C. Council Directives 91/492 and 91/493, which set health standards for production and marketing of live bivalve mollusks and fishery products, respectively. In response to controversy regarding quality of seafood products available on the market, the E.C. has enacted these directives originally planned to be in place by 1 January 1993, although in reality 1993 has been more of a transition period. The concern has been over quality deterioration arising from post-harvest handling and storage. One of the purposes of the directives is to remove disparities in quality regulations existing between Member States.

Also among the requirements is that third countries, for example, the United States, "name a competent authority or authorities to monitor and certify fishery product exports to the E.C." (E.C. Commission, 1991a). In addition, the E.C. requires that an approved list of companies be compiled, each with its own approval number and accompanying mark indicating that the competent authority has found it and its products in compliance. Health certificates must accompany every shipment to the E.C., with a second health certificate guaranteeing that products are disease-free in the case of aquaculture. The plan is based on a state-of-the-art inspection system, Hazard Analysis Critical Control Point, or HACCP.

The issue from the U.S. perspective is that it has not, to this date, determined that a comprehensive seafood inspection system is necessary. In contrast to meat products, there is no comprehensive, mandatory inspection system for seafood at the federal level. In response to consumer groups' insistence, past sessions of Congress have proposed legislation to create a national mandatory inspection program for seafood, for example, the Consumer Seafood Safety Act of 1992, a Senate bill. This act proposed the administration of a national seafood safety program designed to set tolerances for contaminants in seafood, monitor growing areas and fishing grounds for water pollution, and devise processing and handling requirements and an inspection system. To date, none of these bills have become law, partially due to the apparent lack of a widespread safety problem but also due to conflicting political interests. One controversy concerns which federal agency should be the lead agency, the USDA, the Food and Drug Administration that inspects imported seafood, or the National Marine Fisheries Service (NMFS, part of the U.S. Department of Commerce under the National Oceanic and Atmospheric Administration), which is the primary regulatory body governing the harvest of fishery resources.

There have been several impacts of these directives on trade relations between the two regions. A problem for the United States in exporting to the E.C. becomes one of meeting requirements of the E.C. regulations. For example, determination of who is the "competent authority," given there is no comprehensive inspection program, has been difficult. The FDA has taken the most aggressive initiative by launching an HACCP program jointly with NMFS. Given this progress, in 1993 the E.C. recognized NMFS as the competent authority. In addition, individual plants that export product to the E.C. must be certified by NMFS. There are literally hundreds of seafood processors who ship product to the E.C.; thus to complete all inspections will take time. Since the process began in both the E.C. and United States, everyone involved is finding it costly. In the United States, the processors must pay for inspection and these costs will at some point be passed on to consumers. Thus, these E.C. policies have imposed added uncertainty, risks, and costs on those who export seafood to the E.C., although consumers worldwide should ultimately benefit from a higher-quality seafood supply.

Aquaculture—Protectionist Policies Revisited?

World aquaculture production has experienced tremendous growth in the last 20 years. Aquaculture products include salmon, trout, shrimp, catfish, tilapia, hybrid striped bass, mussels, clams, and many others. In fact, aquaculture production of finfish has grown from 2.6 million metric tons (mt) in 1975 to 8.4 million mt in 1990; crustaceans from 29.7 thousand mt in 1975 to 715 thousand mt in 1990; and mollusks from 2.0 million mt in 1975 to 3.0 in 1990 (FAO, 1990c). The largest producer of aquacultured seafood is Asia, with 8.6 million mt in 1988, followed by Europe with 1.1 million mt and North America with 0.42 million mt (FAO, 1990c). In addition, Asia cultured 3.6 million mt of seaweed in 1988.

From the perspective of the United States, Canada, the E.C., and Norway, the salmon aquaculture industry has led to the most contentious trade issues. World production of farmed Pacific and Atlantic salmon rose 4454 percent from 7,149 mt in 1980 to 325,563 mt in 1991. Norway's share of farmed Atlantic salmon production was 52 percent in 1991, and virtually all of it was exported (USDC, 1992). Other major producers and exporters of farmed salmon are Canada and Chile, although the United States has a small industry in the states of Maine and Washington and the E.C. has some production in Ireland and Scotland. This tremendous growth in farmed salmon production has coincided with a simultaneously large increase in the production of wild salmon. Figure 21.3 shows the growth in salmon production by species from 1973 through 1991. The rise in Atlantic salmon from 1983 through 1991 reflects the increase in farmed salmon, most of which is Atlantic salmon.

Due to an extensive marketing program that distinguished Norwegian farmed salmon as a uniquely high-quality product, Norway was extremely successful in exporting salmon to the United States and E.C. at premium prices. Along with product, Norway exported production and feed technology to other producing nations.

In 1989, a world glut of salmon generated by record production of farmed salmon as well as record production of wild salmon in Japan, Alaska, and British Columbia, Canada, caused a significant decrease in prices for all types of salmon. The farmed salmon industry in the state of Maine alleged that the price decline for farmed Atlantic salmon in the U.S. market had been caused by Norwegian dumping of product, causing

FIGURE 21.3 World Harvest of Salmon, by Species.

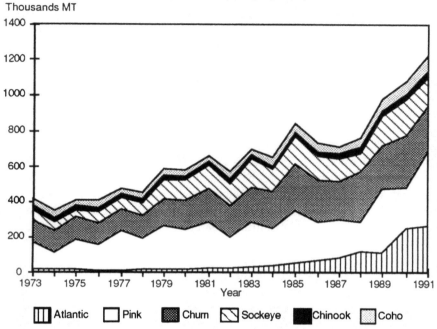

material injury to the U.S. salmon aquaculture industry. In February 1990 these farmers asked the U.S. International Trade Commission (USITC) to investigate the dumping charge and to institute a countervailing duty to counteract subsidization of the farmed salmon industry by the Norwegian government. Similar charges were filed with the E.C. Commission by Scottish and Irish farmers.

The burden of proof in the USITC case pivoted upon the definition of "like product" (USITC, 1991). In other words, what is a like product for Norwegian fresh farmed Atlantic salmon? The U.S. farmed salmon industry claimed like product is other fresh farmed Atlantic salmon only. With this definition, the U.S. coalition of salmon farmers argued that Norwegian imports were the cause of the price decline since Norway was the dominant producer, holding the largest share of the fresh farmed salmon market in the United States. The Norwegians, on the other hand, argued that all salmon in fresh form are a like product and therefore substitute for Norwegian salmon. This point was crucial, because, as mentioned above, prices fell for all Pacific salmon species in 1989.[3] The Norwegians thus used the argument that prices were falling due to an increased supply of all salmon.

USITC findings were that premium-quality fresh farmed salmon is a like product (USITC, 1991). The basis for this finding was that, even though certain species of Pacific salmon are frequently named as substitutes for Atlantic salmon, the majority of Pacific salmon is harvested wild, is ultimately frozen, and generally receives lower prices than Atlantic salmon. In addition, fresh high-quality wild salmon appear in the market during different times of the year from farmed salmon.

As a result of the USITC ruling, a 2.3 percent countervailing duty was placed on Norwegian fresh salmon entering the United States, based on the finding that Norwegian producers were unfairly competing in the market because of government subsidization (USITC, 1991). Norway has consistently claimed that any subsidization that has occurred were not export subsidies but rather a means of maintaining viable employment for citizens in rural areas, including fishermen displaced from work due to declining wild fish stocks. The USITC determined that Norwegian regional development loans and grants, bank loans, capital tax incentives, and other government grants conferred subsidies on salmon farmers. Thus, an additional anti-dumping duty of 26 percent on average was placed on Norwegian salmon. Figure 21.4 shows the effects of the anti-dumping and countervailing duties imposed on fresh Norwegian salmon by the United States on Norwegian exports. A GATT dispute panel has since upheld the USITC ruling on Norwegian salmon, although the tariff rates have recently been lowered. The E.C. began its own anti-dumping and countervailing duty investigation into Norwegian export practices, but, because of ongoing negotiations between the E.C. and EFTA, agreed to refrain. Instead, minimum import prices were imposed on Norwegian salmon.

Figure 21.4 shows the growth in Norwegian salmon exports to the E.C. during the last 10 years. From 1980 to 1990, the United States saw its share of the fresh and frozen salmon market in the E.C. fall from 43 percent to 11 percent (FAO, 1990b; USDC, 1992). Meanwhile, Norway's export share has increased from virtually zero to over 50 percent during the same time period (FAO, 1990b; Norwegian Central Bureau of Statistics). Recently, an effort has been coordinated by Scottish and Irish farmed salmon producers to form a producers' organization that may include Norwegian producers. POs are E.C.-approved organizations that allow producers to collectively coordinate production through production quotas, exchange market information, and, if necessary, apply countermeasures when prices fall too low for producers. The likelihood of such a cartel forming may increase if Norway joins the E.C. If so, this will certainly prove to be a contentious issue between the United States and E.C.

FIGURE 21.4 U.S. and E.C. Imports of Fresh Norwegian-Farmed Salmon.

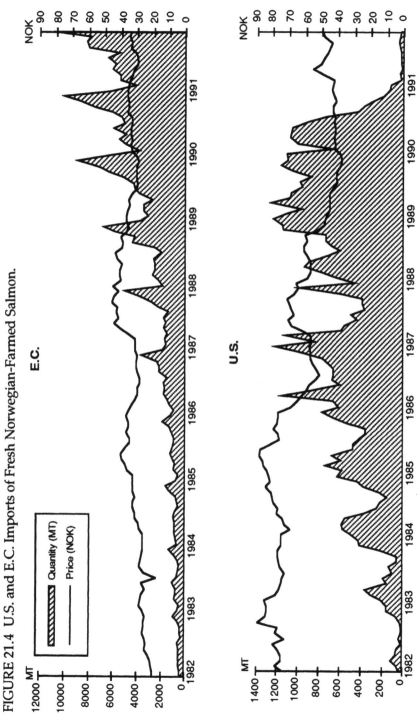

Source: Norwegian Central Bureau of Statistics.

Conflicts Between Fisheries/Environmental Management and Free Trade

Fisheries Management or Trade Barrier?

At the inception of the Uruguay round of the GATT, the United States proposed that issues related to fish and agricultural products be jointly negotiated. The E.C. agreed but proposed that the 200-mile Exclusive Economic Zone is a trade barrier and hence should also be negotiated in the Uruguay Round. The United States and Canada strenuously disagreed. Thus, fish and agricultural negotiations were separated.

This is not the only case of international fisheries law conflicting with policies regarding free trade. Since enactment of the U.S.-Canada Free Trade Agreement, conflicts between fisheries management policies and international trade agreements have generated considerable acrimony between these two nations. The resolution of these disputes have considerable implications for global trade.

A major dispute occurred over banned trade in unprocessed salmon and herring from Canada to the United States (McDorman, 1990). Prior to 1989, Canadian regulations prohibited export of unprocessed salmon and herring, ensuring that all salmon and herring caught in Canadian waters be landed and processed in Canada. The United States argued that these regulations were inconsistent with the GATT.

The basis of these regulations was the Canadian equivalent of the U.S. Magnuson Act, both of which are domestic laws consistent with an international treaty, the 1982 United Nations Convention on the Law of the Sea (LOS Convention). In 1987, the United States complained that Canadian regulations were contrary to the GATT. However, Canada argued that these regulations were not export restrictions, but rather multipurpose measures to facilitate regulatory measures dealing with landing, inspection, weighing, grading, and collecting harvest data and were admissible under Article XI of the GATT, which excepts those export restrictions necessary for application of quality standards. A GATT dispute panel did not accept this argument, stating that Canadian regulations disallow exports even in situations where unprocessed fish met quality standards.

In 1989, Canada replaced the ban on unprocessed exports with a requirement that all salmon and herring be landed in Canada. Once fish were landed, they could be transshipped to U.S. processors. The United States again lodged a complaint, noting that this added unnecessary costs to fish going to export markets and thus constituted an export restraint. Rather than use a GATT dispute panel, the United States and Canada agreed to arbitration by a USCFTA dispute panel, although GATT articles were again used as a basis for the rulings. Canadian arguments were similar to those in the previous case, where the requirement was a necessary component of data collection for fisheries management purposes. In addition, Canada argued that the landing requirement applied equally to fish destined for both domestic and export markets. However, the panel ruled in favor of the United States, citing that alternative measures could be taken to achieve the data collection. The two nations negotiated a compromise where a percentage of Canadian fish may be landed directly in the United States.

In another important case, in 1989 Canada and the United States were at odds regarding a U.S. decision to restrict imports of live Canadian lobster (McDorman, 1991). The U.S. lobster management plans do not allow lobster below a minimum size to be harvested for stock management purposes. Lobsters below this size are not allowed to be marketed live in the United States, regardless of origin, as stipulated in the Mitchell Amendment to the Magnuson Act. The minimum size for lobsters is smaller in Canada than the United States. The justification of including all lobsters, regardless of origin, is the need to remove the possibility of cheating by U.S. lobster fishermen and to make enforcement of the conservation measure easier.

Canada and the United States again agreed to utilize the dispute settlement process of the USCFTA, although the issues themselves involved interpretations of GATT. The Canadian position was that, because of different water temperatures, Canadian lobsters mature at a smaller size. The United States argued that the size restriction applies to exports as well as imports and thus is nondiscriminatory, and that if not upheld the U.S. market would be forced to give more favorable treatment to Canadian lobster than its own. The majority membership on the FTA panel agreed with the United States. This was important to U.S. fishermen, who felt that it is unfair to compete in the market with Canadian lobsters given that U.S. lobster harvest requirements are stricter than Canadian, thus placing U.S. fishermen at a comparative disadvantage.

These conflicts are examples of debates that frequently arise in many disputes over environmental regulations that differ between nations. At issue is the apparent comparative advantage that is bestowed upon other nations when domestic environmental regulations are more costly to comply with than those elsewhere. It is clear that this type of debate will occur time and again in the future. Without progress in GATT negotiations, it is less clear how they will be resolved.

Marine Resource Conservation or Trade Barrier?

Another example of how environmental regulations can instigate a trade dispute is in the well-known conflict between several members of the E.C., United States, and Mexico over dolphin-safe tuna. This conflict stems from a controversial practice of the United States, which uses import restrictions on fishery products as a means to force other nations to comply with U.S. marine resource policy. Concern for whales, tuna, sea turtles, and dolphins has led the United States to enact laws that contain in them prescribed actions against third nations designed to force them to adopt the U.S. view of appropriate conservation and management practices. The goal of these laws is to encourage other nations to enter into or adhere to bilateral or multilateral agreements for the conservation and management of the particular species, or to have other countries adopt fisheries management programs and standards equivalent to those existing in the United States. The failure to fulfill U.S. standards might, and in some cases must, lead to the imposition of unilateral trade sanctions by the United States against the offending nation.

Several laws in the United States fall into the above category, including: the 1971 Pelly Amendment to the 1967 Fisherman's Protective Act; the 1979 Packwood-Magnuson Amendment to the 1976 Magnuson Fishery Conservation and Management Act (FCMA); the 1988 Marine Mammal Protection Act (MMPA); the 1989 Sea Turtles Amendment to the Endangered Species Act of 1973; and Driftnet Control Act of 1990 (McDorman, 1992). The Pelly Amendment grants the President discretion to prohibit imports of any or all fish or fish products originating in a country that is diminishing the effectiveness of an international fishery conservation program.

The Marine Mammal Protection Act stems in part from concerns about the effect of tuna fishing on dolphins. The killing of dolphins by tuna harvesters has led to Federal legislative efforts, which have in turn led to complaints to the GATT. The negotiations over NAFTA have also been affected by this issue. The reason for the controversy lies with the production process involved in capturing yellowfin tuna. For reasons that are not entirely clear to biologists, dolphins frequently associate with yellowfin tuna in the Eastern Tropical Pacific ocean (ETP). Fishermen use purse seine nets that encircle both the dolphin school and yellowfin swimming below in tuna harvesting.

The MMPA is designed to reduce incidental taking of marine mammals in the course of commercial fishing operations. To extend this policy beyond waters directly under U.S. jurisdiction, it also provides for the imposition of trade restrictions on other nations that use production processes that result in an incidental killing exceeding U.S. standards. In early 1992, an import embargo on yellowfin tuna from Mexico, Venezuela, and Vanuatu as nations that violate U.S. standards for the production of tuna in a dolphin-safe manner was instituted (USITC, 1992). Later in 1991, an embargo was placed on five nations (Costa Rica, France, Italy, Japan, and Panama) for exporting to the U.S. tuna products that had originally been harvested by nations that did not certify their production to be dolphin-safe.

Mexico filed a complaint with the GATT in January 1991. Briefly, there were three major arguments that the United States used to defend the trade restrictions as consistent with the GATT (USITC, 1992). First, the United States argued that the measures treated imported products no less favorably than products of domestic origin. However, the GATT panel pointed out that the MMPA focuses on production processes rather than tuna; thus, imported Mexican tuna was being discriminated against. Second, the U.S. position was that the sole purpose of the MMPA was to protect dolphin life and health. Furthermore, there was no alternative measure reasonably available to the United States to achieve this objective. The GATT panel again disagreed, finding that the United States had failed to exhaust other options such as international cooperative agreements regarding these production processes. Third, the United States argued that the MMPA is entirely consistent with the GATT exception relating to the conservation of exhaustible resources (Article XX(g)). Once more, the GATT panel disagreed, having decided that this exception only applied to the conservation of exhaustible natural resources within the United States. Efforts to conserve exhaustible natural resources outside the jurisdiction of the United States falls outside the scope of the exception. Mexico deferred a request for a GATT Council ruling on the panel report, instead choosing to address this issue within the negotiations over NAFTA and other cooperative agreements.

The economic effect of the dolphin-safe controversy on the world tuna market has been widespread and significant for all sectors of the market, harvesting through retail. Trade patterns have altered substantially, with Thailand, Indonesia, and the Philippines playing a bigger role as harvest has shifted away from the ETP toward the Western Tropical Pacific. In the E.C., due to pressure from environmental groups, Spanish, French, and Italian canners all expressed intentions not to buy "dolphin-unsafe" tuna (FAO, 1992b). E.C. legislation requiring an import embargo on tuna not harvested using dolphin-safe practices failed to pass (American Seafood Institute, 1992). However, in response to low prices on imported canned tuna from Southeast Asia, the E.C. has instituted references prices on imported canned tuna and imposed a quota on canned tuna imported from nations other than those covered by the Lomé Convention (FAO, 1993). Germany and the United Kingdom, which import a majority of their canned tuna from Southeast Asia, are most negatively affected. However, Côte d'Ivoire, Senegal, and the Seychelles benefit since their exports to the E.C. are not subject to the import quota. France is hurt the least by this policy and possibly benefits, since France imports primarily from these West African nations in addition to owning a majority of the canneries in this region (FAO, 1993).

Another recent controversy that involves the United States is a result of the Packwood-Magnuson Amendment to the Magnuson Act. This amendment requires the President to impose trade sanctions pursuant to the Pelly Amendment if a country is diminishing the effectiveness of the International Whaling Convention (IWC) (McDorman, 1992). This issue has recently strained relations between the United States and Norway, as Norway resumed limited commercial harvest of minke whales in 1993. As a member of the IWC, Norway agrees to follow the recommendations of the scientific committee of the IWC regarding allowable catch of the various whale stocks. In May 1993, scientific committee (made up of scientists from all over the world) recommended that limited harvest of minke whales could begin. The scientific committee based these recommendations on their study, which had concluded that there exist approximately 760,000 minke whales in the Antarctic and 114,000 in the North Atlantic, enough to allow a limited harvest. Norway proposed to harvest a total of 296 whales in 1993. Based on the recommendation of the scientific committee, Norway would not be violating international law or the law of the IWC by harvesting minke whales. However, a majority of the member countries declined to adopt the recommendations of the scientific committee, prompting the chairman of the scientific committee to resign (Royal Norwegian Embassy, 1993).

The United States threatened to embargo seafood imports from Norway if it persisted beginning commercial harvest of minke whales. Norway did resume whaling. President Clinton, under mandate from the Pelly Amendment to act on this issue, stated in a letter to the U.S. Congress on October 4, 1993, that while the United States is deeply opposed to commercial whaling, "I believe our objectives can best be achieved by delaying the implementation of sanctions until we have exhausted all good faith efforts to persuade Norway to follow agreed conservation measures." (U.S. Congress, 1993). However, the President has directed that a list be made of seafood products that could be subjected to import restrictions at a later date.

This problem is certainly not resolved. While the E.C. has not placed a formal embargo on products from Norway, the matter will almost certainly arise as Norway's membership to the E.C. is negotiated. In the meantime, if either the E.C. or United States decides to impose an embargo on imports of Norwegian fish and fish products, it is likely that Norway will lodge a complaint with the GATT. It is unclear how the GATT would rule on this issue. However, the resolution of the dispute between the United States and Mexico over dolphin-safe tuna may provide an indication, since whales are also highly migratory and any products that may be subject to embargo will not be whale products.

Implications for U.S.-E.C. Seafood Trade Relations

It is apparent from this brief and cursory discussion that the trade issues affecting seafood are complex and wide-reaching, compounded by the fact that fish are not a homogenous commodity, in addition to varying substantially in production areas, harvest methods, and markets. Aquaculture production practices are similar to those in agriculture and, as a result, mimic some of the same trade issues that other food markets face. Further complicating these industries are the interactions of markets for aquacultured species with wild harvests of the same. In turn, wild fisheries are generally subject to many domestic and international harvest regulations, due to their common property nature. These regulations at times conflict with international agreements regarding free trade.

The implications of these issues for future U.S.-E.C. trade relations lie in part in the progress made in current and future GATT negotiations. As subsidization of agriculture is decreased through repeated GATT negotiations and CAP reform, CFP reform will no doubt follow. Likewise, this will decrease the probability that aquaculture will become as subsidized and protected as agriculture currently is. Progress in better defining dumping and countervailable subsidies through continuing GATT negotiations will discourage the use of additional tariffs. However, conflicts between marine resource management and free trade are likely to continue. As noted by Patterson (1992), Petersmann (1993), and Runge (1990), the treatment of environmental management and protection must be clarified within the GATT. Alternative policies that both protect the resource yet have no trade-distorting affects must be developed. Without progress in all of these areas, conflicts in international seafood trade relations between the United States and E.C. are likely to continue to emerge.

Notes

Partial funding was provided by USDA/CSRS Grant No. 93-34276-6963 and the Rhode Island Agricultural Experiment Station, RI/AES No. 2902. The authors would like to thank James L. Anderson for his helpful comments.

1. Fisheries products are classified into edible versus nonedible products. Nonedible products include fishmeal, a very important commodity that may substitute for soybean meal as an animal feed product.

2. However, fishermen in the United States have begun to ask their congressmen and senators why fishermen are not treated as farmers, with all the benefits that entails.

3. There are six species of Pacific salmon: chinook, coho, sockeye, chum, pink, and cherry. Cherry is only produced in small amounts by the Japanese and Russians and is not traded on the world market. The other five species are

produced by Canada, the United States, Japan, and Russia, with the United States being the dominant producer of all except chum. Significant quantities of chum and pink are canned and exported to the E.C.; virtually all of the sockeye harvest is exported frozen to Japan from Alaska. Chinook and coho have been argued to substitute most closely with farmed Atlantic, although this greatly depends on the market, for example, Japan versus the E.C. versus U. S. domestic markets, and restaurant versus retail markets (Anderson and Bettencourt, 1993).

References

American Seafood Institute Report. 1992. "E.C. Acts on Dolphin Issue." 3: 13.

Anderson, J. L., and S. Bettencourt. 1993. "A Conjoint Approach to Model Product Preferences: The New England Market for Fresh and Frozen Salmon." *Marine Resource Economics* 8: 31-49.

Commission of the European Communities. 1991a. *Council Directive 91/493/EEC.* Brussels, 22 July.

———. 1991b. *The Common Fisheries Policy.* Brussels, March.

Food and Agriculture Organization. 1990a. *Yearbook on Fisheries Statistics, Catches and Landings.* Rome, Italy.

———. 1990b. *Yearbook on Fisheries Statistics, Commodities,* Rome, Italy.

———. 1990c. *Aquaculture Minutes,* No.8, August, Rome, Italy.

———. 1992a. *The State of Food and Agriculture,* Rome, Italy.

———. 1992b. *Globefish Highlights.* Fisheries Industries Division 3: 13.

———. 1993. *Globefish Highlights* Fisheries Industries Division 1: 10.

McDorman, T. L. 1990. International Trade Law Meets International Fisheries Law: The U.S.-Canada Salmon and Herring Dispute." *Journal of International Arbitration* 7: 107-121.

———. 1991. "Dissecting the Free-Trade Agreement Lobster Panel Decision (Lobster from Canada, Final Report of the Panel [May 25, 1990] 3T.C.T. 8182)." *Canadian Business Law Journal* 18: 445-458.

———. 1992. "The 1991 U.S.-Mexico GATT Panel Report on Tuna and Dolphin: Implications for Trade and Environmental Conflicts." *North Carolina Journal of International Law and Commercial Regulation* 17: 461-488.

Norwegian Central Bureau of Statistics. Various issues. "Monthly Bulletin of External Trade." Oslo, Norway.

Patterson, E. 1992. "GATT and the Environment—Rules Changes to Minimize Adverse Trade and Environmental Effects." *Journal of World Trade* 26: 99-110.

Petersmann, E. U. 1993. "International Trade Law and International Environmental Law—Prevention and Settlement of International Disputes." *Journal of World Trade* 27: 43-82.

Royal Norwegian Embassy. 1993. "Norway Resumes Traditional Small-type Coastal Whaling." *News of Norway* 50: 1-2.

Runge, C. F. 1990. "Trade Protectionism and Environmental Regulations: The New Nontariff Barriers." *Northwestern Journal of International Law and Business* 11: 47-61.

U. S. Congress. Office of the Press Secretary. 1993. Letter to the U. S. Congress from President William J. Clinton. Washington D. C., Oct. 4.

U. S. Department of Agriculture. Economic Research Service. 1991. "Foreign Agricultural Trade of the United States," Calendar year 1990 supplementary tables. Report No. FATS-91, Washington, D.C.

U. S. Department of Commerce. NOAA/NMFS. *Fisheries Statistics of the US.* Washington, D.C., various years.

———. 1992. *World Salmon Aquaculture Report.* Washington, D.C.

U. S. International Trade Commission. 1991. *Fresh and Chilled Atlantic Salmon From Norway: Determination of the Commission in Investigation No. 701-TA-302 and No. 731-TA-454 (Final).* USITC Publication No. 2371, Washington D.C., April.

———. 1992. *Tuna: Current Issues Affecting the U.S. Industry.* USITC Publication No. 2547, Washington, D.C., August.

22

The Impact of Agricultural Policy Reforms and a GATT Agreement on the European-North American Durum Wheat Markets

Richard Gray, Gary Storey, and Brent Zacharias

Introduction

In this chapter we examine the international market for durum wheat. Durum is one of several classes of wheat that is used primarily for the manufacture of pasta products and couscous. The highest per capita consumption is found in the Mediterranean region, particularly in Italy and North Africa. It is a spring wheat produced mainly in the Mediterranean region and in the semi-arid parts of the northern great plains of North America. The ability of durum producers to grow other varieties of wheat has made the location of durum production and the patterns of durum trade very sensitive to government policies.

How the world durum market has been shared and how price has been arrived at has not been well understood. Various articles on the wheat industry provide insights (McCalla, 1966, 1970; Taplin, 1969; Alaouze *et al.*, 1978; deGorter and Meilke, 1985; Carter and Schmitz, 1992), but these tend not to be specific to durum. Specific studies on durum appear to be limited (Tewari, 1982; Dhaliwal, 1984; Storey *et al.* 1988; Carter and Schmitz, 1992). These studies have modeled the wheat economy from an industrial organization or structuralist approach, which determines both behavior and performance. This approach requires that the analyst be sensitive to changing conditions that are often the result of policy changes by one or more of the major exporters and/or importers.

A major structural change in the world durum trade resulted from the

E.C. becoming a significant exporter in the mid-1980s. This situation would appear to have resulted from the specific nature of how the E.C. applied its Common Agricultural Policy (CAP) to durum in comparison to ordinary wheat and other crops. Exports from the E.C. had to be made with restitution payments to E.C. exporters and this resulted in the United States retaliating with its Export Enhancement Program (EEP). The trade warfare being engaged between the United States and the E.C. over durum has resulted in the anomalous situation of Canada exporting durum to the United States. In similar fashion policies and actions have affected the trade patterns within the E.C. Italy has shifted some of its sources of durum to France.

The durum industry in all regions is facing an uncertain future, as it depends on the result of E.C. reforms and a settlement of the current GATT negotiations. This could be further affected by changes to domestic agricultural policies. What adds complexity is that various policy changes in the countries in question are interrelated. What happens in the E.C. could considerably affect policy actions in the United States such as the use of EEP. What implications will various policy changes have for the production and price of durum, and for market shares, production, and trade patterns?

Objectives and Scope of the Study

The purpose of the chapter is to determine how the agricultural policies of Canada, the United States, and the E.C. have affected the international durum economy and to examine how changes to these policies will affect the durum market in the future. The specific objectives of the chapter are:

1. To describe and discuss the dynamics of the international durum industry from a structuralist perspective,
2. to develop a model to determine the structural impacts of key policies, and
3. to measure how a GATT agreement, E.C. policy reform, and U.S. policy change would affect the location and level of production, trade, and the price of durum.

The scope of the chapter is limited to durum and the durum trade of the E.C., Canada, the United States and the rest of the world (ROW). The chapter thus does not specifically examine the implications for the North African countries, Japan, and the former USSR as major durum importers, nor for Argentina and Australia as both former and thus potential exporters. The processing of durum into semolina and pasta products and the market for these products was seen to be beyond the scope of the chapter.

The Structural Dynamics of the Durum Economy

The purpose of this section is to provide the basis for understanding the evolution of the durum wheat economy in terms of how policies have affected pricing, production, and trade patterns. We present the data on acreage, yields (production), government program prices, market prices, stocks, and trade for the four components of the model. We utilize this data along with structural assumptions to examine the behavioral actions of the key actors in the durum economy and their implications.

Market Shares

We start by examining the world durum market and the market shares of the major exporters over the last 30 years (see Table 22.1). Overall, the world durum trade has grown from 3.2 million tonnes for the period 1970-71 to 1974-75, to 4.8 million tonnes for the period 1990-91 to 1992-93. The trade data shows that although Canada and the United States dominated the world market they shared it with Argentina, which had 18.7 percent of the market for the period 1965 to 1970. Canada had only 27.3 percent of the market, compared to the U.S. share of 45.1 percent. These three countries controlled over 90 percent of the market.

A significant structural change took place in the 1970s, when Canada replaced Argentina in the world durum market. By the end of the 1970s Argentina's durum production had fallen so that it essentially ceased being an exporter. Canadian durum production increased as did its exports so that by the early 1980s Canada's market share rose to over 50 percent. In 1982-83 and 1983-84 Canada's market share was 61 percent in

TABLE 22.1 The Market Share of Regions in the Durum Market (Percent)

	Canada	U.S.	Canada/U.S.	E.C.	Argentina	Others	World
1965/66 to 1969/70	27.3	45.1	72.4	1.1	18.7	7.8	100
1970/71 to 1974/75	40.0	45.8	85.8	.4	12.5	1.3	100
1975/76 to 1979/80	46.9	44.4	91.3	.8	5.2	2.7	100
1980/81 to 1984/85	56.0	38.6	94.6	5.3		2.3	100
1985/86 to 1989/90	47.9	30.4	78.3	16.9		4.7	100
1990/91	63.4	21.0	84.4	14.5		.9	100
1991/92	54.5	28.3	82.8	16.0		3.3	100
1992/93	53.1	22.4	75.5	20.4		4.1	100

Source: International Wheat Council (IWC).

both years. However, just three years later its share had fallen to 42 percent.

In the early 1980s, although the E.C. still remained as a large net importer of durum, its production was increasing so that it was beginning to export. In the period 1980 to 1985 the E.C. captured 5.3 percent of the export market share. Canada's market share increased to 56.0 percent. It was the United States that suffered a loss in share, which fell to 38.6 percent. U.S. exports continued to decline with its share falling further to 30.4 percent in the period between 1986 and 1989. Canada's market share also declined somewhat to 47.9 percent. It was in these years that the E.C. expanded its net exports with its share increasing to 16.9 percent. This pattern has continued into the 1990s with Canada holding over 50 percent of the market. The E.C. is forecast to increase its share to 20 percent in 1992-93 with the United States holding only slightly more than 20 percent.

Shifting Competitive Advantage—Policies and Technical Change

The durum acreages for Canada, United States, and the E.C. are outlined in Table 22.2 for the period 1971-72 to 1992-93. It shows wide fluctuations in durum acreage in both Canada and the United States. The patterns, however, are different. In Canada durum acreage has tended upward, while in the U.S. durum area tended to increase reaching a peak in 1981-82 when 2.3 million hectares were harvested; two years later U.S. durum area had fallen to 1.0 million hectares. In 1991 and 1992 durum area in the United States had returned to levels similar to those of the early 1970s. By comparison Canadian acreages were nearly double those of the early 1970s. What is the explanation for this significant change in the export structure of the world durum economy?

The answers probably lie with the production characteristics of durum wheat and changing agricultural policies. As shown in Figure 22.1 the shift in acreage could be attributable to both relative prices and changes in genetic stock.

Changes in Genetic Stock. In Canada over 80 percent of the durum produced is grown in the province of Saskatchewan, especially in areas with low rainfall (250mm to 375mm per year) that lie in the southwest region of the province. In these regions the typical crop rotation is wheat—fallow and over 90 percent of the planted crops are wheat. Farmers will substitute readily between hard red spring wheat and durum wheat depending on the differences in expected price, farm held stocks, and market opportunities. The husbandry of growing durum and hard spring wheat are nearly identical, with the main difference being that durum wheat is longer strawed, requires a few more days to mature, and tends to sprout quicker than hard red wheat given a wet harvest. These are the main reasons that durum is not more readily grown in the areas with a

TABLE 22.2 Area of Durum Wheat: Canada, United States, E.C., and Rest of the World

Year	Canada (000 ha)	Percent	United States (000 ha)	Percent	E.C. (000 ha)	Percent	ROW (000 ha)	Percent	TOTAL (000 ha)
1971/72	919	5.7	1,159	7.2	1,974	12.3	11,948	74.7	16,000
1972/73	1,279	6.8	1,032	5.5	1,969	10.5	14,420	77.1	18,700
1973/74	951	5.3	1,167	6.5	1,903	10.6	13,879	77.5	17,900
1974/75	1,153	6.2	1,659	8.9	1,925	10.3	13,963	74.7	18,700
1975/76	1,473	7.6	1,894	9.8	2,020	10.4	14,013	72.2	19,400
1976/77	1,413	7.2	1,856	9.5	2,095	10.7	14,236	72.6	19,600
1977/78	728	4.3	1,224	7.2	1,586	9.4	13,362	79.1	16,900
1978/79	1,477	7.9	1,628	8.8	1,994	10.7	13,501	72.6	18,600
1979/80	1,133	6.2	1,591	8.7	1,966	10.8	13,510	74.2	18,200
1980/81	1,255	6.6	1,958	10.4	2,057	10.9	13,630	72.1	18,900
1981/82	1,699	9.0	2,289	12.1	2,201	11.6	12,719	67.3	18,908
1982/83	1,477	8.3	1,690	9.5	2,267	12.8	12,266	69.3	17,700
1983/84	1,416	8.4	1,006	6.0	2,356	13.9	12,122	71.7	16,900
1984/85	1,606	9.7	1,303	7.8	2,423	14.6	11,268	67.9	16,600
1985/86	1,740	10.2	1,252	7.4	2,486	14.6	11,522	67.8	17,000
1986/87	1,845	10.8	1,164	6.8	2,782	16.3	11,309	66.1	17,100
1987/88	2,186	11.4	1,327	7.3	2,855	15.8	11,732	64.8	18,100
1988/89	2,266	13.4	1,152	6.8	2,727	16.1	10,736	63.5	16,900
1989/90	2,811	15.7	1,446	8.1	2,825	15.8	10,818	60.4	17,900
1990/91	2,113	11.7	1,419	7.9	2,961	16.5	11,507	63.9	18,000
1991/92	1,295								
1992/93	971								

shorter growing season such as in the northern prairies or in wetter regions. Some of the varieties introduced during the 1970s and 1980s have shorter straw, mature earlier, and are more sprout resistant than traditional varieties. Many of these varieties have the same yield as spring wheat varieties. The lack of genetic progress in hard spring wheat varieties and the progress in durum varietal development has expanded the area where durum can effectively compete with spring wheat into slightly more humid areas of the region.

In the United States about 80 percent of the durum is grown in North Dakota, adjacent to Saskatchewan south of the 49th parallel. Here cropping practices are similar to those in southern Saskatchewan, although the area is slightly more humid with more frost-free days. One could speculate that the reduction in durum area in this region may, in part, be due to the successful adaptation of semi-dwarf hard spring and winter wheat

FIGURE 22.1 Changes in Wheat and Durum Production.

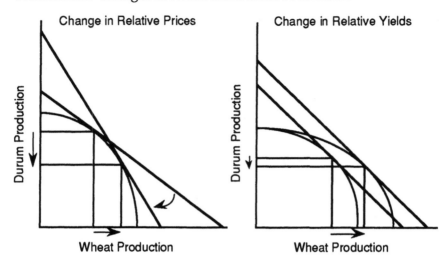

varieties that are able to displace durum acreage. Richard Frohberg, a spring wheat breeder from North Dakota, suggested that several years ago whereas durum varieties tended to outyield spring wheat varieties, while the reverse now tends to be true.

The changes in relative genetic potential for durum and other wheats in the E.C. is an issue that requires further study. Given the long growing season and the genetic advances in soft and hard wheats one would suspect that the genetic advances have been in favor of the other classes of wheat.

Relative Government Support for Durum and Other Wheat. The relative economic return for wheat versus durum will also be determined to a large extent by the relative support for wheat versus durum. Durum acreage is very sensitive to relative market prices.

Tewari estimated Canadian durum acreage to be a function of the ratio of the expected price of durum to spring wheat, and the ratio of previous farm deliveries of durum compared to hard spring wheat. Both variables were statistically significant. The corrected R^2 was .776 for the period 1964 to 1980. The differences in Canadian Wheat Board (CWB) initial payments were taken into account as were differences in delivery opportunities between durum and spring wheat as reflected by different quota delivery levels. Government programs have also played a role in the acreage of durum in Canada. While most programs provide the same level of per acre support for both wheat and durum, the notable exception to this is the 1991 GRIP program, where each crop was supported at 70 percent of a 15-year indexed moving average price. This program supported durum at a price 15 percent higher that wheat prices in a year when anticipated prices for durum were below spring wheat. In 1992 the GRIP program was modified to remove this bias in Saskatchewan. Now all producers in an area receive the same per acre support no matter what crop is grown.

Tewari (1982) specified U.S. durum acreage to be a function of the ratio of the cash Minneapolis price of durum to dark northern spring in the first calendar quarter of the crop year and the ratio of ending farm stocks of durum to other wheat for the end of the first calendar quarter of the crop year. Both variables were significant at the 5 percent level and the corrected R^2 was .798.

A summary of the EEP, U.S. support prices, and market prices is shown in Table 22.3. The table shows that the United States has lowered its support prices for wheat over the last several years. For example, the U.S. loan

TABLE 22.3 U.S. Export Subsidies and Price Supports for Wheat ($US/t)

Year	Target Price	Loan Rate	Deficiency Payment	EEP Non-durum	EEP Durum
1970/71	—	45.93	57.68		
1971/72	—	45.93	59.89		
1972/73	—	45.93	49.23		
1973/74	—	45.93	24.98		
1974/75	75.32	50.33	—		
1975/76	75.32	50.33	—		
1976/77	84.13	82.67	—		
1977/78	106.55	82.67	23.88		
1978/79	124.92	86.34	19.10		
1979/80	124.92	91.85	—		
1980/81	133.37	110.22	—		
1981/82	140.00	117.57	55.11		
1982/83	148.80	130.43	18.37		
1983/84	157.98	134.10	23.88		
1984/85	160.92	121.24	36.74		
1985/86	160.92	121.24	39.68	27.60	26.97
1986/87	160.92	88.18	72.75	26.90	34.25
1987/88	160.92	83.77	66.50	37.74	37.85
1988/89	155.41	81.20	25.35	33.53	19.94
1889/90	150.63	75.68	11.76	18.53	17.45
1990/91	146.96	71.64	47.03	14.20	37.29
1991/92	146.96	74.95	54.01	36.45	49.02
1992/93	146.96	81.20		47.22	37.45

Source: USDA, ERS, Wheat Situation and Outlook Yearbook, various issues. National Grains Bureau

rate reached a peak at $134.10 per tonne ($3.65 per bushel) in 1983-84. In 1986-87 the United States reduced the loan rate to $88.18 per tonne ($2.40 per bushel). The loan rate was further reduced to $71.64 per tonne ($1.95 per bushel) for the 1990-91 crop year. In the last two years it has been increased to $81.20 per tonne ($2.04 per bushel) for the 1992-93 crop year. The United States has not differentiated durum and other classes of wheat in its farm programs. The EEP programs have also been very similar for durum and other classes of wheat. From 1985-86 to the end of the 1991-92 crop year the average EEP for all wheat excluding durum was $31.51/t whereas the average EEP for durum was $33.75/t. The Conservation Reserve Program (CRP) has idled almost 40 million acres from grain production. A disproportionate number of these acres are in the semi-arid durum growing regions, perhaps contributing to the decline in durum acreage.

These factors outlined above may not fully explain the differences in the durum acreage patterns between Canada and the United States and the E.C. Other factors such as the lack of a futures market may be contributing to the decline. That is, the U.S. farmers find it easier to forward price dark northern spring wheat, where there is a futures market, than durum where there is none. Based on the substitution principle as discussed above, Prentice and Storey (1988) explained the changing patterns for world flaxseed using what they called "the theory of crowding out." They suggested that a commodity, analogous to the product life cycle theory, can get crowded out of a farm rotation where it fails to provide as high a return as another crop, especially over a period of years. The same principle may exist at the demand level where there are products that are close substitutes. This applies to durum where there are other types of wheat that can be used to manufacture pasta. Durum area in the E.C. has steadily increased over the last 20 years. The area planted to durum has increased from approximately 2.0 million hectares in 1971-72 to 3.0 million hectares in 1990-91. This was almost equally matched by a decline of 1.0 million hectares planted to other wheats. This suggests a substitution of durum for other wheats (and possibly other crops) on farms in the E.C. This can be explained by the differences in the CAP as it was established for durum.

In the E.C., durum is treated differently from other wheats. Although the E.C. was a large net importer of durum, it was not the goal of self-sufficiency but social policy that largely determined how durum was handled under the CAP. Coincidentally the lowest farm incomes are to be found in southern Italy and southern France where durum wheat is produced. A concession was made to the farmers in these regions by establishing higher support prices for durum compared to soft wheat. That is, the target and intervention prices were set at a higher level. A comparison of the prices of soft and durum wheat in the E.C. including the level of production aid is outlined in Table 22.4. The prices have been

TABLE 22.4 E.C. Support Levels for Durum and Soft Wheat ($US/tonne)

Year	Intervention Price			Durum Production Aid* (per hectare)
	Durum	Soft Wheat	Difference	
1970/71	117.09	98.40	18.69	34.64
1971/72	121.13	101.79	19.34	34.84
1972/73	125.31	112.26	13.05	39.51
1973/74	131.67	117.96	13.71	41.51
1974/75	198.79	131.11	67.68	34.88
1975/76	250.13	165.32	84.81	32.72
1976/77	226.68	147.01	79.67	23.62
1977/78	236.97	158.27	78.70	49.52
1978/79	273.89	184.78	89.11	44.85
1979/80	316.25	213.34	112.91	52.06
1980/81	351.95	236.86	115.09	43.85
1981/82	296.81	198.64	98.17	41.93
1982/83	284.35	170.85	123.50	45.64
1983/84	275.55	162.97	112.58	48.24
1984/85	254.35	148.93	105.42	30.21
1985/86	242.27	139.30	102.97	33.29
1986/87	308.67	185.24	123.43	45.08
1987/88	359.28	221.10	138.18	56.89
1988/89	339.06	220.16	118.90	67.00
1989/90	279.48	192.08	87.40	—
1990/91	279.24	199.47	79.77	—
1991/92	273.11	202.97	70.94	—
1992/93	264.92	196.10	68.82	—
1993/94*	149.29	149.29	0	—
1994/95*	137.81	137.81	0	—
1995/96*	127.60	127.60	0	—

*Intervention price calculated at the current US$/ECU exchange rate of $1.276/ECU.
Source: Cap Monitor

converted from European Currency Units (ECUs) to U.S. dollars. What the table shows is an increasing difference between durum and soft wheat intervention prices. In 1987-88 the difference was $138 per tonne ($3.76 per bushel U.S.). Provisions had to be established to ensure that varieties suitable for pasta production were planted. The combination of higher support prices and the production aid were instrumental in increasing durum production by a combination of increased hectares and higher yields.

Price Determination and Market Structure

Prior to 1972 world wheat prices were relatively stable. From 1949 to 1968 International Wheat Agreements were in existence that tended to reduce uncertainty for both exporting and importing countries. In addition to the major exporting countries, Canada and the United States, before 1968 and after that Australia held large stocks relative to export levels. Prices were supported at the U.S. loan rate for many years. These stocks provided security for importers and prevented any sharp increase in price. The stock levels were managed directly by year-to-year adjustments in acreage and price support programs (United States) and indirectly in Canada by the CWB quota delivery system.

Price determination in the wheat market has been analyzed and described by McCalla (1966) in an oligopolistic framework. He modeled the wheat market as a cooperative duopoly between Canada and the United States in the period up to the mid 1960s. Other exporters, Australia, France, and Argentina, were modeled as competitive fringe as in a dominant firm model. As these countries did not have the same ability to store grain they tended to undercut Canadian and U.S. prices until their excess supplies beyond domestic requirements were sold. Thus Canada and the United States were seen as facing a residual demand for exports that they had somehow to share. McCalla saw the relationship as a leader-follower Stackelberg model with Canada being the price leader and the United States as a follower. McCalla argued that the United States was not in a position to be the leader as it had to set export subsidies as its own internal price supports exceeded the world price. It was easier for U.S. administration to let the CWB set the daily offer price and follow with its offer of export subsidies. The United States was seen to demand a minimum market share, beyond which it would be content to share the market. That is, the United States was prepared to cooperate with other exporters as long as it could meet its own objective function. The CWB was seen as attempting to set price along the residual demand curve facing Canada and the United States so as to maximize total revenue, which would be where demand was unitary elastic.

Taplin (1969) developed a similar framework but depicted the residual demand curve as kinked at the point of unitary elasticity. By this he theorized that the United States as follower would not follow if the CWB tried to set price above the point of unitary elasticity but would match all price cuts below the point of unitary elasticity.

Increases in wheat production by some of the traditional importers and thus declining export markets coupled with increased wheat production by Australia destabilized the wheat market in the mid 1960s. Australia's policy of undercutting the market price in order to eliminate its surpluses led to price wars in 1965-66 and 1968-69. McCalla (1970) and Alaouze,

Watson, and Sturgess, (1978) (AWS) made a case that the price wars that the United States engaged against Australia led to the formation of a triopoly involving the United States, Canada, and Australia. Australia had increased its ability to store wheat and thus had the ability now to cooperate in sharing the residual export market. The United States was content to resort to being a follower after it had acted as the policeman in the market to restore an order under which it was willing to operate.

The period after 1972 through into the 1980s is characterized by increased and unstable prices. The price escalation in 1972 was triggered by low carryover and the unexpected entry of the USSR in the market that led to a period of panic buying by importers. It was a period in which world wheat trade expanded. The expanded market was largely filled by the United States, which was able to return idled acreage to production. It probably served to give the United States a new level of market share, which it would feel was its right and thus provide a level over which it was prepared to defend. For example, the U.S. share of the world wheat market reached 53 percent in 1973 and its exports rose to 1.8 million bushels in 1981. However, when U.S. exports declined to just 909 million bushels in 1985 and its wheat carryover rose to a record 1.9 billion bushels the United States was forced to make a drastic policy change. While maintaining its target price level it slashed its loan rate by $33 per tonne. It signaled that it was not prepared to unilaterally be the residual exporter and be the only country willing to manage production in the face of declining export markets. It was not willing to carry burdensome stocks in an attempt to maintain market prices. In particular it was not prepared to let the E.C. enter the market as a major exporter and go unchallenged. It was for this reason that it resorted to export subsidies that had been abandoned in 1974.

The return to export subsidies in 1984 marked the beginning of a new period in trade relations, in this case one of trade and hence price warfare. It was a situation where both the E.C. and the United States would present very dissimilar positions to the GATT Round. Both the E.C. and the United States would attempt to maintain policies to protect their farmers while making it exceedingly difficult for other exporting countries, in particular Australia, Argentina and Canada, to maintain similar income support for their farmers.

The models, although they were developed for wheat in general, have applicability for durum. Tewari presented the durum economy as one of a duopoly between the United States and Canada. As outlined above, once Argentina ceased to be a significant exporter in the 1960s this left the durum market almost entirely to the United States and Canada. It is likely that Canada and the United States treated Argentina as a fringe supplier. Argentina did not hold stocks (see Table 22.5). In the period 1970 to 1974

TABLE 22.5 End-Of-Year Carryover, Durum: Canada, United States, E.C., Argentina (000 tonnes)

Year	Canada	United States	E.C.	Argentina	Total
1970/71	2,255	1,591	508	138	4,492
1971/72	1,653	1,879	618	111	4,271
1972/73	1,470	1,006	310	13	2,799
1973/74	1,232	762	150	29	2,173
1974/75	959	708	866	57	2,590
1975/76	1,537	1,442	1,324	84	4,387
1976/77	2,328	2,504	922	50	5,804
1977/78	1,170	1,823	433	24	3,450
1978/79	2,260	2,341	503	50	5,154
1979/80	1,689	1,660	313	30	3,692
1980/81	1,165	1,633	548	40	3,348
1981/82	1,233	2,885	822	10	4,740
1982/83	1,174	3,701	658	19	5,533
1983/84	764	2,694	993	44	4,451
1984/85	524	2,722	1,511	41	4,757
1985/86	554	3,293	1,300	NA	5,147
1986/87	1,610	2,586	2,449	NA	6,645
1987/88	1,541	2,259	3,101	NA	6,901
1988/89	828	1,633	1,799	NA	4,258
1889/90	1,352	1,361	1,618	NA	4,331
1990/91	1,600	1,700	1,900	NA	5,200
1991/92	2,100	1,500	4,600	NA	8,200
1992/93	1,600	1,400	3,700	NA	6,700

Source: IWC, *World Grain Statistics*.

Argentina's average durum carryover was only 69.6 thousand tonnes, and more importantly only 12 percent of its average production in this period. Although the E.C. held .5 million tonnes, on average this represented only 14.7 percent of E.C. production. By comparison Canada held an average of 1.5 million tonnes of durum, which was 87.1 percent of its production in this period. For this five-year period the United States held an average of 1.2 million tonnes of durum, which represented 57.8 percent of its production. Fifteen years later the situation had reversed. First, Argentina almost ceased producing durum. For the five-year period 1985 to 1989 Canada's average carryover had fallen to 5.9 million tonnes, which represented only 36.9 percent of its production. In contrast U.S. carryover of durum rose to an average of 2.1 million tonnes—93.7 percent of its production. By this time the E.C. had become a net exporter. The E.C.'s average carryover for this same period was 10.3 million tonnes which represented 30.6 percent of its production. In 1990-91 the E.C.'s closing stocks were 4.6 million tonnes, equal to the level of the annual world durum trade. It would appear that the E.C. was attempting to take some responsibility for its surplus production and not to expand its use of export subsidies to capture further market share to rid itself of its surplus durum stocks. Little action, however, has been taken to address the source of the increased production in the E.C.

Not until the E.C. entered the export market in the 1980s was it necessary for either Canada or the United States to fight for market share. In this case the United States was fighting for retention of its market share for all wheat including durum. As a result the EEP was applied to durum as well as to other wheats. The problem for the United States was that its production of durum fell in recent years when it needed increased production to continue to engage the E.C. in the trade war as part of it attempt to influence the GATT negotiations. What resulted was a shortage of durum for the U.S. domestic market, thus affording the CWB the opportunity to fill that market. The anomaly is that it allowed the CWB to give up markets where it was faced with lower prices from the application of the EEP by the United States and to move this durum to the U.S. market where it did not have to face EEP. It could be hypothesized that U.S. trade practices could give Canada higher overall returns.

Empirical Model and Estimation

Examining the incidence of domestic polices on the international durum market requires an understanding of the production, consumption and trade flows of the major countries with some notion of equilibrium in the market place. This section of the chapter describes a simple model that was estimated for this purpose. The model estimates supply and demand for Canada, the E.C., and the United States, excess demand for durum in the rest of the world (ROW), and a world stock holding equation as well as identities consistent with market-clearing conditions.

Equations, variables, data requirements, estimation procedure, statistical tests, and hypotheses are described below. First the notation and data sources:

Endogenous Variables:

A_C	Annual durum acreage in Canada, 000 hectares, *IWC*.
A_{US}	Annual durum acreage in the United States, 000 tonnes, *IWC*.
A_{EC}	Annual durum acreage in the E.C., 000 tonnes, *IWC*.
A_{ROW}	Annual durum acreage in ROW, 000 tonnes, *IWC*.
Y_C	Annual durum yield in Canada, tonnes/hectare, *IWC*.

Y_{US} Annual durum yield in the United States, tonnes/hectare, *IWC*.

Y_{EC} Annual durum yield in the E.C., tonnes/hectare, *IWC*.

Y_{ROW} Annual durum yield in the ROW, tonnes/hectare, *IWC*.

D_C Domestic demand for durum in Canada, 000 tonnes, *IWC*.

D_{US} Domestic demand for durum in the United States, 000 tonnes, *IWC*.

D_{EC} Domestic demand for durum in the E.C., 000 tonnes, *IWC*.

D_{ROW} Domestic demand in the ROW, 000 tonnes, *IWC*.

WORELP   (MINNPD / MINNPW) Relative world price of durum to wheat, USDA ERS, *Wheat Situation and Outlook Report*.

CANRELPL   (CANPd / CANPw) Canadian relative final realized price of durum to wheat where, CANPd = Final realized price of No. 1 Amber Durum and CANPw = Final realized price of NO. 1 Red Spring Wheat, *CWB Annual Report*

CANSTKDL   Lagged Canadian stocks of durum, 000 tonnes, *CWB Annual Report*.

ECPdL   ([ECINVPd + ECACPAY]*UsEcu) Lagged equivalent price paid to E.C. farmers for durum, $U.S./tonne, where, ECINVPd = Intervention price, ECU/tonne, *CAP Monitor*, ECACPAY = Acreage payments,ECU/tonne, *CAP Monitor*, UsEcu = $U.S./ECU, *International Financial Statistics*.[1]

ECPwL   (ECINVPw * UsECU) Lagged equivalent price paid to E.C. farmers for wheat, $U.S./tonne, where, ECINVPw = Intervention price, ECU/tonne, *CAP Monitor*.[1]

ECSTKDL   Lagged E.C. stock of durum, 000 tonnes, *IWC*.

MINNPd   Cash Minneapolis, No. 1 Hard Amber Durum, $U.S., USDA ERS, *Wheat Situation and Outlook Report*.

MINNPw   Cash Minneapolis, Dark No. 1 Spring, $U.S., USDA ERS, *Wheat Situation and Outlook Report*.

SK_t (CANSTKDL + USSTKDL + ECSTKDL) World stock levels of durum, 000 tonnes, *IWC*.

T   Trend variable.

USRELP   (MINNPd / MINNPw) U.S. relative price of durum to wheat, $U.S., USDA ERS, *Wheat Situation and Outlook Report*.

USSTKDL   Lagged U.S. stocks of durum, 000 tonnes, *IWC*.

USSTKWL   Lagged U.S. stocks of wheat, 000 tonnes, *IWC*.

The Model

(1) $X = (SK_{t-1} + AC * YC + AUS * YUS + AEC * YEC + AROW * YROW)$

(2) $Y = (D_C + D_{US} + D_{EC})$

(3) $Z = (D_{ROW})$

$$\text{(4)} \quad SK_t = (X - Y - Z)$$
$$\text{(5)} \quad P_D = (a + b \, SKt)Pw$$

The estimated equations are reported in Table 22.6.

Estimation Procedure

The estimated equations required for the supply and demand equations are reported in Table 22.6. Equations 6 through 17 had exogenous right-hand side variables and were estimated using ordinary least squares (OLS). They were corrected for autocorrelation where it was found to be

TABLE 22.6 The Estimated Equations

Eq. No.	Depen. Variable	Intercept (t-values)	Coefficient Estimates {t-values}	R^2	DW
6	AC	970.85 {1.53}	+839.75 CANRELPL – .239 CANSTKDL {2.12} {-1.95}	0.68	1.77
7	AUS	638.57 {1.13}	+351.16 USRELP+.019 USSTKWL–.337 USSTKD⌐ {2.52} {3.15} {-3.75}	0.84	1.47
8	AEC	1,752.40 {4.51}	+9.54 ECPdL -9.79 ECPwL + .105 ECSTKDL* {1.74} {-1.45} {.99}	0.77	1.68
9	AROW	13,274.00 {61.6}	-105.59 T {-5.90}	0.70	1.90
10	YC	1.73 {8.97}	-0.0087 T {-0.5}	0.02	1.62
11	YUS	1.80 {8.73}	+.011 T {.62}	0.03	1.28
12	YEC	1.44 {10.15}	+0.063 T {4.89}	0.61	2.06
13	YROW	0.97 {17.8}	+0.018 T {3.76}	0.49	1.80
15	DC	236.52 {2.33}	+30.61 T {3.37}	0.43	1.57
16	DUS	1,179.60 {13.13}	+15.70 T {1.95}	0.20	1.35
17	DEC	4,035.20 {12.81}	+49.54 T {1.75}	0.17	2.16
18	DROW	1,256.60 {1.86}	-8.99 MINNPd + 10.05 MINNPw +138.41 T {-.65} {0.48} {5.01}	0.34	1.79
19	WORELP	1.50 {14.64}	-0.000095 SKt {-3.26}	0.42	1.74

Source: Authors' estimates.

*Although the sign on the durum stock variable is positive rather than the expected negative sign, the coefficient is not significant.

significant. Equations 18 and 19 were estimated using 2 stage least squares. Given the large number of equations, and the limited number of observations, SUR and 3 stage least squares were not employed.[2]

Policy Simulations

The estimated model was modified for the purpose of policy simulations. The lagged supply and the stockholding equation makes the model inherently dynamic. Determining optimal strategies in a dynamic model can be done but requires the specification of a whole set of dynamic actions and reactions. For the purposes of this chapter, i.e., to simulate the effect of policy change on the world durum market, the estimated model was modified to reflect long-run equilibrium conditions. The model was then used to perform comparative statics to move from one static equilibrium to another.

In the static equilibriums, production was equal to consumption and markets cleared with prices being endogenous. Finding this equilibrium involved selecting a particular year, setting lagged prices equal to current prices, removing the stock equation (as stocks neither contribute nor detract from current demand), and finding the prices where markets clear given the polices being simulated.

The trade flows were established using market clearing conditions. The E.C. imports from North America and exports excess supply to the ROW. The U.S. exports to the E.C. at the U.S. commercial or domestic price. The U.S. exports to the ROW at the U.S. price minus the EEP bonus level. It was assumed that Canada, operating through the CWB, exported to the United States, E.C., and the ROW with the objective of maximizing returns for Canadian producers.

The price in the E.C. and the United States is higher than the EEP subsidized prices in the ROW market. There is a need to restrict the volume of exports shipped to these high-priced markets to reflect the quantities shipped, because the E.C. and the United States export their surpluses to maintain the price differential. Without restriction on quantity, arbitrage would force all Canadian exports through these markets producing somewhat incredible results. To restrict the quantities that flow through these premium markets a basis was added to these trade flows. The price received for Canadian durum shipped into the United States was the U.S. commercial price minus a basis of $20 per million tonnes shipped. This could be due to either a basis increase or a recognition of the possibility of U.S. trade retaliation. The quantity of Canadian durum shipped to the E.C. is limited in a similar fashion with a large basis ($100/ MMt) that increases with volume. One could argue this basis is more likely a reflection of the limited demand for Canadian durum. The U.S. shipments are restricted to one-third of the Canadian exports to the E.C.

The equilibrium in this market including the CWB market allocations are solved using a nonlinear optimization model created within the "solver" routine of the Microsoft Excel™ (Ver. 4) spreadsheet program.

The Base Case

To validate the model and this approach we found the equilibria consistent with the policies and the supply and demand curves for the 1985-89 period. The model generated results consistent with the patterns that existed during the period. For the 1985-89 equilibrium the EEP was set at $33 per tonne and the E.C. had a farm support price of $228 per tonne (the averages for the 1985-89 period).

As shown in Table 22.7, these policies resulted in the United States importing .5 MMt of durum from Canada and exporting 1.1 MMt. Canada exports nearly 2 million tonnes, and the E.C. is a net exporter of .5 MMt.

The Effect of Increased EEP

In this case we simulated the effect of an increase in the EEP for durum from $33 to $55 per tonne. These results are reported in Table 22.9, which can be compared to the summary of the Base Case reported in Table 22.8. As expected U.S. exports increase, European net exports decrease somewhat. Export subsidy expenditures increase for both the United States and the E.C. This is an amazing case from Canada's perspective. The ability to ship to the U.S. market and the ability to price discriminate leaves Canada better off in terms of market revenue with even a large increase in the EEP. The additional revenue created in the U.S. domestic market more than offsets the decline in revenue in the ROW. The gains are particularly apparent when the reduced cost of the reduced requirement for export subsidies are considered.

The Durum Trade with E.C. CAP Reform

The third objective of the chapter was to examine the future of the durum industry. We looked at this in two perspectives. The first way was to extrapolate the status quo with a 15 percent reduction in the E.C. support levels.[3] We suggest this represents the status quo or the most likely situation. These results are shown in Table 22.10. In this case world prices of durum increase somewhat allowing Canada and to some extent the United States to regain market share. Note, as long as the price levels remain high, durum shipments continue to the United States.

TABLE 22.7 Simulated Durum Market: The 1985-89 Base Case*

	Area	Yield	Quantity	Price	Net Sales
CANADA					
Supply					
Production	1,790	1.59	2,848	152	
Demand					
Domestic			726	152	110,465
U.S. exports			325	156	50,762
E.C. exports			171	167	28,522
ROW exports			1,626	150	243,392
Excess			0		433,140
UNITED STATES					
Supply					
Production	1,067	1.98	2,108	163	
Canadian imports			325	167	-54,207
Demand					
Domestic			1,431	163	232,786
EC exports			85	163	13,910
ROW exports			916	130	118,851
Excess			0		311,341
E.C.					
Supply					
Production	2,191	2.45	5,363	228	
Canadian imports			171	167	-28,522
U.S. imports			85	163	-13,910
Demand					
Domestic			4,828	228	1,100,342
ROW exports			792	130	102,679
Excess			0		1,160,589
ROW					
Excess demand				130	
Exports to row			3,334		
ROW excess			0		
World excess			0		

Notes: Year =1987
    EEP durum subsidy ($/t) = 33
    EEP wheat subsidy ($/t) = 31
    EC support price ($/t) = 228.00
    Canadian WGTA Subsidy ($/t) = 21.00

The Durum Trade With General Trade Reform

The other possibility we examined is a reduction in the export subsidies of Canada, the United States, and the E.C. consistent with the now defunct Dunkel proposal. These results are shown in Table 22.11. As one might expect general trade reform leads to slightly higher prices, less production in the E.C. and the United States and slightly more production in Canada. All of these effects are modest.

TABLE 22.8 Summary Table for the Base Case

	E.C.	U.S.	Canada	ROW
Domestic Price (US$/t)	228	163	152	130
Production (000t)	5,363	2,108	2,848	
Consumption (000t)	4,828	1,431	726	
Imports (000t)	256	325	0	3,334
Exports (000t)	792	1,002	2,122	
Market Revenue ($1000 US)	1,160,589	311,341	433,140	
Export Subsidy ($1000 US)	52,571	30,241	37,735	

Source: Authors' estimates.

TABLE 22.9 Summary Table for the $55/t EEP*

	E.C.	U.S.	Canada	ROW
Domestic Price (US$/t)	228	175	152	122
Production (000t)	5,363	2,173	2,849	
Consumption (000t)	4,828	1,431	726	
Imports (000t)	407	825	0	3,400
Exports (000t)	942	1,567	2,123	
Market Revenue ($1000 US)	1,145,851	318,697	433,572	
Export Subsidy ($1000 US)	56,529	75,895	27,253	

*Notes: Year =1987
        EEP durum subsidy ($/t) = 53
        EEP wheat subsidy ($/t) = 31
        EC support price ($/t) = 228.00
        Canadian WGTA Subsidy ($/t) = 21.00

Source: Authors' estimates.

Summary and Conclusions

Durum wheat is an important crop in the semi-arid wheat growing regions of the world. Like other types of wheat, the durum market is subject to a great deal of government intervention. However, because of the agronomic similarities with other types of wheat, the acreage of durum is very sensitive to prices, policies and technology which determine the comparative and competitive advantages of the crop.

The world durum trade has been characterized by large changes in market shares including the loss of some exporting nations such as Argentina. In the last two decades durum acreage has been increasing in Canada and particularly in the E.C. and falling in the United States. These changes can be attributed in part to relative genetic improvements in durum and substitute crops but in general are driven by government policies. In the

TABLE 22.10 The Durum Trade with E.C. Reform*

	E.C.	U.S.	Canada	ROW
Domestic Price (US$/t)	196	196	185	163
Production (000t)	4,612	2,280	3,130	
Consumption (000t)	4,828	1,431	726	
Imports (000t)	216	325	0	3,037
Exports (000t)	0	1,174	2,404	
Market Revenue ($1000 US)	901,824	407,715	578,530	
Export Subsidy ($1000 US)	-7,126	36,363	43,654	

*Notes: Year =1987
　　　　 EEP durum subsidy ($/t) = 33
　　　　 EEP wheat subsidy ($/t) = 31
　　　　 EC support price ($/t) = 194
　　　　 Canadian WGTA Subsidy ($/t) = 21

Source: Authors' estimates.

TABLE 22.11 Trade Patterns with General Trade Reform*

	E.C.	U.S.	Canada	ROW
Domestic Price (US$/t)	194	194	193	172
Production (000t)	4,577	2,272	3,198	
Consumption (000t)	4,828	1,431	726	
Imports (000t)	251	0	0	3,062
Exports (000t)	0	841	2,471	
Market Revenue ($1000 US)	888,382	424,705	616,252	
Export Subsidy ($1000 US)	-5,518	16,666	34,601	

*Notes: Year =1987
　　　　 EEP durum subsidy ($/t) = 22
　　　　 EEP wheat subsidy ($/t) = 20
　　　　 EC support price ($/t) = 194
　　　　 Canadian WGTA Subsidy ($/t) = 14

Source: Authors' estimates.

E.C., high government support levels have increased the durum area. In the United States, farm programs have failed to maintain the historical premium durum prices enjoyed in the 1970s. In Canada, durum is treated as a separate product from wheat in terms of marketing, but government programs and policies have been almost neutral with respect to durum.

The pattern of trade that developed during the late 1980s and has continued to the present is also very much a function of policy. Two points are worth noting. The E.C. has become a small net exporter of durum due to its production subsidies. The second anomaly is that Canada now ships significant quantities of durum to the U.S. market. "Hauling coal to Newcastle" only makes sense in the presence of large EEP subsidies creating a premium market in the United States. In our empirical model we show that larger EEP levels can leave Canadian producers slightly better off given that they have access to the U.S. market.

The world durum industry will continue to be dominated by government policy. If the current situation persists, the U.S. durum industry will continue to decline; however, if the CAP reforms are implemented world prices for durum will again rise to a premium allowing increased planting in North America. Finally, we show that a general trade reform package would create patterns of trade similar to those that existed in the early 1980s.

Notes

The authors wish to thank Mr. C. Gillen of the Canadian Wheat Board for his assistance in obtaining data and general advice.

1. From the 1987-88 to 1989-90 season ECINVPd and ECINVPw = buying in price minus Coresponsibility levels. Buying price was set at 94 percent of intervention price as of the 1987-88 season. Coresponsibility levels were 5.38 ECU/ tonne up to the end of the 1989-90 season.

2. The small sample properties of these estimators are ambiguous.

3. The choice of this percentage reduction is somewhat arbitrary. Obviously, large commercial producers will receive a larger reduction, while smaller producers in the regions where durum is concentrated will see little reduction in direct farm support.

References

Alaouze, C. M., A. S. Watson, and N. H. Sturgess. 1978. "Oligopoly Pricing in the World Wheat Market." *Amer. J. Agric. Econ.* 60: 173-185.

Carter, C., and A. Schmitz. 1992. "Effects of U.S. Durum Wheat Imports." Unpublished Paper, University of California, Davis.

———. 1979. "Import Tariffs and Price Formation in the World Wheat Market." *Amer. J. Agric. Econ.* 61: 518-522.

Dhaliwal, N. S. 1984. "An Analysis of Alternative Forecasting Methods of the International Durum Wheat Market." Unpublished Masters Thesis, Department of Agricultural Economics, University of Saskatchewan, Saskatoon.

de Gorter, H., and K. D. Meilke. 1985. "The EEC's Common Agricultural Policy and International Wheat Prices." International Trade Policy Division, Agricultural Canada, July 8.

International Wheat Council. *World Wheat Statistics.* London, Annual Reports.

McCalla, A. F. 1966. "A Duopoly Model of World Wheat Pricing." *Journal of Farm Economics* 48: 711-727.

————. 1970. "Wheat and the Price Mechanism." Paper Presented at Seminar on Wheat, Department of Agricultural Economics, University of Manitoba, October, 177-204.

Prentice, B., and G. G. Storey. 1988. "Flaxseed: Victim of Crowding Out or Potential Cinderella Crop." Paper presented at Canadian Agricultural Economics and Farm Management Society Annual Meeting, McGill University, Montreal, July.

Storey, G. G. *et al.* 1988. "An Economic Profile and Analysis of the Canadian and International Durum Wheat Industry." Department of Agricultural Economics, University of Saskatchewan, Saskatoon, RR: 88-04, October.

Taplin, J. 1969. "Demand in the World Wheat Market and the Export Policies of the United States, Canada, and Australia." Ph.D. Thesis, Cornell University.

Tewari, D. D. 1982. "An Econometric Forecasting Model for the International Durum Wheat Market." Unpublished Masters Thesis, Department of Agricultural Economics, University of Saskatchewan, Saskatoon.

Zacharias, B. E. 1993. "The Impacts of Foreign Agricultural Policy on the Canadian Durum Industry." Unpublished BSA Paper, Department of Agricultural Economics, University of Saskatchewan, Saskatoon.

About the Editors and Contributors

Giovanni Anania, Associate Professor, Department of Economics, University of Calabria, Italy.

Kym Anderson, Professor, Department of Economics and Centre for International Economic Studies, University of Adelaide, Australia.

Neil Andrews, Australian Bureau of Agricultural and Resource Economics (ABARE), Canberra, Australia.

Robert E. Baldwin, Hilldale Professor of Economics, Department of Economics, University of Wisconsin, Madison, U.S.A.

Giuseppe Barbero, Professor, Department of Sociology, University of Rome "La Sapienza," Italy.

Richard R. Barichello, Associate Professor, Department of Agricultural Economics, University of British Columbia, Vancouver, Canada.

Jonathan Brooks, OECD, Paris, France.

Colin A. Carter, Professor, Department of Agricultural Economics, University of California, Davis, U.S.A.

Nadia Cuffaro, Assistant Professor, Department of Economics, University of Cassino, Italy.

Michele De Benedictis, Professor, Department of Public Economics, University of Rome "La Sapienza," Italy.

Fabrizio De Filippis, Associate Professor, Department of Economic Sciences, University of Tuscia, Viterbo, Italy.

Brian S. Fisher, Executive Director, Australian Bureau of Agricultural and Resource Economics (ABARE), Canberra, Australia.

Walter H. Gardiner, Economic Research Service (currently on leave at OECD, Paris, France), United States Department of Agriculture, U.S.A.

Bruce L. Gardner, Professor, Department of Agricultural and Resource Economics, University of Maryland, College Park, U.S.A.

Richard Gray, Assistant Professor, Department of Agricultural Economics, University of Saskatchewan, Canada.

Eckart Guth, Directorate-General for External Economic Relations, Commission of the European Communities, Brussels, Belgium.

Hervé Guyomard, INRA, Station d'Economie et Sociologie Rurales, Rennes, France.

Stephen Haley, Agricultural Economist, Agriculture and Trade Analysis Division, Economic Research Service, United States Department of Agriculture, U.S.A.

Lisa Hardy-Bass, Agricultural Attaché, U.S. Mission to the European Communities, Brussels, Belgium.

Dermot J. Hayes, Associate Professor, Center for Agricultural and Rural Development, Iowa State University, U.S.A.

Michael D. Helmar, Assistant Scientist, Center for Agricultural and Rural Development, Iowa State University, U.S.A.

Michael T. Herlihy, Leader of the Western Europe Section, Agriculture and Trade Analysis Division, Economic Research Service, United States Department of Agriculture, U.S.A.

Susan Hester, Australian Bureau of Agricultural and Resource Economics (ABARE), Canberra, Australia.

Tim Josling, Professor, Food Research Institute, Stanford University, U.S.A.

Larry Karp, Associate Professor, Department of Agricultural and Resource Economics, University of California, Berkeley, U.S.A.

Dale J. Leuck, Agricultural Economist, Agriculture and Trade Analysis Division, Economic Research Service, United States Department of Agriculture, U.S.A.

Peter Liapis, Agricultural Economist, Agriculture and Trade Analysis Division, Economic Research Service, United States Department of Agriculture, U.S.A.

Mary Lisa Madell, Economist, Western Europe Section, Agriculture and Trade Analysis Division, Economic Research Service, United States Department of Agriculture, U.S.A.

Louis P. Mahé, Professor, Department of Social and Economic Sciences, ENSA, Rennes, France.

Mary A. Marchant, Assistant Professor, Department of Agricultural Economics, University of Kentucky, U.S.A.

Marina Mastrostefano, Assistant Professor, Department of Economics, University of Cassino, Italy.

Alex F. McCalla, Professor, Department of Agricultural Economics, University of California, Davis, U.S.A.

William H. Meyers, Professor, Center for Agricultural and Rural Development, Iowa State University, U.S.A.

Giancarlo Moschini, Associate Professor, Department of Economics, Iowa State University, U.S.A.

Steven A. Neff, Economist, Commodity Economics Division, Economic

Research Service, United States Department of Agriculture, U.S.A.

Pier Carlo Padoan, Professor, Department of Economic Sciences, University of Rome "La Sapienza," Italy.

Tonia Pankopf, Directorate-General for External Economic Relations, Commission of the European Communities, Brussels, Belgium.

Michel Petit, Director, Agriculture and Natural Resources Department, The World Bank, U.S.A.

Terry L. Roe, Professor, Department of Agricultural and Applied Economics, University of Minnesota, U.S.A.

Cathy Roheim Wessells, Assistant Professor, Department of Resource Economics, University of Rhode Island, U.S.A.

George E. Rossmiller, Chief of the Situation and Policy Studies Service, Policy Analysis Division, Food and Agriculture Organization of the United Nations, Rome, Italy.

Luca Salvatici, Assistant Professor, Department of Public Economics, University of Rome "La Sapienza," Italy.

Spiro E. Stefanou, Associate Professor, Department of Agricultural Economics and Rural Sociology, Pennsylvania State University, U.S.A.

Gary Storey, Professor and Assistant Dean for Agriculture, Department of Agricultural Economics, University of Saskatchewan, Canada.

Daniel A. Sumner, Frank H. Buck, Jr. Professor of Agricultural Economics, Department of Agricultural Economics, University of California, Davis, U.S.A.

Stefan Tangermann, Professor, Institute of Agricultural Economics, University of Goettingen, Germany.

Secondo Tarditi, Professor, School of Economic and Banking Sciences, University of Siena, Italy.

David Vanzetti, Australian Bureau of Agricultural and Resource Economics (ABARE), Canberra, Australia.

Petter Wallström, Graduate Research Assistant, Department of Resource Economics, University of Rhode Island, U.S.A.

Mei Xiao, Research Assistant, Department of Agricultural Economics, University of Kentucky, U.S.A.

Brent Zacharias, Department of Agricultural Economics, University of Saskatchewan, Canada.

Annalisa Zezza, Senior Researcher, Italian National Institute of Agricultural Economics (INEA), Rome, Italy.

About the Book

Agricultural trade, always a source of international friction, will remain a contentious issue in the years to come. The GATT agreement achieved only partial trade liberalization; recognizing this, the agreement calls for a continuation of the negotiation process to achieve the long-run goal of a "substantial reduction in agricultural support and protection." In any case, it is clear that U.S.–European Union (EU) agricultural trade relations will remain central to any future negotiation.

In this volume, leading experts present a comprehensive set of analyses of the U.S.-EU agricultural trade conflict. The discussions provide a unique perspective on the U.S.-EU agricultural trade confrontation in recent years and offer insights into both the final GATT agreement and forthcoming agricultural issues.

Presenting a broad historical context, the book focuses on changes in U.S. and European trade and agricultural policies, looking at the implications of these changes for bilateral relations and global agricultural markets. Providing U.S., EU, and third-party perspectives, the contributors analyze the negotiation process in the Uruguay Round of the GATT. Finally, the book explores several additional dimensions of the U.S.-EU agricultural trade conflict, including the consequences of the EU integration and enlargement processes, the environmental impact of the Union's agricultural policies, and the mechanisms and forces that determine agricultural policy formation in both the United States and in Europe.